Literature and the
Young Adult Reader

Literature and the Young Adult Reader

Ernest Bond

Salisbury University

Boston   Columbus   Indianapolis   New York   San Francisco   Upper Saddle River
Amsterdam   Cape Town   Dubai   London   Madrid   Milan   Munich   Paris   Montreal   Toronto
Delhi   Mexico City   Sao Paulo   Sydney   Hong Kong   Seoul   Singapore   Taipei   Tokyo

Vice President and Editor-in-Chief: Aurora Martínez Ramos
Series Editorial Assistant: Meagan French
Executive Marketing Manager: Krista Clark
Production Editor: Mary Beth Finch
Editorial Production Service: Omegatype Typography, Inc.
Manufacturing Buyer: Megan Cochran
Electronic Composition: Omegatype Typography, Inc.
Cover Designer: Elena Sidorova

Library of Congress Cataloging-in-Publication Data

Bond, Ernie.
   Literature and the young adult reader / Ernest Bond.
         p. cm.
   Includes bibliographical references.
   ISBN-13: 978-0-13-111695-5
   ISBN-10: 0-13-111695-9
   1. Young adult literature—Study and teaching.   2. Young adult literature—History and criticism.   3. Young adults—Books and reading—United States.   4. Youth—Books and reading—United States.   I. Title.
   PN1008.8.B65   2010
   809'.892830712—dc22

                                                                    2010019791

Printed in the United States of America

10 9 8 7 6 5 4 3 2 1   RRD-VA   14   13   12   11   10

www.pearsonhighered.com

ISBN-10: 0-13-111695-9
ISBN-13: 978-0-13-111695-5

ABOUT THE AUTHOR

Dr. Ernest Bond is the co-chair of the Department of Teacher Education and an associate professor at Salisbury University. Bond is the 2007 Maryland Professor of the Year (Carnegie Foundation and the Council for Advancement and Support of Education) and the recipient of the 2006–2007 Maryland Regent's Award for Teaching Excellence. Dr. Bond is the co-author of *Interactive Assessment* and has written chapters in *Harry Potter's World*, articles in *Theory into Practice* and the *Journal of Children's Literature*, and book reviews for *Bookbird* and the *School Library Journal*. He was the 2010 U.S. jurist for the Hans Christian Andersen Award and serves on the jury for the U.S. Professors of the Year. Bond is also one of the founders of the Green Earth Book Awards for books that inspire environmental stewardship in young readers. For his service on this award he was recognized with the President's Gold Volunteer Service Award (2010). In the summers he teaches International Children's Literature courses in various countries around the world including New Zealand and Australia.

CONTENTS

4   From the Campfire to the Stage: Traditional and Scripted Literature for Young Adults   141

8   Poetry   343

PREFACE

> Readers are made not born.
>
> —Aidan Chambers

Literature and the Young Adult Reader introduces the reader to the wide array of literature now available to young adults, allowing them to make informed decisions both about how to choose books for the classroom and the library and how to best integrate these books into a learning environment for young adults. This book advocates a student-centered, constructivist approach to literacy that is reinforced through the technology links and critical thinking strategies introduced in the various chapters.

Each chapter includes an overview of the genre or topic, then moves into discussions of issues and implications for authors and readers and literary explorations in the classroom, the library, or the home. Each chapter also includes special features such as Author Spotlights, Technology Links, In the Field, and Literary Theory.

Several aspects of this text stand out:

1. Sample themed literature sets accompany each chapter.
2. The book emphasizes diversity both in the literature and in the potential audience, including insights into making literary experiences more beneficial for English language learners (ELL) and students with special needs.
3. Best practices in the integration of technology are infused throughout, including ideas for meaningful enhancements.
4. In the Field examples of best practices using literature with young adults are provided.

When working with middle and secondary students I recommend using a variety of book sets with a range of perspectives and styles, lists of choice books with an even more diverse range to accommodate varied interests and needs, and an occasional whole class read to enhance discussion. Because I strongly advocate modeling, I suggest that courses that use this text also use appropriate young adult reading choices. Each chapter includes booklists and the end of the book contains a broader bibliography of recommended titles to choose from. Some wonderful books are undoubtedly not mentioned—over 5,000 titles are published for young people every year and only a sampling of those can be included here. However, tips for locating additional and current titles are provided throughout the text.

I also strongly advocate performance-based assessments and the dialogue and interactions they can promote. Student comprehension of the history of young adult literature, the characteristics of a particular genre, and understandings of literary theory and adolescent development might be tested to a certain extent, but this only provides a fleeting snapshot of the student's knowledge and abilities. I recommend an array of assessments with the most important component being that all assessments reinforce and feed back into learning.

Acknowledgments

This book is written in the hopes that my own children Nicolas and Nathan will have the potential to read a variety of high quality books in school and for pleasure when they are young adults.

The manuscript could never have been finished without the persistence of Linda Bishop and Cynthia Parsons, the resolve of the team at Omegatype Typography, the support of Margaret Bolovan, and the participation of all of the incredible authors, illustrators, and experts who contributed their voices. James Hessen and Brittany Krempel helped greatly with the editing. Thanks to those who helped by providing permissions and graphics for the book. The authors, illustrators, experts, and young adults who contributed their words and their works make the book what it is. I would also like to thank the following reviewers for their helpful comments on the manuscript: Bonnie Armburster, University of Illinois, Chicago; Karen Coats, Illinois State University; Ward Cockrum, Northern Arizona University; A. Waller Hastings, Northern State University; Ruth Oswald, University of Akron; Peggy Rice, Ball State University; and Alice Trupe, Bridgewater College.

My mother Adrienne and my grandmother Violet instilled in me a great love of literature. Mentors including Janet Hickman and Rudine Sims Bishop taught me everything I know about exploring books with young people. Special thanks to the childlit community for being an essential forum for discussion, and especially to Michael Joseph for his feedback on the literary theory.

1

Literature for Young Adults

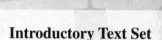

Introductory Text Set

Afterlife by Gary Soto

The Breadwinner by Deborah Ellis

Monster by Walter Dean Myers

Rats Saw God by Rob Thomas

The Sisterhood of the Traveling Pants by Ann Brashares

A Step from Heaven by An Na

The Wanderer by Sharon Creech

Whale Talk by Chris Crutcher

What Happened to Lani Garver by C. Plum-Ucci

Diverse Voices Text Set

The Absolutely True Diary of a Part Time Indian by Sherman Alexie

Ask Me No Questions by Marina Budhos

Beacon Hill Boys by Ken Mochizuki

Born Confused by Tanuja Desai Hidier

Buried Onions by Gary Soto

Call Me Maria by Judith Cofer

Harlem Hustle by Janet McDonald

Thief of Hearts by Laurence Yep

Classroom Scene I

A college student doing her field placement for a secondary education/English course has been told by the professor to inventory the literature used in a tenth-grade classroom. A bookcase behind the mentor teacher's desk holds 30 copies of several titles as well as assorted dictionaries. After determining that the students read four novels in common and use an anthology with a variety of excerpts and short stories, she asks the teacher what else they read to reach the state curricular goal of "the equivalent of twenty-four novels" during the year. The mentor teacher gives her an incredulous look and answers, "Honey, we're lucky if they read these four!"

Classroom Scene II

A college student doing her field placement for a secondary education/English course has been told by the professor to inventory the literature used in a tenth-grade classroom. The room has several shelves loaded with a wide variety of novels, anthologies, and nonfiction books. The walls are covered with author studies, poems, and student projects. On top of the corner bookshelf a half dozen books are on display with a sign "Recommended Books of the Week." When asked about the state curricular goal of 24 novels during the year, the mentor teacher smiles and replies, "Oh sure! We have two whole-class reads and four literature circle sets. Then we do a poetry unit. But the majority of the readings come from the two books per month that they have to select to read and journal on."

Library Scene I

A 16-year-old boy required to read two novels over winter vacation has gone to the public library. He has a list of books recommended to him by friends and by his teacher. When he uses the computer catalogue he discovers that only three of the books are available. Two are in the children's section. Glancing over at the kids and parents milling about in "Children's Books" he decides to try for the third book, which is located in the adult section. After a thirty-minute search he hurriedly grabs the book off the shelf, noticing only that it seems from the cover to be about a dog and a boy. "Oh man," he thinks. "Whatever! I'm not spending any more time in here."

Library Scene II

A 16-year-old boy required to read two novels over winter vacation has gone to the public library. Approaching the Teen Scene section he sees a group of young adults lounging on sofas reading books and magazines. The young adult librarian, who is straightening the graphic novel display, asks a young woman walking by if she plans on coming to the meeting of the Teen Advisory Council to go over new book orders. The young man slides the booklist he is carrying back into his pocket when he notices the display of new acquisitions. He begins to browse through the books and ends up leaving with three interesting novels.

There are numerous ways professionals who work with young adults can help them make connections with literature. However, in order to do so effectively these professionals need to know something about the developmental and social needs of young adults. And it goes without saying that they need to know a lot about the literature available. The obvious place to start such an exploration is by taking a look at what we actually are referring to when we use the term *young adult literature.*

Defining Young Adult Literature

Though at first many readers would imagine defining young adult (YA) literature to be a matter of common sense, distinguishing literature for children, young adults, and adults is actually the subject of much debate. Are these categories based solely on age? Reading level? Interest? Do we mean books written for a particular age range, books marketed for this group, or books read by a certain number of people in this demographic?

When asked about their favorite books from their high school years, undergraduates in my courses tend to mention a diverse mix of popular adult books, classics, older works of young adult fiction, and novels that are really marketed for readers in the middle grades. Some undergraduates will include more recent YA titles, but this is far from the norm. By and large they simply have not encountered many of these books in the schools they attended. In most school districts, the elementary grades are much more likely to integrate age-appropriate literature than are their secondary counterparts. A majority of my students who are familiar with recent YA literature know these works from sources outside of school.

Getting teens and tweens to read for pleasure is not always a simple process. Finding books that hold their interest can be essential. Photo by Jennifer Seay.

What does this mean in terms of defining YA literature? First of all, it would serve us well to remember that teenagers are going to enjoy a wide range of reading materials. If a student is excited about Kurt Vonnegut or Alice Walker, there is certainly no reason to discourage this interest. If they are just at this age discovering Jerry Spinnelli's *Maniac Magee* or J. K. Rowlings's *Harry Potter and the Sorcerer's Stone,* these books are much more likely to enhance their reading skills than to detract from them. The fact that students are engaging with text is more significant than pigeonholing their reading level. Many ninth graders will in fact be challenged and excited by these books, and if they help build an interest in reading, the effects can be far reaching.

At the same time there is a specific array of literature written or marketed for a teen audience. These are the books that, in a growing number of libraries, are housed in a "Young Adult" or "Teen" section. The literature that falls into this more specific category are the works we are most concerned with in this text. The following attributes frequently identify literature as being YA:

- Written for young adults
- Read by young adults
- Teenage protagonist
- Young adult perspective

Written for Young Adults

Most young adult books were written and marketed for a teen audience. However, there are many exceptions. *The Chocolate War* (1974) by Robert Cormier, a staple of young adult literature, was initially written for an adult audience but wisely marketed by the publisher in a juvenile collection. *Ender's Game* (1985) by Orson Scott Card is a science fiction title written and marketed for adults, but (like many fantasy and science fiction novels) it holds themes that are extremely popular with some young adults. In fact, because so many adult books have appeal for young adults, the Alex Awards have been created specifically to honor these books. *Imani All Mine* (1999) by Conni Porter and *A Long Way from Home: Memoirs of a Boy Soldier* (2007) by Ishmael Beah are just two of the books that have received this award. Both could easily have been marketed as YA books.

Quite a few authors who are best known for their YA literature did not have that audience in mind when they wrote their first books. Rob Thomas did not consider *Rats Saw God* to be a YA novel until a publisher saw the potential for a teen audience. The idea that a publisher would make such a vital decision is actually not that uncommon. "Such distinctions are necessary for publishers," asserts author Julius Lester, "but not for me as a writer. I write and let the publisher figure out what age group it fits" (see Lester interview, p. 73). Indeed, many authors of young adult literature insist that they are not thinking of audience as the primary consideration when they write. The characters and the storyline seem to be much more significant. An Na suggests that "it's up to the characters or the story to unfold in the way that it needs to. Thinking about the audience seems to be jumping ahead of oneself" (see Na interview, p. 18). Aidan Chambers asserts that when he first started writing, he did think explicitly about audience. He was a teacher writing with his own students in mind. However, he then "made the shift from being a *writer* to being an *author*" (see

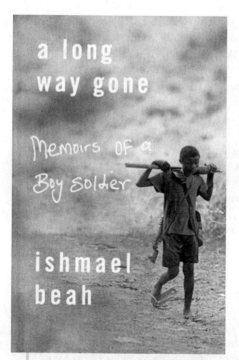

Ishmael Beah's *A Long Way Gone* (2007) is one of many mainstream adult books popular with young adults. Jacket design by Jennifer Carrow from *A Long Way Gone: Memoirs of a Boy Soldier* by Ishmael Beah. Jacket design copyright © 2007 by Jennifer Carrow. Jacket photograph copyright © 2007 by Michael Kamber/Polaris.

Chambers interview, p. 182). Writers, he suggests, focus on the reader, whereas authors focus on the text.

At some level though, literature is generally affected by the audience. "I write my first draft without thought to my audience at all," states Donna Jo Napoli. "Then, once I know what my story is (something I do not know until I've finished that draft), I consider the audience and that consideration often leads me to develop certain scenes more than others" (Napoli, 2006). Editors also tend to keep a focus on audience, both when reviewing a manuscript and when making the choices about which manuscripts to accept for publication. In the introduction to *Places I Never Meant to Be,* Judy Blume discusses an editor's influential concerns over the situations and language that appear in her books. The same editor who had been so supportive when she was writing *Are You There God? It's Me, Margaret* became much more hesitant about working with controversial material in the 1990s. Even Blume, an established author, found herself caving in and removing mature lines from *Tiger Eyes.* Imagine the changes many less established authors have accepted as editors attempt to make their literature more "appropriate" for the intended audience.

One related trend in which audience is explicitly considered can be found in the growing popularity of adapting books originally written for adults to the YA market. Da Chen's *China's Son: Growing Up in the Cultural Revolution* is an adaptation of a section of his bestselling adult book *Colors of the Mountain.* The adult trade edition of *American Patriots: The Story of Blacks in the Military* by Gail Buckley was adapted for a YA market by Tonya Bolden. So although the age of the intended audience is often significant, the borders are quite fluid and frequently traversed with marketing and editorial decisions playing an important role in determining what is classified as YA.

Read by Young Adults

A number of critics have argued that the YA label should be applied to those works of literature that are actually read by young adults, including works written for adults or children that have become favorites of young adults. With some books this is practical, but the question arises—how many young adults need to read a book to classify it this way? What do we do with the book that is written for young adults but primarily read by preteens, or books like *Harry Potter and the Sorcerer's Stone,* read by everyone from second graders to retirees?

Patrick Jones asserts that publishers have started to realize that (or have even helped create the idea that) there are actually several overlapping YA markets: the 10- to 14-year-olds who are the traditional YA book readers and a new market of 14- to 20+-year-olds looking for edgier books—"for the adults in young adults" (1998, n.p.). The lines are often

Alyce Shirleydaughter

Author LouAnne Johnson (alias Alyce Shirleydaughter), the teacher featured in the book and film *Dangerous Minds*, purposefully wrote two versions of her novel, wanting to have an authentic narrative for young adults to read but also knowing that the cleaner version of the book would be used in more schools. Now *Yo! Eddie!* (2007) and *Alternative Eddie* (2007) exist in a third version, *Muchacho* (Knopf, 2009). © LouAnne Johnson, 2006. Reprinted by permission.

blurred and we see novels like Block's Weetzie series being cross-marketed to adult audiences. In fact the term "cross-marketing" is being discussed openly in some publishing houses with plans to release "two editions of a title—one still aimed at the library YA market, with another aimed at bookstores and [the twentysomething] coffee shop hang out crowd" (Jones, 1998, n.p.). Generally the only difference between these two editions is in the marketing and perhaps the cover illustration. Occasionally a book like *Yo Eddie* by LouAnne Johnson will be published with an adult edition (*Alternative Eddie*) that does have stronger language and more explicit scenes.

In Britain, books in the Harry Potter series have been printed in a special adult edition, with the only real difference being the cover. The change is meant to add appeal for the mature audience. Garth Nix's fantasy novel *Ragwitch*, which was published as an adult fantasy by Tor Books, has been remarketed by HarperCollins Children's Books with a cover that will catch the eye of younger readers. This type of cross-marketing sometimes defies logic. Jennifer Armstrong's *In My Hands: Memories of a Holocaust Rescuer* was published in hardback for young readers (Knopf), but the paperback was published on an adult list (Anchor).

Teenage Protagonist

The majority of books read by young adults have characters of roughly the same age or slightly older than the readers. Many authors who did not really consider audience when writing their novels suggest that the age of their characters is actually more significant. Chris Crutcher, for example, asserts, "Adolescence is such a raw time that it's ripe for stories. I don't usually think of myself as writing for young adults as I do writing about young adults" (see Crutcher interview, p. 29). Rob Thomas also builds on this idea: "At its best, YA literature isn't much different than adult fiction except in the age of the protagonists and the choice of themes. I think the best YA writers don't try to write to teens; they write about them" (personal correspondence, 2006).

However, although this is generally true, it certainly is not always the case. The protagonist might be an adult, a 300-year-old vampire, or a dog, or there might be 16 protagonists, as in Paul Fleischman's *Bull Run,* some of whom are adult and some adolescents. Still, the narrative is more likely to appeal to the young adult audience if they can relate to the characters, so youthful protagonists are the norm in YA books.

On the flip side, many novels marketed for adults also have teen protagonists. As Donna Jo Napoli suggests, sometimes the only distinction is who publishes the book: "*The Bluest Eye*

We were getting our stuff from our lockers at the end of the day, and Rowley came up to me and said—

WANT TO COME OVER TO MY HOUSE AND PLAAYYY?

I have told Rowley at least a billion times that now that we're in middle school, you're supposed to say "hang out," not "play." But no matter how many noogies I give him, he always forgets the next time.

I've been trying to be a lot more careful about my image ever since I got to middle school. But having Rowley around is definitely not helping.

18

Diary of a Wimpy Kid (Abrams, 2007) is being read by third graders and eighth graders. The humor seems to work well across age groups though the character is facing middle school problems and issues. Reprinted by permission of Abrams.

could as easily have been published as a YA, but it was published by an adult press, so it's considered an adult book" (see Napoli interview, p. 163). Many coming-of-age novels marketed for an adult audience have been discovered by teen readers and the people who work with them. Again there are no facile distinctions between adult and young adult books, but there are generalities, such as that young readers often like to read about young characters.

Young Adult Perspective

Young adults, like all readers, are much more likely to read a book that deals with issues and problems relevant to their lives. Some authors do undoubtedly think about their audience and what they would be interested in reading; others enter into what Aidan Chambers calls "young adult consciousness," meaning that

> young adult literature is written in the consciousness of a young adult. It isn't just a question of "seeing life through young adult eyes." It is much more than that. The entire book is controlled by the young adult consciousness of the narrator (who might or might not be a character in the story). (see Chambers interview, p. 182)

Many authors who are popular with young adults suggest that they actually enter into the character of the protagonist as they write. Mary Casanova asserts, "Like an actor on stage, I try to step as fully as possible into the shoes of my character. When I do this, the narrative seems to come pretty naturally from my character" (see Casanova interview, p. 262). Other authors draw on the worldview they remember or that they see expressed by the young people they encounter, and they create their literary worlds from within this worldview. Some authors are more successful at this than others; often when a reader balks at a preachy or overly didactic scene in a book, it is because the author has stepped outside of this young adult consciousness.

Young adults are going through a number of developmental changes that influence their reading interests: their social identity is developing; they are necessarily negotiating new roles in their families and in their work and leisure; love becomes an issue for them; peers are becoming increasingly important, resulting in peer pressure and conformity as major issues; and teens are becoming sensitive to the complexities of life. There is much written on the developing literacies of young adults. A good place to start is with NCTE's "Adolescent Literacy: A Policy Research Brief," which can be downloaded from NCTE's website at www.ncte.org/collections/adolescentliteracy.

All of these developments are reflected in the literature young adults read. As An Na suggests, "YA literature really deals acutely with the issues and emotions that speak to the lives of young adults" (see Na interview, p. 18). It should be stressed, however, that there is wide variation in physical development, especially in the middle school years, and enormous variation in social development and life experiences—all of which makes it extremely difficult to choose a single novel that will appeal to every eighth grader in a class.

The backgrounds and perspectives of young adults are diverse and if a narrative is not pertinent or the perspective does not ring true, the book is less likely to be read.

> *To Consider*
> When seeking books to use with young adults, how significant do you feel it is that these books be written and marketed for that age group?

These characterizations are not universally true of young adult books, but for every book that might be considered young adult literature, some combination of these elements holds true. Ultimately the term "YA" is a classification that allows librarians to create a section of interest to many young adults, teachers to locate appropriate reading material for middle and secondary students, scholars to explore trends and issues, and publishers to reach out to particular audiences.

Technology Links

Young Adult Library Services Association

The Young Adult Services Division of the American Library Association (ALA) was formed in 1957 and later evolved into the Young Adult Library Services Association (YALSA) in 1992. YALSA's website is one of the premier online resources for information about young adult literature.

The booklists alone make this site a must for anyone serious about young adult literature. The annotated lists include Printz Award winners, Alex Award winners, Quick Picks for Reluctant Young Adult Readers, Popular Paperbacks for Young Adult Readers, and Selected Videos and DVDs for Young Adults. There is also information about YALSA activities, such as Teen Read Week and the Great Book Giveaway contest. One section specifically for young adults, Teen Reading, includes the Teen Top Ten and recommended readings. The site reaches out to teens with a blog, a wiki, and podcasts, as well as through Twitter.

Much of the information and resources on the YALSA website are free and open to the public, though for members there are added resources such as the most up-to-date booklists with annotations. For anyone serious about staying on top of books and media for young adults, membership in YALSA is essential.

For more information visit the YALSA website at www.ala.org/yalsa.

The logo for the Printz Award. Used with the permission of the Young Adult Library Services Association, a division of the American Library Association.

The Printz Award

In 1999, the Michael L. Printz Award for Excellence in Young Adult Literature was established by the American Library Association to identify stellar literature that appeals specifically to the young adult reader. The Printz Award is presented annually to a book that exemplifies literary excellence in young adult

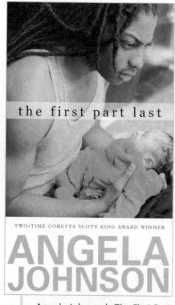

the first part last

TWO-TIME CORETTA SCOTT KING AWARD WINNER

ANGELA JOHNSON

Angela Johnson's *The First Part Last* (2003) was the recipient of both the Printz Award and the Coretta Scott King Award in 2004. Reprinted by permission of Simon Pulse.

literature. The prize is named in memory of a Topeka, Kansas, school librarian who was a longtime active member of YALSA.

Before 1999, literature for young adults was considered alongside literature for children in awarding the Newbery Medal (also an ALA honor). The distinction between the two was certainly welcomed by advocates for YA literature, as it is difficult to compare the literary merits of books for third graders to books for teens. Following is a list of Printz Award winners:

- 2000—*Monster* by Walter Dean Myers
- 2001—*Kit's Wilderness* by David Almond
- 2002—*A Step from Heaven* by An Na
- 2003—*Postcards from No Mans Land* by Aidan Chambers
- 2004—*The First Part Last* by Angela Johnson
- 2005—*How I Live Now* by Meg Rosoff
- 2006—*Looking for Alaska* by John Green
- 2007—*American Born Chinese* by Gene Luen Yang
- 2008—*On the Jellico Toad* by Melina Marchetta
- 2009—*Going Bovine* by Linda Bray

For the full list including honor books visit www.ala.org/yalsa/printz.

Author Spotlight

Photo courtesy of Walter Dean Myers.

Walter Dean Myers

Walter Dean Myers was born in West Virginia in 1937. His mother died when he was 3 and he went to live with the Dean family in Harlem, where he spent most of his youth. At 17 he quit high school and joined the army. Afterward he worked for the New York State Department of Labor, the post office, and a rehabilitation center, all the while writing for periodicals and magazines. In 1984 he graduated from Empire State College. A major change in his writing career came when he won a contest sponsored by the Council on Interracial Books for Children for his book *Where Does a Day Go?* (1969). Since that time he has written numerous books for young adults, as well as poetry, picture books, and nonfiction. Myers was awarded the Margaret A. Edwards Award in 1994, which honors a living author for a distinguished body of young adult literature, and was the U.S. nominee for the Hans Christian Andersen Award in 2010. Visit his website at www.walterdeanmyers.net.

SELECTED BOOKLIST

The Autobiography of My Dead Brother (HarperCollins, 2005)
The Beast (Scholastic, 2003)
Blues Journey, Illus. by Christopher Myers (Holiday House, 2003)
Dope Sick (HarperCollins, 2009)
Fallen Angels (Scholastic, 1988)
Harlem (Scholastic, 1997)
Jazz, Illus. by Christopher Myers (Holiday House, 2006)
Malcolm X (Scholastic, 1993)
Monster (HarperCollins, 1999)
Scorpions (Harper, 1988)
Shadow of the Red Moon (Scholastic, 1995)
Slam (Scholastic, 1996)
Somewhere in the Darkness (Scholastic, 1992)
Sunrise over Fallujah (Scholastic, 2008)

ON HOW HE BEGAN WRITING FOR YOUNG PEOPLE

I began writing for myself. I did not think of myself as a writer for young people. I thought of myself just as a writer, but I wrote about teenagers. Someone said to me, "Oh, this is a young adult book." I said, "What's a young adult book? What does that mean?"

For the picture books there was a contest I saw in the mail. I was living in Queens, New York. I came home one day for some work and my house had been burglarized. Typical New York story. So I was reading a *Writer's Digest* waiting for a carpenter to come repair the door; I saw a contest for black children's writers that was run by the Interracial Council for Children's Books. I said, "Black people don't read this magazine. This is not a black publication, so maybe I have a chance." So I composed a story, sent it off, and it won the contest. Previous to that I had been writing newspaper articles and short fiction, and again much of this fiction dealt with teenagers.

ON WHAT HE ENJOYED READING AS A YOUNG ADULT

My reading was always directed by schools. When I was quite young, I loved *Robin Hood,* all the adventure stuff, *The Three Musketeers,* anything with an adventure. When I got to be an older teenager, 14 and 15, I went to a good high school in New York and the English teacher there turned me on to Balzac and Thomas Mann. . . . That was a major step up for my reading, but I loved it. When I was coming up, no one spoke in New York City schools about the Harlem Renaissance or about black authors.

I didn't actually become a reader of African American literature until I was around 22 or 23. That was because I did not know much about it. As a young man I was deadly serious and wanted the best literature. Then I happened upon *Sonny's*

Blues by James Baldwin. I just found it and I was absolutely taken with it. He was writing about my neighborhood and he was writing in a way that I could say, "Well this is literature!"

ON DIVERSITY AND THE PUBLISHING INDUSTRY

It has expanded (over the last 20 years). The idea that we still categorize is true though. If someone is going to do a sportsbook, for example, they will have one good sportswriter, and he will be *their* good sportswriter. I worked for a publishing firm for 7 years actually, and we had one sportsbook on the list. Someone said, "Well, let's do another one." They said, "Good, but not on this list."

Unfortunately, people of color also are categorized, so you may end up with one or two black books. Occasionally, there is more flexibility. There is more flexibility now than there was 10 years ago. There are fewer publishing companies. So instead of doing eight books with one black author per year, now a publisher might do 50 books with two or three black authors.

But the big difference and what has created the demand is the use of multicultural literature in schools. When the multicultural literature was only in bookstores and libraries, that made a fairly slow market, but now that more and more schools are using books, that makes all the difference in the world. If a school district in Cincinnati includes your book on their reading list, that's more sales to a publisher than if all the libraries in the city bought copies. So that inspires the publishers.

Right now the public school system is predominantly minority in many places. Even in a city like Dallas where the population might only be 30 percent minority, the public schools are more like 70 percent minority. That makes a big difference. That has created a market.

ON WHETHER CULTURAL OUTSIDERS CAN WRITE AUTHENTIC NARRATIVES ABOUT CULTURES OTHER THAN THEIR OWN

What I think happens is that the cultural outsider sees part of the culture and they often misidentify what's going on. You might see an African American family and you can put in the collard greens and they're sitting around the table, and that's just the surface. All families are more intricate than that. One of the real problems I have with some of the writing about other cultures is that so much of the literature is based upon the idea of "Look, I'm accepting another culture!" But yeah, so what?

I don't want to read any more stories about the desperate little black girl that nobody was interested in saving or understanding except the kindly, liberal, white woman. You see so much of that.

I think that when I write about black culture, it's about the people that I know, and the story is not about accepting the people, it's not about saying as a black person you're OK, I don't mind you even though you are black. But it doesn't bother me that other people write about black culture because I feel that if I'm going to write about black culture and can't do a better job than an outsider, then that's my problem.

ON WHETHER HIS OWN LIFE APPEARS IN HIS FICTIONAL WORK

My values are in all the books. I can make up a story about anything, but my values are always there. My values—the values of my family. My sisters read my books and say, "Yeah, well, OK. I know where you got this from and I know where you got that from."

I'm thinking of my son Christopher's work. To see his work and meet Christopher you may not recognize him as my son, but you'll recognize the same values. He is an accumulation of my values and those of his mom (who is an artist). Collaborating with him was a really easy thing to do. He has a lot more formal education than I have. He's full of himself. He is bright and I respect that and he respects me. There are so many things that we do not ever have to discuss and that's going back to that value concept. Our values are more or less the same. Our methods of approaching them are very different, but it is stimulating to work with him. I think I get more out of it than he does. He has this young point of view, sometimes wrong, but always stimulating. He is fun to work with and he challenges me, so it's good.

ON THE IMPACT OF BEING THE FIRST
RECIPIENT OF THE PRINTZ AWARD

At first I thought it had no impact but then I realized that it had. It attracted an awful lot of attention. The book has been published in Turkish, Dutch, Japanese. The book is being published all around the world. That was a very enjoyable thing. And I think the Printz Award emphasizes good literature for a certain age group. Also receiving the distinction has given me, I think, more freedom with my writing. It has been one of the happiest publications of my life.

Young Adult Literature in Schools

Many teachers of young adults, especially at the high school level, feel that they have the duty to expose young people to the classics, the literature that has withstood the test of time and represents the best that Western civilization has to offer. Even in many school systems where very creative things are done with literature in the early years, in high school English classes teachers get down to the business of preparing students for college by reading Shakespeare, Poe, and Dickens. Although these are certainly great authors and many colleges would expect their students to be at least somewhat familiar with their works, there are some problems with this scenario.

First and foremost, we have to question our motives for teaching literature. Is the overarching idea to help teens become lifelong readers? If so, what would be the best means of achieving this goal? Teacher's Discovery, a publisher from Michigan, started the Red Readers series that publishes versions of classics with contemporary translations. In *Romeo and Juliet* the famous speech "But soft! What light through yonder window breaks? It is the east and Juliet is the sun" is translated as "Juliet is a hotty!" Some teens might read and enjoy this dual language edition. They will certainly get the basic storyline, even if they only read the "translations," and it is always possible that the humor will entice them to read the original. The larger question concerns what we are hoping teens will learn from reading literature. If we just want to make sure they know the basic storylines of a handful of classics, we could google the SparkNotes and be done with it. But if we are interested in developing readers, there are scores of beautifully written YA novels that use language in inventive ways and engage readers in critical thought and in the pleasures of language.

The common refrain heard from college students is "I haven't read a book that wasn't assigned for a course in years." At the beginning of the semester students in my young adult literature course moan that they will never be able to read 12 or 13 novels in a semester, but by the end of the session a majority of them have sought out sequels, other books by an author they enjoyed, or books recommended by other students! They tend to read beyond the requirements for the course. We discuss this phenomenon in class and especially how this same enthusiasm for reading might affect young adults in their middle and secondary school years. For example, the following benefits have been asserted for YA literature:

- Can reconnect young people with the idea of reading for pleasure
- Engages readers in literary worlds and so helps develop the imagination
- Involves narrative that reflects the way young people construct and communicate their realities
- Provides vicarious experiences and new perspectives
- Reveals patterns of experience and insights into the human condition
- Cumulatively enhances reading and writing skills
- Builds vocabulary and literary discourse at an appropriate level
- Enhances grammatical understanding
- Helps develop familiarity with story structures and conventions
- Introduces facts and cultural knowledge embedded in the story

So what does literature for young adults look like? The reading preferences of any two 12-year-olds can be quite distinct. The reading interests of a 12-year-old and an 18-year-old can be worlds apart. So it should come as no surprise that there is an enormous variety in the types of books that appear under the classification of young adult literature. For example, recent popular YA books that have received critical praise include the following varied stories:

- A young girl in Taliban-controlled Afghanistan who has to dress as a boy to support her family after her father is arrested. (*The Breadwinner,* Ellis, 2001)

- An athletic teen who dislikes organized sports but still helps his English teacher create a swim team made up of some of the biggest outsiders at his high school. (*Whale Talk,* Crutcher, 2001)

- A young Korean immigrant who thinks she is moving to heaven when she comes to America but soon discovers that life is much more complicated. (*A Step from Heaven,* Na, 2001)

- A young man who is murdered within the first few pages of the book and then spends the rest of the story learning something about himself and maybe even falling in love. (*The Afterlife,* Soto, 2003)

- A newcomer to an island community (who might be a boy or a girl or maybe even an angel!) helps the teen narrator (who is in remission from cancer) gain control of her life, but is attacked (maybe even murdered) by local ruffians. (*What Happened to Lani Garver,* Plum-Ucci, 2002)

- A high school senior, former A student who is an outsider in his new school and estranged from his astronaut father, is given a chance to keep from failing if he will write a 100-page essay about his life. (*Rats Saw God,* Thomas, 1996)

- The summer adventures of four girls who though separated stay connected through a magical pair of blue jeans. (*The Sisterhood of the Traveling Pants,* Brashares, 2001)

- A young man, referred to by his prosecutor as a "monster," who is on trial for being an accomplice to murder, which he may or may not have done, tells his own story, alternating between journal entries and a movie script. (*Monster,* Myers, 1999)

- A young woman who sets out to cross the Atlantic in a boat with her uncles and two cousins. (*The Wanderer,* Creech, 2000)

> *To Consider*
>
> If you are going to provide young adults with a wide array of books to choose from, how significant is it that you as the teacher or librarian have read all of the books before putting them on the shelf or adding them to the list?

Different readers might get interested in a particular book based on the topic, the cover, what they have heard about the book from peers, and so on. Although many young adults might find that they actually enjoy reading all of the books listed, having a choice in at least some of what they read is a significant element in becoming a lifelong reader (Moore et al., 1999). The very idea that people might read for pleasure is a foreign concept for many teens, and it will remain so unless they encounter books that are relevant to them.

Booktalks

Many teachers and librarians have found that booktalks will not only guide students to quality literature but will actually hook them, getting them excited about reading. A booktalk typically involves introducing the book and why it is a compelling read without revealing too much about the plot. For instance, a booktalk on Walter Dean Myers's *Monster* might start with the following introduction:

> Imagine you are a good student who has managed to stay out of trouble—even though there is trouble all around you. You have family members who care, friends who stand by you, teachers who know you will do well—now imagine that was yesterday. Today you stand accused of being an accomplice to murder, of being—as the prosecutor refers to you—a monster. While awaiting your trial you are put in prison, not juvie but the real thing . . .

edited by **Jon Scieszka**

Jon Scieszka has been a moving force behind Guys Read, an effort to help male readers find material they can get excited about reading. Part of this effort has been to edit *Guys Write for Guys Read* (2005), which brings together stories with reluctant male reader appeal by some of the best storytellers. Reprinted by permission of Penguin Group (USA).

Generally the booktalk will include at least one passage from the book. I have watched the faces of reluctant ninth-grade readers change from passive to enthralled as they listen to the beginning of *Monster:*

> The best time to cry is at night when the lights are out and someone is being beaten up and screaming for help. That way even if you sniffle a little they won't hear you. If anybody knows that you are crying, they'll start talking about it and soon it'll be your turn to get beat up when the lights go out. (p. 1)

Likewise a booktalk on *What Happened to Lani Garver* by Carol Plum-Ucci could not fail to grab many readers' attention with the following:

> It was during an Indian summer spell in early November that Lani Garver first came to Hackett. And in the frosty, windy, fogless hours between Indian summer and an impending ice storm, I watched a bunch of guys try to drown him. I watched Lani sink in the murky waters of the harbor, and I never saw him resurface. (p. x)

Then you reel them in with a line like "If you want to know what happens next you will need to read the book!" Reluctant readers will often ask for more and afterward hurry to the library shelf. One of the greatest joys of working with young adults is to see that young person who never willingly picks up a book nonchalantly work their way over to the shelves after a booktalk, looking for a title that caught their attention. Teachers, media specialists, and students can serve as literary agents by recommending and sharing loved books to and with each other.

In the Field *Joni Richards Bodart on Booktalks*

Joni Richards Bodart is an internationally known expert on booktalking. Since 1977, Bodart has written around 20 books on the subject of booktalking. She has taught at both Emporia State University and the University of Denver. Since 2006 she has been in the School of Library and Information Science at San Jose State University, where she is in charge of the youth curriculum and also teaches in the areas of reader's advisory and collection development. Her most recent title is Radical Reads 2: Working with the Newest Edgy Titles for Teens *(Scarecrow, 2010), which examines recent controversial titles for teens. For more information and a wide collection of booktalks, check out Bodart's website at www .thebooktalker.com.*

ON CREATING AN EFFECTIVE BOOKTALK

A lot of things go into creating an effective booktalk: choosing an intriguing aspect to focus on; good writing techniques that help hook the kids; excellent presentation skills to put the content across; and, perhaps the most important thing, the booktalker's connection with and enthusiasm about the book—that's really what sells it, in the final analysis.

ON THE RESPONSE OF YOUNG ADULTS TO BOOKTALKS

I've always found that teens respond positively to booktalking, but they show their response in different ways, based on their age and "coolness" levels. High school students always have a less obvious response than younger kids, but that doesn't mean that they aren't listening or won't want to read the books you talk about. Middle school students are more overt in their response, and more likely to want to actually pick up and look at the books and talk with the booktalker when the presentation is over, whereas high school students, by and large, are too cool for that. But with both ages, the books do get checked out—and that's the ultimate measure of success!

ON THE FORMAT AND LENGTH OF BOOKTALKS FOR YOUNG ADULTS

I like to vary the type and length of the booktalks I use in a presentation for teens. However, I'm more likely to use longer talks with older teens, and include talks on adult titles that I think they will respond to. Using different types of talks, changing the focus from character to plot to mood, makes my presentation more lively and dynamic, just like using talks of different lengths. With younger teens, I use more short talks, and allow more time at the end of the presentation for them to come up and look at the books. That isn't really necessary for older kids, who don't generally tend to want to do that. I do make sure that I mention the title and author of the book when I begin my talk, and repeat at least the title when I end it, sometimes working it into the last sentence of the talk. I also make sure that I display the cover so everyone can see it, both at the beginning and the end of the talk. If they can recognize the cover later, when they come to the library, they won't have to ask anyone for it, but can just pick it up.

I think it's better to do a group of talks on a variety of titles, so there's "something for everyone." Doing just one talk at a time won't interest everyone in the group, and doing several on different genres or topics will do two things: interest more of the audience, because they won't all like the same thing, and the presentation itself will build excitement and energy as it goes on, something that won't happen when you stop after just one. As for how often should a specific group hear booktalks, that really depends on a huge number of factors—how much time does the booktalker have to devote to booktalking; how much time will a specific teacher donate to booktalking, given that most teachers feel that they already have too much material to present in too little time; what are the needs of the group that are being met by booktalking; how available are the titles being presented; and what are the goals of the booktalker and the teacher. Most of the time, in my experience, if I am going to individual classrooms, I won't be able to visit any one of them more than twice a semester, because I just don't have enough time. In addition, many teachers aren't interested in more than one visit per class per semester. In a school where I don't go to classrooms, but talk to several classes at once in the school library, I generally go about once or twice a month, but even in that situation, I don't see the same kids more than twice a semester, and usually only once.

ON CHOOSING BOOKS TO BOOKTALK

I know I have to hook the group with my first talk, so it's one I really enjoy, and one that has a definite hook to it—something intriguing or gory or scary or controversial—something that will make them want to find out more about it. The main part of the presentation can be structured any of several ways, including mini-theme groupings of books, alternating books for boys and girls, varying talks by length and type, and so on. And then I always try and end with another book that I'm sure will stick in their minds afterwards, one like the first title I talked about.

YA literature has so many good authors writing about so many relevent issues that teens have to face today, and I don't want kids to skip over them to go on to adult titles too quickly. Most fiction for teens today is actually better written than fiction for adults. Adults will put up with poor quality more easily than teens will. If the author doesn't get their attention right away, and write in a style that will keep their attention, teens will put down the book and go on to something else. Adults are more likely to just keep reading, just so they can finish the book. Teens don't have time for that and so demand more from their authors.

In addition, YA literature covers subjects that are difficult and controversial, ideas that some adults, including some parents, are uncomfortable talking to teens about, even though teens need to hear about them. Drugs, sex, abuse, betrayal, bullies, prejudice, anger, and isolation are not easy topics to discuss, and today's YA literature is full of these and other problems, so teens can get the intellectual and emotional information they so badly need.

I look for the best in YA literature to share with teens; at the same time I also look for titles with strong characters that my audience will feel a connection with, a plot that will interest them, and a dynamic writing style that will intrigue them. And of course, the book has to be one that I responded strongly to, or I'll never be able to convince anyone to read it. Of course, the next question is what if you have to do a talk on a book you don't like? The answer is to find something about it that I DO like and focus my talk around that quality or character. And that can be really hard. Unless I have to, I avoid titles I don't really enjoy talking about because it is so hard to put them across effectively.

ON THE REWARDS OF BOOKTALKING

For me, booktalking is without a doubt the most fun and most effective way of persuading kids to read. For some, it comes quickly and easily; for others, learning the techniques means lots of hard work. But in either instance, the rewards for both the booktalker and the audience of teens are more than worth it. I've found it to be more than addictive, and when I don't have time to do it for a while, I begin to feel the need to get back to it, even though it means taking time to read more, write more, and practice more. Watching kids hang on every word, scribble down titles, and come up to snatch up the books afterward is a rush that can't be forgotten. And it's not just kids. Just yesterday, in a Denver middle school, I was doing talks when another teacher walked into the back of the room. She obviously was going to talk to the teacher who'd invited me, but decided to wait a minute until I finished or got to a stopping point. Once she started to listen, she was just as interested as the kids, and ended up staying for the rest of the class and writing down the titles she wanted to read. I just had to grin inside. "Gotcha!"

Author Spotlight

Reprinted by permission of Penguin Putnam.

An Na

An Na was born in Korea and grew up in San Diego. She graduated from Amherst College and received an MFA from Norwich University. Before becoming a full-time writer she was a middle school teacher. *A Step from Heaven,* her first novel, was the 2002 winner of the Printz Award. The novel follows the life of Ju as she grows from a toddler in Korea to a high school graduate in California. Before coming to America the young girl envisions her new country as heaven. In reality her family faces many obstacles, not the least of which is balancing her desire to be all American with her parents' demand that she retain her Korean heritage. Visit her website at www.anwriting.com.

SELECTED BOOKLIST
The Fold (Putnam, 2008)
A Step from Heaven (Front Street, 2001)
Wait for Me (Puffin, 2007)

ON HOW SHE BECAME AN AUTHOR OF YA LITERATURE

This was quite accidental. I entered the MFA in Writing Children's Literature at Vermont College with the idea that I would be doing picture books. But during my time there, I became involved in writing vignettes in the style of Sandra Cisneros, *The House on Mango Street.* With the encouragement of my advisor, I sent it off to Front Street who really specialize in YA literature and they accepted the manuscript.

ON WHETHER SHE WRITES WITH A PARTICULAR AUDIENCE IN MIND

I don't write with an audience in mind. Rather, it's up to the characters or the story to unfold in the way that it needs to. Thinking about the audience seems to be jumping ahead of oneself. If the story is good, there will be an audience for it.

ON THE INSPIRATION FOR HER STORIES

I had read *The House on Mango Street* in college and loved the way Cisneros captured childhood through such poetic means. I wanted to be able to capture the immediacy of Young Ju's childhood along those same lines. When I read good books, I am inspired. My first love will always be reading. Growing up, reading was my escape, my teacher, my heart. Good stories fueled my imagination, made me believe in other worlds and lives. I still get that high when I run across a good story, a good book that won't let me go. It makes me want to aspire to create worlds that entrap others.

ON THE EXTENT TO WHICH HER OWN LIFE STORY APPEARS IN HER WORKS

Some of the vignettes are definitely inspired by my own memories. For instance, the vignette about getting a perm before coming to America. That actually happened! But I don't remember the specifics of how that all took place. Rather, I have a faint recollection and a picture of myself with curly hair. Drawing on that one idea, I imagined what it might be like for this character, Young Ju, to experience the transformation from straight to curly hair and the meaning that holds for her. I think all writing to a certain extent draws on one's own life and experiences. Even the stories that seem the most remote or different, the writer must still infuse the heart of the character with emotions that are real and keen in order for the story to be believable to a reader. A good story draws from the blood of the writer into its work.

ON WHAT DISTINGUISHES YOUNG ADULT LITERATURE

I think YA literature really deals acutely with the issues and emotions that speak to the lives of young adults. To teenagers that balance between the world they are leaving behind, childhood, to a world that isn't quite accepting or accessible to them, the adult realm.

ON WHAT MIGHT HELP YOUNG ADULTS DEVELOP AS WRITERS

Read read read. Learn from those who are better than you. Learn from loving stories. And write write write. Stories, thoughts, musings, sketches. Whatever you want. Just because it doesn't have structure, it doesn't mean that isn't good writing. Sure, stories have coherence, but most stories begin with writing that speaks, and to give your writing a voice, you must practice.

ON WHETHER AUTHORS CAN WRITE CONVINCINGLY ABOUT CULTURAL EXPERIENCES THAT ARE NOT THEIR OWN

I think an author can try. Sometimes that is good enough and other times it falls short. However, in the attempt to write outside of one's own culture or voice, it is imperative that your motivations and research be thoroughly examined. As with any kind of writing, the character must be developed with thoughtfulness, not just because it would be exciting to have the character be black or Asian or a different gender than one's own. Why are you choosing to write outside of your experience? Does it do anything for the story? Could you write the same story with a character of your same gender or cultural background? If the answer is yes, then I think it's important to consider the reasons why you want to write outside your "experience." If you still do decide to create a character of a different culture or background, make sure the research is right on. If you were going to write historical fiction, you would want to make sure that all the facts are in place. While I certainly believe in artistic license, one must also consider the issue of power. Race, class, gender, sexuality, these are all loaded issues. If you are a male, wealthy, straight man trying to write from the perspective of a poor black woman, what is the power dynamic there? Similarly, if you are taking folktales from other countries and other cultures, who's directly benefiting from these tellings? Why not choose to retell or investigate folktales from one's own culture? Certainly, giving voice to stories that we might not be aware of has benefits to all, but in the end, whose story is it to tell? I mean, are these "other" folktales or perspectives coming out because there is a certain sense that the dominant culture or voice is bankrupt in terms of newness and thrill factor? Could it be a form of colonialism to take these stories? It's a hard call, I think. On the one hand, if these stories and perspectives were not out there, just making the general public aware of them could open the door to other writers who are from that background. And yet, if the writing is not done in such a way as to be sensitive and thoughtful, you could be doing more harm than good. To walk that fine line, awareness of your own motivations and of the other culture or background is crucial.

ON WHETHER THERE ARE TOPICS THAT AUTHORS FOR YOUNG ADULTS SHOULD AVOID

I have one word for that question: television. Honestly, I think all topics can be dealt with if it's done with sensitivity. Many young adults are aware of topics that even adults can't handle. I find that writers are oftentimes in the role of trying to undo some of the damage that has been done by movies and television.

ON HOW WINNING THE PRINTZ AWARD IMPACTS HER WRITING

Well, I've been thinking about retirement lately. The Printz Award for a first novel? How do I top that? I can't. I just have to keep going, keep writing, and find the characters that speak to me. To have my first novel be recognized with the Printz was tremendous and also extremely lucky. In the end, I don't write for awards, I write because I am moved to tell a story.

An Introduction to Audio Books

Teachers, librarians, parents, and teens seek out audio books for a variety of reasons. Of course, some narratives simply beg for reading aloud and with the right reader this can be a pleasurable experience in and of itself. For some students the audio version makes the literature more accessible. People with visual impairments, students who are learning English as a foreign language, and students with special needs, for example, might benefit greatly from the availability of audio books.

Some teachers have used audio books quite effectively to discuss narrative interpretation. The oral "reading" adds new layers of meaning through elements such as intonation, voice, and the use of background music. These elements set the mood, create or reinforce tension, and define character. Many of the same critical elements discussed in Chapter 4 concerning young adult drama come into play when comparing the written text with its oral interpretation. Lists of some selected audio books are included throughout *Literature and the Young Adult Reader.* You might want to start by taking a look at the following list.

Audio books have become quite popular with some teens. Some schools and media centers now have books preloaded on MP3 players for patrons to check out. Photo by Diallo Sessoms.

To Consider

Individual students might listen to audio books at home or even with headphones in class, perhaps as they read along with the text, but are there any benefits to using audio books with the whole class?

Audio Books

Diversity and Literature

The Breadwinner by Deb Ellis; read by Rita Wolf. (Random House, 2002)

Buried Onions by Gary Soto; read by Robert Ramirez. (Recorded Books, 2001) (Y)

Habibi by Naomi Shihab Nye; read by Christina Moore. (Recorded Books, 1999) (Y)

Homeless Bird by Gloria Whelan; read by Sarita Choudhury. (Listening Library, 2001) (N)

Jesse by Gary Soto; read by Robert Ramirez. (Recorded Books, 1999) (Y)

Monster by Walter Dean Myers; read by a full cast. (Listening Library, 2000) (A, Y)

Parrot in the Oven: Mi Vida by Victor Martinez; read by the author. (Harper Audio, 1998) (Y)

The Sisterhood of the Traveling Pants by Ann Brashares; read by Angela Goethals. (Listening Library, 2001) (A, Y)

A Step from Heaven by An Na; read by Jina Oh. (Listening Library, 2002) (Y)

The Thief Lord by Cornelia Funke; read by Simon Jones. (Listening Library, 2005) (N)

The Wanderer by Sharon Creech; read by John Beach and Dana Lubotsky. (Listening Library, 2000)

Whale Talk by Chris Crutcher; read by Brian Corrigan. (Listening Library, 2001) (Y)

Zazoo by Richard Moser; read by Joanna Wyatt. (Listening Library, 2002) (Y)

    A—Audiofile Earphones Award

    N—ALSC Notable Children's Recording

    Y—YALSA Selected List of Audiobooks

In the Field · *Pam Spencer Holley on Audio Books*

Pam Spencer Holley is a retired school librarian and former president of YALSA. She has served on the Audio Book and Media Exploration Committee and has chaired the Printz Award Committee. This article was originally published by Listening Library in Books on Tape 2007.

Look around. Teens everywhere seem to have headphones on or in their ears. This fact, together with studies showing a positive correlation between listening to audio books and reading improvement, is leading teachers and librarians to use audio books in their classrooms and libraries. With this increase in audio book usage, I reviewed the literature (various articles, presentations, and conversations) to compile a list of the reasons why teen listening is important, beyond just the enjoyment factor. Here is that list:

Ten Top Educational Benefits of Teen Audio Book Listening

  10. Removes any stigma of lower reading levels or "uncool" genres

   9. Increases vocabulary skills

   8. Improves speaking and writing skills

   7. Introduces storytelling, an important tradition in human history

   6. Engages imagination by allowing teens to create mental images of the story

   5. Improves listening skills—essential in this multimedia world

   4. Makes mundane, yet necessary tasks (exercising, dishwashing, room cleaning) more tolerable

   3. Keeps teens informed of popular books or latest releases from favorite authors

   2. Improves ability to multitask and complete assignments simultaneously

   1. Listening is an important step for becoming a life-long reader

Librarians and educators are in agreement that teens should, and do, listen to audiobooks—but are teens listening for all of the educational benefits stated in the literature? To answer this question, I left the literature behind and asked a small group of teens (and a preteen) to complete an informal survey. This survey yielded the following information:

Top Ten Reasons Why Teens *Really* Listen to Audio Books

10. Listening is easier than reading
 9. Listening is faster than reading (though this was eventually overruled by the majority of the teens)
 8. Can do other stuff while listening—running, driving, beading
 7. It's safer to listen and drive than to read and drive
 6. Narrator adds excitement to the book
 5. Easier to understand a book after listening to it
 4. Different voices keep listener's attention and help concentration levels
 3. Enjoy the shared experience of two or more listening together and then discussing
 2. Removes the embarrassment of having to read aloud in class
 1. You can pretend not to hear your parents when they talk to you

Several items struck me when comparing and contrasting these two lists. First is that teachers are successfully using audio books in the classroom. Second, teens recognize that they comprehend more about a book when reading *and* listening rather than when they do either task in isolation. Next, teens are discovering that tedious tasks can be enlivened when listening to a book. Teens are internalizing the message that books are important and that the perfect time and place for reading versus listening may differ.

Teens are also realizing that a good narrator will enhance and create excitement in their audio book experience. They are becoming aware that the quality of an audio book production will be affected by the narrator's ability to imitate a variety of voices, vary tempo and inflection, and mimic dialects. These qualities are important to teens. They are gaining the listening skills needed to connect the right voices to the telling of a story.

The most intriguing finding was that most teens wanted to listen together in a small group. In contrast, adults often regard listening as a solitary experience. In one case a mother–daughter pair mentioned how much they enjoy listening and discussing an audio book when they're in the car together. This illustrates how valuable the audio book experience can be during the turbulent teen years when it's hard to establish a dialogue with one's child; let the audio book serve as the gateway to family chats.

Photo by Diallo Sessoms.

Educators and teens didn't come to exactly the same conclusions about the benefits of listening but many items on their lists are alike. Teens mention that listening to an audio book in class saves them, or another student, from the embarrassment of reading aloud. Educators state a similar idea by mentioning that the stigma of reading choices can be hidden when listening to an audio book.

But, to be fair, I must compare the top educational benefit discussed in the literature versus the top reason why teens say they listen. Librarians and teachers naturally consider audio books to be important in the process of becoming a lifelong reader. Just as naturally, teens have discovered that audio books serve as a new foil for tuning out parents—what mom or dad can challenge listening to a classic work for an English class? It's understandable that teens are unaware (or unwilling to admit) that they are improving listening and writing skills when tuned in to an audio book. Yet, that's exactly what is happening. Combining the listening and reading experience is helpful to teens, though they don't feel a great need to figure out why—they just know it works.

Pam's Pointers for Increasing Teen Listening in Your Library or School

1. Ensure that a varied collection of audio books is available, from titles on school reading lists to the latest works of YA and adult authors.
2. Have the necessary listening equipment available for checkout—CD players, MP3 players, Playaways.
3. Subscribe to a service that offers digital downloads to patrons and students.
4. Set aside areas for joint or shared listening.
5. Allow listening to an audio book as an acceptable basis for a book report, perhaps even letting students record their reports.
6. Highlight narrators by organizing a display or providing listening opportunities to the stars of the audio book industry.
7. Build your collection with award-winning audio books selected by ALA committees for the Odyssey Award, the ALSC Notable Children's Recordings, and YALSA Selected Audiobooks for Young Adults (www.ala.org).
8. Share reviews so students understand the qualities that make a good audio book production.
9. Suggest audio books that will further classwork, such as biographies of authors or historians, works about major events in American history, or titles recorded in a foreign language.
10. Let students see you listening as you walk to lunch, work in your office, or head to a school event.

Selecting and Evaluating Young Adult Literature

Even librarians and teachers who are interested in providing the widest array of young adult literature possible are going to find that they are only able to select a certain number of books from the increasing number of YA titles published each year. So what should be involved when determining which books to choose? After taking into account budgetary and spatial constraints, three major considerations tend to come into play when selecting books for the classroom or library: pleasure, quality, and appropriateness.

Pleasure

Will young adults enjoy reading this book? There are many reasons that readers enjoy particular books and although this is often hard to predict, you can look for a wide variety of books that young adults do enjoy. You can begin by thinking about whether you enjoyed reading the book. Does a book share traits with other books young adults you work with have enjoyed in the past? Does the book have themes that might be of interest to young adults? Is the book well written? If the answer to more than one of these questions is yes, then there is a good chance the book will be well received. Still, the greater the diversity of books provided, the more chance you have that young adults will be able to find the right book at the right time.

Quality

Many elements go into creating a quality narrative including voice, style, character development, plot, theme, tone, point of view, mood, pace, design, accuracy, and setting. Among the questions to consider are the following:

- Is the story well written, well illustrated, and engaging?
- Does the work contain an authenticity of voice and setting?
- Are elements such as style, character development, plot, theme, tone, point of view, mood, pace, dialogue, and design effective in enhancing the storyline?
- How does the book compare to other books by the same author and illustrator?
- How has the book been received by reviewers (professional as well as young people)? Do you agree with these reviews?
- Do graphic elements work effectively with the storyline?

Ideas about quality might sound fairly commonsensical if you belong to the cultural community deciding on the criteria, but it is difficult to find even two critics who will agree on every book. Of all of the books nominated for the American Library Association's "Best Books for Young Adults," only around 10 each year are unanimously selected for the list. It can certainly be argued that committees of adult scholars, teachers, and librarians actually reward books that give well-educated adult audiences the most pleasure or that appeal to an adult sense of what young people should read and are therefore deemed of high quality. The point is that although every teacher, librarian, or parent will want to make available a certain percentage of books they judge to be quality books, their notions of quality might exclude many worthwhile works. The issue of variety still outweighs having a specific canon of literature.

Appropriateness

Appropriateness is another sticky issue. Is this the right book for the context? Will it appeal to this individual or group? Will it provide a pleasurable educational experience? Are the topics or language too difficult (or too simple or too banal) so that reading becomes frustrating? The same books may not be appropriate at a particular time for any two readers in a class or age group. For many books you can make a good guess as to the general profile of an implied reader, but that does not mean that an individual fitting that profile will enjoy the book. Some books are more likely to appeal to a whole class as a read-aloud, but numerous contextual factors determine whether a group enjoys a particular book. The exact same book used with two different groups that fit the same general profile can elicit drastically different responses.

Then there is the question of who decides what is appropriate for the classroom or for the library. In many school districts there are approved reading lists and a book not on that list is not to be used for direct instruction. Depending on the system, adding a book to the list can be a long process. Parental groups, church organizations, and other community groups often want to get involved, either in the selection process (which might be beneficial), or in the de-selection process (censorship, which is rarely beneficial). Unfortunately, books of interest to many young adults are often objectionable to one interest group or another. So selecting books based on pleasure, quality, and appropriateness is not as simple a process as it might have first sounded. The best compromise might be to strive for a balance of popular and engaging books with works that offer high quality and diverse literary experiences.

In the Field   *Sheila Mikkelson on Serving Young Adults in the Library*

Sheila Mikkelson is the director of the Seymour Public Library District in Auburn, New York. Previously she was the director of the Dover (Delaware) Public Library; the Young Adults' Services manager at the Allen County Public Library in Fort Wayne, Indiana; and the young adult coordinator at the Cumberland County Public Library and Information Center in Fayetteville, North Carolina. She also served on the Young Adult Library Services Association (YALSA) Board of Directors. Under her maiden name, Anderson, she is the editor of Serving Older Teens *(Libraries Unlimited, 2004) and* Serving Young Teens and 'Tweens *(Libraries Unlimited, 2005) and is the author of* Extreme Teen: Library Services to Nontraditional Young Adults *(Libraries Unlimited, 2005).*

ON CREATING A SPECIFIC SPACE FOR YOUNG ADULTS

Young adults are not children, but they are not adults, either. They need their own space in libraries. They are typically too big to fit in the furniture in the children's department, and they do not feel welcome in a space appropriate for small children. In the adult section, they sometimes feel lost and overwhelmed. People experiencing adolescence are typically very social and they spend lots of time with their friends. They need a place to hang out. This is especially true of younger teens who cannot have a job yet and are not bogged down with tons of school work like teens in the middle and late stages of adolescence. Besides comfortable and appropriate seating, YA spaces should have appropriate library collections for teens, including both print and electronic materials. Because the teen years span such a huge range—from 11, 12, or 13 through age 18 or 19, the collection needs to have materials for all types of reading levels. The teen area should include some type of decorations that teenagers have actually assisted with in planning and implementation so that they feel a type of ownership. YA spaces are not a totally new thing. Although more libraries may be creating YA spaces, many have had them for years, such as the Allen County Public Library in Fort Wayne, Indiana. The former YA area was a 4,500-square-foot room with a collection of 40,000 materials and nine staff members. The department included the full range of Dewey along with fiction and many types of nonprint materials (software, music, videos, DVDs, etc.) For more information about teen spaces, please consider using the library journal *Voice of Youth Advocates* because it includes a "YA Spaces of Your Dreams" column.

ON THE SELECTION PROCESS

In Fayetteville, my budget was somewhat limited. Therefore, I made sure that we had fiction that was critically acclaimed (award winners, Best Books for Young Adults, etc.) as well as appealing books, such as R. L. Stine titles (please note that this was in the late 1990s). Appropriateness for the age group is always a factor, but book reviews typically include this information. In Allen County, I had a very large budget, approximately $70,000 just for materials. The library keeps every last copy of all books, except for duplicates, so we also had an extensive historical YA fiction collection in storage. We bought almost every single YA fiction book published each year. Before I managed the department, paperbacks were not a priority. I changed that and put lots of paperback series on standing order because I believed that popularity of items should be a factor in collection decisions as well. Again, appropriateness for the age group was a consideration. Because the entire library was well funded, if we found something that we wanted for the collection but we were unsure of age appropriateness, we could always request that another department (children's services, business, music, etc.) purchase the item. In Dover, the YA collection was extremely weak when I began as the director in 2001. I was somewhat starting from scratch. During the first few years in Dover I purchased a mixture of popular items and award winners for the purpose of building a strong collection.

ON ATTRACTING A YOUNG ADULT CLIENTELE

In Fayetteville I held an R. L. Stinefest that attracted a large crowd. That would probably not attract a lot of people now because he is not as popular. We also had a YA summer reading program in Fayetteville called "Teen Read" that was very popular. When the Internet first became popular, on Sunday afternoons we offered training sessions called "Sundae Surfing" where teens could eat ice cream sundaes, wash their hands, and then surf the Internet. (No sticky fingers on the keyboard!)

In Fort Wayne, during the school year, we had many groups of students visit the library with teachers. Even classes from the surrounding counties visited the library. We provided bibliographic instruction to the groups. The department seated 100 people, so space was not an issue. We also had a summer reading program in Fort Wayne with a huge budget. The prizes included passes to area attractions, such as the city swimming pools, bowling, miniature golf, etc. We had a chess tournament each year that attracted a lot of teens. We formed a Teen Advisory Board that met each month and they began reviewing books as part of the YALSA Teen Top Ten project. Also, they filmed public service announcements for the summer reading program. Access Fort Wayne, the local public access station, was housed in the library, so we had unlimited publicity for library events.

Programming is number three on my list for attracting teens to the library, though. Number one is accepting them as they are and providing good customer service. In Dover, all of my staff went through training called "Customer Service to Youth" and we explored how to make children and teens feel welcome in the library. We discussed issues such as stereotypes, developmental stages, redirecting negative behavior, and dealing with overbearing parents. I think that if you make teens feel glad to be in the library in the first place, they will most likely return.

Second on my list is having a decent library collection. Do not shy away from magazines, graphic novels, comic books, game code books, and other types of materials that are popular with teens. Also, make sure that you replace the books about sex that are missing—and do not weed them, even if they have not been checked out. Chances are, some shy teen has pored through the pages of the book in the stacks, but he or she was too embarrassed to actually check out the book and take it home. One day a teen male walked out of the library and set off the alarm. He turned around and it was obvious that he had a book shoved down his pants. I let my male staff member handle the situation, figuring that it would be less embarrassing. The book was about sex. My male staff member had me speak with the teenager. I politely but firmly let him know that if he wanted to take the book home, he had to check it out. He said no and left. I did not mention the topic of the book or scold him in any way. I realized that he was just trying to gain information. I could tell that he knew he was wrong. If the patron had been an adult, I would have handled the situation in an entirely different manner. I would have called the police and he or she would have been arrested for theft.

Booktalking is also a way to bring teens into the library. As a young adult librarian I frequently visited middle schools, high schools, and a detention center (in Fort Wayne) where I would perform booktalks. Booktalking is a way of promoting books to teens without giving away the ending. It is similar to storytelling, but not the same. Booktalkers typically use some type of "hook" to get the audience interested in the story. This will often draw teens into the library who would not normally visit the library. Teenagers are usually impressed to see librarians out of the library role for a change. In Fort Wayne we had an outreach program with detention centers and we had deposit collections at six area agencies—detention centers, foster care, etc. I really enjoyed working with incarcerated teens and it is what I miss the most about my former position.

> *Keys to Attracting a YA Clientele*
> - Accepting young adults as they are and providing good service
> - Having a decent, diverse collection
> - Programming—teen advisory board, reading programs, Internet events, etc.
> - Booktalking outside of the library to pull them in

Topic Focus

What Do Young Adults Choose to Read?

It quickly becomes evident to librarians and teachers that the books chosen by critics are not necessarily the same books chosen by young readers. So what are the favorites of teens? One place to look for the answer is the Young Adults' Choices Project, sponsored by the International Reading Association. Each year since 1987 around 4,500 students in grades 7 to 12 have participated. They read books published in the previous year that received at least two positive reviews. Then they vote on the best books from the year. An annual list of the titles with the most votes (approximately 30 each year) is published in the November issue of the International Reading Association's *Journal of Adolescent & Adult Literacy*. As noted on the IRA website (IRA, 1994), the project has three main goals:

- To develop an annual annotated reading list of new books that will encourage young adults to read

- To help teachers, librarians, booksellers, parents, and others find books that young readers will enjoy
- To provide middle and secondary school students with an opportunity to voice their opinions about the books being written for them.

This list has become influential with teachers searching for new books to use in their classrooms. The types of literature chosen vary greatly. Contemporary realistic fiction carries the most titles, but young adults also select a wide array of books from various genres. What is perhaps most essential for professionals who work with young adults to realize is that there are high-quality books out there that appeal to young readers and that in order to get more teens interested in literature you first have to prove to them that there is something worth reading!

Some books hold interest because of the themes they address, whereas other books gain interest because of context: a movie related to the book, a fad, world events. *The Breadwinner* is a good example of outside influences creating high interest. Deborah Ellis, a Canadian author, has crafted a beautifully written narrative and a captivating story, but before 9/11 the book was relatively unknown in the United States. *The Breadwinner* is the exciting and inspiring story of Parvana, a young girl growing up in Afghanistan, as she struggles to make a life for herself and her family under the harsh rule of the Taliban. By 2002, it was difficult for U.S. librarians to keep a copy on the shelves. The first printing sold out and a second edition had to be issued. The quality of the writing and the adventure aspect of the narrative will likely keep it in circulation for some time, but it was world events that really propelled it into popularity and led to two sequels.

To Consider

There is often a mismatch between the books praised by critics and those that are popular with young adults. To what extent is quality of writing an issue with young readers when choosing a book to read?

Author Spotlight

Photo by Kelly Halls.

Chris Crutcher

Chris Crutcher is originally from Cascade, Idaho. He now resides in Spokane, Washington. His novels and short stories inevitably show up on the ALA Best Books for Young Adults lists. In 2000 he received the Margaret A. Edwards Award for lifetime achievement in writing for teens. For 10 years he directed an alternative school for inner-city children in Oakland, California. In addition to writing, he currently works as a family therapist. Crutcher's experiences with young people come through in his insightful prose. In his novel *Ironman* a character remarks that if you want to see how something works, look at it broken, and that is what Crutcher often does in his narratives. He presents broken lives, allowing the reader to discover ways in which their own world might actually work. Visit his website at www.chriscrutcher.com.

SELECTED BOOKLIST

Angry Management (Greenwillow, 2009)
Chinese Handcuffs (Greenwillow, 1989)
The Crazy Horse Electric Game (Greenwillow, 1987)
Deadline (HarperTeen, 2007)
Ironman (Greenwillow, 1995)
King of the Mild Frontier (Greenwillow, 2003)
Running Loose (Greenwillow, 1983)
The Sledding Hill (HarperTeen, 2005)
Staying Fat for Sarah Byrnes (Greenwillow, 1993)
Stotan! (Greenwillow, 1986)
Whale Talk (Greenwillow, 2001)

ON HOW HE BECAME AN AUTHOR OF YA LITERATURE

I did write one "adult" novel in the early nineties called *The Deep End* and I intend to write more. My first book was about a teenager, however, and it did fairly well and I was working with teenagers at the time, so good stories about them were all around me. Adolescence is such a raw time that it's ripe for stories. I don't usually think of myself as writing for young adults as I do writing about young adults.

ON WHETHER HE WRITES WITH A PARTICULAR AUDIENCE IN MIND

I purposely do not have an audience in mind, because I think that would affect my narrative in a negative way. I try to tell the best story I can to myself, and let it land where it lands.

ON THE INSPIRATION FOR HIS STORIES

I usually get the inspiration from something that has happened. I may see it on the news or I may hear about it from someone. A good idea can come from anywhere. When I was writing *Whale Talk* I was very interested in outsiders because of the media attention on school shootings and because of the "zero tolerance" epidemic that was sweeping the country.

ON THE EXTENT TO WHICH HIS OWN LIFE STORY APPEARS IN HIS WORKS

Different stories, different extents. I'll use anything out of my own life if I believe it fits the story and can make the audience laugh or cry. I'm always aware of my own history when I write, though there are very few scenes in any book that happened exactly that way in life. The imagination is what makes reality into good fiction.

ON WHAT HE ENJOYED READING AS A TEENAGER

To Kill a Mockingbird and cereal boxes.

ON WHAT HE ENJOYS READING CURRENTLY

It varies. I like some of the coming-of-age fiction out now; the good tough stuff of Lois Lowry and Terry Davis and Will Weaver. Terry Trueman's *Stuck in Neutral* is a great read. I'll read anything by Christopher Paul Curtis, can never wait for something new by Walter Dean Myers. A young Australian guy named Markus Zusak has a book out called *Fighting Ruben Wolfe,* which I think is pure poetry. Every time I think of a name I think of someone I'm leaving out and this could get really long. I still read Kurt Vonnegut regularly because you can learn to write while you're having the time of your life. I think there has been no better book in the last 50 years than *The Things They Carried* by Tim O'Brien. *The Color Purple* by Alice Walker, *The Prince of Tides* by Pat Conroy, and *I Know This Much Is True* by Wally Lamb are a few others that I think are masterpieces.

ON WHAT DISTINGUISHES YOUNG ADULT LITERATURE

The age of the protagonist, more than anything.

ON WHAT MIGHT HELP YOUNG ADULTS DEVELOP AS WRITERS

Something I didn't do. Read like crazy and write like crazy. It works just like athletics. The more you practice the better you get.

ON WHETHER AN AUTHOR CAN WRITE CONVINCINGLY ABOUT ANOTHER CULTURAL EXPERIENCE

I'd be a fool to say no because so many have done it. I think you have to be careful and I think you have to take your imagination with you, but the truth is that humans are far more alike than different across cultures and backgrounds.

ON THE ENDING OF *WHALE TALK*

There are a lot of ways that story could have turned out. The price of redemption didn't have to be so high. It just was. I was focused on the brutality of racism and the astonishing power of hate. I remember when the Randy Weaver stand-off was going on not far from here at Ruby Ridge, a zealot had jumped onto a bus somewhere in the country and ridden all the way here to support Randy Weaver and his beliefs. In the Spokane bus station, he came upon a mixed race couple and, on impulse, shot them.

Understanding Cultural Context and Authentic Narrative

If diverse voices are explored in every chapter of this book, as well they should be, then why do we need another section devoted to diversity? There is clearly a need to have narratives that reflect the realities of the world they know available for young people to read (Sims, 1982). Students do not always want to read about themselves and the problems they face, but to never see characters who think like you, live like you, or talk like you in the literature reinforces the notion that reading fiction is not for you—that it is something written by and for other people.

At the same time, literature is one of the best ways for young adults to experience other ways of knowing and thinking about the world around them. As our realities become more and more interconnected around the globe one hopes that future generations gain empathy for and understanding of how other people live. One good way to look at different cultures and how they interact with mainstream U.S. culture is in books about young people from different countries whose families immigrate to the United States. The following list shows several good examples.

- *Ashes to Roses* by Mary Jane Auch (Ireland)
- *Behind the Mountains* by Edwidge Danticat (Haiti)
- *Esperanza Rising* by Pam Muñoz Ryan (Mexico)
- *Fresh Girl* by Jaira Placide (Haiti)
- *Journey of the Sparrows* by Fran Leeper Buss and Daisy Cubias (El Salvador)
- *An Ocean Apart, A World Away* by Lensey Namioka (China)
- *Red Midnight* by Ben Mikaelsen (Guatemala)
- *A Step from Heaven* by An Na (Korea)
- *Tonight by Sea* by Francis Temple (Haiti)

It should be noted that there are still huge gaps in the voices being heard and the images being represented in the available literature. The Printz Award is a good indication of the quality of diverse literature being written for young adults. In the few years since its creation winners have included African Americans, a Korean American, a Chinese American, Australians, and British authors. Does this signal a change in terms of what is being published? Perhaps, though authors and characters of color still make up a disproportionately small percentage of what is published.

In 2001 Sandy Guild and Sandra Hughes-Hassell published a study in *The New Advocate* looking at students' reactions to depictions of urban minorities in young adult literature. The most revealing aspect of the study is that for the entire decade of the 1990s they were only able to locate 20 novels with the following criteria: The main protagonist is a minority young adult; the setting is urban; the novel is realistic fiction; and the book is marketed for young adults, still in print, and favorably reviewed. OK, that's a lot of criteria—but only 20 in a decade out of the more than 5,000 books being published each year for children and young adults. Out of these 20 only one had an Asian American protagonist and none were identified with a Native American protagonist. There are still major gaps in who is represented in YA literature. Although humans of all cultures are more alike than different, teens who do not find cultural and physical reflections of themselves in books are less likely to read for pleasure.

Culturally Specific versus Color-Me-Brown

Though there are as many opinions on this topic as there are people you ask, authors of color often make several similar points that really stand out in the dialogue about authenticity. First, many authors whose cultural background is outside the mainstream will say that they became writers because when they were young they could not find themselves in books. They did not see themselves or the people they loved in what was being read at school, and they wanted to fill that gap so that kids like them in the future would feel a connection with literature.

Second, when asked who has the right to tell stories about characters of a certain culture, many authors from outside the mainstream culture say that anyone can try, and if they do a convincing job, then they have been successful. The truth is that it is hard to write convincingly outside of the realities you know. If you are a cultural insider you know the nuances, the details of daily life. The narrative will not ring true if an author does not know a culture intimately, especially to a reader who is a cultural insider.

Imagine (for those of you who are not Cajun) trying to depict what life is like in a Cajun household. What do you have for breakfast? What do the children call their mom and dad? What do you talk about at the dinner table? Well for some Cajun families the answers might well be Cheerios, mom and dad, and "American Idol." But many families will have styles of talking, customs, and ways of relating to each other that are at least somewhat culturally distinct. Someone who doesn't know Cajun culture intimately will get some of those details wrong and might at times even draw on stereotypes.

Joseph Bruchac speaks about the idea of non-Native writers who create stories with Native American characters:

> I am very dissatisfied with the majority of YA books "about" Native Americans that have been written by non-Natives. I think a lot of Indian people today are not happy with the way they and their cultures have been (and continue to be) treated by non-Native writers. The stereotypes and attendant blindness about the truth of Indian realities are so engrained that few non-Indians are able to avoid making the sorts of mistakes that make Indians groan. (Interview with Bruchac, p. 145)

It is certainly difficult for authors not to make mistakes when writing about realities they have not lived.

A related issue involves authors who attempt to create culturally neutral characters and then describe one of them as African American, or Latino, or Chinese American. A few cultural specifics might be thrown in but basically these characters are included to make the book diverse without dealing with issues of diversity. Basically, what you have in some of these books are color-me-brown characters with no culturally rich detail involved in character development, simply the physical descriptions.

Why is this significant? Well, for one thing there are questions of power to consider. Mainstream white voices have been well represented in American literature, so much so that many times we forget that we are seeing the world through a cultural lens when reading this literature. At times we use terms such as "universal

---

To Consider

Think of an acquaintance who comes from a cultural background distinct from your own. Try to imagine that person at their parents' or relatives' home for the holidays. What is the household like, how do people interact, what do they do in the evenings, at dinner time. Imagine writing an essay about a day in this person's life. Now imagine that you have to let that person read the essay you have written. Are you worried that some of your statements might be viewed as stereotyping? Do you think your descriptions are fairly accurate or at least possible? What would you have to do to create a more authentic essay?

Literature both reflects and influences our perceptions. In this book from Germany in the late 1930s, stereotypes are clearly part of the storyline. The narrative suggests that although poor Inge has been warned by her League of German Girls leader to avoid Jewish doctors, her mother foolishly sends her to be examined by one anyway. All of the images in *Der Giftpilz* reinforce stereotypes that helped justify the events of the Holocaust. Illustration from *Der Giftpilz* by Ernst Hiemer (1938).

Hinter den Brillengläsern funkeln zwei Verbrecherangen und um die wulstigen Lippen spielt ein Grinsen.

themes" and values to describe mainstream ways of knowing when we are actually talking about a culturally specific worldview. After Lonnie, the young character in Jacqueline Woodson's *Locomotion,* writes a poem about a white Beaver Cleaver–type family he sees on a TV commercial, his teacher asks, "Lonnie, what does race have to do with it?" Lonnie reflects that his teacher does not understand what it is like never seeing your own life reflected in the media:

> How if you turn on your TV that's what you see—people with lots and lots of stuff not having to sit on scratchy couches in Miss Edna's house. And the fact is a lot of these people are white. Maybe it's that if you're white you can't see all the whiteness around you. (p. 13)

Certainly one of the big issues involved when a member of a culture of power writes about characters of other cultures is that, despite the best intentions of "color blindness," the result is often a real blindness to issues of diversity.

Diversity in the USA

Coming to terms with issues of identity is a main focus of adolescence. Resolving who we are and where we come from with the common teen longing to be something else, something more is a conflict that many young adult characters struggle with. Conflicting expectations of peers, family, and mainstream culture are central in adolescents' lives. Despite the fact that her mother is Chinese American, Stacy in Laurence Yep's *Thief of Hearts* has never felt that she is different. When a Chinese immigrant comes to her school, Stacy discovers that not everyone sees her as a "regular" American. Her comfortable identity is shattered and she has to discover who she is again.

Novels such as Sherman Alexie's *The Absolutely True Diary of a Part-Time Indian* (2007) and An Na's *A Step from Heaven* (2001) tell stories about individuals within a specific cultural context written by authors who can fill the narratives with authentic detail because they know the intricacies of the experiences the characters are living. *The Absolutely True Diary of a Part-Time Indian* reprinted by permission of Little, Brown and Company. *A Step from Heaven* published by Front Street, an imprint of Boyds Mills Press. Reprinted by permission.

In Rita Williams-Garcia's *Fast Talk on a Slow Track,* Denzel also thinks he knows who he is—the academic success story. He has forged an identity with the help of his family and community as the school valedictorian. Now, with his acceptance to Princeton, he is on track to be the role model, the poster boy. But when Denzel attends the Princeton summer program for minority students, he leaves his support system behind and finds that he is having to re-create his identity. The pressure becomes too much and the fear of failure too strong.

The impact of cultural heritage on any person's identity is a complex and extremely diverse experience (Derrickson, 2003, p. 1). People rarely belong to just one culture; we have varying levels of competency in several cultures and especially when we are teens there is a fluidity of identity as we seek to discover who we are. All youth have to learn to master the rules of the cultures in which they operate, cultures that are already filled with a variety of contexts and subcultures.

Sunita, in *The Sunita Experiment* (Perkins), has led a fairly comfortable existence but when her grandparents arrive for a lengthy visit from India her world becomes confused. With her mother acting like a different person and her Indian heritage so obvious, the identity that she had created before is thrown into upheaval. In the end she finds a new balance that includes pleasure in her heritage.

Young adults who are outside the mainstream are often "marked by language, ethnicity, economic and social factors as *los otros,* the outsiders" (Cofer, 2003, p. vi). In *Born Confused* (Hidier), Dimple Lala has resisted Indian tradition and her parents' ways all her life, but suddenly when she attends high school, Indian is trendy. Now her parents are trying to set her up with a suitable Indian boy. When the boy turns out to be totally cool, that's great—or is it?

Young adults commonly feel the constriction of other people's expectations; this is exacerbated for teens who have "felt isolated by language, skin color, or anything else that did not fit the big picture" (Cofer, 2003, p. viii). In African American books there is a pattern of looking at today's conditions as a continued part of the struggle that has included and is benchmarked against slavery and the civil rights movement (Guild and Hugh-Hassell, 2001). Issues of racism, stereotypes, and societal inequities certainly are part of the discourse in these novels. For instance, in *If You Come Softly* (Woodson, 1998), school administrators assume right off the bat that Miah should be placed in remedial math classes despite the records from his former school:

> It just seems like more than a coincidence when it happens to me. Like what made them think I needed remedial anything. Nobody tested me. Nobody asked me. They just threw me in it and then looked surprised when I knew it all. I mean, it makes you wonder—is it my hair? (pp. 75–76)

On the flip side it is generally by reconnecting with community or with cultural history that these characters navigate the search for identity that comes with being an adolescent. Oftentimes, a teacher of color helps instill a sense of pride. This is clearly evident in *The Skin I'm In* (Flake) and *Babylon Boyz* (Mowry), for example.

Toswiah in *Hush* (Woodson) actually loses her identity and watches her family disintegrate because of inherent racism. Her father, the only African American police officer in his precinct, witnesses fellow cops shoot an unarmed black kid. When he testifies to what he saw, the family has to go into the witness protection program. Now she is Evie and has to create a new identity. One question raised is to what extent other people's preconceptions already define her.

Going to college is often an identity challenging experience. Ellen Sung in *Saying Goodbye* (Lee) has always been the only Korean American in her school; when she goes away to college, she is suddenly exposed to diversity. She revels in being away from the confines of home, able to explore and discover new interests, and create her own self. Part of this is learning Korean for the first time, which her parents had discouraged. Unfortunately she also learns that racism is part of life in this world, and the decisions she makes about who she is and what she will stand up for are not always easy.

These emotionally powerful glimpses of human beings in the process of becoming mature adults entice adolescent and adult readers alike. In this way literature is important because it helps us understand the inner lives of others. Even within a cultural group the realities of young adults vary tremendously, as Gary Soto writes about in *Buried Onions:*

> I glanced over my shoulder, slowing but not stopping, because if you stopped and it was your enemy, your life could spill like soda right on the black asphalt, spill before you could touch your wound. I never ran with the gangs, never kicked it with the weasel-necked vatos locos, but you had to be careful, quick as a rabbit. (p. 6)

Certainly this sense of imminent threat is not a reality all teens have experienced. Whether they have ever felt fear of this kind, if the narrative pulls them in they will soon not only root for Eddie as he struggles to make it in junior college, they may even come to understand something of what his life is like.

Author Spotlight

Photo courtesy of Judith Cofer.

Judith O. Cofer

Judith Ortiz Cofer was born in Puerto Rico, raised in Paterson, New Jersey, and now makes her home in Georgia. She is the author of poems, novels, short stories, and essays. She has received numerous awards and honors for her writing. In 2005, *Call Me Maria* was selected as one of two texts to receive Honorable Mention for the Américas Award. Additionally, *The Meaning of Consuelo* was selected as one of two winners of the 2003 Américas Award and included on the New York Public Library's "Books for the Teen Age 2004 List." Her young adult short story collection, *An Island Like You,* received the inaugural Pura Belpré Prize from the American Library Association in 1996. Judith Ortiz Cofer is currently the Regents and Franklin Professor of English and Creative Writing at the University of Georgia. She lives in Athens, Georgia, with her husband, John Cofer, a fellow educator. Visit her website at www.english.uga.edu/~jcofer.

SELECTED BIBLIOGRAPHY

Call Me Maria (Orchard, 2004)
An Island Like You: Stories of the Barrio (Scholastic, 1995)
The Meaning of Consuelo (Farrar, Straus & Giroux, 2003)
Riding Low on the Streets of Gold: Latino Literature for Young Adults (Pinata, 2003)
Silent Dancing: A Partial Remembrance of a Puerto Rican Childhood (Arte Público, 1997)

ON WHAT LED HER TO WRITE A BOOK FOR YOUNG ADULTS

I have been aware for some time that essays from *Silent Dancing* were being used in high school classrooms. And that I did have a YA audience, but it was a by-product. I used to get letters from high school teachers and young people telling me that they have read these coming-of-age essays, but I had not thought about writing for young adults. The first time that I thought about it was when I did a reading in New York and an editor from Little, Brown (she's still my editor though with a different house) said that she had become aware of my work and that I have young characters that interested her. Would I be interested in doing a young adult book? And I said maybe and she continued to pursue me for two years and I finally agreed. I didn't want to do a young adult novel because I didn't know that I could sustain a young character for that length of time. So, we agreed on a group of stories and I was to imagine the protagonists being the children of my adult characters who lived in my building from my novel *The Line of the Sun*.

I just drew from my experiences growing up in New Jersey and actually the characters also include a melding of my daughter's sensibilities. And I found that I was enjoying writing about these kids, but my deal with the editor was that I wasn't going to think in terms of censoring my language or in any way limit my writing style. And she agreed to that, and of course at the editing stage she felt free to tell me that "I don't think that a young person will understand this." So we had a lot of arguments and discussions. But I absolutely wanted to not talk down to young people. To just tell the stories the same ways I would tell them if I wasn't thinking of a young adult audience.

There were some instances where I gave in. Where she said that this wasn't appropriate, or whatever. But I am not a writer who needs expletives a lot. I am a former Catholic, so the prohibition is already in place for most infringements and violations, so it wasn't that so much, as she questioned, "Will a 14-year-old get this?" And I fought for that because one of the things that I understood from having a daughter myself and from reading to young people is that they would rather stretch and get it than to be talked down to. With "Matoa's Mirror," which is about a kid who does drugs, she thought it ought to be a little more explicit, and more moralizing. I said that I think they will get it. I think that they will see that what I am saying is that you always have a chance to use drugs but then that you lose self-control and that is all I want to say. I am not going to moralize. I also didn't want to devoid the world that I was creating of characters who are absolutely a part of the world of teenagers today. I wanted to write about a gay character, and we discussed this a lot and I finally showed her that what I wanted to do you would have to be a real prude or real reactionary to object to the character of Rick. I understand that in some schools they won't use this book because of the gay character. But it doesn't matter to me! I wanted to populate my world with real people. And many schools are using this book. So it is satisfying.

ON WHERE THE "MULTIPLE VOICES FROM A COMMUNITY" FORMAT IN *AN ISLAND LIKE YOU* CAME FROM

I was thinking in terms of influences after the fact. I had been teaching multicultural American literature and was using Erdritch's *Love Medicine*. That book was interesting to me because it was tribal, it was a bunch of voices from the community. I think of the barrio as that. I think of it as a beehive, a vertical island. I wanted the kids to know each other; I did not want these to be isolated stories. I wanted them to be a part of the barrios. It starts out with that poem with the kid on the roof which says that everyone is an island. You don't know what's really going on inside them. Each has an inner life. Even the toughest kid can fall in love. The shy kid can imagine herself flying. Or the one who is tormented for being different is heroic like Arturo. I was thinking in terms of the communal voices of the barrio. I wanted them to be related but to also each have an integrity.

In *An Island Like You* each story is separate and I intended for each of these stories to be able to stand on their own. I tested them out by sending them out on their own. Several were placed in publications first. The harder part was making them work together.

If you read "Arturo's Flight," you could read it as a story; put him back in the book and he is part of this group. I don't see the book as a novel in stories; I see it as a story cycle with each part removable. In the same way with *Call Me Maria* it's a little different in that it has an overall narrative structure but there are some stand-alone poems. I think to get the full experience with what I intended to do (create a community) reading the whole book is best. If there is a kid who feels isolated, Arturo's story will speak to him. However, it would be a fuller experience to read Arturo in terms of where he lives.

ON WHETHER AUTHORS CAN WRITE AUTHENTICALLY OUTSIDE OF THEIR OWN CULTURES

The only criterion is can you pull it off. It's like asking, "Do you think everyone can try tight rope walking?" Well, everyone can try it but if you can't get to the other side—I know that there are some people who scream if you have an African American character and you are not African American yourself. That would be so constraining to me; yes all of the kids in my stories are PR but I wasn't into drugs and I didn't run away from home. All of the situations are invented and each one of them is an individual. If I had chosen to make one of the characters African American or white I would have done so. But if I were to write in the character of one of my husband's students (he teaches in a rural high school in Georgia) it would be my duty to immerse myself into that culture or I come off sounding like an imposter.

I did do something. In my book *Call Me Maria* I have a biracial character, Whoopie Dominguez, who likes to rap. Whoopie likes to take over for the teacher when he leaves the room. One day he is doing the imperative tense and she takes over the lesson plan and does it in rap. First I tried it out on my daughter; she'd say not yet, mother. Then at the risk of my life I tried it out with English teachers. If I cannot imitate a biracial rapper successfully then I know that I have reached the limitations of my talent.

One often hears the question, why should I read the words of an African American woman speaking in black dialect when I'm a white guy with German ancestry? Mainly it's because I need to understand that you have an inner life before I can be sympathetic to you. You need to get past the language barriers and idiosyncracies, get past the fact that the character is black to see that the story is about love or hate or suffering, that the characters in the story share the basics of humanity.

LITERARY THEORY

Young Adult Literature

It is impossible to teach or learn literature: what one teaches or learns is criticism.

—Northrop Frye

Does "critical" talk about football or baseball kill the pleasure of those sports for their adherents? Does the critical discussion of wine or clothes spoil the pleasure for people who enjoy those things? Of course not. We all know such shared discussion enhances the pleasure.

—Aidan Chambers

Teachers and librarians inevitably approach literature from a position that has been influenced by the theoretical perspectives of those from whom they have learned. College professors, high school teachers, parents, authors, and librarians have all shown them something about the relationships that exist among author, reader, and text. For some teachers it is essential that students discover certain themes, structures, or information. For others it is more important to examine and interpret, or to expose stereotypes and inconsistencies. Still others see the ultimate goal of reading literature to be enjoyment of a well-told story—after all, if a person enjoys reading, they will do more of it, and the more they read the more proficient they will become. All of these conceptions of literature and reader are value-laden and connected to theoretical notions of what literature is.

Many readers have never really thought about why they approach literature in one manner or another. They assume that this is simply the way reading is done. "Reading" does not always include thinking critically about what has been read. One of the major contentions of this text is that young adults can engage in critical analysis of literature (and that they can enjoy doing so) if they are provided with the necessary background and rhetoric. Children and young adults need the chance to develop into informed readers. Unfortunately in secondary English classes there is often an insistence that there is one correct answer and this can "poison" the students' disposition for literature (Miall, 1996).

Would students become more interested readers if they were helped to read critically? Certainly interpretation can be an exciting but at the same time demanding process that adds another level of engagement with text. There can also be real pleasure in literary critique. As for teachers and librarians, knowing how literature works will provide insight into how it will affect young people and what it might mean to them both consciously and unconsciously (McGillis, 1996, p. 206).

Each chapter of this text includes a discussion of an approach to understanding literature, a lens used by some critics to view the literature they are discussing. Students who have access to these lenses are not only more likely to be able to discuss and respond to literature in interesting ways but also are more apt to enjoy reading. There is no way to do justice to a literary theory in one or two pages so suggestions for further readings are provided in each of these sections.

Reader Response Theory

In the realm of K–12 education reader response is the literary theory that most teachers and preservice teachers have knowledge of from courses in reading and language arts methods. Louise Rosenblatt is the single biggest influence on reader response theory. Her work was first published in 1938 but had a major impact on the field beginning in the 1960s. Rather than view the text as the authority, reader response looks at the reader's engagement with text and how meaning is constructed as part of the reading process. A number of elements come together in a "never-to-be-duplicated combination" that impacts the reading:

- Personality traits
- Memories of past events
- Present needs and preoccupations
- The particular mood of the moment
- The particular physical conditions (1938, pp. 30–31)

Meaning derives from the transaction between the text and the reader within a specific context, so each reading is a unique event. Even the same reader will never experience the same text in the exact same way again.

There are two basic interrelated ways of responding to the text: efferent (what is the text saying) and aesthetic (how does this relate to me). Stanley Fish (1980) has added to this equation the interesting idea that readers "mispreread" texts. This builds on the notion that people "shape the words they read to fit prior assumptions about both the world and the literature they are reading" (p. 16). Reader response is further complicated by read-alouds, class discussions, and teacher comments, factors which tend to create an interpretative community in which readers move towards a certain level of shared meaning (though some members of the discussion might react against consensus).

One simple activity that can really lead to better understanding of reader response is to have students look at several personal reactions to a single text and discuss similarities and differences in how the readers responded. The following excerpts are from the responses of three preservice teachers to Deborah Ellis's *The Breadwinner:*

Student 1

The Breadwinner reveals the difficulties of the harsh conditions men, women, and children are facing in Afghanistan today. I would recommend this book for 5th grade students and up. This fact-filled novel would be well suited for a current events social studies lesson. The teacher could have the class bring in news articles, which chronicle the events in Afghanistan (or any other breaking news stories). Because Parvana lived in a constant state of fear the teacher could ask the class to keep a journal while reading *The Breadwinner,* expressing their concern for Parvana. Additionally, they could write about what they would do if they were in a similar situation. This would also be a great language arts lesson because the class would have to use their reading, writing, and critical thinking skills.

Student 2

I found it interesting that Deborah Ellis, a Canadian, got the idea for this book while talking to women and girls in Afghan refugee camps in Pakistan, conducting research for the purpose of writing a nonfiction book about the lives of women living under oppression in

Afghanistan. The storyline that has 11-year-old Parvana earning a living and feeding her family after her father is snatched away by the Taliban was adapted from bits told to Ellis by the women she interviewed. While in Pakistan, Deborah Ellis received a death threat and returned shortly thereafter to Canada. *The Breadwinner* gives the world a view inside another culture and also gives back to the Afghani people; proceeds from its sale are donated to a fund for the education and betterment of the lives of Afghan girls in refugee camps.

Student 3

I was hooked on *The Breadwinner* after the very first page, and I hated not being able to read it in one sitting. It was one of those books where the climax kept climbing, and yet the story remained very realistic. I have almost gotten immune to the recent news because you hear something about the Taliban almost everyday, but the book provokes my interest in Afghanistan and makes me want to seek additional information on the topic. I do not think that you could ask anything more of fiction.

Here we see one reader talking primarily about how the book might be used in the classroom, another discusses what they learned about the author/book relationship, and still another explores the personal impact of the narrative. How do you judge whether one of these responses is more on target, insightful, or "correct"? With preset criteria or a directed question to respond to, you could assess these reactions accordingly, but still the question remains—did one of these students learn more from reflecting on the book than the others? Or did each of these readers react in ways that fit his or her needs, assumptions, and outlooks of the moment? Reader response theory does not mean "anything goes" when interpreting literature, but it really does make us reconceptualize the relationship between text and reader.

For Further Reading

Beach, R. *A Teacher's Introduction to Reader-Response Theories.* NCTE, 1993.

Benton, Michael. "Readers, Texts, Contexts: Reader-Response Criticism." In Peter Hunt (ed.), *Understanding Children's Literature.* Routledge, 2005.

Cooper, Charles Raymond (ed.). *Researching Response to Literature and the Teaching of Literature: Points of Departure.* Ablex, 1985.

Farrel, E., and J. Squires (eds.). *Transactions with Literature: A Fifty Year Perspective.* NCTE, 1990.

Fish, Stanley. *Is There a Text in This Class? The Authority of Interpretative Communities.* Harvard University Press, 1980.

Iser, Wolfgang. *The Implied Reader: Patterns of Communication in Prose Fiction from Bunyan to Beckett.* Johns Hopkins University Press, 1974.

Rosenblatt, Louise. *Literature as Exploration,* 5th ed. Appleton-Century, 1995. (Original work published 1938)

Tompkins, Jane (ed.). *Reader-Response Criticism: From Formalism to Post-Structuralism.* Johns Hopkins University Press, 1980.

2

The History of Young Adult Literature and the Role of the Classics

History of Young Adult Literature Text Set

The Chocolate War by Robert Cormier

The Contender by Robert Lipsyte

The Day They Came to Arrest the Book by Nat Hentoff

Dinky Hocker Shoots Smack! by M. E. Kerr

Dragonwings by Laurence Yep

The House of Dies Drear by Virginia Hamilton

The House on Mango Street by Sandra Cisneros

Killing Mr. Griffin by Lois Duncan

North Town by Lorenz Graham

The Outsiders by S. E. Hinton

The Pigman by Paul Zindel

Roll of Thunder, Hear My Cry by Mildred Taylor

Classics Revisited Text Set

Dateline Troy by Paul Fleischman

Dating Hamlet: Ophelia's Story by Lisa Fiedler

Edgar Allan Poe's Tales of Mystery and Madness

A Mystery for Thoreau by Kim Platt

Ophelia by Lisa Klein

Orfe by Cynthia Voigt

Othello by Julius Lester

The Playmaker by C. B. Cheaney

Romiette and Julio by Sharon Draper

The Shakespeare Stealer by Gary Blackwood

Shakespeare's Romeo and Juliet by Michael Rosen

Troy by Adele Geras

Your Own Sylvia by Stephanie Hemphill

Investigating Historical Texts and Trends

If it is true that young adults are most responsive to contemporary narratives (as much evidence would indicate), then the question might be asked: Is it important for people who work with young adults to study the history of YA literature? Or perhaps this is a side issue primarily of concern to historians and scholars.

One need look no further than the National Endowment for the Humanities summer reading list (2003) to discover that at least some of our culture bearers believe that historical works of literature should play a pivotal role in a young reader's development. Interestingly, in the category for young adults most of the recommended books on this list are historical works written for an adult audience. There are certainly some valid reasons for investigating the history of any literary tradition, as shown by the following list of benefits of learning about the history of young adult literature.

- Historical texts and trends offer insight into how ideas about youth and education have changed over time.
- Historical literary trends and traditions shape perceptions about what YA literature is and influence the writing, publishing, and perception of new works.
- Exploring books that were popular in a certain era but no longer appeal to young adults can provide interesting information about societal trends, linguistic changes, and the shifting wants and needs of young adults.
- Some books have withstood the test of time and are still popular reads.
- With some classics of YA literature, the word craft and literary merit are so great that to not introduce these books to young adults would be doing them a disservice.

I STOOD LIKE ONE THUNDERSTRUCK

It would probably take a good deal of persuasion to cajole a class of tenth graders into reading *St. Elmo* by Augusta Jane Evans Wilson, a novel which was extremely popular in 1867 and for decades thereafter. *St Elmo* is a domestic novel and the language and values would likely seem stilted, the issues raised no longer relevant, and the characters difficult to relate to. But if students were put into the role of experts investigating how the book both reflected and influenced its era's values, writing styles, and preconceptions, then it is possible that students would have an incredible critical and literary experience with the novel.

Crusoe's first encounter with "Friday" might be read without any background information but knowledge of the historical context helps the reader understand the stereotypes included. Illustration from *Life and Adventures of Robinson Crusoe* (T. Nelson and Sons, 1876). Courtesy of Salisbury University's Blackwell Library.

Other historical works like *Robinson Crusoe* and *Alice's Adventures in Wonderland* would likely find a wider appeal because their storylines still resonate with many young people. But the "story" (in movie format and adaptations) might actually hold more appeal for many young people than the original narrative does. Blasphemy, you say! I am not suggesting that persuading young people to read these books is not a wonderful thing. Of course it can be. A person who reads and enjoys an array of survival books for young people can easily become interested in reading *Robinson Crusoe* and hopefully will have someone willing to discuss why "Man Friday" is depicted the way he is. The brief chronology of young adult literature in the Appendix provides a nice overview of historical works that have been read by teens over the centuries. Many historical texts need to be looked at in context, whereas others simply no longer have enough appeal to get young people excited about reading because the language, issues, and societal norms are outdated. If getting teens to actually read these books is on the agenda, it will often take substantial preparation.

A Brief History of Young Adult Literature

Oral Literature

The vast majority of literature throughout history has been oral. Ballads, legends, epics, folktales, poetry, drama, religious stories—even long after the advent of writing only a small percentage of literary pleasure was afforded through silent reading. It would be extremely hard to separate out something that might be deemed "young adult" from this vast body of traditional literature. For one thing the concept of adulthood itself has shifted; in past centuries, people married, went to work, and went to war at earlier ages. Most of this oral literature was either specific to the very young (nursery rhymes) or intended for a general audience (though storytellers tend to mold the story to fit the audience at hand). Myths and legends were learned throughout life, though it should be noted that in many cultures some stories and songs are associated specifically with the initiation into adulthood. The "Epic of Sundiata," for example, was told by griots (storyteller/historians) in Mali to young men as part of their rite of passage.

Vast numbers of traditional tales, stories, songs, and legends have been retold in a written format (see Chapter 4). Some of the earliest printed fairy tales in Europe were collected by Charles Perrault in the 17th century—including "Cinderella," "Sleeping Beauty," and "Little Red Riding Hood." However, these are not necessarily the same child-friendly versions common today and would likely have been listened to by audiences of various ages, including people in their teens.

Young Adults and Reading

Bennett Brookman (1985) contends that there was no separate literature for young people in the middle ages "apart from pedagogical texts designed to teach them to read, to write, to cipher, and to behave civilly" (p. 18). Until the 18th century, young people in the Western world tended to be viewed as "deficient adults," and so they were given religious and didactic material to read. Gilliam Adams (1998), on the other hand, asserts that literature for young people did exist but was not clearly labeled and needs to be rediscovered just as much as the historical literature authored by women has been rediscovered in the past few decades. Either way, the period between childhood and adulthood was not recognized as a separate stage of growth.

Literate teens tended to read either works aimed at children or literature written for a general audience. Still it is probable that there have always been works of literature that, despite not being labeled as such, have appealed directly to teen audiences. One can easily imagine, for example, that young adults in Renaissance England might be drawn to *Romeo and Juliet,* with its young characters and themes of love, death, and family estrangement.

Throughout history many young people learned to read and write (if they ever did) in their teens, using reading materials designed for that purpose. In school settings reading materials included hornbooks, battledores, and primers. Hornbooks were wooden panels with the alphabet, vowels, or the Lord's Prayer printed on parchment. The name came from the thin transparent plates of horn that covered the panel. Hornbooks first appeared in the 1440s and lasted for several centuries as a tool for teaching reading. Similar to hornbooks in terms of usage and content were battledores, which were often paper-based and could therefore contain more illustrations and a larger amount of text.

Primers were small, simple books that introduced young people to the alphabet, generally followed by prayers. Religious in nature, primers first emerged in the 16th century and were often accompanied by illustrations after the 1650s. By the late 18th century primers began appearing that were less religious but used the same general format to introduce various simple topics. *The New England Primer* (circa 1690), believed to be authored by Benjamin Harris, was the most commonly used book for teaching young people to read in the United States for almost a century.

Outside of school, price alone kept most literature out of reach of the average young adult reader. However, there was at least one type of literature that common folk could afford. Chapbooks were folded paper booklets sold by peddlers (chapmen). These inexpensive books, illustrated with woodcuts, appeared in England in the 1580s (though not called chapbooks until the 19th century). Some told stories such as "Who Killed Cock Robin" and "Jack the Giant Killer," stories that are still being retold in picture book format today. Others were much more bawdy and aimed at a variety of age groups. Popular books, such as *Robinson Crusoe,* were also abridged as chapbooks. Chapbooks were an early example of an inexpensive mass-produced form of literature created as pleasurable reading material.

As society became increasingly urban, youth spent more time in school before working, and a greater variety of reading materials were needed to engage specific audiences. Also, as changes in printing technology made mass-produced books a possibility, new markets were sought. British publisher John Newbery (1740s–1760s) is often credited with pioneering the children's book industry. He published books that were actually appealing for young people, effectively connecting illustrations with text. Books like *Little Goody Two Shoes* are not often read anymore, but they have had a lasting impact on literature and society. Even as this pleasurable literature for youth evolved, however, many highly moralistic, didactic tales continued to be published.

Girls' series books, or family stories, were the accepted norm for young women in the late 19th and early 20th centuries. The Elsie Dinsmore series, for example, with 28 volumes (1860s), was extremely popular. Many of these books would be a hard sell today because

The company went together to the sea shore and planted
the signal . . . .

The Young Marooners on the Florida Coast
(James Claxton, 1852) by F. R. Goulding
is one of the many Robinsonades aimed
at young audiences. Goulding's book
was extremely popular and went though
10 editions. Courtesy of Salisbury
University's Blackwell Library.

they are quite moralistic, and most young readers would find the language and themes to be dated. However, a few of these family stories have survived, such as *Little Women* (1868) by Louisa May Alcott. Even the Elsie Dinsmore books have been republished recently by a small religious press and several enthusiastic websites provide ebook versions of these novels.

Boys' series books from the same era tended to be adventure stories. Some of these adventures were originally written for adults but became favorites of young men (and young women). Although not written as a book for young readers, *Robinson Crusoe* quickly became a favorite and sparked centuries of geographical adventure novels, many of which were actually spinoffs or retellings of *Robinson Crusoe*. There were so many in fact that they were grouped in a new category of literature referred to as "Robinsonades." *The New Robinson Crusoe* by German author Henrich Campe (1779) was one attempt to make the story more appropriate for young readers by adding Jean Jacques Rousseau's influence. Swiss pastor Johann David Wyss added religious piety to the storyline in *The Swiss Family Robinson* (1812). However, during the Victorian era there was a shift back to Robinsonades that stressed the excitement and danger of the adventure story over didactic intent. Many of these books replaced the adult figure with a group of young protagonists. Ballantyne's *The Coral Island* (1858), Taylor's *The Young Islanders* or *The School Boy Crusoes* (1849), and Goulding's *The Young Marooners* (1862) are among the many examples.

Not every adventure book concerned marooned survivors of course. *The Last of the Mohicans* (Cooper, 1826), *Ivanhoe* (Scott, 1820), and *Treasure Island* (Stevenson, 1883) were all popular with young adults in their day and still retain a level of popularity. Howard Pyle, Horatio Alger, and G. A. Henty are well known for their series aimed specifically at boys and young men. Henty alone authored more than 70 adventure stories, and over 25 million copies of his books were sold prior to 1914. Occasionally, a young person will still come across a book such as Pyle's *Robin Hood* and become entranced, but most readers will never encounter a Horatio Alger story (though they might hear the phrase in a politician's speech—these stories inevitably involved a protagonist who pulled himself up by the bootstraps to become a successful member of society).

School stories were another popular type of literature targeting boys. Thomas Hughes's novel *Tom Brown's Schooldays* (1857) was among the first of many explorations of the school context. These school stories tended to be extremely moralistic. Talbot Reed's *The Master of the Shell* (1894), for example, was published by the Religious Tract Society. But it was set in a secondary school with a heavy stress on sports and despite the didacticism was quite popular. These school stories continue to influence literature for youth today; even the Harry Potter books have been impacted by the school story tradition.

DEATH OF THE PIRATE RUGGIERO MOCENIGO
Page 100

G. A. Henty (1832–1902) wrote novels that tended to include a young male protagonist paired with a heroic adult figure. Illustration by Gordon Browne from G. A. Henty's *Orange and Green* (Blackie, 1888).

THE BALL ROSE AND FLEW DIRECTLY FOR THE BASKET.
Gir's of Central High at Basketball   *(Frontispiece)—Page* 90

Although young women were expected to read certain types of books, characters in girls' series books sometimes break the gender norms. Illustration from *The Girls of Central High School* (Grosset and Dunlap, 1914). Courtesy of Salisbury University's Blackwell Library.

The dime novels of the 1860s, with characters such as Deadwood Dick and Nick Carter, had an impact on many teen readers as did some of the Edward Stratemeyer series books, including Soldiers of Fortune and Nancy Drew. The 1930s to 1950s saw the advent of the Junior novel, and the precursors of the young adult novel appeared, including *Seventeenth Summer* (Daly, 1942), *Hot Rod* (Felsen, 1950), and *Johnny Tremain* (Forbes, 1944).

Some of these historical works that are considered classics will be reprinted from time to time, and most are in the public domain, so any publisher can print a new edition. New illustrations and introductions by contemporary authors are sometimes added to enhance the appeal. When *The Adventures of Tom Sawyer* was reprinted in 2002 by Kingfisher Classics, a foreword by Katherine Paterson was included. Young people familiar with her works might be enticed to read *Tom Sawyer* with her endorsement, and professionals might choose this edition over others because of her foreword.

To Consider

Why does one book fade into obscurity whereas another continues to be read and enjoyed by young people?

Hot Rod by Henry Felsen (Bantam, 1950). Reprinted by permission of Penguin Group (USA).

The Cherry Ames series by Helen Wells starts with 18-year-old Cherry embarking on a nursing career. The first one, *Cherry Ames, Student Nurse,* came out in 1943 (Grosset and Dunlap). Courtesy of Salisbury University's Blackwell Library.

The Emergence of Young Adult Literature

As for what critics have considered young adult literature, there are several turning points in literary history in the United States. The first novel considered by many critics to be specifically YA is Maureen Daly's *Seventeenth Summer,* published in 1942. Here was a book that was not for children, nor was it an adult book that appealed to teens; this novel was for and about young adults. A number of series that commenced in the early 1900s such as Cherry Ames, Student Nurse and Nancy Drew were widely read by teens and preteens alike, but *Seventeenth Summer* was more directly aimed at the high school audience and so is considered by many as a benchmark.

Still, the girl series books should not be discounted. Nancy Drew solved her first mystery in 1929 and is still going strong. Over 40 million copies have been sold in North America and the books have been translated into 17 languages. Sixteen-year-old Nancy was a girl being raised solely by a father in the 1930s. Not only was this nontraditional family situation unusual but Nancy held enormous responsibility for running her household. To a large extent the issues and relationships in these books often seem most appropriate for preteens, but many teens past and present have enjoyed reading them.

For other critics the term *young adult literature* did not take on real meaning until 1967 and the publication of S. E. Hinton's *The Outsiders.* This was something new! Hinton's writing was influenced by the life she was living as a teenager, a reality that she had not been able to find reflected in the books she encountered. *The Contender* (Robert Lipsyte) also came out that same year, and both met with great success. A number of books followed that held a similar hard edge of realism and dealt with themes relevant to many young adults. *Soul Brother and Sister Lou* (Hunter, 1968) and *The Pigman* (Zindel, 1968), for example, appealed directly to adolescent readers, not just to their teachers and parents. Judy Blume introduced preteens and teens to the female coming-of-age novel in *Are You There God? It's Me, Margaret* (1970), which broke new ground in books for youth. In this new edgier young adult milieu Robert Cormier's editor marketed his book *The Chocolate War* (1974) for young adults, and what we recognize today as YA literature was in full swing.

The 1970s and 80s were filled with so-called "problem novels," as formerly taboo topics were brought to the literary realm. These novels tended to deal with adolescents confronting alcohol, homelessness, abuse, and other social ills. The term "problem novel" is often used today with negative connotations, calling to mind melodramatic after-school specials. Patrick Jones (1998) asserts that much of this literature actually lost its edge and became rather formulaic during this time. However, some excellent works of literature such as *Dicey's Song* (Voigt, 1983), and *The Pigman* (Zindel, 1968) are also generally included as problem novels, but these are exceptions. In many of these books, though the characters are teens, the mindset of the writing reflects teens decades behind the times, or as Jones puts it, "absurdly out of whack with the youth zeitgeist," making the literature less likely to appeal to the age group they address. Indeed, many novels with protagonists aged 12 to 16 were being read by kids in the fourth or fifth grade. Nevertheless, a number of these YA novels from the 1970s and 80s are still being read in schools today, some because teachers feel comfortable using the books they know, others with enthusiasm because they remain relevant to contemporary YA readers.

In the Field *Age-Appropriate Literature in the Classroom*

June Harris is currently associate dean for academic affairs at the University of Arizona South. She has over 40 years experience in public education and has taught every grade level from fourth grade through graduate school. This essay was originally posted on the childlit listserv of which Harris is an active member.

Way back in the dark ages when I first discovered YA lit, my ninth-grade classes were required to read a novel as part of the curriculum, and *Silas Marner* was the one on the list. I was new to high school teaching, and I didn't have much notion of how I might interest my students in a book they saw as having nothing to do with them or their lives. Consequently, I managed to talk the department head into letting me buy a class set of S. E. Hinton's *The*

Outsiders. The problem I had then was that the students had to read the book in class; we had one class set that was shared by five classes. The students got into the book so much that they started stealing copies. I had to number the books and assign numbers to the students so I could track the copies. Then they went out and bought their own copies. My students wanted to read more than the one class hour per day would allow. Nobody ever stole *Silas Marner.* I'd swear, in fact, that I had more copies at the end of the year than I'd had at the start (maybe they were bringing them from home to toss into the book box).

Over the years I managed to acquire other class sets of YA books. Paul Zindel (*My Darling, My Hamburger; Confessions of a Teenage Baboon*) was popular, as were other books by Hinton. I had so much more success with the YA fiction than with the classics that I started to see the YA books as a way to introduce the classics. Once the students learn the characteristics of the novel with a book whose plot they do not have difficulty negotiating, they can apply what they've learned to more difficult fiction. I learned about "pairing" novels—that is, using a YA to introduce a classic, matching them according to theme, plot line, setting, etc. I've paired *Roll of Thunder, Hear My Cry* (Taylor) with *To Kill a Mockingbird* (Lee); and I've used *The Witch of Blackbird Pond* (Speare) to introduce *The Scarlet Letter* (Hawthorne). It seemed to work for me, and my students seemed to like it as well.

Author Spotlight

Photo courtesy of Arnold Adoff.

Virginia Hamilton and Arnold Adoff

Arnold Adoff was born in the East Bronx, New York City. It was while working as a teacher in Harlem in the 1960s that Adoff discovered the need for an anthology of poetry focused on African American authors, and this was the impetus for *I Am the Darker Brother* (1968, revised 1997). He has since authored and anthologized over 30 books for young people. Adoff is well known for his use of shaped speech stylings in his poetry. In 1988 he was the recipient of the NCTE Award for Excellence in Poetry for Children, and he has received numerous other distinctions and awards, including an American Library Association Best Book for Young Adults citation for *Slow Dance Heartbreak Blues.* Visit his website at www.arnoldadoff.com.

SELECTED BOOKLIST

All the Colors of the Race (William Morrow, 1982)
Chocolate Dreams (Lothrop, Lee, and Shepard, 1989)
I Am the Darker Brother (Collier, 1968)
OUTside/Inside Poems (Harcourt Brace, 1981)
Slow Dance Heartbreak Blues (Lothrop, Lee, and Shepard, 1995)

Photo by Carlo Ontal, courtesy of Arnold Adoff.

Virginia Hamilton was one of the most prolific writers of and advocates for children's and young adult literature. She began publishing in 1967 and had on average a new book published every year until her death on February 19, 2002. Hamilton was born in 1936 and grew up on a family farm in Yellow Springs, Ohio. Her parents were both storytellers, and she attributed her love of traditional literature and storytelling methods to their influence. Among her numerous distinctions are the Edgar Allen Poe Award in 1968 for *The House of Dies Drear,* the Newbery Medal in 1974 for *M. C. Higgins the Great,* the Laura Ingalls Wilder Award in 1995, the Coretta Scott King Award in 1996 for *Her Stories,* and the international Hans Christian Andersen Award in 1992. Virginia Hamilton and Arnold Adoff were married in 1960. They have a daughter Leigh and a son Jaime (author of *The Songs Shoot Out of My Mouth* and *Names Will Never Hurt Me*). Visit her website at www.virginiahamilton.com.

SELECTED BOOKLIST

Bluish: A Novel (Blue Sky Press, 1999)
The Girl Who Spun Gold (Blue Sky Press, 2000)
Her Stories (Blue Sky Press, 1995)
The House of Dies Drear (Simon and Schuster, 1968)
In the Beginning (Harcourt Brace, 1998)
M. C. Higgins the Great (Simon and Schuster, 1974)
The Planet of Junior Brown (Simon and Schuster, 1971)
Second Cousins (Philomel, 1990)
Timepieces (Blue Sky Press, 2002)
Zeely (Simon and Schuster, 1967)

ON WRITING FOR YOUNG ADULTS IN THE 1960s

I started as an anthologist with *I Am the Darker Brother,* what we called Negro poetry back in 1967, when Virginia started with *Zeely.* Many of Virginia's books, even the extraordinary ones, extraordinary in terms of structure and in complexity, like *Aurelia Sundown* and *The Magical Adventures of Pretty Pearl,* were classified by publishers as children's books because there was usually quite an antipathy towards the YA novel. Even people like John Donovan—*I'll Get There But It Better Be Worth the Trip* (1969)—and other groundbreakers who opened up young adult literature in the sixties, they could talk about being gay, they could talk about death, or drugs, but very subtly, tangentially, treading softly.

ON CHANGES IN THE DIVERSITY OF VOICES IN YOUNG ADULT LITERATURE

There is such a long way to go!

Publishers absolutely consciously disregard the social context to the extent that a kind of tokenism exists; I can't tell you how infuriating it is to see the smaller numbers, and the numbers are shrinking. There is no question that it's so much more than it was when we began and so much more than when I began teaching in the late fifties. There are more Asians coming in, Korean-American Linda Sue Park won the Newbery Medal. Publishers are opening up the doors. There are a few soliciting, like Jump at the Sun and Lee & Low—those did not exist back in the sixties, that specifically aim for publishing people of color, of parallel cultures.

But my yardstick is very simple; tell me that there are 7,000 new titles every year for children, young adults, and I say, "Show me 700 by and about African Americans" because that's 10 percent of the population. Then let's talk about other people as well, you know, Hispanic Americans, Mexican Americans, Puerto Rican Americans, Dominican Americans, Cuban Americans, and you could only name handfuls, not dozens. So there is still a tremendous hole culturally in a white male-dominated power structure that controls this very conservative and conventional field which is children's literature or youth literature.

ON EXPANDING YOUNG PEOPLE'S WORLDS THROUGH LITERATURE

Virginia and I really aimed to do things for young people that would get inside their heads and try to make progress from point A to point B. Virginia was always like that. We would sometimes call her novels like *M. C. Higgins* survival novels so it wasn't always race and she broadly went beyond race and color and America to the things that had to do with the environment, that had to do with gender, that had to do with kinds of family relationships. The universals were extraordinary, the specifics most of the time may have been African American, but it only allowed for her work to be far more relevant.

She really was so deeply, deeply grounded in creating superb literature, in becoming the best fictionist. But on the other hand, even with something like *The Girl Who Spun Gold,* where she found this Caribbean version of Rumpelstiltskin and wrote it over and over again until it was readable for today's audience, she subtly developed the character of a young woman creating a kind of a modern-day sensibility and independence in her consciousness.

ON USING YOUNG ADULT LITERATURE IN SCHOOLS

The high school class is a hard place to go. Not the school library anymore, and certainly never the public library. But how can you have a kid in high school who hasn't read a Jacqueline Woodson novel and why shouldn't the teacher bring that in or a Virginia Hamilton novel? High school teachers by and large are afraid to use things that are not on the list because they are afraid of parents coming in, and censorship, and losing their jobs. By and large that's the trend, and by and large youth literature is an extremely conventional art form, an extremely conventional publishing program. There's just a long, long way to go—like using live writers in a high school class, like bringing in nonwhite writers, like bringing in YA novels, everything you look at is a stick of dynamite in a community. It only takes one—look at what happened in Queens, New York, for God sakes with *Nappy Hair*. The point is a book is inflammatory and so these teachers by and large take the conventional route because of the education that they got in education schools themselves.

ON WHY THEY WRITE FOR YOUNG PEOPLE AS OPPOSED TO WRITING FOR ADULTS

We met in '58. When we were married in 1960, our marriage was illegal in 28 states. This is the America we lived in. It was a different time. So in the midst of hatred and in the midst of violence and riots and counterrevolution and Nixon's years and Reagan's years, everything that energized us really had to do with young people, children's librarians, and children's lit professors and colleges and teachers and people who became our friends and became the support group, and children's book editors. And the more you delve into history, the more you realize that the adults are just going to have to fend for themselves, and maybe by the time they got to be adult, it was too late.

ON WHETHER A PERSON CAN WRITE AUTHENTIC NARRATIVE ABOUT A CHARACTER FROM A CULTURE OUTSIDE OF THE AUTHOR'S OWN PERSONAL EXPERIENCES

The simple answer that Virginia would always give is if you're a white woman and if you can create a black kid with a black voice that's as good as one that I can do or one that Jackie Woodson can do or Walter Dean Myers can do, then you did it and you're certainly entitled. And if you didn't do the research or if you don't have the ear or if you can't create that kind of character that stands alongside one that is as absolutely authentic and real as something that a black writer could create, then you failed and you failed as a writer, and you don't deserve to have that published and it has nothing to do with racism, reverse racism, or anything else. And that's really what it comes down to in the end: literary excellence.

ON COLLABORATION BETWEEN TWO CREATIVE FORCES

There was a great deal of collaboration. Our marriage lasted until she died—that was 42 years. And we'd known each other a year and a half before. The one time that we tried to do the same book was a cookbook that someone wanted us to do and we couldn't get past arguing about the first recipe. How to cook the chicken. And the green beans would have been the next one and that would have been a battle. So there's Eurocentric recipes, there's southern black and white recipes that are geographic as well as cultural, and we realized then that it would have been a huge mistake and it was as far as we got, it was just impossible.

I was her agent and manager and trip organizer for over 30 years. She never answered the phone, and when she was traveling she would answer and pretend to be her own secretary most of the time. She was a writer rather than a talker. She was a shy, quiet girl from a family in Ohio and she had to develop a public persona to go out and give speeches and thank people for awards and present some of her political and literary points of view. We were collaborators in the sense that she would read to me always each new chapter. We talked about the business all the time to the point where the kids at the dinner table many times would have to say, "Enough already! Let me tell you what happened in school."

Historical Texts in the Classroom

Knowing about the history of literature has its own value, but the question of how these historical texts might benefit our middle and secondary school students is also significant. As already mentioned, some of these books can be enticing reads in and of themselves. In the contemporary adventure novel *Wild Timothy* by Gary Blackwood, a reluctant camper becomes stranded in the wilderness. One of the things that helps Timothy get through it all is the book he finds stashed in his coat pocket, *The Call of the Wild* by Jack London. Certainly London's novel is one of the quintessential adventure stories and it is still enjoyed by many people of all ages. The book was recently reissued by Aladdin Classics for its 100-year anniversary with a new forward by Gary Paulsen, the author of another great adventure novel, *Hatchet*. Another version published as part of the Scribner Classics series has beautiful illustrations by Wendell Minor.

In addition to simply being read for pleasure, these books might be explored as historical documents and investigated for the insights they provide on assumptions about gender and race from certain time periods; ideas about family, war, or dating; the way language was used; and how young adults were depicted, to name only a few of the many possibilities.

If there were few contemporary books in the early 1960s that appealed specifically to young adults, realistic books portraying African American youth were extremely rare. Lorenz Graham's books *South Town* (1958) and *North Town* (1965), the first two of four books in a series, accomplished both and so were pioneering in several ways. This series has recently been reissued by Boyds Mills Press with a foreword by Rudine Sims Bishop that does an excellent job contextualizing the books historically and socially. The story remains relevant thematically—anyone who has been in a high school cafeteria knows that the effects of racism and segregation are far from over as an issue for young adults. In terms of exploring the context of the 1950s and 60s, Graham creates characters who manifest "the range of attitudes and behaviors that were prevalent among both Black and white citizens," and places these characters in positions where they must "grapple with the issues

Huckleberry Finn, considered one of the great American novels, is an adventure story in the picaresque tradition. Mark Twain's *The Adventures of Huckleberry Finn* (Chatto and Windus, 1884).

and decide what is the right thing for them to do" (Sims Bishop, 2003, p. xi).

A novel such as *North Town* might be part of a wonderful historical study comparing the book to nonfiction of the time period, to recent historical fiction about the late 1950s and 60s, to the representation of blacks (or lack thereof) in other books for young people from the era, or even to a more recent work of fiction about a student of color transferring to a predominantly white school (*The Beast* by Walter Dean Myers or *The Warriors* by Joseph Bruchac). All of these explorations could lead to beneficial dialogue and critical thought.

With older historical works, exploring the context is often essential. *Huckleberry Finn,* for example, is still used in schools around the country, but it is often challenged and sometimes removed from schools and libraries, primarily because of the depiction of Jim and the use of the word "nigger" throughout. Reasoned and heartfelt arguments have been made that the book can be devastating to African American students in the class and can reinforce stereotypes held by other students. Julius Lester, for example, asserts that *Huckleberry Finn* is not a selection he would make as a parent: "While I am opposed to book banning, I know that my children's education will be enhanced by not reading *Huckleberry Finn*" (1995, p. 342).

Some teachers have addressed this issue head on, and if they decide to use the book do so within a broader examination of social and historical issues. The Cherry Hill School District in New Jersey, for example, put together a wonderful unit wherein students explore the context in which the book was written and then role-play a debate about whether the book should still be used in the curriculum. Rather than bystanders, the students have been placed in the role of experts concerning the book (www.pbs.org/wgbh/cultureshock/teachers/huck).

Monica Edinger at the Dalton School in New York has found another interesting way to integrate historical texts. Her classes have taken Lewis Carroll's *Alice's Adventures in Wonderland* (1865), which like most literature written over 75 years ago is in the public domain, and created their own electronic version in which the original text is accompanied by student created illustrations (www.dalton.org/ms/alice/content.html). This project was done with elementary school students but similar projects could be done at the middle and secondary levels.

In a project of this sort, the students gain some ownership of the text and are more likely to be excited about reading and understanding the storyline. This type of activity could easily be replicated at the secondary level with any number of books. The first

To Consider

Books in the public domain may be easily accessible but teachers need additional reasons for choosing to use these historical works. What rationale would you use to explain your choice to administrators and parents?

*Some Excellent Repositories
of Public Domain Books*
- Children's Literature Web Guide—
  www.ucalgary.ca/~dkbrown
- Net Library—www.netlibrary.com
- Online Books Page—http://onlinebooks
  .library.upenn.edu
- Project Bartleby—www.bartleby.com
- Project Gutenberg—www.gutenberg.net

step would likely be to have students explore some of the different versions and compare how the illustrator's vision of the storyline influences the reader's response. Some versions like Otto Seibold's or Sabuda's pop-up book at first seem more suited to a younger audience, though each has layers of sophistication. However, a quick look through Barry Moser or Ralph Steadman's renderings will quickly convince many YA readers that the story has a level of depth that they might enjoy exploring.

Technology Links

Historical Works Online

One of the most enticing reasons for using historical pieces of literature in the classroom is that many of these works are available in the public domain and can be used by teachers without worrying about copyright issues (though you should always double-check to make sure the book is in the public domain first). There are a number of depositories of historical works of literature online where the full texts of these books can be accessed.

The University of Calgary's Children's Literature Web Guide is a convenient resource for accessing many of the best known historical works for young people. *White Fang* (London), *Robinson Crusoe* (Defoe), *Huckleberry Finn* (Twain), *War of the Worlds* (Wells), and *The Call of the Wild* (London) can all be found here. Some are provided simply with the text; others include illustrations from historical editions. They come in various formats including html, rich text, or pdf. Among the numerous repositories of public domain books, the Online Books Page, which has been operating since 1993, is one of the largest with over 20,000 books, making it a good source for locating more obscure works.

Author Spotlight

Photo courtesy of Lois Duncan.

Lois Duncan

Lois Duncan was born in Sarasota, Florida, the daughter of respected photographers, Joseph and Lois Steinmetz. She had her first story published when she was 13, and she began writing magazine articles in her teen years. She has written over 300 articles and short stories and around 50 books. Duncan received the Margaret A. Edwards Award in 1992, which honors a living author for a distinguished body of adolescent literature. She is well known for her suspenseful fiction such as *Gallows Hill*, and *I Know What You Did Last Summer*, as well as for her nonfiction book *Who Killed My Daughter?* (the story of her search for the truth behind the brutal murder of her daughter Kaitlyn). For more information see Duncan's DVD "A Visit with Lois Duncan" (Silver Moon Productions) or visit her website at http://loisduncan.arquettes.com/index.htm.

SELECTED BOOKLIST
Don't Look Behind You (Delacorte, 1989)
Gallows Hill (Delacorte, 1997)
I Know What You Did Last Summer (Little, Brown, 1978)
Killing Mr. Griffin (Little, Brown, 1973)
Songs from Dreamland (Knopf, 1989)
Stranger with My Face (Little, Brown, 1981)
The Terrible Tales of Happy Days School (Little, Brown, 1983)
Who Killed My Daughter? (Delacorte, 1992)

ON HOW SHE BECAME AN AUTHOR OF YOUNG ADULT LITERATURE

I started submitting stories to magazines when I was 10, and made my first sale at 13. Throughout my teens, I continued to write regularly for young people's publications, primarily *Seventeen Magazine*. So when I wrote my first novel at 20, it was natural to write about what I knew about and was used to writing about, which was young adult subject matter.

ON THE INSPIRATION FOR HER STORIES

I'm the mother of five children, with 16 years between the oldest and the youngest. There was never a lack of inspiration.

ON THE EXTENT TO WHICH HER OWN LIFE STORY APPEARS IN HER WORKS

In my nonfiction book, *Who Killed My Daughter?*—the true story of my youngest child's unsolved homicide and our family's ongoing battle to fight the police cover-up—my "own life story" is everything in the book (see www.kaitarquette.arquettes .com). In my fictional novels, characterization and background are reflections of my own life experiences, although the plots are primarily products of my imagination.

ON WHAT SHE ENJOYS READING CURRENTLY

I still enjoy novels and poetry. But since my daughter's homicide, I find myself reading (and writing) a lot more nonfiction.

ON WHAT DISTINGUISHES YOUNG ADULT LITERATURE

YA literature utilizes mature subject matter (which children aren't ready to comprehend), but—in my opinion, at least—should do so with sensitivity. Although my suspense novels, by the nature of the genre, may sometimes include violent situations, I don't sensationalize violence or present it as titillating. Which is why I was so upset by the fact that my 1970s novel, *I Know What You Did Last Summer,* was turned into a slasher film. And I don't write explicit sex scenes.

ON WHAT MIGHT HELP YOUNG ADULTS DEVELOP AS WRITERS

That they sit down every day and put words on paper. Writing is a self-taught craft. There are no shortcuts, and nobody can do it for you.

ON THE APPEAL OF SUSPENSE NOVELS

Today's young people have become conditioned by television. They tend to have short attention spans and are used to switching channels if something doesn't "happen" immediately. Suspense novels come closer to fulfilling their TV-oriented expectations of instant entertainment than most other genres.

Topic Focus

Selection and Censorship

In our system, it should not be the role of teachers or librarians or principals to restrict ideas but rather to illuminate and analyze them, good and bad, so that students learn how to do that for themselves for the rest of their lives. I mean, so that students will learn how to think for themselves.

—*The Day They Came to Arrest the Book* by Nat Hentoff

Of the thousands of titles published each year, a teacher or librarian can only afford to select a limited number, and this selection is guided to an extent by the process adopted by the school system or library. Most school systems have an established procedure for adding titles to the approved reading list and another procedure for procuring titles in the school media center.

There are of course both frustrations and benefits involved in having a set selection process. Tales of it taking up to a year to add a single book to the approved reading list in a school district are not uncommon! However, once the book is approved, there is generally better support within the system in case the book is challenged. This is a serious consideration because in recent years book challenges have become more widespread. When we think of book bannings, certain topics might immediately come to mind: sex, drugs, violence, and racism, at least until recent years (the Harry Potter series has pushed fantasy to the forefront with charges of satanism), were the most common censorship red flags. Yet it might be surprising to find the range of issues that are cited, and the reasons for a particular book being challenged can change over the years.

The Adventures of Huckleberry Finn has been on challenged booklists since the year of its publication. Objections in the 19th century tended to view the novel as negative in the depiction of southern whites, or simply lacking in good morals. *The St. Louis Globe-Democrat* wrote of Huck Finn:

> It deals with a series of adventures of a very low grade of morality; it is couched in the language of a rough dialect, and all through its pages there is a systemic use of bad grammar and an employment of rough, coarse, inelegant expressions. It is also very irreverent. . . . The whole book is of a class that is more profitable for the slums than it is for respectable people. (March 17, 1885)

Over time, the objections have shifted to focus on negative stereotypes in the portrayal of Jim.

A quick check on the books listed in the recommended historical text set that accompanies this chapter reveals that all of the books on this list are included in the ALA Banned Books list with the exception of *North Town* (which has not been widely used in schools). Among the hundreds of challenges:

> Paul Zindel's *Pigman* was challenged as suitable curriculum material in Harwinton and Burlington, Connecticut (1990), because it contains profanity and has subject matter that sets a bad example and gives a negative view of life.
>
> S. E. Hinton's *The Outsiders* was challenged in George Washington Middle School in Eleanor, West Virginia (2000), because of the focus on gangs and gang violence.
>
> Harper Lee's *To Kill a Mockingbird* was banned from the Lindale, Texas, advanced placement English reading list (1996) because it "conflicted with the values of the community."
>
> Nat Hentoff's *The Day They Came to Arrest the Book* was challenged in the Albemarle County school system in Charlottesville, Virginia (1990), because it offers an inflammatory challenge to authoritarian roles.
>
> Mildred Taylor's *Roll of Thunder, Hear My Cry* was removed from the ninth-grade reading list at the Arcadia, Louisiana, High School (1993) because of its "racial bias."
>
> Robert Cormier's *The Chocolate War* was challenged by the Grosse Point, Michigan, school district (1995) because it deals with "gangs, peer pressure, and learning to make your own decisions."

Source: Banned Books by Robert Doyle, American Library Association, 2001

> *To Consider*
> Are there books that you feel strongly enough about that you would fight to keep them in your classroom or library? Under what conditions would you allow these books to be removed?

Some of the reasons given for wanting to remove books, for example, "learning to make your own decisions," might seem ludicrous until you have to face these challenges in your own school. Both the NCTE (www.ncte.org) and the ALA (www.ala.org) offer a wide range of materials on their websites and through their publications to assist schools and libraries as they deal with this issue.

Young Adults and the Classics

> It's not as easy as it once was to take for granted that Shakespeare's reputation—and Beatrix Potter's—depend on the inherent superiority of their work rather than on the insistence of powerful people and institutions that their work is superior.
>
> —Perry Nodelman and Mavis Reimer

The books discussed in the first part of this chapter are in many ways the new classics of young adult literature, but with the exception of a few crossovers (such as *Huckleberry Finn*), these books are not generally considered to be "classics" of the Western literary canon. So what is a classic and why do we have young adults read them anyway?

Almost two decades ago, Arthur Applebee (1989) surveyed 322 secondary schools and found that the most commonly used books were

1. *Romeo and Juliet*
2. *Macbeth*
3. *Huckleberry Finn*
4. *To Kill a Mockingbird*
5. *Julius Caesar*
6. *The Pearl*
7. *The Scarlet Letter*
8. *Of Mice and Men*
9. *Lord of the Flies*
10. *Anne Frank: The Diary of a Young Girl*

He also found that students did not particularly enjoy what they were reading. Though this study is somewhat dated, the reading lists at many secondary schools have not changed drastically. So two questions arise: Why don't young adults get excited about reading most of these books? And why are they still being used? As for the first question, keep in mind that not many of the "classics" were originally intended for a young audience, and they generally have themes, styles, and dialects that would appeal most directly to an adult audience of a certain time period (Anne Frank's diary is certainly an exception here). It can be extremely difficult to get young people who are reluctant readers to engage with any text; give them something that is outdated, irrelevant (on the surface at least) to their lives, with unfamiliar syntax and vocabulary, and you have a recipe for Cliff Notes (or SparkNotes). To further complicate things, three of the books on Applebee's list are actually scripts meant to be seen on stage rather than read, but for the most part in schools they are read and analyzed as if they were prose.

So why are these particular books used? The concept of "Great Works" is nothing new. In centuries past, to be educated meant that you could read literary works in a language long since dead. To read or write in English, French, or German was seen as vulgar. Refined people read classic works in Latin. This is part of a complicated phenomenon which involves the construction and perpetuation of an educated elite. Once people have determined that educated people should know certain information or have read certain books, it is difficult to decide that this knowledge or these particular books might not actually be the absolute best choices for all occasions and all times.

Other factors include the belief that colleges want applicants to know these books, that many anthologies include these works, teachers are familiar with these texts and feel more prepared to teach with them, the works have withstood the test of time, and they are part of our literary tradition and cultural knowledge.

John Bushman and other proponents of YA literature have argued passionately that classical literature was by and large written for an educated adult audience and does not "provide the answers that young people are seeking" (1997, p. 35). Bushman thinks teaching *Julius Caesar, The Iliad,* and *The Old Man and the Sea* to eighth and ninth graders is totally opposed to good educational practice. Interestingly, in Bushman's survey of the literature actually being used in classrooms around the country, he found that sixth and seventh graders were being exposed to some (mainly older) works of YA literature, but by the eighth grade, only 6 of the 48 most widely used books were for young adults (again older works). From the ninth to twelfth grade, YA literature was almost nonexistent on the lists of the most widely used books. One exception was Walter Dean Myers's *Fallen Angels,* which was in the top 10 books used at the twelfth-grade level. Perhaps the most interesting detail of Bushman's study is that the amount of pleasure reading done by secondary students in his survey also decreased as they moved from freshman to senior year.

Related to this, the National Endowment for the Humanities in 2003 put out a "classics" summer reading list for grades K–12. For younger children, most of the recommended readings are historically significant picture books, but as you move up through the grade levels, works for youth are systematically replaced by "classic" books written for an adult audience. By the ninth- to twelfth-grade levels, there are almost no books included that were originally published for young people. There are some crossover books like *Huckleberry Finn, Catcher in the Rye,* and *Treasure Island,* which over the decades have become staples of what young adults read. Some diversity is also mixed in, including *Things Fall Apart* by Nigerian author Chinua Achebe. The organization's stated goal is to promote the classics, but it is interesting that for children they emphasize classics of children's literature, but for young adults they ignore the entire body of young adult literature.

Selecting developmentally appropriate reading material is one of the key concepts stressed in reading methods courses, yet we subject even the youngest of teens to literature which in the past was read primarily by elite, educated adults. This remains the case despite studies like Arthur Applebee's (1994), which found that English classrooms are most successful when they integrate not only young adult literature but also comic books, song lyrics, and other forms of reading that appeal to young readers.

It has also been suggested that lists of classics are really rather arbitrary. Even with books that have become classics of youth literature, there are often no clear reasons as to why certain works are included. "Why *Anne of Green Gables* and not *Emily of New Moon*?" asks Sarah Ellis. "One does not seem better written than the other" (2000, p. 56). In fact, some works considered classics are not especially well written. British children's book editor Julia MacRae has asserted that *Treasure Island* is "long-winded, unconvincing, badly written, and just plain irritating" (Ellis, 2000).

Even so, in each of these works there is something that has appealed to a reading public. As Gary Blackwood suggests, "Classics are classics because they have themes and issues that people of various ages and times and places can relate to" (see Blackwood interview, p. 64). The key it seems is to first decide whether particular classics can be read with pleasure by the young people you work with and then with books you choose consider which strategies will make them more accessible to young readers. Historical works and classics might be used effectively, but this will often require more preparation and encouragement on the teacher's part. As Julius Lester asserts, "The classics depend on having good teachers to unlock them" (see Lester interview, p. 73) One question teachers and librarians constantly confront when selecting books is which works of literature will be most beneficial for and appealing to the particular readers being served.

Audio Books

Historical and Classic Connections

Are You There God? It's Me, Margaret by Judy Blume; read by Laura Hamilton. (Bantam Books-Audio, 2000) (N)

Around the World in 80 Days by Jules Verne; read by Jim Dale. (Listening Library, 2005) (Y)

The Chocolate War by Robert Cormier; read by Frank Muller. (Listening Library, 1998)

Hatchet by Gary Paulsen; read by Peter Coyote. (Random House, 1992) (N)

The King of Shadows by Susan Cooper; read by Jim Dale. (Bantam Books-Audio, 2000) (E, P)

Roll of Thunder, Hear My Cry by Mildred Taylor; read by Lynne Thingpen. (Bantam Books-Audio, 2001) (N)

A Separate Peace by John Knowles; read by Scott Snively. (Audio Bookshelf, 2002) (Y)

Troy by Adele Geras; read by Miriam Margolyes. (Random House, 2003) (AA, Y)

AA—Audie Awards	P—Parent's Choice Audio Award Winner
E—Booklist Editor's Choice	Y—YALSA Selected List of Audiobooks
N—ALSC Notable Children's Recording	

In the Field   *Read-Alouds at the Gary Public Library*

Audio books and read-alouds are not something teachers typically think of using with young adults. However, there are some very good reasons for getting teens to listen to a variety of literature being read aloud. An effective reading adds a level of interpretation to the story that includes the use of voice, pacing, and dramatic elements.

Anne Paradise, an extension librarian at the Gary, Indiana, Public Library, has found that certain types of literature work very well as read-alouds with young adults. Essentials include short chapters, a plot that is easy to pick up on the fly, and a good fit in persona between the reader and the narrator. For whole-class read-alouds it also helps if the book contains humor and a good bit of dialogue.

In her library, Paradise reads around two chapters per week at the scheduled time and a small core group comes to most of these sessions, along with a handful of drop-ins.

She has used a wide range of young adult literature; most recently she read Joan Bauer's *Squashed* and she is working with a special needs reading teacher to present a read-aloud of Karen Cushman's *The Midwife's Apprentice* to a whole class. However, she has a special affection for reading aloud versions of the classics. She has found some classics to be quite effective, including *A Midsummer Night's Dream*. As a spin-off to the read-alouds Paradise plans in the future to present stick figure puppet plays of shortened versions of *A Midsummer Night's Dream* and the story "Dionysus and the Pirates."

The question remains as to what is accomplished by reading the classics out loud to young adults? Jim Trelease asserts that young people listen at a higher level than they read, so with read-alouds students are being introduced to vocabulary and structures that they would not have access to when silently reading on their own. Young adults who listen to the story of *A Midsummer Night's Dream* are likely to understand more, to learn something about narrative structures, and, if they have an enjoyable experience, to be interested in reading more about the characters and situations.

The Gary, Indiana, Public Library is not the only institution interested in making read-alouds available for young adults. The Middle Grade Reading Network in Indiana is one of many efforts across the country that emphasizes reading aloud with older students. There are many arguments for presenting good oral readings to young adults:

- Exposing listeners to the enjoyment of reading
- Allowing them to see how others respond to literature
- Modeling fluent English
- Enhancing their understanding of structures such as dialogue, voice, and intonation, which might improve both their oral and silent reading skills
- Revealing differences between oral and written language
- Expanding vocabulary
- Increasing students' listening skills
- Helping students think about audience

Author Spotlight

Reprinted by permission of Penguin Putnam.

Gary Blackwood

Gary L. Blackwood was born and raised in rural western Pennsylvania. He went to school in a one-room schoolhouse. His school had few books, which made those they had very valuable to him. At an early age, he became interested in writing stories and began submitting to magazines in his teens. By the time he was 19 he had sold his first story. Blackwood has since published over 20 books, a half-dozen plays, and numerous articles and stories. In addition to writing, he has taught courses in writing for young people as well as playwriting.

SELECTED BOOKLIST

The Great Race around the World (Abrams, 2008)
The Shakespeare Stealer (Dutton, 1998)
Shakespeare's Scribe (Dutton, 2000)
Shakespeare's Spy (Dutton, 2004)
Wild Timothy (Atheneum, 1991)
Year of the Hangman (Dutton, 2002)

ON HOW HE BECAME AN AUTHOR OF YOUNG ADULT LITERATURE

Just lucky, I guess. When I started writing with publication in mind, I didn't know what I was best at, or what was likely to sell, so I tried some of everything—plays, science fiction, nonfiction, short stories, poems, "true confessions," TV scripts. It just happened that the first thing I sold was a children's story. When I moved on to novels, I ran the gamut again, from historical novels to westerns to fantasy to mystery to an autobiographical novel—some for adults, some for kids. The first thing I sold was a book for middle readers, so I figured why mess with success? I'm very glad now that it worked out that way. It seems to me that young readers aren't as locked into genres as adults are; they're open to anything, as long as it's good.

ON THE INSPIRATION FOR HIS STORIES

That sounds suspiciously like the standard question that kids ask: "Where do you get your ideas?" I won't give my smart-aleck answer ("There's a store in town that sells them for ten bucks apiece"). The truth is, there is no good answer. Ideas come from everywhere—a newspaper article, a historical site, my nonfiction research, something someone says—or from nowhere, from my unconscious. The trick is to recognize the good ones.

Though I enjoyed studying Shakespeare in college and relish his plays, I wouldn't have thought of using him or his times as the basis for a book if I hadn't stumbled across a reference to a 16th-century system of shorthand. That, and not the Elizabethan theatre, was my starting point.

ON WHAT HE ENJOYED READING AS A TEENAGER

Though my reading, like my writing, has always been pretty eclectic, I went through two main phases in my teens—my historical fiction phase and my science fiction phase. It's hard to say when or why I got interested in theatre. I wasn't really exposed to it until high school, when I acted in two mediocre plays. But that motivated me to write my first work for the stage—a full-length musical, no less! Thankfully, it was never performed.

ON WHAT DISTINGUISHES YOUNG ADULT LITERATURE

As far as I can see, there is no clear dividing line. Most young adult books have teen protagonists, of course, but so do countless adult coming-of-age novels. And there are plenty of children's books with adult protagonists. Adults who have read my books often express surprise that they could enjoy something that was written for young readers. But the elements that appeal to kids and young adults—lively prose, a compelling plot, believable characters—are the same ones that make up a good adult book.

ON WHAT MIGHT HELP YOUNG ADULTS DEVELOP AS WRITERS

A lot of young authors tell me they're frustrated because their stories so often fizzle out somewhere in the middle. It's natural to want to start writing as soon as inspiration strikes you, but it usually works best—for me, at least—to do some serious planning first, to get a handle on who the main character is and what his problem is and how he's going to go about resolving it. If you know where you want to go with a story, you're a lot more likely to get there.

ON HOW NARRATIVE IN DRAMA DIFFERS FROM PROSE NARRATIVE

There are a couple of practical concerns with plays that you don't have with novels. One is that, ordinarily, there is no exposition. Unless you use a narrator (like the Stage Manager in *Our Town*), everything has to be conveyed through dialogue and action. The other is that, while anything (realistic or fantastic) can happen in a book, anywhere on (or off) the planet, with any number of characters (human or otherwise), there are limits, both physical and financial, to what you can do on the stage. Fortunately, the playwright has the collaboration of the audience, in the same way a novelist has the collaboration of the reader. In a book, you don't have to describe everything down to the last detail; the reader will use her imagination. By the same token, you don't have to try and reproduce real life on the stage; the audience will fill in the blanks.

ON CREATING AN AUTHENTIC HISTORICAL NARRATIVE

The hard part was locating a copy of Dr. Bright's book on shorthand. There was certainly no shortage of material about Shakespeare and Elizabethan London. I love doing research; not only does it provide all those nitty-gritty details that give the reader the feeling of Being There, it also yields up things—people, events, facts—that actually determine the course of the story, things that I never would have thought of on my own. I can never hope to incorporate everything I learn into my book, of course, not even when I'm doing nonfiction. With fiction, it would bog the story down hopelessly. I just try to absorb as much of it as I can and then squeeze out a few drops here and a few there, as needed.

ON THE CLASSICS

As with the question about young adult books versus adult and children's books, I don't see a clear distinction between classics and contemporary books. Classics are classics because they have themes and issues that people of various ages and times and places can relate to.

Revisiting the Classics

Publishers, authors, and teachers have approached the classics in numerous ways in the hopes of enticing young readers. Some of these works still resonate with young readers and have been reissued in new editions. Many classics are freely available on the Internet, so new editions tend to be inexpensive and sometimes beautifully rendered. *Treasure Island* by Robert Louis Stevenson with illustrations by N. C. Wyeth (1882–1945) still catches the reader's attention and is part of the Scribner Storybook Classics series, a wonderful collection of reprints. The series also includes *The Last of the Mohicans, Robinson Crusoe,* and *Robin Hood,* all with Wyeth's illustrations. Other books have forewords added by contemporary authors to lure the reader in. For example, Rudyard Kipling's *Just So Stories* was rereleased in 2002 by Aladdin with a new foreword by Janet Taylor Lisle, and Candlewick released a version in 2004, *A Collection of Rudyard Kipling's Just So Stories,* with illustrations by eight incredible artists.

Other reissuings such as *North Town,* discussed earlier in this chapter, or Aladdin's edition of Harriet Beecher Stowe's *Uncle Tom's Cabin* in 2002 add historical and contextual information, knowing that teachers who use these books are likely to discuss their historical relevance in class. Still another form of reissue that occurs with short stories and poetry involves organizing materials in a new way, or collecting selections that will appeal to a young adult audience. For example, Edgar Allan Poe's *Tales of Death and Dementia* is a collection of Poe's work presented with illustrations by Gris Grimly.

Abridgements, Retellings, and Adaptations

Often classics are retold in a way that makes them more accessible or more interesting to the contemporary audience. This might involve simplifying the story, modernizing the language, or even adding a new twist to the original. Perhaps the most common way to retell a classic for a young audience is to abridge it.

Abridgements and simplified versions are not at all new. There are dozens of simplified versions of books, such as *The Pilgrim's Progress in Words of One Syllable* (1869) and *Robinson Crusoe in Words of One Syllable* (1867), both retold by Lucy Aikin (aka Mary Godolphin). The simplified version of Robinson Crusoe actually uses one-syllable words throughout with the exception of the names:

> I was born at York on the first of March in the sixth year of the reign of King Charles the First. From the time when I was quite a young child, I had felt a great wish to spend my life at sea, and as I grew, so did this taste grow more and more strong; till at last I broke loose

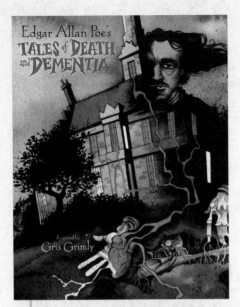

Edgar Allan Poe's Tales of Death and Dementia, illustrated by Gris Grimly (Atheneum, 2009), presents several of Poe's classic stories slightly abridged. The addition of macabre illustrations that beautifully complement the storyline will lure many contemporary teen readers into Poe's work. Reprinted by permission of Atheneum.

from my school and home, and found my way on foot to Hull, where I soon got a place on board a ship. (p. 1)

The original version *The Life and Strange, and Surprising Adventures of Robinson Crusoe* (1719) tells this same portion of the narrative in a little over two pages of text, part of which includes the following paragraph:

> Being the third Son of the Family, and not bred to any Trade, my Head began to be fill'd very early with rambling thoughts: My Father, who was very ancient, had given me competent share of learning, as far as House-Education, and a Country-Free-School generally goes, and design'd for the Law; but I would be satisfied with nothing but to go to Sea, and my inclination to this led me so strongly against the Will, nay the Commands of my Father, and against all the Entreaties and Perswasions of my Mother and other Friends, that there seem'd to be something fatal in Propension of Nature tending directly to the Life of Misery which was to befall me. (pp. 1–2)

This is a rather drastic comparison; most abridgements do not limit themselves to words of one syllable! Still a quick look brings up some of the issues of contention. On the one hand, the original is rather dense and difficult for many young adults to follow. However, on the other hand, much of the story, the voice of the narrator, and the style have been lost in the abridgement.

Critics of abridgements believe that they rob the work of word craft, drop away layers of meaning, and lose emotional and aesthetic force. However, one needs only read some of the more artful abridged versions, such as *The Hunchback of Notre Dame* by Tim Wynne-Jones for example, to see that skillfully crafted abridgements are possible. Wynne-Jones is quoted by Sarah Ellis as saying that some classics "are simply unbelievably great stories, which is why they have survived their transformations into movies, cartoons, and classic comics" (p. 56). He suggests that many classics have been synthesized into our culture by mass media and become like folklore—open for abridging, rewriting, and fracturing.

Retellings

In *Othello,* Julius Lester creates a retelling which is a skillful blending of old and new, emphasizing Othello's Africanness while retaining the major themes of Shakespeare's version. Lester asserts, "The driving force behind retellings for me is making literature accessible which has become inaccessible for a variety of reasons" (Lester interview, p. 73). The themes involved—jealousy, love, and betrayal—do not go out of style. In fact, Shakespeare himself was retelling a Spanish novel when he penned *Othello*.

Many retellings are quite similar to abridgements. Michael Rosen and illustrator Jane Ray have created a beautiful illustrated retelling in *Shakespeare's Romeo and Juliet*. Some of the most famous lines are used word for word and the whole way through the lines are linked to act and scene references provided in the borders. Bruce Coville has crafted a beautiful but even briefer retelling in *William Shakespeare's Romeo and Juliet,* with illustrations by Dennis Nolan. Although it is a picture book, the themes, the age of the protagonists, and the storyline all make it a book for older readers.

In 1807, Charles and Mary Lamb retold some of Shakespeare's best-loved dramas in a collection of stories entitled *Tales from Shakespeare.* Over a century later, Tina Packer in her *Tales from Shakespeare* (2004) adds a beautiful twist to the retellings of 10 of Shakespeare's best-known works. The stories are enhanced with illustrations by a dozen of the best artists in the industry.

Some retellings focus on only a part of a classic story, Margaret Hodge's *Gulliver in Lilliput* only retells that section of *Gulliver's Travels* that takes place in Lilliput. Similarly, Barbara Cohen's adaptation, *The Canterbury Tales* with illustrations by Trina Schart Hyman, includes the stories of four of the characters from Chaucer's original: the Nun's Priest, the Pardner, the wife of Bath, and the Franklin. Other retellings are more distinctive in that they give different perspectives, provide a new context, or alter the resolution. *Dating Hamlet: Ophelia's Story* by Lisa Fiedler retells *Hamlet* from Ophelia's perspective as she searches for a way to save her betrothed from deceit, depression, and madness. Gloria Skurzynski in *Spider's Voice* tells the story of the 12th-century French lovers Abelard

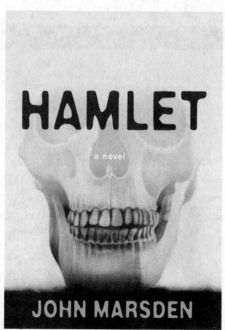

John Marsden retells the story of Shakespeare's ultimate angst-ridden hero in *Hamlet* (Candlewick, 2009). Reprinted by permission of Candlewick Press.

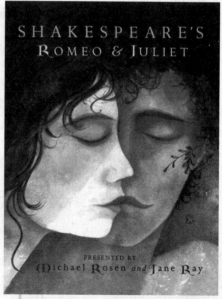

Shakespeare's Romeo and Juliet (Candlewick, 2003) by Michael Rosen with illustrator Jane Ray is a retelling with drawings that many teens find appealing. Reprinted by permission of Candlewick Press.

and Eloise from the perspective of a servant called Spider. Because of the language and the youthful perspective the narrative is more accessible than the original, but it is still a tangled, complex tale. *Wendy* by Karen Wallace tells the story of Wendy Darling before her encounter with Peter Pan. Each of these novels makes for an enjoyable story on its own, but they also might be used as part of an exploration of the fictional world of a classic. *Pride and Prejudice and Zombies* retains the mannerisms of the Jane Austin novel but Seth Grahame-Smith adds a farcical horror twist to the storyline.

Moby Dick retold by Lew Sayre Schwartz and illustrated by Richard Giordano is a graphic novel adaptation of Herman Melville's classic. This is definitely not the simplified Cliff Notes introduction to the novel that one might imagine. The narrative is beautifully written, the art intricately executed. The book also includes information about Melville and the whaling industry. Another graphic novel retelling that has received much attention is Will Eisner's *Fagin the Jew,* which tells the perspective of the villified character who was rather stereotyped in Dickens's novel, a fact that even Dickens recognized and apologized for afterwards.

Eisner has suggested that *Fagin the Jew* is definitely not a children's book. His intended audience is adults. Yet the book, illustrated with theatrical flair, has found a place on YALSA's list of Best Books for Young Adults.

Retellings can also take the form of film adaptations or films based on classics. Some examples are given in the following list.

Books to Film

Classics

Emma by Jane Austen (Movie: *Clueless.* Paramount Pictures, © 2005)

Emma by Jane Austen (Movie: *Emma.* Miramax Films, © 1999)

Little Women by Louisa May Alcott (Movie: *Little Women.* Radio Pictures, directed by George Cukor, © 2001)

The Outsiders by S. E. Hinton (Movie: *The Outsiders.* Warner Home Video, © 2005)

Pride & Prejudice by Jane Austen (Movie: *Pride & Prejudice.* Focus Features, © 2006)

Rumble Fish by S. E. Hinton (Movie: *Rumble Fish.* Universal Home Video, Inc., © 1998)

The Taming of the Shrew by William Shakespeare (Movie: *Ten Things I Hate about You.* Touchstone Home Video, © 1999)

Myths and Epics as Classics

Works related to Western mythology are often considered to be classics, though the myths themselves are also part of traditional literature (Chapter 4). Greek and Roman mythology certainly appear in both literary realms and figure prominently in the secondary school curriculum. Written epics connected to these mythologies, such as *The Odyssey* and *The Aeneid,* are generally included in discussions of the "Great Works of Western Civilization," but are also good examples of storylines and themes that young adults might get excited about reading. However, the original texts can be difficult to access. Retellings of classic mythological

Sharon Draper's *Romiette and Julio* (Simon Pulse, 2001) places the themes of *Romeo and Juliet* in a contemporary Ohio setting. Reprinted by permission of Simon Pulse.

tales include *Quiver* by Stephanie Spinner, which recounts the myth of Atlanta, a female warrior who could outrun any man in Greece; Cynthia Voigt's *Orfe,* a contemporary version of the myth of Orpheus; and Clemence McLaren's *Waiting for Odysseus,* which tells the events of Homer's story from the perspective of four of the major female characters involved.

Pairing

One way of integrating the classics and young adults is to pair books with similar themes (Wilder and Teasley, 1998). Joan Kaywell in her series *Adolescent Literature as a Complement to the Classics* (1993) provides lists of possible pairings. Some books are such obvious pairs that publishers have already created combined editions. For example, Romeo and Juliet and West Side Story are coupled together in an edition by Dell Laurel-Leaf. Shakespeare's play is again paired with a screenplay of a film adaptation by Craig Pearce and Baz Lurhman in *William Shakespeare's Romeo and Juliet: The Contemporary Play.* This work has the script of the film alongside the original play, which allows students insight into the differences between two forms of performance-based narrative.

Romiette and Julio by Sharon Draper is a contemporary retelling of Romeo and Juliet. In Draper's novel, Romiette is African American and Julio is Latino. The two young lovers must deal with their parents' (and society's) prejudices as well as with a local gang. Reading the play and the novel together allows for a comparison of the themes, which can reinforce understandings of both storylines.

With pairings such as Thoreau's *Walden* and *The Island* by Gary Paulsen, the teacher might assign chapters of Paulsen's book to be read at home and then read aloud before making comparisons to *Walden* in the classroom. Similarly, with Shakespearean pairings there is a wealth of interesting possibilities. Students might read *Dating Hamlet* at home and watch a production of *Hamlet* at school, comparing the two over several weeks. Or one week students might read aloud from the play, the next week watch scenes from a movie version, and the next week look at a live production. This would allow students to work not only with retellings but also with a variety of media.

A set of novels providing different perspectives on a classic work could be used to great effect. When covering *The Iliad,* the classic might be used in the classroom with students each reading one of the following novels at home:

- *Black Ships before Troy: The Story of the Iliad* by Rosemary Sutcliff
- *Dateline Troy* by Paul Fleischman
- *Inside the Walls of Troy* by Clemence McLaren
- *Troy* by Adele Geras

The story of the Trojan War is told by Helen and Cassandra in McLaren's *Inside the Walls of Troy*. The epic poem is retold in beautiful prose accompanied by color illustrations in *Black Ships before Troy*. Fleischman's *Dateline Troy* juxtaposes scenes from the Trojan War with newspaper clippings from recent history, showing that the themes are not outdated. In *Troy* Aphrodite has become bored after 10 years of war and intervenes. Having students discuss and give insight into these four retellings could broaden everyone's understanding of the original.

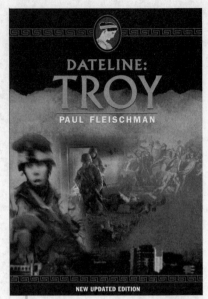

In *Dateline Troy* (Candlewick, 2006), Paul Fleischman finds connections between contemporary events and the themes of the Trojan War. Reprinted by permission of Candlewick Press.

Possible Pairings

- *Black Ships before Troy* by Rosemary Sutcliff with *The Iliad*
- *Dating Hamlet* by Lisa Fiedler with *Hamlet*
- *The Island* by Gary Paulsen with *Walden*
- *Othello* by Julius Lester with Shakespeare's *Othello*
- *Romiette and Julio* by Sharon Draper with *Romeo and Juliet*
- *Waiting for Odysseus* by Clemence McLaren with *The Odyssey*
- *Wild Timothy* by Gary Blackwood with *Call of the Wild* by Jack London

Bridging

Bridging is another frequently used method of making beneficial connections between contemporary literature and the classics. In a thought-provoking article, Linda Tebers-Kwak and Timothy Kaufman (2002) suggest that picture books might be used to scaffold readers into Shakespeare's works. For example, they suggest having ninth graders rewrite *A Midsummer Night's Dream* for a fourth-grade audience using the Burdett series of picture book adaptations as a model. In this way the ninth graders are introduced to the plot, the characters, and the relationships among characters in easy-to-grasp narrative while they are positioned as the experts imparting the story to younger students. Along the way the ninth graders also have to think about audience, voice, and the other elements of writing as they adapt Shakespeare's work.

Bridging might happen the week before or even several years in advance of reading the novel or play. *The Shakespeare Stealer* by Gary Blackwood and the sequels *Shakespeare's Scribe* (2000) and *Shakespeare's Spy* (2003) provide valuable information about the Globe Theatre and the Renaissance. They are also exciting, well-written adventure stories, which might also create an interest in reading Shakespeare's plays. Similarly, J. B. Cheaney's *The Playmaker* explores Shakespearean London and the theatre through the eyes of a young playmaker in a story filled with intrigue and adventure.

Younger middle school students might enjoy *Crushing on a Capulet* by Tony Abbott, a book in which two middle school students are magically transported into the middle of Romeo and Juliet and gain a new appreciation of the play and the historical setting. Contextual nonfiction and even film might also be used effectively as a bridge. Books such as *Shakespeare: His Work and His World* (Rosen) or *Welcome to the Globe: The Story of Shakespeare's Theatre* (Chrisp) provide insight into Renaissance England and Shakespeare's theatre to help create background and interest before a "classic" work is read.

Suggestions for Bridging

- *Crushing on a Capulet* by Tony Abbott as a bridge to *Romeo and Juliet*
- *The Day They Came to Arrest the Book* by Nat Hentoff as a bridge to *Huckleberry Finn*
- *Jason's Gold* by Will Hobbs as a bridge to *Call of the Wild*
- *The Shakespeare Stealer* by Gary Blackwood as a bridge to any Shakespearean drama
- *The Sword of the Rightful King* by Jane Yolen as a bridge to *Le Morte d'Arthur*
- *The Wreckers* by Iain Lawrence as a bridge to *Kidnapped*

SHANA NORRIS

In *Troy High* (Amulet Books, 2009) Shana Norris recasts Homer's *Iliad* as a rivalry between two football teams, the Trojans and the Spartans. Cover reprinted by permission of Abrams.

Author Spotlight

Photo courtesy of Julius Lester.

Julius Lester

Julius Lester was born in Missouri in 1939. He has worked as an author, a radio talk show host, a musician, and a professor of both African American and Judaic studies. His career as an author was established when his collection of slave narratives and commentaries *To Be a Slave* (1968) received a Newbery Honor. He has authored over 30 books, including poetry, picture books, folklore, and fiction. Visit his website at http://members.authorsguild.net/juliuslester.

SELECTED BOOKLIST

Cupid (Harcourt, 2007)
Day of Tears (Hyperion, 2005)
Guardian (Amistad, 2008)
On Writing for Children and Other People (Dial, 2004)
Othello (Scholastic, 1995)
Pharaoh's Daughter (Harcourt, 2000)
Sam and the Tigers illus. by Jerry Pinkney (Dial, 1996)
To Be a Slave (Longman, 1968)
When Dad Killed Mom (Harcourt, 2000)

ON WHETHER HE WRITES WITH A PARTICULAR AUDIENCE IN MIND

When I'm working on a picture book I do keep audience in mind. The language needs to be simpler, for one thing. And for another, the picture book is a hybrid and ideally, words and images should work together to create a whole. So there is sometimes the need to adjust the text for the sake of the images. Other than picture books, however, I do not have the audience in mind. I have never been able to distinguish between a book for a middle school reader and one for a high school reader. Such distinctions are necessary for publishers, it seems, but not for me as a writer. I write and let the publisher figure out what age group it fits.

ON THE INSPIRATION FOR HIS STORIES

I seldom get inspired. Often an editor or someone else will present me with an idea for a book. If it strikes a chord within, then I'll consider it. I don't get inspired, though, I muse.

ON THE EXTENT TO WHICH HIS OWN LIFE STORY APPEARS IN HIS WORKS

The life of my emotions appears in my fiction quite a bit.

ON WHAT HE ENJOYED READING AS A TEENAGER

Mystery novels and westerns.

ON WHAT HE ENJOYS READING CURRENTLY

I still love mystery novels. My favorite author currently is, however, Orson Scott Card.

ON SUGGESTIONS FOR YOUNG ADULTS TO HELP THEM DEVELOP AS WRITERS

READ! READ! READ!

ON WHETHER A PERSON WHO IS NOT A CULTURAL INSIDER CAN WRITE AUTHENTICALLY ABOUT CHARACTERS THAT ARE

An involved and complex question. Generally, I don't think a writer must belong to a culture to write authentically about it. However, that writer better know that culture inside and out before seeking to write from within it. I used to have a hard time writing white characters before I had lived among whites for a lot of years.

ON WHAT DISTINGUISHES YOUNG ADULT LITERATURE

I think such distinctions are artificial. Adults and children read Stephen King, Orson Scott Card, and others. The only distinctions I make are between good books and not so good books.

ON HIS RETELLINGS

In the case of *Sam and the Tigers* young audiences didn't know it was a retelling since they had never been exposed to *Little Black Sambo*. The driving force behind retellings for me is making literature accessible which has become inaccessible for a variety of reasons. In the case of *Othello* and *Uncle Remus* the language obscured the stories.

ON THE CLASSICS

I wonder if too much is made of the so-called classics. All too often they are taught in such a way that young people are unable to connect them to their own lives. But this may be because many teachers teach the classics because they are told to, not because they understand or care about them. The classics depend on having good teachers to unlock them and such teachers seem to be in short supply.

ON WHETHER THERE ARE TOPICS THAT AUTHORS FOR YOUNG ADULTS SHOULD AVOID

No.

Topic Focus

Literature Circles and Journaling

Literature circles are basically small-group discussions in which the members pool their knowledge and their responses to construct meaning connected to the literature they have read. In many of these book discussions, especially when a teacher is first introducing the concept to the class, each group member is assigned a certain task such as Discussion Director, Investigator, Illustrator, or Word Master. Harvey Daniels describes their roles and benefits in his widely used book *Literature Circles: Voices and Choice in Book Clubs and Reading Groups* (2001). Teachers often use these roles to facilitate student familiarity with collaborating and dialoguing in circles. However, many teachers quit directly assigning roles after students become familiar with the process. Either way, groups read and discuss the novel over the course of several weeks and then generally engage in some sort of culminating activity or presentation. Following are some of the roles Daniels describes:

- *Discussion director.* Poses open-ended questions concerning the reading
- *Literary luminary.* Reads aloud key passages from the text
- *Illustrator.* Creates graphic images inspired by the text
- *Connector.* Finds links between the work of literature and the wider world
- *Summarizer.* Produces a brief summary of the text
- *Vocabulary enricher.* Selects and defines significant words from the text
- *Investigator.* Locates background information on topics related to the reading

Literature circles are organized in a variety of ways (visit the online Literature Circle Resource Center at www.litcircles.org) but the role that the teacher plays tends to involve being either a silent observer or a roaming facilitator. One features that all literature circles have in common is that they are meant to encourage collaboration, dialogue, and the enjoyment of literature. In most literature circles students will have some choice in what they read—though they choose from a teacher-selected text set. These text sets tend to be designed around a theme or genre but generally also contain literature to meet a variety of interests and reading levels. The small groups also tend to have a lot of control over what exactly they will discuss at each meeting, though again all of this occurs within boundaries predefined by the teacher.

Numerous activities and assessments might be connected to literature circles, including teacher observations, student self-assessments, and presentations of finished projects. However, for many teachers journaling is the key assessment. The teacher learns much about the student's understanding of the literature being read from the journal entries, but what is so productive about journals is that they are not just an assessment but can also serve as an important learning tool. The journal is an excellent platform for learning about one's personal response to literature and to explore the meaning one takes from a text. At the same time, journaling allows readers to organize their understandings of an idea or concept, perhaps using story quilts, storyboards, maps, and other ways of retelling the storyline.

In the Field   *Literature Circles with Janine King*

Janine King is a middle school literacy coach in Seattle Public Schools. Before this she was a sixth- through eighth-grade teacher at Brighton School in Lynnwood, Washington. She is co-author of Literature Circles in Middle School: One Teacher's Journey *(2003).*

In Janine King's seventh-grade class, students discuss six books during the school year using the literature circle format. Students coming into the class have not necessarily participated in literature circles before, so they begin the year with a whole-class read to simplify things while focusing attention on the logistics of literature circles—including having good discussions, writing journal entries, and creating meaningful extension projects. What they read and explore for the first literature circle is a paired set: Jack London's classic novel *Call of the Wild* and Will Hobb's *Jason's Gold*.

Other literature circles throughout the year are thematic or topic based, with students choosing from a short list of books. King has everyone write down their first, second, and third choice and she does her best to honor everyone's preferences while still creating balanced groups. In the spring the class returns to a whole-class novel, because by then "things are usually a little raggedy and we need to revisit the literature circle skills we focused on in the fall."

ON WHY SHE ALTERNATES WHOLE CLASS READS AND TEXT SETS

One reason I do whole-class novels is that sometimes a book is just too good to limit to one group. A good example of this would be *The Outsiders*. Every seventh grader loves reading this book. It's like a rite of passage. The reason I don't do all-class novels with every unit is because students love having a choice in what they read.

ON WHOLE-CLASS READS

Some books, such as *Goodnight, Mr. Tom* (Magorian), I like to do as a whole class because of the sensitive issues involved. I like to work through them together as a class. Sometimes when I choose books to highlight a social issue, such as bullying, that I feel we need to work on, I want the whole class working with the same characters and events. When weaving in drama, such as tableaux, it is fun to be able to work with the whole class at once working with the same elements.

ON THE DOWNSIDE TO WHOLE-CLASS READS FOR LITERATURE CIRCLES

Whole-class novels can work well if all the students in the class have fairly similar reading levels and interests. I rarely see this. Most classrooms are filled with students representing such a wide range of reading abilities that many students would not be able to access a grade-level novel. Now I create literature circle units that include books that offer choices to match all students' reading abilities from the highest to the lowest. Richard Allington has done so much research that backs the importance of kids being in "just right" books, and I have seen too many students either sit and pretend to read or just give up altogether when they constantly are being asked to read books they can't access.

ON PAIRING YOUNG ADULT NOVELS WITH THE CLASSICS

All students read both *Call of the Wild* and *Jason's Gold.* These two work wonderfully together for a variety of reasons. One of the biggest skills we focus on in this unit is comparing and contrasting. Because *Call of the Wild* was written 100 years ago, we compare the difference in classic versus contemporary literature. There are many other obvious comparisons, too, such as one book is written from the point of view of a dog and one from the point of view of a teenager. Being able to analyze these differences spills over into the choices my students make in their own writing. Finally, there is this old-fashioned English teacher in me that makes me think it is important that students be exposed to the classics. This is an enjoyable, digestible way to do it!

ON *THE OUTSIDERS* AS A WHOLE-CLASS READ

The students almost see reading this book as a rite of passage. They love how cool and tough the characters are. Although many of the words, the clothing, etc. are outdated, the adolescent issues are universal, so yes, it does still hold relevance. We will always have the rich and the poor, the haves and the have-nots. Adolescents will always be searching for where they fit in, feeling insecure, concerned over their appearance, being an individual, etc. etc. My students are always inspired by the fact that S. E. Hinton wrote this novel when she was 16. It makes them see the possibilities of becoming writers themselves.

ON HOW JOURNALING FITS IN WITH THE LITERATURE CIRCLES

Since I don't give tests or worksheets during literature circle units, I like to have some kind of concrete evidence of what students are learning. Also, during discussions, I am floating around from group to group so I don't hear everything that is said. In addition, some students are very shy or intimidated during discussions and feel much more comfortable sharing their ideas on paper. During discussions, I leave things wide open for students to talk about what they are compelled to talk about. Often with journals, I will request some of the entries to be about certain topics so that I can assess students' understanding, especially if it is something new I have just introduced (such as foreshadowing, conflict, importance of setting, point of view, etc.). Finally, students keep their journals here at school. They are wonderful pieces of evidence of growth over time for me, their parents, and for the students themselves.

ON HOW MUCH STUDENT CHOICE IS ALLOWED IN THE ARRANGEMENT OF CIRCLES

When I use whole-class novels, the orchestration of the groups is entirely my doing. I try to balance the groups by gender, ability, personality, etc. On the other hand, when there are choices of books, I try to give every student their first choice regardless of the above-mentioned factors. The only time I interfere is to create groups of four or five for each book, because I want all the books to be a part of the unit, and I only have enough books to create groups of this size.

ON THE PURPOSE OF INCLUDING THE EXTENSION PROJECT AS PART OF WHAT STUDENTS DO IN THE CIRCLE

The beauty of including reading, discussing, writing, and art or drama in every unit is that it levels the playing field. Many students who struggle with reading and writing are able to express their comprehension of the book through art or drama.

ON WHETHER STUDENTS TAKE ADVANTAGE OF THEIR RESPONSIBILITY IN SETTING THEIR OWN PACE

Students get to set their own pace for how many pages they read in a day, or in a week, but I set the date when they need to be finished with the novel. This, along with the fact that their group members make life hell for them if they come to the discussion and are behind in their reading, keeps students from taking advantage of the responsibility I'm giving them. Also, as a teacher and a parent, I find that the tighter adults try to control everything, the more adolescents want to take advantage of situations.

ON WHETHER CIRCLES MEET AT THE SAME TIME AND WHAT OTHER STUDENTS DO WHEN THEIR CIRCLES ARE NOT MEETING

Currently, I have all my students involved in discussions at the same time. Previously, when that seemed overwhelming to me, the students who weren't involved in discussions were busy reading their books and writing in their journals. I had to lay down some very clear expectations for noise level and responsibilities, but it was time well spent, because it worked.

LITERARY THEORY

New Criticism

New Criticism was the dominant form of literary theory in the 1940s and 50s and as such has had a lasting impact on how literature is taught in the United States. Teachers who were in college in this era have tended to teach with this theoretical lens to students, many of whom have in turn taught this way to their own students.

> ### To Consider
> Why might New Criticism be more easily applied to poetry than to prose?

One of the key tenets of New Criticism is the privileging of the order and unity of the literary text. A work of literature is seen as a self-contained object complete within itself, written for its own sake, and unified in its form. Critics are not concerned with context (historical, biographical, psychological, or intellectual) but rather with the language and unity of the text. The personal input of the writer and the emotional effect on the reader are also not seen as significant. Because of its emphasis on text and form New Criticism is regarded by its proponents as objective criticism.

In New Criticism the reader does not need to transact with the text, but instead searches for the truths already there. The reader constructs an informed and empirical reading of the literary work looking for the evidence within the text. Furthermore, only the expert reader can discover how these conventions of literature work in the textual unity. Ordinary readers are not always capable of interpreting the text, but they can understand the true meaning of the text when informed of that meaning by scholars or are trained in close textual analysis.

The ideas of New Criticism have impacted English teachers in several ways. First, teachers were to teach the skills of close reading, emphasizing technique and form, and because not all teachers were expert critics, they were provided with teachers' manuals that gave them the correct answers. Second, because great literature was identifiable, a canon of good texts could be created from which teachers could find books to use.

Not many New Critics were concerned with works of literature written for youth, because they were interested primarily in "Great Works"—what would today be called "the Canon." However, there were New Critical readings of *The Adventures of Huckleberry Finn*. Unlike the debate earlier in this chapter on censorship, these studies did not search for social or historical significance but were instead interested in style and form. The big question was: Does the unity of the work make this a great piece of literature? And there was enormous disagreement about this, mainly due to the ending of the novel in which Tom Sawyer overshadows Huck in a series of whimsical escapades. A number of New Critical reviews describe the novel as a masterpiece up to the disastrous ending! However, T. S. Eliot, who was not a New Critic but whose ideas were extremely influential among them, was a defender of the novel, again in terms of structure. Huck, he argues, gives the book style and the river gives it form but both are without beginning or end:

> Hence he can only disappear; and his disappearance can only be accomplished by bringing forward another performer to obscure the disappearance in a cloud of whimsicalities. (Phelan and Graff, 1995, p. 288)

Tom, T. S. Eliot suggests, plays an important role in the beginning of the novel and his resurfacing at the end adds to the overall unifying structure. Interestingly, he argues that this all happened unconsciously and that Mark Twain wrote a much "greater work than he could have known he was writing" (Phelan and Graff, 1995, p. 289).

For Further Reading

Daniels, Harvey. *Literature Circles: Voice and Choice in Book Clubs and Reading Groups.* 2nd ed. Stenhouse, 2001.

Hill, Bonnie Campbell, Katherine Noe, and Janine King. *Literature Circles in Middle School: One Teacher's Journey.* Christopher Gordon, 2003.

Hill, Bonnie Campbell, Katherine Noe, and Nancy Johnson. *Literature Circles Resource Guide.* Christopher Gordon, 2001.

Ransom, John Crow. *The New Criticism.* New Directions, 1941.

Richards, I. A. *Practical Criticism.* Routledge, 1964. (Original work published 1929)

Richards, I. A. *Principles of Literary Criticism.* Routledge, 1970. (Original work published 1924)

3

Illustrated Literature for Young Adults

Picture Books Text Set

Alice's Adventures in Wonderland by Lewis Carroll; illus. by Robert Sabuda

The Always Prayer Shawl by Sheldon Oberman; illus. by Ted Lewin

The Arrival by Shaun Tan

Blues Journey by Walter Dean Myers; illus. by Christopher Myers

Casey at the Bat by Ernest Thayer; illus. by Joe Morse

Collector of Moments by Quint Buchholz

A Day, a Dog by Gabrielle Vincent

Faithful Friend by Robert San Souci; illus. by Brian Pinkney

Home of the Brave by Allen Say

January's Sparrow by Patricia Polacco

John Coltrane's Giant Steps by Chris Raschka

Leonardo's Horse by Jean Fritz; illus. by Hudson Talbott

Love Story: Amiri and Odette by Walter Dean Myers; illus. by Javaka Steptoe

Middle Passage: White Ships/Black Cargo by Tom Feelings

The Old African by Julius Lester; illus. by Jerry Pinkney

Patrol by Walter Dean Myers; illus. by Ann Grifalconi

Pink and Say by Patricia Polacco

The Red Tree by Shaun Tan

Rosa by Nikki Giovanni; illus. by Bryan Collier

So Far from the Sea by Eve Bunting; illus. by Chris Soentpiet

The Stinky Cheese Man by Jon Scieszka; illus. by Lane Smith

The Three Pigs by David Wiesner

The Wall: Growing Up behind the Iron Curtain by Peter Sís

The Wolves in the Walls by N. Gaiman; illus. by D. McKean

Woolvs in the Sitee by Margaret Wild; illus. by Anne Spudvilas

Illustrated Book Set

Autobiography of My Dead Brother by Walter Dean Myers; illus. by Christopher Myers

Chess Rumble by G. Neri

Coraline by Neil Gaiman; illus. by Dave McKean

Diary of a Wimpy Kid by Jeff Kinney

Emily the Strange: The Lost Days by Rob Reger, Buzz Parker, and Jessica Gruner

Happy Face by Stephen Emond

Hugo Cabret by Brian Selznick

Keeping the Night Watch by Hope Anita Smith; illus. by E. B. Lewis

Leviathan by Scott Westerfield

Metamorphosis by Betsy Franco; illus. by Tom Franco

Riding Invisible by Sandra Alonzo and Nathan Huang

The Savage by David Clements; illus. by Dave McKean

Graphic Novel Text Set

9–11 Artists Respond from Dark Horse Comics

The Adventures of Tony Millionaire's Sock Monkey by Tony Millionaire

Amy Unbounded: Belondweg Blossoming by Rachel Hartman

Batman: The Dark Knight Returns by Frank Miller and Klaus Janson

Bone: Out of Boneville by Jeff Smith

The Books of Magic: Bindings by John Rieber and Peter Gross

Castle Waiting: The Curse of Brambly Hedge by Linda Medley

Clan Apis by Jay Hosler

Courtney Crumrin and the Night Things by Ted Naifeh

Deogratias: A Tale of Rwanda by J. P. Stassen

A Distant Soil: The Gathering by Colleen Doran

The Essential Spiderman by Stan Lee and Steve Dirko

Fagin The Jew by Will Eisner

The Good Neighbors: Kin by Holly Black and Ted Naifeh

The Hardy Boys: The Ocean of Osyria by Scott Loddell, Daniel Rendon, and Lea Hernandez

Herobear and the Kid: The Inheritance by Mike Kunkel

Hikaru No Go by Yumi Hotta and Takeshi Obata

Hopeless Savages by Jen Van Meter and Christine Norris

I Kill Giants by Joe Kelly

Initial D by Shuichi Shigeno

Jax Epoch and the Quicken Forbidden: Borrowed Magic by Dave Roman and John Green

Mage: The Hero Defined by Matt Wagner

Maus: A Survivor's Tale by Art Spiegelman

Meridian: Flying Solo by Barbara Kesel, Joshua Middleton, Dextor Vines, and
    Michael Atiyeh

Nat Turner by Kyle Baker

Palestine by Joe Sacco

Pedro and Me: Friendship, Loss, & What I Learned by Judd Winick

Persepolis by Marjane Satrapi

Rosemary's Backpack by Antony Johnston and Drew Gilbert

Sidekicks by J. Torres and Takeshi Miyazawa

Spirited Away by Hayao Miyazaki

Still I Rise by Roland Laird, Taneshi Laird, and Alihu Bey

Superman: Peace on Earth by Alex Ross and Paul Dini

Tale of One Bad Rat by Bryan Talbot

Twilight: The Graphic Novel by Stephenie Meyer and Young Kim

Understanding Comics by Scott McCloud

Usagi Yojimbo: Demon Mask by Stan Sakai

When I ask the undergraduates in my young adult literature courses to envision literature in which the graphics are at least as important as the words, most of them think initially of young children reading picture books. Moving further with the concept they might recall images of teens with collections of X-Men or Batman comics wrapped in plastic covers.

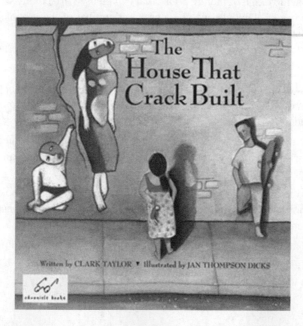

The House That Crack Built (Chronicle, 1992) uses a pattern commonly seen in books for young children but while doing so it explores themes more appropriate for a mature audience. The parody has the effect of making the messages even more striking because of the contrast. From *The House That Crack Built* © 1992 by Clark Taylor (text) and Jan Thompson Dicks (illustrations). Used with permission from Chronicle Books, San Francisco. Visit chroniclebooks.com

By this point in the term most of the students have come to the conclusion that there actually is some high-quality literature out there for young adult readers. The phrase "Where were these books when I was in school?" has been overheard several times. But then I mention picture books and graphic novels for young adults, and suddenly we are back at square one. A sea of skeptical faces greets the idea that the last two decades have seen a boom in both picture books and comics for a YA audience.

I have had several students assure me that one of these formats is not age appropriate and that the other can barely be considered literature! Yet as we discuss whether any of them read illustrated literature or sequential art in high school, someone admits that they received Dr. Seuss's *Oh the Places You'll Go* for high school graduation; another collects *Spiderman* comics; one student drew cartoons for his high school paper; another mentions that she loves *Doonesbury* or *Garfield* and we are ready to take the plunge.

Using Picture Books with Young Adults

Depending on the classroom context, there can often be resistance to using picture books, even with upper-elementary school students. The initial response is that books with a heavy emphasis on graphics are inappropriate for readers above a certain age. However, as with novels, authors of picture books are often more interested in telling a good story than in appealing to a particular age group, and Jon Scieszka is not atypical when he states that he likes to make "books funny enough, and multilayered enough, and intelligent enough to connect with readers of all ages and educations" (Scieszka interview, p. 173)

Generally, after exploring a range of picture books, college students need no further convincing because they have found several books that they really enjoy reading—for the story, the art, and the unique narrative that these elements create together as a work of literature. In addition to the wide range of picture books that can be used effectively with young adults to introduce themes or elements of style, a growing number of these books are also being published specifically for older readers.

There are, in fact, numerous valid reasons for using some illustrated literature with young adults:

- It is amazing how excited young adults can get about picture books when approached in appropriate ways, and pleasurable reading experiences are the greatest encouragement to become lifelong readers.

- There are plenty of illustrated books with complex themes and story structures that can get young adults thinking critically, and perhaps more significantly, there is an interplay of word craft and imagery that can spark their imaginations.

- Because text and image work together to create narrative in a picture book, readers are introduced to the notion of story as more than just words. Some great connections can be made between picture books and the concepts of media and visual literacy.

- Picture books contain wonderful examples of narrative and artistic techniques.

- Young adults who are familiar with picture books and how to read them will be prepared for reading with their own children.

Narrative and the Picture Book

> The best picture book narratives are poems, minimal brushstrokes, the bare elegant bones of a story. In a picture book you have to leave space for the illustrator. You don't need to describe how things look—readers can see that for themselves.
>
> —Scieszka interview, p. 173

First of all, we should define what is meant by the term *picture book.* There are certainly young adult novels that include graphic elements. Walter Dean Myers's *Autobiography of My Dead Brother,* a novel enjoyed by many young adults, has occasional illustrations. In Adam Rapp's *33 Snowfish,* a book at the older end of YA literature, one of the main characters tells his side of the story solely through illustrations. In 2007 a novel, Brian Selznick's *The Invention of Hugo Cabret,* even won the Caldecott Medal. However, illustrated books and books that include occasional illustrations are quite distinct from picture books. In an illustrated book several illustrations scattered throughout the narrative might enhance the storyline, in contrast to a picture book, in which the graphics and words create the storyline together. Julius Lester asserts that "the picture book is a hybrid and ideally, words and images should work together to create a whole" (Lester interview, p. 73). He feels strongly enough about this that sometimes after an artist has created the illustrations, he will go back and adjust the text.

The picture book category is broad enough to include alphabet books, counting books, and concept books. The term *picture storybook* is sometimes used to refer to books in which the two narrative elements of illustration and writing work simultaneously to tell a story. Finally, the term *picturebook* with no space between the two words, is used by some critics to emphasize the integral relationship between illustrations and words in particular books such as Margaret Wild's and Anne Spudvilas's *Woolvs in the Sitee.*

According to Perry Nodelman, a picture book actually contains three stories: the story of the words, the story told by the pictures, and the story that comes from combining the two (1996). In the ideal picture book the combination of text and graphics works so well that the reader cannot help but recall the illustrations when thinking about the narrative (Klemin, 1966). As Gerald McDermott describes it in his Caldecott acceptance speech, the medium makes it possible "to create a dynamic relationship between the visual and the verbal" (1975). This relationship affords a new pleasure that expands the aesthetic consciousness of the reader in both spatial and temporal ways.

A wide variety of literature employs the picture book format. Many of these books would only be used with high school students under special circumstances. Baby/board books, Mother Goose and nursery rhymes, alphabet books, and counting/number books might all be beneficial for secondary students to read in preparation for engaging in service learning projects where they work in daycare centers or mentor elementary school students (or for reading with their own kids). Occasionally, an alphabet book such as *Alphabeasts* (Edwards), with its bizarre, surreal illustrations, or *The Disappearing Alphabet* (Wilbur), with its sophisticated word craft, might be engaging for young adults, but the vast majority of these picture books are for young children. At the same time, there is also a growing number of picture books that operate on multiple levels, books with illustrations and narratives that are complex, interesting, and thematically relevant for young adult readers.

Author Spotlight

Reprinted by permission of
Penguin Putnam.

Patricia Polacco

Patricia Polacco was born in Lansing, Michigan, in 1944. Much of her young life was spent in the company of her grandparents, which has greatly influenced her work. When she was 14, one of her teachers discovered that she had dyslexia, a discovery that impacted her learning (and which eventually led to the book *Thank You, Mr. Falker*). Story and art have always been at the center of her life. Polacco was raised in a family of storytellers and she wrote stories for her two children, Steven and Traci, as they were growing up. She also earned a Ph.D. in art history and worked restoring ancient pieces of art for museums. It was not until around the age of 41 that she began writing down and illustrating her own stories for publication. After several years in Florida and 37 years in Oakland, California, Polacco again resides in Michigan. Visit her website at www.patriciapolacco.com.

SELECTED BOOKLIST

The Butterfly (Philomel, 2000)
Chicken Sunday (Philomel, 1992)
January's Sparrow (Philomel, 2009)
Pink and Say (Philomel, 1994)
Thank You, Mr. Falker (Philomel, 1998)

ON WHAT SHE ENJOYED READING AS A TEENAGER

J. D. Salinger, C. S. Lewis, Dickens. I was into drama and theatre and liked to read the other works by the playwrights we were dramatizing.

ON HER FAVORITE AUTHORS AND GENRES CURRENTLY

I still love children's books—Annie Dillard, David Small, Sarah Stewart, Bob San Soucci, Jerry Spinelli, Lois Lowry. I have also been known to read a Stephen King book or two.

ON WHETHER SHE WRITES WITH A PARTICULAR AUDIENCE IN MIND

No, I write for myself.

ON THE POTENTIAL FOR YOUNG ADULT READERS
TO ENGAGE WITH SOME OF HER BOOKS

I see potential for YA readers and everyone else, for that matter, to enjoy and find children's books and picture books engaging. If I had to choose one of my books, probably *Pink and Say* was my first book to offer a dramatic narrative that might appeal to older kids.

ON HER SUGGESTIONS FOR YOUNG ADULTS TO HELP
THEM DEVELOP AS WRITERS OR ILLUSTRATORS

As an artist draw, draw, draw!!!!! Carry a sketch book with you and catch things as you see them. As a writer, journaling is the best way to keep practicing with words.

ON THE WAYS HER PICTURE BOOK NARRATIVES DIFFER
FROM THE NARRATIVES FOUND IN NOVELS

We have to be more concise. We have to develop characters much quicker, get right to the point. It is quite difficult to say what you want in as short a space as possible.

ON HER APPROACH TO THE DUAL NARRATIVE
OF ILLUSTRATIONS AND TEXT

It depends on the story. Sometimes they appear as pictures first, sometimes the story comes first.

ON THE INFLUENCES ON HER ART

The impressionists—Lautrec, Klimpt, Schiele.

ON THE WAY SHE BECAME AN AUTHOR/ILLUSTRATOR
FOR YOUNG PEOPLE

It was kind of an accident. I came from a family of storytellers, that mixed with the art. I always did books or "fat cards" for my kids on special occasions. One thing led to another and the next thing I know I'm in New York meeting with publishers.

ON THE EXTENT TO WHICH HER WORKS REFLECT
HER OWN LIFE STORIES

Almost all of my stories are based on my family or my life experiences. Keeping stories close to home, close to things you really know helps keep them authentic.

Picture Books for Young Adults

Although there are many picture books that can be enjoyable and beneficial reads for young adults, the themes in some books make those narratives particularly well suited for young adults. A book such as *The Middle Passage* by Tom Feelings might be used with mature upper-elementary students, and it will certainly appeal to many adults, but the theme, the symbolism, and the use of visual storytelling make this an extremely engaging book for the YA audience. Feelings evokes the pain of the middle passage in ways that words might not capture.

   Pink and Say by Patricia Polacco is a hard-hitting story set during the Civil War. A wounded Yankee soldier named Say is saved by Pink, who is a member of a Negro regiment. Say is taken to Pink's mother, who nurses him back to health but is subsequently killed by a band of outriders. While returning to the warfront the young men are captured, Pink is executed, and Say is sent to Andersonville prison camp. The format and the vocabulary make the book accessible to some younger children, but thematically it is certainly appropriate for older readers.

   In *Brundibar*, Tony Kushner and Maurice Sendak retell a Czech opera that was performed by children imprisoned in the Terezin concentration camps. Younger children reading the story need not know all of the details, and indeed the context is not explicit in the narrative. But YA readers might read the book with deeper understanding after discussing how most of the children who took part in the play died in Auschwitz. On one level, the story is simple enough; a brother and sister go to town to get milk for their sick mother. In order to buy the milk they plan to sing on the street for money, but Brundibar, a bully of a hurdy-gurdy man (who somewhat resembles Hitler), does not allow other street musicians to perform. The brother and sister befriend three talking animals and a crowd of schoolchildren who help them defeat the bully. Young adult readers would have much to explore, as the book is full of symbolism and intertextual references to Sendak's other works.

   In *So Far from the Sea* (Bunting) a young Japanese American girl tells how she and her family visit the site at Manzanar, which for a time housed close to 10,000 prisoners. The narrator's father was interned at Manzanar as a child in 1942, and her grandfather Iwasaki died while interned there. To create the two time frames, the illustrations of wartime are done in sepia shades, almost like old newsreel, and the contemporary scenes are in color. The book could serve as a good introduction to the idea of

Patricia Polacco evokes intense emotion and tension in this illustration from *January's Sparrow* (Penguin, 2009) through the contours, the positioning, and the juxtaposition of the figure on the white space. Image copyright Patricia Polacco. All rights reserved. Used under authorization. Unauthorized duplication is a violation of applicable law.

The character in Bryan Talbot's *Tale of a Bad Rat* (Dark Horse Comics, 1995, p. 11) decides that she will no longer suffer through the pain of abuse with the symbolic shattering of that world. Reprinted by permission of Bryan Talbot.

Japanese internment during World War II before exploring the topic in depth.

Slavery, war, death, the Holocaust, Japanese internment during World War II—these are all topics that might be approached with younger readers. However, they are complex issues, and these books reflect that complexity in ways that might entice young adults.

The age of the characters is also a factor in deciding whether a young adult will choose to read a picture book for pleasure. In Patricia Polacco's *Pink and Say* the characters are young adults, as is the case in Michael Rosen's *Shakespeare's Romeo and Juliet.* The fact that connections to the play are given in the borders and that the costumes and architecture are authentic to 16th-century Italy make the abridged version of *Romeo and Juliet* a wonderful choice for young adults. *The Faithful Friend* (San Souci), *The Always Prayer Shawl* (Oberman), and *Home of the Brave* (Say) are among many picture books with young adult characters.

The sophistication of the narrative and artistic techniques might also make a picture book appropriate for young adults. In *Home of the Brave* reality and dream overlap, creating a poignant message. The use of light and dark adds to the dreamlike quality of the surreal paintings. After passing through an underground tunnel the character thinks he has found an Indian reservation when he sees two children sitting by an adobe ruin. But the children have Japanese features and nametags indicating that they are from a camp. Soon the reader discovers that they are in fact from an internment camp, and thousands of nameless children cry out to be taken home. Suddenly searchlights come on and the main character must flee. Young children might be confused by much of what occurs in the book. The historical context and the imagery together make the work more suited to a YA reader.

In *John Coltrane's Giant Steps* Chris Raschka's characters combine with other elements to perform a visual rendering of the song "Giant Steps." The narrator's voice introduces, focuses, and directs the sheets of sound. The raindrops are the tempo, the snowflakes, the harmony, the box is the bass, and the kitten, the melody. Raschka (Children's Literature, 2005) asserts,

> It's more a visual experimentation to see what happens if you follow principles that are developed in music and try to translate them into graphic materials.

A clear plastic dustjacket emphasizes the idea that the kitten/melody overlays the other elements. The kitten takes "some giant steps across the page." But problems occur and the narrator/conductor calls a halt. "People, people! What happened? Okay, okay, let's take a look at some trouble spots." Eventually the layers come together in a Coltranesque

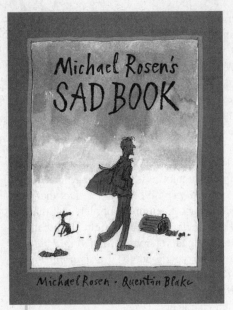

Michael Rosen's *Sad Book* (Candlewick, 2002) is a picture book for all ages but the strong theme of loss and depression after the death of a loved one might be especially appealing to mature readers. Reprinted by permission of Candlewick Press.

shaping of color and sound. Clearly, although some children will enjoy the storyline, readers who understand musical concepts will be more likely to find pleasure in the narrative.

An activity involving young adults and literature that merits special attention is cross-age reading. Working with young adults who are engaged in reading literature with elementary school students can be one of your most rewarding educational experiences. Generally, it is advantageous to work with the young adults first on book choice, on how to read with kids, and on how younger children might respond. When engaged in this type of activity, the young adult readers begin to think more about story, performance, appropriateness, and audience. Of course, the younger children gain immensely from the reading as well as from the modeling that occurs (Burns, 2006; Jacobson et al., 2001; Whang, 1995). Depending on the ages and individual preferences of the students involved, a wide variety of literature might be utilized. Some books seem ready-made thematically for such a project. *My Man Blue* by Nikki Grimes (illus. by Jerome Lagarrigue) presents a realistic bond of friendship between young Damon and a caring adult named Blue who lost his own boy to the streets. When Blue meets Damon, he is determined to be there for him. This is a nice example of a book that might serve several purposes when used in a cross-age reading context.

Wordless (and Almost Wordless) Picture Books

Wordless picture books tend to have a well-defined narrative structure because they must convey the emotions, characters, and plot development entirely through the illustrations. The storyline, of course, is given in the sequence of graphics, but there are also multiple layers of meaning, tangential stories, and emotions conveyed. In *A Day, a Dog,* Vincent manages to evoke the confusion and pain of the abandoned dog in her simple black-and-white line drawings. In *Middle Passage* each page is rich with symbolism. Wordless books provide an opportunity for students at any level to work with narrative structure, and many of these books make ready prompts for creative writing (Cassady, 1998; Osborn, 2001; Smith, 2004). In *The Arrival* the wordlessness serves a symbolic purpose as well. In the absence of written description the reader is planted firmly "in the shoes of the immigrant character" (Tan, 2008).

Wordless (and Semi-Wordless) Books

- *Age of Reptiles: Tribal Warfare* by Ricardo Delgado*
- *The Arrival* by Shaun Tan
- *A Day, a Dog* by Gabrielle Vincent
- *Flotsam* by David Wiesner
- *Lamouche* by Lewis Trondheim*
- *Middle Passage* by Tom Feelings
- *Monkey vs. Robot* by James Kochalka*
- *Museum Trip* by Barbara Lehman
- *The Other Side* by Istvan Banyai
- *Sector 7* by David Wiesner
- *The Snowman* by Raymond Briggs
- *Time Flies* by Eric Rohman
- *Yellow Umbrella* by Jae-Soo Liu

*Graphic novels

Wordless picture books like Gabrielle Vincent's *A Day, a Dog* and Shaun Tan's *The Arrival* are wonderful not only for the art but also for their visual storytelling. Seemingly simple line drawings capture movement and space beautifully in *A Day, a Dog* (Editions Casterman/Front Street, 1995). *The Arrival* (Arthur Levine, 2008) tells an amazing complex story of immigration with a fantasy setting, but with concepts that reflect common experiences. *A Day, a Dog* by Gabrielle Vincent © Casterman S. A. Reprinted by permission. *The Arrival* reprinted by permission of Arthur Levine.

In the Field *ELL Writing with Wordless Picture Books*

At the summer Migrant School in Princess Anne, Maryland, one of the most effective techniques utilized by preservice teachers has been to engage English language learners in creative writing using wordless picture books. The fact that the narrative is accessible in the illustrations for students regardless of their level of proficiency in English allows them to build on the story using the English they know, rather than struggling to understand the story and to find the English words to explain their understanding at the same time (National Center for Family Literacy, 2006).

The preservice teachers found that collaborative writing was very beneficial, partially because students could pool the vocabulary and structures they knew and so were able to create a richer story with a higher level of English language. At the same time, it allowed them to dialogue about the story and about their understandings of various language structures. All of the students in this particular school spoke Spanish as their first language and had varying levels of fluency in written and spoken English, so a good bit of peer translation occurred as well. One student who had only been in the United States for a few weeks was extremely creative in his interpretation of *Time Flies,* but he spoke no English. The other two members of his group teamed up to translate and rewrite his narrative, and together they constructed a wonderful story to go along with Eric Rohman's illustrations. So the ELL readers reconstructed a narrative together, learning English vocabulary and language structures while working with quality literature.

Elements of Illustration and Graphic Design

One major drawback to illustrated literature for young adults is that they often view these books as being for little kids. The best way to avoid this problem is to position YA readers as experts in the field. Providing them with understandings of the artistic and narrative elements can greatly enhance both the readers' interest and their ability to read critically, as can showing them how the format and design of the book are integrally connected to the reader's engagement with text, pleasure of reading, physical act of reading, and interpretation of the storyline. Perhaps of primary concern is the recognition that the narrative exists in multiple formats and that these various forms utilize different techniques that affect the reader's response. Thus, an effective approach to using picture books with young adults is to help them learn to recognize the design and graphic elements and the possible effects these have on reading and appreciation. Empowered with this knowledge young adults can approach illustrated literature and other graphics as experts. When used appropriately, these understandings add to the pleasure of the reading.

Action

The pictures in books are motionless images, yet through a variety of techniques, illustrators can create the feeling of movement. Sometimes distortion or movement lines are used. Raymond Briggs adds movement in *The Snowman* through the use of blurred lines. In Gabrielle Vincent's *A Day, a Dog,* simple yet stylistically appealing movement lines and blurred figures both create a sense of action. The position of the legs and the road narrowing into the angled distance add to the captured sense of movement.

Molly Bang in *Picture This: How Pictures Work* (1991) suggests that vertical shapes in general can add energy to an illustration, and diagonal shapes tend to imply motion. Other times, movement is implied. Joe Morse masterfully captures the intensity of freeze-framed action in *Casey at the Bat* (Thayer). One of the most compelling literacy aspects of picture book illustration is that there are numerous gaps in the action that is depicted, which the reader learns to fill in, thus constantly participating in the authoring of the visual narrative.

In this image from *Casey at the Bat* (Kids Can Press, 2006) the incomplete action is beautifully conveyed. Morse discusses his art at www.youtube .com/watch?v=vOaEOrHut_s. Image from *Casey at the Bat* by Ernest L. Thayer with illustrations by Joe Morse is used by permission of Kids Can Press Ltd., Toronto. Illustration © 2006 Joe Morse.

Book Size and Shape

Publishers generally use a typical rectangular shape for their books because the cost of nonordinary covers can be prohibitive. Sometimes the use of shape is effective yet hardly noticeable. It makes sense, for example, in Stephen Gammel's *Ride* that the book has a short but wide rectangular shape to mirror the space inside the car. Other times the shape and size really complement the contents of the book. In Hudson Talbot's *Leonardo's Horse* (Fritz), the domed shape of the book works beautifully with the illustrations, enhancing the theme, mood, and historical context.

Borders

Borders on individual pages of a picture book can be used to highlight, foreshadow, or even extend the story. In Anthony Browne's *Willy the Dreamer* the pictures during the dreams are all framed to emphasize the surreal paintings that serve as intertexts. Although this picture works for young kids, only older readers will be able to appreciate the connections to Picasso or Magritte. In *Snowflake Bentley* some of the thin black frames (which bring to mind the photographs for which Bentley is known) contain sidebars with nonfiction information. In *Pish, Posh Hieronymous Bosch* Leo and Diane Dillon use an intricate silver, bronze, and brass frame (sculpted by Lee Dillon) around each full-page illustration.

The dome shape in *Leonardo's Horse* fits perfectly with the storyline, adding to the Renaissance feel of the book. Jean Fritz's *Leonardo's Horse* illus. by Hudson Talbott (Putnam, 2001). From *Leonardo's Horse* by Jean Fritz, illustrated by Hudson Talbott, copyright © 2001 by Hudson Talbott, illustrations. Used by permission of G. P. Putnam's Sons, a division of Penguin Young Reader's Group, a member of Penguin Group (USA) Inc., 345 Hudson Street, New York, NY 10014. All rights reserved.

Codes, Symbols, and Metaphors

Picture books often operate on multiple layers. Authors and illustrators sometimes intentionally allude to other stories and other meanings in their works. At the same time, meanings that were not necessarily intended can also be found. Often these allusions and hidden layers are more accessible to an older reader, and this is one of the reasons that many picture books can be enjoyed by young adults. In *Tibet: Through the Red Box* by Peter Sís, the mazes and the family pictures with the father whited-out evoke a quite sophisticated imagery. Holocaust symbolism in *We're All in the Dumps with Jack and Guy* (Sendak), Japanese internment in *Home of the Brave* (Say), the image of the clutched hands in *Pink and Say* (Polacco) are all complex in their imagery, and if younger readers are to understand the various nuances of meaning, some background information would have to be provided. On the other hand Shaun Tan writes specifically in an essay on *The Arrival* that symbolism is not about "standing for" something else but is more about intuitive resonance—when we know that something is being referenced even though we might not be able to articulate what it is exactly.

The colors Anne Spudvilas uses in *Woolvs in the Sitee* (2007) help create a mood of doom and danger. From *Woolvs in the Sitee* by Margaret Wild and Anne Spudvilas. Front Street, 2007. Reprinted with permission by Boyds Mills Press.

Color

The ways hues, shades, and colors are used help create mood. Green, for example, is often used to create a sense of peace and blue might evoke serenity, though certainly these effects will be shaped by cultural norms and context, and not all readers will have the same response to particular colors. Color is a major narrative element in *Woolvs in the Sitee*. Every page triggers an emotional response even before the images take shape in the reader's mind.

In *The Red Tree* color is used in complex ways to add to the symbolism and the mood. Red as a foreshadowing of danger is used in many stories from *Little Red Riding Hood* to Peter Sís's *The Wall* to *Schindler's List*. In *Rosa* (Giovanni), yellow is used to denote the southern heat but it also emanates from Rosa Parks like she is a guiding light.

The lack of color can also be used to good effect. The textured black and white images in C. B. Mordin's illustrations for *Silent Movie* (Avi) help capture the style and look of silent movies. In *So Far from the Sea* color illustrations are used for the contemporary settings, whereas black and white drawings are used for the scenes from the past. Both sets of illustrations are photographic, which adds to the effective use of color for creating the historical context. In *The Always Prayer Shawl* a similar technique is used; the first half of the book, which depicts the past, is illustrated in gray tones and then mid-book a full-page spread counterposes the young boy in black and white with the grown-up man in color, after which the contemporary color illustrations take over.

Continuous Narrative

Multiple sequential pictures on the same page can be used to convey action, to add perspective or depth, or to show contrast with a technique known as continuous narrative. Sometimes this continuous narrative is unframed, sometimes it reflects the paneling frequently found in the sequential art of comic books, as in *The Snowman* or *The Arrival*.

Cover and Dustjacket

The illustrations on the cover can create expectations for the content, and of course they play a tremendous role in attracting a young reader's attention to the book. Often a picture from inside the book is used, but sometimes the cover picture extends the story. In *Brundibar,* for example, the cover picture is very similar to an internal illustration found near the end of the book, but there are subtle differences. For one thing whereas the bucket is empty on the cover, in the internal picture the bucket is full of milk.

The actual cover of a picture book is often hidden beneath a dustjacket. Some covers have the same images as the dustjacket, but this is not always the case. In Peter Sís's *Tibet: Through the Red Box* the cover is quite different from the dust jacket, which is covered with maps, symbols, writing, and ancient mazes. The cover itself is mainly white with one small maze representing Tibet at its center. Kate Hovey's *Arachne Speaks* has a strikingly different illustration on the cover. *John Coltrane's Giant Steps* uses a transparent dustjacket with an illustration of a cat overlaying the illustrations on the actual cover. This effect ties in beautifully with the musical theme of the book. Unfortunately, many libraries make sure that the dustjackets cannot be removed in an effort to protect the book.

Design

Picture books all tend to share several elements in common. They all are illustrated throughout, and they generally have either 32 or 28 pages (always multiples of four). However, numerous other elements such as the use of borders, the placement of illustrations, the placement of text, the color and size of the fonts used, the stock of the paper, the shape of the book—all make the book distinct and help determine the reader's response. These collective elements add together to create design effects. It should be noted that some of these decisions are being made by the various employees at the publishing house rather than by the author or illustrator.

In Dave McKean's illustrations for David Almond's *The Savage* (Candlewick, 2008) the reader sometimes sees from the perspective of the savage. In this case the zoom-in emphasizes what this character is looking at. Art copyright Dave McKean from *The Savage* by David Almond. Candlewick, 2008.

Endpapers

The endpapers are the double-page spreads attached on one side to the inside of the front or back cover and on the other side to the first or last page of the book. Sometimes the endpaper is colored paper matching the tone of the story; other times the endpapers have a patterned design or even illustrations. In Bryan Collier's endpapers for *Rosa* we are presented with a sepia-toned scene from the book. In *The Arrival* the endpapers are filled with photorealistic images of immigrants from around the world—perhaps the best indication in the book that this fantasy tale is a metaphor for the common immigrant experience.

Focus

Sometimes the use of focus directly mirrors cinematic techniques. Mordan's *Silent Movie* will show a character in one panel and then in the next panel zoom in or out on that same picture in a way that recalls silent films.

Front Matter, Title Page, and Dedication Page

The front matter (which occasionally is actually found in the back of the book) includes all of the vital information about the work, including the ISBN, copyright information, and sometimes a summary. Additional information such as the media and technique used by the illustrator is also provided at times. There is generally both a separate title page and dedication page, though in some books these pages might be combined in various ways. The material on these pages is not usually part of the narrative, but the illustrations or other elements found there might enhance the story. Jerry Pinkney in his version of Hans Christian Andersen's *The Nightingale* uses detailed landscapes in his title page and front matter. In *Pink and Say* the pictures on the title and copyright pages show parallel partings as each boy leaves his family to go to war.

The title page in *Black and White* (Macaulay) includes a warning: "This book appears to contain a number of stories that do not necessarily occur at the same time. Then again, it may contain only one story. In any event, careful inspection of both words and pictures is recommended." On the title page of *John Coltrane's Giant Steps,* rather than authored and illustrated by, the credits read "remixed by Chris Raschka." So tie-ins and connections to the narrative are sometimes included in these otherwise utilitarian pages.

Lettering

The size, color, and style of the font tends to be chosen in ways that complement the art. In *The Wolves in the Wall* by Dave McKean the font and the positioning of words on the page add to the effect. In some instances, the lettering might actually be considered to be part of the illustration. For instance, the words are an integral part of the art in Stephen Gammell's *Ride.* Even in a novel such as *The Knife of Never Letting Go* (Ness) fonts can serve a narrative purpose.

In Patrick Ness's *The Knife of Never Letting Go* (Candlewick, 2008), the variety of fonts helps represent the barrage of different thoughts coming from the village. Reprinted by permission of Candlewick Press.

Light/Shadow

The interplay of light and shadow can impact the entire story. In Chris Soenpiet's *Something Beautiful* shadow is used effectively to emphasize the state of disrepair and even implies a level of threat in the neighborhood. Books such as *Home of the Brave* (Say) and *The Polar Express* (van Allsburg) use light and dark to add to the dreamlike quality of the narrative. Allen Say utilizes an interesting technique in which sunlight and searchlights reflect off of and illuminate various aspects of the illustrations. Chris van Allsburg uses chiaroscuro (the interplay of light and shadow) to add a three-dimensional effect to his illustrations.

Mood and Atmosphere

The overall mood of a book is created by a combination of aspects, including color, design, and media. Most books for young people have an upbeat or at least hopeful ending, but a surprising number include sadness, anger, confusion, or a certain level of somberness along the way. The amazing

atmosphere E. B. Lewis creates in *Night Boat to Freedom* (Raven) with the darkness and the shadowy blurry background combines with the tension and fear in the body posture and the facial features—the protagonist's feet invisible, his journey impossible.

Perspective and Point of View

The angle from which the reader sees events helps guide the reader's reception of the work. Does the reader have a bird's-eye view, or are they face to face with the characters? In Wiesner's *Tuesday* the reader sees the story unfold from a variety of angles, which helps convey the overall chaos. In Chris Van Allsburg's *The Widow's Broom* the reader is placed in a position of looking up at the witch's face, adding to the sense of vulnerability.

Related to the angle of perspective is the point of view from which the reader sees events. The first time the two title characters meet in *Pink and Say,* readers see Pinkus approaching as if they are laid out on the ground with Say. In one illustration from *Smoky Night* (Bunting) the reader is actually looking out of the window with the character. Both perspective and point of view can affect the reader's relationship to the storyline and the characters. In Jane Yolen's *Encounter* the reader sees Christopher Columbus from a perspective perhaps never considered, that of indigenous people already living in the "new" world.

The use of frames in *Arachne Speaks* by Kate Hovey (Margaret McElderry, 2001) emphasizes the idea of the Greek chorus that comments on the action. The chorus reacts in shock when Arachne challenges the gods of Mt. Olympus. Reprinted by permission of Margaret McElderry.

Artistic Style

Most illustrators are not creating within one clearly defined artistic style or tradition. Illustrators who are distinctly impressionistic, for example, would not be the norm; an illustrator is at least as likely to be eclectic with a variety of influences. Still, just as with the written word, style is borrowed, reworked, and echoed in what is sometimes referred to as *stylistic referencing.* Occasionally, the influences on an illustrator's work are easily recognizable. Anthony Browne, for example, draws heavily on the surrealist tradition. At other times stylistic elements surface in ways that are more implicit. Patricia Polacco, whose work is often discussed as folk art, regards the impressionist painters as her greatest artistic influences.

It can be important to at least introduce readers to some of the traditions that are likely to have influenced picture book illustrators, because style itself is a combination of conventions that create an effect. With art, narrative, film, and other media the reader or viewer will be impacted by the style whether or not they understand the effects and the traditions out of which it arises.

The humor of Old Tom has cross-age appeal. This illustration appears in *Old Tom, Man of Mystery* by Leigh Hobbs (Peachtree, 2005). Copyright Leigh Hobbs. Used by permission.

The term *cartoon art* originally referred to line drawings. Today the concept is used more broadly, but art identified this way still tends to have distinctive lines that create movement and humor. Typically cartoon art also reflects other conventions of the sequential art found in comic books, including dialogue bubbles and multiple frames on a page. Maurice Sendak, David Macaulay, and Jeff Smith all use cartoon art in their work.

The term *expressionism* refers particularly to an artistic style of the late 19th and 20th centuries that sought to depict subjective emotions in response to objects and events. Bright shocking colors are utilized with rapid brush strokes that in works like Stephen Gammel's sometimes look as if the artist actually threw the paint on the canvas. Proportions are often skewed as the emphasis is on what the artist feels rather than what is seen; therefore, distortion and exaggeration are common. When some of these elements are present, as in Gary Kelley's *Black Cat Bone,* critics will often refer to a work as expressionistic.

Folk art is defined in various ways, but it is generally seen as reflecting an artistic style tied to a particular cultural tradition. Artists identified in this way tend to be self-taught and connected to the life of a community. *Tar Beach* (Ringold), which draws on African American quilting in technique and theme, is a good example. Many picture book folktales draw on the folk traditions of the culture from which they have emerged. However, it should be noted that there are also plenty of schooled styles (i.e., professionally learned) from non-Western cultures; the key element is that the art reflects a form of cultural expression learned in the community rather than in an institute.

Impressionism is a style associated with French painters of the late 19th century, such as Monet and Pisarro. The impressionists sought to capture first impressions before the intellect and emotion could define or change the images. These painters used dabs or strokes of primary colors to simulate reflected light, with the result often being soft and dreamy. Impressionist paintings are also typified by unfinished edges, hazy images, and textured surfaces. *A Blue Butterfly: A Story about Claude Monet* by Bijou LeTord uses impressionistic art to tell this biographical story about one of the major impressionists. Ted Lewin's watercolors catch every nuance of light and shadow playing off of the water, buildings, and brightly clad pilgrims in *Sacred River: The Ganges of India.* Patricia Polacco, asked about the influences on her art, said, "the impressionists—Lautrec, Klimpt, Schiele" (Polacco interview, p. 86). In these instances, the interested reader might look directly at the works of these painters to see whether they can discern any similarities.

Naturalism and romanticism are in some ways easily recognizable styles. Some illustrators present the world as they actually see it, often with an almost photographic quality. Yet there are many schools, some direct reactions against others, which for the uninitiated might be difficult to differentiate. Thomas Locker's paintings reflect an identifiable style, the Hudson River School, which although very realistic in many ways present a pastoral romantic vision of the world. Realism and in particular naturalism arose as a school in

A surreal illustration from *Gaven* ("The Present"), published by Gyldendal, Denmark, in 2007. Copyright © Gyldendal and Søren Jessen, 2007.

reaction to romantic sentiments and tends to focus on the everyday, the gritty, the real. The art in both cases resemble photographs, and so are often used in contemporary realistic and historical fiction where the "real" is strived for, but the sentiments and moods evoked can vary drastically.

Surrealism, on the other hand, combines realistic elements with bizarre juxtapositions, creating fantastic or incongruous imagery. The style refers to an avant-garde movement of the early 20th century. In Buchholz's *Collector of Moments,* beautifully detailed watercolor paintings with photographic qualities are taken beyond realism when elements that should not be there are included. In *Imagine a Night,* Rob Gonsalves beautifully captures that moment between sleeping and waking time. Anthony Browne, David Wiesner, and Chris van Allsburg all add elements of the surreal to their illustrations.

Of course, this is only the tip of the iceberg in terms of stylistic influences. For instance, many illustrators find their inspiration in non-Western artistic styles. Raschka's style in *Giant Steps* was influenced by Chinese painters of the last two centuries, especially in terms of the fat brushes used. Ed Young has drawn on many of the old Chinese masters. Some illustrators are more influenced by styles that reflect other media, like Mordan's *Silent Movie.* Furthermore, many illustrators are influenced by other picture book artists more than by a particular school of art, so the stylistic echoes often surface in distinct and interesting ways.

Artistic Media and Graphic Techniques

Acrylics are a type of paint with a synthetic base to which colored pigments are added. Acrylics tend to have brilliant colors and an opaque finish. The bright colors often have an effect on the overall mood created by the illustrations. Susan Guevara's *Chato and the Party Animals* and Jerome Lagarrigue's paintings for *My Man Blue* are good examples of the use of acrylics. Other artists who use this medium include David Shannon, Carole Byard, Barbara Cooney, William Joyce, Dav Pilkey, and Jeanette Winter.

Charcoal is basically made from burnt wood, which can be applied in fine lines or in thick broad strokes. A number of artists use charcoal for preliminary sketches. Thomas Allen's use of charcoal in the book *In Coal Country* (Hendershon) relates directly to the

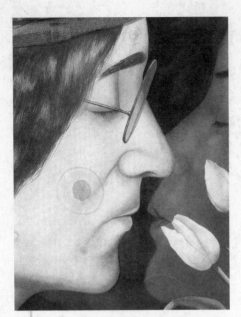

Bryan Collier's collage art from *John's Secret Dreams* (Hyperion, 2004). Tulips are often symbolic of perfect love. Art copyright 2004 by Bryan Collier, used in *John's Secret Dreams* by Doreen Rappaport, Hyperion, 2004. Used by permission.

content of the story. Other artists who use this medium include Ian Falconer in the Olivia books and David Wiesner in *Night of the Gargoyles* (Bunting).

Collage involves assembling paper, fabric, wood, and other materials to create illustrations. Collage allows artist and reader to explore the relationships among shapes. In *Smoky Night* (Bunting) David Diaz uses "found" materials as part of the collage to effectively evoke the aftermath of the riot in the story. In *John's Secret Dreams* Bryan Collier uses a collage technique that involves cutting or tearing patterns from magazines and from paper on which he has painted in watercolor and then assembling these parts on the page. Other artists who use collage include Jeannie Baker, Romare Bearden, and Susan L. Roth.

Cut paper illustrations consist of two-dimensional images that are strategically cut and arranged so that they take on a three-dimensional quality. These illustrations can be simple, as in Lois Ehlert's *In My World* (which includes layered cut paper and die-cuts), or very complex, as with David Wisniewski's *Golem*. To create the intricate cut paper layering in *Golem*, Wisniewski used as many as 100 blades on this one book. The three-dimensional quality is enhanced by using double-stick foam tape and matboard. Robert Sabuda uses cut paper and paint on papyrus in *Tutankhana's Gift*. Sabuda also takes cut paper in another direction with his pop-up books. Other artists who use this medium include Grayce Bochak and Amy Walrod.

Artists have used a variety of fabric and needlework art to illustrate picture books. Chue and Nhia Cha in *Dia's Story Cloth* (Che) and Faith Ringold in *Tar Beach* employ needlework techniques to create narrative and art in ways that are tied to a particular cultural heritage. Hmong story clothes and African American quilts hold important places in these artistic traditions. Both art forms have also traditionally served as narrative forms. Ringold's *Tar Beach* was originally a story quilt made with acrylic on canvas paper with fabric borders. The picture book adaptation stuck with this same technique. Other artists who use fabric and needlework to illustrate include Marthe Jocelyn, Salley Mavor, and Yoshi.

Gouache ("gwash") is French (from the Italian *guazzo*) for a particular type of watercolor paint to which chalk has been added to give it an opaque finish distinct from that of typical watercolors. *A Place to Grow* (Pak) illustrated by Marcellino Truong is a wonderful example of this technique. David Diaz uses gouache paintings in *Smoky Night* backed by photographic collages. Other artists who sometimes use gouache to illustrate include Frané Lessac, Marisabina Russo, Marcia Sewall, and Diane Stanley.

Oil paints are created by mixing colored pigments with an oil base. They come in varying thicknesses but in general dry slowly so that color must be added in layers. This allows previous layers to show through. Artists who use this medium include Thomas Locker, Eric Rohmann, Lane Smith, Don Wood, and Paul O. Zelinsky. Domitila Dominguez experiments with mixing marble dust into the oil paint to create an interesting effect in *The Story of Colors: La Historia de los Colores*. The book was written by Subcomandante Marcos, the leader of the Mexican Zapatista guerrilla movement. Though younger children reading the book need not know anything about Mexico, for the young adult reader the story will take on another level of meaning as they explore why the leader of a guerrilla army might have written this narrative.

Pastels consist of pigments that are molded into manageable sticks that can be either soft or hard, depending on the effect the artist wants to create in the final images. They are similar to crayon but not as greasy. Pastels can be rubbed and altered for effect. Artists who use this medium include Stephen T. Johnson, Nina Laden, Phoebe Stone, and Sharon Wilson.

Pencil and ink can both create a distinctive look in terms of texture and line. Quite often pencil is used in conjunction with other media. Tom Feelings uses pen and ink with tempera on rice paper to create the evocative illustrations in *Middle Passage*. Other artists who use this medium include Peter McCarty and Brian Wilcox. A number of illustrators use ink as part of the media, often to create distinctive lines. Dave McKean in *The Day I Swapped My Dad for Two Goldfish* (Gaiman) uses ink quite effectively. In *Blues Journey* Christopher Myers creates a blues riff using blue ink, white paint, and brown paper bags.

Photography can be used in many ways, and numerous effects and techniques can be connected to this medium. Archival photographs from the Civil War are combined with J. Patrick Lewis's *The Brother's War* to beautiful and at the same time disturbing effect. Artists who utilize photographs include Charles R. Smith, Jr., and Nic Bishop. Other artists like David McKean will sneak an occasional photograph into their illustrations.

David Almond's *The Savage* (Candlewick, 2008) with illustrations by Dave McKean explores the inner turmoil of a young man. The washes of color add to the mood but it is the pen-and-ink drawings that make the book stark and edgy. Reprinted by permission of Candlewick Press.

Scratchboard is a process that includes scratching the illustration into the black paint or ink covering a white board. Colors may be placed underneath the black media beforehand or added afterwards. Artists who use scratchboard include Susan Guevara and Michael McCurdy. Brian Pinkney uses a distinctive form of scratchboard. Starting with a whiteboard covered with black ink, he scratches a drawing and then adds color with oil or oil pastels in *Faithful Friend* (San Souci).

Tempera is similar to watercolors, except colored pigments are mixed with a sticky base, such as egg yolk. Tempera paint dries very quickly. Artists who use this medium include Judith Brown, Ashley Bryan, and Richard Jesse Watson. The tempera creates depth in the images of *The Middle Passage* (Feelings).

Watercolors are finely ground pigments with a natural or chemical base that are mixed with water. They tend to create soft muted color. Cornelius Van Wright and Ying-Hwa Hu use watercolors in *Jingle Dancer* by

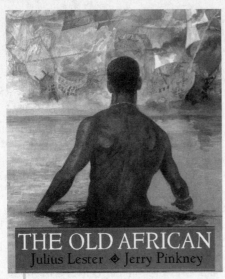

The Old African (Dial, 2005) illus. by Jerry Pinkney. Reprinted by permission of Penguin Group (USA).

Cynthia Leitich Smith to create a warmth and vitality. The type of paper used can also have an effect on the final product. In *Lizards, Frogs, and Polliwogs* Douglas Florian paints with watercolors on primed brown paper bags! Other artists who use watercolors include Jerry Pinkney, Ted Lewin, Allen Say, and Chris Raschka.

Woodcut illustrations are printed from engraved wood or linoleum. The engravings are traditionally carved into the wood, then covered with paint and pressed to paper. The result is often thin lines and bold shapes with the grain of the wood contributing to the contours of the illustration. David Frampton's woodcut illustrations in *Rhyolite: The True Story of a Ghost Town* add to the haunting mood of the story of a gold strike in Nevada. Mary Azarian, who won the Caldecott for her woodcuts in *Snowflake Bentley* (Martin), sketches illustrations onto a basswood block and then cuts out the engravings. After pressing the woodcuts she handcolors them. Keizaburo Tejima in *Owl Lake* uses Japanese-style woodcuts, which would make a wonderful comparison to Azarian's style. Other artists who use this medium include Betsy Bowen and Christopher Manson.

Another form of engraving involves the use of copperplate etchings. Arthur Geisert is building on 500 years of tradition when he uses tools and acid to scratch pictures into copperplates. Thick ink is then placed on the metal and it is run through a press. Because the engraving process creates a mirror image on the paper, the pictures have to be etched backwards. This process is described in *The Etcher's Studio* by Geisert. (A slideshow with pictures of the process is available at the Reading is Fundamental website at www.RIF.org.)

As is the case with techniques and styles, many artists utilize multiple media in creating their illustrations. Chris Raschka uses the mixed media of watercolor and ink to great effect in *John Coltrane's Giant Steps*. Sims Taback in *Joseph Had a Little Overcoat* mixes watercolor, gouache, pencil, ink, and collage as well as die-cut holes. David Wiesner uses watercolor, gouache, colored inks, pencil, and colored pencil in *The Three Pigs*. In *Wolves in the Walls* Dave McKean uses painting, line drawing, and photographs. In fact, McKean often starts with a canvas of color photographs and paper collage; this way there are already "interesting textures, colors and shapes" and then he paints the characters on top of that (www.apple.com/pro/design/mcken/index2.html). Often he scans the materials onto the computer and then blends them together. Other artists who tend to use a variety of mixed media include Lisa Campbell Ernst, Patricia Polacco, and Yumi Heo.

Books about the Art of Picture Books

- *A Caldecott Celebration: Six Artists and Their Paths to the Caldecott Medal* by Leonard Marcus
- *Children's Book Illustration and Design II* by Julie Cummins
- *Picture This: How Pictures Work* by Molly Bang
- *Side by Side: Five Favorite Picture-Book Teams Go to Work* by Leonard Marcus
- *Talking with Artists: Conversations with Illustrators* by Pat Cummings
- *Ways of Telling: Conversations on the Art of the Picture Book* by Leonard Marcus
- *Wings of an Artist: Children's Book Illustrators Talk about Their Art* by Julie Cummins

A number of novels are coming out now with illustrations interspersed. *The Graveyard Book* by Neil Gaiman was actually published in two different editions in England, one with illustrations by Dave McKean (2008) for adults and one with illustrations by Chris Riddell (2008) for children. In the United States only the McKean version was published but it was marketed for young readers. Art copyright Dave McKean from *The Graveyard Book* by Neil Gaiman. Subterranean Press, 2008. Art by Chris Riddell from *The Graveyard Book* by Neil Gaiman. Bloomsbury, 2008, UK cover.

Technology Links

Virtual Insight into the Illustrator's Studio

One of the most beneficial aspects of the Internet is access to information. For young adult literature this means information about the books, their creators, and ideas for exploring and extending storylines with young adults. Among the most exciting resources are those that provide direct looks into the author or illustrator's studio. There are certainly many sites with print interviews of illustrators. Achuka, School Library Journal, and Cynthia Leitich Smith's website are among the many online sources where you can access written interviews with some of the best illustrators and authors.

As beneficial as these interviews are, there are other websites that take advantage of the multimedia possibilities of the Internet. Students can listen to Jon Scieszka on Scholastic Teacher Radio, Peter Sís on NPR, or Robert Sabuda on Loose Leaf. The literature discussions on Loose Leaf are thematically based with a handful of authors, illustrators, editors, and scholars addressing a particular theme. The interviews can be listened to or printed, making this a valuable resource.

Some sites even have visuals. Reading Is Fundamental provides brief but excellent slideshows on the artistic techniques of leading illustrators like Chris Raschka. The Cooperative Children's Book Center (CCBC) has posted a number of videos, including Uri Shulevitz's acceptance of the Charlotte Zolotow Award.

The online resources mentioned thus far are free, but some high-quality sites are being created that require a subscription. One of the most beneficial of these services,

TeachingBooks.net, provides links to hundreds of sites such as the ones just mentioned, and in addition they have created high-quality glimpses inside the studios of some top-notch illustrators and authors. You can see firsthand how Bryan Collier, for example, creates his unique watercolor and collage illustrations. In another video David Wiesner demonstrates the four-step process he uses when creating a picture book and discusses his love of wordless books. Still another focuses on Denise Fleming, who walks the viewer through her process for creating pulp paper illustrations. Each of the Author Up-Close movies is accompanied by movie transcripts, in-depth interviews, book guides, bibliographies, and links to numerous related websites.

TeachingBooks.net is ideally suited for purchase by a school system or library. Individuals can also purchase a subscription for just over $100 per year. Fortunately Teaching Books.net and other sites of this kind tend to offer trial periods so that individual users can sign up for several weeks to investigate the resources offered. If your school or library has the money for a subscription you will find the collected materials to be a wonderful asset. TeachingBooks.net also contains audio book readings, thematic booklists, and an exhaustive number of links related to literature for young people.

Achuka (www.achuka.co.uk)

CCBC website (www.education.wisc.edu/ccbc)

Cynthia Leitich Smith (www.cynthialeitichsmith.com)

Reading Is Fundamental (www.rif.org)

School Library Journal (www.schoollibraryjournal.com)

TeachingBooks.net (www.teachingbooks.net)

Author Spotlight

Bryan Collier and members of the After School Achievement Program. Photo courtesy of Bryan Collier.

Bryan Collier

Bryan Collier was born on the Eastern Shore of Maryland. He says that though he was a reader as a young adult, he was not really a leisure reader until after college. Then he rediscovered picture books and fell in love with this form of literature, mainly because of the illustrations. Anyone who needs an example of an older person actually becoming a leisure reader because of picture books need look no further. Currently he browses the shelves of bookstores searching out exciting titles like Ntozake Shange's *Ellington Is Not a Street,* about which he says, "the dualities in it really hit me and of course the art is wonderful." Visit his website at www.bryancollier.com.

SELECTED BOOKLIST

John's Secret Dreams by Doreen Rappaport (Hyperion, 2004)
Martin's Big Words by Doreen Rappaport (Jump Sun, 2001)
Twelve Rounds to Glory with Charles Smith (Candlewick, 2007)
Uptown (Henry Holt, 2000)
Visiting Langston by Willie Perdomo (Henry Holt, 2002)

ON HIS ARTISTIC INFLUENCES

The main influence was my grandmother who I lived with for a big part of my life. We would do things like cook together, and she would make quilts. All of these things are interrelated. I always make the connection between collage and cooking when I talk. Collage is like cooking; it's very ordinary but then these extraordinary things happen when you put these ordinary things together. I try to break down the myth of being an artist and recognize that creativity is that thing that we do every day. We all do it, so I'm not different from you. I am searching for common ground.

ON PICTURE BOOKS FOR YOUNG ADULTS

Young adults will be surprised because they think that picture books are for kids. But if they really look into it and look at the metaphors, there are things hidden within the graphics which expand the text and make it more relevant. You'll find yourself in the text and it becomes magical and wonderful then.

ON THE PROCESS OF ILLUSTRATING SOMEONE ELSES'S WORDS

First the text will be sent to me by the editor and I have to decide if it moves me. I work closely with the editor as well as the art director. I'll do a story board, which is a loose attempt to show them what I think, where the art should flow on the page. My job is to bring the visual storyline to the text. Setting, mood, time frame—the illustrations help bridge all of these things together. Words create images, and the images compound each other. I try to balance all of these things.

In *Uptown,* which I authored and illustrated, the words and the images evolved together. I knew that I wanted to bridge old Harlem and today's Harlem.

ON HIS USE OF COLLAGE

I use a combination of watercolor and collage. I cut from old magazines, wall-paper, and other patterns. There is no routine. Sometimes I use more watercolor, sometimes more collage. I love the vibrant movement of color. I hear the art. In a way it all goes back to my grandmother's cooking. These ordinary ingredients come together to create something extraordinary.

Guidelines for Selecting and Evaluating Illustrated Literature for Young Adults

In addition to the general selection criteria for young adult literature, you may want to consider the following questions when working with illustrated books:

- Do the text and illustrations work together to create a well-developed setting, characters, and themes?
- Are the illustrations integral to the story?
- Is the narrative complemented and extended by the illustrations?
- Do the style, mood, and media of the illustrations fit with the storyline? Why has the illustrator chosen to illustrate this way?
- Do graphic elements (including layout, coloring, lettering, and dramatic impact) work effectively with the storyline?
- Do other elements of the format (such as font, endpapers, cover and jacket design, size and shape of the book) add to the aesthetics and meanings conveyed?

Topic Focus

English Language Learners and Literature

A teacher who has not had much experience with nonnative English speakers often leaps to certain assumptions on hearing that an English language learner (ELL) will be in the class. However, the term encompasses students from anywhere in the world (including in the United States) for whom English is not their first language. The diversity among ELLs is so rich that it is difficult to determine standardized strategies for helping them learn to read English. A number of literacy and background factors are going to influence reading abilities and preferences, including cultural norms; literary traditions with which they are familiar; previous schooling; home ties; school attendance; family literacy background; whether they are native born, legal immigrants, illegal immigrants, or refugees; proficiency in first language; living conditions; personal experiences; and personal reading preferences.

Teachers often bemoan the fact that ELLs are not going to be able to read the literature everyone else in the class is using. Even worse, some teachers make the assumption that they should be providing ELLs with more worksheets while the rest of the class reads. So why is it essential to use literature with all students, and in particular with those learning the language?

- Well-written books model language that is meaningful, natural, useful, and relevant.
- Literature supplies contextualized language.
- Read-alouds give an opportunity to listen to the structures and tones of the language.
- Meaningful narrative is more likely to lead to dialogue.
- Literature can provide natural and meaningful language at a variety of levels.
- Picture books include visual cues that also give access to the narrative.
- Illustrations can provide contextual and narrative information that supplements the written text.

A young adult reader. Photo by Kathy Pusey.

Picture books can often serve as a great vehicle for exploring narrative, which can benefit the entire class while serving the particular needs of ELLs. My students have in the past worked with students in migrant schools as well as ELLs in mainstream classrooms and have found the following strategies to be most significant:

- Choose books from diverse cultural perspectives.
- Use read-alouds even with older readers.
- Offer bilingual and primary language books when available.
- Provide peer translation when possible (but without putting the translator on the spot).
- Arrange various forms of oral and written expression to respond to the literature.
- Write in groups.
- Work on various forms of artistic work in small groups to allow students to create visual representations and discuss understandings.
- Employ manipulatives and hands-on activities frequently.
- Include storytelling, puppetry, song, and other narrative forms tied to oral tradition.
- Publish and exhibit.

However, their most significant finding is that all these techniques will enhance the learning environment for the entire class but might have special benefits for many ELLs.

Sequential Art: Graphic Novels and Comics for Young Adults

What Is a Graphic Novel?

Art Spiegelman, the only graphic novelist to win a Pulitzer, has referred to graphic novels/comics as the "Bastard hunchback dwarf of the Arts" (2002, n.p.). Of course detractors of the format have called it far worse. Sequential art is after all a literary/artistic format that has suffered through both Senate hearings and the creation of a stringent Comics Code Authority! The history of comics and graphic novels is intriguing to say the least.

When I first included graphic novels in my YA literature course, the reaction of preservice teachers and school librarians was not especially positive. I had created a text set with works like *Sandman* (Gaiman), which is a rather sophisticated read, and *Ghost World*

The autobiographical book *Blankets* (Top Shelf, 2003) by Craig Tompson was listed in *Time* magazine as one of the Top Ten Graphic Novels of all time. This book about growing up evangelical, mental disabilities, and first love received the Harvey Award and the Eisner Award, among others. The topics have caused the books to be challenged in several libraries but they have also made it a favorite of many teens. Reprinted by permission of Top Shelf.

(Clowes), which centers on two cynical young women who are graduating from high school. Both of these books are popular with some older young adults, but many of my students thought that these works were too edgy to use in the classroom. In fact, a majority of the preservice teachers were already wary of using "comics" in the classroom at all.

Several intertwined issues emerged. First, of my secondary education and library services majors, only a few had ever been avid comic book readers. Some were familiar with superhero comics (or at least with these characters' roles in popular culture), and a few had read Art Spiegelman's *Maus*. But the majority simply did not have the background literacies and associations that would give them access to enjoyment of the literature. Spiegelman has asserted, "Comics can be hard to learn, but they are a self-teaching machine" (Reid, 2000, p. 44). Indeed readers who are interested in the illustrations or the content might struggle a bit discovering how to fit the pieces together, but they work their way through and before long they are easily following the narrative flow. However, many adult readers seem to have already prejudged the format as trash literature and so lack the motivation to trace the narrative sequence.

The second issue is that preservice teachers are already somewhat resistant to using literature with young readers about topics such as sex, gender, violence, or abuse. The visual element that graphic novels add to the literature only magnifies the strong reservations about exploring these controversial topics. The same holds true for different reasons with fantasy elements (as will be discussed in Chapter 5).

Some teachers and librarians also fear parental reaction to images that might be deemed inappropriate.

Adding to all this resistance is the notion that comics simply are not high-quality literature—that they might be a corrupting influence. This is not a new idea. In the early 1950s there were 35 publishing houses specializing in comics and it is estimated that 80 percent of children in the United States read comic books. In 1954 Frederic Wertham's *Seduction of the Innocent* was published. What was causing juvenile delinquency in America, Wertham asks. Not poverty, or drugs, or even communism—but, you guessed it, comics! Wertham's book was taken very seriously, prompting the Senate that same year to hold hearings. As a result, the industry created a Comics Code Authority (CCA), with rules like the following:

- In every instance good shall triumph over evil and the criminal will be punished for his misdeeds.
- Profanity, obscenity, smut, vulgarity, or words or symbols that have acquired undesirable meanings are forbidden.
- Although slang and colloquialisms are acceptable, excessive use should be discouraged and wherever possible good grammar shall be employed.
- Suggestive and salacious illustration or suggestive posture is unacceptable.
- All characters will be depicted in dress reasonably acceptable to society.
- Illicit sex relations are neither to be hinted at nor portrayed.
- The treatment of love/romance stories shall emphasize the value of the home and the sanctity of marriage.

These rules do not apply just to comics for children but all comics. Imagine if this were applied to soap operas, music videos, theatre, or any other genre or format of literature for that matter! Initiation of the CCA shattered the comic book industry, and within a year only nine publishers were left standing. Over the decades the language in the CCA has been revised and only a few publishers still seek the seal of approval (Marvel Comics stopped taking part in 2001 but DC still participates).

With all this stacked against comics and graphic novels, why is there a move by young adult librarians and teachers to incorporate this literature into the reading material offered to young people? A number of significant reasons are explored in the following pages, but foremost is the fact that a substantial group of young adults are already hooked on this format. They read this literature, write fan fiction, create fan art, wait impatiently for the next installment, collect it, and discuss it. Teachers and librarians who can harness this energy and enthusiasm can really expand student literacies.

Sequential Art Definitions

- A *comic book* is a collection of sequential art in a single-issue publication of generally less than 36 pages. Comic books are often published on a monthly or quarterly basis.
- *Manga* is the Japanese term for comic book (literally "motionless picture entertainment"). In the United States the term refers specifically to Japanese comics. Many children and young adults become interested in manga through animé (animated cartoons), which have the same style and often the same characters.
- Coined by Will Eisner in 1978, the term *graphic novel* refers to a self-contained story in a comic book format. Graphic novels are trade books intended as literature, as opposed to comics, which are considered more ephemeral and likely to be collected, traded, or discarded after being read. In the United States, these books sometimes take years to complete, published first in serial form and only later coming out as a complete self-contained unit.
- Collections of previously published comic books reprinted together in bound editions are generally referred to as *trade paperbacks*. Graphic novels and comic trade paperbacks tend to be lumped together in most bookstores and libraries.

Graphic novels have a long and involved history, highlights of which are provided in the chronology that appears in the Appendix. The development of sequential art was impacted profoundly by the 1954 publication of *Seduction of the Innocent.* Between 1902 and 1953 comics had become extremely popular, with peak U.S. readership at 80 percent of young people. There was a wide variety as well: Superhero, detective, science fiction, horror, western, war, and romance genres all had an active readership. But Frederic Wertham's book fueled an already growing anti–comic book crusade that blamed sequential art for the delinquency of young people, and within a year the number of publishers creating this literature had drastically declined. In the United States, mainstream comics were stifled for several decades.

In Japan, on the other hand, the popularity of the format has increased dramatically since World War II. Over 30,000 comic book rental shops operate there. Fortunately, crime rates remain low in Japan, and reading comics does not seem to have created a nation of delinquents there. In France "bandes dessinnées," which are considered the ninth art, are prominently featured in bookstores and libraries. The same holds true for much of Europe.

Among the comics that remained in the United States after the CCA was established, superheroes became popular again and soon were the big genre, but an interesting trend also occurred. Whereas most of these superheroes had been almost godlike before, now new heroes appeared who had teen angst and other real-world problems. At the same time, another big trend was the underground comix movement. Many writers and artists did not want to submit to the CCA, and independent, unauthorized publishers began to appear. Some incredible art and literature came out during the underground comix movement of the 1960s and 70s. These trends and other factors have led to the interesting culture of the sequential art industry, perhaps the only literary realm in the United States where someone might self-publish and still end up in stores and at conventions across the country (zines and poetry chapbooks also have followings but not nearly to the same extent).

A graphic novel differs from a comic book in more than length. The comic book is generally considered either collectible or disposable. A graphic novel is a trade book meant to be placed on a bookshelf. Sometimes a collection of comics is put together into a trade paperback and sometimes a graphic novel is first published as a series of issues, so the distinctions become fuzzy, but the graphic novel tends to tell one lengthy story, whereas the collection of comic book issues might read more like a series of connected short stories.

A Contract with God by Will Eisner is considered by many to be the first graphic novel. However two groundbreakers that young adult readers are more likely to have read appeared in the mid-1980s. In *The Dark Knight Returns,* Batman has been retired for 10 years and the world has gone to hell in a handbasket. Batman is in a crisis as to whether he should go back to crime fighting. The other major graphic novel from the 1980s, *Maus,* a book with cats as Nazis and mice as Jews, is based on Art Spiegelman's own life and that of his father who survived the concentration camps. These two books really affected the way critics and retailers look at graphic novels, and for many, this was when graphic novels gained some legitimacy. Today there are around 120 publishers of comic books, most of them small independent companies.

Author Spotlight

Photo courtesy of Colleen Doran.

Colleen Doran

Colleen has been a professional artist since age 15. She has worked as a writer, penciler, inker, colorist, industry consultant, designer, letterer, painter, editor, and publisher. Her list of credits includes *Sandman, Amazing Spiderman,* Walt Disney's *Beauty and the Beast, Wonder Woman,* Clive Barker's *Hellraiser, X-Factor, Star Wars Galaxy,* and *Captain America.* She owns and operates Colleen Doran Studios, her own production company, where she creates *A Distant Soil* (Image comics). She is the only female cartoonist producing a series for a major U.S. publisher. More than 500,000 copies of Distant Soil comics and graphic novels have been sold. There are three Distant Soil graphic novels in print—*The Gathering, The Ascendant,* and *The Aria,* and over 35 comic book issues have appeared in the series. Doran is featured in the book *Comic Book Rebels.* She received the Amy Schultz Memorial Award for using the Distant Soil series to heighten public awareness of child abuse. In her spare time she enjoys gardening, kickboxing, reading, and hiking. Visit her website at http://colleendoran.com.

SELECTED BOOKLIST
A Distant Soil: The Aria (Image, 2001)
A Distant Soil: The Ascendant (Image, 2001)
A Distant Soil: The Gathering (Image, 2001)
Girl to Grrrl Manga: How to Draw the Hottest Shoujo Manga (Impact, 2006)
*Manga Pro Superstars Workshop: How to Create and Sell Comics
    and Graphic Novels* (Impact, 2007)
Orbiter by Warren Ellis (Vertigo, 2004)

ON WHERE SHE GETS HER INSPIRATIONS

Everywhere. I read incessantly. I spend a heck of a lot more time studying now than I ever did as a kid in school. I read a great deal of nonfiction, especially histories of royal families and anthropology and the like, so I can get a hook on the complex alien cultures I am trying to develop.

I also put a lot of my own life into the work. My book *A Distant Soil* is the story of a young girl who is born the heir to an alien religious dynasty. She has incredible paranormal powers and various groups of people are trying to either help her or exploit her. I identify strongly with her and with another character in the book, who is called an Avatar, a young man who is caged and exploited, treated like a piece of valuable property. I felt like that when I was younger. I became a professional illustrator when I was only 15 and I also did some acting and singing as a girl. Some publishers saw the seminal work I was doing on *A Distant Soil* at that time. I was so young and inexperienced that I was often taken advantage of in business dealings and treated pretty badly by some of the adults with whom I was working. I put a lot of that angst into my book. There are entire conversations and experiences from my life that have been dropped right into the story. All I did was add some paranormal elements, but the actual conversations and experiences were real.

ON THE POPULARITY OF GRAPHIC NOVELS AND COMIC BOOKS

I hear graphic novels are the most stolen books in libraries. Well, if they are being snitched it is because they are wanted! This should be taken as a good sign!

They are popular because they are entertaining. When I was a kid, there was a great deal of stigma associated with reading for entertainment. Teachers and librarians behaved as though if kids didn't read Kierkegaard, they were going to rot their brains. This was inane logic. If kids don't learn to read for entertainment, they never learn to read at all. Graphic novels are much more entertaining and can be enjoyed by a wide variety of people, even those who don't usually enjoy reading. Reading for pleasure improves overall reading skills. Comics are a reflection of pop culture, a more visually oriented modern culture and people can relate to them. They can relate to stories that combine words and pictures because they have spent their lives watching films and television, mediums which are visual and verbal. It is easy to make the leap to graphic novels from that, even if one doesn't normally enjoy reading.

ON NARRATIVE IN GRAPHIC NOVELS

Well, a graphic novel is written in much the same way as a screenplay. A lot of people who try to write graphic novels have some difficulty because they don't realize that the pictures tell part of the story and that it isn't necessary to use captions and exposition to describe what the reader can see. Captions and dialogue should only be used to describe what the reader cannot see or experience from the pictures. If you can see the sun rising, it is not necessary to write a caption telling the reader that the sun is rising. That is redundant. If you are going to write a caption describing the sunrise, the caption should describe something that the reader cannot see with their own eyes. Perhaps you could describe the heat of the sun, or the smell of the morning dew, or the sound of the birds singing or the mounting traffic in the streets. There are a number of famous writers who have bombed as comic or graphic novel writers because they don't know when to stop writing. They cram the pages with unnecessary captions and descriptions that do not move the story along or add anything to the reader's experience because they cannot remember that the pictures tell the story with the words. The visual and verbal information should be integrated. In a narrative, naturally, everything must be told in words. In a comic, the pictures carry a great deal of the responsibility of the storytelling process. If the writer does not remember to let the pictures tell their part of the story, then they are failing as a graphic novel writer. Just because one can write beautiful prose does not mean that one can write a graphic novel. The writer has to be able to be verbal and visual at once. Not every writer has this skill.

ON USING GRAPHIC NOVELS IN THE CLASSROOM

Let the kids decide. Let them read for themselves. Don't choose for your students what you want them to read every time; otherwise they may never read at all. If you force them to read only what you want and never give them an option, they will reject reading entirely. I have seen this happen again and again. I had a very forward-thinking teacher in high school who once let the class vote on what we wanted to read that semester, as long as the teacher also had some say in what we read. The teacher chose *To Kill a Mockingbird* for us, and the students voted to read some schlocky novel. We read them both as a compromise. At the end of the class, remarkably, all the students but one agreed that the teacher's choice was the better book. We enjoyed the classic novel more than the schlocky one we had all wanted to read. But we all read them both, and willingly, because the teacher let us have our way while having his way. Yet when other teachers forced the kids to only read the teacher's choices, many of the kids didn't even do the assignment. Reading shouldn't always be a chore. Reading is fun. Reading is entertaining. Teachers continually extol the virtues and joys of reading, but berate and belittle their students' choices in reading material. What better way to turn kids off to reading than to tell them they have bad taste or that their choices are stupid! You know, I was reading great classics when I was a very little girl. My father introduced me to Plato, Aristotle, and Marcus Aurelius by the time I was 12 years old. But I also enjoyed reading *Wonder Woman* comics! In fact, I read *Wonder Woman* because I enjoyed all the classic Greek mythology in the stories! Let kids read for fun, and you can bet that their reading skills will improve and that they will move on to more complex material at their own pace. And some of that complex material will be found in some remarkably mature and sophisticated graphic novels. Don't say no to a kid who wants to read, just because you don't think the material is lofty enough. Teachers should dance in the streets every time they see a kid who actually wants to read a book.

ON PORTRAYALS OF FEMALE CHARACTERS IN COMIC BOOKS

Well, when I first got into the comic book business, I was pretty much alone. I was a teenager and the only young girl around. There were some women adults, but they were usually the wives or girlfriends of people in the business. It wasn't a very hospitable environment back then. But things have changed a lot. There are plenty of young women entering the field and there are a lot of new opportunities for women creators. Old attitudes are changing. In fact, one male editor who had always given me a hard time, called me into his office last week to tell me that he was sorry for underestimating me and my work because he really liked what I was doing on my new book and he respected me. That meant a lot. In the past, he had always vetoed me on projects because he didn't believe there were any good women artists in comics, but I was able to change his mind with the calibre of the work I am doing on my new book. Even some of the old-timers in the business are getting over their old prejudices.

However, it is still a male-dominated industry, in part because most [comic book] readers are men and boys. More and more girls and women are reading comics and as they do, the people that do them will reflect that new environment.

A lot of the women drawn in comics are sexpots, mannequins who are meant to look good in tights while they jump across rooftops beating people up. You know, I don't have a problem with the beautiful women drawn in comics. That's part of what attracted me to comics in the first place. I wanted to be a big, strong, beautiful, and powerful woman when I grew up, someone that helped people and had a lot of adventures. Boys dreamed about being Superman and I dreamed about being Supergirl.

A lot of men just assume that if women are objecting to a woman character it must be because they are jealous of her beauty, but that is silly. Many of the women have such grotesquely exaggerated physical features that they look ridiculous and painful in their silly costumes. Beauty doesn't offend me in the least. The bad drawing does.

Why Use Graphic Novels with Young Readers

Comic book characters have become important symbols in Western society, adapted for every imaginable medium from newspaper comic strips to radio, to movies, television, and magazines. Partly because of this, comic book art is often regarded as part of pop culture, which for many teachers means it is not part of what is done in the classroom. This is unfortunate as there are a number of compelling reasons for making at least some age-appropriate graphic novels available to young adults.

- The format is extremely popular with many young readers.
- Comics have unique art and sophisticated narrative structures that combine illustration and text to create a whole.
- Sequential art often appeals to reluctant readers and can also be an excellent resource for English language learners.
- Graphic novels might be used to introduce literary elements and artistic techniques.
- Many international works in this format have cross-cultural appeal.
- Sequential art might stimulate interest in illustration skills and techniques.
- In part because of the visual element, graphic novels tend to utilize a higher level of vocabulary than other formats do, while still being accessible to young readers.

The lines dividing comics for children, young adults, and adults are very wavy. Some graphic novels might be identified as appealing to certain age groups based on the sophistication of art and narrative, the age of the protagonists, and of course who the content might be most appropriate for or likely to appeal to. For example, Torres and Miyazawa's *Side-*

kicks: The Transfer Student, about a high school for young superheroes, seems to be most popular with younger teens, so it would be logical to classify this as a YA book (though 9- to 14-year-olds would be the most likely readership). However in general, the boundaries when they can be drawn at all tend to be extremely fluid.

Many graphic novels deal with themes similar to YA novels, but at the same time with a special appeal for some readers because of the graphic elements. Even though only a segment of the YA population has regular contact with sequential art in trade books, there tends to be both a casual and a devoted audience, and many of those books are among the most popular in any YA collection.

It should be noted that graphic novels are not a genre of literature but rather a format. Just as with picture books, there is a wide variety aimed at different ages in assorted genres. One big difference between picture books and some graphic novels is that, especially when the illustrations are in color, a team of two, four, or even more people might actually work on the art in a graphic novel. For example, in *Negation: Bohica* Tony Bedard is the writer, Paul Pelletier is the penciler, David Maikis is the inker, James Rochelle is the colorist, and Troy Peteri is the letterer. Furthermore, in Chapters 1 and 2 there was a co-writer and in Chapter 6 a different penciler, inker, and colorist were used. The credits in a graphic novel can sometimes read like movie credits.

Illustration from *The Tale of One Bad Rat* (Dark Horse Comics, 1995) by Bryan Talbot. The literacy skills involved in reading sequential art have to be learned through experience like any other literacy skill, but the art itself often guides us as we learn to navigate the panels. Reprinted by permission of Bryan Talbot.

Of course, many techniques are utilized in sequential art, some quite similar to those used in picture books. Perspective, mood, angles, movement, and many other factors will be similar to picture book art. One distinction in many instances can be found in the use of panels and all the related design elements such as placement, pacing, overlays, and borders. Even a short graphic novel of 40 pages will often have six or more images in panels on a page; in contrast, most picture books are limited to 32 images or 16 double-page spreads. It is the sequencing on the page that is probably most demanding for people who have not developed the literacies involved in reading comic books. With multiple panels on a page, one of the major considerations concerns how the placement of images influences the flow of narrative. On page 23 of *Buffy the Vampire Slayer: Ring of Fire,* Ryan Sook leads the reader's eyes through the panels with the use of foreground elements and angles. Sook has asserted, "Whenever I can I like to have a vertical gutter going the length of the page. That line cutting the page in half pulls the reader's eyes from left to right" (Allie, 2000, p. 10). Other artists use a variety of different techniques, with the basic movement being from left to right, top to bottom.

In the illustration showing a page from *The Tale of One Bad Rat* the reader who is used to scanning from left to right will have no problem finding the narrative flow.

The left-to-right pattern of Western literature is reinforced by the diminishing size of the images in boxes at the bottom of the page as they move from left to right, coupled with the zoom-in effect.

Readers are always active in the literary experience, but participation is especially strong in sequential art. In film the images are given to you and though there will be gaps when the viewer tries to figure out what has happened, the majority of the details are provided. In a novel the reader creates a visual narrative in the mind's eye based on the descriptions given, and, unless something in the text contradicts the images created, the reader can continue to create a visual narrative based on what is read (though filtered through the reader's own past experiences). In sequential art the visual images are provided in a series of snapshots (often full of action) but with a constant series of gaps between the panels. The reader takes the given images and extends them to fill in the spaces between panels. So the reader is constantly internalizing and predicting to bridge those gaps.

Looking at graphic novels can also be an effective way to bring media literacy into the classroom, used here as in the expanded definition given on the Center for Media Literacy website: "Media Literacy is a 21st century approach to education. It provides a framework to access, analyze, evaluate and create messages in a variety of forms—from print to video to the Internet. Media literacy builds an understanding of the role of media in society as well as essential skills of inquiry and self-expression necessary for citizens of a democracy."

Ray Harryhausen and John Landis (1996) see little distinction between the sequential art of comics and the continuity drawings or storyboard sketching done for cinema. Landis writes, "Since the days of silent films, storyboard artists have been used to help the director visualize a sequence, especially in the areas of action and special effects" (n.p.). Richard Delgado for example is a storyboard artist who makes a smooth transition into graphic novels with *Age of Reptiles.*

Questions about how color affects the mood, the use of stereotypes in the illustrations, point of view, the effects of style on perception—are all ripe for discussion. The illustrator is consciously thinking about style, audience, and effect. Bryan Talbot, for example, writes

> The story dictated the illustration technique. This is true for every comic I've worked on; I've always tried to adapt my drawing style to project the different atmospheres required by each individual story. With Bad Rat, this meant a drastic stylistic change. Because of the content and the mainstream nature of the story, I felt that it needed to be clear and accessible, easily readable by those without an acquired knowledge of comics grammar. (1995, n.p.)

Talbot used models and scenes from real locations, and to create the abused character's dialogue about her feelings he borrowed from transcripts of actual victims.

Lavin (1998) suggests that reading graphic novels actually requires more complex cognitive skills than other forms of literature. There are sophisticated narrative structures in both the words and illustrations, as well as the combined narrative created by the sequencing and design of words and graphics together. All of this might help "develop much needed analytical and critical thinking skills" (Versaci, 2001, p. 62). Critics and artists such as Colleen Doran have even suggested a correlation between the high literacy rate in Japan and the proliferation of manga/comic books there (2002).

As with novels, some titles are not well written or illustrated, and some are inappropriate for the classroom for various reasons, but many are high quality and a powerful body of art and literature has been created. Among signs that graphic novels are gaining in acceptance are reviews in *Library Journal, School Library Journal,* and *Kirkus;* the increased space bookstores are devoting to them; and the appearance of titles in Scholastic Bookfair lists. Furthermore, a growing number of picture books with graphic novel formats are being published by the large publishing houses. *The Wolves in the Walls* was billed as a graphic novella. The Little Lit books edited by Art Spiegelman are reminiscent of picture book versions of *Mad* magazine but created by some of the best sequential artists from around the world. Raymond Briggs (*The Snowman*), Will Eisner (*The Princess and the Frog*), and Jules Pfeiffer (*Meanwhile*) all have created books that can be cross-marketed as both picture books and graphic novels. Several bandes designées from France have recently been published as picture books in the United States (*Little Vampire Does Kung Fu*). Harcourt's Silver Whistle division has put out several graphic novels along the lines of *Amelia Earhart: Free in the Skies.* And a new imprint called Doubleday Graphic Novels offers several graphic novels, including Eisner's *Fagin the Jew,* a retelling of the story of Oliver Twist.

In the Field *Graphic Novels and Manga in the Library*

Rachel Jones was a library associate at the Wicomico County Public Library in Salisbury, Maryland, from 2000 to 2007. She redesigned the young adult area of the library to include comfortable seating, artwork, and popular material such as magazines, DVDs, music CDs, and graphic novels. After a request from teen customers, Rachel started a monthly Teen Animé Club where members get together to talk about their favorite sequential art, chat, and of course eat! (Animé is basically the video equivalent of manga; animé clubs tend to look at both the print and the video versions of Japanese comics.)

ON THE POPULARITY OF GRAPHIC NOVELS

They fly off of the shelves! Including graphic novels and manga in our teen collection has increased circulation tremendously. We also see more teens hanging out in that section of the library—reading, looking at displays, asking for new titles. The success of graphic novels in the teen area of the library led us to build a collection for adults as well.

ON THE CURRENT INTEREST IN SEQUENTIAL ART

I think sequential art appeals to a wide range of interests and a diverse group of readers. I think some reluctant readers are drawn to the familiar comic book style of graphic novels; others are drawn to the subject, whether it be superheroes, fantasy, romance.

ON WHAT'S POPULAR

Manga series like Inu Yasha and Fushigi Yugi are very popular with young adults of both genders. Superhero titles are also in demand. The Hopeless Savages series has also been a big hit here.

ON THE SELECTION PROCESS FOR GRAPHIC NOVELS AND MANGA

As the person responsible for purchasing all materials for teens, I began looking into manga and graphic novels after talking to our teen customers. I take suggestions from them and read professional reviews in VOYA [*Voice of Youth Advocates*] and other journals. The Graphic Novels in Libraries listserv www.topica.com/lists/GNLIB-L has been helpful in choosing new series and keeping up with what's happening in the world of GNs. Graphic novels are as much a part of the collection as traditional fiction. I've received grants to update the collection and purchase shelving. Graphic novels have labels and are searchable in the library catalog. Library staff (both public service and administrative) have been educated about graphic novels and why they have a place in our building. All of these steps promote the format as an important part of the library's holdings.

ON THE TEEN ANIMÉ CLUB

The Teen Animé Club started in the summer of 2000, after I held a book discussion session focusing on manga and graphic novels. The teens were interested in starting a monthly club. Students get together once a month to talk about their favorite animé, manga, and graphic novels. The core group of teens also recommended new titles for the library to purchase.

ON THE IMPORTANCE OF INCLUDING ILLUSTRATED
LITERATURE IN THE TEEN SECTION OF THE LIBRARY

It's important to respond to the needs of our customers, especially teens. It can be difficult to establish a relationship with this age group; if we can find out what they want and make an effort to have it available, it shows that we value their input.

Author Spotlight

Photo courtesy of Jeff Smith.

Jeff Smith

Jeff Smith gained a love of comics early in life. As a college student Jeff drew comic strips for Ohio State University's student newspaper. Then he co-founded the Character Builders animation studio in 1986. In 1991 Jeff launched *Bone,* which was an immediate cult favorite. *Bone* is now printed in 13 languages across the globe. Smith received the Eisner award for Best Writer/Artist—Humor in 1998 and the Harvey Award the same year for Best Cartoonist. He has also been honored with international awards including Italy's Yellow Kid Award for Best Author and Finland's Lempi International for Best International Cartoonist. Visit his website at www.boneville.com.

SELECTED BOOKLIST

Bone: Crown of Horns (Graphix, 2009)
Bone: Eyes of the Storm (Graphix, 2006)
Bone: Ghost Circles (Graphix, 2007)
Bone: Old Man's Cave (Graphix, 2008)
Bone: Out from Boneville (Graphix, 2005)
Bone: Rock Jaw Monster of the Eastern Border (Graphix, 2007)
Bone: The Dragonslayer (Graphix, 2006)
Bone: The Great Cow Race (Graphix, 2005)
Bone: Treasure Hunters (Graphix, 2008)
Rose with Charles Vess (Cartoon Books, 2002)

ON WHAT HE READ AS A TEENAGER

When I was a teenager I really enjoyed books like *Tarzan,* and Doc Savage, and Conan, things that were like fantasy pulp.

As far as comics went, or cartoons of any kind, what I really enjoyed was reprints of comic strips from the newspaper. I loved *Peanuts* and *Pogo.* You could get reprints of old Donald Duck, Scrooge stories that were drawn by this one artist who never signed his work—Karl [Parks], but amongst fans everybody knew him as the good duck artist. I was very big on Gary Trudeau's *Doonesbury.*

ON FAVORITE AUTHORS AND FORMATS CURRENTLY

It's surprising. I read so much fiction when I was growing up and even as an adult. And then when I was 31, I started writing this Bone story. I serialized it as a comic book and once a year collected into sort of like an ongoing chapter. But it's one big story that I am telling. It will be a 1,300-page novel when it's done. Since I started that, I have been almost unable to read fiction. I think that's interesting. I don't really know why that is. So all I read now is nonfiction. I read a lot of books on science, on history. I do a lot of reading that I use as research for my work, you know. So if I need to look up certain kinds of armor or weaponry, or what does a horse-drawn hay cart really look like, how does the harness work on the horse, and how does it connect? I mean things like that. I read that all the time. As far as like my contemporaries in graphic novels, there are quite a few. The list would be really long. Just quickly I'll say Bryan Talbot who did *The Tale of One Bad Rat, Hundred Percent* by Paul Pope, *Goodbye Chunky Rice* by Craig Thompson. I like the newer non-superhero graphic novels.

ON WHETHER HE WRITES AND ILLUSTRATES
WITH A PARTICULAR AUDIENCE IN MIND

I do not. It may sound like a cliché, but I write and draw for me. I write it so that I'm interested and that it makes me laugh and it's what I would like to read.

Having said that, I'm a 42-year-old man, but I'm writing the comic that I wanted to read when I was 9. So even though I'm the only audience I'm kind of covering an age group from 9 years old to 40.

ON WHY GRAPHIC NOVELS AND COMICS ARE POPULAR

Well, I think it's pretty obvious. I think Americans love cartoons. I think they love comics. What kid doesn't?

ON HOW COMIC AND GRAPHIC NARRATIVES DIFFER FROM PROSE NARRATIVES

I think overall I can honestly say there is no difference. I don't believe, and not everyone agrees with me on this, but I don't believe there's anything that you can't tell in comics. There's nothing you can do in a novel you can't do in a comic. And there are people who definitely disagree. They might think that comics are incapable of creating pathos or certain kinds of drama and conflict. But that's completely not true, you can. It has been done. I've seen it, I have attempted to do it myself. As far as the actual differences between writing, that's a really good question. And all I can say is that even when I was young, even when I was about 9 or 10, when I read a comic, even then I knew that some of the story information was contained in the pictures. It's not a bunch of little word dialogue balloons with illustrations just to explain what they're doing. Now some comics are just that. You know, they're just kind of simply made, they're not very artistic, they're not very well done. But good, well-made graphic novels will have a balance between the verbage and the visual communication.

ON THE LONGEVITY OF BONE

The eighth collection just shipped, as we speak, less than a month ago, and I envision the entire thing being a nine-book, nine-graphic-novel set. And it is one story from Volume 1 all the way through to the end of Volume 9. It's one giant *Le Mort d'Arthur,* which is in a lot of ways one of my main models for this story.

ON THE INSPIRATION FOR THESE STORIES

I'm writing for myself, I'm trying to create the comic I wanted to read when I was 9. And even as a youngster I was reading books like *Moby Dick* and I wanted, I really wanted a character, a comic book character like Donald Duck or Pogo to go on a big odyssey, to participate in the *Iliad*. Pretty much that's what I've done. I have attempted to take these 3 Bone cousins, which are very typical three-fingered, big foot, big nose cartoon characters and inserted them into an epic adventure. And I've modeled that on *Moby Dick,* and *Huckleberry Finn,* and *Le Morte d'Arthur,* and the *Lord of the Rings.*

ON TEACHER RESISTANCE TO USING SEQUENTIAL ART IN THE CLASSROOM

The idea that comics are just cheap crap for children is a long-engrained notion in our society. It's difficult to shake off. What I would say to them is that that's just not true. You just can't judge a book by its cover. There is just as much cheap crap in prose books and in music and in films as there is in comics. The good stuff is truly good. The good stuff rises easily to the level of any novel that has ever been written. And probably most importantly, to a librarian who wants to view this as literature, it is clear to me that looking at a graphic novel is reading. You start at the upper left, you go left to right, and then you go back down and go left to right again. Left to right, top to bottom, it is just like a book. It is reading. It has its own language which doesn't exist anywhere else but in comics, but it is familiar, it is reading.

The Bone books were originally published by Cartoon Books but gained widespread accessibility when republished by Scholastic. They are often referred to as all-ages books because they have appeal to many children, teens, and adults. Copyright Jeff Smith. Reprinted by permission.

ON ADVICE FOR ASPIRING AUTHOR/ILLUSTRATORS OF COMIC BOOKS

They just need to read a lot of them and practice writing and drawing them. Then you can see all the mistakes that are possible to make.

ON THE PROCESS OF WRITING AND ILLUSTRATING GRAPHIC NOVELS

In general terms when you think of comics, you think of *Spiderman* or *Batman* or something like that. And that's generally done by a team. One person writes it, another person pencils it, inks it, letters it, etc. And it's usually overseen by the company's editor that owns the trademark on the character. But more and more there are quite a few of us who want to be the writers and the artists, who have a story and a vision that we want to share. And it's becoming commercially possible to do that in the comic book market.

ON THE HISTORY OF GRAPHIC NOVELS

In 1986 we had *Dark Knight, Maus,* and *Watchmen,* and that really changed things because not only were they commercially successful, but they were critically acclaimed. And then you had Neil Gaiman's *Sandman* and *Bone,* two of the first actual graphic novel series. It's exciting, man. This is the new deal in comics, I think.

A Survey of Graphic Novels for Young Adults

Graphic novels are not a genre of literature but rather a literary format. Superhero comics have long been the most popular genre of comics with young adults, but there are also science fiction, fantasy, humor, realistic fiction, action/adventure, horror/supernatural, life stories, and manga (which has a following easily as devoted as that of the superheroes). Of course, many graphic novels defy these labels and do not fit comfortably into one genre. *The Barefoot Serpent* by Scott Morse, for example, is difficult to categorize. The central portion of this narrative concerns a family, especially a young girl, coming to terms with the death of her brother. The narrative in art and words is simple yet evocative. This portion of the book would likely be considered by many to be a children's story about a spiritual journey. However, the central story is framed by a biography of the famous Japanese director Kurosawa. The two narratives actually fit together beautifully but push the reader to think in terms of sophisticated allegories and cinematic parallels. Like many graphic novels this book is neither for a set age group nor confined to a particular genre. Still it can be helpful to understand the distinctions and similarities between these broad literary categories to help young adults locate books they might be interested in reading.

Superheroes

The most popular genre of sequential art has been superheroes since 1938 and the appearance of Superman. Kurt Busiak's *Astro City* (Kurt Busiak and Brent Anderson, 2000/1996) is a wonderful tribute to the golden age of superhero comics. His tales of the superheroes of Astro City are all his own, but they draw on the best elements of the early superhero comics. Superhero comics fell out of fashion for a time following World War II, but today they are again the backbone of the comic book industry, with several hundred active superheroes currently in print.

The first trade book in this genre to receive major critical attention was *Batman: The Dark Knight Returns* (Frank Miller and Klaus Janson, 1997/1987) which is now considered a milestone for graphic novels. Originally issued in comic book format, it tells the story of Batman at age 50, struggling with coming out of a 10-year retirement to save Gotham City. Similar in many ways is *Kingdom Come* (Mark Waid and Alex Ross, 1998/1996), in which Superman has been out of action for 10 years and most of the old heroes have disappeared. Superman is pulled back into action in this sophisticated story.

In another groundbreaking superhero comic from 1986, *Watchmen,* Alan Moore and Dave Gibbons (Warner Books, 1995) create a world where Richard Nixon never resigned and superheroes are outlawed. This graphic novel explores the notion of the burdens of power. The popular X-Men series has always dealt with the concepts of the outcast, bias, and prejudice. In *The Dark Phoenix Saga* (Chris Claremont and John Byrne, 1990) intricate themes of the corruption of power are explored.

J. Torres / Takeshi Miyazawa

Many superhero comics appeal to teen readers. Some like *Sidekicks: The Transfer Student* by J. Torres and Takeshi Miyazawa (Oni, 2002) are actually focused on the young adult experience. Reprinted by permission of Oni.

Many of the best known superhero comics are collected in trade paperbacks. *The Essential Spiderman* (Stan Lee and Steve Dirko, 1996) is part of a series of "Essential" volumes reprinting classic comics in black and white. Spiderman would also fit nicely into the theme of "responsibilities of power." The first villain he lets escape kills his beloved uncle. For the most part the public thinks that Spiderman is a menace, yet he goes on saving them.

Depending on the students in the classroom, a teacher might have wonderful results using a set of graphic novels to explore the topic "A Question of Power." Are there inherent responsibilities for anyone who holds incredible power? What happens when this power becomes corrupt or is misused? Is it always easy for someone with power to determine the right course of action?

Part of the appeal of Spiderman and some of the other superheroes popular among young adults is that they are young adults themselves. Some less well-known graphic novels, such as *Sidekicks: The Transfer Student* (J. Torres and Takeshi Miyazawa, 2002), which tells the story of a teenage girl who enrolls at a school for young superheroes, might be well received for the same reason.

The superhero genre first and foremost can be a pleasurable read for many young adults, but teachers and librarians might also occasionally want to take advantage of the genre's intertextual connections to add interest to other literary explorations. Jack Kirby was the co-creator of some of the biggest name superheroes, such as the Fantastic Four and Captain America, but he gained the most critical acclaim for *Jack Kirby's New Gods* (1998) a saga that originally appeared in the 1960s chronicling the war between the demi-Gods of New Genesis and their evil counterparts from Apokolips. The book is a modern attempt at a mythological world and could be compared in interesting ways to various world myths. It also might be used to explore the way mythological structures inform contemporary literature in general. Rumor has it that Star Wars borrowed extensively from the New Gods storyline. Interesting connections might be found with numerous fantasy novels that also draw heavily on mythology (see Chapter 5).

Matt Wagner's *Mage: The Hero Defined* is great fun, with contemporary characters who seem to be reincarnations of various heroes from legend and myth, including King Arthur, an Olympian hero, and a trickster god. This band of heroes fights trolls, goblins, and harpies in a struggle between good and evil. Unlike *New Gods,* which creates a whole new mythology, *Mage* recycles past myth. Exploring how these contemporary characters are similar to their past incarnations would be a great way to bring out the essential character traits of various traditional figures. The trickster character would be particularly interesting as he seems to be an amalgam of numerous tricksters, and that raises the question of what mythological characters like Anansi, Loki, and Coyote (all trickster figures) actually have in common.

Imagine a story in which the Invisible Man, Dr. Jeykl, Captain Nemo, Alan Quatermain, and Nina Murray-Herker team up to fight against the evil Fu Manchu. This is exactly what Alan Moore and Kevin O'Neil do in *League of Extraordinary Gentlemen.* Sure many young adults will only know these names from movies, but this great cast from Victorian pulp fiction creates a thrilling adventure even if the characters are new to the reader (and with the recent movie version many teens will already know the storyline). Using this graphic novel might open the door to an exploration of Victorian literature.

Other superheroes who are outside of mainstream comics, like Scott McCloud's *Zot* and Paul Chadwick's *Concrete,* appeal to some readers because while they have amazing powers, the story explores their human side. Michael Chabon introduced the world to two comic book creators in the Pulitzer-winning *Amazing Adventures of Cavalier and Clay.* He followed up with *The Escapist,* a graphic novel in which the comic strip from the novel comes to life.

Action and Adventure

One drawback to using older comics, many of which are currently being reprinted as trade paperbacks, is that stereotypes were often more explicit in years past. The comics collected in *Dragon Lady* (2000) are from the series Terry and the Pirates by Milton Caniff, originally published in the 1930s. The action-packed spy storyline and the illustrations which have been so influential on subsequent sequential art also include the offensive caricature of the Chinese manservant Connie. Herge's *Tintin,* which has remained popular since the first one was published in 1929, is another good example of a great storyline hampered by stereotypes. The young hero and his dog travel around the world battling evil and interacting with people from many lands. Looking at these books in historical context might actually be a great way to bring these stereotypes to the surface for discussion. Written literature from these time periods often holds similar caricatures, but stereotypes are harder to ignore when graphics are included. Making these images overt can shed some light on stereotypes past and present.

Parts of the action-packed Interman series can be read on the website of author Jeff Parker at www.theinterman .net. Jeff Parker's *The Interman* (Octopus Books, 2003). Reprinted by permission. Copyright Jeff Parker.

As with the superhero genre, graphic novels that might be classified as action books are wide ranging and many actually overlap with superhero, crime, fantasy, and science fiction. *The Interman* by Jeff Parker, for example, revolves around a genetically enhanced spy created during the Cold War who now freelances. When the CIA discovers him, they decide he is a threat and seek to eliminate him. *City of Light, City of Dark* (Avi) is an exciting adventure from an author many young adults will already know from his numerous novels for young readers. This adventure story takes place in an alternate universe in which two youngsters have to save New York City from a power-hungry villain.

Initial D by Shuichi Shigeno has a story that is a bit far-fetched, but the action shines through in the way downhill driving is brought to life on the page. A young man named Tak used to be the top downhill racer in his town, but he has given that up and now he runs deliveries for his father's food stand. Secretly his father is forcing him to make faster and faster deliveries down the treacherous mountain roads. Soon he has unwittingly become the fastest downhill racer in the region, and his skills are put to the test.

Hopeless Savages by Jen Van Meter is one of the hippest graphic novels of late, with real young adult appeal. When two aging punk stars are kidnapped, their teenage children must come to the rescue. This premise could easily have been contrived, but instead it is subtle and effective. As for the art, Christine Norrie does the main narrative, and Chynna Clugston-Major illustrates the flashbacks. The whole thing adds up to great fun. For the middle school student *Allison Dare: Little Miss Adventures* by J. Torres and J. Bones might be a good choice. These fun action-packed stories revolve around a young female Indiana Jones–like character with some teen problems mixed in.

Some of the most popular action titles are adaptations like *Lara Croft: Tomb Raider* (1999) and *Tarzan*. After the immense success of the film version of *Crouching Tiger Hidden Dragon*, Comics One released a graphic novel series authored by Andy Seto based on the original novels by Wang Du Lu. The comics begin before the action that takes place in the film and extend the story as well. This leads to another popular subgenre, that involving the martial arts. Comics One has initiated over seven Kung Fu series, most of which seek to capture the action of the Hong Kong martial arts cinema. *Usagi Yojimbo: Demon Mask* by Stan Sakai is another interesting martial arts–related graphic novel that crosses boundaries into the realm of fantasy. The story is strongly tied to elements of Japanese folklore and legend. The setting is based on 17th-century Japan but with anthropomorphic animal characters and folkloric encounters. Most of all, it is an action-packed adventure story.

For the uninitiated, reading sequential art, like any literary skill, can take some getting used to, but these narratives allow for an interesting combination of visual and textual storytelling. The panels, like cinema, allow multiple perspectives, forms, and angles that shape the reader's reception. *Usagi Yojimbo: Gen's Story* by Usagi Studios, 2003. Reprinted by permission of Fantagraphics.

Detective/Crime/Mystery

DC, one of the largest comic book publishers, gets its name from its earlier incarnation as Detective Comics, which started up in 1937. Crime comics had a boom after World War II. One series alone, *Crime Does Not Pay,* sold more than 4 million copies per month in the late 1940s

(Duin and Richardson, 1998). Dick Tracy is likely the longest-running detective comic. *The Dick Tracy Casebook: Favorite Adventures 1931–1990* (1990) is filled with adventures that capture some of the many faces of Dick Tracy.

When Wertham published *Seduction of the Innocent,* it was primarily crime comics he was objecting to, and quite a few of them did contain gruesome violence. There are not nearly as many crime comics today as there were in the 1950s, and they are generally less gory. *Ruse* from CrossGen is one crime comic (though it straddles several genres) that might appeal to young adult readers.

The Opera House Murders is the first volume in The Kindaichi Case Files about the genius crime solver Hajime Kindaichi, who is actually the grandson of a famous fictional Japanese detective, Kousuke Kindaichi. In this volume the members of a high school drama club are being murdered as they prepare a production of *The Phantom of the Opera.*

Several others that are really for adult readers might also find a ready YA audience. *Kissing Chaos* by Arthur Dela Cruz is sure to appeal to some young adults with mystery, adventure, and romance; it is also sure to be avoided by many teachers because of the law breaking, violence, and romance. *From Hell* is a cross between mystery and horror, with some well-researched history thrown in. This retelling of the story of Jack the Ripper casts the murderer as a metaphor for the modern age. Teens who are fans of Johnny Depp will have seen the movie and so might be drawn to the book. *Torso* by Brian Michael Bendis and Marc Andreyke is about America's first known serial killer. Many have heard of Eliot Ness, the man who triumphed over Al Capone, but it is less well known that he moved to Cleveland to take over their corrupt police force and soon found himself defeated by a still unsolved string of murders. *Torso* tells about the investigation from the perspectives of Ness and the two main detectives involved in the case. The storyline focuses as much on the interrelationships as on the murders. Actual photographs and newspaper clippings are integrated throughout.

Westerns

In post–World War II America, western comics also became quite popular. Titles such as *Blaze Carson, Tom Mix Western, Roy Rogers,* and *Gene Autry* all had lasting readerships, even after the Comic Code Authority. Perhaps the most influential western series was Jean-Michel Charlier and Jean Girard's Blueberry series about a Confederate soldier who heads west. The series ran from 1963 to 1986.

Like crime comics, most westerns have ridden off into the sunset. Still a few good possibilities for young adults have been published in recent years. *Blaze of Glory: The Last Ride of the Western Heroes* and the sequel *Apache Skies* by John Ostrander and Leonardo Manco tell the story of the summer of 1885 and the hail of gunfire that resulted when Marvel's legendary western heroes like the Outlaw Kid, Kid Colt, and Reno Jones come together.

Lost Cause: The True Story of Famed Texas Gunslinger John Wesley Hardin by Jack Jackson (1998) is another recent western that some young adults might enjoy. *Lost Cause* is a well researched docudrama that reads like a movie. The biographical narrative follows the life of Hardin as he makes the transition from outlaw to law enforcer.

Fantasy

Fantasy (and speculative fiction in general) is certainly one of the most prolific genres for sequential art. It is also a genre with frequent crossovers among age groups. Some fantasy will appeal to the whole family. Titles like *La Mouche* (1995) by French artist Lewis Trondheim and *Herobear and the Kid* by Mike Kunkel (2003) could easily be read by fourth graders, but they are witty enough and the art sophisticated enough that they can be enjoyed by young adults and adults as well.

La Mouche is a whimsical wordless comic about a fly who is on a journey of self-discovery. *Herobear and the Kid: The Inheritance* commences with Tyler's grandfather passing away. His family inherits the house, which means going to a new school. Tyler inherits a teddy bear and a broken watch. Tyler is not at all pleased with the turn of events, but things are not as simple as they seem, and he discovers that the stuffed animal can transform into Herobear. Soon Tyler and Herobear are battling school bullies and saving the world.

Jeff Smith's *Bone* series is another great graphic novel for "all ages." *Out from Boneville* is the first volume in the misadventures of the exiled Bone family. The Pogo-like characters in this series are not exactly sweet and innocent, but they are heroes when it comes down to it. *Rosemary's Backpack* by Antony Johnston and Drew Gilbert is another title that might be appreciated by older elementary students but will also cross over to younger teens. When Rosemary, a girl who typically confines herself to her room with her computer, bumps into someone on the way to school and ends up with the wrong backpack, she embarks on an amazing adventure. For those who love animal fantasy, *Mouseguard* and the graphic novel version of *Redwall* should not be missed.

Dave Roman and John Green's *Jax Epoch and the Quicken Forbidden: Borrowed Magic* (AiT/PlanetLar, 2003). Copyright John Green and Dave Roman. www.yaytime.com and www.johngreenart.com

All of these fantasy graphic novels can work very well with young adults, and fantasy is one of the genres with the most crossover, but there are also a growing number of fantasy graphic novels that have teen characters and address specific teen concerns. Several of the most exciting take a contemporary teen who somehow enters a world of magic. In *Jax Epoch and the Quicken Forbidden: Borrowed Magic* (by Dave Roman and John Green) a dissatisfied teen accidentally passes into another dimension while the magic all leaks into her world. When she returns to her world, she is blamed for causing all of the chaos. *The Books of Magic: Bindings* (Rieber, Amaro, and Gross) is another fantasy that starts in the real world and then moves the reader into the fantasy world. Sure he looks like Harry Potter, and like Harry, he is a magician who doesn't know his own potential as he enters the world of magic, but that is not all this book has going for it. This is an extremely sophisticated story where reality and myth

Jax Epoch and the Quicken Forbidden: Borrowed Magic by Dave Roman and John Green (AiT/PlanetLar, 2003). *Borrowed Magic* is the first in this speculative fiction series with a female teen heroine. Like a modern-day Alice, Jax follows the rabbit down the hole into another universe. These panels show the normalcy of Jax's life before she enters the magical world. For teens who are not already big fantasy readers, having a character from the real world enter the fantasy realm with them can be a great way to introduce them to the genre. To read *Jax Epoch* in full color visit Quicken Forbidden on the Internet at www.quickenforbidden.com. Copyright John Green and Dave Roman. www.yaytime.com and www.johngreenart.com

merge in a plot conceived by Neil Gaiman and a foreword by Jane Yolen.

Some works of fantasy take place entirely in a speculative world. In *Amy Unbounded: Belondweg Blossoming* by Rachel Hartman, the title character is coming of age in the town of Goredd. Her mother is a Barbarian, and she is friends with a dragon. In *Meridian: Flying Solo* after her father dies, teenage Sephie must defend the floating city of Meridian with powers that are just awakening. *Castle Waiting: The Curse of Brambly Hedge* by Linda Medley (1996) and the sequel, *Castle Waiting: The Lucky Road* (2000), flow directly out of folklore and are full of recognizable characters.

Some fantasy graphic novels that have been marketed primarily for an older audience might also be of interest to young adults. Neil Gaiman's Sandman series has a large readership, receiving rave reviews from critics. Gaiman draws extensively on world myth and tells compelling stories about human fragility. These are sophisticated stories. Because there are young adult readers who are very interested in the series, some libraries have placed them in the YA section, but because of the mature content many others have kept them with the adult books.

For readers who have become excited about the Lord of the Rings, *The Hobbit* by J. R. R. Tolkien (retold by Dixon, Denning, and Wenzel) is a popular title. The same audience might enjoy *Sojourn: From the Ashes* by Ron Marz, Greg Land, Drew Garaci, and Caesar Rodriguez (2002), a high-fantasy adventure with a female protagonist. The warlord Mordath has returned from death and gathered his troll army, and only Arwyn and her band can stand against him. Also of interest is *Elfquest: The Hidden Years* by Wendy and Richard Pini (1994), in which a race of elves search for their home.

At the more surreal end of the fantasy spectrum, one can find *The Adventures of Tony Millionaire's Sock Monkey* by Tony Millionaire. With talking toys and animals, this series seems like it might be for young kids, and indeed a children's version has been published, but the original has a sophisticated and often rather bizarre humor better appreciated by an older audience. Also among the bizarre is *Colonia* by Jeff Nicholson, with characters like Lucy the Talking Duck and Teela the Mermaid.

Science Fiction

Among the most popular science fiction graphic novels are adaptations from movies, including *Aliens*, *Predator*, *Star Wars*, *Star Trek*, and *Terminator*. As with fantasy, there is a lot of crossover, and it can be difficult to label these science fiction graphic novels as young adult or adult. *The Adventures of Barry Ween, Boy Genius* by Judd Winick, for example, will definitely appeal to many teen readers but includes some crude humor (somewhere between Jimmy Neutron and South Park), which might make many teachers wary of using it in the classroom.

Most science fiction graphic novels seem to fall into two categories, robots and space adventures. *Astro Boy* by Osamu Tezuka is one of these graphic novels that is appropriate and appealing even to children; he is also one of the best-known cartoon characters in the world (though not as well known in the United States). This young robot boy was originally created by a scientist to replace his lost son, but then he ends up in a circus and finally becomes a hero who protects the world. Despite being cartoony and often humorous, there are a wide range of beautifully crafted emotions, including longing and pain, which is part of what has made *Astro Boy* so popular. As with other older comics one concern would be with stereotyped characters.

Jason and the Argobots by J. Torres and Mike North is one of Oni Press's comics for all ages, about a boy who digs up a giant robot that at first seems like the perfect toy but becomes much more. Similarly, *Big Guy and Rusty the Boy Robot* by Frank Miller and Geoff Darrow involves robots who battle to save the world. A good allegorical flipside to this is *Monkey vs. Robot* by James Kochalka. *Monkey vs. Robot* is rather simple on the surface—robots fight monkeys—technology versus nature, the future versus the past—but it is so expressive and clever that it has become a big hit.

Chobits is written and illustrated by CLAMP, a group of female artists, though looking at the cover, this would be the last thing you might imagine. The big eyed cherub in the miniskirt looks like so many other manga, but there is much more going on here. This doll girl is actually a robot, a persocom. When a boy finds her in the trash, he takes her to a genius friend who fixes her operating system by linking her to an experiment called CHOBITS. Though it looks on the surface like numerous other manga for preteen girls, it is clever and at times sophisticated.

Another good science fiction story with a twist involves a beautiful android who is a painter and "normal" girl but who faces prejudice from people, who see her as a soulless semihuman. In *The Complete Geisha* by Andi Watson this android girl must work as a bodyguard in order to make money because no one will buy her art.

That's a lot of robots! Surprisingly, robots seem to outnumber any other science fiction theme, even space adventures. Yet there are still some interesting aliens for young adults. In *Soulwind: The Kid*

To Consider

In *The Complete Geisha* the android's adopted brother smokes cigarettes and his band plays music in crowded bars filled with drinking, bar fights, and eccentric characters. Scenes like this are not uncommon in YA literature (and fairly standard on TV and in movies) but the visual elements make them more likely to be challenged in schools and libraries. To what extent would the visual elements affect whether you select a book for your YA collection?

Andi Watson's *The Complete Geisha* (Oni, 2003) is not what many readers might expect from science fiction. The main character, who is an android, wants to be an artist but is up against prejudice and societal expectations. Reprinted by permission of Oni.

The cigarettes alone might keep this out of many schools but the futuristic prejudice in Andi Watson's *The Complete Geisha* provides an interesting twist. Reprinted by permission of Oni.

from Planet Earth by Scott Morse, a boy is plucked from his home and taken to a distant planet where it has been foretold that he will save the inhabitants from an evil dictator. *Wake: Fire and Ash* by Jean Morvan and Phillip Buchet (2003) is the story of the only surviving human from a spaceship that ends up on Wake. In *Negation: Bohica!* (Bedard, Pelletier, Meikis, and Rochelle) 100 "people" from across the galaxy have been gathered together as prisoners by the evil empire of Negation. A soldier named Obregon Kaine is one of these prisoners, and he attempts to lead an uprising. *A Distant Soil* by Colleen Doran is a multipart saga, an epic some have called it, about two children of an alien freedom fighter. These two siblings have powers that might allow them to overthrow the powerful Ovanan empire, but of course this makes them a prime target of imperial force.

Horror and Supernatural

The first horror comic came out in 1947, published by Eerie Comics. After World War II, when superheroes lost their appeal, horror was one of the genres that became very popular.

Ted Naifeh's *Courtney Crumrin and the Night Things* (Oni, 2003). Reprinted by permission of Oni.

Crypt of Terror, Tomb of Horror, Chamber of Chills were among plenty that were extremely imaginative and quite a few that were rather crude.

Today, several horror graphic novels are geared specifically toward young adults. In Ted Naifeh's *Courtney Crumrin and the Night Things* a young girl's family moves into her uncle's strange old mansion, and they aren't the only ones there. The book deals with the supernatural, but at the same time the focus is on school outcasts and the cruelty the young can inflict on one another. In *Leave It to Chance* (James Robinson and Paul Smith) the 14-year-old daughter of a famous paranormal investigator wants to follow in his footsteps. When he lets Chance know that he thinks the profession is too dangerous for her, she sets out on a great adventure to prove she is capable. *The Book of Jack* by D. P. Filipi and O. G. Boiscommun is another graphic novel that should not be missed. While attempting an initiation into a street gang, Jack's world is turned upside down, and he becomes a werewolf. The medieval setting is beautifully rendered.

For the teen reader, Buffy the Vampire Slayer is one of the most popular supernatural/ horror series. *Ring of Fire* (2000) is among the best GNs based on the Buffy world. The narrative for *Ring of Fire* was written by Doug Petrie, who also writes for the TV series, so it ties in nicely with what viewers already know about these characters. The art by Ryan Sook is very moody and cinematic in the use of angles, close-ups, and long shots.

Terry West and Steve Ellis offer another series, similar in many ways to Buffy, but a bit more light-hearted in the Confessions of a Teenage Vampire books. In the first one, *The Turning,* average Lily is chosen by the 400-year-old founder of her village to join the ranks of the undead!

Hellboy: Seed of Destruction, another popular but more mature horror series, is bound to face some challenges for the name alone, but it can be a very fun read. The premise is that the Nazis were engaged in a mystical experiment when they were interrupted by the Allied forces; their experiment turns out to be Hellboy, who now handles bizarre X-File–type top-secret assignments

Adaptations and Spin-Offs

Proust, Kafka, Melville, Kipling—yeah, we've got that too! A wide range of classic books, movies, and even TV shows have been adapted into graphic novel formats. Some books have been adapted with the original text intact. For example, *Rudyard Kipling's Jungle Book,* illustrated by P. Craig Russell (1997), is a beautiful rendition

To Consider

Immediately following World War II the public lost interest in superheroes and crime, and western and horror comics became popular genres. Why do you think this occurred? How does the historical context influence the reading habits of American youth?

Will Eisner's *Fagin the Jew* retells the story of *Oliver Twist*. Jacket cover from *Fagin the Jew* by Will Eisner. Used by permission of Doubleday, a division of Random House.

of the classic "wild man" story, predating Tarzan. The illustrations might indeed add to the pleasure of the reading for some young adults, but the book might also be explored in terms of how the graphic interpretation affects the reader's understanding of the story.

Many other classics have been adapted or abridged. *Moby Dick* has been retold by Lew Sayre Schwartz and illustrated by Richard Giordano. The graphic novel adaptation includes information about Melville and the whaling industry. Another retelling that might be of interest to young adults and has already proven to be popular among teachers is Will Eisner's retelling of *Oliver Twist,* which presents the story of the often vilified character *Fagin the Jew.*

Not many young adults have developed an interest in Proust or Kafka. So one would think that teachers in college prep courses would be anxious to get their hands on Proust's *Remembrance of Things Past: Combray* and *Give It Up! And Other Stories* by Franz Kafka (illustrated by Peter Kuper). Kuper's illustrations, which have the look of woodcuts, add to the sense of alienation found in Kafka's stories but also make them more approachable for many young readers.

Some adaptations from TV and movies have already been mentioned. The world of Star Wars has seen numerous graphic novel spin-offs. Some of these, such as *Star Wars: Dark Empire,* follow the movie scripts rather faithfully. Others extend the story in various ways. *Darth Maul,* for example, tells the story of this enigmatic character about whom little is known from the movies.

An interesting opportunity presents itself with the Star Wars graphic novels. The same storyline has been adapted from George Lucas's *Star Wars: A New Hope* script by artists in both the United States and in Japan, and the two versions are now available through Dark Horse. Differences arise in the two interpretations due to the individual artists as well as the stylistic traditions of comic book art in the two countries. Comparing and contrasting the two versions can highlight the ways illustration, pacing, design, and other artistic elements are influenced by the cultural milieu. When my 6-year-old son first saw Hisao Tamaki's Star Wars adaptation, his response was "Why are the Pokemon dressed up like Star Wars?" His experience with manga is very limited, which makes it even more telling that the stylistic elements are so recognizable! The scene in which Obi-Wan gives Luke his light saber and they listen to Princess Lea's message stored on R2D2 is one section that might effectively bring out the stylistic differences. Look at the facial expressions, sound effects, body postures, sequencing of panels, relationships between characters. Some things are very similar, and other elements quite distinct. Why did Tamaki change Princess Leia's trademark hair? Is Luke kneeling down at the table to get a closer look at the hologram or in deference to Obi-Wan? Would an American audience have accepted the expression on Luke's face when Obi-Wan tells him he is coming to Alderan?

Another type of adaptation that might lead to interesting comparisons is graphic novel to movie. A number of graphic novels have been made into movies in recent years, including *League of Extraordinary Gentlemen, Persepolis, Spawn, Ghost World, Hellboy,* and *The Road to Perdition,* and of course superhero movies are hot again, especially angst-ridden Marvel heroes like Spiderman and the X-Men.

To add to the joy and confusion, there are some interesting novels set in comic book worlds. One of the best recent works of this sort is *Mary Jane* by Judith O'Brien (2003). Tangentially, the novel tells the story of the young Spiderman from Jane's perspective. But the focus is more on Jane's relationship with her mother, her anorexia, love, and peer pressure.

Contemporary Themes

When looking at prose fiction, contemporary realistic novels tend to be among the most popular with young adults. However, with graphic novels this does not necessarily hold true; superheroes, science fiction, and fantasy all have larger audiences among those who read the sequential art format. Still there are some excellent works that explore contemporary life. The first graphic novel to receive a Printz honor is *American Born Chinese.* Though it mixes in storylines that seem bizarre and fantasy-like at first, one learns that this indictment of racism and internalized stereotypes is mainly taking place inside the main character's head.

The Tale of One Bad Rat by Bryan Talbot (1995) was written in Britain, but it is also well known in the United States. In this story a young woman who is being molested by her father hits the road in search of safety. A well-developed Beatrix Potter connection adds to this thoughtful read.

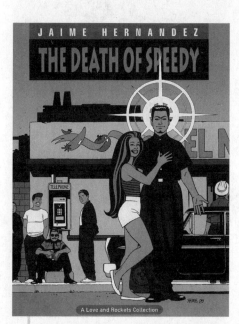

Jaime Hernandez's *The Death of Speedy* (Fantagraphics, 2001). Reprinted by permission of Fantagraphics.

Daniel Clowes's *Ghost World* centers on Enid and Rebecca, two cynical teens about to graduate from high school and trying to figure out what to do as adults. Likewise *The Death of Speedy* by Jaime Hernandez will appeal to some young adults but the subject matter will keep it out of many classrooms. This slice of life from the LA barrio is both brutal and humorous.

Chris Ware, author/illustrator of *Jimmy Corigan: The Smartest Kid on Earth,* was included in the prestigious Biennial Exhibition at the Whitney Museum of American Art in New York in 2002. His art is hot and relevant for many teens in its exploration of family relationships and absentee fathers.

Romance is a subgenre of contemporary realistic fiction that has not really caught on yet in the United States, but internationally *Mars* by Fuyumi Soryo, for example, is a best-seller. Two totally different high school students, Kira, the introvert female artist, and Rei, the popular rebel with a Ducati motorcycle, meet and fall in love in this high drama love story filled with violence and death. At the opposite end of the spectrum, Jeanne Mortinet has created a gem in *Truer Than True Romance,* in which the author takes scenes from the romance comics of an earlier generation and adds new dialogue to create a humorous storyline.

Life Stories

There are some beautifully rendered biographical and autobiographical stories in the graphic novel format. Some of these titles might be of high interest to young adults. *The Amazing "True" Story of a Teenage Single Mom* by Katherine Arnold is a semi-autobiographical story of a teen tackling single parenthood. Judd Winick's *Pedro and Me: Friendship, Loss, & What I Learned* concerns the author's friendship with Pedro Zamora, a young man dying of AIDS. Winick and Zamora were on MTV's "The Real World" together, which gives the book added YA appeal.

Ritchie Kill'd My Toads by Scott Getchell, like many of these graphic novels, is not necessarily written for a youthful audience, but it is about young boys. Teens (and adults) who fought, crushed insects, and terrorized the neighborhood as third graders will get a kick out of this book. Drawn from the author's own boyhood, this book will explain a lot to young women trying to figure out what's up with these bizarre male creatures.

Some life stories refuse easy classification. *The Complete Maus* by Art Spiegelman (1997), which has been called "arguably the most important piece of comic art ever pub-

Nate Powell's *Swallow Me Whole* (Top Shelf, 2008). Reprinted by permission of Top Shelf.

Many readers are surprised to find biography in the sequential art format. There are wonderful life stories portrayed in books such as *King* (Fantagraphics, 2008). Reprinted by permission of Fantagraphics.

lished," is somewhere between biography, historical fiction, and fantasy (Weiner, 2001). The narrative focuses on the lasting impact of his father's experiences in a concentration camp during World War II. Raymond Briggs's *Ethel and Ernest* (1998) is also written primarily about the lives of the author's parents but at the same time the narrative chronicles 50 years of change in England. In *King* Ho Che Anderson has created a complex biography of Martin Luther King Jr., which incorporates an interesting mix of media, including photographs.

Persepolis is Marjane Satrapi's memoir of growing up during Iran's Islamic Revolution (early 1980s). Satrapi grew up during Iran's most turbulent years, but although the big events serve as a backdrop, it is the everyday occurrences that are emphasized in the book. The youthful perspective is beautifully complemented by the black-and-white illustrations that resemble woodcuts.

Manga

Manga is simply a Japanese term for motionless sequential art, or comics. In the United States the term is applied to any comic book art with the style associated with most of the material coming from Japan, and because 40 percent of the literature published in Japan is manga, there is lots of it. Even young kids can generally discern this style once they have a familiarity with it. There is, of course, a wide variety of literature that falls under the umbrella term *manga*.

The Four Immigrants Manga is one fascinating historical work that reads like historical fiction but was actually written as a contemporary piece in the early 20th century. This graphic novel explores the life of four immigrants in San Francisco from 1904 to 1924. Irony and humor is mixed into the stories of these immigrants from Japan to the United States; for example, the Japanese characters speak fluently while the mainstream Americans speak in broken English. This might seem strange at first but from the immigrant perspective it makes perfect sense.

Many YA librarians shared anecdotes about manga at a YALSA preconference to the ALA convention (Atlanta, 2002). Manga, some say, is the most frequently stolen material

Notice that flipping does not just change the flow of the narrative but also the relationships among details in the image. *Star Wars: Episode IV—A New Hope* Manga Volume 1 © 1998 Lucasfilm, Ltd. All rights reserved. Used under authorization. Unauthorized duplication is a violation of applicable law.

at the library. Others assert that some teens are attempting to learn Japanese so that they can read the original material (before it gets translated). One of the most interesting anecdotes deals with the concept called "flipping." In Japan literature is read from right to left, and so the story flows from what for readers of English would be the back of the book to the front. Die-hard fans are appalled by "flipping" because it doesn't just change the flow of the narrative, it also flips the illustrations.

Osamu Tezuka, creator of *Astro Boy,* which has already been mentioned, is known in Japan as the god of manga. However, in the United States it is likely that books like Kazuki Takahashi's *Yu-Gi-Oh!* typify the image that comes to mind when most young readers think of manga. There are, of course, major connections between manga and animé. It should be pointed out that in the case of *Yu-Gi-Oh!* the manga is really aimed at readers who are a bit older than viewers of the animé might be. The protagonist, who is in the tenth grade, is a bit of a sadist when it comes to dealing with his opponents. This book also retains its Japanese right-to-left format, which takes some getting used to.

The top grossing animé movie of all time, *Spirited Away,* has been turned into a series of manga-style graphic novels in five parts called *Miyazaki's Spirited Away*. The English version has not been flipped and is a great example of the flow of manga. The use of paneling is beautifully done. Even sound effects are included in the form of *katakana* (a set of phonetically based Japanese characters).

Another interesting manga series from Japan is *Hikaru no Go* by Yumi Hotta and Takeshi Obata. Go is a traditional Japanese game, and the story involves a sixth grader who finds an old Go board inhabited by the spirit of a noble, Fujiwara-no-Sai, who was a Go champion. The boy is the only one who can see Sai, and he reluctantly agrees to help Sai play the ultimate game. Slowly the boy becomes excited about the game for his own sake and becomes a professional player. The series has started a Go craze in Japan and has won awards not only for the art and story but also for the preservation of heritage.

Iron Wok Jan! by Shinji Saijyo is not your typical manga. The 16-year-old grandson of the former "Master of Chinese Cuisine" is out to claim the title back for his family, but before he can challenge the current champion, he must first face the champion's granddaughter, Kiriko, who is interning in the same kitchen. From what I understand the information about cooking throughout is legit.

Historical Fiction

It would be difficult to identify any of the following titles of historical fiction as specifically young adults. However, they are all thought-provoking works that might be of interest to young readers.

Vittorio Giardino is a legend in Italian comics; in his *A Jew in Communist Prague: Loss of Innocence* the year is 1951 and Czechoslovakia has been under Soviet rule for 3 years. Jonas Finkel's father has been arrested, and Jonas is barred from college for antisocialist activities (they are Jewish and bourgeois). The book chronicles the slow disintegration of his life under the Stalinist regime.

Joan: Book 1 by Yoshikazu Yasuhiko commences after the death of Joan of Arc. A young girl named Emil is being raised by the same knight who trained Joan. Eventually she takes up the battle to unify France, and like Joan of Arc she has visions (or madness),

Days Like This by J. Torres and Scott Chantler (Oni, 2003). Reprinted by permission of Oni.

though she is guided by Joan herself. The cinematic illustrations are done in attractive watercolors.

Not all historical fiction is weighty. *Days Like This* by J. Torres and Scott Chantler (2003) takes a look at the pop music industry of the early 1960s but is also about women heading out on their own in an era when that was not the norm.

Nonfiction

Most people would never think to include nonfiction trade books and graphic novels in the same sentence, and yet there are some incredible works of nonfiction sequential art. One of the most widely read graphic novels of all time is *The Cartoon History of the Universe II* by Larry Gonick (1994). Although humorous, the book is filled with information. A great history of life in the United States from an African American perspective can be found in *Still I Rise: A Cartoon History of African Americans* by Roland Laird, Taneshia Laird, and Elihu Bey (1997). Among excellent graphic novels related to current events, *9-11: Artists Respond* and *9-11: Emergency Relief* are from a group of works by well-known artists who responded to the heroism, fears, and hatred that followed the events of 9-11.

Nonfiction works can be found for the whole range of YA readers from *Amelia Earhart: Free in the Skies* by Robert Burleigh and Bill Wylie (2003), which might be used with readers as young as the fifth grade, to *Introducing Kafka* for the "I've Got to Get Them into College" honors teacher. The second book could easily be justified to parents and school boards for the mature teen, but it also has some appeal for the rebellious young adult, as the art is by the same person who created Fritz the Cat of underground comix fame.

For science (with a touch of fantasy thrown in) *Clan Apis* by Jay Hosler is a wonderful narrative infused with scientific information. The story follows a honeybee named Nyuki from larva to mature worker bee in the clan community of Apis. Hosler's storytelling expertise is equal to his scientific ability. *Fallout: Robert Oppenheimer, Leo Sziland and the Political Science of the Atom Bomb* (Ottaviani) is an interesting combination of science, political science, and social commentary. *Dignifying Science* and *Two Fisted Science* by Jim Ottaviani are also strong works that merge literature and scientific exploration.

Another interesting form of nonfiction can be found in the comics journalism of Joe Kubert and Joe Sacco. Kubert offers *Fax from Sarajevo*, which is based on actual faxes received by Kubert during the war in the former Yugoslavia. They tell the story of Ervin Rustemagic and his family trapped in Sarajevo when it is under siege in a book that won the Harvey Award, the Eisner Award, and Le Prix France INFO Award for Best Nonfiction Book.

Sacco's books *Palestine* and *Safe Area Gorazde* should not be missed. *Palestine* was originally published as a nine-part comic book series. The complete edition, for which Sacco won an American Book Award in 1996, includes a foreword by Edward Said (a prominent postcolonial critic and respected authority on Middle East conflicts). The book provides a good introduction to the motivations and perspectives of the Palestinians. At the

Palestine by Joe Sacco (Fantagraphics, 1996/2002) was honored with the American Book Award in 1996. Reprinted by permission of Fantagraphics.

same time, the book is about comic journalism. Sacco is the protagonist, and the reader gets to come along as he does his research. Text boxes and dialogue bubbles allow several narratives to mingle with the visual narrative.

A final and very popular form of nonfiction consists of books about sequential art. There are literally dozens of "how to draw" books. The *How to Draw Manga* books by the Society for the Study of Manga Techniques are among the most sought-after titles in many YA collections. For the history of comics in the United States, *Comics between the Panels* (Duir and Richardson, 1998) is an excellent reference. However, for young adults investigating how sequential art actually works, the source to turn to is *Understanding Comics* by Scott McCloud, which uses the comic medium to explore the format.

Although comics and graphic novels have traditionally been placed in with adult nonfiction at public libraries, the issue of where to house these works is still much debated: by the Dewey decimal system, alphabetically by author's name with other works of that genre, or in a separate section specifically for YA sequential art and animé. It often becomes very muddled. One local library with an extensive collection has some graphic novels on a separate shelf in the YA section; yet many (especially older works) that might appeal to young adults are in adult nonfiction, some are mixed in with YA fiction, and a few can be found in with the intermediate fiction—and it should be noted that the divisions have little to do with logic but are based mainly on which librarian happened to order them.

Online Comics

Technology Links

Quite a few publishers of comics and graphic novels now offer some materials online. Some post the first installment of a title online as a promotion. Other publishers actually have a number of comics that are specifically being published online (e.g., Top Shelf Comix), and Marvel Digital Comics Unlimited offers access to thousands of comics for as little as $4.95 per month, with 250 comics available for free on the site.

Still the comics mentioned so far are basically handheld comics posted online. There are also some interesting comics being created specifically as online comics that exploit the possibilities of the technology. A great place to discover some of the most exciting comics online is through the links page of Scott McCloud, author of *Understanding Comics*. His website features a page of links to a number of the most exciting online comics—though before sending any young adults to explore, first check them out; the comics linked to are frequently updated and not necessarily appropriate for young readers. The Google of online comics is OnlineComics.net, a database of links to hundreds of works of sequential art being published online. A great example of one that appeals to young adults is Footloose, about a half-human who must learn to defend herself.

Footloose (www.footloosecomic.com/footloose/01_01.html)

Humble Comics by Gene Yang (www.humblecomics.com)

Marvel Digital Comics Unlimited (www.marvel.com/digitalcomics)

OnlineComics.net (www.onlinecomics.net/pages/comics.php)

RealmsEnd Comics (www.RealmsEnd.com)

Scott McCloud's personal website (www.scottmccloud.com)

Top Shelf Comix (http://TopShelfComix.com)

LITERARY THEORY

Postmodernist Literary Criticism

The term *postmodern* has connections with, and is sometimes used to encompass, a number of other theoretical ideas, including deconstruction and poststructuralism. Here we will look at the idea of the postmodern as applied to literature that is open to the term, specifically to authors and illustrators who consciously use postmodern concepts in their books.

The postmodern understands truth and meaning as historically constructed and seeks to expose the mechanisms by which this production is hidden and "naturalized." In books for young people this is often accomplished through parody. Numerous picture books utilize parody to poke fun at the content and structure of the text, thereby exposing the narrative to scrutiny. In order for this to work, the reader of parody must be an active participant.

Another important concept for the postmodern is *bricolage*—using bits and pieces of older artifacts to produce new works of art. When these intertextual references are noticed, they expose the elements of the text as a construction. Also important for the postmodern analysis is the concept of *metafiction*—wherein the characters are aware that they are characters. Wiesner's *The Three Pigs* has a wonderful zoom-in of a pig looking out at the reader saying, "I think . . . someone is out there." Later in the book the characters pick up the fallen letters of the traditional narrative and use them to rewrite the ending of the story. The image from Sacco's *Palestine* makes evident to the reader that the observer is not only also being observed but that the shifting focus of the narrative is always in question.

Deborah Stevenson has called Scieszka and Smith's *The Stinky Cheese Man* "the classic postmodern picture book" with "self referential irony, in both text and illustration" (1994, p. 32). One of these postmodern elements is the fracturing or disordering of the story. One could argue that this process does more than just entertain. In both *The Stinky Cheese Man* and *Squids Will Be Squids* Scieszka and Smith subvert accepted meanings by making elements that do not belong integral to the story. When the reader recognizes the altered elements, the accepted storyline and structures are also revealed as constructs, so the reader learns to challenge the construction of meaning in the narratives they read.

Playfulness with book conventions is another essential element of the postmodern. By altering elements "that kids do not even know, or do not know that they know; often the

What is achieved by the author/character's shadowy figure growing larger in each panel? People outside the window in the panels definitely notice Sacco; he is watching them but many of the people are also looking at him warily, expectantly as he looms ever larger. He is the Western observer in an unfamiliar reality, but he is not a neutral party—he is drawn in and we see the events from his subjective perspective. *Palestine* by Joe Sacco (Fantagraphics, 1996/2002). Reprinted by permission of Fantagraphics.

book teaches convention by subverting it" (Stevenson, 1994, p. 33). David Macaulay's *Black and White* is one of the most obvious examples of this postmodern playfulness. Four narrative strands, each using different stylistic techniques, are told simultaneously with each double page spread divided into four parts. The four stories seem to be just that—four separate stories, but the reader begins to see connections before long and quite a few inferences can be made about a larger story of which each strand is merely a part. Rather than any final closure the reader is left thinking about possibilities and relationships. Postmodernists sometimes envision themselves as engaged in a struggle against a hegemonic tradition whose beneficiaries produce or position literature as prima facie justification for their privileges, and New Criticism was seen as part of that—a rhetoric or code that maintained the inequities of society for the elitists.

For Further Reading

For a fuller treatment of postmodernism see General Introduction to the Postmodern, www.sla .purdue.edu/academic/engl/theory/postmodernism/modules/introduction.html

Anstey, M. "'It's Not All Black and White': Postmodern Picture Books and New Literacies." *Journal of Adolescent & Adult Literacy, 45,* 2002, 444–457.

Coles, M., and C. Hall. "Breaking the Line: New Literacies Postmodernism and the Teaching of Printed Text." *Reading Literacy and Language, 35,* 111–114.

Dresang, E. T. *Radical Change: Books for Youth in a Digital Age.* H. W. Wilson Company, 1999.

Goldstone, B. P. (2004). "The postmodern picture book: A new subgenre." *Language Arts, 81*(3), 2004, 196–204.

Gregson, I. *Postmodern Literature.* TransAtlantic, 2004.

Head, Patricia. "Robert Cormier and the Postmodernist Possibilities of Young Adult Fiction." *Children's Literature Association Quarterly, 21*(1), Spring 1996, 28–33.

"Postmodernism and the Postmodern Novel" The Electronic Labyrinth. http://jefferson.village .virginia.edu/elab/hfl0256.html

Stevenson, Deborah. "If You Read This Last Sentence, It Won't Tell You Anything: Postmodernism, Self-Referentiality, and the Stinky Cheese Man." *Children's Literature Association Quarterly, 19*(1), Spring 1994, 32–34.

Yearwood, Stephenie. "Popular Postmodernism for Young Adult Readers: *Walk Two Moons, Holes,* and *Monster.*" *ALAN Review, 29*(3), Spring/Summer 2002, 50–53.

4

From the Campfire to the Stage
Traditional and Scripted Literature for Young Adults

"Rapunzel" is a story about a girl locked in a tower by her mother. It's a story of abuse, physical and psychological. There's no way that story should be limited to little children.

—Donna Jo Napoli

Traditional Literature Text Set

Novels

Bound by Donna Jo Napoli

East by Edith Pattou

The Eye of the Warlock by P. W. Catanese

I Am Morgan LeFay by Nancy Springer

Just Ella by Margaret Haddix

The Lightning Thief by Rick Riordan

Not the End of the World by Geraldine McCaughrean

Skeleton Man by Joseph Bruchac

Straw into Gold by Gary Schmidt

Sword of the Rightful King by Jane Yolen

Collections

Can You Guess My Name? by Judy Sierra

Favorite African Folktales ed. by Nelson Mandela

Her Stories: African American Folktales, Fairy Tales, and True Tales by Virginia Hamilton

Momentos Magicos/Magic Moments by Olga Loya

Red Riding in the Hood by Patricia Marcantonio

Spirit of the Cedar People by Chief Lelooska

The Troll with No Heart in His Body and Other Tales of Trolls from Norway by Lise Luge-Lason

Dramatic Script Text Set

3 Girls and Clorox by Belinda Acosta*

The Analysis of Mineral #4 by Moses Goldberg*

Anne Frank and Me by Cherie Bennett*

Center Stage: One-Act Plays for Teenage Readers and Actors ed. by Don Gallo

Day of Tears: A Novel in Dialogue by Julius Lester

Eddie Mundo Edmundo by Lynn Alvarez*

The Effect of Gamma Rays on Man in the Moon Marigolds by Paul Zindel

Esperanza Rising by Pam Muñoz Ryan*

Goodbye Marianne by Irene Watts*

A Heart Divided by Cherie Bennett and Jeff Gottesfeld

The Lost Boys of Sudan by Lonnie Carter*

Mother Hicks by Suzan Zeder*

Nerdlandia by Gary Soto

Pied Piper of New Orleans by Jeff Church*

Playing Juliet by Coleen Jennings*

Plays for Young Audiences ed. by Max Bush

The Shape of a Girl by Joan MacLeod*

Skellig: The Play by David Almond

Snapshot Silhouette by Kia Corthron*

With Their Eyes: September 11th ed. by Annie Thoms

A Woman Called Truth by Sandra Asher*

Zap by Paul Fleischman

Ms. McKenzie's eighth graders are comparing versions of the Cinderella story. The students have recently finished reading *Just Ella* and are three chapters into Donna Jo Napoli's *Bound*. In literature circles they are charting the similarities and differences among picture book variants of Cinderella from around the world. "I really don't understand why *Yeh Shin* would be a Cinderella story," says one student. A young woman in the circle jumps in. "Well, she does fit the profile—underdog character gets magical help to find love—what I don't get is why they need a prince at all!" A third student says, "I like the way in *Raisel's Riddle* that she finds love but on her own terms. She's not so needy like other Cinderellas."

The students all began the unit with certain notions about what the Cinderella story entailed, based on the images they have encountered in books, movies, and media. They soon discover that these stories are older and more multifaceted than they had ever realized.

Indicates a script that would need to be purchased from the publisher.

After determining what it is that makes a Cinderella story identifiable despite cultural variation and stylistic differences the students in this circle begin to create a scripted version of Cinderella set in the present day. At the end of the term the eighth graders will present their plays to elementary school students.

From the Oral Tradition to the Written Word

When using the term *traditional,* literary scholars are generally referring to literature passed down orally that reflects the imagination of a culture, community, or family. This broad category denotes a wide range of literature, including folklore, myths, legends, epics, campfire stories, family histories, religious stories, and urban legends. Throughout history, and still in many parts of the world, oral literature has been the predominant form of literature young people come into contact with.

Because these narratives are part of an oral tradition and already exist in multiple forms, when a writer publishes a version of a traditional narrative, we tend to say it is "retold by" or "adapted by" rather than "written by" that person. Theoretically, in its purest form traditional literature has no identifiable author, though the distinctions are often blurry and many contemporary versions actually base their retellings on previously written versions. Today many authors and publishers are mindful of including information about the known origins of the narrative and the cultural and literary tradition being represented. Still it is important to remember that there is a wide range of retellings from the fairly authentic to loose adaptations to literary tales that utilize motifs and character types from mythology and folklore but are the creations of individual authors.

For the most part, traditional literature is told, with details of the narrative changing to fit the context. Oral literature is carried by storytellers from place to place, and each teller makes some changes (with one big exception being certain religious stories that are considered sacred and meant to be repeated verbatim). Protagonists in traditional narratives tend to be archetypes rather than well-developed characters, but they tell stories of the human experience and often convey a rich sense of culture and context. Interestingly, folktales, legends, and myths from around the world share many of the same basic literary elements known as motifs and these motifs are constantly being echoed in written literatures as well.

Many people assume that traditional narratives are generally meant for young children and indeed they are often retold in picture book format. Yet oral literature was generally told by a storyteller who molded the telling to meet the needs of the audience at hand, and these tales were by no means meant solely for children. In fact historically, folklore has never really been considered a "children's genre" (Zipes, 1997, p. 3). Likewise, contemporary storytellers do not always envision children as their only audience. Donna Jo Napoli for example asserts,

> Traditional fairy tales come from oral literature—people sitting around telling stories in the evening by the fire. Adults and children together. They appeal to all ages. (Napoli interview, p. 163)

In Donna Jo Napoli's *Bound* (2004), a Cinderella figure has been placed in the 17th-century Ming dynasty. Napoli combines Chinese versions of the tale with Western versions and with historical fiction to create an exciting storyline. Reprinted by permission of Simon and Schuster.

Indeed when exploring the older written versions of these stories, it becomes obvious that many have elements more appropriate for a mature audience.

> "Rapunzel" is a story about a girl locked in a tower by her mother. It's a story of abuse, physical and psychological. There's no way that story should be limited to little children. "Beauty and the Beast" is a story about a man trapped in a beast's body—with all the soul-rending compromises that accompany that physical torture. Again, why should such drama be limited to little children? (Napoli interview, p. 163)

Many of the best-known tales focus on coming of age and romance. This is especially true of those stories often referred to as *fairy tales* and specifically *rise tales,* like "Cinderella," in which a character is magically elevated from poor to wealthy/aristocratic in the course of the story (generally through marriage). In these tales there is traditionally a "focus on the crucial period of adolescence, dramatizing archetypal female dilemmas and socially acceptable resolutions" (Rowe, 1989, p. 212).

Mature elements often find their way into picture book retellings as well. One need only look at Sarah Moon's *Little Red Riding Hood,* where the rape metaphor is apparent for most teen readers, to see how folktales can have meanings for older readers that might not be readily apparent to children. In Paul Zelinsky's *Rapunzel* the teenager in the tower becomes pregnant with twins after being visited by the prince. Most young readers will barely even register that fact but for a teen reader this might totally alter their understanding of the text: Was the witch really that evil or might she just have been overprotective? The symbolism in these books is often sophisticated. Angela Barrett's illustrations for *Snow White* commence on the endpapers with a symbolic drop of blood on the pure white snow. What is this going to signify to a 7-year-old? Not that any of these elements precludes the use of these stories with younger children, but they certainly hint at the possibility that these stories might have some potential with older audiences as well.

Still the question arises, why bother using traditional literature with young adults? A number of reasons are typically given. The pleasure that can be gained is foremost. These stories, legends, and myths would not have survived if they did not entertain certain audiences. They have kindled the imaginations of listeners for centuries. Bruno Bettelheim in *The Uses of Enchantment* (1976) suggests that tales help listeners/readers feel less alone in the world because others have felt extreme emotions just like they have. These tales are symbolic of human fears, needs, and desires.

To Consider

Why do you suppose folktales with mature themes are often retold as picture books and marketed for young children?

When Soviet officials forbade the use of folklore in the classroom, Russian poet Kornei Chukovsky pointed out that children who are deprived of these stories will make up their own to meet their emotional needs (Blatt, 1993, p. 3). And this is not just true of children; any authentic retelling expresses the dreams of at least a segment of a culture. In some instances, similar tales have arisen in diverse places because they express common needs or desires. In other instances, tellers have refined these tales to reflect diverse human experiences. Either way these stories contain the rich heritage of story—the narrative structures, motifs, and stylistic elements that inform the literature being written today. In a very significant way traditional literature serves as the foundation, or building blocks, for contemporary literature. Traditional narratives

- Provide entertainment
- Contain the rich heritage of story
- Tell stories of the human experience
- Kindle the imagination
- Offer a window on diverse cultures
- Serve as the building blocks for contemporary literature/framework for literature

Author Spotlight

Reprinted by permission of Penguin Putnam.

Joseph Bruchac

Joseph Bruchac was born in 1942 in the Adirondack foothills of New York. He received a B.A. from Cornell University, an M.A. in Literature and Creative Writing from Syracuse, and a Ph.D. in Comparative Literature from the Union Institute of Ohio. Today he lives with his wife Carol in the same house where his maternal grandparents raised him. Bruchac has written over 60 works for young people and is one of the best-known contemporary Native American storytellers. Abenaki is the part of his cultural heritage (which also includes Slovak and English) that he draws on most frequently in his writing. In addition to writing and storytelling, he and other family members perform traditional and contemporary Abenaki music with the Dawnland Singers. With his wife, Carol, he is the founder and co-director of the Greenfield Review Literary Center and The Greenfield Review Press. His numerous honors include a Rockefeller Humanities fellowship and the Lifetime Achievement Award from the Native Writers Circle of the Americas (1999). Visit his website at www.josephbruchac.com.

SELECTED BIBLIOGRAPHY

Bearwalker (HarperCollins, 2007)

Bowman's Store (autobiography) (Sagebrush, 2001)
Code Talker (Dial, 2005)
Hidden Roots (Scholastic, 2009)
Pocohontas (Silver Whistle, 2003)
Sacajawea (Silver Whistle, 2000)
Skeleton Man (HarperCollins, 2001)
The Warriors (Darby Creek, 2003)
The Winter People (Dial, 2002)

Folklore

Heroes and Heroines, Monsters and Magic (Ten Speed, 1985)
Native American Animal Stories (Fulcrum, 1992)
Native American Stories (Fulcrum, 1997)
Native Plant Stories (Fulcrum, 1995)

Audio

Iroquois Stories (Good Mind, 1997)

ON RETELLINGS OF TRADITIONAL LITERATURE

Well, first of all, there are some stories that I simply will *not* put down into writing—stories that are restricted in one way or another. I always do my best to both acknowledge sources and gain proper permission before writing down such stories. For example, in *The Winter People*, I obtained permission from the descendants of one of my characters based on a real person to include my translation of a song she sang in Abenaki during Rogers' Raid.

As regards the difficulty of "translating" from oral to written form, I have to say that I "talk" my stories onto the page and then read them aloud again to see if they still have the sound of a told tale.

ON BEING FAITHFUL TO "ORIGINAL" VERSIONS OF THE TALE

I may use my own words and add descriptive language, but I stay true to the heart and bones of the story. This, by the way, is a traditional approach for most classes of stories in Native oral traditions—aside from certain "formula stories," which like Dine (Navajo) healing "Ways" must be learned exactly and repeated accurately.

ON CREATING AN AUTHENTIC HISTORICAL NARRATIVE

Historical accuracy is deeply important to me. I just finished a novel about Pocahontas and John Smith in which I alternated first-person chapters between the two characters. Part of my work involved immersing myself in both the Powhatan language (and other related Algonquin tongues) and in the post-Elizabethan language of John Smith and his peers. Language appropriate to your character, accurately used can take you much further toward understanding people and events of the past. Storytelling does it, too. I have always thought of stories as being like time machines, transporting you out of this reality. Story is also, for me, one of the best ways of telling history. (I was deeply impressed early on by the novels of Robert Graves, such as *I, Claudius*.) I try to just include enough historical detail as is needed to both bring the reader into the setting and strengthen the tale.

The research I conduct is always of two kinds—on the ground, actually being physically in the places where the story happened, and in the words that have been written previously about the event. For *Sacajawea*, I both visited most of the sites (over a period of years) and also read the entirety of all the surviving journals from the expedition (thousands of pages). I also familiarized myself with the oral literature of the Native peoples encountered in the book. Indians are still telling stories that were told in the early 19th century and also telling some stories about the Lewis and Clark expedition itself!

ON WHETHER AN AUTHOR CAN WRITE CONVINCINGLY ABOUT A DIFFERENT CULTURAL EXPERIENCE

It depends on two things. The first is how you define "insider." Just because you are born into a certain culture does not make you an absolute expert. The second is how deeply someone is writing about a particular character. Deep knowledge requires years of study and experience.

Having said these things, I also have to add that I am very dissatisfied with the majority of YA books "about" Native Americans that have been written by non-Natives. I think a lot of Indian people today are not happy with the way they and their cultures have been (and continue to be) treated by non-Native writers. The stereotypes and attendant blindness about the truth of Indian realities are so engrained that few non-Indians are able to avoid making the sorts of mistakes that make Indians groan.

Traditional Narrative Forms and the Young Adult Reader

Folklore

Numerous folktales have been retold in multiple written versions, some paying strict attention to particular oral traditions, others creating looser or even new alternate retellings. Contemporary authors generally make a conscious attempt to maintain the traditional narrative framework. Donna Jo Napoli asserts:

> I try to be faithful to the framework handed to me by tradition. I am reverential of tradition. Those stories have stood the test of time—they grab hearts. There's no way I'm going to deviate from them and risk losing their truth, their power. (Napoli interview, p. 163)

In *Red Riding in the Hood* (2005) 11 tales are retold with a Latino twist. In *Spindle's End* (2001) Robin McKinley reimagines and extends the story of Sleeping Beauty, a young woman destined to die on her 21st birthday. Illustration by Renato Alarcão from *Red Riding in the Hood* by Patricia Santos Marcantonio. Illustration © 2005 Renato Alarcão. Used by permission of Farrar, Straus and Giroux, LLC. Cover of *Spindle's End* reprinted by permission of Penguin Group (USA).

At the same time authors also tend to make some changes in their retellings to suit the audience at hand, to add new connotations, or simply to tell a good story. Paul Zelinzky asserts that there is really no way for an author to stick strictly to a traditional retelling, as any decent storyteller will make the story his or her own.

Some critics suggest that authors often go to the other extreme and actually write stories that only vaguely resemble the traditional story. This can become problematic when publishers market these tales as authentic. Retellings of this sort have been referred to as "fakelore" (Dorson, 1976; Singer, 2004), a concept that brings into question whether authors/publishers are striving to be true to cultural versions of a tale or are simply using the label of authenticity to sell more books. The key contention here is not whether the picture books in question are well written or enjoyable, nor even whether authors should have the right to create new retellings of a folktale; rather, the focus is on whether authors and publishers are doing a disservice to readers when they misrepresent a folktale as belonging to a certain cultural tradition and then change it so much that it loses any cultural value it might have had. The question of authenticity gains in significance when the story is likely to be used as part of a cultural study. When a teacher integrates a folktale into the social

> *To Consider*
>
> Why might it be important for young adults to learn to question labels of authenticity? If young adults do not know a culture intimately, how can they critically consider a tale's authenticity?

studies curriculum, in a Native American unit for example, we might naturally assume that either the tale in question is authentic or that it will be examined through a critical lens. Unfortunately, this is not always the case.

There are many subgenres or classifications of folklore. In practice not all tales fit neatly into one category, yet these classifications still serve the function of helping distinguish the types of characters and motifs that are frequently encountered.

The *cumulative tale* makes extensive use of one of the common tools of storytelling—patterned repetition. The cumulative repetition used in a story like Lulu Delacre's *The Bossy Gallito* makes it a wonderful tale to use with young listeners, as well as with older language learners. The fact that this book is bilingual, in English/Spanish, adds to its potential benefits with English language learners or Spanish learners. Still, by and large, cumulative tales are primarily for young children. An occasional fractured cumulative tale, like *The House That Crack Built* (Taylor), uses the cumulative pattern effectively for a young adult audience.

Stories in which at least one of the main characters is an animal with some human characteristics are known as *beast tales*. These creatures might inhabit an animal world where no humans exist, and as in "The Three Billy Goats Gruff," effectively take the place of humans. Or they might be a unique animal like "Puss in Boots" who enters a world otherwise inhabited by humans. Many *trickster tales* also have an animal protagonist: Coyote, Raven, Anansi, Reynard, and Brer Rabbit are well-known examples. Trickster tales generally involve a relatively small, "weak" character like Brer Rabbit or Anansi the Spider, who defeats a more powerful enemy by using wits and cunning. Some of these tricksters, such as High John the Conqueror or Jack (from the Appalachian Jack tales) are human. Virginia Hamilton provides a wonderful collection of these trickster tales from around the world in *A Ring of Tricksters*.

Every culture has created tales that explore why the natural world is the way it is. These stories, referred to as *pourquoi tales,* are attempts to explain elements of the natural world. Most picture book examples like *How Turtle's Back Was Cracked* (Gayle Ross) and *How the Chipmunk Got His Stripes* (Joseph and James Bruchac) are primarily for a younger audience. Pourquoi tales are often told tongue in cheek, but some of these stories are sophisticated and tied to the mythology of the culture from which they arose. Occasionally a pourquoi tale, such as Subcomandante Marcos's *The Story of Colors/ La Historia de los Colores,* is particularly suitable for young adults.

The term *fairy tale* is often used interchangeably with *folktale.* However, this term more specifically denotes stories that deal with the fantastic, with magic, and generally with love. These stories are commonly referred to by folklorists as *wonder tales.* "Cinderella," "Sleeping Beauty," and "Snow White" are popular examples of tales of wonder or fairy tales. These stories are sometimes called *marchen* from the German term popularized by the Grimm brothers. *Marchen* also tend to involve enchantments, transformations, and magical figures. Interestingly wonder tales have often become or even started as literary tales. In fact the term *fairy tale* can be confusing because it is also used to refer to written literature that has many of the same characteristics as traditional tales of wonder. A critic named Ruth Bottingheimer caused an uproar among folklorists in 2009 when she asserted that the rise tales of European tradition were all actually literary tales as opposed to oral tales from the "folk." Her research convinced her that these stories simply did not exist before and authors created them.

There are also some folktales that have fairly realistic (at least in relative terms) characters and contexts. *Realistic tales,* such as *The Lost Horse* by Ed Young, have characters who are sketchy and undeveloped like those in most folklore, but there is nothing magical or fantastic about them.

Many books are recognizable as spin-offs on the basic structure of a traditional story. These mixed-up versions with alternate perspectives, contemporary contexts, or simply unexpected twists are referred to as *fractured folktales*. Scieszka's *The True Story of the Three Little Pigs* is among the best known of this story type. Fractured tales work best as parody when the story is recognizable, so even authors who write this type of retelling pay attention to detail. Jane Yolen, for example, asserts,

> I try to stay close to the intent of the story, but sometimes I fracture even that. But I always give the background of the original—its name, address, and serial number as it were—so that the reader can go back and find it and compare it with what I have done. (Yolen interview, p. 156)

So even in a fractured tale such as *Sleeping Ugly,* Yolen knows the folktale intimately before reworking it. If the fractured tale is recognizable as a spin-off of traditional versions, then it will be understood within the context of the preexisting storyline.

Some Common Classifications of Folktales

- Cumulative tales
- Beast tales
- Trickster tales
- Pourquoi tales
- Wonder (fairy) tales
- Fractured folktales

Literary Tales

Some contemporary stories might easily be mistaken as folklore because they are written in the style of traditional tales. Julius Lester's *Shining* reads like a folktale but is entirely the creation of its author. Classic literary tales, like those written by Hans Christian Andersen, are often confused with folktales. Andersen's *The Ugly Duckling* and *The Little Mermaid* were created in the folk tradition but have a known author and were not part of the repertoire of storytellers before he published them. As with folktales, new adapted versions of Andersen's stories continue to be published because they have now become a part of that pool of literature that numerous storytellers draw on. Jerry Pinkney, for example, has created beautiful new illustrated versions of *The Little Match Girl*, *The Ugly Duckling,* and *The Nightingale*. Lisbeth Zwerger has created stunning illustrations for a recent edition of *The Little Mermaid*, and John Alfred Rowe provides a zany version of *The Emperor's New Clothes*. Occasionally, these literary tales are retold with new contexts and sometimes fractured in the same ways as folktales. Alain Vaes for example offers an interesting adaptation of *The Princess and the Pea* in which the princess is also an auto mechanic and very much an independent woman.

This returns us to possible distinctions between literary tales and folktales. A look at the history of some fairy tales reveals that the distinction is not as clear-cut as we might imagine. Fairy tales were actually quite popular with adult audiences in French literary salons. "Beauty and the Beast" is a good example of a written story that has worked its way into the folk tradition. Madame de Beaumont (1756) wrote this literary fairy tale for the salon and its adult audience, but over time the tale was recast into the story we recognize today (Griswold, 2004). The Comtesse d'Aulnoy authored an entire collection of tales, *Contes des Fées* (1697–1698) which retold traditional stories but with the distinct style of an individual author. Other literary tales were written by Giovanni Francesco, Giambattista Basile, and Charles Perrault, all of whom were inspired by folklore.

But if we think of the Grimm brothers' tales as being somehow purer than the literary tales of the salons, we should take another look. Zipes (1997) has eloquently discussed how Wilhelm Grimm recreated tales, making major changes in the tone, in character traits, and in the turn of events to add what he deemed to be German morals to the stories he collected. It is also interesting to note that some of these tales were collected from aristocratic families of French Huguenot descent. These collections of stories came out in a series of revised editions, so scholars have looked closely at the changes made over time as they were transformed into "German" tales. It would be difficult to argue that these are "pure" traditional stories.

Theoretically, the folktale is oral, communal, and malleable in the retelling whereas the literary tale has an identifiable author and a fixed form. These distinctions work well as a guide, but in terms of practice it can sometimes be difficult to distinguish between traditional tales (*Volksmarchen*) and literary tales (*Kunstmarchen*).

When considering picture book versions of folktales, a number of elements might indicate the potential of these books with young adults. Because of their length, folktales, in general, are an excellent means of presenting a theme or for exploring intertextual connections. Teen characters, sophisticated narrative and imagery, and mature themes are all indicators that certain picture book retellings might be appropriate for young adults. *The Faithful Friend* by Robert San Souci has young adult characters who are dealing with love and jealousy. In *Sleeping Boy* (Craddock) the character avoids militarism, war, and the partitioning of Berlin as he sleeps. Both of these picture book retellings might be used with younger children, but they are at least as appropriate for young adult readers.

Fables

The fable is another genre of traditional literature that often appears in a picture book format. Fables tend to be short narratives that provide an explicit moral. Historically fables have not been intended solely for the young, but most picture book adaptations are aimed at young children. The following are a few fables that might be used effectively with young adults.

- *Aesop's Fables* illus. by Jerry Pinkney
- *Aesop's Fables: A Classic Illustrated Edition* compiled by R. Ash
- *The Boy Who Cried Wolf* by B. G. Hennessey
- *Squids Will Be Squids* by Jon Scieszka and illus. by Lane Smith
- *The Wolf Who Cried Boy* by Bob Hartman

Novelized Folktales

For young adults the novelized folktale is one of the most popular forms of literature related to the traditional. These novels are extended versions of folktales with added detail, embellished storylines, and fleshed-out characters. The novelized folktale is really more than a retelling; it takes a 5-minute story and transforms it into a narrative several hundred pages in length. Many of these books are in fact categorized as fantasy novels in libraries and bookstores. Novelized folktales are such a popular concept that the types of stories being told might be broken down into several broad categories: retellings, retellings from alternative perspectives, extensions, and connected stories. The following list shows some examples of these types of books:

- Retellings—*Rose Daughter* (McKinley), *East* (Pattou), *Ella Enchanted* (Levine), *Bound* (Napoli)
- Retellings from alternate perspectives—*Zel* (Napoli), *I Was a Rat* (Pullman), *The Rumpelstiltskin Problem* (Velde)
- Extensions—*Just Ella* (Haddix), *Straw into Gold* (Schmidt), *The Thief and the Beanstalk* (Catonese)
- Connected stories—*Skeleton Man* (Bruchac), *Chinese Cinderella* (Mah), *The Amah* (Yep)

One of the first novelized retellings of this type was Robin McKinley's *Beauty* (1978), an extended version of "Beauty and the Beast." Two decades later McKinley revisited the tale in a longer, more introspective retelling entitled *Rose Daughter*. The fact that one author could create two critically praised novel-length versions of the same tale is indicative of the fact that the story still resonates with contemporary readers. *East* by Edith Pattou, which retells the related Norse story "East of the Moon, West of the Sun," was a Printz honor book in 2004. Each of these retellings embellishes and extends the story. Likewise, "Cinderella" is often retold. *Ella Enchanted* by Gail Carson Levine (a crossover from children's literature) is one of the most popular retellings, though many young adults who enjoyed the novel were disappointed by the movie adaptation because it was aimed at a much younger audience. Some retellings like *Bound* by Donna Jo Napoli might be less recognizable as Cinderella stories for an American audience, though there are enough similarities that astute readers with the necessary background knowledge will quickly note connections.

Among the most interesting retellings are those that recount events from a new perspective, looking at events through a different lens. Often it is the villian's perspective we hear in these retold folktales. For instance, *Zel* by Donna Jo Napoli (1996) tells the story of Rapunzel from several perspectives, including the witch's point of view as she keeps the beautiful girl locked in the tower. Other times, we discover more about a character who had only a minor role in the popular versions. *I Was a Rat* by Phillip Pullman tells the story of one of the rats from "Cinderella" who somehow remains a human after the stroke of midnight. Vivian Vande Velde also works with perspective

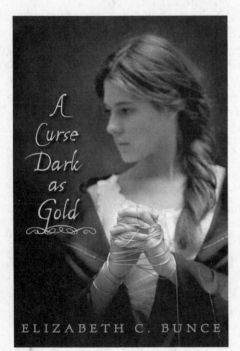

Novelized extensions of folktales elaborate on the storylines. Telling an extended narrative with all the twists and elaborations that involves, as happens in Elizabeth Bunce's retelling of "Rumpelstiltskin," can really shed light on the story. *A Curse as Dark as Gold* (2008) reprinted by permission of Arthur Levine.

in a collection of short stories called *The Rumpelstiltskin Problem*, in which each story tells the events from a different point of view and within differing contexts so that rather than finishing the story with a set conception of events, the reader comes away with an array of possibilities.

Another interesting concept in novelized folktales involves extending the tale beyond the traditional ending. *Just Ella* takes up where Cinderella ends, only the prince in this case turns out not to be all that charming. Gary Schmidt in *Straw into Gold* explores what might have happened if the queen had failed to guess Rumpelstiltskin's name and her baby was taken from her. This narrative takes place 12 years later, when we meet two orphan boys on a quest, one of whom just might be the queen's baby. In *The Thief and the Beanstalk* by P. W. Cantonese, a young thief is forced to raid a mansion, where Jack (now an old man) gives him magic beans. A new adventure begins that allows the character to revisit the past tale and chart his own future.

Still other novels recast the frame of the story in a contemporary context. *Skeleton Man by* Joseph Bruchac situates a Native American folktale within a modern story. The Mohawk tale serves as both an intertext and a framing narrative for a spooky contemporary tale. *Chinese Cinderella* by Adeline Yen Mah explores the similarities between Mah's own life and the motifs of the Cinderella story. In Laurence Yep's *The Amah* the protagonist is not only given the role of stepsister in a dramatization of Cinderella, she also actually starts to feel like an ugly stepsister when her mother becomes an Amah (nanny) for a girl her own age. In each of these instances the reader revisits the traditional story while at the same time using the folktale as a lens for examining other events or situations.

Collections

There are numerous collections of folklore appropriate for young adults. Many are thematically based and cover an amazingly wide range of topics. Collections that have become popular generally owe their success to the themes and emotions they explore.

Jane Yolen's *Not One Damsel in Distress* offers stories from around the world of strong young women, as do Katrin Tchana's *The Serpent Slayer* and Kathleen Ragan's *Fearless Girls, Wise Women, and Beloved Sisters.* Other collections of stories from around the world focus on themes as diverse as giants in Paul Robert Walker's *Giants,* bird tales in Howard Norman's *Between Heaven and Earth,* and magic in Patricia Wrede's *Book of Enchantments.*

Judy Sierra in *Can You Guess My Name? Traditional Tales around the World* argues that classic folktales address universal concerns, such as "Can I survive on my own?" and "Will I marry the right person?" In this collection Sierra provides three quite diverse variations on "The Three Pigs," "The Bremen Town Musicians," "Rumpelstiltskin," "The Frog Prince," and "Hansel and Gretel" from a total of 13 countries.

Many of the retold stories in collections for young adults have twists in their plots, shedding new light or adding a new perspective to the retelling. Among the most interesting retellings are those in direct response to problematic aspects of the traditional tales. Jack Zipes for example in *Don't Bet on the Prince* offers a collection of contemporary feminist fairy tales for young adults and older readers. Other interesting collections include Francesca Lia Block's *Rose and Beast,* James Finn Garner's *Politically Correct Bedtime Stories,* Priscilla Galloway's *Truly Grim Tales,* Vivian Vande Velde's *Tales from the Brothers Grimm and the Sisters Weird,* Patricia Marcantonio's *Red Riding in the Hood,* and Ellen Datlow and Terri Windling's *Wolf at the Door and Other Retold Fairy Tales.* As with other works of folklore many of these collections have appeal for a variety of age ranges, but these particular collections are most appropriate for readers with a certain level of maturity.

Some collections focus on tales from a particular culture or region. Virginia Hamilton, for example, has several collections of folktales, including *Many Thousand Gone, The People Could Fly,* and *Her Stories,* all of which are connected by the broad cultural spectrum of the African diasporic tradition. Some works, like Lulu Delacre's *Golden Tales,* draw from a large region (Latin America). Others are more specific in terms of the cultural tradition represented. Bruchac and Jacob's *The Boy Who Lived with the Bears and Other Iroquois Stories* only includes stories from the Iroquois tradition. Still others such as Lise Luge-Lason's *The Troll with No Heart in His Body and Other Tales of Trolls from Norway* hone in on a particular type of tale from a specific culture.

Collections that focus on tales from a particular region tend to have a strong focus on rich cultural detail, partly found in the language and the storytelling rhetoric from the cultural tradition. For example, an authenticity of voice comes through in the English translations of Olge Loya's *Momentos Magicos/Magic Moments.* Furthermore, the 15 tales from Latin America are also told in the original Spanish. To actually capture the language and rhetoric of the spoken tale it would, of course, make the most sense to include an oral version of the story. This is exactly what Chief Lelooska does in *Spirit of the Cedar People.* A CD is included that allows readers/listeners to actually hear the stories told by the author, who is a native storyteller.

Other elements might also add to the accessibility and cultural value of the stories. In *Favorite African Folktales* Nelson Mandela writes that folklore might help readers "enlarge their earthly dwelling place with the magic of stories" (2002, p. 15). The 32 stories in this collection are told and illustrated by people from various African countries. Although they are rich in cultural detail, the stories are accessible to a wide audience, partly because the stories are well chosen to have wide appeal and partly because of formatting that includes a synopsis of each story as well as a glossary.

Legends

Legends have shaped the way we think about heroism, adventure, and romance. Many legends are at least ostensibly based on a person who actually lived, though the stories of their courage and deeds have been elaborated and extended in various ways. Legends arise around people as diverse as Johnny Appleseed (*The Sun, the Rain, and the Appleseed* by Lynda Durrant) and *El Cid* (retold by Geraldine McCaughrean). As legends move from oral to written and then back again, or to drama and movies, the details and values change but enough traces remain that one often recognizes a modern Robin Hood even if he is different in drastic ways from his predecessors. One of the most interesting retellings of legend is Napoli's *Breath* that tells the story of the Pied Piper of Hamelin in a way that makes it more like historical fiction than legend. The superstitions and the pestilence of medieval "Hameln" are masterfully rendered.

King Arthur

Among the most popular legends in the Western world are the Arthurian stories. There are an extraordinary number of contemporary novels connected to King Arthur and the Knights of the Round Table. Jane Yolen suggests that Arthurian legends are still popular because they "have *everything* in them to make a great story: compelling characters, love, honor, courage, truth, loyalty, and betrayal" (see Yolen interview, p. 156). Numerous authors and illustrators have found this to be true and a handful of new novels related to King Arthur are published each year. Some examples include

- Retellings—*Sword of the Rightful King* (Yolen)
- Alternate perspectives—*I am Morgan le Fay* (villain) (Springer), *Parsifal's Page* (added characters) (Morris)
- Extensions—*The Lost Years of Merlin* (Barron)
- Connected stories—*The Seeing Stone* (Crossley-Holland)

A historical survey of Authurian legends for YA readers would be extensive. Stories such as Katherine Paterson's *Parzival: A Quest of the Grail Knight* retell and extend stories already well known and well explored. Jane Yolen in *Sword of the Rightful King* puts a new spin on the King Arthur tale. Arthur has already been crowned, but treachery is everywhere. Merlinus devises a plan wherein he magically sticks a sword into a rock and then lets it be known that whoever draws forth the sword out will be the rightful king. The plan is that after so many others try unsuccessfully, Arthur will step forward and pull out the sword and everyone will proclaim him king. However, things unfortunately rarely go as planned.

In *I Am Mordred, a Tale of Camelot* by Nancy Springer (2002), the son of King Arthur is destined to kill his own father, a destiny he struggles to change. Reprinted by permission of Penguin Group (USA).

Just as with folklore, some retellings of legend tell the story from different perspectives. In Nancy Springer's *I Am Morgan le Fay,* Morgan is thrown into a world of chaos when her father is murdered and her mother taken away by Uther Pendragon. She must be strong and learn to harness the magic inside her; when she does, she will change the fate of Britain. The storyline is similar to many versions of King Arthur that readers might be familiar with, but the perspective and connotations are quite different.

Some of these new tellings focus on a character who was absent from or voiceless in the traditional stories. Through the eyes of a page, a squire, or a damsel we are presented with a new story connected to the Knights of the Round Table. In Gerald Morris's *The Savage Damsel and the Dwarf,* the protagonist Lynett travels to King Arthur's court to find a knight who might rescue her older sister. As companions she has a dwarf and a kitchen knave.

In Elizabeth E. Wein's trilogy, which commences with *The Winter Prince,* the story of Arthur is extended to his offspring. Medraut is the eldest son of Artosking of Britain and should have been heir to the throne, but when his younger brother Lleu is chosen, the embittered young man joins Morgause and plots to take the kingdom. Some other Arthurian spin-offs expand the story into the past, serving as prequels to the story with characters and situations in the tradition of the legends but of the author's own invention. T. A. Barron and Jane Yolen each have a series of books focusing on the young years of Merlin.

Finally, a few books, such as *The Seeing Stone* by Kevin Crossley-Holland, use the King Arthur legend as a major intertext while telling a connected story. *The Seeing Stone,* which is the first in a trilogy, tells the story of a young man named Arthur in the 13th century. The boy has a seeing stone that allows him to connect with the adventures of the first King Arthur. In this compelling story the character is able to contemplate his own life as reflected in King Arthur's story without the trick of the seeing stone ever becoming overbearing.

Some Popular Versions of the Legend of King Arthur
- *Arthur: High King of Britain* by Michael Mapargo, illus. by Micheal Foreman
- *I Am Morgan le Fay* by Nancy Springer
- *King Arthur and the Legend of Camelot* by Molly Perham
- *The Once and Future King* by T. H. White
- *Parzival: A Quest of the Grail Knight* by Katherine Paterson
- *The Savage Damsel and the Dwarf* by Gerald Morris
- *The Seeing Stone* by Kevin Crossley-Holland
- *Sword of The Rightful King* by Jane Yolen
- *The Winter Prince* by Elizabeth E. Wein
- *The World of King Arthur and His Court: People, Places, Legend and Lore* by Kevin Crossley-Holland (nonfiction)

Author Spotlight

Photo courtesy of Jane Yolen.

Jane Yolen

Jane Yolen was born in New York City. She earned her B.A. from Smith College and an M.Ed. from the University of Massachusetts. She currently resides in Hartfield, Massachusetts. As the author of more than 200 books, she is one of the most prolific writers in the United States, having written for young adults, children, and adults in diverse formats and genres. One would be hard pressed to say whether she is best known for her novels, her poetry, her retellings of traditional literature, or her picture books. Among many distinctions, she has received the Regina Medal (1992) and the Kerlan Award. Illustrator John Schoenherr was awarded the Caldecott for his illustrations of her story *Owl Moon.* All of her children have been involved in at least one of her books. Her son Adam Stemple created musical arrangements for *Sing Noel.* Jason Stemple is the photographer for several of her poetry anthologies, and Heidi Stemple is the co-author of *Dear Mother, Dear Daughter: Poems for Young People.*

SELECTED BOOKLIST
Armageddon Summer (with Bruce Coville) (Harcourt Brace, 1998)

Dear Mother, Dear Daughter (with Heidi Stemple) (Boyds Mills, 2001)
The Devil's Arithmetic (Viking, 1988)
Dragon's Boy (HarperCollins, 1990)
Girl in a Cage (with Robert Burns) (Philomel, 2002)
Sleeping Ugly (Coward McCann, 1981)
Sword of the Rightful King (Harcourt Brace, 2003)
The Young Merlin Trilogy (Harcourt, 2004, 1996, 1997)

ON HOW SHE BECAME AN AUTHOR OF YOUNG ADULT LITERATURE

A story whispered in my ear and off I went. I do that with all my books.

ON WHETHER SHE WRITES WITH A PARTICULAR AUDIENCE IN MIND

Never. I write with the particular story in mind. The audience is within my own breast. If it does not please me, I do not write it.

ON THE INSPIRATION FOR HER STORIES

Inspiration—ideas—are cheap. What one then does with them is the real coin of our province. I have gotten inspiration from landscape, from old stories, from my own past, from history, from eavesdropping, from dreams. I have gotten inspiration from songs old and new, from photographs, from newspapers and magazines, from editor suggestion, from my children and grandchildren, from my husband.

ON RETELLINGS OF TRADITIONAL LITERATURE

I try to stay close to the intent of the story, but sometimes I fracture even that. But I always give the background of the original—its name, address, and serial number as it were—so that the reader can go back and find it and compare it with what I have done.

ON THE EXTENT TO WHICH HER OWN LIFE STORY APPEARS IN HER WORKS

More than even I know.

ON WHAT SHE ENJOYED READING AS A TEENAGER

I read Dostoevsky, Conrad, Isak Dinesen, James Thurber, and Leon Uris, who was popular at the time.

ON WHAT SHE ENJOYS READING CURRENTLY

I am a big reader of magical realism, biography, and mystery. Just finished reading Alice Hoffman's *Blue Diary* (no magic, alas, except for her gorgeous prose), a biography about Robert Louis Stevenson, and a nonfiction book about the Pacific Northwest Makah Indians who went on a modern whale hunt. And am just now dipping into a big collection of fantasy short stories by women.

ON WHAT DISTINGUISHES YOUNG ADULT LITERATURE

Usually a young adult protagonist. Usually a shorter book than those doorstops disguised as adult books. Usually about the emotional concerns of young adults, which as far as I can make out are snogging, clothing, beer, and the perennial questions who-am-I-and-how-do-I-fit-into-the-universe?

ON WHAT MIGHT HELP YOUNG ADULTS DEVELOP AS WRITERS

Read great books. Write every day. Don't take no from any teacher or parent or other adult who says writing is not a life choice.

ON WHY TRADITIONAL LITERATURE IS SUCH A STRONG INTERTEXT IN HER WRITING

I don't know—maybe because it is such a part of my own breathing.

ON WHY ARTHURIAN TALES ARE STILL SO POPULAR IN YOUNG ADULT LITERATURE

They have *everything* in them to make a great story: compelling characters, love, honor, courage, truth, loyalty, and betrayal.

Robin Hood

As with the King Arthur stories, the tales that feed into the legends of Robin Hood can be traced in many directions, and contemporary retellings are also affected by the numerous previous literary retellings. Influential retellings of Robin Hood include those by John Keats, Alfred Lord Tennyson, and Howard Pyle. Robert Louis Stevenson's *The Black Arrow* also has characters that many readers quickly identify as Robin's Merry Men. Some others include

- New tellings—*The Outlaws of Sherwood* (McKinley)
- Alternate perspectives—*In a Dark Wood* (villain) (Cadnum), *Forbidden Forest* (added character) (Cadnum)
- Extensions—*Lionclaw: A Tale of Rowan Hood* (Springer)
- Connected stories—*Robin of Sherwood* (Morpurgo)

Some retellings of Robin Hood take the basic storyline of the legend and elaborate and rework it. Robin McKinley's *The Outlaws of Sherwood* is a fine example of this. Others add new life to the story by telling different perspectives on what transpires. Michael Cadnum has explored the legend from both the Sheriff of Nottingham's perspective *(In a Dark Wood)* and that of Little John *(Forbidden Forest)*. Jane Yolen offers an edited collection of Robin Hood stories called *Sherwood: Original Stories from the World of Robin Hood,* in which eight authors provide diverse perspectives on the legend.

For tweens there are several series that add youthful protagonists and extend the storyline. In Nancy Springer's *Rowan Hood: Outlaw Girl of Sherwood Forest,* Rosemary disguises herself as a boy after her mother dies so that she can search for her outlaw father, Robin Hood. She ends up starting her own small band of merry teens. The story continues in a series that includes *Lionclaw: A Tale of Rowan Hood* and *Outlaw Princess of Sherwood.* This series and another by Theresa Tomlinson (beginning with *The Forestwife*) are perhaps most appropriate for 10- to 14-year-olds, but older young adults are reading them as well, both as bridging books for more sophisticated Robin Hood retellings and as exciting adventure stories in their own right. Finally, there are connected stories, such as Michael Morpurgo's *Robin of Sherwood* that tells the story of a contemporary boy who, after finding a skull, is pulled into a dream/vision of Robin Hood.

For the most part, the legends explored in YA literature of the United States come from European cultures. Some that are less familiar to the mainstream American audience can help expand students' cultural knowledge. Evangeline Walton, for example, has retold a connected series of Welsh legends in her Mabinogion series. The four novels, published separately in the 1970s, were republished as The Mabinogion Tetralogy in 2004. Excellent examples of legends from non-European sources have also gained in popularity. *Shadow Spinner* by Susan Fletcher and *The Storyteller's Daughter* (Dokey) are both wonderful explorations of the Arabian Nights. *Fa Mulan,* known primarily in the United States through the Disney retelling, is revisited by Robert San Souci in a version largely based on the ballad "The Song of Mulan" from imperial court anthologies collected during the Tang Dynasty (A.D. 618–907). The illustrations by Jean and Mou-Sien Tseng are done in the tradition of a Chinese scroll. There is much in this classic legend of a young woman who dresses as a man to go to war that might appeal to teens. Laura Gallego Garcia's *The Legend of the Wandering King* is inspired by an actual legend but the author's retelling is a literary crafting of history, the poems of pre-Islamic Arabs, and her own imagination.

Epics

An epic is basically a lengthy narrative poem that is heroic in nature and episodic in form. Generally, epics are connected to myth. Among the best-known epics in the Western world are the *Iliad* and the *Odyssey,* as well as Virgil's *Aeneid,* each of which have been retold numerous times (see the discussion in Chapter 2 on the classics). Novels such as Rosemary Sutcliff's *Black Ships before Troy,* Padric Colum's *The Trojan War and the Adventures of Odysseus,* and Rosemary Sutcliff's *The Wanderings of Odysseus* are excellent reads as well as good companion books for the *Odyssey.* Eric Shanower's *Age of Bronze* is a wonderfully researched graphic novel retelling that recounts the story of the Trojan War in a narrative reading more like historical fiction. In terms of traditional literature one of the most interesting retellings for young adults is Kate Hovey's *Voices of the Trojan War,* which returns to the poetic roots of the epic.

The story of *Beowulf* has fired the imaginations of many illustrators, including Gareth Hinds (Candlewick Press, 2007) and Christopher Steininger (AAM/Markosia Enterprises, 2007). Reprinted by permission of Candlewick Press and AAM/Markosia Enterprises.

In the secondary school context *Beowulf* is one of the most commonly read epics. Kevin Crossley-Holland, Robert Nye, and Charles Kegin have all retold versions that are accessible to many young adult readers. John Gardner in *Grendel* offered a retelling from the monster's perspective. The story of Beowulf is also an important intertext in novels such as Nancy Farmer's fantasy *The Sea of Trolls* and Michael Crichton's novel for adult audiences *Eaters of the Dead*.

Gilgamesh, an epic from Mesopotamia, has been retold in Geraldine McCaughrean's widely used *Gilgamesh the Hero*. It is also available in a trilogy of illustrated books by *Ludmila Zema: Gilgamesh the King, The Revenge of Ishtar,* and *The Last Quest of Gilgamesh*. The great epic tale from India *The Ramayana* has been retold in novel format by Jamake Highwater in *Rama: A Legend* and in Jessica Souhami's picture book *Rama and the Demon King*. One of the greatest epics from Africa has become well known in America through D. T. Niane's *Sundiata: An Epic of Old Mali*. Will Eisner has also retold this epic in a graphic novel format as *Sundiata: A Legend of Africa*.

Myth

Mythology is basically about making sense of the universe. It is a reflection of a belief system that is essentially religious in nature. Myths are stories that explain the origins of the world and all that is in it, including people, animals, and natural phenomena. The study of mythology is significant both because myths highlight a culture's worldview and because literature, in general, is full of mythological allusions. Mythology is often approached in nonfiction as a belief system and a number of books such as Sheila Keenan's *Gods, Goddesses, and Monsters: An Encyclopedia of World Mythology* can be used to further explore both the literary and religious aspects of myth. When dealing with living cultures one must be especially sensitive to this fact. In North America students primarily learn about ancient mythologies, especially Greek, Roman, Norse, and Egyptian systems.

The search for mythic intertexts at times can make simple picture books educationally appropriate for young adults. Christopher Myers's *Wings* and Arthur Yorinks's *Hey Al* both allude to the myth of Icarus. Myers uses the myth of Icarus to examine social intolerance in a book that is open to some wonderful explorations with young adults. *Hey Al,* on the other hand, is more about escapism and dissatisfaction with one's life, a topic that is also likely to hold relevance for many young adults. Despite its picture book format, Kevin O'Malley's *Mount Olympus Basketball* is more meaningful for readers having some familiarity with mythology. For teens who have explored Greek mythology the humor and the allusions will resonate.

Some wonderful recountings of myths tell these stories in ways that are accessible for a wide age range; Leonard Fisher's *Jason and the Golden Fleece* and Dorris Orgel's *Ariadne, Awake!* are good examples. Some others are specifically considered YA books. Kate Hovey's *Arachne Speaks,* for example, is a complex and poetic account of the war between Athena and Arachne.

Many of these renditions of myth for a young adult audience explore the story from an alternate perspective. Donna Jo Napoli's *Sirena* is a love story concerning a young siren and her sisters who pine away on an island because the only way they can gain immortality is by making a human fall in love with them. Whenever they call to a ship, luring the men in with their voices, the ship crashes on the rocks and the men drown. Sirena manages to rescue one of the warriors from drowning and then sets about trying to make him fall in love with her. This is most assuredly not a "children's" book, but the themes and the situations are of interest and appropriate for many teen readers.

A few YA novels tell a contemporary story with a mythological intertext. In *Orfe* Cynthia Voigt retells the myth of Orpheus in a modern rave context. Priscilla Galloway in *Snake Dreamer* offers a modern-day twist on the legend of Medusa. The 16-year-old protagonist Dusa dreams of snakes and travels to Greece in search of a cure. Rick Riordan's *The Lightning Thief* is the first in a series that brings mythical characters into today's world, and has become one of the most popular series today. The contemporary retellings of myth can be good pleasure reads and they are handy for bridging and pairing with the classic myths (for more on these concepts see Chapter 2).

Some Other Myths Retold

- *Atlanta's Race: A Greek Myth* by Shirley Climo
- *Dora's Box* by Ann-Jeanette Campbell
- *The Great God Pan* by Donna Jo Napoli
- *Persephone and the Pomegranate* by Kris Waldherr
- *Theseus and the Minotaur* by Leonard Fisher

Collections of Myth

Many mythology collections are organized by culture or by region, such as Mary Pope Osborne's *Favorite Norse Myths* and *Favorite Greek Myths,* Neil Philip's *Odin's Family: Myths of the Vikings,* Alice Low's *The MacMillan Book of Greek Gods and Heroes,* and Jacqueline Morley's *Egyptian Myths.* Other collections of mythic tales are connected by theme, including Virginia Hamilton's *In the Beginning: Creation Stories from around the World* and Ellen Datlow and Terri Windling's *The Green Man: Tales from the Mythic Forest.* These two books offer a good contrast as Hamilton's stories are all retold by one author, whereas the various nature myths explored in *The Green Man* are more loosely adapted by different authors including Jane Yolen, Neil Gaiman, and Tanith Lee. Throughout the ages, mythology has also been explored by visual artists. In *Art Tells a Story: Greek and Roman Myths,* Penelope Proddow makes connections between myths and the art they inspire.

Religious Stories

Though most public schools will likely avoid religious stories, some excellent collections are available for young adult readers. Among the most beautifully done are *Journeys with Elijah: Eight Tales of the Prophet* by Barbara Diamond Goldin with illustrations by Jerry Pinkney and *A Time to Love: Stories from the Old Testament* by Walter Dean Myers and Christopher Myers. The themes and situations make these stories especially meaningful for teens. *A Time to Love* focuses on the complexities of love among friends, lovers, brothers, parents, and children.

Barry Moser's wood engravings highlight this collection of stories, some of which are creepy, spooky, or disturbing, by authors such as Bram Stoker, Joyce Carol Oates, and Stephen King. From *Scary Stories.* Illustrations © 2006 by Barry Moser. Introduction © 2006 by Peter Glassman. Used with permission from Chronicle Books, San Francisco.

An intriguing retelling of the story of Noah, entitled *Not the End of the World* by Geraldine McCaughrean, received the prestigious Whitbread Award in 2005. With added characters (such as Noah's 14-year-old daughter who narrates much of the story) and multiple perspectives often showing people in a harsh light, the novel is sure to raise some controversy. But the story is part of both oral and written literature, appearing not just in the Old Testament but also orally as an important part of the Medieval Mystery Play cycle.

Scary Stories

Scary stories are among the most challenged books in the United States while also being favorites for many listeners and readers of all ages. Patricia McKissack has collected ghost stories drawn from the African American oral tradition in *The Dark Thirty: Southern Tales of the Supernatural.* In *Mysterious Tales of Japan* Rafe Martin retells an assortment of supernatural stories from Japan. Perhaps the most popular of these collections is *Scary Stories to Tell in the Dark* (Schwartz) that revisits many of the stories still told around campfires in the United States. Interestingly, the Scary Stories series is also listed on the American Library Association's 100 most frequently challenged books.

Guidelines for Selecting and Evaluating Traditional Literature

In addition to the general guidelines for selecting and evaluating literature, when working with traditional storylines the following issues of quality should be considered:

- How does the retelling relate to earlier written and oral versions? Is this relationship explained (in a foreword or author notes, for example)?
- Is cultural and historical information given on the source of the tale?
- Are aspects such as orality and cultural storytelling traditions reflected in the retelling?
- Do the illustrations reflect the cultural and artistic traditions of the story?

Author Spotlight

Photo courtesy of Donna Jo Napoli.

Donna Jo Napoli

Donna Jo Napoli is both a linguist and a writer of children's fiction. She lives outside Philadelphia and has five children and a cat named Taxi. She received her Ph.D. in romance languages and literatures from Harvard (1973) and has since taught linguistics at universities around the world (currently at Swarthmore College). In addition to authoring literature for children and young adults, Napoli has written and edited a number of scholarly works in the field of linguistics. She also writes essays about literature for children and young adults. She has received numerous recognitions, including the New Jersey Reading Association Award (1997), the Golden Kite Award from the Society of Children's Book Writers and Illustrators (1998), and the Sydney Taylor Book Award from the National Association of Jewish Libraries (1998). Visit her website at www.donnajonapoli.com.

SELECTED BIBLIOGRAPHY
Bound (Atheneum, 2004)
Breath (Atheneum, 2003)
Daughter of Venice (Wendy Lamb, 2002)
Hush: An Irish Princess' Tale (Atheneum, 2007)
Sirena (Scholastic, 1998)
The Smile (Dutton, 2008)
Stones in Water (Dutton, 1997)
Zel (Dutton, 1996)

ON WHAT DISTINGUISHES YOUNG ADULT LITERATURE

With regard to the adult versus YA distinction: nothing more than who publishes it. That is, *The Bluest Eye* could as easily have been published as a YA, but it was published by an adult press, so it's considered an adult book. With regard to the YA versus children distinction: Here I think the issue is who wants to read the book. If children want to read it, if they find that it speaks to their needs and interests, then it's probably a children's book, even if young and old adults also love reading it. But if only adults want to read a book, then it's an adult book, not a children's book. The issue is who it appeals to.

ON RETELLINGS OF TRADITIONAL LITERATURE

I try to be faithful to the framework handed to me by tradition. I am reverential of tradition. Those stories have stood the test of time—they grab hearts. There's no way I'm going to deviate from them and risk losing their truth, their power.

ON WHETHER FOLKTALES APPEAL TO YOUNG ADULTS

"Rapunzel" is a story about a girl locked in a tower by her mother. It's a story of abuse, physical and psychological. There's no way that story should be limited to little children. "Beauty and the Beast" is a story about a man trapped in a beast's body—with all the soul-rending compromises that accompany that physical torture. Again, why should such drama be limited to little children?

Traditional fairy tales come from oral literature—people sitting around telling stories in the evening by the fire. Adults and children together. They appeal to all ages. I write for anyone, regardless of age—so fairy tales are a natural for me.

ON GIVING VOICE TO ALTERNATE PERSPECTIVES FROM TRADITIONAL TALES

When my children were little, my husband and I used to turn off the light in their bedroom at night and sit in the middle of the floor, with all of them (we have five) in their beds, and we'd take turns telling stories. Sometimes we'd all tell the same story, from different characters' perspectives. It was fun. And enlightening. Take two witnesses to a crime and ask them what happened. They won't agree on at least some of the details, and maybe not even on some of the major points. We all see things differently. That interests me a lot. I want to bring that to my reader.

ON CREATING AN AUTHENTIC HISTORICAL NARRATIVE

I do a lot of research on all my stories, whether they are labeled historical fiction or fantasy. I grew up poor, and I didn't travel much beyond my hometown. But books carried me all over the world, and way back into the past, and way forward into the future. They expanded the world for me. That's something I want to do for my readers—bring them into another world, let them taste and smell and hear and see and feel what it was like to be in Israel in the first century (as in *Song of the Magdalene*) or to live in the sea (as in *Sirena*) or to be a prisoner in a work camp during a war (as in *Stones in Water*). If possible, I visit the places I write about and walk the land my characters walked. I listen to music, look at art, and read literature from those times. With *Stones in Water*, I interviewed men who had been in the work camps and I read reports of children in the work camps that I found in the archives of the International Red Cross in Geneva, Switzerland. I consult with scholars of the periods I'm writing about, and sometimes I'm lucky enough to get them to give me feedback on early drafts. Right now I'm working on a story set in Germany in 1280, and I visited the town this summer and felt the doorknob on the church in my story and sat and looked at the stained glass windows my character stared at. So I do whatever I can.

But, really, I am living in this day, in this place, and I can never know another day and another place that I have never lived. I try hard to get into the sensibilities of the people of the time and place I'm writing about, but I am me, not them; I am the product of the world as I know it—a world with computers and airplanes and knowledge about the universe. So I have no idea how nearly accurate or woefully inaccurate my work is. But I certainly learn as much as I can and I never ignore what I have learned.

Audio Books

Traditional Literature

Beast by Donna Jo Napoli; read by Robert Raminez. (Recorded Books, 2001)

Cupid by Julius Lester; read by Stephen Henderson. (Listening Library, 2007)

I Am Mordred: A Tale from Camelot by Nancy Springer; read by Stephen Crossley. (Recorded Books, 1999) (Y).

I Was a Rat by Phillip Pullman; read by Phillip Pullman. (Full Cast Audio, 2001)

Just Ella by Margaret Haddix; read by Alyssa Bresnahan. (Recorded Books, 2001)

The Seeing Stone by Kevin Crossley-Holland; read by Michael Maloney. (Bantam Books-Audio, 2001) (Y)

The Seven Songs of Merlin by T. A. Barron; read by Kevin Isola. (Listening Library, 2002)

Spirit of the Cedar People by Chief Lelooska; read by Chief Lelooska. (DK, 1998)

Troy by Adele Geras; read by Miriam Margolyes. (Listening Library, 2002)

Y—YALSA Selected List of Audiobooks

The Question of Culture and Fakelore

Many contemporary authors make an effort to infuse authentic cultural elements into their retellings of traditional literature. This literature can therefore provide a window on diverse cultures, and the use of traditional literature in the classroom often revolves around cultural investigation. Certainly cultural information exists both in the elements of story (character types, narrative structures, ways of relating to others and to the world, language use, etc.) and in the detail provided by the artist (the setting, body postures, clothing, artistic style, etc.). This, of course, assumes that the author and illustrator each knows the culture intimately, a problematic issue that was explored in Chapter 1.

Perhaps the most essential issue related to culture lies in the distinction between fakelore and folklore (Singer, 2004), an issue that might be explored with great educational benefit by young adults. In general, the publisher is seeking to market a commercially viable book, not necessarily to capture historically and culturally authentic oral traditions. Yet teachers and others who work with young people constantly use these loosely adapted folktales as cultural artifacts.

Picture books such as Tomie dePaola's *The Legend of the Indian Paintbrush* and John Steptoe's *Mufaro's Beautiful Daughters* have little to do with a particular culture's traditional literature. Steptoe's story is often used in units on Africa with teachers and students discussing it as a fine example of a folktale from Zimbabwe, when actually it is a literary tale inspired by the author's reading of a collection of folklore from Zimbabwe called *Kaffir Folklore* (Theal, 1886). *Mufaro's Beautiful Daughters* is a wonderful, beautifully illustrated story filled with folkloric motifs, but the question remains whether we are misinforming students when we use it to teach about Zimbabwe or Africa.

At times publishers and even authors add to the illusion that their literary tales are authentic by labeling the story "retold by" and adding a subtitle such as "A Cherokee Tale." Glossaries, notes about the sources, and a foreword about the culture can all express the idea that these are indeed authentic tales, despite the fact that the authors "did not learn these stories as members of traditional communities and have never told these stories as part of those communities" (Singer, 2004, n.p.).

Still, although it is true that numerous published tales might be viewed as whitewashed, westernized, and romanticized versions of traditional stories, not many critics would go so far as to argue that modern versions of literary tales should not be used with young readers. The bigger issue is that these stories are often packaged and used as something they are not. Exploring this concern with young adults can certainly feed into critical discussions about the relationship among authority, misinformation, and story.

Although there are some great reasons for not making the folktale and festival approach to diversity the centerpiece of your multicultural program, there are excellent reasons for looking at the connections between cultural traditions and folklore. Many authors and illustrators do incorporate rich cultural detail in the stories they retell. Shonto Begay captures the artistry of sand paintings in *Ma'ii and Cousin Horned Toad*. Michael Lacape's style has been influenced by southwestern pottery and basketry in *The Magic Hummingbird: A Hopi Folktale*. P. J. Lynch prepared to paint *East o' the Sun and West o' the Moon* by spending hours in the Norwegian National Art Gallery, consciously seeking to reflect the traditional styles. Regardless of the artists' motives, their renderings will leave an impression on the reader as to what it means to be Norwegian or Hopi. If these are the only images the reader has to draw on they will carry more weight.

At times narratives reflect not only the visual arts but also the heritage of storytelling itself. Folktales are, of course, traditionally

To Consider
To what extent should a story that is identified as belonging to a particular cultural tradition be accountable for authenticity?

oral and many authors attempt to retain this convention. Joseph Bruchac, for example, asserts,

> As regards the difficulty of "translating" from oral to written form, I have to say that I "talk" my stories onto the page and then read them aloud again to see if they still have the sound of a told tale. (see Bruchac interview, p. 145)

The rhythms of speech, the storytelling rhetoric, and the dialect all add to the power of the story. Occasionally, other storytelling elements tied to cultural heritage will also be included. In *The Lost Horse,* which is a Chinese variant of a popular proverb, Ed Young includes three beautifully crafted paper puppets. Puppetry has been used to tell Chinese tales and stories for at least a thousand years and is a great way to reconnect the folktale to traditional storytelling techniques. In Young's book the story is also retold in Chinese calligraphy at the beginning of the book, so connections can be made to both the language of origin and the cultural form of storytelling.

Power, Nationalism, and Folklore

In many contexts literature and politics are integrally tied together. In *The Woman Who Outshone the Sun,* Alejandro Cruz Martinez retells the legend of Lucia Zenteno, a story associated with the struggle over access to water. The author/reteller of this story was actually involved in organizing the Zapotecs of Mexico to regain their lost water rights. The two efforts were intertwined. Martinez published the story in picture book format in 1986 and was assassinated in 1987. The connections among words, power, and culture are not often so explicit in the United States, but it is wise to remember that the relationships between literature and power can be strong.

One of the most common ways of exploring folklore with young readers is to celebrate the culture conveyed. Many scholars have argued that folktales can show us something about differing world views and distinct cultural styles (Darnton, 2000). At the same time, questions have been raised regarding whether folklore actually represents a national or cultural character. The Grimm brothers, for example, felt they were holding up a mirror for the German people to see their national identity, a mirror that would not simply reflect but also help define Germany's character. On the flip side, in the decades following World War II, the German folktale was attacked and condemned for promoting nationalism and sadism among Germans. Claims concerning the negative nationalistic properties of German folktales continued appearing, even as recently as 1978 (Snyder). Both the idea that folklore encapsulates a culture and the notion that folklore can confine and limit our worldview are normative conceptions of folklore. They share in common the notion that folktales have a strong influence on how we think and act.

Interestingly, the Grimm brothers did not provide authentic unaltered tales of the folk. Many of their stories were collected from aristocratic informants or from literary sources (Zipes, 1986). The Brothers Grimm published their tales in 1810, 1812, 1819, 1843, and 1857. In each edition there are stylistic and sometimes major plot changes in individual stories. If there is one story that many Americans might readily identify as German, that tale would be "Hansel and Gretel." Yet this tale was collected by the Grimm brothers from a woman of French Huguenot descent. In early editions the children were nameless and they lived with their mother and father. In later editions the children were given German names and an evil stepmother replaced the mother. The Grimms unabashedly wanted to project a certain image of what it was to be German but this required modifications of the tale. According to Zipes during the 47 years the Grimm brothers worked with "Hansel and Gretel," the major changes included

- Embellishments of the text
- The introduction of Christian themes
- Changes in the social reality reflected
- The erasure of the mother and the depiction of the witch

By 1857, the text literally became twice as long as in the first edition, with many of the additions borrowed from literary tales.

Topic Focus

Examining Folktale Variants

One activity that has real potential with a young adult audience involves the exploration of multiple variants of a particular tale. Many folktales have been collected and adapted numerous times throughout the world, and writers and publishers have taken many liberties with the storylines (Zipes, 1997). As Donald Haase suggests, this is a great opportunity for students to "discover individual ownership" of these tales (Haase, 1993). If this is a classroom objective it might be necessary to provide a wide variety of retellings of a familiar story and to encourage their creative reception. Obviously, here is a great opportunity for young adults to deconstruct the tale and examine possible interpretations. When examining variants it can be productive to first have the students look at the commonalities—what it is that identifies this tale as a version of the Cinderella story. Then in looking for the contrasts readers can delve deeper into cultural and artistic variations that might shed light on the folktale, on society, and on narrative in general.

In a recently overheard conversation among a group of tenth graders who were comparing "Hansel and Gretel" variants, someone pointed out that in three of the four versions the mother/stepmother is dead at the end when the children are reunited with their father. "Do you think that means something?" one of the students asked. "Or is that just part of the happy ending?" "Ha, ha. It's sexist if you ask me. Why does the stepmother always get abused?" said another student. "What happens to her? Does it say in any of the books?" They looked closely at the texts and after a few minutes, one of them held up Susan Jeffers's *Hansel and Gretel* (1980). "Look," she said. "The witch and the stepmother could almost be the same person!" Indeed there is a distinct similarity in dress and physical characteristics between the stepmother and the witch. Suddenly they were talking about the story on a whole new level, excited about what they had discovered.

Different sets will work better for investigations into cultural variations, differences in artistic renderings, or retellings that change connotations and perspectives. Depending on what students will be exploring, you may want to choose the sets yourself ahead of time. However, if you are interested in open-ended explorations, students could certainly search for variants on their own.

Examining Cultural Variation in the Cinderella Story

In terms of cultural versions there is probably no tale more widespread than the Cinderella story. As early as 1951, Anna Poth explored over 700 versions. There are more picture book retellings of "Cinderella" than any other story. Most of these versions share several key motifs: a good and deserving but poor, overworked girl, a wicked stepmother and usually a stepsister or two, a magical helper of some sort, and a very eligible bachelor (in a few versions genders are reversed).

The fact that there are so many distinct cultural versions can actually make choosing difficult. More significantly, it is not always easy to determine whether a version is authentic to the culture represented, and if cultural variation is what is being explored, this is significant information. In such instances you might consider letting the students start by researching reviews of the picture books to discover what critics have said about their authenticity, or alternately they might explore the cultural aspects and form their own opinions.

The two written versions responsible for Cinderella's fame in the Western world are the retellings by the Brothers Grimm in Germany (1812) and Charles Perrault in France (1697). Nonny Hogregian provides a beautiful picture book rendition of the Brothers Grimm's *Aschanputtel*. This German version is very recognizable, though with some rather grim twists which younger readers have not likely encountered before, such as the stepsisters' toes and heels being chopped off. K. Y. Craft has created a lavish retelling in *Cinderella* (2000), based on Perrault's version. The paintings resemble 17th-century French art with borders and ornamentation. Some cultural aspects come through in the narrative, as well as in the artistic renderings in both these versions. These books serve as a good base for starting an investigation as they demonstrate that some of the key elements of what we consider the "traditional" story are actually from the Disney adaptations.

Ed Young's *Yeh Shin* is a retelling of a Chinese version of the tale based on what is arguably the oldest written version of a Cinderella story, dating back to 850 B.C.E. (though there is an Egyptian version that might predate it). The Chinese literary and cultural tradition make the tale seem quite distinct at first, but on closer inspection it does have the motifs of the poor, overworked girl, the wicked stepmother, a magical helper, and a king searching for a wife.

What really makes the Cinderella story so interesting as a variant set is that there are so many distinct cultural versions from around the globe. In Silverman and Gaber's *Raisel's Riddle,* Cinderella is a Jewish orphan in a Polish city. After the death of her grandfather she is hired to help in the house of a distinguished rabbi. The cook in the household is jealous and tries to make Raisel miserable. When Raisel gives food to an old woman, she is granted three wishes. Rather than a ball, she attends a Purim celebration, and rather than a glass slipper, she leaves behind a riddle. The rabbi's son searches for the young woman who asked the riddle. When he finally finds her, he asks for her hand in marriage. She agrees, but only if he can provide the answer.

The versions recounted so far have art and narrative that reflect the culture out of which they arose. But there are other retellings that take a tale and recast it in a new historical or cultural context. Roberto Innocenti places his retelling inspired by Perrault in 1920s London. The clothing, style of speech, and architecture are all beautifully and lavishly depicted. Those who still believe that folktales are only for children might want to examine the last page of Innocenti's *Cinderella,* which makes viewers rethink traditional understandings of the stepmother. Robert San Souci's Creole version, *Cendrillon,* builds on the familiar European versions of the tale but in a New World context. This variant set in the Caribbean is narrated by the godmother (a washerwoman) who helps Cendrillon find true love. The story in words and art (by Brian Pinkney) is filled with French Creole cultural detail. In each of these variants, whether the story arose from within a culture or was simply retold from within a new context, the rich cultural detail enhances both the telling and our understanding of the story.

Additional Versions of Cinderella

- *Ashpit* retold by Joanne Compton
- *Cinder Edna* retold by Ellen B. Jackson
- *Cinderella* retold by Roberto Innocenti
- *Cinderella* retold by Charles Perrault; illus. by Susan Jeffers
- *Cinderella* retold by Ruth Sanderson
- *Cinderella* retold by Christine San Jose
- *Cinderella* retold by William Wegman
- *Cinderella: An Art Deco Love Story* retold by Lynn Roberts
- *Cinderella: A Fairy Tale* by Charles Perrault, trans. by Anthea Bell; illus. by Loek Koopmans
- *Cinderella Penguin* by Janet Perlman
- *Cinderella's Dress* by Nancy Willard; illus by Jane Dyer
- *CindyEllen* by Susan Lowell; illus. by Jane Manning
- *If the Shoe Fits: Voices from Cinderella* by L. Whipple; illus. by L. Beingessner
- *The Irish Cinderlad* retold by Shirley Climo; illus. by Loretta Krupinski
- *Little Gold Star/Estrella de Oro* by Joe Hayes; illus. by Lucia Angela Perez
- *Lovely Vassilisa* by Barbara Cohen; illus. by Anatoly Ivanhoff
- *Prince Cinders* by Babette Cole
- *The Rough Faced Girl* retold by Rafe Martin; illus. by David Shannon
- *The Turkey Girl: A Zuni Cinderella* retold by Penny Pollock; illus. by Ed Young

Novels
- *Bound* by Donna Jo Napoli
- *Chinese Cinderella* by Adeline Yen Mah
- *Cinderella 2000* by Mavis Juke
- *Ella Enchanted* by Gail Carson Levine
- *I Was a Rat* by Phillip Pullman
- *Just Ella* by Margaret P. Haddix

Examining Variation in Artistic Renderings of "Rapunzel"

Another beneficial examination of variants might emphasize the ways artistic renderings affect the retellings. Many of the artistic elements will certainly be tied to culture, but other stylistic choices are determined by the illustrator's interests or by the mood of the story itself. When Paul Zelinsky's version of *Rapunzel* was awarded a Caldecott there were some who questioned the appropriateness of the story for young readers. Zelinsky retold a traditional version of the tale that includes some mature elements: The teen character gets pregnant and has twins and the prince gets blinded, for example. Although even many young children see more inappropriate material every day on TV, this is a good example of the fact that neither picture books nor folktales are exclusively for children.

Zelinsky captures the flavor of the Italian Renaissance, not just the setting and the clothes but also the Fresco Renaissance-inspired style. There is a certain classic romance feel to the mood throughout. This might be contrasted with Berenzy and Maja Dusikova's retellings of German versions of the tale. In Berenzy's story, a fairy named Mother Gothel confines Rapunzel to the tower. After finding out about the elopement, she cuts Rapunzel's hair and casts her into a desert and then blinds the prince. Mother Gothel is drawn with sharp edges that enhance the feeling of harshness. The illustrations are done on black paper with colored pencils and gouache, and the interplay between light and dark is beautifully captured, especially the dark interiors of the tower. The prince, on the other hand, is dressed in green, like the spring he brings into her life. Maja Dusikova's version also comes from the Grimm brothers. She uses a dark background, in this case done in charcoal. The harshness of the landscape is created with dreamy dark watercolors and misty landscapes that, together with the addition of birds, butterflies, and cats who observe the unfolding story, mellows the mood to an extent.

Several recent renderings stand in sharp contrast to the versions so far explored. *Rapunzel: A Groovy Fairy Tale* (Roberts) sets the story in a modern context. The art is cartoon style with at least an element of humor. But the mood conveyed is mixed and the use of symbolism is strong. An air of coming of age, alienation, and angst appears throughout, despite the comic relief. A scene such as the page where Rapunzel stands alone on the balcony is deceptively simple, yet full of images of puzzles, traps, and a longing for freedom.

Falling for Rapunzel (Wilcox) is also done in a cartoon style, with an even lighter tone. The acrylic and collage illustrations use bright colors and bold patterns to accentuate the exaggerated features. Unusual background details (such as the computer in the tower) add to the silliness. The princess is not weeping about being locked in the tower, but rather about the state of her hair. The prince, believing she is distraught, seeks to rescue her. She can't hear him, and when he says throw down your hair, she throws down her underwear. So goes the story with her misunderstanding and sending down the wrong things, until finally he says braid and she sends her maid. The maid and the prince ride off together.

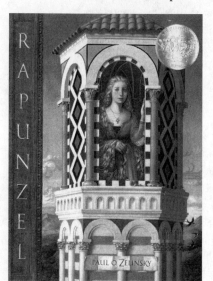

Zelinsky's *Rapunzel* (1997) drew from various sources for his retelling of the story, but he relied mainly on the Brothers Grimm. Reprinted by permission of Penguin Group (USA).

Although the cultural comparison mentioned previously allows young adult readers some perspective into the intersections of beliefs, values, and traditions with narrative, the focus on artistic variation can lead into some great discussions on aesthetics and encourage investigations into visual and media literacies. Other variant sets might emphasize the shifting connotations of a tale. *Sleeping Ugly* (Yolen), *Sleepless Beauty* (Minters), *Sleeping Boy* (Craddock), and *Sleeping Bobby* (Osborne and Osborne) each consciously changes the connotations of a popular tale in interesting ways. Or the comparison might concentrate on differences in the ending of a tale. Comparing the final scenes of Trina Schart Hyman's *Little Red Riding Hood* with versions of the tale by Beni Montresor, Sarah Moon, and Ed Young could lead to some amazing discussions.

Sometimes rather than looking at variants of a particular tale, you might want to take a look at the various manifestations of a motif. The general theme of transformation, for example, can lead to excellent discussions. A wide variety of tales such as "The Crane Wife," "The Frog Prince," and "Beauty and the Beast" revolve around the theme of transformation. Examining how these transformations take on new meaning in each variation of this theme can be a exciting exploration.

Additional Versions of Rapunzel

- *Falling for Rapunzel* by Leah Wilcox
- *Petrosinella: A Neopolitan Rapunzel* retold by Frederick Warner; illus. by Diane Stanley
- *Rapunzel* retold by Nicoletta Oeccoli
- *Rapunzel* retold by Barbara Rogasky; illus. by Trina Schart Hyman
- *Rapunzel* retold by Paul Zelinsky
- *Rapunzel: A Groovy Fairy Tale* by Lynn Roberts; illus. by David Roberts

Novels
- *The Tower Room* by Adele Geras
- *Zel* by Donna Jo Napoli

Visual Interpretation

When exploring artistic variation in tales, one technique that can add to the success of the project is to start with a visual interpretation. In this approach the reader/viewer looks at the detail in the illustration, makes some possible interpretations, and raises questions about symbolism and structures of meaning.

In *Rapunzel: A Groovy Fairy Tale* one might start by listing the details from the page with the balcony scene: butterflies, a Rubik's Cube (unsolved), a balcony high up, a potted plant (dead or dying), a teenage girl with very long hair, and one could go on about the types of clothes she wears and so on. The next step would be to interpret what has been noted. The butterflies might symbolize freedom, which the young girl longs for. The Rubik's Cube might signify that she is trying to find a solution to her problem. Perhaps the dying potted plant alludes to Rapunzel herself, also perhaps dying undernourished in a constrained space. The fact that the butterfly on her finger has a mirror-image butterfly on the plant certainly supports this interpretation (the third identical butterfly adds to the imagery of the longing for freedom). These images are open to being interpreted in many ways.

This illustration from Lynn Roberts's *Rapunzel: A Groovy Fairy Tale* illus. by David Roberts (2003) is filled with symbolism. Reprinted by permission of Abrams.

Finally, there are likely many questions that the reader/viewer will have after exploring the illustration. What are the pieces of metal on the side of the balcony? Is Rapunzel dressed the way she is because she is poor or is that the fashion? Who is keeping her in the tower? What is she daydreaming about? Why is her hair so long? Once students have raised questions they would like to have answered, they are likely to be more engaged with both the graphic elements and with the story.

When tied to working with folktale variant sets, engaging in visual interpretations can really scaffold young adult readers' analysis of the literature. They will notice many things through close examination of the illustrations, which will enhance their understanding of the narrative. The added bonus is that once they start approaching the book this way they are more likely to keep making exciting comparisons between versions of the tale.

Novels in the Folk Tradition

Just as there are some creative picture books written in the folkloric tradition, there are novels that build extensively on the ideas and motifs of traditional literature. Although generally fitting into the broad category of speculative fiction that will be explored in Chapter 5, it is worth mentioning their existence here as they are a direct link between folklore and fantasy.

William Goldman's *The Princess Bride,* William Brooke's *Teller of Tales,* and Patrice Kindl's *Goose Chase* are three popular examples of novels written with a strong tie to folklore. *Goose Chase,* for example, builds on the theme of the poor but generous young person who offers her bread and water to a hungry old lady. She is "rewarded" for this by being transformed into an incredibly beautiful young woman. What seems at first to be a blessing soon has unexpected consequences. When a prince and a king begin fighting over the goose girl, she just wishes things could go back to the way they were.

Author Spotlight

Photo by James Schuck.

Jon Scieszka

Jon Scieszka was born in Flint, Michigan, in 1954 and grew up in a house with five brothers. He received a M.F.A. from Columbia University in 1980. When Scieszka first started submitting children's books, he was told that they were too sophisticated for young readers and that they would not understand his use of parody and point of view. But he was working as a teacher in New York City with kids from first to eighth grades and he knew that his students could appreciate the postmodern and beyond. When his wife Jeri, an art director, introduced him to illustrator Lane Smith, the two began to collaborate and they have since authored a number of award-winning works together. Scieszka also is the founder of Guys Read, an outreach effort to connect reluctant male readers with literature about which they might get excited. In 2008, the Library of Congress appointed Scieszka as the inaugural "National Ambassador for Young People's Literature." Visit his website at www.jsworldwide.com and Guys Read at www.guysread.com.

SELECTED BIBLIOGRAPHY
Guys Write for Guys Read (Viking, 2005)
Math Curse illus. by Lane Smith (Viking, 1996)
Science Verse illus. by Lane Smith (Viking, 2004)
Seen Art? illus. by Lane Smith (Penguin, 2005)
Squids Will Be Squids illus. by Lane Smith (Viking, 1998)
The Stinky Cheese Man and Other Fairly Stupid Tales illus. by Lane Smith (Viking, 1992)
The True Story of the Three Little Pigs illus. by Lane Smith (Viking, 1989)

ON THE POTENTIAL FOR YOUNG ADULT READERS TO ENGAGE WITH HIS BOOKS

I like to make my books funny enough, and multilayered enough, and intelligent enough to connect with readers of all ages and educations. So it doesn't surprise me that teachers find this in the books and go with it.

ON HOW PICTURE BOOK NARRATIVES DIFFER FROM THE NARRATIVES FOUND IN NOVELS

The best picture book narratives are poems, minimal brushstrokes, the bare elegant bones of a story. In a picture book you have to leave space for the illustrator. You don't need to describe how things look—readers can see that for themselves. The novelist has to paint the complete picture with words.

ON RETELLING TRADITIONAL LITERATURE WITH A TWIST

I've always been a big fan of the humor generated by the friction generated between content and unlikely form. Monty Python, *Mad* magazine, writers Robert Benchley and S. J. Perelman, and cartoonist Tex Avery were masters of this humor. There is also something about the challenge of finding the most unlikely subject for humor (the math in *Math Curse,* for example) and breathing new life into it.

ON HIS EFFORTS WITH GUYS READ

My experience as a guy in the worlds of school and children's books convinced me that we do need to do something to interest boys in reading. The dismal reading test scores and dropping college enrollment of boys are the stats that prove it. Something in our culture and education system is not right when so many boys see school and reading as something that is imposed on them.

I started Guys Read as a program to make people aware that our boys do need help. And I built the website guysread.com to take the first most simple step to help guys read—find out what books guys do like to read and get the word out there.

Technology Links

Digital Storytelling

As already seen there is a wide range of traditional literature available in a written format. Of course one of the key aspects of this literature that is "lost in translation" is its orality. Technology allows for literary formats that can handle oral narrative; it can also provide wider access to these narratives. Young adults today can find excellent audio materials on the Internet. The Moonlit Road, for example, provides a range of ghost stories from the American South told by some of the region's best storytellers. Each month a handful of feature stories are available in streamed audio free of charge, accompanied by text versions and cultural background notes. A larger library of oral tales is available to paying members.

Other sites take advantage of video capabilities, allowing the viewer to not only hear the story but also see how body language and facial expressions add meaning to oral literature. The Australian Museum's Stories of the Dreaming site is a good example with video segments of a half dozen aboriginal storytellers performing traditional tales. Some stories like "The Two Wise Men and the Seven Sisters" include video of a storyteller explaining the meaning and history of the tale. On another clip one of the storytellers, Warren Foster, explains, "The reason that we tell these stories is to know where we're coming from. Gives us an identity of the people. And if we know where we're coming from, we know where we're going. As long as we keep telling these stories we know that our culture is alive and running strong through our veins" (www.dreamtime.net.au).

If technology can be used to view stories, it can also be used by young adults to collect and tell stories. One of the most interesting projects at the intersection between oral literature and technology is The Digital Clubhouse Network. Basically what they do is train young adults to help tell the stories of community members using digital authoring tools. Young adults aged 12 to 15 participate in a program referred to as DAPP (Digitally Abled Producers Program), in which they are taught the technology, communication, and interpersonal skills needed to carry out projects. There is no charge for the courses, but participants must provide an hour of community service for every hour of training. The young adults have worked with veterans of World War II and members of the civil rights movement, among others. One of the newer projects, Digital Griot, seeks to combine "the age old art of storytelling with the power of digital technology so that we can revive, enrich, and communicate the traditions of the African American experience in ways that can educate and inspire people of all backgrounds." In the mini-movies created, the storyteller's own voice is combined with images, music, and other effects to appeal to the audience and bring the story to life.

The Digital Clubhouse Network (www.digiclubnyc.org)

The Moonlit Road (www.themoonlitroad.com)

Stories of the Dreaming (www.dreamtime.net.au)

LITERARY THEORY

Myth and Archetypal Criticism

Looking across cultures at various myths and folktales, it is easy to see sometimes striking similarities in terms of motifs, character types, images, and structures. In the 1940s, 50s, and 60s, some critics noting these patterns postulated an archetypal understanding of how "good writing happens" (May, 1997, p. 20). Proponents of myth criticism focus on recurring patterns within literature. The mainstay of myth criticism is the focus on the heroes' quest for identity in light of these recurring patterns that are believed to relate back to primitive rituals and habits and are manifested over and over again in literature. They shape the way people organize and therefore understand the world and determine story structures and meanings.

Carl Jung suggests that these similarities are archetypes arising from the collective unconscious (imprinted patterns of experience from our ancestors). Claude Levi-Strauss, on the other hand, finds the meaning of myth in the structures of relationships between extremes such as life and death. Northrup Fyre, another major figure in myth criticism, emphasizes that for whatever reason, these patterns do exist and they extend beyond myth to be reenacted in literature and in human imagination.

Examining these traditional patterns can provide students with insights into character traits and story shape. Odysseus, Luke Skywalker, and Frodo Baggins all go on similar life journeys. The hero leaves home, completes a quest, and returns all the wiser for the journey. Joseph Campbell discusses this quest pattern in *The Hero with a Thousand Faces*. The structural patterns begin to signify almost immediately "without needing to be interpreted, because the meaning lies in the repeatability and the deeply laid similarity amongst otherwise apparently diverse stories" (Stephens and McCallum, 1998, p. 62). Familiarity with the hero's quest allows the reader to predict and to compare how a particular journey might be similar to or different from the paths traveled by other heroes.

Though myth critics have typically discussed and studied archetypes as "universals," the theoretical lens has generally been applied to mainstream Western literature. Interestingly, narratives for young people often offer a mock hero fumbling through the quest, creating in effect a parody of the archetypal journey (Stott, 1990). Still, stories as diverse as *Where the Wild Things Are* (Sendak) and Adele Geras's *Troy* can easily be approached using an archetypal analysis.

> *To Consider*
>
> When the protagonist goes on a quest or adventure, archetypal patterns might be discernable, but can this type of literary theory be applied to more introspective stories?

From Page to Stage to Imagination

Drama is another form of literature that is delivered primarily in an oral mode. Drama in education has many literary manifestations. Unfortunately, it is also true that many young people will go through 12 years of schooling without encountering reader's theatre or creative dramatics, and quite a few young adults will never enjoy the wonderful array of professional plays that might appeal to them. The aesthetic and educational potential of drama is enormous, because more than any other literary format it presents the possibility of involving all the senses. In drama students become part of the narrative in ways that draw on multiple literacies.

There are of course some novels with wonderful dramatic connections—Gary Blackwood's *The Shakespeare Stealer* or Gordon Korman's *No More Dead Dogs,* for example. *A Heart Divided* by Cherie Bennett and Jeff Gotesfield serves as a wonderful introduction to script writing. The novel focuses on a young woman from New York who has decided that script writing is her passion. When her family moves from New York to Tennessee, her dream of scripting seems to be shattered, but she persists. The last third of the book is the script that she has finally finished.

Author Spotlight

Photo courtesy of Dramatic Publishing.

Max Bush

Max Bush is a freelance playwright and director whose plays are widely produced on professional, educational, and amateur stages across the country. He's won numerous awards for his work, including the Distinguished Play Award from AATE, the IUPUI National Playwriting Competition, and Individual Artists Grants from the Michigan Council for the Arts. He has been commissioned by Nashville Academy Theatre, Emmy Gifford Theatre (Omaha), Lexington Children's Theatre, Honolulu Theatre for Youth, Karamu House (Cleveland), Idaho Theater for Youth, Hartford Children's Theatre, Portland High School (Michigan), Circle Theatre (Grand Rapids), and the Goodman/DePaul School of Drama (Chicago). In 1995, Meriwether Press published an anthology of ten of his plays. Also in 1995, the American Alliance for Theatre and Education awarded him the Charlotte Chorpenning Cup for a body of work of national significance. Visit his website at http://usaplays4kids.drury.edu/playwrights/bush.

SELECTED SCRIPT LIST

The Boy Who Left Home to Find Out about the Shivers (Anchorage Press, 1999)
Ghost of the River House (Anchorage Press, 1997)
Looking through You (Dramatic Publishing, 2005)
Sarah (Dramatic Publishing, 2000)
Voices from the Shore (Dramatic Publishing, 2005)

ON HOW HE BECAME A WRITER FOR YOUNG ADULTS

It was a natural progression from writing both adult plays and plays for children. Gradually, I seemed to meet both interests in the middle and ended up doing a series of plays for high school actors and audiences. I also taught high school early in my career and have a long, positive working relationship with the age group. Also, that age is a crucible of growth issues, issues which reflect both up and down the ages. Many of the growth struggles we engage throughout our lives are accentuated in young adulthood.

It's also an incredibly dynamic period for all sorts of issues: beginning to separate from parents, beginning to seriously consider an extended future, beginning to seriously engage in extended romantic relationships, beginning to deal more extensively with money issues. And it is a critical period of individuation, identity, and self-knowledge.

ON HOW HE BECAME INTERESTED IN DRAMA

As a teenager I read sports books and science fiction. I saw my first play when I was a sophomore in high school. I was in my first play as a senior—*The Bald Soprano*—and fell in love with the theatre, and have been heavily involved ever since. Really, it was my high school drama director who opened the door and showed me the world of the theatre.

ON FAVORITE AUTHORS AND PLAYS

A little bit: My two favorite authors are Arthur Miller and, of course, Shakespeare. I like Miller because he could write so clearly and (seemingly) simply and he experimented with many different forms. Look at *Salesman* and *After the Fall*. He had a profound understanding of his characters and the ability to have them speak directly and yet expressively. And in both he let the form be shaped by the characters and the content.

Shakespeare's density and poetry are stunning to me still. I recently saw my favorite comedy, *Twelfth Night,* at the Globe in San Diego. Although I've studied the play for years and "know" it well, this production transported me to a beautiful space of dream, romance, poetry, sadness, and grace. Given a good production, the play is able to transcend the study and familiarity and live in the moment in a way only a play can. And at the same time, it is so rich the study is rewarded continuously with fresh emanations from the text.

ON WHAT DISTINGUISHES YOUNG ADULT DRAMA FROM DRAMA FOR CHILDREN OR DRAMA FOR ADULTS

Primarily it is the age of the protagonist. Secondarily, the play deals with issues that face the age group. Other than that, good theatre is good theatre for everyone. In my latest plays for high school theatres (*Sarah, Voices from the Shore, Looking through You*) all or nearly all of the characters are the same age as the protagonist.

ON HOW NARRATIVE IN DRAMA DIFFERS FROM PROSE FICTION

There's a tremendous difference between the sensibility of the prose writer and the dramatic writer. Young writers should read lots of both and write lots of both to find out where their temperament is most clearly suited. I know very few people who write both well. If the young author feels closer to drama, he or she should see many plays, work backstage in plays, act in plays, and *read plays* from different time periods and different styles to see how others have solved the problems of writing for the stage. Also, theatre is much more collaborative than prose.

ON CHANGES OVER THE PAST 20 YEARS IN TERMS OF THEMES AND RECEPTION

I have seen a couple constants: First, the desire to use theatre to educate the young person has not abated; it continues to be the single most destructive element in theatre for young adults and children. Second, most plays written and produced for young adults and children continue to be adaptations from existing prose works. It seems to me that this trend has increased in intensity. Works originally conceived for the stage are fewer and fewer. Thirdly, many more theatres are requesting not only "name" shows (plays with recognizable titles) but "name" shows that tie directly into the curriculums of the surrounding schools. This is a tremendous limiting factor in terms for what plays can be commissioned and produced.

Fourthly, the limits of possible subject matter for plays for young adults have been pushed way back. Almost any subject matter can be treated dramatically. Fifth, censorship, both stated and unstated, is still a very powerful force in theatre for young adults. "Bad" language, non-Christian values, sexual situations are not allowed much.

ON WHERE A HIGH SCHOOL OR MIDDLE SCHOOL TEACHER CAN TURN TO FIND THE BEST NEW SCRIPTS FOR YOUNG ADULT THEATRE

Dramatic Publishing treats the age group with the most respect and publishes more good plays for the age group than anyone else I know. This is why I chose them to publish the acting editions of my young adult plays.

Storytelling

Storytelling is one of the oldest forms of literary entertainment and can definitely stand on its own as a narrative form. At the same time there are many elements held in common with drama. Unlike an oral reading from a book, in storytelling the narrative can change to fit the context and the reactions of the audience. Because of this, dramatic elements such as pace, the use of shifting voices, and vocal expression all become significant. Much has been written about the benefits of the language strategies involved in storytelling (Flynn and Carr, 1994; Fox, 1987; Wagner, 1988).

Folktales, ghost stories, and other forms of traditional literature have already been tested over time as effective for oral retelling. Many narratives are conducive to oral retelling; in fact, storytelling can be an effective way for young adults to extract important dialogue and details from storylines (Mofett and Wagner, 1992). The very act of oral telling can aid in the comprehension and recall of stories (Hamilton and Weiss, 1990). Tips for effective storytelling include

- Read and reread to get the story firmly in mind
- Create a mental sequence
- Use language repetition

Soliloquies and Monologues

A dramatic monologue is basically a speech performed by a single person. When an actor is speaking a character's personal thoughts and motives to herself, this is referred to as a soliloquy. Many plays include monologues or soliloquies within the drama—for example, Hamlet's famous "To be, or not to be" soliloquy.

A few interesting young adult dramas are written as a series of monologues. *With Their Eyes: September 11th—The View from a High School at Ground Zero* is the creation of high school English teacher Annie Thoms and her students. At Stuyvesant High School, only a few blocks from the World Trade Center, students, faculty, and staff had their lives changed on September 11. The students in Ms. Thoms class began collecting oral accounts of that day. The resulting book is a hard-hitting series of dramatic monologues. Students, teachers, staff—a rich tapestry of voices is created to tell the story of 9/11 in an especially authentic way.

Technology Links

The Monologue Database

This database, created by Kellie Powell, is an online resource for scripted monologues. Kelly, a scriptwriter who began publishing plays as a sophomore in high school, has created a database of hundreds of monologues that can be searched by character's name, author, or play. Another key site, though not young adult specific, is the Monologue Search database with over 3000 monologues.

The Monologue Database (http://notmyshoes.net/monologues)

Monologue Search (www.monologuesearch.com)

Julius Lester wrote *Day of Tears* as a series of interior dialogues, yet many teachers have discovered that it works beautifully as a play in monologues. Lester's writing of the text was influenced by several experiences he had with oral delivery of narrative.

When I was in seventh and eighth grade at Northeast Junior High School in Kansas City, Kansas, I belonged to the school's voice chorus, a rather large one, as I recall. We did not sing; we recited poems at school assemblies. The poems were divvied into various timbres of speaking voices. When I started working on *Day of Tears*, that experience of what can be conveyed solely through voices came back to me. And I had a radio show on WBAI in New York for 7 years from 1968 to 1975, and I loved doing radio because it was a medium solely of sound. In *Day of Tears* I tried to keep descriptive passages to the bare minimum so that the emphasis is placed on the voices. (childlit listserv, 2007)

In monologue, everything you discover is mediated by the voice of the character. So the audience is only exposed to the reality of that character. The beautiful thing about *Day of Tears* with all of the different characters is that the realities presented in the monologues intertwine and conflict, forcing the reader/viewer to think critically, creating an informed understanding of the whole. Like *With Their Eyes*, it is a drama in voices, monologues that work together to tell a beautiful story.

Reader's Theatre

In reader's theatre two or more people read aloud from hand-held scripts. With scripts in hand, young adults do not have to worry about forgetting lines and can concentrate on using voice and gestures to develop character. Rather than memorization of lines, readers are concerned with emphasis, pacing, shifting voice for perspective, fluency, and projection. Much has been written about reader's theatre, and the most cited benefits are that it deepens the comprehension of the story (McCaslin, 1980; Stewig, 1983) and enhances the reader's fluency (Black and Stave, 2007).

A few novels, such as Paul Fleischman's *Bull Run*, make excellent reader's theatre. Also, many scripts might alternately be read as reader's theatre. Aaron Shepard has a few scripts on his website (www.aaronshep.com/rt) that are appropriate for young adults, including "Savitri: A Tale of Ancient India" and "Resthaven," a selection adapted from Nancy Farmer's *The Ear, the Eye, and the Arm*. Some teachers have students take a section of a novel and create a script that is then used for reader's theatre. This process has the added benefit of incorporating writing and highlighting the narrative differences between prose and script.

Creative Drama or Improvisation (Story Drama, Process Drama)

There are many different ways of carrying out improvisational dramas in which participants are given a scenario that they must then play out in character. Cecily O'Neil has used the term *process drama* to describe these complex dramatic encounters. In process drama there is no script, no separate audience, and the outcome is unpredictable. This dramatic activity can be used to get students to participate in the storyline, to interpret and reflect.

David Booth has explored using story as a pretext for drama. He asserts, "The action in the story drama develops as the participants solve or work through the dilemma symbolized in the story" (Booth, 2009, p. 107). He encourages readers to experiment with roles and solve problems by entering into and interacting with the imagined world. The original story provides a starting point for these explorations. For example, the scenario of a news show can be used to bring characters from a novel in to interview them. A folktale with numerous variants can be a great pretext. One dramatic activity often carried out involves young adults assuming a role in order to resolve conflict or try out a different perspective. Imagine that the witch from "Rapunzel" is on trial for abuse. What will the various witnesses say? How will the witch explain her actions?

Although literature is not the only possible pretext for process drama, it does provide a firm base for the dramatic encounter. Performing a story is a great way to learn to read, interpret, and negotiate text (Booth, 1994; Booth and Lundy, 1985). A good story drama would have to tighten the story while retaining essential dramatic elements. Many of the objectives of modern education and creative drama are unquestionably shared, including the following:

- Creativity and aesthetic development
- The ability to think critically
- Social growth and the ability to work cooperatively with others
- Improved communication skills
- The development of moral and spiritual values
- Knowledge of self
- Understanding and appreciation of the cultural backgrounds and values of others (McCaslin, 1980, p. 6)

Author Spotlight

Aidan Chambers

Photo courtesy of Aidan Chambers.

Aidan Chambers was born in County Durham, England, in 1934. He was an only child and considered "slow" by his teachers. Ironically, after serving in the Royal Navy, he trained as a teacher and taught high school. He joined an Anglican monastery in 1960. His first plays were published while he was a teacher. Chambers left the monastery in 1967 and a year later became a freelance writer. Six of his novels are part of what he calls the "Dance Sequence." One of these, *Postcards from No Man's Land,* received both the Carnegie Medal and the Printz Award. He and his wife, Nancy, founded Thimble Press and the magazine *Signal* to promote literature for children and young adults. From 2003 to 2006 Chambers was president of the School Library Association in England. Visit his website at www.aidanchambers.co.uk.

SELECTED BOOKLIST

Novels

Breaktime (HarperCollins, 1979)
Dance on My Grave (HarperCollins 1983)
Now I Know (Harper and Row, 1988)

Postcards from No Man's Land (Dutton, 2002)
This Is All (Bodley Head, 2005)
The Toll Bridge (Laura Geringer, 1992)

Scripts

The Dream Cage (Heinemann, 1982)
Only Once (Line by Line, 1998)
De Tolbrug (Ibycus, 2000)

ON HOW HE BECAME AN AUTHOR OF YOUNG ADULT LITERATURE

Though I'd intended to be a professional fiction author from the time I was 15 years old, I could not get published and became a secondary school teacher in order to earn my living. I found I enjoyed teaching very much. My second job involved running the school library, which I had to start from scratch. After 3 years of building it up, many of the pupils still complained they could not find the kind of fiction they wanted to read. One day I asked them to describe the books they wanted. Which they did. That evening two thoughts came together: I wanted to be a writer of fiction but couldn't get published; they wanted books I couldn't find; why shouldn't I try and write the kind of book they wanted? In fact, during the next 2 years I wrote two short novels (they wanted short books), and, at the same time, three plays for the same pupils to perform. The novels and the plays were all published. I'd found an audience, a voice, and characters that seemed natural to me, and so almost by accident—contingency in fact—I became a young adult author.

ON WHETHER HE WRITES WITH A PARTICULAR AUDIENCE IN MIND

When I first started writing young adult fiction, I did: the pupils I was teaching. But after ten years of that kind of writing, the first of what I think of as "my own books" happened. This was *Breaktime*. None of my fiction since then has been written "for" a particular readership or with a particular audience in mind. With *Breaktime*, I made the shift from being a "writer" to being an "author." (Writers write for a known audience: They are reader focused. Authors write in order to make an object—a novel or poem: They are text focused.) "My own" novels are written in the young adult consciousness. They look at the world through the adolescent state of being. They make no concessions in language, form, or content. They are read by anyone who is prepared to enter that state of being. I sometimes try to explain it by saying I write adult books for young people and youth books for adults.

ON THE INSPIRATION FOR HIS STORIES

All my youth novels, beginning with *Breaktime*, belong to a sequence, a family. So they share a genetic make-up. I've known that this was so since the second book,

Dance on My Grave. So each book thereafter was in a sense predictable. Not in detail or even in plot, but in what had to be written. I won't go into the details, which I've written about elsewhere and which can be found on my website if you're interested. When I came to *Postcards*, I knew that the story needed to be set in a city with a fairly liberal attitude to behavior, needed to be set in a foreign country where they speak English well but their own language is not much taught in British schools, and needed a Second World War battle. Holland had all of these and also gave me Rembrandt and Anne Frank, which played into the thematic needs of the story perfectly. Once I identify the right location for a story—its home—and once I know the names of the principal characters, the story then seems to make itself. The necessary "raw material," so to speak, seems to be lying around everywhere just waiting to be used. In fact, I always have much more material than I need or use. The rest is hard steady work and the patience to allow the story to reveal itself to you. A novel, to me, is an organism: it grows according to its genetic structure and must be allowed to grow in its own way.

That said, an essential to me as a writer is reading. I read far more than I write, and could not write if I did not read. Reading is the generator, the source of energy and stimulus. If you like, reading is my inspiration. I'm always aware of what the authors I admire have produced, and though I never believe I can match them, I always want to try. I am a writer because I am a reader.

ON WHAT DISTINGUISHES YOUNG ADULT LITERATURE

Quite simply, that young adult literature is written in the consciousness of a young adult. It isn't just a question of "seeing life through young adult eyes." It is much more than that. The entire book is controlled by the young adult consciousness of the narrator (who might or might not be a character in the story). In adult literature, young adulthood is perceived by "looking back at it." In children's literature, a young adult is merely observed as a child would observe a teenager. The controlling fact is the way the language is used and precisely what and how the narrator chooses to relate in the story. It is about selection and focus of attention and where the "center of gravity" is placed. In truth, there are very few adult writers who actually achieve this completely. Most slip in and out of the young adult consciousness during the course of the story.

ON HOW GAINING INTERNATIONAL ACCLAIM AFFECTS HIS WRITING

[Chambers has been awarded the Carnegie Medal, the Printz, and the Hans Christian Andersen Author Award]

The most obvious impact is on sales and critical attention. The awards have increased both. On myself, the encouragement of such recognition helps keep me going and supports my confidence (which is always fragile). But on what I write or how I write it, there is no impact at all. I continue to write what I would have written and in the way I would have written it.

ON HOW THE NARRATIVE OF DRAMA COMPARES WITH PROSE NARRATIVE

A big (and fascinating) subject! Plays are about social interactions. They are not good at exploring the interior life of people, which is the strength of the novel. There are technical problems to be kept in mind which do not occur when writing a novel—what an actor can and cannot do, the running time of a scene or a play, the possibilities and otherwise of lighting and props and stage effects. Writing a novel is a solitary activity. There is only the writer and the blank page. Writing plays is a communal activity. No play is finished until it has been performed; and no play script is finished until it has gone through the hands of many people—director, actors, designers, technicians—all of whom cause changes to be made and contribute to the finished result. (There is an old theatre joke: If you go into a rehearsal room and see someone sitting in a corner, looking as if he or she is being murdered, that's the author.) When writing plays I think almost exclusively in dialogue and visual and dramatic images. When writing a novel I think much more in narrative flow—telling the tale—and it is the interior life of the characters that interests me. A play has to be much more tightly constructed than a novel and cannot deal with as many themes or threads of ideas as a novel can. It's a "quicker" business. Everything must be to the point and succinct and you have to learn how to pack a great deal of meaning into very few words and actions. (His skill at doing all this is one of the qualities that makes Shakespeare preeminent among all writers.)

ON YOUNG ADULTS AS LITERARY CRITICS

Does "critical" talk about football or baseball kill the pleasure of those sports for their adherents? Does the critical discussion of wine or clothes spoil the pleasure for people who enjoy those things? Of course not. We all know such shared discussion enhances the pleasure. The primary feature is that the participant must first enjoy the activity for its own sake. (I detest football. Talk about it of any kind bores the pants off me.) So the first step is to make reading enjoyable. (How we do this is another large question.) But once we enjoy it, sharing our opinions and views, our likes and dislikes, the things we have found puzzling and the things we understand, increases our pleasure.

As a teacher the first rule is "Begin where the pupils are and with what they know and like, then lead them on from there." After that, knowing how to encourage critical talk of a kind that increases pleasure is a matter of teacherly skill. It is also true that readers are made by readers and nonreaders are made by nonreaders. No one is born not wanting to read. On the contrary. The fact is, people who dislike reading have been taught to dislike it. They have been conditioned by parents, teachers, an antireading culture. Unless a teacher truly loves reading for its own sake and is passionate about it, he or she is unlikely to be a good teacher of reading to anyone, much less to reluctant young people. As you say, I've written at length about these things and cannot repeat it all here.

K-Gar Ollie (Namir Smallwood), A. I. Josh (André Samples), and T-Mac Sam (Samuel Roberson, Jr.) discover, for the first time, modern conveniences like refrigerators and Cheetos in their Fargo apartment in the world premiere of *The Lost Boys of Sudan* on The Children's Theatre Company's Cargill Stage in 2007. Photo by Rob Levine. Reprinted by permission.

Professional Plays

Viewing drama can be more than just entertainment. As spectators, young adults "become involved vicariously in the adventures of characters on the stage" (McCaslin, 1980, p. 4). When watching professional productions, viewers are presented with models for oral delivery. Meaning is coming at them from all of the senses. When viewing drama each audience member chooses where to place their attention—on the words of a speaking actor, on the scenery, on the interactions between characters, or on the body language of an individual.

There are certainly many adult plays that are interesting and relevant to some young adults. August Wilson's *Fences* and Neil Simon's *Biloxi Blues,* for example, have appealed to many young viewers. Less well known but more in tune with the wants and needs of many teens are scripts aimed at young adults. Some of these plays are written for teens to perform, but there are also many that are specifically created for young adult viewers. In Gary Blackwood's *The Shakespeare Stealer,* the choreography of the sword fights and the complicated scenery indicate that at least originally this was meant to be a professional play for young adults. Many of these dramatic productions demand an entire crew: "playwright, director, actor, costume designer, choreographer, set designer, and so on" (Parker-Webster and Van Horn, p. 10). Some of the popular fantasy titles for children and young adults that have been professionally produced as theatre in Britain in recent years, including *Skellig* and *His Dark Materials (The Golden Compass),* are huge productions that would be extremely difficult to carry out at the high school level.

Partaking in Drama

Performing arts help children experience literature in new ways and provide bridges to story writing (Jett-Simpson, 1989; Kardash and Wright, 1987). In drama, story is conveyed by all of the senses becoming more concrete for students, allowing them to draw on multiple literacies. Many mainstream plays can be effectively performed by teen actors. In *Beyond the Bard*, Joshua Rutsky introduces a diverse selection of 50 plays to use in high school. There are also many dramas written directly for young adults, which tend to have the following characteristics:

- Relatively short, taking no more than 50 to 70 minutes
- Relevant, with YA topics
- Flexible casts
- Contemporary settings

Fashion designers Roberto (left, Robert Verhoye) and Jasper (Traci M. Allen) take to the runway to present their collections in the final taping of the reality TV show *Fashion 47*, a world premiere at The Children's Theatre Company in 2007. Photo by Rob Levine. Reprinted by permission.

Some of these scripts are published as trade books: Paul Zindel's *The Effect of Gamma Rays on Man in the Moon Marigolds,* Gary Soto's *Nerdlandia* (a Latino version of *Grease*), and David Almond's *Skellig* (script version) can all be purchased in bookstores. However, most scripts for young adults are published by companies that specialize in dramatic scripts. Copies of the scripts themselves are generally very cheap compared to trade books. Where the publisher and author actually make money is from royalties when the play is performed.

In the Field *Marilee Miller from Anchorage Press Plays*

Marilee Miller directed and produced plays professionally for 30 years before becoming publisher at Anchorage Press Plays, a major publisher of and agency for plays for young people. Miller holds a B.A. in secondary education from Baylor University and a master's degree in theatre.

ON WHAT MAKES A POPULAR DRAMA FOR YOUNG ADULTS

A good story. It helps if the story has relevance to their lives but it doesn't have to be a contemporary reflection of themselves. The story can be in the past, present, or the future. It is the truth of the character that is the test. Young adults are exposed to quality writing through books, film, and quality television. A character in a play must speak with an authentic "voice," not a pedantic lesson.

ON TRENDS IN YOUNG ADULT DRAMA

Today's young adult requires less exposition of character and can assimilate a nonlinear story. The action of the play can begin almost immediately, even if one knows nothing about the background of that character. That's a change from their great grandparents' playwright, Bernard Shaw, who wrote act one just to introduce the characters. Television shortened the character exposition needed for their parents and MTV, sampling, and nonlinear editing have rewired the young adult's brain to be able to pick up the character and the story from almost any point and still process it as a whole.

ON THE QUALITY OF YOUNG ADULT THEATRE BEING WRITTEN

The best stories are being told in the youth/young adult drama field. The writers, readers, and the audience still "believe" that they can make a difference in the world. Hope, bravery, discovery, friendship, and love are still possible—even when there is conflict and especially when there is conflict!

ON SUGGESTIONS FOR YOUNG PEOPLE ENTERING THE FIELD

A play is living language. The words that the character speaks should carry forward the action and the story. They must create as many character voices in their writing as there are characters. Let the characters live a story rather than telling the story. Too often the telling of the story becomes a lecture and the characters only an excuse for narrative.

ON WHAT TEACHERS NEED TO KNOW ABOUT PURCHASING AND ROYALTIES

Scripts are just paperback books when they are purchased for reading. (The same copyright rules apply to a script as to any copyrighted book regarding copying or reproduction.) If scripts are purchased for reading in a class, they are still just paperback books. It is when the reading or performance includes reading or presenting to others from outside the class that it becomes performance. The use of the script has changed and it has become the text of a performance. There is a special performance licensing required called royalty or performance royalty to secure permission (rights) for using the author's words and story in performance. To secure this permission a teacher or director contacts the publisher or agent indicated in the play script and asks for permission and usually is required to pay a per performance fee (royalty). The cost of the purchase of the script and this fee is the writer's pay for the use of their creativity.

ON THE VALUE OF READING SCRIPTS

I see benefit in reading scripts in the English classroom, in the social studies classroom, in the Science classroom, and there are even scripts that help students learn math! Reading scripts silently for exercise is good—but following that use with reading them aloud is even better. Students get to use visual, aural, and kinesthetic learning at the same time! More students get the opportunity to participate. Reading a script silently or aloud needs some introduction for the student who has never experienced it. A little time needs to be spent to introduce the different layout of a script and to explain that there is action and interaction going on that may not be described in detail. Play scripts give more opportunity for young adults to be creative in filling in the blanks with their own interpretation.

In the Field *Workshopping a Play*

William Strauss is a co-founder of Cappies, a national high school theatre program that stresses writing reviews of dramatic productions by other high schools. Strauss is co-author of nine books, including Millennial Rising *(2000). He is also playwright of three musicals:* MaKiddo, Free-the-Music.com, *and* Anazazi. *He is also well known for his work with the Capital Steps, which he co-founded and directs.*

A really cool concept that a few high schools have gotten involved in is workshopping a play still in progress. William Strauss and his publisher Crimsonblue Productions have offered schools that chance with great success through two musicals: *MaKiddo* and *Free-the-Music.com.* Working with a play this way can be very intense, because the participants' transactions with text help create the final script. *Free-the-Music.com* (then called *Stopscandal.com*) was workshopped at Osborne Park High School in Virginia. The play is very topical, dealing with young adults who were caught uploading and downloading music. A big corporation tries to stop them and the battle moves to the U.S. Congress. The focus then turns to corruption in the Congress and the ability of a large music company to influence the political process. The workshopping idea was so successful in this instance that the high school students took the play on the road to the off-Broadway Maverick Theatre in New York.

ON THE INTEREST IN WORKSHOPPING NEW YOUNG ADULT DRAMA

One of my interests has been in trying to construct teen musicals that are not about the 1950s or 60s. I see these high schools doing *Bye Bye Birdie* and *Grease*. They don't speak to teenagers anymore; they are about their grandparents' experience. And there has been nothing on Broadway in the last couple of decades that has spoken to the contemporary teen experience. That's what I was trying to address in these two shows in different ways.

They feel as though they are not going to sell tickets unless it's a familiar name. Which I think is incorrect; I'm not sure people only want to see movies they've seen 12 times. I'm for something new. The idea of a brand new fresh musical on a contemporary topic should draw a crowd; you just have to market it that way. I would personally support a constitutional amendment banning *Bye Bye Birdie* from being produced anymore. It's a bit painful to watch teens singing about Ed Sullivan. I'm for something new!

ON WHAT KINDS OF CHANGES TO THE PLAY OCCURRED DURING THE WORKSHOPPING

Oh, there were all the script changes and musical changes. This is how you develop a musical. You have to set it up. We have developed two shows now (*Free-the-Music.com* and *MaKiddo*) through a series of high school productions. Both of those shows are now completed with set scripts and scores. We developed them that way through high school shows. In one case, *Free-the-Music.com,* we had a show at a college as well. But it's mostly high school.

ON THE PROCESS

I listened to how they shifted some of the lines into their own vernacular and I encouraged them to adjust the dialogue in ways they found useful. And of course I watch to see what directors do and learn from that and from the director's notes. It gives you ideas for fixing scenes and fixing dialogues. You don't change the music as much.

In the Field *Playwriting at the Key School*

Chip Lamb is the department chair at the Pomfret School in Connecticut. Previously he was the director of the theatre program at the Key School, an independent PK–12 day school in Annapolis, Maryland. In addition to teaching playwriting and acting, he has directed nearly 30 productions at Key. He has taught at the University of New Hampshire, Brandeis University, and the Pomfret School in Connecticut, where he served as an adjunct faculty member for 10 years. Lamb holds an A.B. from Kenyon College and a M.F.A. from Brandeis University. He is a member of the Actor's Equity Association.

Playwriting is not a language art that has received much attention in schools, though there are several awards for student playwrights, most notably the Michael Kanin Playwriting Awards Program (www.keene.edu/events/actf/playwriting.cfm). Before becoming the chair of the drama department at the Pomfret School, Chip Lamb taught an introduction to playwriting course at the Key School in Annapolis, Maryland. The course was multiage for grades 10 through 12. At the end of the year the course culminated in a production. Students engaged in writing life story monologues. Lamb asserts, "These kids have something to say that's not just about trivial things, but about things that are really important to us as human beings. . . . They think very seriously about themselves, about their family, about society" (Lamb, personal correspondence, 2004). His students used theatre as a way to communicate. A one-act play written by one of the students was performed by professional actors at the Center Stage in Baltimore.

The playwriting course used Aristotle's six elements of drama as a template. Each element was defined and explored through readings of published plays. The playwrights were then expected to demonstrate the use of the elements in dialogue or monologue form, usually in a five- to seven-page short play or scene. In addition to these ongoing writing assignments, each student was expected to complete a 10-minute play at the end of the first quarter and a fully realized one-act play at the semester's conclusion. The last 2 or 3 weeks of the course took a tutorial form as the playwrights revised their drafts of the one-act. Then, all the one-acts were read for a small invited audience.

Four of these one-acts were chosen for production. After a 5-week rehearsal period, the plays were given three public performances. The scriptwriting course was offered in the fall; the productions were rehearsed and performed in the spring. Their production schedule also included a fall play just before Thanksgiving and a musical performed with a full orchestra in early March.

The original impulse for the creation of this course was a lack of creative writing opportunities in the Upper School. As consumers of theatre, television, and film, the students were quite familiar with different forms of dramatic writing. The course allowed the students to use theatre as a place of self-expression and a forum for their ideas, aspirations, and dreams. Also because theatre is a collaborative process, each writer worked in a communal environment where his or her work was constantly shared with others. This sharing served to validate the individual creativity of the playwrights and strengthened their bond with each other.

In the production of the one-acts the writer worked with the director Lamb to shape the play into a cohesive and compelling performance. The actors were energized by creating a role for the first time and collaborating with both a director and a writer. The playwright's text was given the ultimate test by the process of rehearsal and performance, which informed future writing attempts.

Selection Criteria

In addition to the general criteria for selecting and evaluating literature for young adults, when looking at dramatic scripts one should consider the following:

- Is there lively and credible development of story and characters?
- Is the story shown in the dramatic action and not just told?
- Are the characters believable?
- If there is a message, is it part of the character development?
- Are stage directions incorporated to aid with production?

Survey of the Literature

A wealth of dramatic scripts are aimed at young adults either as the audience, the cast, or both. The following lists might be a good start to finding the best scripts for your needs, and it introduces the wide variety of titles that are available.

Novio Boy: A Play by Gary Soto is a humorous tale about dating, providing multiple perspectives. Novio Boy, copyright © 1997 by Gary Soto, reprinted by permission of Houghton Mifflin Harcourt Publishing Company.

Classical

Mark Twain's Huckleberry Finn by Rita Grauer and John Urquhart. A retelling of Twain's classic. Anchorage, 1999.

The Odyssey retold by Gregory Falls and Kurt Beattie. A quite faithful retelling of Homer's classic. Music, mime, and theatrical effects enhance the drama. Anchorage, 1978.

Othello or Tracking the Green Eyed Monster adapted from Shakespeare by Nancy Linehan Charles. A retelling of Shakespeare's story of jealousy and pride. Storytellers narrating from the sidelines keep the plot on track and encourage the audience to participate. Dramatic Publishing, 2000.

Traditional

Androcles and the Lion by Aurand Harris. A musical retelling of Aesop's fables. Anchorage, 1964.

Cinderella by Charlotte Charpenning. Dramatic retelling of "Cinderella." Anchorage, 1940.

The Crane Wife by Barbar Carlisle. Retelling of a popular Japanese folktale using Japanese theatre conventions. Includes the role of a signer (American sign language). Musical scenes and dancers are used to good effect. Anchorage, 1997.

Ezigbo, the Spirit Child by Max Bush and Adaora Nzilibe Schmiedl. Based on an Igbo (African) folktale about a spirit child who is torn between the people she loves and the spirit world. Anchorage, 2001.

Hansel and Gretel: The Little Brother and Little Sister by Max Bush. Based on the Brothers Grimm story. Anchorage, 1995.

The Oldest Story Ever Told by David Eliot. Dramatic retelling of "Cinderella." Anchorage, 2000.

The Pied Piper of Hamlin dramatized by Tim Wright. Close retelling of the legend we know. Anchorage, 2003.

Rapunzel by Max Bush. Retelling of "Rapunzel" that includes a song, Rapunzel's lament. New Plays for Children, 1986.

Selkie by Laurie Brooks. Based on Celtic myths of the ocean creatures who look like seals but can transform into human form. In the collection *Theatre for Young Audiences* ed. Coleman Tennings. Anchorage Press, 1997.

The Trial of the Big Bad Wolf by Joseph Robinette. A fractured retelling with folkloric characters who have secrets to hide. A comedy that could be performed by children, but would make a wonderful production for children. Dramatic Publishing, 1999.

Speculative Fiction

The Ghost of the River House by Max Bush. A ghost story about a girl, her father, a fishing trip, and a ghost. Anchorage, 1997.

Liza and the Riddling Cave by John Urquhart. Set in Appalachia in the 1930s. Siblings searching for their father have to match wits with a pair of ghosts. Anchorage, 1999.

Contemporary Themes

The Analysis of Mineral #4 by Moses Goldberg. A science mystery drama that takes place in a high school chemistry lab. Anchorage, 1982.

Black Butterfly, Jaguar Girl and Other Super Hero Girls, Like Me, Columba by Luis Alfaro et al. A one-act play with five female characters who basically come of age, progressing from 12 years of age to 16. Play scripts forthcoming.

Deadly Weapons by Laurie Brooks. A thriller involving three teenage friends who decide to take the law into their own hands. They are forced to confront the consequences of their actions. Dramatic Publishing, 2002.

The Effect of Gamma Rays on Man in the Moon Marigolds by Paul Zindel. Story of a dysfunctional family. Harper & Row, 1971.

Nerdlandia by Gary Soto. A comical look at love. Putnam, 1999.

Newcomer by Janet Thomas. A young refugee named Mai Li who is a newcomer to high school meets Benny, a popular Chinese American student who is asked to be her guide to campus but refuses. Anchorage, 1987.

The Pinballs adapted by A. Harris from the Betsy Byers novel of the same name. Three children abused and abandoned are bounced around like pinballs from foster home to foster home. Anchorage, 1992.

Private High by Thomas Martin. Five former students from a high school return to share their thoughts on alcohol at a school assembly. Becomes more complex when it turns out that one of the former students is lying. Anchorage, 1987.

The Shape of a Girl by Joan MacLeod. Based on the 1997 murder of a schoolgirl by her peers. The main character attempts to understand what has happened at her school. Talon Books, 2002.

Historical Fiction

Across the Plains by Sandra Asher. Follows the Donner Party's 19th-century migration from Illinois to California and is based on the actual letters, diaries, and newspaper accounts of the journey. Dramatic Publishing, 1997.

And the Tide Shall Cover the Earth by Norma Cole. The story of a girl and her grandmother in the Appalachia of the 1930s. The Wolf Creek Dam has been built and hard rains are falling. Farms and homes are being flooded and people have to move. A young girl and her grandmother clash over whether to go. Anchorage, 1994.

Conestoga Stories by Susan Beck. The storylines are taken directly from the letters of men and women who traveled the Oregon Trail in the late 19th century. The characters brave blizzards, disease, and hardship on their journey to Nebraska territory. Music by Jonathen Cole. Anchorage, 1995.

Goodbye Marianne by Irene Kirstein Watts. The story of one Jewish family in Germany starting in 1938. Marianne befriends a boy named Ernest but when she finds out that he is a Hitler Youth and he discovers that she is Jewish things get complicated. Her parents decide to send her away to Britain in what would come to be called the "Kindertransportes." McClelland Stewart, 1998.

Lincoln's Log (Or Better Angels) by Barry Kornhauser. A sick 18-year-old Tad Lincoln reminisces on the Civil War and his time in the White House. Aesthetically complex with puppets, shadows, period music, and projection of archival photographs. Anchorage, 1999.

Esperanza (Erin Nicole Hampe) longs for her mother (Melanie Rey) in the world premiere of *Esperanza Rising*, based on the award-winning novel by Pam Muñoz Ryan, at The Children's Theatre Company in 2006. Photo by Rob Levine. Reprinted by permission.

Mother Hicks by Susan Zeder. Set in Illinois during the Great Depression. The narrator uses sign language to tell the story and a chorus and other characters interpret what he is saying. Anchorage, 1986.

Paper Lanterns, Paper Cranes by Brian Kral. A young woman shows up in a Japanese hospital and appears to be suffering from exposure to fallout from the bombing. Anchorage, 2002.

The Rose of Treason by James DeVita. A group of German university students form an underground movement after learning about the atrocities Nazis are committing during the war. Anchorage, 2003.

Biographical

Jim Thorpe, All American by Saul Levitt. About the Native American athlete who won two gold medals at the 1912 Olympics. Anchorage, 1980.

A Woman Called Truth by Sandra Asher. Celebrates the life of Sojourner Truth from the day the young Sojourner is sold away from her family to her speeches as an abolitionist and women's rights advocate. Dramatic Publishing, 1991.

Differences between Dramatic Narrative and Prose Narrative

One productive exploration that is often used with young readers to highlight dramatic script is to carry out a comparison between prose and scripted narrative. There are a number of texts that have been written in both formats that allow a ready comparison of the characteristics of both. Generally speaking, scripts will include the following:

- More dialogue and less narration
- Sets and staging as important factors to be considered
- Shorter length—meaning if it is adapted from prose, something will have to be cut
- Dramatic tension and action combined to reveal character
- A different way of transacting with text in which all of the senses are impacted

Comparisons can be made between any two prose and script texts, but the most effective comparisons can be made with a storyline that has been written in both formats. In the case of *Anne Frank and Me* (Bennett) the novel and the dramatic script are written by the same authors.

ANNE *(both scared and brave)*: Nicole, if you're from the future and you really read my diary, then you know what happens to me.

NICOLE: No—

ANNE: Yes. You can tell me.

NICOLE *(chagrined)*: I never finished it.

ANNE: You never— *(She bursts out laughing)*. Peter put you up to this!

NICOLE: But I did read a very juicy part about you and him, how you loved him and didn't think you needed to wait until you were "a suitable age"—

ANNE: I'm a free thinker!

NICOLE: You sound like my little sister. She's planning to run away with Clark Gable.

ANNE: Don't tell Peter, but I don't think he's the perfect boy for me after all. I'd like to break a million hearts, wouldn't you?

NICOLE: Oh, yes!

ANNE: And see the whole world—

NICOLE: And have a million adventures.

ANNE: I want to see Paris!

NICOLE: Oh, it's wonderful—after the war I'll take you everywhere. The Louvre, and the Eiffel Tower —

ANNE: Where do you want to go?

NICOLE: Oh, I don't know. Palestine, maybe.

ANNE: Really?

NICOLE: I think a friend of mine is there.

ANNE: Then we'll go there. Everything is possible. Don't you see?

Nicole heard the tremor in Anne's voice as the train slowed. "Nicole, I want to ask you something. If you really are from the future, and you read my diary, then you must know what happens to me."

"No—"

"You can tell me," Anne insisted. "Please."

Nicole hesitated. "I never finished it."

"You never—?" Anne burst out laughing. "Very funny. Now I know that Peter put you up to this!"

"I did read a very juicy part about you and him, how you loved him and didn't think you needed to wait until you were 'a suitable age.'"

Anne grinned mischievously, "I'm a free thinker!"

"You should like my little sister. She's planning to run away with Clark Gable."

Anne leaned close, a conspiratorial gleam in her eye. "Don't tell Peter, but I don't think he's the perfect boy for me after all. I'd like to break a million hearts, wouldn't you?"

"Oh, yes."

"And see the whole world—"

"And have a million adventures."

"I want to see Paris!"

"It's wonderful—after the war I'll take you everywhere," Nicole promised. "The Louvre, and the Eiffel Tower—"

"Where do you want to go?"

Nicole thought for a moment. "Palestine, maybe."

"Palestine? Really?"

(ANNE stares into NICOLE's eyes giving her the gift of faith. Finally, in a tiny, quavering voice, NICOLE begins to sing the Zionist anthem, "Hatikva." ANNE, her voice just as tiny, joins in. They do not get very far into the song when the train's brakes squeal, then a loud, slamming sound. The stage might go to black except for a search light—which could swing over the audience. The sound of the cattle car door being opened. *Note:* Some Gestapo voices can be pre-recorded, as well as additional voices of people screaming and crying through this scene change.)

From the script *Anne Frank and Me,* pp. 77–78.

"I think a friend of mine is there."

"Then you'll go there." Anne squeezed Nicole's hand. "Everything is possible. Don't you see?"

Anne's eyes searched Nicole's, and Nicole saw herself reflected in them—grimy, hungry, lice-ridden. But this moment she knew: She would not change places for a moment with the people who had made her that way.

From the novel *Anne Frank and Me,* pp. 227–228.

Direct comparisons like this allow the reader to better understand how narrative unfolds in prose and script. *Skellig* (Almond), *The Shakespeare Stealer* (Blackwood), and *Esperanza Rising* (Ryan) are among the many narratives available in both formats.

In the Field   *"Cappies" Teen Theatre Critics*

William Strauss (introduced on p. 189), co-founder of the Cappies, discusses the organization and the process of getting young adults to review dramatic productions.

ON WHERE THE CAPPIES IDEA CAME FROM

The idea for Cappies came in part because I was a theatre parent back in the 1990s. All of my kids have been involved in musical theatre (two were very active in theatre) and I noticed that there was no media coverage of their shows and in one case I contacted the paper and said you should review this and they said that they did not have the stringers to cover them. I offered to write a review and they said the production is over, why would we want to review it now and I said the sports games are over too and you write summaries of those. There just wasn't a system in place that made it easy for the papers to do this. In the spring of 1999 I was writing a book called *Millenials Rising* about today's teenagers and Columbine happened on the 20th of April and I was invited to be part of a television panel on C-SPAN about youth violence. And one of the other guests was a high school sophomore. I spoke with her in the green room and asked her what she did extracurricularly, and she told me that she wanted to be a theatre critic, but she couldn't review her own shows because she was usually in them. We talked about how it might be interesting to have students from her school review shows for another school and vice versa. The idea stuck with me. I spoke with the theatre resource teacher Judy Bowns, who has been my co-founder and I brought up the idea of a round robin of schools, of getting some schools who wanted to review other shows to create critic teams. And then to get the papers to publish those. She checked with some theatre teachers and there was some interest. So I called the *Washington Post* and I proposed that we send them 200-word reviews of high school shows that would be written by students from other schools. They said that's too short, how about 300 to 400 words and make it two per show and how about can we send a photographer. It turns out that just a few days before had had a meeting following Columbine about the need to find new creative ways to celebrate positive things teens do other than sports and proms. The timing was good.

I went back to the schools in the area and reported that and they were quite excited. We began in the fall of 1999 with 13 schools from the Fairfax County public school system, plus one parochial school, Bishop Ireton. The first Cappie show had the reviews published and we got full page treatment in the *Post*. We couldn't believe that high school theatre would ever get this kind of coverage, so we got a whole lot of other schools contacting us wanting to join. When that first school year 1999–2000 ended we had 23 schools in the program.

And all along we were promising them a Cappies Gala. I was feeling a little bit like Harold Hill in the boys band. I was promising this big Tonys-like event and I figured I had to move beyond the think method and actually put this on. So we organized that and had the student critics vote for awards. And we had a Cappies Gala in which we filled a 1,400-seat high school auditorium at Hayfield Secondary School. And it was a huge success. Everybody had a wonderful time. They were dressed formally and snippets from the nominated shows were included.

And the school administrators decided that they wanted to do this at the Kennedy Center the next year. So we approached the Kennedy Center, and sure enough they were willing to host it starting in June of 2001. For the 2000–2001 school year we've been having our Cappies Galas at the Kennedy Center Concert Hall with 2,400 seats and enormous festivities. It's kind of like a high school sports championship meets the Tonys.

Very high intensity. Three hours of terrific entertainment. Regional select casting. Opening and closing numbers. Shows that are nominated for the top musical and play awards get to put on pieces from their shows. And we get local dignitaries, school officials, political people, managing directors of major theatres—things like that to present the awards and editors from the papers, publishers. And so that's been quite exciting. We now have about a dozen newspapers that participate. Typically we will have anywhere from four to seven Cappies reviews published of each show that we review. We currently have in our program this year 55 schools, about 350 critics on the roster. At a typical Cappies show there will be usually about 35 to 45 critics and two mentors who are usually theatre teachers or English teachers from participating schools, each of whom are responsible to volunteer twice over the course of the year to lead discussions, to supervise the critics, and then to receive the reviews on an online system and select the reviews that will be published. They'll review a show on a Friday or Saturday night. They're required to submit their reviews by around midday on Sunday.

The mentors screen the reviews, select the top ones for publication, those are edited carefully, forwarded to the *Washington Post*. All reviews are forwarded to the performing school on Monday. So they post usually 35 or 40 reviews on the Web, reviews written by students from around the area. The reviews can be critical, but they stress the constructive side; they praise more than they criticize. Let's say they range from A triple plus to a B minus. We're not closing shows down here. When they criticize, they cannot do it by name.

So they can say the performer sang off-pitch but they can't say that so-and-so sang on-pitch. And it's a quite exciting thing. When Cappie critics come to a show, [there's a Cappies' room that's prepared for them] the parent boosters provide refreshments, there's a special roped-off area where they get complimentary tickets right in the center of the house. They walk in 1 minute before curtain [and they're quite a conspicuous group]. Everybody knows they are there. The cast and crew who are putting on the show are quite excited. And then not only do they write their reviews, but then at the end of the year, after they have seen all the shows, critics who've reviewed five or more shows get to vote as Awards Judges. They do all this on an online system that was developed by a team of students from Thomas Jefferson High School for Science and Technology. They constructed a very modern Web infrastructure for this program and a voting system that would put the state of Florida to shame. It's quite something what they came up with and that's the basis for the nominations and awards. We have 35 awards categories: 3 for critics, 9 for tech, and 23 for performance. It's like an expanded Tonys.

And in the last 2 years the program has gone national. We currently have nine Cappies programs nationwide. Ours is the largest here with 55 schools, but we have other very large ones in places like Cincinnati and south Florida. We've got programs in Baltimore; Orange County, California; Dallas; El Paso; Kansas City; Springfield, Missouri. We help put those together, we construct training tapes, and we stay in touch. We go to their galas, and their program directors come to ours and our annual meeting. And they follow the same framework, with same rules for awards and for review writing.

One further thing about the Cappies: each summer we have the Cappies National Theatre centered at the Kennedy Center here in Washington, D.C. We base it at a local high school and we do shows at the Kennedy Center. Each of our original programs can send the lead actor and lead actress winners in the play and musical categories. So the top four performers from their programs are eligible for this. They become part of a national Cast of Top Cappie award winners who then workshop new material at the Kennedy Center Theatre Lab. We put on a STARZ show, it's a variety show, and then a series of short plays in the second week, and then they workshop a brand new musical in the third week. It's quite an extraordinary cast that we assemble. These are the best young performers of their community from around the country. They stay with host families.

In order to join the Cappies a school system would first have to construct a Cappies Program in their area. To start a Cappies Program you need at least four schools in a region where they can review each other's shows, we recommend trying to find seven or eight schools and even more if you can but you can start at that level. You find four or more schools willing to do it, you appoint a steering committee, and you apply to us. We help the new program go through the process of getting word out about the program, training critics, contacting newspapers, getting reviews published. Everything is done online. They apply online, and the schools in their program apply online. Everything is done through the Web system I described.

The way a group of schools would apply would be by going to our website (www.cappies.com) and applying online. They could go to our homepage and they'll find places to go to learn about the program and to apply. It's all volunteer. We are fueled by volunteers. We got a grant from the William T. Grant Foundation in New York to help a little bit with outreach. On the whole what makes us go is a very large number of people volunteering enormous numbers of hours, including theatre teachers and of course the student critics. The newspapers too. The *Washington Post* hosts our critics' training here and takes an active role in that. We've had tremendous support from the papers here, and in most parts of the country: the *Cincinnati Enquirer*, the *Dallas Morning News*, they've been huge for the Cappies.

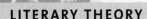

LITERARY THEORY

Critical Literacy

There is actually a wide array of theoretical and practical ideas that fall under the notion of critical literacy. All share in common the following concepts:

- Literacy is a social and cultural construction.
- Its functions and uses are never neutral or innocent.
- Meanings constructed in texts are ideological and involved in producing, reproducing, and maintaining relations of power that are unequal. (Comber and Kamler, 1997)

Perhaps the key to understanding critical literacy is the idea that texts include statements, assumptions, and attitudes that are ideological. A text is produced in a milieu, by a person with political convictions, and so the text always carries with it an ideological stance. All books contain hidden messages and assumptions about the world. Mainstream literature tends to perpetuate the values and cultural conceptions of the ruling group. Even when written with good intentions, no book is free of bias, as Perry Nodelman (1993) suggests: "Because writers assume that their specific view of reality is universal, texts act as a subtle kind of propaganda, and tend to manipulate unwary readers into an unconscious acceptance of their values" (p. 94). Books for young readers, even when not overtly didactic, have served the pedagogical function of reinforcing societal norms. Furthermore, adult authority figures tend to mediate most of the books young adults explore, and the adult mediator is not a disinterested party. The reader also comes to the text with assumptions and convictions, and critical readers might attempt to both demystify the text and recognize the various political agendas (including their own) that are brought to their reading of the book.

Literary study can help readers "notice . . . 'systems of dominance' and 'systems of privilege'" (Edelsky, 1991, p. 12). Literature might even provide "a context for students to become conscious of their operating world view and to examine critically alternative ways of understanding the world and social relations" (Glasgow, 2001, p. 54). How do we make sure that young readers do not unconsciously or uncritically assimilate the encoded messages? Critical literacy seeks to explore how power is exercised in textual practices and help readers learn to ferret out the ideological designs of these books. "Learning to read and write," suggests Anderson, is "part of the process of becoming conscious of one's experience as historically constructed within specific power relations" (Anderson and Irvine, 1993, p. 82). Teaching young adults to read for the ideological messages in books is important if we wish them to be informed readers and, ultimately, to participate intelligently in cultural discourse. Critical literacy is therefore as much a way of socializing young readers as a way of looking at literature.

Readers are constructed and a critical literacy lens will help them make clear "the connection between knowledge and power" (Aronowitz and Giroux, 1985, p. 132). Basically, readers should be empowered to explore and question the assumptions about the world and the values that underlie the literature they read. For example they should be able to question simplistic stereotypes and unequal power relations in society. Ultimately, the goal of critical literacy would be to position students as readers/writers with real power who can engage in critical dialogue with an author or text.

For Further Reading

To begin an investigation into critical literacy as it applies to young adult literature you might commence with the following readings:

Anderson, Gary, and Patricia Irvine. "Informing Critical Literacy with Ethnography." In Colin Lankshear and Peter McLaren (eds.), *Critical Literacy: Politics, Praxis, and the Postmodern*. SUNY Press, 1993, 81–104.

Aronowitz, Stanley, and Henry Giroux. *Education under Siege*. Bergin-Garvey, 1985.

Beck, Ann. "A Place for Critical Literacy." *Journal of Adolescent and Adult Literacy, 48*, 2005, 392–400.

CLIP Podcast, www.clippodcast.com

Comber, Barbara. "Classroom Explorations in Critical Literacy." *Australian Journal of Language and Literacy*, *16*(1), 1993, 73–83.

Comber, Barbara, and Barbara Kamler. *Critical Literacies: Politicizing the Language Classroom*. 1997. www.schools.ash.org.au/litweb/barb1.html

Davens, Lori, and Thomas Bean. *Critical Literacy: Context, Research, and Practice in the K–12 Classroom*. Sage, 2007.

Foucault, Michel. "The Subject and Power." In Hubert Dreyfus and Paul Rabinow, *Michel Foucault: Beyond Structuralism and Hermeneutics*. University of Chicago Press, 1983, 208–226.

Glasgow, Jacqueline. "Teaching Social Justice through Young Adult Literature." *English Journal, 90,* 2001, 54–61.

Lewis, Cynthia. *Literacy Practices as Social Acts: Power, Status, and Cultural Norms in the Classroom*. Lawrence Erlbaum, 2001.

Luke, A., and P. Freebody. "Critical Literacy and the Question of Normativity: An Introduction." In S. Muspratt, M. Luke, and P. Freebody, *Constructing Critical Literacies: Teaching and Learning Textual Practice*. Hampton Press, 1996, 1–13.

Luke, C. "Media and Cultural Studies in Australia." *Journal of Adolescent & Adult Literacy, 42,* May 1999, 622–626.

Pailliotet, A. W., L. Semali, R. K. Rodenberg, J. K. Giles, & S. L. Macaul. "Intermediality: Bridge to Critical Media Literacy." *The Reading Teacher, 54,* 2000, 208–219.

Simpson, A. "Critical Questions: Whose Questions?" *The Reading Teacher, 50,* 1996, 118–127.

Vasquez, Vivian. "Critical Literacy." In Joanne Larson and J. Marsh, *Framing Literacies: Multiple Perspectives on Literacy Learning*. Sage, 2005.

To begin an investigation into myth criticism as it applies to a young adult literature you might commence with the following readings:

Campbell, Joseph. *The Hero with a Thousand Faces*. Commemorative ed., Bollingen, 2004.

Hearne, Betsy. *Beauty and the Beast: Visions and Revisions of an Old Tale*. University of Chicago Press, 1989.

May, Jill. *Children's Literature and Critical Theory*. Oxford University Press, 1997.

Stephens, John and R. McCallum. *Retelling Stories, Framing Culture*. Garland, 1998.

Watson, Jinx Stapleton. "Appreciating Gantos' Jack Henry as an Archetype" *The New Advocate*, *14*(4), 2001, 379–385.

Wolf, Virginia. "Paradise Lost? The Displacement of Myth in Children's Novels," *Studies in the Literary Imagination, 18*(2), Fall 1985, 47–64

Storytelling

Bruchac, Joseph. *Tell Me a Tale: A Book about Storytelling,* Harcourt, 1997.

Lipman, Doug. *Improving Your Storytelling*. August House, 1999.

MacDonald, Margret. *Storyteller's Start-Up Book*. August House, 1993.

Sawyer, Ruth. *The Way of the Storyteller*. Penguin, 1977.

Monologues

Brown, Kent (ed.). *Scenes and Monologues for Young Actors*. Dramatic Publishing, 2000.

Reader's Theatre

Black, Alisa, and Anna Stave. *A Comprehensive Guide to Reader's Theatre: Enhancing Fluency and Comprehension in the Middle School and Beyond*. IRA, 2007.

Black, Ann. *Readers Theatre for Middle School Boys*. Libraries Unlimited, 2008.

Flynn, Rosalind. *Dramatizing the Content with Curriculum-Based Reader's Theatre*. IRA, 2007.

Neill, Dixon, Anne Davies, and Colleen Politano. *Learning with Readers Theatre: Building Connections*. Peguis, 1996.

Walker, Lois. *Readers Theatre Strategies in the Middle and Junior High Classroom*. Meriwether, 1996.

Creative Drama

Booth, David. *Story Drama: Creating Stories through Role Playing, Improvising and Reading Aloud*. Stenhouse, 2005.

Booth, David. *Story Drama: Reading, Writing and Roleplaying across the Curriculum*. Pembroke, 2004.

Heinig, Ruth Beall. *Improvisation with Favorite Tales*. Heinemann, 1992.

Keller, Betty. *Improvisations in Creative Drama*. Meriwether, 1988.

O'Neil, Cecily. *Drama Worlds: A Framework for Process Drama*. Heinemann, 1995.

Schneider, Jenifer Jasinski, Theresa Rogers, and Thomas P. Crumpler (eds.). *Process Drama and Multiple Literacies: Addressing Social, Cultural, and Ethical Issues*. Heinemann, 2006.

Dramatic Performances

Bray, Errol. *Playbuilding: A Guide for Group Creation of Plays with Young People*. Heinemann, 1994.

Cassady, Marsh. *The Theatre and You! An Introductory Text on All Aspects of Theatre*. Meriwether, 1992.

Pura, Talia. *Stages: Creative Ideas for Teaching Drama*. J. Gordon Shillingford, 2002.

5
Speculative Fiction
Fantasy, Science Fiction, Horror

We are tapping into some of the most powerful images and symbols in human culture: the struggle between good and evil, or destruction and growth; the sources of ancient myths and legends, the great hero sagas that inspire people when we need inspiration most.

— *Tamora Pierce*

Speculative Fiction Text Set

Fantasy

Abarat by Clive Barker

Airborn by Kenneth Oppel

The Alchemyst by Michael Scott

The Amazing Maurice and His Educated Rodents by Terry Pratchett

The Amulet of Sumarkind by Jonathan Stroud

Coraline by Neil Gaiman

Creature of the Night by Kate Thompson

The Golden Compass by Phillip Pullman

Harry Potter and the Half-Blood Prince by J. K. Rowling

Hero: A Novel by Perry Moore

Howl's Moving Castle by Diana Wynne Jones

The Hunting of the Last Dragon by Sherryl Jordan

Inkheart by Cornelia Funke

The Legend of the Wandering King by Laura Gallego Garcia

Leviathan by Scott Westerfield

Moribito: Guardian of the Spirit by Nahoko Uehashi

Nation by Terry Pratchett

Repossessed by A. M. Jenkins

The Ropemaker by Peter Dickinson

The Schwa Was Here by Neal Schusterman

The Sea of Trolls by Nancy Farmer

Shamer's Daughter by Lene Kaaberbøl

Summerland by Michael Chabon

Trickster's Choice by Tamora Pierce

Wolf Brother by Michelle Paver

The Year of the Hangman by Gary Blackwood

Science Fiction

Among the Betrayed by Margaret Haddix

Crash Course by Matthew Reilly

The Destiny of Linus Hoppe by Anne-Laure Bordoux

Diary of Pelly D by L. J. Adlington

Dragon and Thief by Timothy Zahn

Feed by M. T. Anderson

Framed by Malcolm Rose

The House of the Scorpion by Nancy Farmer

The Hunger Games by Suzanne Collins

The Knife of Never Letting Go by Patrick Ness

The Last Dog on Earth by Daniel Ehrenhaft

Life as We Knew It by Susan Pfeffer

Little Brother by Cory Doctorow

Rash by Pete Hautman

The Secret under My Skin by Janet McNaughton

Sight by Adrienne Maria Vrettos

Singing the Dogstar Blues by Alison Goodman

The Sterkarm Handshake by Susan Price

Taylor Five by Ann Halam

Horror

A Banquet for Hungry Ghosts by Ying Chang Compestine

Being Dead by Vivian Vande Velde

Bliss by Lauren Myracle

Blood and Chocolate by Annette Curtis Klause

The Boy Who Couldn't Die by William Sleator

Cirque du Freak by Darren Shan

City of Bones by Cassandra Clare

Eternal by Cynthia Leitich Smith

The Forest of Hands and Teeth by Carrie Ryan

Generation Dead by Daniel Waters

The Graveyard Book by Neil Gaiman

High School Bites by Liza Conrad

The Last Apprentice by Joseph Delany

Monstrumologist by Rick Yancey

Peeps by Scott Westerfield

Poison by Chris Wooding

The Presence by Eve Bunting

Revenge of the Witch by Joseph Delany

Skeleton Man by Joseph Bruchac

Twilight by Stephenie Meyer

Wolf Moon by Charles de Lint

Understanding Speculative Worlds

The term *speculative fiction* is used to encompass a wide range of literature, including three sometimes overlapping genres: fantasy, science fiction, and horror. Readers who are not themselves lovers of speculative fiction often gloss over the differences in these genres. In fact, many discussions of literature for young readers tend to emphasize the concept of "modern fantasy," leaving science fiction and horror with only a short discussion within the larger framework of fantastic worlds.

Young adults are often unable to put into words the similarities and distinctions among these genres (which can certainly be fuzzy), but when they start to think about the types of characters they would expect to find in science fiction, fantasy, and horror, the general distinctions become clearer.

Common Characters in Speculative Fiction

Fantasy	*Science Fiction*	*Horror*
Wizards	Aliens	Vampires
Elves	Mutants	Ghosts
Dragons	Robots	Werewolves
Trolls	Androids	Ghouls
Fairies	Time travelers	Monsters
Talking animals	Futuristic humans	Zombies
Unicorns	Clones	Psychos

A quick brainstorming session can lead to great discussions about the possible distinctions and connections in these three genres. Indeed, though they are all based in imaginative worlds, vast differences can exist. Fantasy tends to arise out of the realm of myth, folklore, and magic. Science fiction on the other hand extends the world of scientific possibilities. Of course, character types are not the only distinction; it can be argued that the mood, intent, and the entire philosophy of science fiction is distinct from that of fantasy. Authors who write fantasy, horror, or science fiction have also generally read widely in that genre, so style and themes are often echoed. Each of these genres has developed its own traditions. Whereas horror draws on both of the other imaginative realms, the added pervasive element of fright serves to make it distinctive. Some of the elements of horror are so recognizable that a movie like *Scream* can use them as effective parodies: "Never make love or smoke pot in a horror flick"; "The Black character always dies first," and so on.

It is relatively easy to find examples in which these distinctions are clear, though there are also many books in which these boundaries are arbitrary at best. Suspenseful fantasy and horror tend to have a good bit of overlap, and terms such as "science fantasy" are sometimes used to refer to books that combine elements of the fantastic with scientific or futuristic possibilities.

Despite the overlap, young adults who read science fiction are not necessarily the same ones who read fantasy or horror. One aspect these genres do all share in common is that there tends to be a lot of crossover among books for adults, young adults, and children. Depending on the bookstore, Brian Jacques's Redwall books, *The Lord of the Rings* (Tolkien), *A Wizard of Earthsea* (Le Guin), and Star Wars books might be found in any (or more than one) of these sections! As for libraries, marketing tends to influence where books will be placed, but again that is sometimes rather arbitrary and many of these books are cross-marketed. Some books definitely have more appeal for certain demographics. Books in the Goosebumps series are not likely to be found in an adult or even the young adult section of the library. However, a novel like *The Rover* by Mel Odom (an Alex Award winner), with its halfling librarian who gets thrust into adventure, can be an exciting read for many young adults (and some children). Originally marketed for adults, *The Rover* is a sure bet to be found on the reading lists of fantasy lovers of all ages. The same is true of Orson Scott Card's *Ender's Game,* which has become a staple in discussions of YA science fiction, and marketing efforts by the publisher have reflected this shift.

So what is it about speculative fiction that attracts readers? It has been suggested that fantasy and science fiction are modern responses to a mythless world. Tamora Pierce asserts that these stories tap into the most powerful images and symbols in human culture. Even readers who "never read fantasy" will be familiar with many of the storylines listed in the chronology of fantasy that appears in the Appendix. These narratives often remain compelling for readers over the generations. One thing is sure: For some young readers they spark the imagination and inspire an interest in reading unlike any other genre.

Author Spotlight

Photo courtesy of Tamora Pierce.

Tamora Pierce

Encouraged by her father, Tamora Pierce began writing in the sixth grade. She also become a reader of fantasy at around this age but was unable to find many strong female characters in the books she read. She attended the University of Pennsylvania, majoring in psychology, and while there began to write for publication. After college she worked as a housemother at a group home for teenage girls, and she would read her first fantasy novel, *Song of the Lioness,* out loud to them. Her books have received much acclaim, providing her readers with the strong female protagonists that were lacking when she was young. Pierce lives in Manhattan with her husband, writer/filmmaker Tim, and their assorted animals. Visit her websites at www.tamora-pierce.com and www.sheroescentral.com.

SELECTED BOOKLIST

Protector of the Small series:

First Test (Random House, 1999)
Page (Random House, 2000)
Squire (Random House, 2001)
Lady Knight (Random House, 2012)

The Immortals series

Emperor Mage (Atheneum, 1995)
The Realms of the Gods (Atheneum, 1996)
Wild Magic (Atheneum, 1992)
Wolf-Speaker (Atheneum, 1994)

Song of the Lioness series

Alanna: The First Adventure (Atheneum, 1983)
In the Hand of the Goddess (Atheneum, 1984)
Lioness Rampant (Atheneum, 1988)
The Woman Who Rides Like a Man (Atheneum, 1986)

Trickster trilogy

Melting Stones (Random House, 2004)
The Will of the Empress (Random House, 2005)
Trickster's Choice (Random House, 2003)
Trickster's Queen (Random House, 2004)

Beka Cooper series

Bloodhound (Random House, 2009)
Mastiff (Random House, 2011)
Terrier (Random House, 2006)

ON THE APPEAL OF FANTASY

Part of it, of course, is the spare room for the imagination to spread out. It takes more work to imagine a world that existed in the distant past, or worlds that never existed, and worlds that might exist. The more we exercise our imaginations, the more we expand our own creativity, and the more ways we find to help us fend off the boredom of everyday life. Fantasy also gives many of those who read and write it a chance to toy with some of the most powerful ideas, characters, and events from history, placing them in a different context to see how they might unravel if particular elements were changed. There's a branch of science fiction called "alternate history" which does this more purely (Gary Blackwood's *The Year of the Hangman* is the first YA I've seen with the alternate history label attached to it, but there may be others), but all historical fantasy and even a certain amount of science fiction does this, asking the writer and the reader to reexamine things we might otherwise take for granted.

Also, at least as far as fantasy is concerned, we are tapping into some of the most powerful images and symbols in human culture: the struggle between good and evil, destruction and growth; the sources of ancient myths and legends, the great hero sagas that inspire people when we need inspiration most. My own work brings home to me over and over just how powerful that ancient image of the woman in armor is: It's the one that generates the most enthusiastic response among my readers. Kids are passionate by nature; they want stories and characters who pack a punch on all levels, which leave them with matter for thought and imagination long after the book is set aside. Fantasy, with its theme of powerful, ungovernable energies (magic itself) and characters which draw from the world's ancient lifeblood (folklore, myth, and legend), is a form which speaks strongly to its readers.

There's one other thing: Many people ask me why teens like fantasy so much, when my feeling is one of surprise that more teenagers don't like it. Virtually every fiction book a kid reads, from her or his first board book straight on through beginning chapter books and the classics of children's literature, contains the same elements as fantasy—talking, intelligent animals; wizards and knights; princesses and queens; sword battles, evil oppressors, struggles for ideals, the dangers of giving way to all-consuming appetite, and so on. Children's literature for readers 10 and under is almost *all* fantasy.

I suppose the turning point comes when kids turn from the literature of possibility to books that cast light on their contemporary, concrete lives and problems, but until then, from *The Cat in the Hat* and *Where the Wild Things Are* to the many different colors of *Fairy Book,* what they read in the main is fantasy. They just don't call it that!

ON CREATING A BELIEVABLE SPECULATIVE WORLD

You've presented me with a bit of a problem here. Realism is one of the areas for which the literati out and out reject fantasy and any other form of speculative fiction, unless it contains that thing called "magical realism." When books have magical realism, whatever that means, it is then redeemed from the just-made-up ghetto of fantasy, science fiction, and horror, and welcomed back to the literature shelves again. They also seem to think that "cautionary tales" are not speculative fiction, but literature. Does this attitude sting? Nah. Whyever would anyone think that?

As a developing writer in the ghetto that my mother termed "that junk" (she was an English major and proud of her literary sensibilities), driven to write what I loved to read, I nevertheless found givens in a number of fantasy books that chafed me. Almost no one had a sense of humor. Nobody went to the bathroom. Among the ranks of the dark, evil, twisted, misshapen guys in black and the tall, regal, pale, noble, steadfast people in white, I recognized—no one. I loved what is termed "high fantasy" as a teen—I just didn't recognize anything in it but the passion for things like honor, chivalry, and idealism. My goal became, and still is, this: I want readers to feel they can turn a corner on any street, anywhere, find my characters, and hang out with them for a while. I want them to read of characters who respond badly, grumpily, selfishly, whinily, and sullenly, and somehow find it in themselves to do the right thing anyway, just as we all do. I want characters who tell bad jokes at dreadful moments. (I am at my funniest in hospitals and dentists' offices. As a housemother I was ejected from the room where one of my girls was being checked for false labor pains, because I made her laugh so hard they couldn't accurately monitor her contractions.) I want a reader to be able to sink into one of my books and live it.

As I got older, my reasoning got a bit more sophisticated than "characters should go to the bathroom." I'm aware that to enjoy speculative fiction, readers have to be able to make the considerable suspension of disbelief that allows them to read without stopping every page or so to cry, "But this makes no sense!" My feeling is that it's my job to make everything else that happens as realistic as possible, so that when readers get to my areas that demand extra suspension of disbelief, those which revolve around magic, all of their imaginative energy will be there to help them make the leap; they won't have expended it all in drips and drabs getting past pale, body-function-less, sanitized-for-your-protection kings and princes, and wizened, hissing, gnarled creatures in serious need of braces and a retainer.

It helps if the magic itself works in a systematic way, that it follows rules and there are times when it can and can't be used. In a literary sense it must meet all of the demands of any other system for believability, so that using magic becomes like using any tool or force of the real world. Dramatically the use of fantasy fails if the wizard can resolve everything with a spoken word and a wave of a wand. For there to be drama there must be struggle; people must overreach; they must fail; they must try again or accept their failure and move on. Magic, like weapons, like a weaver's loom, like the distillation of napalm, has to follow rules of some kind if it is to generate good drama and not simply wish fulfillment. I also put to use the things of this world I see as magical: the ability of good needlewomen like my stepmother and sister to turn balls of cloth into afghans, the ability of a gardener to produce food and perfect miniature trees, and the ability of someone to take silica and chemicals and create glass. I find these things magical, and I use them to create magical workings for my books that feel right to me.

I've been called "the fantasy writer for people who don't like fantasy." Maybe it's because I work so hard to make each element of my universes make sense, and to be a logical, theoretical next step for what is true in our world. And maybe it's also because I deal in heroes, as most fantasy writers do. My heroes don't become heroes (I hope) because that's what they're supposed to be because, just like in reality, they have to work really hard, get discouraged, fail, sulk, and try again. In the course of that striving, they deal with their families, friends, people they love, bosses, teachers, the police, politicians, shortages, money, and falling over their own feet. I *think* that's why my books work for so many people; that's why writing works the way it does for me. But you would have to ask readers, and I would bet you anything you care to name that their responses will seldom sound like mine!

A Survey of Fantasy for Young Adults

The terms *high* and *low fantasy* are often used to distinguish two basic types of fantasy. High fantasy refers to the sort of novel some readers of this text thought of when they reached this chapter and muttered under their breath, "Oh no, hobbits and dragons." *The Lord of the Rings* is probably the first book that leaps to mind for many readers when they think of fantasy and Tolkien's trilogy is an excellent example of a high fantasy: a world of mythic archetypes, heroic quests, and magic. The term *low fantasy* is very broad, but one might define it by saying that while high fantasy draws on the epic struggles of mythology, low fantasy gets the majority of its themes, motifs, and character types from folklore.

Within the broad category of low fantasy there are a number of classifications that might be more useful in their specificity. Books that fit into one of the subgenres of fantasy tend to share a number of literary tropes and elements of style, so these distinctions give the reader some information about what to expect from the narrative. However, there are certainly also numerous good novels that do not fall neatly into these categories.

Animal Fantasy

Some of the most well-loved fantasy novels involve animal characters that have human traits. Many of these protagonists, although they are personified in the tradition of *Watership Down*

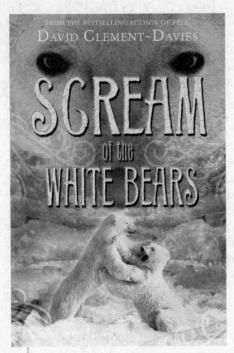

Many popular animal fantasies such as *Scream of the White Bears* (2010) include characters who behave like animals for the most part but take on some human characteristics. Reprinted by permission of Abrams.

(Adams, 1974), still retain their animal characteristics. Avi's Poppy series for example has characters who are very human in their thinking but deep down still behave like the animals they are. Even in the Deptford Mice books, the sewer rats and the evil cat Jupiter behave with identifiable animal traits while at the same time partaking in villainy.

Other animal fantasies focus on the animals but include some human interaction. Some of the most popular animal fantasies for children are of this sort, *Charlotte's Web* (White) and *Babe: The Gallant Pig* (King-Smith) for example (both of which are well known in part due to their film versions). Newbery winner *The Tale of Despereaux* by Kate DiCamillo, set in a vaguely medieval fantasy time, involves intertwining stories of a mouse, a rat, and a princess and is very much a fairy tale, though one that many middle school students enjoy. There are fewer novels in this category for older teens but *The Amazing Maurice and His Educated Rodents* by Terry Pratchett can be an exciting read for many young adult readers. In this reworking of the Pied Piper, it is magical refuse thrown out by wizards that causes the rats and a cat to mutate. Maurice the talking cat travels with a pack of intelligent rats and a young piper. Together they run a scam on towns until they come across much darker villains.

Though there are rodent stories in abundance, other animals also find their way into fantasy literature. In Zizou Corder's *Lion Boy* the protagonist is able to communicate with felines of all sizes, and in their cat-like ways, they aid him in his quest to save his parents. There are also animal fantasies that take place in an alternate world where animals effectively take the place of human characters. The Redwall series by Brian Jacques is accessible to fourth and fifth graders, but the high adventure of these sword-wielding animals appeals to many young adults as well.

Michael Hoeye creates a very different animal world in *Time Stops for No Mouse,* a book that was originally written for an adult audience of one, the author's wife. Hermux Tantamoq is a quiet, hardworking mouse who runs a watch shop, cares for his pet ladybug, and leads a quiet life. But when daredevil aviatrix Linda Perflinger brings in her watch to be repaired, everything changes for Hermux as he is launched into adventure. The sequels are just as witty and sophisticated as the first book. Though an easy read, *The Sands of Time* (the second in the series) can led to some great discussions with teen readers on the themes of censorship and freedom of speech. Although much of the adventure would be appreciated by 10- to 12-year-olds, thematically this an engaging read for young adults and adults as well.

Toy Fantasy

People who claim that they have never been fantasy readers also tend to forget about another subgenre of fantasy that many of them did enjoy when they were young—toy fantasy. Winnie the Pooh and Pinocchio are two personified toys that most readers in the English-speaking world are familiar with. Of course, the original *Pinocchio* is not the Disney story that leaps to mind for many readers in the United States. Sara Fannelli's illustrated version of Carlo Colladi's classic story can be a surprising read for many middle school students. There are not many stories in this category that are specifically for young adults. Although some teens read *The Indian in the Cupboard* (1981) by Lynn Reid Banks (which might also be examined in light of its stereotypic depictions of the toy "Indian") and Ann Martin's *The Meanest Doll in the World,* there are not many toy fantasies specifically for older readers. *Hard Times* by Julian Thompson and *Sweet Miss Honeywell's Revenge* by Kathryn Reiss are two of the few that come to mind. *Hard Times* has a strong dose of contemporary realism thrown in. The teen protagonist has to carry around a surrogate baby doll to remind her not to get pregnant, which is bad enough, but then the doll starts speaking to her! In Reis's novel a cruel governess from the past, Miss Honeywell, attempts to carry on manipulating and controlling others even though she is dead. Both of these novels involve dolls that are possessed. The graphic novels *The Adventures of Tony Millionaire's Sock Monkey* and *Herobear and the Kid* (Kunkel) are more traditional toy fantasies that will likely appeal to some young adults.

Fantasies Focused on Eccentric Characters, Mythical Creatures, or Extraordinary Worlds

One of the most common forms of fantasy aimed specifically at young adult readers involves eccentric characters. In these stories the world is fairly normal until an extraordinary character enters the scene. The converse situation is also quite popular, in which a normal person from our world enters a fantasy realm. Although the character who somehow does not fit in is very common in YA literature in general, in fantasy the outsider is often exaggerated in ways that allow some distancing.

The image of wings, for example, is used in many literary traditions to signify the search for freedom. For the YA character wings can serve a dual purpose. Flight is definitely tied to maturation, finding one's own identity, and searching for freedom, but at the same time the ability to fly sets the character apart. Two of the best examples of the duality of the eccentric character theme can be found in Laurel Winter's *Growing Wings* and Patrice Kindl's *Owl in Love*. In *Growing Wings,* the protagonist in the midst of puberty begins to sprout wings. Sarah, her mother, understands because the same thing happened to her—only her mother had cut the wings off! Sarah has sworn that she will never do such a thing to her own daughter but now that it is happening neither of them is quite sure what to do. The protagonist in *Owl in Love* is a young woman by day but morphs into an owl by night. The 14-year-old's life has always been complicated by her condition, but now puberty is adding to her problems and she has a major crush on her science teacher. Furthermore, a deranged boy has entered her night habitat and is compromising her secret and her safety.

Sometimes, rather than discovering his or her own extraordinary powers, the protagonist discovers a fantastic creature who needs or gives aid of some sort. In David Almond's *Skellig* a bizarre character, perhaps an angel, is discovered in a garage. The creature seems to be barely alive, covered with spider webs, but the young protagonists are able to nurse it back to health.

Many of these eccentric characters are straight out of myth or folklore. The mermaid figure is one that frequently appear in YA literature. Perhaps because she is partly human but noticeably different, readers can see themselves as the mermaid and indulge in

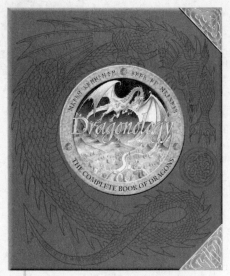

Extraordinary creatures like dragons are quite popular in fantasy for young adults. Fictional fantasy worlds are sometimes extended in related books about their worlds. In the case of *Dragonology: The Complete Book of Dragons* (2003) the "faction" book came first and then a series of novels was created afterward. Reprinted by permission of Candlewick.

the freedom that the water brings, while still evoking the outsider theme. The mercreatures that appear in young adult literature all come more or less from the folklore surrounding the image of mermaids or sirens, the same type of story that inspired Hans Christian Andersen's *The Little Mermaid.* Some other mermaid fantasies include

- *Aquamarine* by Alice Hoffman
- *Indigo* by Alice Hoffman
- *The Mermaid Summer* by Mollie Hunter
- *Sirena* by Donna Jo Napoli
- *Water: Tales of Elemental Spirits* by Robin McKinley and Peter Dickinson

Dragons are among the most popular of fantasy creatures. There is enormous variety in these stories, most of which are rooted in European myth or folklore (*The Hobbit,* Tolkien). Occasionally an eastern dragon will make an appearance (*Dragon of the Lost Sea,* Yep). A few of these dragons even enter the contemporary world (*Hatching Magic,* Downer; *Dragon Rider,* Funke) or take place on other planets (*Dragon Riders of Pern,* McCaffrey).

Many of these dragon stories have readerships that cross several age brackets. Sherryl Jordan's *The Hunting of the Last Dragon* is one that should definitely be on the young adult shelf. The young character, in love with someone he cannot have, feels alone and is struggling to discover who he wants to be. Then when he returns from market in a neighboring town, he finds that his village is gone.

> Only some of the clay block walls of the cottages still stood, and they were black, many cracked and fallen in the heat. Thatched roofs were gone, the little wattle fences between the houses, the wooden sheds where pigs were kept, the ploughs and carts—all gone. (p. 35)

Now he is truly alone. *The Hunting of the Last Dragon* takes place in a world very different from our own but with a protagonist who is very much confronted with the same teen angst we recognize so well. And the author paints such vivid images of his context and his thoughts that it is easy to enter his world with him. Some other recommended dragon fantasies include

- *Dealing with Dragons* by Patricia Wrede
- *Dragon's Bait* by Vivian Vande Velde
- *Dragon's Blood* by Jane Yolen
- *Dragonsong* by Anne McCaffrey
- *Eragon: Inheritance* by Christopher Paolini
- *Here There Be Dragons* by Jane Yolen
- *Searching for the Dragons* by Patricia Wrede

In other stories the world itself that a Dorothy or Alice enters is magical and extraordinary. This is actually a great technique for introducing fantasy elements to the reader, who gets to explore the new world and express disbelief along with the protagonist.

To Consider

Mermaids and girls with wings can easily represent teen outcast characters. The feeling of estrangement that these characters go through fits in nicely with the teen consciousness of the narrative. What role do dragons play in these stories?

In James Gurney's *Dinotopia* two brothers find themselves stranded on an island where dinosaurs still survive on a level of harmony (and disharmony) with humans. The characters are at first quite skeptical about what they see, but slowly they learn more about the land and its history and customs and the reader becomes a part of this world along with them.

Sometimes, as in Chabon's *Summerland,* the "normal kid" has to enter a magical realm to save both that world and his own. Other times the protagonist embarks on an accidental voyage into another world. In *The Divide* (Kay) a young man with a terminal illness is somehow transported to a magical world when he visits the continental divide. Accidental or not the voyage tends to become the vehicle for character growth. One of the most interesting narratives of this sort is Clive Barker's Abarat trilogy. Like her life in the real world, the protagonist experiences a fantasy realm that is fairly brutal but with room for magic and beauty.

Fantasies Involving Magical Powers

Fantasy often revolves around magical elements, a classification that overlaps with many of the other subgenres of fantasy. The Harry Potter series certainly tops the chart in terms of popularity. Although the early books in the series can hardly be considered YA fiction, as Harry has grown older the themes have also matured. Harry, Ron, and Herminone in the latter books deal with real teen problems such as love, jealousy, betrayal, and peer pressure. Younger kids and adults alike read the books, along with young adults.

Other novels with similar themes are more directly aimed at the teen audience. Rose Sabin's *A School for Sorcery* and Diane Duane's Young Wizard series both have young adult protagonists who are learning to harness their magic while they deal with other teen-oriented issues. *A Wizard Alone,* from the Young Wizard series, is especially interesting as one young wizard with enormous powers is also autistic.

Some of these fantasies also might be considered fairy tales. In Jean Ferris's *Once upon a Marigold,* Christian, whose father happens to be a troll, seeks to win the love of a princess. Of course, things are never simple and he has to both win her heart and save her from the queen who is attempting to take over the kingdom. In Juliet Murillier's *Daughter of the Forest,* the heroine has to complete a nearly impossible task to free her six brothers from her stepmother's spell. Diane Wynne Jones creates a magical world with an Arabian Nights flair in *Howl's Moving Castle* and *Castle in the Air,* which have connections to the folkloric tradition of flying carpets and genies. Garcia's *The Legend of the Wandering King* is a literary legend that includes djinns and an incredible magic carpet.

The Artemis Fowl (Colfer) series is quite popular with tweens and the younger end of the YA spectrum. For many readers Artemis is a refreshing antihero. The 12-year-old criminal mastermind is after fairy gold. The true hero is the female fairy police officer who attempts to thwart Artemis's plan. Artemis Fowl is one of many series (like Harry Potter and Abarat) in which a "hidden" magical world exists alongside the real world.

In the best-selling French novel *Quadehar* by Eric L'Homme, the characters inhabit a realm between the real world and what is called the Uncertain world, a wild place with bizarre and dangerous creatures. Robin becomes an apprentice to the sorcerer Quadehar, but soon he and his friends are thrust into the Uncertain world where they must overcome the forces of darkness. In the Bordertown books, including novels by Terri Windling, Emma Bull, and Will Shetterly, a realm between the real world and the world of magic has become accessible and a city filled with uncertainty has arisen.

Other magic-oriented fantasies take place in alternate worlds where magic can be wielded. *Sorcery & Cecelia or The Enchanted Chocolate Pot* by Patricia Wrede and Caroline Stevermer is a fun tale with a Renaissance flavor. The story follows two young women and the parts they play in the magical goings-on in an alternate London of yesteryear. The first of Phillip Pullman's His Dark Materials books also takes place in an alternate world where some things are just slightly different and other things are magical.

In *Wizards of the Game* by David Lubar, Mercer, a teen who loves role playing games, comes up with a great plan to hold a gaming convention at the school's annual fundraiser. Some community members protest that the games are satanic because of the simulated use of magic. Things get out of control when another student writes a newspaper article about the demonic qualities of the game and how it is corrupting the participants. As if that's not enough, a group of actual wizards from another realm shows up wanting Mercer's help.

Harry Potter Fan Fiction

One way readers sometimes respond to the narratives they are reading is through the writing of creative extensions to the fictional world. In the past decade technology has allowed fan fiction to become a huge phenomenon. Fan fiction has quickly developed a culture all its own in which people add to or even change characters and events. They also review each other's narratives and often rewrite based on the feedback they receive. Fan fiction occurs with all types of literature, but none with more frequency than fantasy. And in the realm of fan fiction for young readers no other book or series even comes close to the amount of writing related to the world of Harry Potter.

Some teachers and librarians warmly embrace the concept as it involves built-in motivation, writing for a real audience, peer review, and the use of technology, all excellent skills to develop when working with young adults. However, some publishers and authors oppose the idea and see it as copyright infringement. Also the potential risks are many. Websites to which young people flock are sometimes visited by older fans and unknown browsers who at times post fan fiction with mature themes. Other visitors to these sites might write harsh reviews of the fan fiction they read, devastating the 14-year-old who is submitting fiction for the first time. Some teachers and librarians who entertained the concept at first have begun to avoid the idea altogether. Other facilitators have set up pass word-protected exchanges of fan fiction.

HarryPotterFanFiction.com is not the largest site for writing about the world of Hogwarts and Muggles but is devoted entirely to the cause. In May 2009 it received 39,675,572 hits, housing over 68,000 stories and 1,686,000 reviews! This site is run by primarily adult fans who have learned from the mistakes of the past. The facilitators log the IP numbers of everyone who posts to the site to cut down on the potential risks involved with online exchanges. Fan fiction on this site can be accessed by category (e.g., Action/Adventure, Humor, Romance). There are also featured stories, competitions, and writer's resources all at the click of a button. The quality of the writing and the ages of the authors vary tremendously, but that is half the fun of being a novice writer/reviewer.

Technology Links

A page from the Harry Potter Fan Fiction calendar. Used courtesy of www.harrypotter fanfiction.com.

When asked why he and the other volunteers devote their time to maintaining the site, Jay, the site owner, responded:

> From reading each individual submission to updating the website itself, our staff dedicates hours each day to the site. Composed entirely of volunteers that have their own jobs and families, it takes a unique group of people to work so tirelessly on a site that provides them no physical or monetary reward. While the staffers are all author contributors to the site, they all share a common bond that our other regular members don't: they consider HPFF a stepping stone for young writers and aim to make it a safe, family oriented website that can be an online home for thousands. When we receive an email thanking us for the site or read posts from members who have seen their writing improve due to the resources and assistance we provide them, we are reminded why the site exists and why we spend so many hours at HPFF. In the future, we one day hope to see a published author look back fondly at the site and say, "That's where I got my start!" And that, more than anything, is reward enough for all of us. (personal communication, 2009)

Visit www.harrypotterfanfiction.com to find out more about Harry Potter fan fiction.

Suspense and Supernatural Fantasy

Many suspenseful fantasy novels balance on a fuzzy line with horror. One might typically think of ghost stories as being horror but often it is more about the thrill and mystery than about fright. Sometimes the ghosts aid the protagonist. Peggy in *The Sherwood Ring* (Pope) is orphaned and returns to the family estate where four revolutionary war ghosts help unravel her family's past. Other times the protagonist helps the ghost. Charlotte in *Ghost Sitter* by Peni Griffin is having a great summer in her new home until she discovers that her house is haunted by the ghost of a young girl who thinks she is still alive.

The protagonist in McDonald's *Shades of Simon Gray* seems to be the perfect teen. However, after he crashes into a tree and ends up in a coma, questions arise as to whether he was connected to the recent computer hackings and theft of tests at his high school.

Meanwhile, in his head Simon is conversing with a man hung for murder 200 years ago from the same tree his car has hit.

There are many speculative worlds that are tinged with fright and involve more than ghosts. Mollie Hunter's *A Stranger Came Ashore* expands on the folkloric theme of Celtic selkies who come ashore to lure young women into the sea. Master of suspense Margaret Mahy brings us *Alchemy,* in which Roland finds out that his classmate Jess is delving into ancient magic. Soon Roland discovers that he might also have magical powers. What evolves is an intense and suspenseful thriller.

Many of these books explore the supernatural. *Full Tilt* by Neal Shusterman involves two brothers who enter a bizarre phantom carnival. In *Coraline* by Neil Gaiman, the protagonist finds a door in her new house that is sometimes blocked with bricks but opens up for her, giving access to an alternate universe. *Coraline* plays on our deepest fears as Gaiman takes us through the distorted looking glass. The alternate world contains everything the character has dreamed of, but it also contains horrible marvels.

Time Shift Fantasy

Fiction that explores time shifts, time slips, and time travel might fall into the realm of fantasy, science fiction, or historical fiction and may have elements of all three. Some like *The Devil's Arithmetic* (Yolen), *The Black Canary* (Curry), and *The Grave* (Henegham) read like historical fiction with the fantasy element of time slip used to pull the reader into the past. Other novels, for example those that involve time machines, fit more easily into the category of science fiction. In a few of these books time travel is only a small part of the fantastic world created by the author. In Christopher Tebbetts's Viking series mythological elements are merged with the humorous "historical" Viking world. Vivian Vande Velde's *Now You See It* has an interesting mix of fantasy creatures and time travel. Wendy finds a strange pair of glasses by which she sees that some people at her high school are not exactly what they pretend to be. She can also see portals that allow her to travel to a land populated by dragons and elves. Wendy ends up traveling back in time where she teams up with her teenage grandmother.

> **Additional Time Slip Fantasies**
> - *The 13th Floor: A Ghost Story* by Sid Fleischman
> - Baseball Card Adventure series by Dan Gutman
> - *Both Sides of Time* by Caroline Cooney
> - *Building Blocks* by Cynthia Voigt
> - *A Circle of Time* by Marisa Montes
> - *A Girl Called Boy* by B. Humance
> - *Paperquake: A Puzzle* by Kathryn Reiss
> - *Playing Beatie Bow* by Ruth Park
> - *Rewind* by Jan Page
> - *Something Upstairs* by Avi
> - *A String in the Harp* by Nancy Bond
> - *Tom's Midnight Garden* by Phillippa Pearce

Fantasy Involving Imaginary Pasts and Alternate Histories

In some fantasy there are no major magical or folkloric elements; the fantasy instead involves a time and place that never actually existed. Avi's *Midnight Magic* for example takes place in a medieval-flavored context but in a kingdom that is totally fictional. Although *The Thief* by Meghan W. Turner has minor elements of the supernatural in the characters' interactions with gods, other than these few scenes the book could easily take place in the ancient Mediterranean region.

Many fantasies with a surreal edge are set in an imaginary time and place that is not quite the reality we know. The Lemony Snicket books for example may not involve folkloric creatures or magic wands, but they are beyond the ordinary in many ways. Ken Oppel, on the other hand, creates a totally imaginary alternate past in *Airborn* that is fantastic in some ways but like Lyra's Oxford in *The Golden Compass* contains much that is almost familiar.

On the flip side there are stories steeped in historical detail that play around with the historical possibilities. For instance, Theodore Taylor's *Billy the Kid* begins with many of the well-known details of William Bonney's life but then begins to take liberties. What if things had turned out differently for Billy the Kid? Even a slight change could alter history in interesting ways. Gary Blackwood's *The Year of the Hangman* is a suspenseful alternative history set during the Revolutionary War. It's 1777 and George Washington awaits execution and the rebel leaders who have escaped capture are in hiding or have fled, routed by superior British forces. Benjamin Franklin runs an illegal newspaper, *The Liberty Tree,* in New Orleans. The protagonist, 17-year-old Creighton Brown, has been kidnapped in London and unwillingly forced to spy for the British, so the reader discovers this alternate past along with him. Other good alternate history reads include John Robert's *Hannibal's Children,* which imagines what might happen if Hannibal had defeated the Romans, *The Explosionist* by Jenny Davidson, and *Best Alternative History Stories of the 20th Century,* edited by Harry Turtledove.

Almost Real or Surreal Speculative Fiction

There are also many novels that are not quite fantasy and yet not quite realistic. Some of these books have surreal elements, some delve into magical realism, and some simply include a few unexplainable circumstances that we accept as readers because they are well integrated into the fictional world. A novel like *Holes* (Sachar), which is filled with folkloric structures, is not likely to be found in the fantasy section of the library, but neither is it especially realistic. To a lesser extent the same holds true for Brashares's *The Sisterhood of the Traveling Pants,* in which a group of teenage girls find a secondhand pair of pants that magically fits each of them. Other novels, like *Kit's Wilderness* by David Almond and Edward Bloor's *Storytime,* delve even more into the inexplicable. Bloor's novel takes realistic political/educational trends and skews the world around them in surreal ways.

Two literary trends that have gotten a lot of attention in the young adult field in recent years fit this fantasy category. First, martial arts adventures (which really exists as a genre in its own right) tend to include many folkloric elements in the storyline. In *Wandering Warrior* by Da Chen, for example, a sacred scripture has foretold that the future emperor of China will have five moles on the bottom of each foot. A monk takes an orphan named Luka under his wing, and after discovering the moles on his feet, trains him to be a kung fu wandering warrior. Like many of these martial arts novels, the narrative is historically based but infuses surreal and folkloric elements connected to the tradition. *Tiger* by Jeff Stone and the other books in the Five Ancestors series are adventure stories set in 17th-century China. The extrasensory connections between the young warriors and animals and the amazing martial arts abilities in this novel are beyond the natural but certainly within the norm for martial arts literature. *Sign of the Qin* by L. G. Bass, on the other hand, takes kung fu fully into the realm of legend. Though set in 3rd-century China the story is more inspired by Chinese and other mythic traditions than by historical accounts.

A very different popular fantasy-like trend follows the protagonist into the afterlife. *The Lovely Bones* (Sebold), which was not published as YA fiction, has been very popular with older teens. Similar novels for young adults include Gary Soto's *Afterlife* and Alex Shearer's *The Great Blue Yonder,* both of which involve young people who die and then have to take care of unfinished business.

Modern Fairy Tales

The concept of the modern fairy tale overlaps with traditional literature, as these books are actually somewhere between fantasy and folklore. Some like *Zel* (Napoli) retell the folktale, extending it, adding perspectives and details, filling in the gaps. Other novels take more license and write new stories altogether but which incorporate folkloric characters and motifs. *Pig Tale* by Verlyn Flieger, for example, pulls strongly from Celtic mythology. Flieger has created a story of a pig herder cast out into the wilderness, where she befriends strangers who may be more than human. Likewise, Patrice Kindl's *Goose Chase* takes the motif of the poor girl who helps out a stranger and is then rewarded, in this case with unintended consequences. For more on modern fairy tales see Chapter 4.

High Fantasy

When critics speak of high fantasy they generally have in mind stories like *The Lord of the Rings,* in which a group of unlikely heroes set off on a quest filled with mythic imagery. If fantasy in general draws on folkloric creatures and motifs, then high fantasy works with themes and structures from mythology. In high fantasy the stakes are enormous; generally the fate of a kingdom (or the world) depends on the outcomes of the hero's quest.

In Garth Nix's trilogy the quest begins in *Sabriel* with efforts to free the protagonist's father. By the second book, *Lireal,* the librarian hero is in a battle to save the world when the dead make war on the living. Traditionally, these high fantasies have involved male heroes such as Ged in the Wizard of Earthsea books and Frodo in *The Lord of the Rings.* They are often unlikely heroes, even in contemporary books such as Michael Chabon's *Summerland,* in which a young baseball player named Ethan Feld must somehow save the universe. In recent years quite a few strong female characters have joined the ranks of these unlikely heroes. Blazing the trail with a female hero was Robin McKinley's *Blue Sword* (1982), followed by *The Hero and the Crown* (1984). Tamora Pierce has been the most active writer in following up with female characters who fight dragons and save the world. In both the Song of the Lioness quartet and the Protector of the Small series, Pierce offers female protagonists who, against great odds, become both great warriors and mature women.

> **To Consider**
> Given that genres, subgenres, and other classifications are often very fuzzy, why might it be important to know and be able to talk about them?

Interestingly, despite the fact that high fantasy deals with the triumph of good over evil, it is among the most frequently challenged categories of fantasy. Phillip Pullman was labeled the most dangerous man in the world by Catholic clergy in Great Britain when the third book in the His Dark Materials trilogy was released. This was in part because the mythic constructs that frame the epic battles between good and evil take on religious overtones in this trilogy.

If fantasy in general builds on the tropes, motifs, and characters of traditional literature, high fantasies such as Tamora Pierce's *Alanna: The First Adventure* (2005) and Michael Scott's *The Magician: The Secrets of the Immortal Nicholas Flamel* (2008) use mythology as their foundation. *Alanna* reprinted by permission of Simon Pulse. Jacket cover from *The Magician: The Secrets of the Immortal Nicholas Flamel* by Michael Scott, used by permission of Delacorte Press, an imprint of Random House Children's Books, a division of Random House, Inc.

Many speculative fictions do not fit neatly into one classification or another. Novels such as Dia Calhoun's *Aria of the Sea* and Vivian Vande Velde's *Now You See It* touch on multiple subgenres of fantasy.

In the Field   *Online Student Recommendations*

Rebekah Parker was the sixth-grade humanities teacher at Town School for Boys, an independent K–8 school of around 400 students in San Francisco. Since 2000 the entire Upper School at Town School has been a laptop school. In an effort to enhance excitement for reading in her class Rebekah created an online database of book recommendations written by her students. Rebekah is now the 7/8 English teacher at the American School in Barcelona, where she plans to keep working with online student book recommendations.

I chose to have my students write book recommendations because I feel they give the reader a voice. It forces them to be critical readers, consider who would like the book (even if they didn't), and focus on the positive aspects. They are also far more interesting to write and more appealing to read, as opposed to reports or plot summaries, which are so boring, they risk ruining the book for the reader.

Also, I hoped that students would use the database when they were at a loss for what to read next. They could search it by a number of criteria: genre, author, or by reviewer. Their friends' recommendations speak to them more than an adult's and might inspire reluctant readers and maybe even make reading "cool."

My students were visibly relieved to learn they didn't need to write the same kind of summaries that they were used to doing. A few asked how they were supposed to recommend a book if they didn't like it themselves (classic sixth-grade question!), but because we do this with free-reading books—of their own choosing, read outside of class—I told them to put it down if they weren't enjoying it. The best reactions came when they saw the database for the first time. They all frantically searched for their own recommendations and then for their friends', and had meltdowns if they didn't find them at first!

Individual students visit the database on their own time. Occasionally I'll have my class peruse the site by giving them 10 minutes to check out their friends' latest reads, to remind them that the database exists and perhaps inspire them.

In my 5 years of teaching at Town, fantasy has been the genre of preference for the majority of the class. A high number of Redwall books appear in the database, partially due to the fact that for summer reading, they are required to read at least one book from the series. Many of my students choose to read the whole series, or at least several of the books. They like the animal personifications, great accents, and of course, all the fighting and action. Harry Potter craze aside, I think fantasy is especially appealing to boys. When I asked my students why they like fantasy so much, their response was that there is a lot more adventure and action and a wider range of possibilities for the plot. I also feel despite, or most likely, because of the fantastical nature of the characters, the boys are able to safely relate to them on an emotional level.

Before we began the school's laptop program, I used to have my students write their recommendations on 4×6 notecards. We kept them in a box in the classroom. It was hardly ever used, and because they had to write them by hand, they didn't have the advantage of editing and spell checking their writing with the word processor. We had them sorted by category but because the majority are fantasy, they were really hardly sorted at all. On the other hand, the sort feature on the online database works quite well and makes the information much more accessible and easier to follow. Plus, my students enjoy using their computers, and having the recommendations posted online makes them that much cooler.

For their summer reading before starting sixth grade, my students are required to read at least three books of their choosing. For each book, they are also required to submit a recommendation. That jumpstarts the database. Then each quarter more are added as my students are required to read at least one book besides the books we read as a class. However, some choose to submit more than the required seven per year (three over the summer, four during the school year).

The first day I meet with my students and assign them their summer reading assignment, we spend some time discussing the proper tone for a recommendation. I read amazon.com editorial reviews out loud, and I provide them with a sample that I wrote for

The Phantom Tollbooth, a book they all read in earlier grades. Throughout the year, they also hear me booktalk our class books and read-alouds, so they become increasingly comfortable with the language and tone associated with recommendations. Most of them tend to be quite comfortable with this type of writing.

Audio Books

Speculative Fiction

The Bad Beginning by Lemony Snicket; read by Tim Curry. (Random House, 2001) (A, N, Y)

Blood and Chocolate by Annette Curtis Klause; read by Alyssa Bresnahan. (Recorded Books, 1998) (Y)

Dealing with Dragons by Patricia Wrede; read by Words Take Wind Repertory Company. (Listening Library, 1990) (B)

Eragon by Christopher Paolini; read by Gerard Doyle. (Listening Library, 2003)

Feed by M. T. Anderson; read by David Aaron Baker, with John Beach, Josh Lebowitz, Tara Sands, and Anne Twomey reading the "feeds." (Listening Library, 2003)

The Folk Keeper by Franny Billingsley; read by Marian Tomas Griffin. (Random House, 2000) (N, Y)

Gathering Blue by Lois Lowry; read by Katherine Borowitz. (Random House, 2000) (A, Y)

The Golden Compass (A, AA, N, Y, P), *The Subtle Knife* (AA, N, Y), and *The Amber Spy Glass* (A, AA) by Phillip Pullman; read by the author and a full cast. (Random House, 1999)

Harry Potter and the Goblet of Fire by J. K. Rowling; read by Jim Dale. (Listening Library, 2000) (AA)

Have Space Suit, Will Travel by Robert Heinlein; read by a full cast. (Full Cast Audio, 2003)

Kit's Wilderness by David Almond; read by Charles Keating. (Listening Library, 2006) (N)

The Last Book in the Universe by Rodman Philbrick; read by Jeremy Davies. (Listening Library, 2001) (Y)

Life As We Knew It by Susan Beth Pfeffer; read by Emily Bauer. (Listening Library, 2006)

Mattimeo by Brian Jacques; read by the author and a full cast. (Recorded Books, 2004)

Running Out of Time by Margaret Peterson Haddix; read by Kimberly Schraf. (Listening Library, 1998) (N)

Sabriel by Garth Nix; read by Tim Curry. (Listening Library, 2002) (Y)

Sandry's Book (Circle of Magic 1) by Tamora Pierce; read by the author and a full cast. (Full Cast Audio, 2002)

Time Stops for No Mouse and *The Sands of Time* by Michael Hoeye; read by Campbell Scott. (Listening Library, 2002) (Y)

Tomorrow, When the War Began by John Marsden; read by Suzi Dougherty. (Bolinda Audio, 1999) (Y)

AA—Audie Awards	N—ALSC Notable Children's Recording
A—Audiofile Earphones Award	P—Parent's Choice Audio Award Winner
B—Ben Franklin Audio Award	Y—YALSA Selected List of Audiobooks

Books to Film

Speculative Fiction from Books

The Bad Beginning by Bradley Silberling (Movie: *Lemony Snicket's a Series of Unfortunate Events*. Paramount Pictures, directed by Brad Silberling [DVD], © 2005)

Fahrenheit 451 by Ray Bradbury (Movie: *Fahrenheit 451*. Enterprise Vineyard Film, directed by Francois Truffaut [DVD], © 2003)

The Fellowship of the Ring by J. R. R. Tolkien (Movie: *The Fellowship of the Ring*. New Line Cinema, directed by Peter Jackson [DVD], © 2001)

Harry Potter and the Goblet of Fire by J. K. Rowling (Movie: *Harry Potter and the Goblet of Fire*. Warner Home Video, directed by Mike Newell [DVD], © 2006)

The Hitchhiker's Guide to the Galaxy by Douglas Adams (Movie: *The Hitchhiker's Guide to the Galaxy*. Touchstone Pictures, directed by Garth Jennings [DVD], © 2005)

I, Robot by Isaac Asimov (Movie: *I, Robot*. 20th Century Fox, directed by Alex Proyas [DVD], © 2004)

The Princess Bride by William Goldman (Movie: *The Princess Bride*. MGM Home Entertainment, directed by Rob Reiner [2001], © 1987)

Stardust by Neil Gaiman (Movie: *Stardust*. Paramount, directed by Matthew Vaughn [DVD], © 2007)

The War of the Worlds by H. G. Wells (Movie: *The War of the Worlds*. Dreamworks, directed by Steven Spielberg [DVD], © 2005)

The Melancholy of Haruhi Su-zumiya (2009) from Japan builds on both Japanese fantasy and the literary motifs of manga/animé. Reprinted by permission of Little, Brown and Company.

Suspending Disbelief

When working with a fictional world that is so obviously not real, perhaps the most crucial question involves how the author makes fantasy work for the reader. One thing to keep in mind is that speculative worlds tend to merge the real with the imagined. Even in the most bizarre fantasy narrative there are aspects that readers will recognize from our world. The emotions conveyed, the ways of talking, relationships between characters—although the setting and the characters might be unrecognizable, there will always be a certain amount of the familiar. Those elements that the reader can relate to everyday experience allows the suspension of disbelief.

One technique frequently used is to first place the protagonist in the realistic world to ease the reader into the fantasy. In *Tuck Everlasting* (1975) by Natalie Babbitt, the narrator is a realistic character who stumbles on a fantastic situation. When she finds the fountain of youth and a family who guards it, the fantasy elements are similarly encountered by the young narrator and the reader, who both react with initial disbelief. We struggle through the situation with her and this allows us to grow to accept the premise.

The same holds true in Michael Chabon's *Summerland*. The reader is eased into the fantasy world from a hometown

American setting in Clam Island, Washington. Clive Barker's young character in *Abarat* fits neatly into contemporary realistic fiction until she starts to encounter bizarre creatures and is thrown into the world of Abarat. *Sea of Trolls* by Nancy Farmer might be mistaken at first for historical fiction until gradually more and more mythological elements creep in. Starting in the real world and moving into a fantasy land allows the reader to encounter these unbelievable occurrences through the eyes of the narrator, who is also seeing them for the first time and who often has doubts.

Fantasy also works because people enjoy envisioning alternative realities. Peter Dickinson suggest that people have, in fact, evolved "to speculate about possibilities" (Dickinson interview, p. 224) As an adaptive strategy humans constantly consider even absurd alternatives, providing "spare room for the imagination to spread out" (Pierce interview, p. 204) If this is the case, then certainly invention and discovery are connected to the same type of thought that allows for fantastic speculation.

Perhaps the most crucial element in allowing readers to fully engage with speculative worlds is to ensure that the created elements are consistent. Peter Dickinson suggests that all of the real-world elements in fantasy have got to be right. Furthermore, the fantasy elements have to mesh with them and just as solidly with each other. Tamora Pierce adds that all of the realistic elements help readers suspend disbelief when they reach those elements that revolve around the fantastic. The way the characters themselves respond to the magic also helps the reader suspend disbelief.

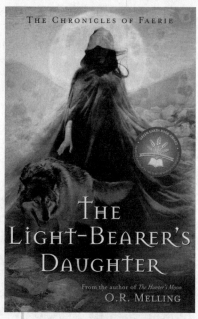 

Fantasy often draws directly on characters and motifs from traditional literature. *The Light-Bearer's Daughter* by O. R. Melling (2008) draws on Irish myth and legend. *Moribito: Guardian of the Spirit* by Nahoko Uehashi (trans. Cathy Hiraro) (2008) is fantasy that draws on both Japanese myth and legend. *The Light-Bearer's Daughter* reprinted by permission of Abrams. *Moribito* reprinted by permission of Arthur Levine.

At the same time, it is crucial that the magic itself be systematic and consistent in the way it is presented. The reader has to be able to make sense of the rules and relationships in order for the story to be "good drama and not simply wish fulfillment" (Pierce interview, p. 204). Keep in mind that although fantasy speaks metaphorically, it is often addressing topics that are quite meaningful for many readers. The distancing involved in fantasy can allow the narrative to address issues of the real world.

Technology Links

Fanart, Trailers, and Wizard Rock

One great indication of the popularity of the fantasy genre is the amount of creative fan interaction with the fictional world. Currently there is no fictional world that has as many readers engaging in storyline creation as the Harry Potter books. The term *fan fiction* as previously discussed is used generally to denote the reader-created narratives that build on an author's fictional work. There are numerous other ways to extend fictional worlds, and the multimedia capabilities of the computer have allowed readers to respond using multiple literacies. Fanart is at least as popular as fan fiction. Readers are creating portraits of characters, sketches of scenes, and maps to visually depict fantasy worlds.

Fanlyrics and fansongs are also quite popular, and the ultimate extension of songwriting for the fantasy world can be found in the phenomenon called *wizard rock*. There are currently around 300 bands that devote their time to singing music inspired by the Harry Potter world. They go by names such as Harry and the Potters, The Hermione Crookshanks Experience, and the Parselmouths. Not all of the bands are ready for *American Idol* but often they create wonderfully insightful lyrics. The Parselmouths sing in character as slightly air-headed, slightly mean Slytherin girls. In their song "Oh Dumbledore" they actually delve into the conflicted emotions these characters might actually feel.

Finally, trailers are a very interesting trend that both lovers of fan fiction and publishers have become excited about. Professional videos like the Lemony Snicket trailer (Harper-Collins) are posted on many publisher sites. These might be used effectively to get young adults excited about reading a book. More relevant are the trailers for books and works of fan fiction created by young adults themselves. In order to make an effective trailer, many literacy skills have to come into play. The director has to excite interest in the themes and capture the mood of the work of fiction without giving away too much of the storyline. If

Harry and the Potters, one of the original wizard rock bands (formed in 2002), on tour in Alaska. Photo courtesy of Joe and Paul DeGeorge.

On *Wizards and Muggles Rock for Social Justice* some of the best wizard rock comes together, creating fantasy-inspired music. Visit the Cheap Rent site on myspace for more information (www.myspace.com/cheaprent). Courtesy of Dave Roman (the artist) and The Whomping Willows (wizard rock band).

well planned, the trailer will incorporate visual, aural, and dramatic elements all designed to entice the viewer into becoming a reader.

Songs

- "Bonjour Fleur" from *How to Write with a Feather* by The Hermione Crookshanks Experience (Kristine Thuna) (www.myspace.com/hermionecrookshanks)
- "Dumbledore Is Gay" by Justin Finch-Fletchley & The Sugar Quills (www.myspace.com/justinfinchfletchley)
- "Oh Dumbledore" from *Illegal Love Potion* by The Parselmouths (Brittany Vahlberg and Kristina Horner) (www.myspace.com/theparselmouths)
- "Save Ginny Weasley" from *Harry and the Potters* by Harry and the Potters (Joe DeGeorge and Paul DeGeorge) (www.myspace.com/harryandthepotters)

Video Trailers

- Lemony Snicket at HarperCollins (www.harpercollins.ca/trailers/snicket.html)
- "Silent Screams: A Harry Potter Fanfic Trailer" by Lindsay Langford (www.youtube.com/watch?v=RYj1E9Rx9xo)
- "Yellow Charm, Green Indifference" (Founders Fanfic) Phoenixproductions05 (www.youtube.com/watch?v=sbUyiALDHIo)

Websites

- Ginny Potter.com. (www.ginnypotter.com/phpnuke/index.php)
- The Leaky Cauldron (www.the-leaky-cauldron.org)
- Harry and the Potters (www.eskimolabs.com/hp/p)
- Real Wizard Rock by Tess (realwizardrock.com)
- Tealin Raintree's Fan Art (www.nocturnalsoldier.org/Tealin)
- Wizrocklopedia (www.wizrocklopedia.com)

Author Spotlight

Photo by Iva Helm.

Peter Dickinson

Peter Dickinson lives in Hampshire, England, with his wife, Robin McKinley. He is a two-time winner of the Carnegie Medal and has also twice received the Whitbread Children's Award. His book *The Ropemaker* was a Printz honor book, the first fantasy novel to hold that honor. He was born in Africa but spent most of his school-age years in England. Visit his website at www.peterdickinson.com.

SELECTED BOOKLIST

A Bone from a Dry Sea (Loose Leaf, 1995)
Eva (Delacorte, 1989)
The Kin (Puffin, 2003)
The Ropemaker (Delacorte, 2001)
The Tears of the Salamander (Wendy Lamb, 2003)
Water: Tales of Elemental Spirits with Robin McKinley (Putnam, 2002)

ON HOW HE BECAME AN AUTHOR OF YOUNG ADULT LITERATURE

I was writing my first book, a crime novel, and got stuck for several months. I then had a nightmare with a sort of SF basis, and to get myself back to sleep retold the story in my head, making it come right. I finished up with a real story, so I thought I'd try to write it as the sort of book I used to enjoy as a young teenager (and still do, to be honest). I hoped doing that would unblock my other book. Which it did, so I finished up with a crime novel and a YA book, *The Weathermonger,* as a by-product. I'd had a great time writing both books, so I decided to carry on like that.

ON WHAT HE ENJOYED READING AS A TEENAGER

Science fiction. I had a supply of "golden age" pulp magazines from the United States. Crime novels, light romance, etc. Not "serious" novels—I detested Dickens, etc. I also liked the sort of old-fashioned poetry that rhymes and scans and sounds good. I still do.

ON THE APPEAL OF SPECULATIVE WORLDS

I believe we have evolved to speculate about possibilities. It's a very useful survival tool for a species expanding into new and different terrains. We still go on doing it because our minds are that shape.

ON CREATING A BELIEVABLE SPECULATIVE WORLD

By fully imagining it as concrete and coherent. If you're reading a realistic novel and you come across something that isn't so in the real world, it has the effect of turning that scene—perhaps the whole book—into cardboard. Almost all fantasy has real-world elements in it. They've got to be right. And the fantasy elements have to mesh with them, and just as solidly with each other. I find fantasy harder to write than realistic fiction.

ON WRITING IN MULTIPLE GENRES

On the whole I don't think about this sort of thing. All I know is that I find it stimulating to try something I haven't done before. In fact, if I get an idea and start saying to myself, "This is my kind of story," I can be pretty sure I'm going to have trouble with it. But if I say, "I wonder if I can do this," there's a very good chance it will come out OK.

Guidelines for Selecting and Evaluating Speculative Fiction

In addition to the general selection criteria for young adult literature, when working with fantasy, science fiction, and horror, you may want to consider the following questions:

- How has the author made the story believable? Does the narrative encourage readers to suspend disbelief?
- Is the speculative world consistent and logical within the world created?
- Is the plot original?
- How are elements of folklore and myth, scientific principles, or terrifying possibilities integrated into the narrative?

Science Fiction for Young Adults

Orson Scott Card, author of *Ender's Game,* has written on the distinction between the two main genres of speculative fiction. "If a story is set in a universe that follows the same rules as ours, it's science fiction. If it's set in a universe that doesn't fit our rules, it's fantasy" (Card, 1990, p. 22). Fantasy, as we have seen, creates its own rules of logic that, as long as they are consistent, do not necessarily have to correspond with those governing the real world. With science fiction, on the other hand, everything is based on scientific possibility. Everything that happens in the fictional world should be at least theoretically possible. As Charles Sullivan asserts, good science fiction "provides a believable extrapolation" from known theories and descriptions of science and technology (1999, pp. 2–3). A quick scan of the chronology of science fiction titles in the Appendix will reveal the diversity of themes, from speculations that have become at least partially realized (space travel, robots, cloning) to ideas that seem more improbable but still leave us wondering.

Science fiction is about testing and experimenting with scientific possibilities. Generally, in science fiction the world we know is disrupted by an invention, an alien intruder, a technological accident, or an experiment gone wrong. The author imagines what might happen after this accident/discovery/catastrophe. In a good work of science fiction the drama often comes from seeking a resolution to the disruption that has occurred. This has led Mendlesohn to assert that science fiction might be considered "an argument with the universe" (Mendlesohn, 2004, p. 290).

Like fantasy, science fiction is a crossover genre. Many teens read science fiction marketed for adults, and many titles are cross-listed. Science fiction is often also considered to be boy's fiction, but this is of course not necessarily true. Despite this, the stereotype is strong enough that author Alice May Norton wrote under the name Andre Norton so that science fiction readers would not be discouraged from choosing her books.

A distinction is sometimes made between science fiction and "hard" science fiction. All science fiction deals with scientific possibilities to a certain extent (though often exploring matters that are only vaguely theoretically possible), but much of what is published for children and young adults uses the future or outer space as a backdrop for a family story or an adventure tale. There simply is not much science involved in *Among the Hidden* (Haddix), one of the most popular futuristic titles for young readers. Much of the near future fiction such as *How I Live Now* (Rosoff) or John Marsden's Tomorrow series are more about social speculation than about scientific possibilities, and they read more like contemporary realistic fiction than science fiction. In hard science fiction the scientific detail is much richer and more intrinsic to the plot development. One is certainly not better fiction than the other, but this distinction often comes into play when looking at the reader's response to the narrative.

Some critics do not consider much of what might be labeled utopian/dystopian literature to be science fiction. Donelson and Nilsen (2005), for example, suggests that Lois Lowry's *The Giver* is somewhere between fantasy and science fiction, with literary traits particular to the utopian subgenre of speculative fiction. To an extent it can be argued that all literature is speculative and great debates can be had concerning what constitutes a genre and whether books could or should be classified in these ways at all. The young adult who can engage in reasoned discussion about these issues will gain a firmer grasp of the literature in question, regardless of the outcome.

Aliens and Space Travel

Science fiction certainly existed before the 1938 broadcast of H. G. Wells's *War of the Worlds*, but the excitement of that event sparked a popular interest in alien fiction. Since then numerous works of science fiction have explored alien invasions; in fact, the extraterrestrial is one of the most popular themes in science fiction. Often these aliens have malign reasons for their visits to earth. John Christopher's *The White Mountains* (1967) was the first of four books about the Tripods, an alien species that takes over the earth in the future. In *The Dark Side of Nowhere* by Neal Shusterman the aliens have been disguising themselves as humans, but their eventual plan is to rule the earth. The same is true of *The Angel Factory* (Blacker), in which the young protagonist's perfect life starts to unravel when he discovers that not only is he adopted but that he is also involved with aliens from a distant planet who have plans for earth. Obviously, most of these books have a rather serious tone to them but occasionally humor is tied to the theme. William Sleator's *Interstellar Pig* and the sequel *Parasite Pig* take a somewhat comic situation and still manage to create an action-packed story, as an unlikely teen hero named Barney plays a board game in an attempt to save the earth from aliens.

Some of the most interesting alien fiction deals with culture (species) conflict and relationships rather than conquest. The science fiction context can allow for rather typical themes to be explored in a suspenseful storyline. A visiting alien disrupts life for the protagonist in Margaret Mahy's *Aliens in the Family* (1986). In Logue's *Dancing with an Alien,* a young alien from another planet has been sent to earth to find a mate because on his planet the females have been killed off by disease. Similarly, in Kate Gilmore's *The Exchange Student,* an alien student is looking for someone to help him repopulate his planet. In *Singing the Dogstar Blues* by Alison Goodman, Joss has no clue as to why the alien student has chosen her as a study partner at the Centre for Neo-Historical Studies. The social dynamics involved in coexisting with aliens can allow interesting themes to be explored.

One of the most interesting aliens in all of YA fiction is Tall John in Walter Mosely's *47.* The novel is set in the 19th-century South and for much of the story seems to be like historical fiction. At first, Tall John seems to be a figure of legend, but soon the reader discovers that he has actually come from a planet far away in search of a young slave called 47 who holds the destiny of the universe in his hands.

Space Adventures and Space Odysseys

Although aliens on earth seem to have more shelf space in YA literature, the type of storyline that most likely comes to mind when people first think of science fiction involves space travel. There are many variations on the space travel theme, though the two biggest categories are social relationships in strange new worlds and heroic odysseys. In either case survival tends to be a key concern.

In the Mars Year One trilogy by Brad Strickland and Thomas Fuller, a colony has been started on Mars. When chaos erupts on Earth, those on Mars lose all radio contact. The Mars colony is not really ready to survive without supplies from Earth, but now they are going to have to try. There is adventure involved but most of the drama revolves around social dynamics in a stressful situation.

Some space adventure novels focus primarily on the relationship between humans and other species. In *Dragon and Thief* (Zahn), for example, a young human thief teams up with a dragon-like warrior refugee from a distant solar system. The warrior can only exist in a symbiotic relationship and his partner has been killed, so he needs the

Nothing new about foul-mouthed, oversexed teens, but Clint in *My Summer on Earth* (2008) is actually an alien disguised as a human. Reprinted by permission of Simon Pulse.

young man to survive. As it turns out the human protagonist is also very much in need of a companion/family.

In what are often referred to as space odysseys, heroes become involved in epic struggles to survive or to save the world or universe. Perhaps the best-known space odyssey, Star Wars, exists as a series of movies and books. The Star Wars novels are written by a variety of authors. One of the best in the series is *Episode 1: The Phantom Menace,* written by Terry Brooks.

Some space odysseys are ranked among the most popular science fiction novels. Orson Scott Card's *Ender's Game* (1985) was originally written for adults but is now cross-marketed explicitly for young adults. "Ender" Wiggin is a student at Battle School training to fight the aliens known as Buggers. Due to events beyond his control he has to go fight earlier than expected.

Karin Lowachee has authored an exciting space odyssey titled *Warchild.* In this novel young Jos Musey's childhood ends when he is taken by pirates from his parents' merchant ship. Jos escapes only to be captured for a second time by a group of aliens called *strints,* who are at war with humanity. The strints train him to be a spy but he has his own agenda.

Utopian/Dystopian Fiction

Throughout history in literature and sometimes in practice, people have attempted to create new communities without discord, places where everyone is equal and happy. These utopian societies are perhaps the grandest of the experiments projected on futuristic worlds.

In *The Giver* (Lowry) a seemingly utopian community is actually a stifling dystopia. In this world there is no war or disease, no starvation or bullies. Children are closely observed and given jobs based on their abilities and personalities. All of these utopian ideals have been "achieved" but at a high price. Interestingly, the companion book *Gathering Blue* and the sequel *The Messenger* are less utopian and read more like fantasy than science fiction.

In Rodman Philbrick's *The Last Book in the Universe,* one part of the world is inhabited by "proovs" who seem to live in a utopian society, but it is only "perfect" for them because the rest of humanity (the "normals") live in the squalor of urban areas filled with social decay and ruled by gangs. In general, these novels explore the concept that any society's idea of perfection is going to come at a price, raising many questions. Is it worth it? Who benefits? Who pays the price?

Time Travel

Time travel has already been mentioned as a subgenre of fantasy and although in some of these novels, time travel involves magic or the unexplained, other novels concentrate on the scientific aspects of time and therefore might be classified as science fiction. Of course, science fiction novels will have a rational explanation for the movement through time, often involving the invention of technology for time travel. Even if you have read none of these books, you can imagine the potential for peril. In H. G. Wells's *The Time Machine,* Simon goes back in time to carry out a secret mission, but he is sidetracked in the past when he falls in love. In Michael Crichton's *Timeline,* modern scientists travel back to the year 1357 and face the dangers of the time as well as the dangers of the imperfection of the technology used. Though there are dangers involved in time travel, there are also possible treasures. In Susan Price's *The Sterkarm Handshake,* time travelers raid the past for its riches.

The Mind's Potential

Whether you consider telekinesis, ESP, and so on as scientific possibility or as fantastic speculation depends to an extent on your personal beliefs. Either way, there are numerous novels that explore the potentials of the human mind. In *Hidden Talents* by David Lubar, the protagonist uses scientific experimentation to prove to his friends that they do, in fact, have some telepathic abilities. In Adrienne Vrettos's *Sight* the main character can only see into someone else's mind when he or she is faced with death, which leads to a very suspenseful mystery.

Numerous science fiction novels include alien characters with natural abilities to communicate, locate, or even move objects with their minds. In *Dragon and Thief* (Zahn), for example, the symbiotic relationship between the human character and the alien creates a bond that allows some feelings to be transmitted between them. Whether science possibility or science fantasy, the special powers of the mind is a theme that often appears in novels considered to be science fiction.

The Future

Technology

The vast majority of science fiction takes place in some future time. There are some good adventure novels whose settings in the future add to the excitement and pleasure of the narrative. Matthew Reilly's Hover Car Racer series appeals to some reluctant male readers who may not otherwise be science fiction readers. The Traces series by Malcolm Rose involves futuristic forensic crime investigations. Young readers of both science fiction and crime novels are likely to enjoy these stories. Generally, in the possible future of science fiction novels, some type of disruption occurs in the narrative world. Although futuristic, these narratives often effectively place contemporary problems in this context so they can be dissected from a distance. Many times the problem involves the use of technology that has unforeseen consequences.

Sometimes it is the technology itself that gets out of control and has to be reigned in, as in *I, Robot* (Asimov) or Philip K. Dick's *Do Androids Dream of Electric Sheep?* (adapted as the movie *Blade Runner*), in which a bounty hunter chases after a group of androids. The technology often has a negative effect on a personal level, as in Dan Gutman's *Virtually Perfect.* In this novel, a teen uses his father's computer to create a virtual character who somehow breaks free to the real world, dates his sister, and tries to become human. Other times the ramifications are global. In Ben Bova's *Dueling Machine* (1971), for example, a machine that was originally created to settle disputes is turned into a weapon of war.

The technology problem might be the result of an accident, as in Andrew Clements's *Things Not Seen.* Or the problem might be the consequence of unethical new technology. In *Be More Chill* (Vizzini), the protagonist purchases a squip (a mini supercomputer) on the black market to help him be cool. It goes without saying that the squip does not work as planned. Other times the problem might be technology that is systematically misused by society. In *The Bar Code Tattoo* (Weyn), a technology that is supposed to make our lives simpler is actually being used for profit by a multinational corporation tracking and monitoring everyone. In each case, the social consequences of technology are actually explored more directly than the technology itself.

Experiments

Sometimes the technological advances involve humans themselves, usually in pursuit of the extension of life. In Margaret Haddix's *Turnabout,* two elderly ladies are victims of an experimental treatment that reverses their aging. Soon they will be too young to take care of themselves and have to find someone else to take care of them. El Patrón in *The House of the Scorpion* (Farmer) tries for immortality in a different way. He is at least 150 years old, living for so long by using the body parts of clones for transplants. Some experiments are carried

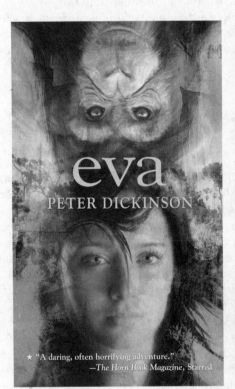 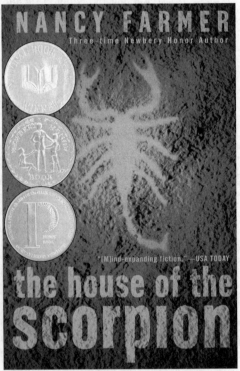

In *Eva* (Random House, 1990), a 13-year-old girl wakes up in the hospital to find that her "neurone memory" has been transplanted into the body of a chimpanzee, saving but also drastically changing her life. Imagine finding out that you are a clone, then imagine finding out that you were created for body parts! This is exactly what happens to Matt in *The House of the Scorpion* by Nancy Farmer (2002). Jacket cover from *Eva* by Peter Dickinson. Used by permission of Laurel-Leaf, an imprint of Random House Children's Books, a division of Random House, Inc. *The House of the Scorpion* reprinted by permission of Atheneum.

out not so much to extend life as to escape death. In *Eva,* a girl wakes up in a hospital after a car crash to discover that her brain has been transplanted into the body of a chimpanzee.

Other experiments are performed to create superior humans. In Nicole Luiken's *Violet Eyes* when two teens try to discover why they are so much alike, they find that they have been injected with "Renaissance" genes and are a new subspecies of human. Scott Westerfield's *Uglies* imagines a society where plastic surgery is commonplace. When young people reach 16, it is normal for them to undergo an operation that makes them supermodel gorgeous. Being pretty is all Tally has been waiting for, but when the time comes she is faced with a choice whether to betray her best friend or remain an Ugly forever.

In each of these instances the futuristic context and even the experiment itself creates an interesting storyline in which ethical issues can be explored. One of the most discussed examples of a futuristic context being used to critique the present is *Feed* by M. T. Anderson. The novel is set in a future world where the Internet is connected directly into people's brains at a young age, resulting in a nightmarish version of instant messaging. People have information at their fingertips, but they are also constantly bombarded with consumerism.

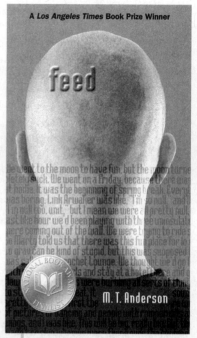

Many science fiction novels such as *Feed* by M. T. Anderson (2002) explore a possible dystopic future. Reprinted by permission of Candlewick.

In *Feed,* the most popular sitcom is called "Oh? Wow! Thing!" and girls have to retire to the ladies room a couple of times an evening because hairstyles have changed; hideous lesions have become fashion statements. During spring break on the moon, Titus (who in Shakespeare symbolized the "absurdity of modern life") meets a young lady who has never had an implant. Titus is intrigued by this outsider and he starts to reconsider the world he knows. While a bit over the top in its presentation of consumerism, teenspeak, and fads, the novel serves as an interesting critique of society today.

> *To Consider*
> If authors are critiquing contemporary society, why would they bother cloaking their criticisms in the context of futuristic worlds?

Cloning

The type of experimentation that has likely received more attention than any other in recent fiction is cloning. The possible implications of human cloning have appeared in science fiction since at least the 1970s and *The Boys from Brazil* (Levin, 1976), though the possibility was envisioned even in Aldous Huxley's *Brave New World* (1932).

Most of these books reject the possible benefits of cloning and instead present the negative social implications. Hillary Crew (2004) suggests that in many if not most science fiction novels for a young adult audience "human cloning is represented as being doomed to failure" (p. 216). Part of the problem stems from the reason for cloning in the first place, generally to replace the original person or to just be there in case the original needs a transplant. Nancy Farmer writes of Matt in *The House of the Scorpion,* "He understood he was only a photograph of a human, and that meant he wasn't really important. Photographs could lie forgotten in drawers for years. They could be thrown away" (p. 84). It is not surprising that the clones themselves question whether they even have free choice. Miranda in *Cloning Miranda* (Matas) struggles with the central question for many of these clones, wondering "when I make a choice," is it her or her "programming"? (p. 127). In *Taylor Five* (Halam) as Tay survives in the jungle she keeps reminding herself that she is a replica of a remarkable person. At the same time she wonders if she can even be considered human.

Although human cloning seems doomed to failure in most of these novels, the protagonists tend to be quite sympathetic. In *The House of the Scorpion,* Matt is a sweet, intelligent, thoughtful young man who discovers that he was made as a depository of body parts for an aging drug lord. The whole idea is abhorrent but now that he is here, is he less than human?

In the Regeneration series by L. J. Singleton, Varina says, "I wasn't the product of two loving parents but the result of experimental science" (*Regeneration,* p. 140). In both novels about cloning and in YA literature in general "individual identity and differentiation" are significant themes (Crew, 2004, pp. 206–207). Teen clones are especially confused and angry about identity and how they relate to other people.

Catastrophes and Societal Changes

Many science fiction narratives explore the potential for things to go wrong in the future. In Margaret Haddix's *Among the Hidden,* readers are introduced to a world facing overpopulation. The government has imposed a strict two-child policy. Luke, an illegal third child, has been relatively lucky living on a rural farm. Though unable to attend school or meet anyone outside of the immediate family, he has at least spent his childhood playing outside—until a new development is built next to his house. Now he must hide away. One day he notices that there appears to be another hidden child in one of the new houses and for the first time Luke meets someone outside of his family. The storyline is especially hard-hitting and not that far-fetched in light of current policies in China.

In the companion book, *Among the Betrayed,* Nina Idi is arrested for treason. She is told that she can get clemency if she will turn in three other children. Even more than the first book in the series, this novel deals with graphic and emotionally charged issues such as torture:

> Nina's wrists and ankles were rubbed raw from the handcuffs and ankle cuffs that chained her to the wall. The skin had been whipped from her back; even the slightest touch of her shirt against her skin sent pain shrieking through her body. (2002, p. 2)

Nina determines to somehow save the children and herself. Haddix's series has proven to be extremely popular, even with readers who say they would never normally choose science fiction. Other science fiction titles look at natural or manmade catastrophes. Nancy Farmer's *The Ear, the Eye, and the Arm* is set in a futuristic Zimbabwe. Hazardous waste sold to the African country by the West over the years has led to some interesting mutations, including the three heroes of this novel.

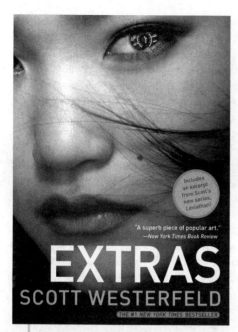

"A superb piece of popular art."
—*New York Times Book Review*

EXTRAS
SCOTT WESTERFELD
THE #1 NEW YORK TIMES BESTSELLER

Readers will recognize so much of today's world in the futuristic pop reality created in *Extras* by Scott Westerfeld (2007). Reprinted by permission of Simon Pulse.

For several decades the most popular world disaster was nuclear war. In a number of postnuclear books of the 1970s and 1980s everybody dies. Robert O'Brien's *Z for Zachariah* (1975) and Robert Swindell's *Brother in the Land* (1984) are among books of this sort that have had a lasting readership. In O'Brien's novel, after a nuclear catastrophe the protagonist finds herself alone in a valley with one other survivor, which as it turns out might be worse than being totally alone. Among the best of the nuclear holocaust stories is Caroline Stever's *River Rats,* in which a group of young survivors live in an old riverboat.

In K. A. Applegate's Remnants series a group of humans escape an impending asteroid impact by blasting off into space. When they wake up they find that they have been asleep for 500 years and an alien ship has recreated an environment based on information from earth's art galleries that is surreal and dangerous.

And then there are the diseases. In *The Last Dog on Earth* by Daniel Ehrenhaft, a mysterious virus is crossing the country, turning dogs into vicious predators. People have started shooting dogs on sight whether they have the disease or not. For Logan this is an emergency, because his dog Jack is the only one who always sticks by him. Soon Jack and Logan are on the run. As luck would have it, Logan's father is one of the few scientists who might be able to find a cure for the disease.

The Kindling by Jennifer Armstrong and Nancy Butcher is the first book in the Fire-Us trilogy. These novels present a world laid waste by terrible illness. Set in 2007, 5 years after a virus wipes out all of the adults (and it seems everyone but them), a group of young people in Florida have banded together to form a family of their own. But then a teen boy arrives trying to convince them to go on a quest to Washington, DC. Another standout is Pete Hautman's *Hole in the Sky,* in which a mutant virus has devastated the world.

Of course, potential futures often involve war as well. John Marsden, an Australian author, has an incredibly popular series known as the Tomorrow series that commences with *Tomorrow, When the War Began* and runs through a seventh action-packed novel, *The Other Side of Dawn.* In these books Australia has been invaded and a group of teens hides out and resists the invaders.

Ethics, Humanity, and Science Fiction

Critics such as Farah Mendlesohn have argued that one cannot just replace elves and dragons with robots and spaceships to create science fiction; the differences are greater than that. Mendlesohn asserts, "Science fiction is less a genre than a mode. It is a way of writing about things, events, and people, rather than a description of which things, events, and people should be written about" (2004, p. 287). In fact, science fiction in this conception is ideological.

Science fiction for young adults often deals with control—of emotions, sexual urges, and identity. In fact many of these books are obviously cautionary tales. The young characters are experimented on, but they are also experimenting with life, and in these books the mistakes that teens make can be deadly. Clones for example tend to feel alone and more cut off than the typical teen. They have to grapple with what it means to be human and what it means to be an individual. "I don't want to be Anna Zimmerman," says Anna after finding out that she is a clone of Zimmerman. "I want to be someone else. Me" (p. 110). These characters are often depersonalized further by being marked as experiments (Ostry, 2004). Matt in *The House of the Scorpion* actually has "Property of the Alacrán Estate" stamped on the bottom of his foot. When the world does not consider these characters to be human, any misstep can be fatal.

Memory itself might be taken away from people or at least from a segment of the population in a futuristic society. Drugs of one kind or another are used to keep people from questioning the way things are. In *The Giver* all adolescents take a pill that suppresses sexual feelings. Angel, from the Regeneration series, has a loyalty chip installed in her head. The eejits in *The House of the Scorpion* have implants installed that turn them into unquestioning work machines.

The beginnings of a chart of themes in YA science fiction might look something like this:

Science Themes	Humanity Themes	YA Themes
Space odyssey	To what extent can we change the world?	The search for identity
Aliens		Coming of age
Technology	How can we balance ethics and our human desires?	Being an outsider
Future		Relating to family
Experimentation	What does it mean to be human?	Peer pressure
Cloning	What is our role in the universe?	Taking responsibility
Future catastrophe	How do we relate with the natural world?	Sexual awakening
Utopia/dystopia	Are we alone?	Control of one's own destiny
Time travel		
The mind's potential		

In the novel *Boy Proof* (Castellucci), a contemporary realistic fiction novel about a girl who is a science fiction geek, the protagonist meets a young man who understands her love of the genre because "they talk about taboo issues and open up a conversation about them" (p. 9).

It is quite common that these books explore ethical problems associated with scientific experimentation. In *Turnabout* (Haddix), scientists seek to reverse the natural process of aging. In *Be More Chill,* Ned Vizzini plays around with many young teens' dreams of having a device that makes them know how to act and what would be cool to say in every instance. Many teens feel like aberrations to a certain extent. In *Eva* (Dickinson) doctors transplant a girl's brain into a chimp's body and she becomes an exaggeration of teen fears. Even worse, the media attempts to make Eva a commercial product, getting her to wear name brand clothes and do commercials. Experimentation and exploitation often seem to

To Consider

We are all conditioned to an extent by society and by our parents and teachers. To what extent are we programmed to act the way we do, and to what extent do we have choice? Can biomachines, clones, aliens, or chimps with human brains be human? What does it mean to be human?

go hand in hand. In Carol Matas's *Cloning Miranda,* the protagonist discovers that she is the clone of her dead "sister" and that another clone was made to use for transplants should she need them.

In so many of these novels the young protagonist discovers that adults and often parents have been lying to them, that their family and society in general are not what was promised. Instead, they realize they are mutants, clones, or experimental products who always feel that they are utterly alone, that they do not know who they are, or who to trust. "Everyone I had ever met had lied to me on a fundamental level," says Angel in *Violet Eyes* (p. 85). Over and over these characters discover that the most important aspects of their lives or identities are lies.

In *Shade's Children* (Nix) everyone is killed at age 14 and turned into biomachinery. Again this is an exaggeration of how many teens actually feel, as they are controlled, cajoled, and enticed into the ideas their parents, teachers, and counselors have chosen for them. Given that these characters often do not fit in, it is a major dilemma for them when they discover that they have remarkable powers. They vacillate between feeling less than human and feeling superhuman.

A number of near future books have appeared in recent years that examine consumerism and the loss of personal freedoms. In Suzanne Weyn's *The Bar Code Tattoo* most people have willingly gotten a tattoo placed on their arm that takes the place of credit and ATM cards, driver's licenses, and other forms of ID. It turns out that the multinational corporation/political group that now controls the nation is tracking more than anyone knows.

A Survey of Horror for Young Adults

A timeline of horror fiction, like any attempt to classify literature by genre, can be difficult. Most of the early books listed in the chronology of horror literature in the Appendix would have influenced the evolution of what today would be called horror but one could hardly call *The Divine Comedy* or *Dr. Faustus* "horror" novels. Even *Frankenstein* is generally regarded as science fiction rather than horror. But these books have profoundly affected the development of the genre. Most of the books on this timeline were not written specifically for young adults, but a large portion of horror readers are young adults.

Ultimately, genre allows us to understand how a piece of literature relates to other books and aids the reader in making inferences and connections. It even allows us to appreciate a writer's fracturing of a literary trope. So if fantasy creatures, motifs, and situations are pulled from traditional literature, and science fiction finds its roots in scientific possibilities, what can we say about the origins of horror? Vampires, witches, and ghosts are as much a part of folklore as fairies and elves, but alien pod people or mutants created by a nuclear spill are creatures of our imagination triggered by what could go wrong in the universe we know. So it seems that horror draws from both realms of speculation. What sets it apart initially is the added value of fright.

It is often very difficult and perhaps simply a matter of rhetoric to decide whether a book such as *Gallows Hill* by Lois Duncan is in fact suspenseful fantasy, supernatural thriller, or horror. In this novel, Sarah discovers that she can see into the future; soon she is facing accusations of being a witch. It turns out that she is not the only one; several students at her school are reincarnations of people killed during the Salem witch trails. Does this type of ghost/witch story have the fear factor that would cause us to label it horror? If made into a movie (as was Duncan's *I Know What You Did Last Summer*), it is likely that even more horror elements would be added, making the story easier to classify.

Whatever the elements are that set horror apart from other genres, they tend to be popular with some young adults. Perhaps teens who read this fiction seek "to integrate their known sense of developing self with the unknown self that pushes from the darkness" (O'Quinn, 2004, p. 51). Part of the attraction is that they speak to the "hunger inside us," as Darren in *Cirque du Freak* (Shan) suggests. Many young adults can certainly identify with M. T. Anderson's teenage vampire in *Thirsty,* who is filled with "unnamed feelings that percolate until they feel like a dam about to burst" (p. 26).

Author Spotlight

Photo courtesy of Annette Curtis Klause.

Annette Curtis Klause

Annette Curtis Klause was born in Bristol, England. She received both her B.A. and her M.L.S. from the University of Maryland, College Park. In addition to being an author she is in charge of Children's Services at the Aspen Hill Community Library in Maryland. Visit her website at www.childrensbookguild.org/klause.htm.

SELECTED BIBLIOGRAPHY

Alien Secrets (Bantam, 1993)
Blood and Chocolate (Delacorte, 1997)
Freaks: Alive on the Inside (McElderry, 2006)
The Silver Kiss (Delacorte, 1990)

ON THE EXTENT TO WHICH SHE DRAWS ON TRADITIONAL TALES AND OTHER LITERATURE WHEN CREATING HER CHARACTERS

Well, the werewolves are a good example. I drew upon fiction and folklore, and also the movies I had seen, but I also did some research to see if I had missed some good info, and what I didn't find to support my story, I made up, but logically, based on the tradition. Changing to a wolf at the full moon is traditional, but I let my werewolves change at other times—only under a full moon they have less control. I found that there were many persecutions of people as werewolves in the Middle Ages, like there were witchcraft trials in America, and most of this took place in France and Germany. That gave me the idea that my werewolves were descended from people who fled these persecutions and ended up in America, and that's why they have mostly French and German names, some of which I stole from those historical records. I have to make my fantasies grounded in reality for them to work for me and for the reader. Many of the stories and films I had seen seemed to make werewolves loners, but that didn't make sense to me. If they were part wolf then they should have packs. If they had packs, then they would have a social order similar to wolves. If they had a society then they would probably have folklore and religion of their own. These myths would probably involve the moon, since the moon has such an influence on them. So I created ceremony and myth and religion for them to refer to.

The same with vampires—I took from the mythology, and the literary tradition, but also made up some of my own lore to explain such things as why vampires are afraid of running water. But I based these explanations on the folklore.

ON THE SENSUAL ELEMENTS OF HORROR THAT OFTEN LEAD TO CHALLENGES IN LIBRARIES AND CLASSROOMS

I like to tell people that these feelings are there in teenagers, and I would be dishonest if I didn't acknowledge them and I would lose the trust of my readers. Acknowledging sensuality does not mean encouraging sexual behavior, however. There is a difference between having feelings and acting on those feelings, and between acting on those feelings responsibly or irresponsibly. Teenagers have a right to have their feelings validated and be given an arena in which they can explore in their imagination the possible consequences of acting on those feelings. Reading a book that talks about sex doesn't mean that a young person will run out and have sex; it means that they will have more of a basis to evaluate the situation should it arise. If a character in a book has irresponsible sex and gets into trouble, or is obviously a less than admirable role model, this is giving the reader cues about behavior right there. A teenager in a book may not always do things adults will approve of, but the way the character responds to the consequences of his or her choices is an opportunity for the reader to learn about life. Teenagers in books should be allowed to agonize about and take joy in the same things real teenagers do, and use the imaginary experience to put real-life situations into context.

Vampires

The most popular subgenre of horror fiction is the vampire story, of which there are two basic types. First are novels that feature vampire protagonists, invariably dealing with themes such as immortality with a price or the internal conflict between humanity and an unquenchable thirst. *Thirsty* by M. T. Andersen and *Cirque du Freak* fall into this first category. Although both of these books address the topic with humor, they also beautifully capture the teen angst of the estrangement from family as all of the teen vampire's monstrous urges awaken.

The second type of vampire novel is more centered on the human attraction to the unknown and the sensual, especially when contrasted with the mundane reality of everyday

life. Annette Curtis Klause's *The Silver Kiss* and Vivian Vande Velde's *Companions of the Night* are about hopeless romance as much as they are about the undead, and there is a definite correlation on these novels between love and death, often with sensual overtones.

The novels of Amelia Atwater-Rhodes should be noted here. Atwater-Rhodes was only 13 when she wrote her first vampire novel, *In the Forests of the Night.* Her vampire character Risika faces the same general internal conflict between morality and her vampire instincts, but there is an acute lack of erotic undertones, which make it a good introduction to the topic for tweens. Atwater-Rhodes's *Demon in My View* adds an interesting twist. The main character is actually a teen novelist who discovers that the vampire stories she writes may be more than fiction, and the vampires are not too happy that she is giving away their secrets.

Another notable author is Stephenie Meyer, whose Twilight series has brought horror and especially vampire literature to the forefront in the popular media. The themes involved in the Twilight books fit with the tradition but they also possibly cause us to rethink the connections between horror, romance, and teen angst.

Ghosts

Ghosts are quite popular in literature for young readers. A typical storyline involves a young person moving into a new house with a haunted history. As previously mentioned, ghost stories often lie on the boundary of suspenseful fantasy, horror, and another subgenre that might be called paranormal or supernatural fiction. In *Look for Me by Moonlight* by Mary Downing Hahn, the protagonist goes to live with her father, who is staying in a historic and haunted inn in Maine. In *Jade Green: A Ghost Story* by Phyllis Reynolds Naylor, 15-year-old Judith moves into her uncle's old house complete with blood stains, noises in the attic, and gossip about a girl who supposedly died in the house.

Ghosts tend to be waiting around for a purpose, and the young adult protagonists often aid them in solving a mystery or completing a task. In Brenda Seabrooke's *The Haunting of Swain's Fancy* two stepsisters, upset about having to stay together on vacation in a strange house, discover a ghost looking out of the attic window and try to solve a Civil War murder mystery.

Ghosts can be frightening but they tend to evoke sorrow as well. As in *The Bagpiper's Ghost* by Jane Yolen, the sense of horror might be outweighed by compassion. At other times the unknown and elements of evil can make ghost stories rather scary. In *The Presence* by Eve Bunting, which involves a girl haunted by the death of her best friend, the protagonist is approached by a ghostly looking stranger who says he can help her communicate with her friend. Scenes in this story are every bit as terrifying as those in a vampire novel. Collections such as Vivian Vande Velde's *Being Dead* and Aidan Chambers's *Favorite Ghost Stories* include the full range of stories from the touching to the creepy to the chilling and can serve as a good introduction to ghost stories.

Various Frights

Ghosts and vampires may be the easiest horrific creatures to find but they are not alone. Werewolves, witches, zombies, and other creatures of myth and legend inhabit our nightmares and find their way into literary worlds. The Night World series by L. J. Smith investigates love stories between creatures of the so-called Night World and the reality known to humans. The problem here is that the laws of Night World strictly forbid such relationships, as they would reveal Night World's existence to humans.

Many of these horror novels tend to complicate the dichotomy of good versus evil. In *Wicked: Spellbound* (Holder and Viguie), for example, there are good witches and bad witches. In *Blood and Chocolate* (Klause) Vivian, who happens to be a werewolf, just wants to have a normal relationship with a "meat boy." The underlying themes are often connected to the teen desire to fit in and still be unique. In *The Wolving Time* (Jennings), which takes place in 16th-century France, Lazlo and his pack of werewolves just want to live in peace. If anyone is evil it is their pursuers who want to destroy them just for being different.

LITERARY THEORY

Psychoanalytic Criticism

Fundamentally the psychoanalytic is concerned with the articulation of desire and sexuality in language. As such, it would likely be of interest to young adults, although many who work with teens might find it problematic to discuss with them. At the same time, it would be impossible to consider the theoretical study of young adult literature without exploring the impact of psychoanalytic theory. In its broadest articulation, psychoanalytic criticism examines how our dreams and fantasies are expressed in story.

Sigmund Freud read the unconscious allusions found in text as symptoms of the author, whose sexual desires come into conflict with the norms of society. The creation of story, like the imaginative play of children, provides therapeutic release for the author (Bosmajian, 2005; Freud, 1993). Building on Freud, numerous critics have read literary constructs as tropes for the unresolved problems of the author (Greenacre, 1955).

Psychoanalytic criticism since Freud has explored a range of psychological issues as they relate to the authors, characters, or readers. All of these theories share in common the idea that story might offer a roadmap to the unconscious. Post-Freudians in general have been more concerned with the reader's transactive relation to the text. Combining what has been theorized about the psyche with the concepts developed by reader response theory, critics have suggested that when you read, you have a transaction with the core fantasies and symbolic foundations of the text on the unconscious or the subconscious level.

Along these lines there is so much that might be explored in stories like the Harry Potter series. Even on the surface level there is a large amount of wish fulfillment. Harry has been a nobody living in abusive conditions under the stairs in his relative's house, but all of a sudden he is the chosen one, the most powerful and popular! All of Freud's significant dream symbols are to be found in Potter's story: flying, trains, unicorns. The first magic he engages in involves freeing a large snake. He acquires a powerful magic wand and soon is given the fastest broomstick.

The phallic imagery is abundant. Of course the wish fulfillment need not be sexual. Some kids might read Harry's story and fantasize that the people they live with are not their real parents (who were really cool people and who loved them so much they died for them and now protect them from the grave). However these novels can certainly be read in terms of gratification and desire. Along with the awakening sexuality of the characters (and by extension the reader or even the author) is the fear that the father/mother/society forbids such desire. Similarly, in *Growing Wings* (Winter) the protagonist discovers that when her mother was coming of age her wings were literally cut off by her own mother! The analogy might seem a little obvious, but it does reflect the way that many young women feel and the fears that they might have.

Among the many psychoanalytic critics since Freud, few have been as influential as Jacques Lacan, whose focus was on the construction of self. Lacan asserts that a mirror stage exists during which the child sees him- or herself reflected in the other and creates a "fictional" identity. Perhaps the ultimate realization of the mirror stage can be found in stories of cloning. Anna in *Anna to the Infinite Power* (Ames) confronts a mirror image—or perhaps she is the mirror image, an image even closer to the source than a mother would be. In fact, the person from whom she is cloned is so much like her that she becomes unable to find herself. Returning to the psychoanalytic possibilities of Harry Potter, when Harry looks in the mirror of desire he sees his parents rather than seeing himself. Harry's parents are absent but still present. When he sees his parents in the mirror, this reinforces the idea that they live on in him. Whether the psychoanalytic reading looks at the psyche of the characters, the author, or the reader, it can shed interesting light on both teen angst and developing identity and on the narrative itself.

> *To Consider*
>
> When adult authors write about teenage identity and sexual awakenings in speculative worlds, to what extent are they reflecting the realities young adults experience, as opposed to simply reinforcing societal ideas about teen development?

For Further Reading

To begin an investigation into psychoanalytic criticism as it applies to a young adult literature you might commence with the following readings:

Bosmajian, Hamida. "Reading the Unconscious: Psychoanalytic Criticism." In Peter Hunt (ed.), *Understanding Children's Literature*, 2nd ed. Routledge, 2005.

Gallop, Jane. *Reading Lacan*. Cornell University Press, 1985.

Gay, Peter (ed.). *The Freud Reader*. Norton, 1989.

Gilman, Todd. " 'Aunt Em: Hate You! Hate Kansas! Taking the Dog, Dorothy': Conscious and Unconscious Desire in the Wizard of Oz." *Children's Literature Association Quarterly, 20*(4), Winter 1995–1996, 161–167.

Gose, Elliott. *Mere Creatures: A Study of Modern Fantasy Tales for Children*. University of Toronto Press, 1988.

McGillis, Roderick. "Another Kick at La/can: 'I Am a Picture'." *Children's Literature Association Quarterly, 20*, 1995, 42–46.

Mitchell, Claudia, and Jacqueline Reid-Walsh. "Mapping the Dark Country: Psychoanalytical Perspective in Young Adult Literature." *Children's Literature Association Quarterly, 25*(2), Summer 2000, 6–23.

Patterson, Nancy-Lou. "Angel and Psychopomp in Madeleine L'Engle's 'Wind' Trilogy." *Children's Literature in Education, 14,* 1983, 195–203.

6

Contemporary Realistic Fiction

Contemporary Realistic Fiction Text Set

An Abundance of Katherines by John Green
Autobiography of My Dead Brother by Walter Dean Myers
Ball Don't Lie by Matt de la Peña
Big Mouth & Ugly Girl by Joyce Carol Oates
Boot Camp by Todd Strasser
Born to Rock by Gordon Korman
Evolution, Me, & Other Freaks of Nature by Robin Brande
The First Part Last by Angela Johnson
Inexcusable by Chris Lynch
Just Another Hero by Sharon Draper
Lord of the Deep by Graham Salisbury
The Misfits by James Howe
November Blues by Sharon Draper
Peak by Roland Smith
Rain Is Not My Indian Name by Cynthia Leitich Smith
Red Kayak by Priscilla Cummins
Schooled by Gordon Korman
Slam by Nick Hornby
Speak by Laurie Halse Anderson
Stay with Me by Garrett Freyman-Weyr
Sunrise over Fallujah by Walter Dean Myers
The Warriors by Joseph Bruchac
The Watcher by James Howe

International Text Set

Camel Rider by Prue Mason
Chanda's Wars by Allan Stratton

Does My Head Look Big in This? by Randa Abdel-Fattah

Getting the Girl by Markus Zusak

The Illustrated Mum by Jacqueline Wilson

Indigo's Star by Hillary McKay

The Killing Sea by Richard Lewis

A Little Piece of Ground by Elizabeth Laird

On the Jellicoe Road by Melina Marchetta

One Whole and Perfect Day by Judith Clarke

The Other Side of Truth by Beverly Naidoo

Parvana's Journey by Deb Ellis

Smiling for Strangers by Gaye Hicyilmaz

Theories of Relativity by Barbara Haworth-Attard

When I Was a Soldier by Valerie Zenatti

In the Field *Holding a Virtual Author Visit*

Photo courtesy of Cynthia Leitich Smith.

The students in April Todd's ninth-grade class at Washington High School have spent the past 2 weeks reading and exploring the novel *Rain Is Not My Indian Name* by Cynthia Leitich Smith. They have compared images from Indian Country Today (www.indiancountry.com) with more traditional images of Native Americans. They have also discussed their own preconceptions of American Indians and whether those images fit with the characterization of Cassidy Rain Berghoff in the novel.

Today their novel unit will culminate in an online discussion with the author using Instant Messenger. Smith lives over 1,000 miles away and is busy working on her next book, but she is able to sit and talk with this class about the themes of death, friendship, and identity for half an hour. The students are excited. They have written questions in advance but have also worked with their teacher to create a format for virtual literature circles so that they will have more of a conversation than simply a list of preset questions. One student sits at a computer to do the typing, and one person serves as the facilitator (ordering the questions and responses in a way that makes sense). Everyone else is split into four groups who watch the Instant Messenger discussion on a projected screen, discuss what the author says, and decide how best to respond.

After introductions the students move straight to their questions.

WHS200587: What influenced you to write this book?

CLeitichSmith: I was first inspired to write *Rain Is Not My Indian Name* by a tragic experience from my own youth. At the first cross-country meet of high school I watched a boy on my team cross the finish line and then die of a previously undetected heart condition. It was my first close brush with the death of a peer, and I always felt haunted by it. Rain's story was inspired by my nightmare, what if that boy had been someone even closer, my first friend who was a boy and more than a friend.

WHS200587: After you wrote *Rain Is Not My Indian Name* were you more released from this nightmare?

CLeitichSmith: Yes, it was a cathartic experience. While the novel was in progress, I had another loss, the death of my beloved grandfather. And this inspired me to think a lot about my feelings toward the circle of life and families. I now feel more comfortable, less afraid, and confident that I'm doing what I can to honor the memory of loved ones.

WHS200587: What inspired you to have Galen's death on Rain's birthday? Was it a personal experience?

CLeitichSmith: Birthdays have always been really important to me. I was born the day before Rain, on New Year's Eve (my father referred to me for 2 years as his "little tax deduction") but the timing of Galen's death on Rain's birthday was more to convey the idea of life continuing, a theme I tried to further reinforce via Natalie's pregnancy and her decision to name the baby Aiyana, after Rain's mother.

WHS200587: In the note from the author you said, "you hoped those with a loss in their own family got some comfort from this novel." Why did you allow Rain to handle the death the way that she did, by not attending the funeral?

CLeitichSmith: I think that each of us grieves in our own way, on our own timeline. My own mother, for example, has a very difficult time attending funerals. She's not ready then to face her loss in such a public forum. I wanted to let readers know that you don't have to grieve like everyone else, that it can be on your own schedule and in your own way. Ultimately, Rain has a service of her own, in cyberspace, by creating a memorial to Galen that can stay online forever. For her, it better captures their relationship, how long it lasted and how personal it was, than a big event involving interaction with many other in-person mourners.

WHS200587: Why did you have Rain go through all of the changes that she did? Galen's death, her dad, & Natalie, & Fynn?

CLeitichSmith: Really, the big change that Rain goes through is from self-isolating to reaching out to others again. The shift, the opening, in her relationships with her family are all examples of this outreach. Really, they have been there for her all along. She just had to let them in and allow herself to risk her heart, to support them in return.

WHS200587: Were you stronger after writing the novel? Do you feel that Rain is a part of you?

CLeitichSmith: I gained strength with Rain, and she is very much a part of me. One of the hardest things for a writer to do is to end a story. To me, Rain is still here, still speaking to me now and then. Like many Native writers (Sherman Alexie, Louise Erdrich) I will be ultimately creating a world of books that interlink to one another. Rain has made it quite clear that she wants to be heard from again.

The room is just a little chaotic as students hurriedly rush new questions up to the facilitator, but amazingly everyone is on task! Everyone is interested!

Technology Links

Virtual Chat with Cynthia Leitich Smith

A number of authors have started engaging in virtual classroom visits. Depending on the technology available at a particular school, and the technology an author is familiar with, communication software as diverse as Instant Messenger, Skype, or Second Life might be used to bring readers and authors together. For many teachers this is extremely practical. When well prepared, these discussions can be exciting for the readers and can really enhance understandings of the literature. Teachers interested in this sort of activity might start with Cynthia Leitich Smith's website, which includes information on carrying out a virtual chat (www.cynthialeitichsmith.com/CLS/events/cyber_speaking.html).

Overview of Contemporary Realistic Fiction

The genre of contemporary realistic fiction ranks high, both in terms of the quantity of titles published and in terms of popularity among young adult readers. In part this is due to the fact that these stories reflect contemporary life, take place in familiar settings, and present common situations with which the reader can identify. To some extent this literature attempts to accurately present life with all of its complexities, and because the characters are teenagers, this reality tends to focus on maturing and finding an identity in relation to the changing world they live in. The strong sense of the real world in a particular context that is conveyed in these books provides windows through which readers can see the world and mirrors in which readers might see themselves.

The author of contemporary realistic fiction tells a story that never happened but could be possible in a present-day setting. The fiction flows from the author's imagination but with a firm foundation in the real world. As fiction these narratives all contain an element of the fanciful and they also convey the perspectives and biases of the author. When successful, the balance between a good story and an author's vision of what might happen in this place and time to these characters creates stories contemporary young people can relate to. Equally important, readers are often able to find out about how other young people might respond to the world around them. In many of the best and most popular of these books readers are able to see both aspects they can identify with and aspects that allow them access to new perspectives on what life is like for people who may not share their culture, gender, or social situation. For many readers it is important that these (seemingly authentic) books present young people with plausible joys, pains, and sorrows.

To an extent all literature can be said to combine elements of the real with the imagined, and there is disagreement about what literature should be included in the realm of

Photo by Jennifer Seay.

contemporary realistic fiction. Some books such as Louis Sacher's *Holes* or Laurie Faria Stolarz's *Project 17* bend the rules of reality, adding some fantasy, folkloric, or supernatural elements to the narrative. Some critics might equate so-called "problem novels" with contemporary realistic fiction, but others define it loosely as any novel presenting a fairly plausible contemporary world. However, mystery, suspense, romance, and detective novels each often have contemporary settings but also have their own literary traditions, narrative structures, and ways of presenting the world.

Rather than draw boundaries, much of what this chapter includes is an overview of the themes and types of literature that are popular in the wider realm of contemporary realistic fiction. For young adults many of these themes reflect concerns in their daily lives, some from personal experiences and some from the realm of imagination. Either way, the fiction based on these themes tends to focus on relatively believable characters and events. Not surprisingly, "coming of age" is one of the most popular themes in YA literature. A quick look at recent popular collections of short stories for young adults provides a good indication of the themes that recur in these books.

- *Dirty Laundry: Stories about Family Secrets* ed. by Lisa Dowe Fraustino
- *Love and Sex: Ten Stories of Truth* ed. by Michael Cart
- *On the Edge: Stories from the Brink* ed. by Lois Duncan
- *On the Fringe* ed. by Don Gallo
- *One Hot Second: Stories about Desire* ed. by Cathy Young
- *Period Pieces* ed. by Erzsi Deak and Kristin Embry Litchman
- *Ultimate Sports: Short Stories by Outstanding Writers for YA* ed. by Don Gallo
- *Working Days: Short Stories about Teenagers at Work* ed. by Anne Mazer

Love, lust, testing the limits, hidden problems—these books appeal to young adults because they can relate to many of the situations and sentiments found in this genre. Unfortunately, this also means that many of these books are challenged by people who do not feel teens should be reading books dealing with these issues. Frank depictions of the problems teens face can make it difficult for educators to get the books onto approved reading lists (Cohn, 2004). Some adults feel uncomfortable discussing the issues because rather than a right or wrong answer, the reader is often confronted with complex ethical dilemmas.

The Appeal of Contemporary Realistic Fiction

Despite the popularity of these books, some literary critics have stereotyped contemporary realistic fiction for young adults as formulaic, didactic, or overly grim literature that is pushed on teens by teachers, librarians, and award committees (Feinberg, 2004). Any genre includes both well-crafted as well as formulaic examples, but the fact remains that many young adult texts scorned by adult reviewers are very popular with young readers (Cart, 1996).

It makes sense that teens might identify with characters who have interests similar to theirs and who must deal with problems similar to theirs. When teen readers recognize situations that they confront in their own lives or that their peers might have encountered, this can make them think in new ways about their world. Rachel Cohn (2004) writes that her books convey "honest depictions of the complicated lives that contemporary teens live—sometimes sad, sometimes harsh, sometimes joyful—but always interesting" (n.p.).

Perhaps the greatest positive benefit of books that young people can relate to is that they get reluctant readers to read. When these struggles are realistic, they present the concept to teen readers that although growing up is never easy, other teens around the world share similar problems and generally manage to struggle through adversity. Young adult readers learn about human problems and human relationships, enlarging their frames of reference and perhaps broadening their interests. In young adult novels such as Judy Blume's *Forever*, teens find a faithful and unvarnished version of true life in all its extremes and emotions (Kaplan, 2003). Through this literature teens experience things vicariously that they might never experience firsthand. Literature can help young adults become more empathetic and critical thinkers (Alsup, 2003). Still, every semester I have a college student who says to me, "Oh yeah, *Forever* (giggle), I must have read that three times when I was younger, but it's not really young adult literature, is it? It's way too graphic."

When Deanna was 13 years old, she made a mistake and 3 years later she is still paying for it in Sara Zarr's *Story of a Girl* (2008). Reprinted by permission of Little, Brown and Company.

Reading literature can be an ethical as well as intellectual process, and as such it can assist adolescents in coping with their tumultuous lives (Kaplan, 2004). YA books, if given the chance, can teach, guide, and mold, through voices and situations to which kids can relate, and hopefully, that adults, too, can appreciate (Cohn, 2004). Critical readings of literature can have an impact on the emotional and intellectual growth of young adults. Teachers of every discipline can help students find good books that address these highly complicated and emotional issues (Alsup, 2003; Kaplan, 2004).

Patti Capel Swartz (2003) believes that classes on young adult literature must include works that discuss racism, classism, ableism, sexism, and homophobia or discriminatory attitudes will never change. English and reading teachers must find these texts and use them in their respective classrooms to motivate young people, especially older adolescents, to talk about these difficult and often explosive issues. They must be read and discussed in high school classes because, whether we like it or not, these and other issues like violence, drug use, and sexuality are real in students' lives (Alsup, 2003). Readers may not always agree with the characters' decisions, but at least they are exposed to possibilities of resolving ethical issues they may not have previously considered. They are provided with choices, and these choices prompt reflec-

To Consider

Imagine a troubling situation you have experienced in the past. How might it have benefited you to have access to narratives about other people who had similar troubles?

tions about their personal beliefs, thereby stimulating their moral development (Bushman and McNerny, 2004).

The possibility that literature can help young readers cope with grief, fear, and anger in the face of adversity has led many to consider using contemporary realistic literature for the purposes of bibliotherapy (Bucher and Manning, 2005). This approach can at times be extremely beneficial. Literature might best serve cathartic purposes when the books are self-selected rather than prescribed as pills: "Oh your mother is an alcoholic, you have to read this book"; "Victim of abuse, here is the perfect book for you!" It doesn't always work like that. Teens do not necessarily want to read about what they are already living through. Professionals trained in bibliotherapy can do some wonderful things with literature, but for the rest of us the best practice might be to simply have many of these books available for young adult readers. Some great sources for professionals who wish to learn more about the potential for bibliotherapy include

- *Helping Teens Cope: A Guide to Teen Issues Using YA Fiction and Other Resources* by Jami Jones (Linworth, 2003)
- *Using Literature to Help Troubled Teenagers Cope with Abuse Issues* by Joan Keywell (Greenwood, 2004)
- *Using Literature to Help Troubled Teenagers Cope with End-of-Life Issues* by Janet Allen (Greenwood, 2002)
- *Using Literature to Help Troubled Teenagers Cope with Health Issues* by Janet Allen (Greenwood, 2000)

History of Contemporary Realistic Fiction

The history of young adult literature is explored in Chapter 2, but in terms of contemporary realistic fiction it is significant to reemphasize that the way the world is represented in books for young readers has changed over time. Early realistic fiction for young adults was filled with a romanticized innocence and tended to depict an all-white world with traditional two-parent families, strong gender roles, and mainstream (WASP) values. Then came the "problem novel" that introduced social issues, and in recent years, books that are both more realistic in their complexity and darker in tone (Kaplan, 2003).

It was in the late 1960s that editors began to publish "serious coming of age stories for teenagers" as part of a movement towards a new realism (Donelson and Nilsen, 1997, p. 113). The impetus behind this movement was at least partially based on the idea that young people would be better adjusted if they were knowledgeable about both the good and bad aspects of their world. Realistic fiction began to depict a more realistic and diverse world in which the issues that teens actually confront took center stage, language began to reflect the way teens actually spoke, and life was not always romanticized.

Though the ages for which they were written and the topics addressed vary tremendously, a look at some of the classics of realistic fiction helps reveal themes that have withstood the test of time: adventures, family stories, the outsider, coming of age, death, experimentation, and love.

Milestones

1826	*Last of the Mohicans* by James Fenimore Cooper	1961	*Where the Red Fern Grows* by Wilson Rawls
1865	*Hans Brinker* by Mary Mapes Dodge	1964	*Harriet the Spy* by Louise Fitzhugh
1868	*Little Women* by Louisa May Alcott	1964	*Zeely* by Virginia Hamilton
1876	*The Adventure of Tom Sawyer* by Mark Twain	1968	*Are You There God? It's Me, Margaret* by Judy Blume
1884	*Heidi* by Johanna Spyri	1971	*Go Ask Alice* by Beatrice Sparks
1911	*The Secret Garden* by Frances Hodgson Burnett	1977	*Bridge to Terabithia* by Katherine Paterson
1938	*The Yearling* by Marjorie Kinnan Rawlings	1980	*Jacob Have I Loved* by Katherine Paterson
1944	*The Black Stallion* by Walter Farley	1983	*Dear Mr. Henshaw* by Beverly Cleary
1948	*King of the Wind* by Marguerite Henry	1999	*Monster* by Walter Dean Myers
1951	*Catcher in the Rye* by J. D. Salinger		

Author Spotlight

Photo courtesy of Sharon Draper.

Sharon Draper

Sharon Draper taught English/language arts to junior high and high school students for more than 25 years. Even before becoming a renowned author, she was nationally recognized for her teaching, including National Teacher of the Year (1997). She holds a Doctor of Humane Letters degree from the College of Mount Saint Joseph in Cincinnati, Ohio, and a Doctor of Arts degree from Cincinnati State University. Her career as a writer began with a challenge from one of her students. She entered and won first prize in a literary contest sponsored by Ebony magazine. Now she is a five-time winner of the Coretta Scott King Award. She has served on the Board of Directors of the National Board for Professional Teaching Standards. She is currently on the Board of the National Commission on Teaching and America's Future. She lives in Cincinnati, Ohio, with her husband and a golden retriever named Honey. Visit her website at http://sharondraper.com.

SELECTED BOOKLIST

The Battle of Jericho (Atheneum, 2003)
Copper Sun (Simon & Schuster, 2006)
Darkness before Dawn (Simon Pulse, 2002)

Double Dutch (Simon & Schuster, 2002)
Forged by Fire (Simon & Schuster, 1997)
November Blues (Simon & Schuster, 2007)
Romiette and Julio (Simon & Schuster, 1999)
Tears of a Tiger (Simon & Schuster, 1994)

ON HOW SHE BECAME AN AUTHOR OF YOUNG ADULT LITERATURE

My students inspired me, some of whom didn't like to read the assigned texts. I wanted to write something that young people could read that would be contemporary and exciting, yet have a solid literary base for teachers to use. I didn't know I was going to write a trilogy. I wrote *Tears of a Tiger,* and it had so much success that I was asked to write a sequel, which is pretty difficult if your main character is dead. So I took the short story that started it all, "One Small Torch" (the one that won the writing contest) and made it Chapter 1 of *Forged by Fire.* I know that when you read the two books, they seem to be out of order. I did not know I was going to write *Forged by Fire,* which, sequentially, happens earlier. That's just how it worked out. The third book, *Darkness before Dawn,* should balance things out a bit. It includes all of the kids from both books and takes them from the first day of their senior year to their graduation in June. The main character is Keisha. In it I tried to answer all the questions not answered in the first two books, including what happens to Gerald and Angel. As I wrote the three, the characters became my friends as well. They grew and developed, and I guess I did too.

ON THE INSPIRATION FOR HER STORIES

I write for young people—teenagers—all of them. I try to deal with topics that are both current and topical. I also hope that by reading it young people can perhaps apply some of the messages to their own lives. Abuse and death are topics that need to be discussed by young people. They are not pleasant, but by talking about the difficult realities of life, perhaps someone can be made stronger. I write about these things because, unfortunately, those are the realities of life for many teenagers today. I hope to say something that will change their lives for the better. I visit dozens of schools every year and the joy on the faces of the students I meet, their fascination with the characters and their lives, and their excitement about reading more is what keeps me going. I'm writing as fast as I can—trying to write stories that young people can enjoy. Sometimes I get them from newspaper articles or events I see on television. Sometimes I get ideas from students who write me or from students that I speak to when I visit their schools. My mind is always buzzing with new ideas for stories. There are thousands of teenagers in schools today. Each one of them has a story.

ON WHAT SHE ENJOYS READING CURRENTLY

Just as when I was a child, I still read voraciously today, not settling on any one author as my favorite. I always skim the first few pages before I buy a book, not to see what it's about, but to see how well it is written. I don't have time to read a thick book full of just plot. I need gentle nuances, poetic expressions, and powerful mastery of words. A good book should paint a picture and I should be able to see the colors in it. A good book should sing to me, and I should be able to hear each note. When I find one, I treasure it. So I've read a wide variety of authors who write well. They make me humble and they inspire me to write better.

ON WHAT DISTINGUISHES YOUNG ADULT LITERATURE

It bothers me when bookstore owners and libraries and even publishers group "children's literature" into one big pile. Literature for young adults is *not* kiddie lit. Teenagers are insulted by such categories and resent the fact that they must go through a doorway of bunny rabbits and butterflies to find a book for themselves. Young adult literature deals with topics that deal with their world as they see it and experience it today, not 5 years before when they were children, and not 5 years hence, when they will be closer to adulthood. YA literature is special, unique, and marvelous in that it exists at all. Our job is to get the books to the young people, through the mediums that reach them—TV, video, cable, etc. They will read if we get their attention. Getting and keeping their attention has been the problem. It is not unsolvable, but a terrific challenge.

ON WHETHER THERE ARE TOPICS THAT AUTHORS FOR YOUNG ADULTS SHOULD AVOID

No, but I think that difficult or controversial subjects should be addressed with skill and delicacy. It is possible to describe a horrible situation, such as child abuse, without using graphic details. Such subjects dealt with in this manner can then be discussed intelligently because it is the ideas and thoughts we want young readers to share, not the experience itself. We are all attracted to tragedy. That's why soap operas and sad movies are so popular. I think there's something within each of us that wants to look at tragedy from the outside so that we don't have to experience it personally. The other difficult issues or social problems I deal with are very real in the lives of many readers. We don't live in a world of sugar plum fairies and happily ever after. Perhaps reading about the difficulties of others will act like armor and protect my readers from the personal tragedies in their own lives.

Literary Elements of Contemporary Realistic Fiction

In contemporary realistic fiction (CRF) the characters, settings, and themes all come from present-day realities but are put together in narratives in ways that both make sense of the world and create an enjoyable reading experience. Among the most significant elements in the creation of fiction are characters, plot, setting, voice, style, and themes.

Characters

A character is a participant in the story, usually a fictional representation of a person, although a character may be any entity that interacts with other characters. In creating a main character, or protagonist, authors generally attempt to accomplish two purposes—present a character with whom readers can identify in order to draw them into the story and who develops or matures in the course of the narrative. The reader comes to know a protagonist in several ways: through the narrative voice's descriptions, through the actions of the character and the ensuing reactions of other characters, through the thoughts or dialogue of the character as revealed in the narrative, and through the thoughts and dialogue of others in relation to the character (Virtualit Interactive, 2007).

Authors often talk about creating characters that are different enough to make us intrigued but familiar enough to make us want to read their stories. Rachel Cohn's fictional Cyd Charisse, from *Gingerbread,* has two eccentric families on opposite sides of the country. As Cohn describes her, "she's been kicked out of a posh boarding school," and "her best friend is an old lady who lives in a nursing home." Not many individual readers are going to identify directly with Cyd's life, so why do so many teen girls relate to her? They relate to her through her "emotions, her vulnerability and quirkiness, her boy craziness, her desire to be independent of her family and yet not alienated from it" (Cohn, 2004, n.p.).

Many teen readers search for characters they might actually know or might want to know. So it is important that the characters are credible and authentic in terms of their interests, the way they talk, what they wear, and how they think. Young adult readers want to be convinced about the sincerity of the character. Are the characters well rounded, and are they maturing and developing during the narrative? It is also important that these characters ring true. It is only in the past few decades that we have had teen characters with sex drives and lives, who may be dysfunctional, and who have real problems such as depression.

Often it is the character that pulls the reader into the narrative and holds their attention. Finding a character that rings true but does not fit the images frequently encountered in the past will often grab a reader's attention. Angela Johnson, for example, writes that young adult readers often inform her that their favorite character of hers is Bobby Morris, a 17-year-old kept busy with an infant daughter. The reason they tend to give is that they had never read a book with a loving, attentive African American teenage male father figure.

Sometimes the character is intriguing because of what we do not know about her. In *Speak* by Laurie Halse Anderson the main character, Melinda, hardly speaks aloud at all, but the reader senses her palpable pain with great sadness and vigor (Alsup, 2003; Kaplan, 2004). The reader wants to know what has happened to this young woman to make her feel this way. In *Luna* (Peters) readers come to understand the protagonist from his sister's perspective rather than hear the story of a transgendered youth from his own perspective. The sister Rachel is so sensitively drawn and her conflicting emotions are so powerful that the reader is drawn into experiencing both Rachel *and* Luna's experiences. Both are complex, fully developed characters.

It is fairly trendy currently to have novels with multiple protagonists, often told in different voices, such as Amy Koss's *The Cheat,* with six protagonists. Most novels also have a variety of

To Consider

Think about protagonists from fiction that really appeal to you. What are these characters like? Are they similar to you in some ways? Why do you think you find these particular characters appealing?

minor or supporting characters who are generally less fully developed and perhaps an antagonist who stands in opposition to the protagonist.

Plot

The plot of a story is the series of events that gives meaning to the narrative. Generally the plot will unfold chronologically, creating a beads-on-a-string storyline. But some authors provide flashbacks intertwined with the current scenes or multivoiced narratives with overlapping time frames.

Plot tends to develop out of conflict between the protagonist and some external experience, antagonist, or internal crisis. As a general rule, a well-constructed plot will have details and events that move forward in a cause–effect relationship, leading to the outcome of the story. The way that the character works through the conflict and other complications that arise creates action around which the storyline develops. Although there are many variations on plot development, stories in the traditional novel tend to include rising action, as the character works through a variety of complications; a climax, when a resolution occurs with the conflict; and falling action from the climax leading to the story's conclusion. Despite the climax and the resolution of action, a well-written story generally does not resolve complex problems with easy answers. Realistic visions of issues and concepts are complex. The way in which the plot unfolds definitely has an impact on the reader. What makes the novel *Speak* so powerful, Alsup (2003) argues, is that the reader does not learn about the central incident that has impacted the character until the very end of the novel, although there is some foreshadowing along the way.

Among the key questions that determine the success of contemporary realistic fiction are the following:

- Is the plot plausible in today's world?
- Are the issues ones that would be of interest to young adults?
- Does the plot appeal to teens and address their hopes and fears?
- Are young adults challenged to think critically about the world?
- Are controversial elements like violence and sex gratuitous or are these elements part of the plot development?

Setting

The setting is the context in which the story takes place. In general, for fiction to be successful the setting must be vivid and believable. The setting might be very detailed or just include a few descriptors to create a sense of the milieu in which the story takes place. The scenery, the weather, the way people dress and talk, the architecture—all are part of the setting. The setting involves the temporal and spatial context but it also involves the social context and the mood. Two stories can be set in almost identical classrooms but the mood created by the authors' descriptions might drastically change the readers' expectations and interpretations of the storyline. Mary Casanova, for example, talks about using settings that she knows well and loves in *When Eagles Fall.* She is very descriptive and her knowledge and even love for the setting comes through in her writing.

Though the setting is not equally significant in all stories, it can have an effect on the events of the plot, reveal character, or create an atmosphere. The details of the setting should

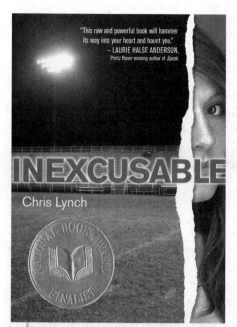

"This raw and powerful book will hammer its way into your heart and haunt you."
– LAURIE HALSE ANDERSON,
Printz Honor winning author of *Speak*

INEXCUSABLE

Chris Lynch

NATIONAL BOOK AWARD FINALIST

Keir is a good guy, so he couldn't have done what Gigi accuses him of—or could he? *Inexcusable* by Chris Lynch (2007). Reprinted by permission of Atheneum.

support the events of the story. Some settings are common in CRF for young adults. School settings, for example, are so popular that there is a whole subgenre referred to as "School Stories."

Voice

The story's voice and the voice of the narrator are generally one and the same. The voice of the story is partly the result of the author's style and is also connected to the tone that is set. Tone refers to the attitude created by the story toward its subject matter. The tone and mood of the story can vary immensely, creating unique voices that may be serious, comic, or sarcastic. When a serious, sincere tone is used in a narrative, the story will take on a different mood than a narrative filled with sarcasm or subtle humor.

One of the biggest issues in YA fiction is capturing a true young adult voice in the writing. Teens respond to young adult literature in part because they can relate to the voice conveyed. Successful young adult literature usually sounds like a real teen talking, whether it's the California slang of Cyd Charrise, the hyper-chaotic rant of Joey Pigza, or the urban hip-hop beat of Janet MacDonald's characters, it is the authenticity of these voices that makes for rich complex narratives. Authors use differing levels of authentic and appropriate slang, dialect, and ways of talking, but some general agreement exists that the way characters talk should reflect contemporary language forms. Janet MacDonald for example had rejected black vernacular English in her own life, but when she began creating narratives set in urban African American settings, she found that her characters had to "speak as truly they would, not as I would have them speak" (MacDonald, 2005).

In an interview with K. L. Going on the Totally YA blog the author asserts that in *St. Iggy* she felt the need "to strike a balance between wisdom and naievete with Iggy's voice and sometimes that was difficult" (2007). In fact, the novel was constructed first and foremost around the voice of the protagonist, Iggy. For Going, because the voice was so clear in her brain, the plot took a lot of hammering out.

Style

Sharon Draper asserts:

> I always skim the first few pages before I buy a book, not to see what it's about, but to see how well it is written. I don't have time to read a thick book full of just plot. I need gentle nuances, poetic expressions, and powerful mastery of words. A good book should paint a picture and I should be able to see the colors in it. A good book should sing to me, and I should be able to hear each note. (Draper interview, p. 248)

The nuances, the colors, and the notes are what make up the style of the narrative. Every writer will construct a narrative with his or her own unique style (Morrell, 2006; Provost,

1988). An author's style will likely be influenced by the genre (romance, mystery, thriller), by current literary trends, and by the social context in which the author is writing. Still, individual authors use language in different ways and the amount of dialogue, the detail provided, the phrasing and diction, and the sentence structures and other language conventions used are wide ranging.

One recent trend involves telling parallel or intertwined stories in multiple voices. Sharon Creech's *Walk Two Moons* with its two intertwined stories is a good example of this. Another example of this is *Snail Mail No More,* in which Paula Danziger and Ann Martin create two distinct narrative voices by each writing from the perspective of a different character in using the format and style of email.

Technology Links

ReadWriteThink

The National Council of Teachers of English (NCTE) and the International Reading Association (IRA) have come together to create ReadWriteThink (www.readwritethink.org), one of the best sources for quality language arts and reading lesson plans. Many of the lessons utilize Internet resources in meaningful ways. For example, "Novel News: Broadcast Coverage of Character, Conflict, Resolution, and Setting" is a creative way to get students to explore literary elements.

Themes

A theme in a work of fiction is a major concept explored in the narrative. Marc Aronson (2001) writes that authors of realistic fiction have to explore the discontinuities of life. Themes are, in some stories, quite explicit, especially in those stories with a didactic intent. But because works of CRF reflect the discontinuities of life these novels tend to contain multiple themes that reflect issues faced by contemporary young adults.

Whether we are talking about sports stories, adventures, romances, or mysteries, if these books have teen characters and appeal to teen audiences, one is sure to find some of the themes common to YA literature. Certain themes are also connected with certain genres of story. For instance, a school story is likely to include bullying, peer pressure, and developing friendships.

Some Popular Themes in Contemporary Realistic Fiction

Families and Home

Many YA novels explore the complex relationships between teens and their family members. Family is extremely important for teens, especially in light of changing relationships with parents/guardians as they move from child to adult. Whereas 30 years ago books for young people were most likely to present a nuclear family, today there is a wide variety of one parent, two parent, extended, and foster families in the literature. Many of these novels demonstrate that adolescents need positive adult role models for support during the many challenges that they face (Bushman and McNerny, 2004).

Young adults frequently face or fear change in their family situations. The topic of parental loss due to divorce and the complex relationships children have with their step-families are explored by Ann Brashares in the novel *The Sisterhood of the Traveling Pants* (2001) and its sequel, *The Second Summer of the Sisterhood* (2003). These two novels feature four teenage friends who are learning to adapt to changing family situations (Bushman and McNerny, 2004).

In some novels characters have to cope with the loss of a parent. In Sharon Creech's *Walk Two Moons,* after her mother disappears, Sal and her grandparents retrace the route taken by her mom. In Tracy Mack's *Drawing Lessons,* Aurora is so close to her father who has taught her all about art that when he leaves the family she is devastated. She uses art as a way to come to terms with life.

Other family novels deal with teens and their parents seeking a way to reconnect. In *Takeoffs and Landings* by Margaret Peterson Haddix, Lori and Chuck's mom has essentially been an absentee parent for the past 8 years. Since their father died she has been working the road as a motivational speaker, leaving them with their grandparents, but this time she brings them along hoping to rebuild the family. Similarly, in Walter Dean Myers's *Somewhere in the Darkness* Jimmy's father, who has been away in prison most of his life, shows up and insists that the boy come with him on a journey.

Sometimes the protagonist does not especially look forward to reconnecting with a family member. In *Gingerbread* by Rachel Cohn, Cyd is sent from the West Coast to stay with her father and his new family in New York. She has to leave behind her surfer boyfriend and the identity she had constructed for herself. In Valerie Hobbs's *Tender,* after the death of her grandmother, with whom she has always lived, 15-year-old Liv must live with her father, who had been absent all these years. The two have definite communication problems. These difficult family situations provide the background for much of the action that takes place in these novels.

As if changes in family are not hard enough to deal with, imagine the difficulties involved when the identity of the entire family changes. In Jack Gantos's *I'm Not Joey Pigza,* Joey's hyper and dysfunctional father returns and tries to change the family after winning the lottery. Not only is the father living with them for the first time Joey can remember but they move to a new home and change their names.

The extended family is another popular theme in YA literature. Several of Chris Crutcher's novels, including *Stotan* (1986), *Running Loose* (1983), *Ironman* (1995), and *Staying Fat for Sarah Byrnes* (1993) feature parents who are either absent or physically or emotionally abusive. In order to find support and make connections with positive adult role models these adolescents must seek out new adults in their lives. In *Stotan, Chinese Handcuffs* (1989), and *Whale Talk* (2001), the abused characters are able to find physical and emotional help from their sports coaches. *Ironman* features Mr. Nak, a community adult who leads an anger management group for troubled teenagers. In *Staying Fat for Sarah Byrnes,* the positive adult role model is a high school English teacher. These caring role models often come from unexpected places. In Deborah Halverson's *Honk If You Hate Me,* Monalisa is basically being raised by the parents of her best friend and the workers at their tattoo parlor.

Stories of kids being moved through a series of foster families, hoping for the one family that clicks are popular with tweens. *Pictures of Hollis Woods* (Giff) and *Home and Other Big Fat Lies* (Wolfson) are among the many examples of such books for young adolescents. For older teens these foster family situations have either clicked in and relationships are solid as in *Whale Talk* or the child has become a casualty of situations that failed as in *America* by E. R. Frank.

Family can also be a significant theme in YA literature by its absence. Being orphaned or separated from parents is a common storyline. In *Can't Get There from Here* Todd Strasser recreates a situation that is altogether too real for homeless teens and runaways who live on the streets. Strasser's heart-wrenching story doesn't moralize or depict young runaways as stupid for running away from some of the situations they are in, but it does show the harsh, dangerous life street children must lead and the choices they might make even when it seems that there aren't any adults in the world willing to help them.

For kids who are already struggling to make it, losing that family structure might be the struggle that puts them down for good. In *America* by E. R. Frank, written for an older YA audience, America had been taken in by the nanny of his foster family and at age 5 felt secure and loved, but when the system allows a visit with his crack-addicted biological mother the boy becomes lost in the system for 11 years. The teen loses his will to live until he finds Dr. B, an adult who actually seems to want to listen.

Peers, Friends, and Social Outcasts

Learning to interact in different social situations is one of the greatest concerns teens have, and peer relations are explored in most YA novels. Peer groups become more and more significant to teens as they become less emotionally dependant on their parents. Often, two friends become close enough that they find themselves sharing their greatest secrets. Such is the case with Sarah Withrow's *Box Girl* and Jacqueline Woodson's *I Hadn't Meant to Tell You This*. Sometimes, one friend helps the other with a problematical situation, as in Chris Crutcher's *Staying Fat for Sarah Burns,* in which "Moby" helps his friend Sarah come to terms with her horrific past.

Some novels focus on changes in friendship, such as in *Sisterhood of the Traveling Pants* when the friends have to go their separate ways for the first summer ever. A fairly common theme involves the oddball friendship between two people who would appear to have nothing in common but end up becoming friends and helping each other through some tough situations. *Fat Kids Rule the World* by K. L. Going, *Stoner and Spaz* by Ron Koertge, and *Define "Normal"* (Peters) are all of this mold, though each is very fresh in storyline.

Along with the importance of peers comes the increasing significance of peer pressure. Characters in YA novels often have to discover who their true friends are. They also often face decisions about going with the crowd or deciding on their own what's right. Some narratives explore how far a character will go in order to have friends. Examples of how negative peer pressure can coerce adolescents into misbehavior are numerous. In *Shopoholic* 14-year-old Taylor is lonely enough to do anything to become friends with Kat. However, Kat loves to shop and Taylor doesn't really have the money to feed this habit. In Lois Duncan's classic novel *Killing Mr. Griffin* Susan's desire for peer acceptance is so great that she agrees to become involved in a plot to kidnap and persecute an English teacher.

Sometimes the main characters resist, or overcome, the negative pressure and ultimately make morally correct decisions. In Chris Crutcher's *Running Loose,* Louis Banks has the bravery to resist going along with the rest of the football team's plan to use cheating tactics during a game. Dan, in Lois Ruby's *Skin Deep* (1994), realizes that the neo-Nazi group he has become involved with might provide him with the sense of acceptance he craves, but that the acceptance would come at the price of the violation of his own moral beliefs (Bushman and McNerny, 2004).

10ᵗʰ ANNIVERSARY EDITION
LAURIE HALSE ANDERSON

speak

CONTAINS ALL-NEW MATERIAL FROM THE AUTHOR

Laurie Halse Anderson's award-winning novel *Speak* (1999) focuses on a ninth grader who has become an outsider and now hardly speaks. Jacket design by Michael Morgenstern from *Speak* by Laurie Halse Anderson. Jacket design © 1999 by Michael Morgenstern. Reprinted by permission of Farrar, Straus and Giroux, LLC.

Walter Dean Myers's novel, *The Beast,* provides the reader with a portrait of a young man who never turns his back on his peers but doesn't let them influence him into a losing lifestyle, either. Anthony "Spoon" Witherspoon returns periodically to his old neighborhood in Harlem from the prestigious and exclusive prep boarding school he attends. Friends, and especially his on-and-off girlfriend Gabi, draw him back into the quagmire of their existence. Meanwhile, his new friends unintentionally pressure him to leave that world behind and join their world of privilege and promise. Spoon learns to navigate the two worlds without abandoning his friends in either (Bushman and McNerny, 2004).

In *Evolution, Me & Other Freaks of Nature* (Brande), Mena became an outsider because of her stand against injustice. The problem is that she has not just become an outcast to her friends; the entire church community, which includes her parents, has also ostracized her—the church that until recently had been her world. A vast number of characters in YA fiction are outcasts, outsiders, loners, or alienated youth. For example, in *What Happened to Lani Garver* (Plum-Ucci), a newcomer doesn't fit with community ideas about gender norms, with dire consequences.

Speak (Anderson, 1999) is a vivid demonstration of the power of both negative and positive peer pressure. When Melinda breaks up an end-of-summer party by calling the police, her friends abandon her and she becomes the high school social outcast (Bushman and McNerny, 2004). The stress of bullying the outsider often leads to calamity, as it does in Todd Strasser's *Give a Boy a Gun.* In this novel, two unpopular kids are tormented unmercifully throughout grade school and junior high. Their response when younger of "I'd like to kill them for treating me like that" evolves into a plan by the middle of high school to get armed and do just that.

The outsider theme often overlaps with the theme of bullying, as in *Buddha Boy* by Kathe Koja. In a school where any difference from the pack is going to result in torment by the jocks, the artsy new kid at school has a shaved head and begs for lunch money in the cafeteria. Justin has to decide whether he can keep ignoring the bullying as he becomes friends with the new kid.

Young adult novels can also demonstrate the positive effects that supportive peer groups can have on adolescents. *The Misfits* by James Howe shows middle-grade readers what the world should be like. At a school where labels are everywhere and there is seemingly no way to escape them, hope is provided by a group of outcasts who decide to start a no name-calling campaign.

To Consider

Some teachers feel strongly that books about bullying and school violence can be used in schools to prevent future violence, whereas others feel that the topic is inappropriate for the classroom and might even serve as a model for students thinking about school violence. How do you feel about this complex issue?

In the Field *The Power of* The Misfits

Richie Partington is a children's literature specialist who has served on YALSA's Best Books for Young Adults committee. His wife Shari is an English and drama teacher at Brook Haven Middle School in Sebastopol, California.

The Misfits is a book that I strongly recommend having your district's middle school teachers take a look at. The story involves four seventh graders who are close friends and who are sick of being called names. Bobby takes abuse for being overweight, and Addie is seen as being too tall and too smart. Skeezie is called names because of dressing in the manner of a 1950s "greazer." Joe is especially a target because he is gay.

Students cannot feel comfortable when they are being harassed because of their gender, their attire, their race, their size or body shape, their religion, or their sexual orientation. My name is Richie Partington, but in middle school several people thought that I should be called Nigger Lips. Thirty-five years later I can still bring back the feelings that resulted from being called that name. Thirty-five years later I can still recall how that led to my having a less than optimal experience in middle school.

What names do kids call each other these days? As part of Shari's curriculum surrounding *The Misfits,* students are asked to submit lists of the names they have been called at school. Here's a sampling from this year's list:

> Slut, skank, chunky monkey, fag, spaz, little meat, pimpette, bitch, blob, butt fucker, whore, screw up, lezbo, anus face, computer john, dweeb, cunt, elf, nigger, lard ass.

The list goes on and on. Does hearing such words, such names, make you uncomfortable? Imagine actually being on the receiving end of such names being spit in your direction. Imagine being a kid and having to wonder if that is who you really are.

Students at Brook Haven have noted that while no one at school was immune to being called names, those kids who are perceived as different for any reason get the worst of it. I applaud any school board for adopting a student conduct policy on bullying and harassment. Gay and lesbian citizens remain targets of an inordinate amount of harassment, both locally and nationwide. I also applaud special efforts to make these students feel

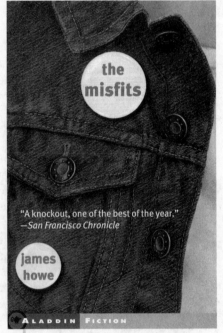

The Misfits by James Howe (2001) inspired the "No Name-Calling Week," which has become popular around the country. *The Misfits* reprinted by permission of Atheneum.

safe in the halls and in the classrooms. I urge school boards to continue working toward making all kids feel comfortable at school.

Special Needs

Teachers and researchers have long advocated for the use of fictional literature as a means to teach students about disabilities (Andrews, 1998; Blaska, 1996; Sridhar and Vaughn, 2000). Twenty years ago most novels cast the special needs character in a secondary role, so readers rarely got to see through their eyes. More recently, Mary Anne Prater (2003) describes research that analyzed 90 fictional books portraying at least one character with a learning disability. In general, Prater writes that fictionalized or true-to-life characters with a known learning disability often serve as role models or as bibliotherapy for children with disabilities. In most fictional books for children and young adults, the learning disabled child is the main character and the story is told from the child's point of view; also, the learning disability had a main impact on the plot (Kaplan, 2003; Prater, 2003) Moreover, most of the characters with learning disabilities are dynamic, meaning they change or grow during the course of the storyline. Following are several books about students with differing types of special needs:

- *Black Eyed Suzie* by Susan Shaw (mental illness)
- *Cut* by Patricia McCormick (self-mutilation)
- *Deaf Child Crossing* by Marlee Matlin (deafness)
- *Head above Water* by S. L. Rottman (Down Syndrome)
- *Humming Whispers* by Angela Johnson (schizophrenia)
- *Inside Out* by Terry Trueman (schizophrenia)
- *Joey Pigza Swallowed the Key* by Jack Gantos (ADHD)
- *Kissing Doorknobs* by Terry Hesser (obsessive-compulsive behavior)
- *The Language of Goldfish* by Zibby Oneal (depression)
- *Not As Crazy As I Seem* by George Harrar (obsessive-compulsive behavior)
- *Of Sound Mind* by Jean Ferris (deafness)
- *Out of the Fire* by Deborah Froese (burn victim)
- *Petey* by Ben Mikaelsen (cerebral palsy)
- *Rat* by Jan Cheripko (birth defect)
- *Stoner and Spaz* by Ron Koertge (cerebral palsy)
- *Stuck in Neutral* by Terry Trueman (cerebral palsy)
- *Tangerine* by Edward Bloor (visual impairment)
- *When She Was Good* by Norma Fox Mazer (mental illness)

Aging and Death

Because many kids today are separated from elderly relatives who go to retirement communities or live apart from their family, young people do not necessarily come into contact with death. However, death is no longer as taboo as it once was in literature. Books such as *A Summer to Die* (Lowry, 1977) and *Tiger Eyes* (1981) by Judy Blume paved the way for a wide range of books that confront the issue today. A few books present a character coming to grips with a terminal illness. Chris Crutcher's *Deadline* involves a character who finds out that he only has a year to live and wants to make the best of the time he has left. *A Time for Dancing* (Hurwin) tells the alternating perspectives of two best friends, one of whom is dying. But much more often these books are about a character going through the grieving process for a sibling, friend, or other family member. Following are several books about young people experiencing the death of someone close to them:

Siblings
- *Blue Eyes Better* by Ruth Wallace-Brodeur
- *Getting Near to Baby* by Audrey Couloumbis
- *Looking for Red* by Angela Johnson
- *Many Stones* by Carolyn Coman
- *When I Was Older* by Garret Freymann-Weyr

Friends
- *Rain Is Not My Indian Name* by Cynthia Leitich Smith
- *Tears of a Tiger* by Sharon Draper
- *A Time for Dancing* by Davida Wills Hurwin

Parents and Grandparents
- *Every Time a Rainbow Dies* by Rita Williams-Garcia
- *Jericho* by Janet Hickman
- *This Isn't about the Money* by Sally Warner
- *Toning the Sweep* by Angela Johnson

Suicide

The Centers for Disease Control (2009) has estimated that suicide was the eleventh leading cause of death in the United States, but the third leading cause of death for people aged 15 to 24.Whatever statistics we look at, it is obvious that suicide is an issue teens deal with and is actually a rather common topic in YA fiction. The following books address suicide:

- *Aimee* by Mary Beth Miller
- *America* by E. R. Frank
- *Because of Lissa* by Carolyn Meyer
- *Blindfold* by Sandra McCuaig
- *Chinese Handcuffs* by Chris Crutcher
- *Earth, My Butt, and Other Big Round Things* by Carolyn Mackler
- *Fat Kids Rule the World* by K. L. Going
- *The Game* by Teresa Toten
- *I Can Hear the Mourning Dove* by James Bennett
- *St. Michael's Scales* by Neil Connelly

Sports

Young adults in the 1950s and 60s had a slew of good romantic sports novels to read, stories that weren't necessarily written for teens but that had plenty of sentimental appeal. In stories such as *The Natural* by Bernard Malamud (1950), the action may revolve around a sport, but there is usually much more going on. For instance, Jan Cheripko's *Imitate the Tiger* focuses on football, but the story is more about the protagonist's drinking problem.

In most of these novels the character develops in some significant way. Numerous excellent sports-related novels are available and when matched with the right reader they are often favorites.

Football

- *Cover Up: Mystery at the Super Bowl* by John Feinstein
- *Damage* by A. M. Jenkins
- *Imitate the Tiger* by Jan Cheripko
- *Roughnecks* by Thomas Cochran
- *Running Loose* by Chris Crutcher

Basketball

- *Hoops* by Walter Dean Myers
- *The Moves Make the Man* by Bruce Brooks
- *Night Hoops* by Carl Deaker.
- *The Outside Shot* by Walter Dean Myers
- *Playing without the Ball* by Rich Wallace
- *Rat* by Jan Cheripko
- *Slam!* by Walter Dean Myers
- *The Squared Circle* by James Bennett
- *Tall Tales: Six Amazing Basketball Dreams* by Charles Smith

Baseball

- *Beanball* by Gene Fehler
- *Bull Catcher* by Alden Carter
- *Dean Duffy* by Randy Powell
- *Striking Out* by Will Weaver

Other Sports

- *Born in Sin* by Evelyn Coleman (swimming)
- *The Brave* by Robert Lipsyte (boxing)
- *The Chief* by Robert Lipsyte (boxing)
- *The Contender* by Robert Lipsyte (boxing)
- *Crossing Jordan* by Adrian Fogelin (track)
- *Iceman* by Chris Lynch (hockey)
- *Runner* by Cynthia Voigt (cross country)
- *Soccer Duel* by M. Christopher (soccer)
- *St. Michael's Scales* by Neil Connelly (wrestling)
- *Stotan!* by Chris Crutcher (swimming)
- *Strike Two* by Amy Goldman Koss (softball)
- *Tangerine* by Edward Bloor (soccer)
- *Tennis Ace* by M. Christopher (tennis)
- *Warrior Angel* by Robert Lipsyte (boxing)
- *Whale Talk* by Chris Crutcher (swimming)
- *Wrestling Sturbridge* by Rich Wallace (wrestling)

Survival Stories

Survival stories seem to have a very strong appeal, especially in middle school. These stories typically involve a young adult or a group of teens who have to survive in a wilderness and somehow grow in the process. Gary Paulsen's *Hatchet* is one of the most popular of these stories. When his plane crashes in the Canadian wilderness, Brian has little besides a hatchet to help him survive. Many of the teens in these novels have major problems before they become stranded in the wilderness and the hardships faced help them put their problems in perspective, as in the following examples:

- *Between a Rock and a Hard Place* by Alden Carter
- *Brian's Return* by Gary Paulsen
- *Brian's Winter* by Gary Paulsen
- *Downriver* by Will Hobbs
- *Far North* by Will Hobbs
- *Hatchet* by Gary Paulsen

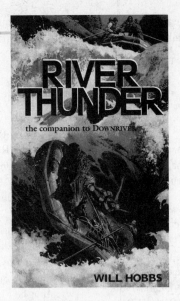

In *River Thunder* (Delacorte, 1997) by Will Hobbs, a group of teens return to the Grand Canyon, planning to raft down the Colorado River, but the river has some surprises in mind. Jacket cover from *River Thunder* by Will Hobbs. Used by permission of Laurel-Leaf, an imprint of Random House Children's Books, a division of Random House, Inc.

- *Rescue Josh McGuire* by Ben Mikaelsen
- *River Thunder* by Will Hobbs
- *Touching Spirit Bear* by Ben Mikaelsen
- *Wild Man Island* by Will Hobbs
- *Wild Timothy* by Gary Blackwood

Eco-Adventures
- *Flash Fire* by Caroline Cooney
- *Flash Point* by Sneed Collard
- *Jaguar* by Roland Smith
- *Lord of the Kill* by Theodore Taylor
- *The Maze* by Will Hobbs
- *Rare and Endangered* by John Dowd
- *When Eagles Fall* by Mary Casanova

Author Spotlight

Photo courtesy of Mary Casanova.

Mary Casanova

Mary Casanova admits to being a reluctant reader as a child. She could only sit still for a story that mattered and was action packed as well. This has led her to be passionate about writing meaningful books that are full of adventure. She lives on the Minnesota–Canada border, a rather remote location with moose, black bear, and wolves, an environment that has greatly influenced her work. *Moose Tracks* is about a boy trying to save an orphaned moose calf from poachers. *Wolf Shadows* pits two friends against each other over wolves. *Stealing Thunder* tells the tale of a girl who is trying to save an appaloosa from danger. *Riot,* which is based on an actual event that occurred in her community, focuses more on human relations. Visit her website at www.marycasanova.com.

SELECTED BOOKLIST

Curse of a Winter Moon (Hyperion, 2000)
The Klipfish Code (Houghton Mifflin, 2007)
Moose Tracks (Tandem, 2003)
Riot (Hyperion, 1998)
Stealing Thunder (Tandem, 2003)
Wolf Shadows (Hyperion, 1999)

ON HOW SHE BECAME AN AUTHOR OF YOUNG ADULT LITERATURE

First, let me say that my novels tend to reach an audience that spans middle grade and young adult readers. I ended up writing books with 12-year-old characters after I stumbled into a weeklong workshop led by author Marion Dane Bauer in 1989 on writing for children. Though I had wanted to be a writer since I was in high school, at 32 that dream had taken a back burner; I was working on a master's degree in English, teaching part-time at the community college, and I thought the two-credit workshop would be enjoyable. It turned my life around. For the first time, I considered writing for young readers. Marion helped me understand how to start using my own emotional experiences in my fiction, and reading Gary Paulsen's *Hatchet* and other authors—such as Natalie Babbitt and Katherine Patterson—opened my eyes to children's and young adult literature.

ON WHETHER SHE WRITES WITH A PARTICULAR AUDIENCE IN MIND

Like an actor on stage, I try to step as fully as possible into the shoes of my character. When I do this, the narrative seems to come pretty naturally from my character, whether it's a contemporary story about Seth, a 12-year-old boy living in rural northern Minnesota, or a story about Cecile, also 12, who is a servant at the court of Louis XIV in 1711. I let the narrative flow from what I perceive to be a certain character's experiences and perceptions. I don't think about the audience I'm writing for as much as the character whose life I'm trying to understand.

So far, I haven't found a piece of history or a topic that is too big, too complex to write about. I don't feel limited by writing for young readers. When I'm aiming for a middle-grade audience, I stay just this side of swearing, violence, and sex. And I guess I manage to keep to this side of that line even with my novels that are more young adult. Through my stories, I've tackled labor disputes, religious wars, animal abuse, environmental issues and ethics, overdrinking, and on and on, all through the eyes and experiences of my characters. Through them, I've come to better understand the world around me. I struggle right along with them, and perhaps that's why I find this field so compelling. At 12 or 13, kids are on the verge of adulthood, but their eyes and senses are wide open to the world around them. They're childlike but very perceptive with a simple wisdom that often goes past adults. And so I've learned to listen to my characters who—like kids and teenagers—are usually wiser than they know.

ON THE INSPIRATION FOR HER STORIES

My novels usually stem from a question or my own experiences. *Riot* stemmed from my need to understand escalating anger when a labor dispute turned violent in International Falls in 1989, where I live. When I was cross-country skiing one day, I came across a fresh wolf kill, and in my attempt to understand wolves and how they could become a wedge between two lifelong friends, I wrote *Wolf Shadows*. My own struggle to understand superstition and intolerance, especially religious intolerance, found its expression in *Curse of a Winter Moon,* set during the Reformation. I spent 2 weeks in southern France as part of my research for Marius's story about struggling to protect his younger brother, Jean Pierre, who other villagers believe is a werewolf or *loup garou.* In *Stealing Thunder,* I drew largely on my own memories of having an appaloosa when I was a teenager. Through the eyes of Libby, I used my love of horses, but perhaps more importantly, my inability to grasp animal abuse. Libby's struggle to speak up against abuse and take action in order to protect a horse she loves parallels my own development from a somewhat shy girl who had a hard time speaking up to the writer I am today who has found her voice.

When *Eagles Fall* weaves in various personal experiences. Like Alexis, I have lost people I love to cancer, my mother-in-law and author and mentor, Pam Conrad. Like Alexis, I struggled to fit in and made some pretty awful decisions at 13, including overdrinking. As an author and parent now, I wanted to understand what makes seemingly "good kids" suddenly turn sharp corners and get in trouble. Pain and loneliness, I knew, drive us to do stupid things sometimes, and I wanted to understand Alexis's story. And finally, I understand how marriages can end in separation or divorce; my husband and I have worked through some difficult times, and when we were hurting, so were our kids. Healing and restoration are important themes to me, both in real life and in fiction. I set the story on my favorite island, Skipper Rock, where I often moor our houseboat in late September, after the eaglets have fledged their island nest. As I wrote the story, I felt completely at ease with the setting, one I know well and love.

In order to write *When Eagles Fall,* I worked with a team of eagle researchers at Voyageurs National Park, here on Rainy Lake where I live, and was part of banding nearly full-grown eaglets from a dozen nests. All the while I was taking notes, photos, paying attention. Great factual material. But on the last nest of our last day of work, when an eaglet was found with a broken leg, suddenly I had story material. I emptied out a manuscript box, we put the eaglet in and shipped it via Northwest Airlines to the St. Paul Raptor center, where it recovered. One month later I had the chance to meet it at the airplane and be part of returning the eaglet to its nest. Like a good story, it ended with a satisfying conclusion.

Mysteries and Thrillers

Mysteries are about solving intriguing problems. Mysteries both provide an escape and the thrill of suspense. Of course, Nancy Drew is one of the longest running mystery series for young readers and it is likely the action and adventure involved that has kept these books in print for all these years. Because the main characters are young adults, these novels tend to hit on several of the other themes mentioned here, but teens who love these books tend to return to the genre for the thrills. The following list provides some good examples of mysteries and thrillers for young adults.

- *Black Mirror* by Nancy Werlin
- *The Body of Christopher Creed* by Carol Plum-Ucci
- *Chasing Vermeer* by Blue Balliett
- *The Creek* by Jennifer Holm

- *Dark Secrets* by Elizabeth Chandler
- *Dead Man in Indian Creek* by M. D. Hahn
- *Playing for Keeps* by Joan Lowery Nixon
- *Sammy Keyes and the Curse of the Moustache* by Wendelin van Draanen
- *Sammy Keyes and the Hollywood Mummy* by Wendelin van Draanen
- *Silent to the Bone* by E. L. Konigsburg
- *Tightrope* by Gillian Cross
- *The Westing Game* by Ellen Raskin
- *When Dad Killed Mom* by Julius Lester

The Edgar Awards recognize the best mystery writing of the year. Following is a list of winners in the young adult category. For more years and the nominated books visit www .mysterywriters.org/pages/awards/winners06.htm.

- 2007—*Buried* by Robin Merrow MacCready
- 2006—*Last Shot* by John Feinstein
- 2005—*In Darkness, Death* by Dorothy and Thomas Hoobler
- 2004—*Acceleration* by Graham McNamee
- 2003—*The Wessex Papers, Vols. 1–3* by Daniel Parker
- 2002—*The Boy in the Burning House* by Tim Wynne-Jones
- 2001—*Counterfeit Son* by Elaine Marie Alphin
- 2000—*Never Trust a Dead Man* by Vivian Vande Velde
- 1999—*The Killer's Cousin* by Nancy Werlin
- 1998—*Ghost Canoe* by Will Hobbs
- 1997—*Twisted Summer* by Willo Davis Roberts
- 1996—*Prophecy Rock* by Rob MacGregor
- 1995—*Toughing It* by Nancy Springer
- 1994—*The Name of the Game Was Murder* by Joan Lowery Nixon
- 1993—*A Little Bit Dead* by Chap Reaver
- 1992—*The Weirdo* by Theodore Taylor
- 1991—*Mote* by Chap Reaver
- 1990—*Show Me the Evidence* by Alane Ferguson

Humor

The majority of the books mentioned in this chapter are somewhat serious but as in life CRF reflects all of the emotions felt by young adults. Although the serious problem novel may be the norm, an occasional humorous novel comes along that stands out, including the following examples:

- *Agnes Parker—Girl in Progress* by Kathleen O'Dell
- *Angus, Thongs, and Full Frontal Snogging* by Louise Rennison
- *A Book of Coupons* by Susie Morgemstern
- *The Canning Season* by Polly Horvath
- *Everything on a Waffle* by Polly Horvath
- *Lizzie at Last* by Claudia Mills
- *Mates, Dates, and Cosmic Kisses* by Cathy Hopkins
- *Mates, Dates, and Inflatable Bras* by Cathy Hopkins

- *No More Dead Dogs* by Gordon Korman
- *Planet Janet* by Dyan Sheldon
- *Sloppy Firsts: A Novel* by Megan McCafferty
- *Surviving the Applewhites* by Stephanie Tolan
- *Trial by Journal* by Kate Klise; illus. by M. Sarah Klise
- *The True Meaning of Cleavage* by Mariah Fredericks

Romance

Romances tend to have happy endings and are often intense in the emotions explored. They involve the story of a person's or a couple's development, but the action centers on falling in love and how the relationship, successful or not, helps the character learn something about self. Some examples include:

- *Forever* by Judy Blume
- *Getting the Girl* by Markus Zusak
- *If You Come Softly* by Jacqueline Woodson
- *I'll Love You When You Are More Like Me* by M. E. Kerr
- *Running Loose* by Chris Crutcher
- *Who Am I without Him? Short Stories about Girls and the Boys in Their Lives* by Sharon Flake

Topic Focus

Teen Romance Fiction*

Romance can be found in most contemporary realistic fiction written for young adults, regardless of genre—whether humor, fantasy, suspense, horror, or something else. For instance, romance can be found in Meg Cabot's popular humorous *Princess Diaries* series, in Holly Black's contemporary fairy tale *Tithe,* and in Angela Johnson's award-winning *The First Part Last.* Romance is always part of the story, but it is never the whole story in contemporary realistic fiction for teens.

In the 1980s, Linda Christian-Smith discovered that young women who read popular teen romance series such as Wildfire and Sweet Dreams were learning to focus on romantic concerns. She argued that romance series, which were constructed for and marketed to teen girls, were intentionally distracting them from plans for college and careers.

In recent years, fewer paperback teen romances have been published. Popular romance series such as Sweet Valley High and Love Stories have disappeared, making way for new examples such as the Gossip Girl series by Cecily von Ziegesar and Cathy Hopkins's Mates, Dates series. Contemporary realistic fiction for teens, including series fiction, could be used in classes as a way to begin discussions about issues teens

*This section contributed by Carolyn Carpan, the author of Rocked by Romance: A Guide to Teen Romance Fiction *(Libraries Unlimited, 2004). She is the Director of Public Services for the Hamilton College Library.*

are dealing with in their everyday lives. After all, romance, and everything that comes with it, is an important part of young people's lives.

Reading young adult fiction gives teens the opportunity to learn about all kinds of romantic relationships. Teens can learn about heterosexual sex by reading Judy Blume's *Forever,* how to get out of an abusive relationship by reading Kathryn Ann Clarke's *The Breakable Vow,* or how to cope with the loss of their first love in Lurlene McDaniel's *Don't Die, My Love.* Teen readers can also learn about gay and lesbian romance by reading Alex Sanchez's *Rainbow Boys* or Sara Ryan's *Empress of the World.* Reading contemporary realistic fiction allows teen readers to learn about dating, communication, sex, sexually transmitted diseases, options for dealing with pregnancy, and how to cope with the end of romantic relationships.

Classroom discussions and exercises could focus on finding out what teens are learning from today's young adult fiction about how to behave in romantic relationships, what kinds of gender roles teens are learning to emulate from the stories, and what, if any, impact these behaviors and roles play in their own lives.

After the Moment (2009) responds directly to the twists and turns of love and the complexities of today's world. Cover from *After the Moment* by Garret Freymann-Weyr. Copyright © 2009 by Garret Freymann-Weyr. Reprinted by permission of Houghton Mifflin Harcourt Publishing Company. All rights reserved.

I would argue that today's teen romance fiction does a better job of promoting strong, smart young women who know they have more choices in life than simply romance, love, and marriage. Although much of teen romance fiction is meant to be recreational reading material, even issues from soap opera series such as Zoey Dean's A-List series or Paul Ruditis's controversial Rainbow Party series could lead to important classroom discussions about gender roles, sexuality, romantic relationships, safe sex, and sexually transmitted diseases. Romantic conflicts found in contemporary realistic teen fiction could also be used to supplement study of classic romantic tales, such as *Romeo and Juliet* or *Wuthering Heights.* Love and romance are central in teens' lives and contemporary realistic fiction can help them learn about these vital parts of life.

School Stories

One of the most popular contexts for YA fiction is the classroom and in fact there is a great tradition of "school stories" with certain themes or motifs that often reappear in these storylines. It is not surprising that one of the primary issues in these school stories is the dilemma of fitting in.

Fitting In

- *All But Alice* by Phyllis Reynolds Naylor
- *Amandine* by Adele Griffin
- *The Beast* by Walter Dean Myers
- *The Girls* by Amy Koss
- *The Misfits* by James Howe
- *Names Will Never Hurt Me* by Jaimie Adoff
- *Slam!* by Walter Dean Myers
- *Stargirl* by Jerry Spinelli
- *The Warriors* by Joseph Bruchac

Teachers

- *Bronx Masquerade* by Nikki Grimes
- *Don't You Dare Read This, Mrs. Dunphrey* by Margaret Haddix
- *Friction* by E. R. Frank
- *The Landry News* by Andrew Clements
- *The Skin I'm In* by Sharon Flake
- *Standing Up to Mr. O* by Claudia Mills

Trouble

- *Alt Ed* by Catherine Atkins

- *Big Mouth & Ugly Girl* by Joyce Carol Oates
- *The Cheat* by Amy Goldman Koss
- *Cheating Lessons* by Nan Willard Cappo
- *Joey Pigza Swallowed the Key* by Jack Gantos
- *Nothing but the Truth* by Avi
- *Rats Saw God* by Rob Thomas

Getting into College

- *All's Fair in Love, War, and High School* by Janette Rallison
- *Catalyst* by Laurie Halse Anderson
- *Perfect Score* by David Levithan

School Milieu

- *Charlie's Story* by Maeve Friel
- *How Not to Spend Your Senior Year* by Cameron Dokey
- *The New Rules of High School* by Blake Nelson
- *The School Story* by Andrew Clements
- *Shattering Glass* by Gail Giles

Controversy: Topics that Frequently Face Challenges

In contemporary realistic fiction there are issues that some parents and teachers will find controversial. Of course numerous themes can cause controversy: political or religious views, stereotypes, profanity, gender issues, or violence, for example. Some teachers believe that school is not the place for these subjects to be addressed, and some parents might argue that explicit sex or drug use is never appropriate in literature for young people. On the other hand, many question whether young people should be shielded from these issues. Perhaps it is more beneficial for young adults to confront these issues head on in literature that provides a safe environment to investigate possible responses.

Photo by Jennifer Seay.

Adults who work with young adults need to stay sensitive to the standards of the community. However, they should also keep in mind that it is not the subject itself that might be inappropriate but how the author treats it. The fear of challenges and complaints will obviously lead some teachers and librarians to avoid controversial texts, but many experts feel that these are the same difficult issues teens are likely to face either firsthand or in their imaginations. So this literature might be a valuable first step in thinking critically about contemporary life (Alsup, 2003; Kaplan, 2004).

Sex

In the late 1960s and early 1970s many of the taboos about sex in YA literature were broken—which is not to say that they weren't challenged and still are to some extent today. *Are You There God? It's Me, Margaret* (Blume) was one of the first books to deal with issues related to female sexuality at all and although the main issue is menstruation, it is still frequently challenged.

More contemporary novels such as *Gingerbread* (Cohn), *Life Is Funny* (Frank), and *Rainbow Boys* (Sanchez) have "hormonal teenagers grappling with issues of sexual identity," but as author Rachel Cohn argues this is also the case in commonly assigned readings such as *Romeo and Juliet, Wuthering Heights,* and *Catcher in the Rye* (Cohn, 2004). It can certainly be argued that teens are going to be thinking about this theme whether they encounter it in literature or not.

Patrick Jones (1998) has asserted, "Sex plays a part in many of these novels, yet also remains just part of the story." Taking a theme out of context can make a book sound like a terrible choice for a teen reader. In *The Facts Speak for Themselves* (Cole), for example, there is a strong theme of abuse and sex but the novel is so honest and beautifully crafted that it received an American Book Award honor.

Novels for young adults present an array of diverse experiences representing contemporary realities. Often this means touchy subjects such as school violence show up in books like *Just Another Hero* by Sharon Draper (2009), creating great interest among many young adults but also causing some teachers to avoid using them in schools. Reprinted by permission of Simon and Schuster.

Novels such as *Speak* (Anderson), *Inexcusable* (Lynch), and *Things Change* (Jones) deal with date rape and date abuse. Many critics and teachers believe that discussion of these issues in school is much more likely to bring awareness and lessen the chance of students committing these crimes or of staying silent when they or someone they know is a victim. Some novels deal with sexual dysfunctions. *Damage* for example by A. M. Jenkins shows sex used in a dysfunctional way for power. In *The Earth, My Butt, and Other Big Round Things* (Mackler) the protagonist follows the "Fat Girl's Code of Conduct," meaning that guys might give her some attention if she lets them do certain things, but they won't want to be seen in public with her. Then there is Remy in *This Lullaby: A Novel* by Sarah Dessen. She has seen how dysfunctional her parents' love lives have become and so has guaranteed herself that she will never fall in love herself. She dates compulsively but cuts all relationships off before the boys can go all "Ken" on her. That is, until Dexter, who refuses to let her go so easily.

More commonly it is the crazy complexities of love that are first becoming a part of daily life during the teen years that are explored in YA literature. Whether it's punker/ravers searching for love in Francesca Lia Block's *Weetzie Bat,* or a beautifully crafted love triangle such as the brother and sister who fall for the same guy in Garret Freymann-Weyr's *My Heartbeat,* these stories are of interest to young adults because they are trying to sort out these feelings themselves.

Sonya Sones's *What My Mother Doesn't Know* is a good example of a teen searching for love. Sophie has a popular

To Consider

Is there a point at which we can say that there is too much sensuality in a novel for it to be considered young adult literature? If a book has young characters doing things that young people do and that teens are interested in reading about, is there a line that cannot be crossed?

boyfriend, a cyber fling, and a secret crush on a geek. The hopeful yet angst-ridden voice in this novel in verse captures the thoughts and feelings of many 15- and 16-year-old girls. Both Wittlinger's *Razzle* and Kate Cann's *Hard Cash* explore the theme of the nice guy who falls for the wrong girl while the right girl is there all along. The age-old Romeo and Juliet love/feud has also lasted through the ages, because it is an extreme version of typical situations. In *Scribbler of Dreams* by Mary Pearson, Kaitlin's dad is in jail for killing a Crutchfield, the family she has grown up hating and with whom her family has feuded for several generations. But romance gets in the way and she finds herself falling for a Crutchfield. *Son of the Mob* by Gordon Korman has a more humorous twist on the Romeo and Juliet scenario. Vince's father is in organized crime, which has caused some problems in his social life, but now he is in love and her father is an FBI agent. All of these novels share the idea that love is not going to be as easy as we might like.

Of course one of the biggest complications involving sex is the possibility of pregnancy. Early books about teen pregnancy include Paul Zindel's *My Darling, My Hamburger* and Richard Peck's *Don't Look and It Won't Hurt.* Interestingly the babies hardly ever appear in the books. Several decades later, babies have actually become characters in such stories as Chris Lynch's *Gypsy Davey* and Rita Williams Garcia's *Like Sisters on the Homefront.* Today there is a huge range of experiences and opinions expressed in the literature. The best of these books do not judge or preach but show teen pregnancy as a multifaceted issue, as in the following examples.

- *Bird at the Window* by Jan Truss
- *Dancing Naked* by Shelly Hrdlitschka
- *Don't Look and It Won't Hurt* by Richard Peck
- *The First Part Last* by Angela Johnson
- *Hanging on to Max* by Margaret Bechard
- *If Not for You* by Margaret Willey
- *Life Is Funny* by E. R. Frank
- *No More Saturday Nights* by Norma Klein
- *Slam* by Nick Hornby
- *Stranger, You and I* by Patricia Calvert
- *That Night* by Alice McDermott

Technology Links

Censorship

A few years back a high school media specialist discovered that many of her students were reading *Angus, Thongs, and Full Frontal Snogging* (Rennison). To meet demand for the book she purchased three more copies. Soon several teachers were reading the book as well and word of mouth made it the most checked out book that term. However, one teacher who saw the book being read by a student during class time complained to the principal that the book had inappropriate content. Soon, several parents complained as well and the principal asked the media specialist to remove the book from circulation. Although the book was never formally challenged, the media specialist gave the books to the public library. Later she said that if she only knew where to go to for help she would have fought to keep the books. With the aid of the Internet, help combating censorship is not so difficult to find.

The Internet has several extremely helpful sources for fighting against book challenges. The American Library Association has a wealth of information, including lists of books that have been challenged, *The Intellectual Freedom Manual* to supply legal information you might need, an Action Guide, and places to go for support.

The National Council of Teachers of English has an Anti-Censorship Center that includes model procedures for responding to a challenge as well as an amazing resource— Rationales for Teaching Challenged Books. Not only do they walk you through how to write rationales for any book, but they also provide on CD-ROM over 300 rationales for books that have been challenged in the past. These rationales are very reasoned explanations of how a book can be beneficial for students to read even though it might have something included that on the surface is objectionable.

The American Library Association's Banned Books Week
www.pla.org/ala/oif/bannedbooksweek/bannedbooksweek.htm

National Council of Teachers of English: Anti-Censorship Center
www.ncte.org/about/issues/censorship

Audio Books

Contemporary Realistic Fiction

Big Mouth & Ugly Girl by Joyce Carol Oates; read by Hilary Swank and Chad Lowe. (Harper Children's Audio, 2002)

Breathing Underwater by Alex Finn; read by Jon Cryer. (Listening Library, 2002) (Y)

Buddha Boy by Kathe Koja. (Full Cast Audio, 2004)

Catalyst by Laurie Halse Anderson; read by Samantha Mathis. (Random House, 2002) (Y)

Cut by Patricia McCormick; read by Clea Lewis. (Random House, 2001) (Y)

Evolution, Me, and Other Freaks of Nature by Robin Brande; read by Kaili Vernoff. (Listening Library, 2007)

Holes by Louis Sachar; read by Kerry Beyer. (Listening Library, 2006) (N, Y)

Hoot by Carl Hiaasen; read by Chad Lowe. (Random House, 2002) (Y)

Loser by Jerry Spinelli; read by Steve Buscemi. (Harper Children's Audio, 2002)

Miracles Boys by Jacqueline Woodson; read by Dule Hill. (Random House, 2001) (Y)

My Louisiana Sky by Kimberly Willis Holt; read by Judith Ivey. (Listening Library, 1999) (A, N, Y)

Seek by Paul Fleischman; read by a full cast; bonus interview with the author. (Listening Library, 2002) (Y)

Slake's Limbo by Felice Holman; read by Neil Patrick Harris. (Listening Library, 2000) (Y)

Snail Mail No More by Paula Danzinger and Ann Martin; read by the authors. (Books on Tape, 2001) (A)

Speak by Laurie Halse Anderson; read by Mandy Seigfried. (Listening Library, 2000) (Y)

Stargirl by Jerry Spinelli; read by John Ritter. (Listening Library, 2001) (B, Y, P)

Stuck in Neutral by Terry Trueman; read by Johnny Heller. (Recorded Books, 2001) (Y)

Touching Spirit Bear by Ben Mikaelsen; read by Lee Tergesen. (Books on Tape, 2001) (Y)

What Would Joey Do? by Jack Gantos; read by the author. Also *Joey Pigza Swallowed the Key* (A, E, N) and *Joey Pigza Loses Control.* (Listening Library, 2002) (A)

When Kambia Elaine Flew in from Neptune by Lori Aurelia Williams; read by Heather Alicia Simms. (Listening Library, 2001) (A, Y)

A—Audiofile Earphones Award

B—Ben Franklin Audio Award

E—Booklist Editor's Choice

N—ALSC Notable Children's Recording

P—Parent's Choice Audio Award Winner

Y—YALSA Selected List of Audiobooks

Books to Film

Contemporary Realistic Fiction

About a Boy by Nick Hornsby (Movie: *About a Boy.* Universal, © 2002)

Bend It Like Beckham by Narinder Dhami (Movie: *Bend It Like Beckham.* 20th Century Fox, © 2003)

Confessions of a Teenage Drama Queen by Dyan Sheldon (Movie: *Confessions of a Teenage Drama Queen.* Walt Disney, © 2004)

Girl Gives Birth to Own Prom Date by Todd Strasser (Movie: *Drive Me Crazy.* 20th Century Fox, © 1999)

Girl, Interrupted by Susanna Kaysen (Movie: *Girl, Interrupted.* Columbia Tristar Home Video, © 2000)

Goal: The Dream Begins by Robert Rigby (Movie: *Goal: The Dream Begins.* Milkshake Films, © 2005)

Holes by Louis Sachar (Movie: *Holes.* Walt Disney, © 2003)

One Flew over the Cuckoo's Nest by Ken Kesey (Movie: *One Flew over the Cuckoo's Nest.* Warner, © 1975)

The Sisterhood of the Traveling Pants by Ann Brashares (Movie: *The Sisterhood of the Traveling Pants.* Alcon Entertainment, © 2005)

Speak by Laurie Halse Anderson (Movie: *Speak.* Showtime Independent Films, © 2005)

That Summer and *Someone Like You* by Sarah Dessen (Movie: *How to Deal.* New Line Cinema, © 2003)

What's Eating Gilbert Grape by Peter Hedges (Movie: *What's Eating Gilbert Grape.* Paramount, © 1993)

Author Spotlight

Photo courtesy of Angela Johnson.

Angela Johnson

Angela Johnson has written picture books, poetry, and novels. Most of her protagonists have been African American girls. Johnson attended Kent State University and has been a freelance writer since 1989. She is a recipient of a MacArthur Fellow and she received the Printz Award for *The First Part Last*. Visit her website at http://aalbc.com/authors/angela.htm.

SELECTED BOOKLIST

The First Part Last (Simon and Schuster, 2003)
Heaven (Simon and Schuster, 1998)
Looking for Red (Simon and Schuster, 2002)
The Other Side: Shorter Poems (Orchard, 1998)
Sweet Hereafter (Simon and Schuster, 2010)
Toning the Sweep (Orchard, 1993)

ON HOW SHE BECAME AN AUTHOR OF YOUNG ADULT LITERATURE

Actually I never thought I'd write a novel. I was content at the time to write nothing but picture books and poetry I didn't believe would ever get published. Cynthia Rylant told me she thought it was time I entertained the idea of trying a novel. I'd done three picture books. One day a copy of *Weetzie Bat* was left on my doorstep. I was blown away by the images, feelings, and voice of the book. I was off.

ON WHETHER SHE WRITES WITH A PARTICULAR AUDIENCE IN MIND

I don't write with any audience in mind except children and teens. I have very little control over what character shows up in my head.

ON THE INSPIRATION FOR HER STORIES

The idea for *The First Part Last* came from a group of sixth-grade girls at the Manhattan School for Children who were asked to talk about their favorite character from my book *Heaven*. They chose Bobby Morris, a 17-year-old with an infant daughter because they had never read a book with a loving, attentive African American teenage male father figure. My editor, Kevin Lewis, asked me if I might entertain the idea of writing a book about Bobby. I initially said no. Until I was invited to New York for a week to speak to kids in an after-school program in Manhattan. The inspiration for *The First Part Last* came from a very young man I saw during that trip on the subway with a baby. I became entranced with him being on the train in the middle of the afternoon (on a school day) with the baby girl he held. I wondered if he was her brother or her father. Suddenly, Bobby was on my mind.

ON THE EXTENT TO WHICH HER OWN LIFE STORY APPEARS IN HER WORKS

It never does cross over. But conversely I tend to use more of my life when I write poetry, which can definitely be more personal.

ON WHAT DISTINGUISHES YOUNG ADULT LITERATURE

To me the only difference between YA literature and children's and adult literature is that you are dealing with a period of human development when all things are ever changing, extremely emotional, and always interesting.

ON WHAT MIGHT HELP YOUNG ADULTS DEVELOP AS WRITERS

I still say the most important thing for a writer to do is to read. It's so important for young people to understand "voice." Once you have heard and been compelled by a distinctive voice, I believe all doors to their own begin to open.

In the end, the one thing that connects us all is the universality of the human condition. If you tell a story that touches many people's hearts you have done just that. It does not matter about the ethnicity, economic background, or gender of the person writing the story if they have indeed convinced the reader of the sincerity of the character. Of course, we are all propelled by where we came from and all our experiences; but that does not preclude any one writer because of ethnicity, gender, etc., to have a lock on certain kinds of stories. I believe in the world theatre where everyone is a part of all things.

Gender Issues and Homosexuality

The door to exploring homosexuality was opened in 1969 with *I'll Get There, It Better Be Worth the Trip* by John Donovan. Since then, numerous books for young adults have included minor characters who are gay. In the 1980s there were many characters discovering that someone they know or love is gay. Many of these homosexuals were portrayed as tortured misfits who paid dearly for their sexual preference—for example, Sarah's brother in *Rumors and Whispers* by Marilyn Levy, Alison's mother in *Breaking Up: A Novel* by Norma Klein, or A. J.'s best friend in *Bad Boys* by Diana Wieler. Still, homosexuality was addressed in beautifully authentic terms as early as 1982 in *Annie on My Mind* (Garden), which has remained one of the most challenged books in YA literature.

Barbara Smith (1999) writes that "homophobia is usually the first oppression to be mentioned, the last to be taken seriously, the last to go. But it is extremely serious, sometimes to the point of being fatal" (p. 112). Schools are "virtual cauldrons" of homophobic discrimination and anger from graffiti on the bathroom wall to the heterosexist bias of most textbooks (Kaplan, 2003). Richard Ramsay has compiled a database of 110 studies indicating that young people with homosexual or transgender tendencies are more likely to commit suicide (2007). Discussion about sexual orientation, she insists, can be brought into the classroom in the same way as any other multicultural issue of diversity through literature, discussion, and writing (Kaplan, 2003). Perhaps having available books which present positive characters with diverse sexual orientations will allow more young adults to find themselves in literature, while providing counter-images to the stereotypes too often found in popular media. Books such as *Boy Meets Boy* by David Levithan, which portrays a gay teenage protagonist as well adjusted and even happy can be a pleasant change from all of the outcasts and victims. Books suitable for young adults include

- *Am I Blue? Coming Out from the Silence* by Marion Dane Bauer
- *Annie on My Mind* by Nancy Garden
- *Athletic Shorts* by Chris Crutcher
- *Baby Be-Bop* by Francesca Lia Block
- *Blue Coyote* by Liza Ketchum
- *Boy Meets Boy* by David Levithan
- *Empress of the World* by Sara Ryan
- *From the Notebooks of Melanin Sun* by Jacqueline Woodson
- *Geography Club* by Brent Hartinger
- *Gravel Queen* by Tea Benduhn
- *Hard Love* by Ellen Wittlinger
- *"Hello," I Lied* by M. E. Kerr
- *The House You Pass on the Way* by Jacqueline Woodson
- *Ironman* by Chris Crutcher
- *Kissing Kate* by Lauren Myracle
- *Love Makes a Family* by Gigi Kaeser
- *Rainbow Boys* by Alex Sanchez
- *Whistle Me Home* by Barbara Wersba

One does not need to be gay, lesbian, or transgendered to empathize with the tension and confusion that many of these characters face as they try to come to terms with who they are and how their peers, family, and society respond to them.

Blood and Guts

Violence has been a part of YA literature from its beginnings. Much of what teen boys have been expected to read, such as *Robinson Crusoe, Last of the Mohicans,* and King Arthur or Robin Hood stories, have contained a certain amount of bloodshed. Many of the books that really sparked YA literature such as *The Outsiders* (Hinton), *The Contender* (Lipsyte), and *The Chocolate War* (Cormier) also have been challenged due to the amount of violence they contain. The first book to win the Printz Award, Walter Dean Myers's *Monster,* was about a young man on trial as an accomplice to murder.

Some have argued that this violence in young adult books has become pervasive, with scenes that are descriptive and disturbing (Isaacs, 2003). Kathy Isaacs asserts that this preponderance of young adult novels with vivid descriptions of violence runs counter to the lives of most teenagers. True violence, she counters, is relatively absent in their daily encounters. It is true that the vast majority of young people in the United States have not been victims of violent crimes.

However, although books like *33 Snowfish* (Rapp) have levels of violence far beyond what most teens will encounter, bullying, gangs, and school shootings are realities in the life of some kids and they are subjects that young adults often want to know more about. Teens can certainly explore the whole question of whether

> *To Consider*
> Do these gritty books with graphic violence represent reality, or are they just representations that authors, editors, and book buyers have bought into to sell more books?

the violence in a novel such as Ron Koertge's *The Brimstone Journals*, reflects reality or is just part of the hype.

In the Field   *Patrick Jones on Creating a Core Collection*

Patrick Jones was a young adult librarian for many years, during which time he wrote the influential A Core Collection for Young Adults *(2003). He is also an author of the YA novel* Things Change.

There is much to consider when putting together a collection of books for the young adult audience, whether we are talking about the public library, the school library, or even the classroom bookshelf. Jones, who is an expert in the field of collection development, asserts

> Collection development is not just about buying new books; it is about mixing new releases with standard titles. It is about weeding and maintaining, not just ordering everything on YALSA's Best Books for Young Adults list. It requires a balancing act between quality and popularity, single copies and multiples, old and new. It has to include books that will generate teen interest to create word of mouth, which means the books are used, discussed, and remembered.

Part of finding the right books for your collection is discovering what YA readers are looking for and one of the key factors here is relevance:

> Relevance to their lives, to their times, and to the questions they are asking. Relevance in terms of the need for recreation, relaxation, or perhaps for a challenging read. That said, when we look at most fiction, not just realistic fiction but also speculative fiction, most teens are looking for stories that relate to the core drives in their lives: independence. For lots of teen boys, reading is the means to reach an end. The end being a fuller understanding, appreciation, and even expertise in a specific area. Girls want to read something; boys want to read about something.

Jones's experience with developing YA collections and discovering what YA readers are looking for in the books they read has directly impacted his own fiction writing:

> The publication of *Things Change* is totally related to my work as a YA librarian. I met the editor of Walker Books for Young Readers when serving on a YALSA committee, and developed a good relationship with her. When I was looking for a publisher, I had a connection. My novel was a negative rejection of teen books which were preachy and filled with happy endings, but also a positive reflection of the best in YA fiction like Rob Thomas, Terry Davis, Chris Crutcher, and Annette Curtis Klause. Knowing the professional field and the target market helped me. After all, the main character in *Things Change is* the type of person who reads lots of YA fiction: a smart young woman searching for role models and release through literature.

Author Spotlight

Photo by Jeffrey Freymann-Weyr.

Garret Freymann-Weyr

Garret Freymann-Weyr was born and raised in New York City. She earned her B.A. from UNC–Chapel Hill and her M.F.A. in film from NYU. She now lives outside Washington, D.C., with her husband. She has written four books for young adults, and *My Heartbeat* won a Printz honor. Visit her website at www.freymann-weyr.com.

SELECTED BIBLIOGRAPHY

After the Moment (Houghton Mifflin, 2009)
The Kings Are Already Here (Houghton Mifflin, 2003)
My Heartbeat (Houghton Mifflin, 2002)
Stay With Me (Houghton Mifflin, 2006)
When I Was Older (Houghton Mifflin, 2000)

ON HOW SHE BECAME AN AUTHOR OF YOUNG ADULT LITERATURE

I don't think of myself as writing for young adults. I write books where, so far, the main characters are 14 to 17. There are some things about that age that are appealing to any writer. A 15-year-old girl is able and likely to sound like she's 9 and then 15 and then 30 and then 11 and finally 9 again, all in the space of an hour. I like the challenge of trying to capture that range. A woman in her twenties sounds like a woman in her twenties. It's not hard (or very interesting) to pin down a static voice.

I am also interested in how and why people make choices. The choices made early are usually made with more care and self-awareness than the ones made later on. My particular preferences (engaging, shifting voices and careful choices) have led to my writing about "younger" characters.

ON WHETHER SHE WRITES WITH A PARTICULAR AUDIENCE IN MIND

I write to satisfy my own standards. I sit down every day knowing I am going to fail in some way. There's always a massive gap between what is in my head and what gets on the page. No one in their right mind would go through this for an audience. It's a private task which every now and then finds outside readers.

ON THE INSPIRATION FOR HER STORIES

I don't know that I am an inspired person so much as I am someone who is willing to work really, really hard to build a story around a phrase or an image or a vague idea.

And I don't know where or how I come upon the phrase or image or idea that will propel me toward my desk and keep me there until I am done. With *My Heartbeat*, I had some vague idea about secrets. And another vague idea about loyalty. And the image of a hidden smile. I guess they all came together in *My Heartbeat*.

ON THE EXTENT TO WHICH HER OWN LIFE STORY APPEARS IN HER WORKS

Certain external details inform my writing. I grew up in Manhattan. My sisters and I were expected to grow up into interesting people. And it was made clear that the way to be interesting was to become and stay interested in "worthwhile" subjects and activities. So my characters tend to be shaped by some degree of a similar experience. In many ways, the city is a force just as expectations are.

ON WHAT DISTINGUISHES YOUNG ADULT LITERATURE

I think the ways in which they are bad are what distinguishes YAs as a group. A good YA novel is just a good novel that gives its "young" characters the same thorough examination that a good grown-up novel gives its "old" characters. A bad grown-up book is badly written. Whereas, a bad YA can be well written, but full of moral lessons about how-to-be-a-good-person. I don't need to give examples. Everybody knows them when they see them.

ON WHAT MIGHT HELP YOUNG ADULTS DEVELOP AS WRITERS

Read. I am always astonished at how many people I meet who want to be writers, but don't read. I never know what to say to them without sounding like a public library campaign, but there it is. Read!

ON WHETHER THERE ARE TOPICS THAT AUTHORS FOR YOUNG ADULTS SHOULD AVOID

No! My feelings about this are so strong that I never escape offending people who disagree with me so let me leave it at no.

Book Buddies: A Cross-Age Dialogue Journal

Most well-written novels are not overly didactic. Rather than preach, they challenge readers to deal with the ambiguities of life. These ambiguities often speak to young adults and even "encourage teen readers to take the next step forward, to express themselves in writing" (Cohn, 2004). One of the great strengths of good young adult fiction is that it can "challenge students to discuss, contemplate, and develop their own moral standards" (Bushman and

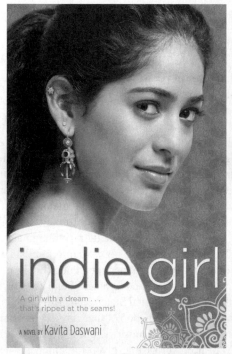
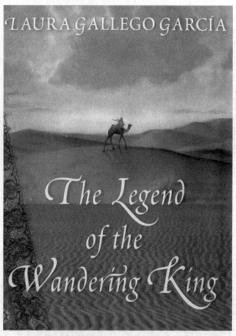

In *Indie Girl* by Kavita Daswani (Simon Pulse, 2007) the Indian narrator has always dreamed of being a fashion reporter. Culture, fashion, gossip, and coming of age come together in this novel. Even books from other countries that are set in the past or in speculative realms are often filled with cultural references. *Legend of the Wandering King* (Arthur Levine, 2005) by Laura Gallego García is from Spain but it is steeped in pre-Islamic Arabian legend. *Indie Girl* reprinted by permission of Simon Pulse. *The Legend of the Wandering King* reprinted by permission of Arthur Levine.

McNerny, 2004). Literary exploration of these books can lead to thought-provoking discussions of mature issues that encourage students to examine critical societal and individual situations from a variety of perspectives.

Of course young people might need assistance both in finding books that will challenge them and in guiding them "through the gauntlet of moral development" (Bushman and McNerny, 2004). One of the best ways to help young adults work through their thoughts on the complex issues they might encounter is through dialogue journals. The typical process is for students to write their reflections (and questions) in a journal as they read the novel. Teachers (or parents) then respond in ways that encourage these reflections. Young readers are able to ask questions and can take the time to reflect on issues that concern them. The adult responder can guide, reassure, and question the reflections made by the teen readers. When effectively done the teacher will learn much about the students' understanding of the narrative as well as the students' background knowledge. The young adult on the other hand will become a more critical, engaged reader. Some teachers have readers engage in dialogue journals with their peers and recently some teachers have utilized student blogs or wikis as a twist on the concept.

International Books

Literature has the potential to reveal to readers the commonality of the human experience. Creating world citizens, as Nussbaum writes, rests in literary creations that enable individuals to comprehend the motives and choices of people different from ourselves. By sharing stories from all walks of life, Nussbaum concludes, readers develop a "narrative imagination" and become more caring people (1997).

Since 2005, the United States Board on Books for Young People (USBBY) has compiled an annual list of Outstanding International Books for Children and Young Adults. The goals of such a list include exposing young readers and those who work with them to quality books from other countries, introducing them to the best authors and illustrators from around the globe, and expanding cultural knowledge and intercultural understandings.

Of course international books in English have always had a major impact on American readers and the literary imagination. Authors like J. R. R. Tolkien, C. S. Lewis, and J. K. Rowling, just to name a few, have really shaped our literary imaginations. Despite this, however, there are surprisingly few international books being published for young adults in the United States. Estimates are that only around 5 percent of books published for young readers in the United States were first published in other countries. The majority of the international books being republished in the United States come from English-speaking countries. In fact, books that have been translated into English only account for around 1 to 2 percent per year. Even more surprising, given the emphasis being placed on multiculturalism and global understandings in society today, very few of the books republished in the United States originally come from non-Western countries.

As Gillian Lathey (2004) suggests, there are at least two reasons for highlighting books from other languages and cultures: so that young readers "don't miss out on the best of international writing for children, and because an appreciation of linguistic and cultural differences is essential in the modern world" (p. 9). Cross-cultural literary experiences widen our horizons and might bridge the language and cultural gaps between groups of people around the world. Readers in the United States tend to know precious little about our neighbors around the globe. Introducing students to world literature might help them understand the diversity of the world and also raise an interest in other countries, cultures, languages, and lifestyles, perhaps even fostering an international outlook.

Still many publishers cite high costs and low profits as the primary reason for not publishing international books, especially translations (Biamonte, 2002). International books have a reputation for not selling well and so are seen as not being worth the investment. It's difficult for publishers to know what narratives are authentic (or even well written) when dealing with cultures or languages the

In *Postcards from No Man's Land* by Aidan Chambers (2002) two thought-provoking stories intertwine in this tale, set in both contemporary Netherlands and occupied Holland during World War II. Reprinted by permission of Penguin Group (USA).

editors do not know. Editors have to rely on people familiar with the literature, cultures, and languages of other countries.

Cheryl Klein, an editor with Arthur Levine, shares how the process generally works at her publishing house:

> The way it usually happens is through the publisher—Arthur Levine will meet with a foreign publisher's international-rights director at the Bologna Book Fair, and based on the director's recommendation/pitching Arthur will ask to see certain books. . . . Or sometimes people just recommend foreign books to us and then we research them. . . . Once we get the books, we send them to readers; if the report is enthusiastic and it sounds like something we'd want to publish, we get sample translations; and if the sample translation is good and we're still enthusiastic, we then acquire it. (Klein, personal correspondence, 2005)

Many publishers believe that audiences like to read about the familiar so when books from other countries are chosen they will most likely deal with "universal" concepts and are often modified to meet the needs of an American reading audience. Some publishers go so far as to hide the fact that the book is not originally from the United States.

Literary texts are cultural texts and they are written and read within cultural positions (Rogers, 1997, p. 97). So our reading of international books might provide us with "a rich and immensely enjoyable literary experience, as well as some understanding of those cultures," but our "engagement and interpretation will be different from that of 'insiders'" (Soter, 1997, p. 215). Being familiar with the political and social context of Israel would certainly help us understand what is happening in *When I Was a Soldier* (Zenatti); however, we can still enjoy, appreciate, and learn from the novel without that background.

Translation is much more than a word-to-word exchange. The multiple meanings, the tone, the sense of style, and the cultural implications must also be captured. The narrative has to be reinterpreted to capture the sense of the author's original intent. Translation is an art form that requires faithful translation, cultural interpretation, and creative authoring. The translator recreates the story, hopefully capturing the tone, the style, and the emotions and characterizations of the original. Translators never translate words in isolation but within

Reading books from another country can be a great way to gain some understandings of both the literary traditions and the cultures of the region. American teens will find much that they can relate to in Suzanne Gervay's *That's Why I Wrote This Song* (2007) and the music video that accompanies this novel (www.sgervay .com/books/thatswhyiwrotethissong .php). Reprinted by permission of HarperCollins Publishers.

contextual situations. They bring to the translation their cultural heritage, their reading experience, and in the case of young adult books, their image of youth (Oittinen, 2000). Translations are cross-cultural communications.

Even books originally published in English, though they are not translated, are often edited and changed in a number of ways—Americanized—in terms of themes and settings. Markus Zusak, speaking about his novel *Getting the Girl,* which was originally titled *When Dogs Cry* in Australia, asserts:

> People down here cringe sometimes when I tell them of the amount of effort that went into reworking the novel, but now I have two different versions for two different countries—and it makes it look like I've come up with an entirely new work. (Zusak interview, p. 282)

Though these changes might make a novel more accessible for U.S. audiences, sometimes readers and teachers would prefer to read the book without losing the international distinctions. Dietlof Reiche's *Ghost Ship* is a good adventure story for tweens, with ghosts and villains, and a male and female character who attempt to solve the mystery behind it all. When you read the book, some readers might notice that some things are off kilter. In the American edition the setting is changed from the North Sea coast of Germany to the coast of New England. The book retains a German flavor despite the translation and editorial changes—it just feels like Germany. But here it is in black and white insisting that the story takes place in New England!

> *To Consider*
> When might young adults be interested in reading books from other countries? In general do you think they might be more interested in reading books that have been Americanized or books that retain cultural relevance?

Author Spotlight

Photo courtesy of Markus Zusak.

Markus Zusak

Markus Zusak has already asserted himself as one of today's most innovative and poetic novelists as the award-winning author of five books for young adults. He was the recipient of a 2006 Printz Honor for excellence in young adult literature. He lives in Sydney, Australia. Visit his website at www.randomhouse.com/features/markuszusak.

SELECTED BOOKLIST
The Book Thief (Knopf, 2006)
Fighting Ruben Wolfe (Arthur Levine, 2001)
Getting the Girl (Arthur Levine, 2003)
I Am the Messenger (Knopf, 2005)

ON WHETHER HE WRITES WITH A PARTICULAR AUDIENCE IN MIND

My biggest concern when I write is not necessarily the audience in terms of age, sex, or anything `of that nature. I'm more asking myself, "Do I believe this?" The beauty of writing anything is making someone believe and live something that isn't real. That's what I'm aiming for, rather than thoughts like "I hope a 16-year-old likes this."

ON THE EXTENT TO WHICH HIS OWN LIFE STORY APPEARS IN HIS WORKS

I guess it's often the starting point. I used to believe that writing was about taking the truth and seeing how much lying you could get away with, but now I think the flip side is that it's actually forming another truth, to form something else believable. It's often the little things that are true, and these small details are what make the rest of it seem authentic. If you can include the small details, it *must* be true.

ON CREATING A YOUTHFUL VOICE

This is something you can't fake, I think. I don't try to keep up with any trends in speech or slang. I write dialogue the way I speak myself, and I want the voice in a book to feel real. In some ways, we all want something we can relate to, but overall, if that means writing something false to try and fit in, I'd be well and truly losing my way.

ON WHETHER THERE ARE TOPICS THAT AUTHORS FOR YOUNG ADULTS SHOULD AVOID

I don't have a problem with people having concerns, but I also think that there are many more books that are quite graphic in comparison. It's also a question of whether the positive aspects outweigh the negative. If there's violence in a novel, as well as love and loyalty (as I hope there is in *Fighting Ruben Wolfe*), the big question must be which is the more powerful. When I think of that book, I think of brotherhood rather than boxing.

Having said that, I don't have to contend with unhappy parents or school boards. In the end, I like to think that a teacher can ask, "Will this book inspire my class?" and if the answer is yes, I hope that he or she is able to go ahead and use it.

ON CULTURAL DIFFERENCES IN READING AUDIENCES

I write in a very Australian way, I think, especially dialogue. If anything, people down here have a bit of inside knowledge into my work in that regard, but overall, I haven't noticed any huge differences in overseas readers. I actually receive more mail from the USA, and in general, I hope that the Wolfe family could really be visualized in many cities around the world. The fact that they live on the non-postcard side of Sydney is only alluded to, and I deliberately avoid describing them in terms of hair color, eye color, and so forth. That way, they're human rather than anything else.

ON CHANGES MADE IN THE U.S. EDITIONS

Fighting Ruben Wolfe has made it to the USA intact. The only necessary changes were Australian slang that Americans just won't understand. Examples are the words like "yobbo" and "westie." These words translate to "idiot" and perhaps "redneck." They appear maybe once or twice in that book. My new book to be released in America has had a change of title. In Australia it is called *When Dogs Cry,* as opposed to *Getting the Girl* in the USA. The new title actually gave me a chance to explore a few other avenues and themes within the book and find several meanings for the title. Some examples are getting the girl as in having her, but then there's getting her as in understanding her, and the question of being okay *without* getting the girl. People down here cringe sometimes when I tell them of the amount of effort that went into reworking the novel, but now I have two different versions for two different countries—and it makes it look like I've come up with an entirely new work. The experience of my books coming out in the USA and Europe has never been a negative one so far. When you're writing your first book in a suburban shack in the outer suburbs of Sydney, you don't really dream that 7 years later, after all of the rejections and procrastination, that you'll be answering questions about the release of your work in the USA. For that reason, and despite all the whining and carrying on that all writers do (myself included), I feel very privileged.

LITERARY THEORY

Polyphony in Feminist and Postcolonial Theory

The concept of polyphony, or heteroglossia, involves looking at the multiple voices in a text. Most theory related to polyphony has built on the writings of M. Bakhtin. The term refers to the underlying voices that inform the way the text is written and the intertextual allusions. Authors tend to build on and be influenced by the books they have read in both conscious and subconscious ways. One might, for example, look for the echoes of James Baldwin in Walter Dean Myers's *The Beast.* If these echoes exist, what then might they mean? Do these voices enhance the narrative or change how readers understand it? Is Myers consciously making references to meanings found in Baldwin's narrative or is he subconsciously echoing elements of Baldwin's literary world because of the impact it had on him as a reader?

Beyond literary allusions there will be other voices from the author's past. You might hear echoes of Myers's mother, his pastor, his third-grade teacher, societal norms from his childhood, an article he read in the newspaper, or even a line from a favorite movie—all of those voices that have made him who he is. One might actually think of polyphony as layers of echoes. And these voices or echoes come together consciously and subconsciously when the author is creating story. On a surface level this is often more apparent in books in which there are multiple narrators but in terms of deep structures, all novels might be looked at this way.

In a consciously multivocal narrative such as Avi's *Nothing But the Truth,* the concept of voices is used by the author to present various sides of an issue so that a reader has to think critically to decide where they stand. On the other hand, Paul Fleischman's *Seek* is written as a radio play in a script format. Rob, a high school senior, is assigned to write an autobiography and in order to do so he listens to tapes of his father (who was a disc jockey). The book would be a great introduction to the concept of polyphony because at its core it is about how voices create identity.

The concept of polyphony is often used to subvert a text's surface meanings by uncovering other voices in the text. An interesting case in point can be found by applying a feminist lesson to the subject of body image. Although common sense would tell us that the image of young women has changed drastically in fiction since the early days of young adult literature, there are some interesting messages about body image that are still prevalent. Beth Younger (2003) provides a comprehensive and provocative read about the role of female body image and sexuality as portrayed in young adult literature written from 1975 to 1999 (Kaplan, 2003).

When the weight of a character is not specified, the reader is most likely to assume the character is thin. Details about weight are only given if the character is considered abnormal, so if a woman's weight is mentioned at all, more often than not, they are called fat or chubby (Younger, 2003). Even more interesting is the idea that there is a link between body image, weight, and sexuality. Almost invariably heavy girls are represented as sexually promiscuous, passive, and powerless, whereas thin characters appear responsible and powerful (Kaplan, 2003). So when reading *The Earth, My Butt, and Other Big Round Things* (Mackler), for example, the teen reader might explore how the narrative reflects societal voices.

Another theoretical lens that has often made use of the concept of polyphony is postcolonial theory, a way of looking at literature related to the cultural legacy of colonial rule. Postcolonialism deals with cultural identity in formerly colonized societies: the dilemmas of developing a national identity after colonial rule; the ways in which writers articulate and celebrate that identity (often reclaiming it from, while still maintaining connections with, the colonizer); the ways in which the knowledge of the colonized people has been used to serve the colonizer's interests; and the ways the colonizer's literature has justified colonialism via images of the colonized as a perpetually inferior people, society, and culture. Postcolonial theory gained in popularity in the 1970s with Edward Said's book *Orientalism.*

Postcolonial theory might be applied, for example, to look at the conflicting voices in a novel written by a British author but set in Nigeria. The critic might use these conflicting voices to deconstruct images of Africa that are based on colonial concepts (such as Africa being "the heart of darkness"), which helped justify colonial practices. Or the postcolonial critic might look at an Indian author's attempt to reconnect with her heritage after being educated in English in British-style schools.

A few years ago the Batchelder Committee selected a beautifully written book set in eastern Africa, *The Baboon King* (Quintana), to honor as the best translated book of the year. Some of the dialogue afterward centered on the fact that though the novel is set in Kenya it was written by a Dutch author. Whether this should be an issue or not, it does gain import when you consider that every adult member of the two African cultures presented in the book is cruel and despicable to the young character, who eventually finds solace by becoming the leader of a troop of baboons. If an author from Kenya had written the story, would the world be presented this way? The postcolonial critic drawing on the concept of polyphony might then look for the echoes of Joseph Conrad's *A Heart of Darkness,* Edgar Rice Burroughs's *Tarzan of the Apes,* and other European portrayals of Africa to help explain where these images come from and then use these echoes to deconstruct the "realities" presented in the novel.

For Further Reading

Polyphony

Bakhtin, M. M. *The Dialogic Imagination: Four Essays.* Edited by Michael Holquist. Translated by Caryl Emerson and Michael Holquist. University of Texas Press, 1981. (Original work published 1930s)

Bakhtin, M. M. *Problems of Dostoevsky's Poetics.* Edited and translated by Caryl Emerson. University of Michigan Press, 1984.

Cadden, Mike. "The Irony of Narration in the Young Adult Novel." *Children's Literature Association Quarterly, 25*(3), Fall 2000, 146–154.

Hunt, Peter. *Criticism, Theory, and Children's Literature.* Blackwell, 1991.

McCallum, Robyn. *Ideologies of Identity in Adolescent Fiction: The Dialogic Construction of Subjectivity.* Garland Publishing, 1999.

McGillis, Roderick. *The Nimble Reader: Literary Theory and Children's Literature.* Twayne, 1996.

Feminist Theory

Clark, Beverly Lyon, and Margaret R. Higgonet (eds.). *Girls, Boys, Books, Toys: Gender in Children's Literature.* John Hopkins University Press, 1999.

Kaplan, Jeffrey. "New Perspectives in Young Adult Literature." *ALAN Review,* Fall 2003. http://scholar.lib.vt.edu/ejournals/ALAN/v31n1/kaplan.html

Lehr, Susan (ed.). *Beauty, Brains, and Brawn: The Construction of Gender in Children's Literature.* Heinemann, 2001.

Paul, Lissa. *Reading Otherways.* Thimble, 1997.

Paul, Lissa. "From Sex Role Stereotyping to Subjectivity: Feminist Criticism." In Peter Hunt (ed.), *Understanding Children's Literature.* Routledge, 2005.

Showalter, Elaine. "Toward a Feminist Poetic." *Feminist Criticism: Essays on Women, Literature, and Theory.* Pantheon, 1985.

Trites, R. S. *Waking Sleeping Beauty: Feminist Voices in Children's Novels.* University of Iowa Press, 1997.

Younger, Beth. "Pleasure, Pain, and the Power of Being Thin: Female Sexuality in Young Adult Literature." *National Women's Studies Association Journal, 15*(2), 2003, 45–56.

Postcolonial Theory

Cesaire, Aime. *Discourse on Colonialism.* Presence Africaine, 1950.

Fanon, Frantz. *Black Skin, White Masks.* Grove, 1967. Reprint of *Peau noire, masques blancs.* 1952.

Fanon, Frantz. *The Wretched of the Earth.* Grove, 1965. Reprint of *Les damnes de la terre.* 1961.

Gilbert, Helen, and Joanne Tompkins. *Post-Colonial Drama: Theory, Practice, Politics.* Routledge, 1996.

Khorana, Meena (ed.). *Critical Perspectives on Postcolonial African Children's and Young Adult Literature.* Greenwood, 1998.

Memmi, Albert. *The Colonizer and the Colonized.* Orion, 1965.

Nkrumah, Kwame. *Consciencism.* Heineman, 1964.

Said, Edward. *Orientalism.* Pantheon Books, 1978.

Wa Thiong'o, Ngugi. *Decolonising the Mind: The Politics of Language in African Literature.* Heinemann, 1986.

7

Literature across the Curriculum
Historical Fiction, Nonfiction, and Life Stories

Those who cannot remember the past are condemned to repeat it.

—*George Santayana*

Historical Fiction Text Set

Blood Red Horse by K. M. Grant

Bull Run by Paul Fleischman

Chains by Laurie Halse Anderson

Day of Tears by Julius Lester

Esperanza Rising by Pam Muñoz Ryan

Fire from the Rock by Sharon Draper

An Innocent Soldier by Josef Hollub

Jason's Gold by Will Hobbs

The Land by Mildred Taylor

Leonardo's Shadow by Christopher Grey

Nightjohn by Gary Paulsen

A Northern Light by Jennifer Donnelly

The Rock and the River by Kekla Magoon

Time Bomb by Nigel Hinton

The Traitor by Laurence Yep

What I Saw and How I Lied by Judy Blundell

The Winter People by Joseph Bruchac

Historical Fiction Text Set: World War II Era

Anne Frank and Me by Cherie Bennett and Jeff Gottesfeld

The Art of Keeping Cool by Janet Taylor Lisle

A Boy at War by Harry Mazer

Elephant Run by Roland Smith

Escaping into the Night by D. Dina Friedman

Eyes of the Emperor by Graham Salisbury

The Fighter by Jean Jacques Greif

Milkweed by Jerry Spinelli

My Brother, My Sister, and I by Yoko Watkins
Run, Boy, Run by Uri Orlev
Soldier Boys by Dean Hughes
Soldier X by Don Wulffson
Traitor by Gudrun Pausewang
Upon the Head of the Goat: A Childhood in Hungary 1939–1944 by Aranka Siegal
Weedflower by Cynthia Kadohata
When My Name was Keoko Linda Sue Park

Life Story Text Set

Bad Boy by Walter Dean Myers
Bowman's Store by Joseph Bruchac
Breaking Through by Francisco Jimenez
Farewell to Manzanar by Jeanne Wakatsuki Houston
Guts by Gary Paulsen
Hole in My Life by Jack Gantos
I Am Scout: A Biography of Harper Lee by Charles Shields
King of the Mild Frontier by Chris Crutcher
A Life in the Wild by Pamela Turner
Lincoln Shot: A President's Life Remembered by Barry Denenberg
A Long Way Gone by Ishmael Beah
Me Me Me Me: Not a Novel by M. E. Kerr
No Pretty Pictures by Anita Lobel
Over a Thousand Hills I Walk with You by Hannah Jansen
Painting the Wild Frontier by Susanna Reich
Seacows, Shamans, and Scurvy: Alaska's First Naturalist by Ann Arnold
Thoreau at Walden by John Porcellino
Three Little Words by Ashley Rhodes-Courter
Tree Shaker: The Story of Nelson Mandela by Bill Keller

Nonfiction Text Set

An American Plague by Jim Murphy
The Battle against Invasive Species by Sneed Collard
Heroes of Baseball by Robert Lipsyte
Hitler Youth: Growing Up in Hitler's Shadow by Susan Campbell Bartoletti
How We Know What We Know about Our Changing Climate by Lynne Cherry and Gary Brausch
Look Closer: Art Masterpieces through the Ages by Caroline Desnoettes
Masterpieces Up Close by Claire d'Harcourt
My Space: Our Planet by Jeca Taudte
Peacejam: A Billion Simple Acts of Peace by Ivan Suvanjieff and Dawn Engle

Quest for the Tree Kangaroo by Sy Montgomery

The Race to Save the Lord God Bird by Phillip Hoose

Soccer: From Beckham to Zidane by Christopher Morris

Thanksgiving: The True Story by Penny Colman

Troy: Unearthing Ancient Worlds by Ann Kerns

Understanding September 11th by Mitch Frank

Unsettled: the Problem of Loving Israel by Marc Aronson

We Are the Ship by Kadir Nelson

Where the Action Was by Penny Colman

Who Was First: Discovering the Americas by Russell Freedman

Two eighth-grade classes at Central Middle School have just finished setting up a museum in the school auditorium. In an interdisciplinary unit they have been reading about and researching World War II. All of the eighth graders have read Harry Mazer's *A Boy at War.* Each student has also read one other piece of historical fiction from a World War II text set as well as an assortment of nonfiction trade books. In literature circles students have collected (and created) artifacts from the time period, they have written newspaper articles and letters from fictional soldiers, and they have brought in everything from model airplanes to speakers from the local VFW. Today the eighth graders will lead the sixth-grade classes through the museum they have created. There is some last minute hustle but not much nervousness; after all, they are the experts who have chosen and created the materials reflecting the time period.

Historical Fiction versus Fictional History versus Historical Nonfiction

I often start my discussion of historical fiction by asking for information from a short historical narrative most of my students know, such as "When did Christopher Columbus sail the ocean blue?" You can imagine the response. The majority of the students shout out "1492."

Then I ask who chopped down the cherry tree. Again most of the students are confident when they answer, "George Washington." However, I then ask, "What year did Washington chop down the tree?" Nobody answers. "Why do you think so many of you remember 1492 but not the date of Washington's lumberjacking?" I ask. Before long they come up with the idea that perhaps when facts are given in a narrative they are more likely to be remembered. Think of all of the information young adults have in their minds: baseball statistics, the powers and attributes of characters in an X-Box game, the social standing of and relationships between everyone at their high school, and so on. Any information that relates to a context that has meaning and significance for them is remembered and analyzed in sophisticated ways. This is a very simple concept that in general does seem to hold true. Narrative structures create a context for detail that aids in recall. Then somebody in the class inevitably points out that the cherry tree story is just a legend that probably never happened, even though school children around the country "know" this detail. So narrativized information is more likely to be recalled whether the information is true or erroneous. This serves as a great segue into the difference between historical fiction and fictional history.

Historical fiction is a fictional narrative set in the past that pays particular attention to historical accuracy and context. Sounds simple enough, yet the term *historical fiction* has been interpreted in a variety of ways by authors and critics. If there is one distinguishing characteristic, it would be that these books tell imagined but possible narratives of the past. As such, historical fiction for children is distinguished from other genres in its attempts to create realistic historical worlds that the author can only discover either through extensive research or from having lived through the time period being described. Historical fiction also differs significantly from the dates, figures, and events approach of history textbooks, because as with other literary genres, in historical fiction the primary objective is to tell a compelling story. In fact, Mingshui Cai has asserted that historical fiction can be "more entertaining than history and more informative than fiction" (1992, p. 107).

Definitions of historical fiction have been quite diverse. Authors of historical fiction and critics often disagree amongst themselves as to what the term actually encompasses and which titles should be classified in this way (Thrall, Hibbard, and Holman, 1999). Although the particulars vary, two characteristics always seem to define the genre: historical context and historical accuracy. Certainly the narrative cannot be set in contemporary times; the action is taking place in a past that is discernable from the present. The authors of historical fiction tend to go to great lengths to create a possible past which not only infuses historical detail but perhaps more significantly only includes occurrences that could possibly have happened during that time period.

Author Spotlight

Photo courtesy of Laurie Halse Anderson.

Laurie Halse Anderson

Laurie Halse Anderson is the *New York Times* bestselling author who writes for kids of all ages. Known for tackling tough subjects with humor and sensitivity, her work has earned numerous ALA and state awards. Two of her books, *Speak* and *Chains*, were National Book Award finalists. Laurie has been honored with receiving the 2009 Margaret A. Edwards Award given by the YALSA division of the American Library Association for her "significant and lasting contribution to young adult literature." Mother of four and wife of one, Laurie lives in Northern New York, where she likes to watch the snow fall as she writes. Visit her website at www.writerlady.com.

SELECTED BOOKLIST

Catalyst (Viking, 2002)	*Prom* (Viking, 2005)
Chains (Simon & Schuster, 2008)	*Speak* (FSG, 1999)
Fever 1793 (Simon & Schuster, 2000)	*Twisted* (Viking, 2007)

ON BALANCING HISTORICAL DETAIL WITH STORYLINE IN HISTORICAL FICTION

I do know how to answer this question, and it requires a lengthy essay <grin>. As a matter of fact, you may want to read the essay "The Writing of *Fever 1793*—A Historical Detective Searches for the Truth," which I wrote for the May 2001 edition of *School Library Journal.*

In a nutshell, I am obsessive about my historical research. Along with spending years reading about the politics, culture, economy, language, dress, architecture, foodways, arts, and worldview of Philadelphia in the 1790s, I consumed all the specific details I could about the epidemic. That included reading newspapers printed in Philadelphia during the epidemic, newspapers reporting on the outbreak from other cities, countless letters, diary entries, government reports, and business account books.

The primary source documents, particularly the letters, gave me the emotional understanding I needed to write about the epidemic and the toll it took on people. The hard part in writing this book was finding the balance of historical detail—too little and my readers would be confused, too much and my readers would be bored. I would like to think I came close to the right amount. I know I left about 60 pages worth of detail on the cutting room floor.

ON HARSH REALITY ISSUES IN BOOKS FOR YOUNG PEOPLE

I have spoken all over America to teachers who are doing just that. *Speak* is becoming required reading in high schools everywhere, and *Fever 1793* is being used in classrooms from grade 4 through high school. (Obviously, nobody is going to use *Speak* with fourth graders. It's all about finding the right book for the right kid at the right age.)

Last I knew, *Speak* had made nineteen state award lists for YA literature, and *Fever 1793* has been placed on twenty-one. Kids want to read books like these because they reflect the real world.

Speak helps kids work through the feelings of isolation and confusion we all go through in high school. It also provides an opportunity to discuss date rape, which is our hidden nightmare, if you ask me. One out of every six women in America has been the victim of an attempted or completed rape—more than 17 million. Nearly half of them are under age 18. You do the math. (For more statistics and information, visit www.rainn.org, an excellent resource.) I know it is hard to talk about rape, but until we adults can find the courage to discuss it, our daughters are going to suffer. I'd like to think we are all ready to take on this issue.

Fever 1793 is a book about fear, courage, and integrity. It uses the backdrop of American history to showcase the story of a kid learning the harshest lessons of life and death. Sad to say, but our country is about two generations past the point where any of us can try to protect children from the real world. We owe it to them to give them the lessons they need in an age-appropriate and caring way, so they can face the challenges of that world with confidence and grace.

Obviously, I have an opinion about this. I know the kinds of pressures schools have to deal with, and teachers and administrators have my unending respect for the difficult and underappreciated job they do. But the role of an artist in any community is to speak up about how she thinks the world can be made into a better place for all. Thanks for listening.

Historical Context

Certainly to be historical fiction the narrative must be set in the past. However, there has been some discussion of just how far in the past the setting must be to distinguish it from contemporary realistic fiction. Drabble (1985) defines the temporal parameters as being set "before the birth of the author." Fleischman (1971), on the other hand, defines novels set two generations ago as historical fiction, whereas those of this generation and the previous one are referred to as "novels of the recent past." Adamson (1987) offers the opinion that historical fiction should be set at least one generation prior to its composition. These and other time frames all have their merits, but without taking other factors into consideration chronology alone cannot define historical fiction.

The sense of place and what Lasky (1990) has called the fabric of the times are equally significant. Historical fiction certainly needs to be set in the past—but more to the point it must emphasize the historical context. If the novel has embedded in it "significant historical content in the sense that the events, people, and the life style in the book" differ from the present, then it should be considered historical fiction (Cai, 1992, pp. 280–281). So one might consider a literary work historical fiction if it places emphasis on the historical period. Perhaps more significant than the historical setting is that the sense of history conveyed "has been isolated from the present flow of time by its uniqueness" (Cai, 1992, p. 281). Therefore, even if the novel is set in the recent past and occurred within the author's lifetime, for instance during the Gulf War or even in Taliban-controlled Afghanistan, we might still consider it to be historical fiction.

There are numerous works of historical fiction that focus on major historical events but other books explore aspects of the time period that are not well known. Walter Dean Myers in *Riot* (2009) uses the race riots in New York City during the Civil War as the backdrop for his story. Reprinted by permission of Egmont USA.

Historical Accuracy

One factor writers of historical fiction tend to stress in analyzing their own work is that they have striven for authenticity

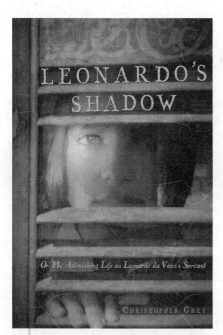

Christopher Grey's *Leonardo's Shadow* (2008) is a well-written, historically accurate fictionalized story. Although the story is fiction, nothing happens that conflicts with what is actually known about Leonardo da Vinci. Reprinted by permission of Simon Pulse.

and have based their literary worlds on historical possibilities. For some this means that historical fiction concentrates on real historical events, whereas others use situations that are imaginary but emphasize placing them in a credible world that could possibly have occurred in the past. Kathryn Lasky adds, "Even though these characters were inventions, the product of my imagination, they had to have as much accountability to their era as the historical figures who actually did exist" (Lasky, 1990, p. 163).

Tomlinson and Lynch-Brown (1993) identify three types of historical fiction:

- Literature in which the main character is imaginary, but secondary characters may be actual historical figures
- Literature in which the past is described in detail but with no historical figures or events
- Literature in which history is mixed with elements of fantasy or time travel

In each of these instances, it is the details of the setting that must ring true for the literary work to be considered historical fiction. Cai (1992) offers as an example *Sarah, Plain and Tall* (MacLachlan), in which there are no special historical events or figures but which nevertheless beautifully captures the time and place of the story. *Dovey Coe* (Dowell) and *A Corner of the Universe* (Martin) are good examples of literature that stays true to a certain time period while primarily focusing on everyday detail rather than historical events.

However, involving a historical figure in fictional adventures is not generally accepted as legitimate (Burton, 1973). Historical personages instead should not do anything that conflicts with what is known or that is out of character. Stories that break this rule are written, but they tend to be looked at as alternate histories (see Chapter 5). This does get problematic, as history is actually quite malleable.

Setting, language, and culture are certainly among the most difficult aspects of history to convey authentically. A balance must be reached between making the language authentic and keeping the narrative accessible to the contemporary reader (Fisher, 1995). Writers have reached a number of different compromises, some more successful than others. Many are satisfied with the occasional period word, whereas others give the rhythm without the use of dialect (Fisher, 1995). Still others, like Gary Paulsen's *Nightjohn,* are wonderful examples of a successful use of strong dialect without making the story incomprehensible.

Everyday People

Of course, to be historically accurate mandates including the unpleasant as well as the pleasant. How do we determine which elements of history are appropriately included in books for young adults? Writers must answer several questions.

1. If you are creating a realistic portrait of history, to what extent do you include murder, genocide, rape, drugs, slavery, and the experience of war?
2. If you are creating an accurate picture of an era, do you include period stereotypes and prejudices?
3. When depicting people of cultures that do not frequently appear in literature for young adults, is there a greater need to stress positive aspects or do you include both positive and negative realistic detail?

There are, of course, no set answers to these concerns. Yet how can history be realistically explored without including multifaceted depictions of the human experience?

To Consider

Accuracy may be a significant consideration for many authors of historical fiction, but as a teacher or librarian who is not so familiar with the time period, how can one possibly determine whether a novel is good historical fiction?

A book like *Roll of Thunder, Hear My Cry* by Mildred Taylor, which includes very moving depictions of racism, also shows courage in the face of adversity. In numerous ways these novels help readers understand and explore the negative aspects of society as part of a historical process that can be confronted and even changed. As for the people "who were left out of the history books," they were not perfect, not always brave and noble. "They were people like us" (Rochman, 1994, p. 161). Yet the fact that they were everyday people does not mean that we can ignore the stereotypes and omissions of the literature we subject children to.

Tone and Perspective

In Mingshui Cai's conception, time and veracity may define historical fiction, but tone and perspective shape it (1992, p. 280). Though this fiction should be steeped in historical detail, there is no prerequisite that it be written in only a serious tone, except when subjects like slavery or the Holocaust might demand it. Several excellent works of historical fiction include heavy doses of humor. *Catherine, Called Birdy* (Cushman) and Catherine Jinks's Pagan series are good examples of appropriate humor. Even a book like Joyce Hansen's *The Captive* includes a number of humorous incidents.

The emphasis on authenticity does not mean that historical fiction presents an unadulterated truth. Although some authors may believe they are unveiling the historical truth to the best of their abilities, many contemporary authors might argue that what they present is simply a perspective on the past. Perhaps more important than making sure all of the historical details are included, which would be an impossible task anyway, the author concentrates on making sure that nothing is "included that contradicts the actual record of history" (Huck, Hepler, and Hickman, 1987, p. 535).

One way authors deal with the limitations of historical knowledge is by utilizing the perspective of a young narrator. In this manner, the event is being seen through the eyes of a participant, and rather than give a definitive account of what occurred, the limited perspective of the protagonist allows the author to write about the past without having to act as an "all knowing" historical source (Burton, 1973). The author can therefore give insight into the historical event without having to state unequivocally that this is the only version of the truth.

Of course, the youthful character also personalizes the situation and the conflict for the reader. Coming of age is something young readers can often identify with even if the setting seems very distant.

Author Spotlight

Photo courtesy of Linda Sue Park.

Linda Sue Park

Linda Sue Park was born in Illinois to Korean immigrants. Her first publication was in a children's magazine when she was 9 years old. She received a B.A. in English from Stanford University, where she was also on the gymnastics team. She has worked in PR and advertising and taught English as a Second Language in London. She lives in upper New York with her husband, two children, and assorted animals. Visit her website at www.lspark.com.

SELECTED BOOKLIST

Archer's Quest (Clarion, 2006)
Keeping Score (Houghton Mifflin, 2008)
The Kite Fighters (Clarion, 2000)
Project Mulberry (Clarion, 2005)
Seesaw Girl (Clarion, 1999)
A Single Shard (Clarion, 2001)
When My Name Was Keoko (Clarion, 2002)

ON WHETHER AN AUTHOR CAN WRITE CONVINCINGLY ABOUT A CHARACTER FROM A DIFFERENT CULTURE AND BACKGROUND

All the historical fiction is outside a person's culture. So absolutely, I mean I have to say that, don't I? I wrote about 12th-century Korea, and I hope the characters were convincing. I think the key for me, whether it's another time or another culture, is respect. For example, in Francis Carpenter's book, *Tales of a Korean Grandmother,* when she presents the idea that girls are not allowed to leave their home, it's horrifying. And that is how I responded as a reader. "Oh it was awful, they were practically barbaric." So this is a great difference in the culture and it is presented as a difference. There is nothing factually wrong with what was presented in the book but there was a complete lack of respect for why the culture might have deemed that a necessary thing, so you have to get beyond that, you have to try to say OK, what is it about the culture, about the time, about the people that made them feel that this was important. The reason was that they believed that girls and women needed to be protected from strange men. Now we feel that way today, we don't want our young people, our girls to be talking to strangers, and they just took it a few steps further then we do. So, with *Seesaw Girl,* I tried hard to put myself in that place, to imagine that I was a part of this culture for which this was a normal idea, not an outlandish one. Perhaps in another couple hundred years, society will have changed to the point where historians say, well in the 20th- and 21st-century America, parents sent their 4- and 5-years-olds for 8 to 10 hours a day to be with people who weren't in their families. This might come to be looked at as a horrifying thing and yet from our perspective it is a reasonable one or some people believe it is a reasonable one, and it is certainly a norm. So can you put yourself there—and that helps me to think about what in our society today is going to be seen as wacko in a couple of hundred years and there were reasons in our culture why we do these things and there must have been reasons in theirs, so I think this fact is huge to get beyond the patronizing attitude of this is barbaric or even isn't that charming. Patronizing or condescension doesn't always have to be negative, but you get the point where you say, well this is normal and therefore there were reasons this was normal. I think that if a writer can get to that point, they can write about another culture or another time.

As far as convincing narrative, I try to focus on setting, and setting not just meaning place but milieu, on the differences in setting that fascinate me. And the similarities and human emotions. I do believe that historical fiction gives us a wonderful opportunity to explore what it means to be human. I think that people do change and are different over time and culture, but I also think there are things about being human that are common to everyone, everywhere no matter what the time, and I think that may be almost biologically programmed—things like ambition and love and the need to find a place for ourselves, those things are just about evolutionary. So I concentrate on the differences in setting, which are so interesting, but also the similarities in emotional response, and I hope that those similarities are what make a narrative convincing.

ON THE ROLE OF HISTORICAL ACCURACY AND PERSPECTIVE IN HER WORK

Obviously, I think research is important; I have done a lot of it for each of my books. I am the type who prefers to get as much of the research done as possible before I begin. I might feel that the story in its entirety including the historical information is coming from inside of me. So to that end, I will read books that—I'm a Post-it fanatic, and I use Post-its like crazy, and I will Post-it whenever I find something that is of interest. When I finish that book, I will go back and reread my "posted-it" pages several times until I feel that the facts are a part of me, that they are in me, that is not to say that I never have to go back, sometimes I do go back, but as much as possible I prefer to have it be coming from inside of me where the rest of the story is also coming from. So the research is very important. For the first three books, the eras that I was writing about, information in English was relatively sparse. It was not as if I had set out to write about the Civil War and had hundreds or thousands of books that I had to look up. It was a question of dozens. So it was possible to read nearly everything that was available in English which helped my confidence some. I wasn't going to know everything, but neither was anybody else. There is also a conscious choice to write fiction which gives you that wiggle room, I do not know whether things were exactly that way but it is my best guess. Therefore, I'm not going to write this as nonfiction and say that this is how it was. Rather this is how I imagine it was, think it was, this was my best guess as to how it was. I haven't had anyone come forward and say that that wasn't the way it was, but it hasn't been published in Korean yet, that's the big test. However, my experiences with *My Name Is Keoko,* which is set in far more recent history, was actually quite comforting. I worried . . . there was a lot more available about World War II and I worried a lot more about this knowing that it wasn't possible to read everything because there was so much more material. When I interviewed my parents and their friends, which I did extensively for that book, I got different versions of things that had happened, which is not really surprising, you know even today you get different news accounts of an event. That was a great comfort to me in that historical truth is not the black-and-white thing we would sometimes like it to be—that things like where you were and who you were and the passing of time can all affect the "historical truth." We've seen this with simple examples like the revisionist interpretations of Columbus—it is not taught anymore the way it was when I was in school. When I came up against researching Keoko, which is far more recent history that people lived through who are still alive, and never got the same story twice from people, I thought well this is great, it's liberating! That means that I can chose what I want, the versions of the facts or the emotional truth that I want to tell. It may not be everyone's truth, it may not be the same as other people's but my experience with interviewing survivors demonstrated there wasn't any one exact version.

Evolution of Historical Fiction

Many of the early books listed in the chronology of historical fiction in the Appendix were not specifically written for young readers but were read by teens and even younger children. *Ivanhoe* (1820) and *Waverly* (1814) by Sir Walter Scott were among the earliest books that might be classified as historical fiction. Though not specifically for children these books were often used in schools and read by many young adults. The distinguishing characteristic of the novels is the attempt to recreate an authentic past.

Charlotte Mary Yonge (1823–1901) was one of the first writers of historical fiction specifically aimed at a young audience. She wrote prolifically throughout her life, authoring nearly 200 works. An 1885 survey of the most popular literature among girls ranked Yonge with Charles Dickens, Sir Walter Scott, Charles Kingsley, and Shakespeare. She is perhaps best known for her domestic family novels steeped in Anglo-Catholic values and ideals. They tend to concern a youth with religious doubts whose faith is renewed. Her historical fiction such as *Caged Lion* (1871) was strongly influenced by the works of Scott.

Two decades later, Howard Pyle offered an exciting depiction of 15th-century England in *Men of Iron* (1891). A pioneer in crafting texts for the intermediate to young adult reader, Pyle not only wrote the text but also illustrated and designed his works. One of his specialties was historical fiction set in medieval times. Pyle portrays the England of this time as a lively place of castles and knights in shining armor. He does not write of disease and raw sewage but he does include castles that are actually lived in and children who seem quite human and real. *Men of Iron* is the adventure of a young English squire during the time of Henry IV, a romantic tale that nonetheless paints a detailed picture of the time.

Pyle's novel focuses as much on the training of youth in medieval times as it does on the storyline of a young man's vindication of his father. This is perhaps what made *Men of Iron* so popular. Though the book is cloaked in romantic notions of chivalry and honor, the characters behave like young people coming of age. They fight, and they sneak away to find adventure; there are rules to be broken, bullies to be bettered, friends to be made, and girls to visit (and not without danger). All of this action is steeped in well-researched historical settings (Pyle was also a celebrated historian).

Although written only 20 years after Yonge's *Caged Lion,* the narrative is so much less formal, less obtrusive, and less moralizing, though it should be added just as romantic. Pyle, like Yonge, tends to combine legend and history and to stress chivalric values and behavior. Medievalism of the sort written by Yonge and Pyle incorporated a serious attempt to infuse the ideas of chivalry into their own Victorian culture—in an effort to correct the present by reintroducing values of the past (Rahn, 1991). This glorification of the past is part of what Taxel identifies as the "selective tradition," wherein societies "define their culture, history and traditions by selectively drawing upon a wider universe of possibilities and then presenting the choices as *the* traditions or *the* significant past" (Taxel, 1983, p. 62).

The style, the language, and the ideals stressed in early historical fiction are quite distinct from contemporary works, but the emphasis on authenticity as well as on well-crafted story are similar as piers of the genre. *Catherine, Called Birdy,* winner of the 1995 Newbery Honor, explores the same general period. Yet Cushman's 13-year-old Catherine lives in a very different England. The 13th century for Catherine is neither home to chivalrous knights and damsels in distress nor a barbaric wasteland. In her Author's Note, Cushman addresses the question of whether we can actually hope to gain an accurate understanding of life in the Middle Ages:

> Can we really understand medieval people well enough to write or read books about them? I think we can identify with those qualities that we share—the yearning for a full belly, the need to be warm and safe, the capacity for fear and joy, love for children, pleasure in a blue sky or a handsome pair of eyes. As for the rest, we'll have to imagine and pretend and make room in our hearts for all sorts of different people. (p. 211)

To Consider

It is fairly easy to look at historical fiction written 100 years ago and see ways these novels romanticize or misrepresent the past. A hundred years from now do you think critics will be saying something similar about contemporary historical fiction?

Cushman stresses that she has done extensive research, yet even with the knowledge of what people wore, what they ate and so on, she wonders whether we can recreate their actual thoughts and sentiments. Indeed, the primary quandaries of historical fiction are the distance of the setting from the author and reader in terms of time, location, and culture and our uncertainty about restoring the "damaged tapestry" of history (Cai, 1992; Fleischman, 1971). Cushman does stay true to historical details without letting them take over the story. Catherine seems to be a possible (though perhaps improbable) authentic medieval character, who nonetheless makes sense and appeals to contemporary readers.

History as a Reconstruction of the Past

To help young people learn to develop historical thinking they must think about how to recreate past worlds, which involves skills such as "determining the credibility of evidence, weighing different kinds of evidence, understanding how historians use evidence to weave a narrative"

(Heyking, 2004, n.p.). Fictional characters placed in this situation can play out the possibilities. Historical figures might be included as well, with attention given to accuracy. Such writing demands much research on the part of the author, to discover not simply the details of life but also the lifestyles, wants, and needs of the characters. As Katherine Paterson (1994) writes,

> Having chosen the setting, the responsibility of the writer, it seems to me, it to be as true to the period and the events and sensibilities of that place and period as she can possibly be. It is my job, as I see it, to create living characters and tell a story about them that really might have happened to people who lived in that world—who experienced those events. (p. 89)

The facts and detail are significant, but it is just as important that the narrative draws the reader in and involves them in the day-to-day existence of the time period.

There are of course quite enjoyable books set in a fictional past that are by no means authentic. Lasky (1990) distinguishes historical fiction from the fiction of history. Historical fiction unveils the time and the people, whereas the fiction of history is a falsification of the past—with the good guys on a white horse.

> What I did not realize at the time was that it was not historical fiction that Hollywood was bringing us; it was, rather, the fiction of history—a subtle but important difference in my mind. One is an unveiling through literary means of a time, of an era, of people and events; the other is a falsification of the past, a cover up, an outright lie. In fictions of history facts are abused, textures erased, and tapestries often unraveled. (Lasky, 1990, p. 159)

Hollywood movies and fictional histories have often distorted the past, telling partial truths and giving an "unbalanced approach to history and to the shading of history" (Lasky, 1990). History in such instances might become a whitewashed world of good guys and bad guys. Though not everyone reacts as negatively to fictional history as Lasky does in this instance, the distinction is certainly an important one to draw. Books, movies, and other media made primarily to entertain can also misinform and distort our understandings of the past. The term *fictional history* is sometimes used to distinguish literature that creates imaginary pasts without historical grounding. Some critics such as Judith Hillman (1995) further distinguish literature having historical detail with the label *historical realistic fiction*.

Author Spotlight

Photo courtesy of Will Hobbs.

Will Hobbs

Will Hobbs is the author of 18 novels for upper-elementary, middle school, and young adult readers, as well as two picture book stories. Seven of his novels, *Bearstone, Downriver, The Big Wander, Beardance, Far North, The Maze,* and *Jason's Gold,* were chosen by the American Library Association as Best Books for Young Adults. ALA also selected *Far North* and *Downriver* for its list of the 100 Best Young Adult Books of the 20th Century. A graduate of Stanford University and former reading and language arts teacher, Will lives with his wife Jean in Durango, Colorado. Visit Will on the web at www.WillHobbsAuthor.com.

SELECTED BOOKLIST

Beardance (Simon & Schuster, 1993)

Bearstone (Simon & Schuster, 1989)

The Big Wander (Simon & Schuster, 1992)

Crossing the Wire (HarperCollins, 2006)

Downriver (Simon & Schuster, 1991)

Down the Yukon (HarperCollins, 2001)

Far North (HarperCollins, 1996)

Ghost Canoe (HarperCollins, 1997) *Go Big or Go Home* (HarperCollins, 2008)

Jackie's Wild Seattle (HarperCollins, 2003)

Jason's Gold (HarperCollins, 1999)

The Maze (HarperCollins, 1998)

River Thunder (Delacorte, 1997)

Wild Man Island (HarperCollins, 2002)

ON WHERE THE IDEAS FOR HIS STORIES COME FROM

Jason's Gold and *Down the Yukon* hearken back to my childhood in Alaska in the 1950s. As a young boy I was spellbound by the rivers, glaciers, mountains, the salmon runs, moose, and the bears. My memories of the winter darkness, the northern lights and rusting gold dredges called out for a story. But the immediate impetus for these historical tales came from a 1996 visit to the Canadian Yukon with my wife, Jean. During our trip we visited the gold rush museum in Dawson City, the destination of the fabled rush. Back home, I delved into a mountain of research and decided I had to try to bring the Klondike to life for kids.

So little is known, I realized, about this amazing last chapter of the Wild West. For example, I hadn't known the details of Jack London's Klondike experience. At the age of 21, he was at the forefront of the rush, leaving California only a week after it started, in July of 1897. Not many made it to the goldfields that fall. London carried 1,500 pounds of supplies on his back more than 20 miles over the Chilkoot Pass, built a boat from timber along with his partners, and succeeded in running 500 miles of the Yukon River, piloting his skiff in the White Horse Rapids and barely beating freeze-up. Did he find gold? Yes, he returned home with four dollars and fifty cents' worth. And a few ideas.

When I learned this and more, I thought that Jack London should be one of the minor characters in the novel. In fact, the personal histories of the real stampeders were so fascinating, I resolved to people the novel mostly with actual historical figures.

My protagonist is fictional. On the first page of *Jason's Gold,* 15-year-old Jason Hawthorn is selling newspapers in New York City. The headline is GOLD IN ALASKA! Within hours, he's jumping trains to try to get to Seattle to catch up with his brothers. He misses them by days, and stows away on a ship heading for Alaska. Little does Jason realize what he's in for—a 5,000 mile adventure that's going to take him 11 months. Along the way he'll meet an adventurous girl named Jamie and of course, he meets Jack London. A novel in the spirit of Jack London would be incomplete without a dog of great character. Jason's constant companion is a husky named King.

Reading about the new gold strike at Cape Nome out on the Bering Sea led to my sequel, *Down the Yukon,* in which Jason and Jamie leave Dawson City together, paddling a canoe heading for Nome. My hope for these stories is that young readers will come away with the sense that history can be incredibly exciting, and that life in any era is filled with adventure, heroism, courage, and love.

Lukacs (1963) asserts that the main character of a work of historical fiction must be an ordinary person because only common people can portray the age. This may hold true as a generality in historical fiction for young adults, though how one defines *ordinary* may differ greatly from novel to novel. If the protagonists of these novels have many of the characteristics of Everyman as Lukacs implies, they also often have extraordinary experiences. An ordinary Catherine in the Middle Ages would most likely have accepted marriage to whomever her father betrothed her. But the title character of *Catherine, Called Birdy* laments that she is not an ordinary village girl. And Adam in *A Boy at War* (Mazer) has to pick up a gun and fight against the invasion of his home—something that for young people in North America is not a common experience. Nonetheless, Catherine and Adam seem real, if not typical. They are characters with whom young adults can connect.

Authors of historical fiction often stress that in their writing they concentrate on the details of everyday life and ordinary people. Rosemary Sutcliff (1973), for instance, who has a talent for making the past come alive through her description, dialogue, and sense of place, writes,

> History is People and I try to teach history. Man's eye view of history, not the God's eye view. It is because history books of necessity take the God's eye view, that they can so often and so easily become dull. (p. 308)

Likewise, Burton's interest in everyday details engages readers and invites them into the story, not just as observers but as participants in history.

> I should be able to see clearly in my mind's eye the houses in which my characters live, the clothes they wear, and the carts and carriages and ships in which they travel. I should know what food they eat, what songs they sing when they feel happy, and what are the sights and smells they are likely to meet when they walk down the street. I must understand their religion, their political hopes, their trades, and—what is most important—the relationships between different members of a family common to their particular generation. (Burton, 1973, p. 300)

Essential details include the material, the emotional, and the ideological—everything that makes up the daily lives of the characters in the novel.

Author's Context and Perspective

History is about the interpretation and reconstruction of the past. Rudman (1994) writes that she was lucky enough to have had a social studies teacher who taught that historians themselves disagree about the facts of the past and that history is about interpretation and reconstruction. Three books representing the life of Christopher Columbus could portray the historical figure in totally different ways—intrepid discoverer, lost explorer, or greedy invader—all based on historical evidence, and each might be a historically valid perspective. Among the many factors to explore, one of the most interesting is how the author's life and times affect the portrayal of history in the novel. There is little doubt that the author's milieu will influence how events are presented. For example, Donna Jo Napoli asserts, "I try hard to get into the sensibilities of the people of the time and place I'm writing about, but I am me, not them; I am the product of the world as I know it—a world with computers and airplanes and knowledge about the universe" (Napoli interview, p. 163).

Whether we are speaking of fiction or nonfiction, the stories of our past have always been written from the point of view of authors who "unconsciously select from the record those facts that support their beliefs while ignoring those that contradict them" (Stanley, 1994, p. 173). A writer of historical fiction like Katherine Paterson (1994) tends to recognize the contrasts and "limitations of time and cultural bias" but despite these limitations seeks to remain as true to "history and human experiences" as they can (p. 91).

Authors' perspectives will also affect (though not necessarily determine) their choice of a historical period to present. Historians and authors are both likely to "use the concerns and preoccupations of their own era as a lens through which to reexamine the past" (Taxel 1983b, p. 35). For some writers this is a conscious occurrence. Paterson (1994) asserts:

> I can see that I have chosen to tell stories set in times however ancient, and places however exotic, that in some way shed light for me on what is occurring in my own time. (p. 87)

But whether conscious or not, the author's perspective will guide the selections made from among the "universe of possibilities" (Cai, 1992, p. 288). Hundreds of small decisions will be made as to what will be included or omitted, from word choice to interpretations to perspective (Stanley, 1994). To an extent all research is biased and positioned by the researcher's knowledge; the best a researcher can do is to recognize what his or her preconceived notions are in the hopes of understanding how they may affect the research.

Joel Taxel (1983a) showed how looking at the way war is perceived in historical novels set during wartime can be very telling. *Johnny Tremain* (Forbes) was written in 1943 when the general sentiment in the United States had become extremely patriotic. War was being discussed as just and necessary and this definitely comes through in this novel about the Revolutionary War.

Another widely read war novel, *My Brother Sam Is Dead* (Collier and Collier) was published in 1974. Public sentiment about war was much more divided during this time, when the Vietnam War had created a state of cynicism in the United States. Sure enough, in *My Brother Sam*

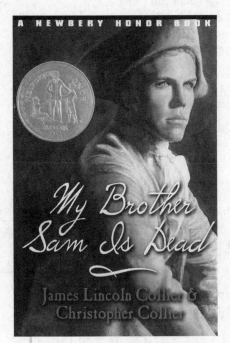

My Brother Sam Is Dead by James and Christopher Collier (1984) is a Newbery Honor book but also one of the most frequently challenged books in the 1990s. Reprinted by permission of Simon and Schuster.

Is Dead, families are divided about which side they belong on, and war is in fact presented as an ugly mess.

Paul Fleischman's *Bull Run,* written in 1993, presents war (in this case the Civil War) from multiple perspectives, with characters who voice very well thought out reasons for taking part in the war and others with very shallow or even cynical reasons. Part of the postmodern experience is the idea that there are numerous stories addressing a variety of "truths" from various perspectives. Although narratives often imply that several versions of a story are possible, they then tend to enlist "the reader's identification with the protagonist's cause" (Levstik, 1993, p. 69). In *Bull Run* the full gamut of emotions and interests are conveyed: the glory of war, the anguish of battle, a yearning for freedom, and fear for loved ones. But even in a deliberately multivoiced novel, the perspectives are all still mediated by the author and the context within which she or he writes. One can make the argument that just as patriotism and cynicism reflected prevalent attitudes toward war in novels mentioned earlier, the diverse realities found in *Bull Run* reflect common sentiments in the 1990s. This sense of the time, or *zeitgeist,* affects not just the perspectives found in *Bull Run* but also the formatting of the book, with its shifting perspectives.

Educational Benefits of Historical Fiction

When the historical detail in a work of fiction is accurate, historical understandings are a likely benefit. Knowledge about the human experience might be gained from the historical knowledge infused in this fiction. Such understandings become possible when stories of the past allow the reader to enter and explore historically viable worlds.

As already suggested there is research that suggests that exposure to historical fiction may actually improve students' knowledge of historical details and their understandings of history as a process (Davis and Hunter, 1990). John Smith and associates have argued based on statistical analyses that

> Subjects whose teachers used historical novels to integrate reading and social studies instruction learned more historical details, main ideas, and total amount of historical information than subjects whose teachers used basal reading materials and social studies textbooks only. (Smith, Monson, and Dobson, 1992, p. 373)

Certainly, it is easier to quantify knowledge of historical data than it is to assess historical understandings, so exact relationships between the reading of historical fiction and the knowledge gained by the student cannot be quantified. Still, there is something to be said for the notion that these novels can enhance the students' perceptions of historical periods.

Narrative not only grounds the historical data in context, it also personalizes history—placing it on a human level, with which students can relate. Young people tend to explain history in terms of human reactions and desires (Hallden, 1986). It is the level of human response found in these novels that allows students to enter into the historical world and understand other people's perspectives (Egan, 1989). Historical narratives provide personal frameworks through which readers can then interpret events of the past. Equally significant, when a reader becomes excited about a novel set during World War II, it might awaken an interest in learning more about the history. At the same time, the themes being explored often reflect contemporary issues, emotions, and relationships while "shedding light on our own time" (Johnson and Giorgis, 2001/2002, p. 400). The brief survey of historical fiction provided in the Appendix is just a taste of the wide range of past experiences recounted in narratives for young readers. These narratives can deepen our understanding of a contemporary issue and help to connect the past to the present.

Guidelines for Selecting and Evaluating Historical Fiction

In addition to the general criteria for selecting and evaluating literature for young adult readers, the following questions should be asked when looking at historical fiction:

- Is historical detail blended into a good story?
- Do themes and language achieve a comfortable balance between the culture and time period depicted and the needs and interests of young adult readers? Can young readers connect with the characters and events?
- Is there a high degree of historical accuracy?
- To what extent do the language of the narrative and the language of dialogue reflect the time depicted?
- Is a context created for readers who have no background in the historical time period?
- Is information included in the book (in an afterword, preface, author's note, or other notification) discussing research and factual detail in the novel?
- Are the characters' beliefs and actions consistent with the time period?
- Are differing points of view about the time period provided in the narrative?

Audio Books

Historical Fiction

Bat 6 by Virginia Euwer Wolff; read by a full cast. (Listening Library, 2000) (A)

Bud Not Buddy by Christopher Paul Curtis; read by James Avery. (Listening Library, 2006) (A, N)

Esperanza Rising by Pam Muñoz Ryan; read by Trini Alvarado. (Random House, 2001) (P, Y)

Fever 1793 by Laurie Halse Anderson; read by Emily Bergl. (Listening Library, 2000) (Y)

The Kite Rider by Geraldine McCaughrean; read by a full cast. (Full Cast Audio, 2004)

The Land by Mildred Taylor; read by Ruben Santiago-Hudson. (Random House, 2001) (A, Y)

A Long Way from Chicago by Richard Peck; read by Ron McLarty. (Listening Library, 1999) (Y)

A Northern Light by Jennifer Donnelly; read by Hope Davis. (Listening Library, 2003)

Nory Ryan's Song by Patricia Reilly Giff; read by Susan Lynch. (Listening Library, 2008) (N)

The Silent Boy by Lois Lowry; read by Karen Allen. (Listening Library, 2003)

A Single Shard by Linda Sue Park; read by Graeme Malcolm. (Books on Tape, 2001) (N)

Soldier's Heart by Gary Paulsen; read by George Wendt. (Listening Library, 1999) (Y)

Witch Child by Celia Rees; read by Jennifer Ehle. (Random House, 2001) (Y)

AA—Audie Awards	P—Parent's Choice Audio Award Winner
A—Audiofile Earphones Award	Y—YALSA Selected List of Audiobooks
N—ALSC Notable Children's Recording	

World War II in Context

Historical appreciation might be enhanced by reading several books set during a certain time period but written from various perspectives. The very process of searching out the variety of perspectives on a historical period communicates that history is a construct and enhances understandings of possible pasts.

This presents problems for teachers both from the limited time available to explore multiple novels addressing one topic and because there is much to be said for leaving many reading choices up to the individual. To address these issues the teacher might create a literature set representing a wide range of historical interpretations on a particular period. If students carry out projects related to these novels and then share their thoughts with others in the class, everyone could benefit from the rich variety of perspectives. By providing opportunities to encounter and reencounter a topic, the teacher is also providing a context for communal construction of meaning.

The first type of book that might be included in a set related to World War II are novels of the home front. These novels show both the time and the effects of war on the lives of young people. For most young adults in North America World War II was about a scarcity of certain comforts, separation from loved ones who were away (*Lily's Crossing*, Giff), heightened prejudice (*The Art of Being Cool*, Lisle; *Under the Blood Red Sun*, Salisbury), and fear of espionage (*Sirens and Spies*, Lisle; *Shadows on the Sea*, Harlow). Most of these books focus on the effects of the war on the everyday lives of the characters. Occasionally one of the narratives will tell aspects of the war that are far from common knowledge. In *Aleutian Sparrow* by Karen Hesse, an Aleutian girl is home visiting her family in the summer of 1942 when the Japanese launch an air attack. The Aleutian population is evacuated by the United States to internment camps, where they are separated from the life they know, facing disease and a lack of freedom, and perhaps most damaging for a culture strongly connected to the sea, with no water in sight. *Eyes of the Emperor* (Salisbury) tells the story of a group of Japanese Hawaiian U.S. army recruits who face prejudice and suspicion as they serve in one of the most degrading programs thought up by the army during World War II. And *Slap Your Sides* (Kerr) tells the little-known story of conscientious objectors during this era.

For Japanese Americans the home front during World War II was a time of drastic change, as can be seen in *Weedflower* (Kadohata). Most homefront novels only touch on the war itself tangentially, but of course Hawaii was the scene for the first big confrontation for American troops and *A Boy at War* covers this homefront violence in a short but gripping story. There were also German prisoners of war brought to the United States during the war, as depicted in *Summer of My German Soldier* (Greene).

On the European front, *Under a War Torn Sky* by L. M. Elliot is the story of a 19-year-old American flyer

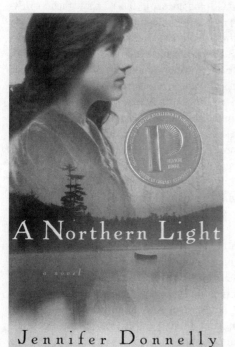

A Northern Light

Jennifer Donnelly

Hopes and dreams and the obstacles to reaching them combine with a turn of the century mystery in *A Northern Light* by Jennifer Donnelly. Copyright © 2003 by Jennifer Donnelly, reprinted by permission of Houghton Mifflin Harcourt Publishing Company.

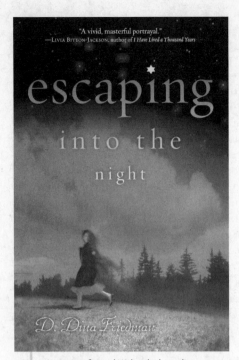

"A vivid, masterful portrayal."
—LIVIA BITTON-JACKSON, author of *I Have Lived a Thousand Years*

escaping

into the

night

D. Dina Friedman

A range of good YA books have been published about the World War II era, including *Escaping into the Night* (Simon and Schuster, 2006). Reprinted by permission of Simon and Schuster.

who is shot down over occupied France. In Dean Hughes's *Soldier Boys* the war is told in the parallel stories of an underage paratrooper from Utah and a member of the Hitler Youth. Both of these young men want to prove their bravery but find that war is not exactly what they imagined. *Soldier X* by Don Wulffson tells the story of the war from the perspective of a 16-year-old German boy. He is drafted into the army and sent to the Eastern Front. It seems that survival is unlikely but he is determined to find a way.

There are some excellent stories of the resistance movements around Europe. Bradley's *For Freedom* is the story of a 16-year-old French spy. *When the War Is Over* (Attema) concerns a 16-year-old about to join his brother and father in the Dutch resistance. *Room in the Heart* by Sonia Levitin and *Number the Stars* by Lois Lowry both focus on the Danish resistance to Nazi occupation and particularly on the rescue of the Jews as the Nazis plot to round them up.

There are quite a few novels that explore life under Nazi occupation. Some are set in the Warsaw ghetto (*Milkweed*, Spinelli) or Nazi work camps and the brutality of the Holocaust (*Torn Thread*, Isaacs; *The Fighter*, Greif); some involve individuals who manage to evade capture (*Run, Boy, Run*, Orlev) or even whole encampments of people who hide out in the forests (*Escaping into the Night*, Friedman).

A smaller number of books present the events of World War II in the Pacific. In *When My Name Was Keoko* Linda Sue Park looks at the lives of a brother and sister during the Japanese occupation of Korea. Kim Sun-hee and her brother Kim Tae-yul are forced to take the Japanese names Keoko and Nobuo. The story alternates between the sometimes conflicting perspectives of the brother and sister. *So Far from the Bamboo Grove* (Watkins) is an excellent complement to Keoko's story, as it follows the life of a Japanese family living in occupied Korea and how their lives fall apart as Japan loses control of the occupied country. Another exciting story is set in World War II Burma. In Roland Smith's *Elephant Run* the teen protagonist is sent to Burma to escape the ravages of war in England. Unfortunately, soon after he arrives the Japanese invade.

Time slip novels combine richly detailed historical fiction with the fantasy element of a contemporary youth traveling back in time to experience events firsthand. Many teachers have found that readers reluctant to choose historical fiction can get interested when following contemporary characters into the past. In *Anne Frank and Me* (Bennett and Gottesfeld) Nicole Burns is a contemporary girl visiting an Anne Frank exhibit when a gunshot leads to chaos and she wakes to find herself in the body of a privileged Jewish girl living in Paris during World War II. At first her new life is great, but as the Nazis tighten their grip on France, she must go into hiding.

A great companion to this would be *If I Should Die before I Wake* by Han Nolan. A contemporary neo-Nazi is riding on a motorcycle with her boyfriend after defacing a Jewish cemetery when they crash. She awakens to find herself in a Jewish hospital. Even more shock-

To Consider

With so many books available on the topic of WWII, which elements would be more important to you as a teacher when putting together a text set for the time period: geographic diversity, multiple perspectives, a range of reading levels, or student interest?

ing she soon finds herself traveling through time into the body of a Jewish girl during World War II. Also *Dreaming in Black and White* by Reinhardt Jung is a time travel novel in which a disabled German boy named Hannes is transported back to the Nazi era where he finds himself labeled as "not worth living." Even worse, in this past his father seems to be swayed by Nazi propaganda.

Some teachers add to the contextual understanding of World War II by including a novel that takes place in the years afterward. *The Legend of Buddy Bush* (Moses), for example, brings to light the fact that African American soldiers were treated with gratitude and with greater civil rights in Europe only to return to their homes to face discrimination and worse. Laurence Yep explores the prejudice and loss of property faced by most Japanese Americans after they were sent to the internment camps. *My Brother, My Sister, and I* (Watkins) presents the chaos of a Japan in defeat after the war.

The United States prior to World War II

- *All the Way Home* by Patricia Reilly Giff
- *Blizzard's Wake* by Phyllis Reynolds Naylor
- *Bud Not Buddy* by Christopher Paul Curtis
- *Dovey Coe* by Phyllis Reynolds Naylor
- *Esperanza Rising* by Pam Muñoz Ryan
- *Witness* by Karen Hesse

The Homefront during World War II

- *Aleutian Sparrow* by Karen Hesse
- *The Art of Keeping Cool* by Janet Taylor Lisle
- *A Boy at War* by Harry Mazer
- *Eyes of the Emperor* by Graham Salisbury
- *Shadows on the Sea* by Joan Harlow
- *Sirens and Spies* by Janet Taylor Lisle
- *Slap Your Sides* by M. E. Kerr
- *Summer of My German Soldier* by Bette Greene
- *Weedflower* by Cynthia Kadohata

Europe during World War II

- *The Book Thief* by Markus Zusak
- *Daniel Half Human: And the Good Nazi* by David Chotjewitz
- *The Fighter* by Jean-Jacques Greif
- *For Freedom* by Kimberly Bradley
- *Number the Stars* by Lois Lowry
- *Room in the Heart* by Sonia Levitin
- *Soldier Boys* by Dean Hughes
- *Soldier X* by Don Wulffson
- *Traitor* by Gudrun Pausewang
- *Under a War-Torn Sky* by Laura Elliott

Eastern Europe during World War II

- *Escaping into the Night* by D. Dina Friedman
- *Malka* by Mirjam Pressler
- *Milkweed* by Jerry Spinelli
- *Run, Boy, Run* by Uri Orlev
- *Torn Thread* by Anne Isaacs
- *Upon the Head of the Goat* by Aranka Siegal

Asia and Oceania during World War II

- *Code Talker* by Joseph Bruchac
- *A Divine Wind* by Gary Disher
- *Elephant Run* by Roland Smith
- *My Brother, My Sister, and I* by Yoko Kawashima Watkins
- *So Far from the Bamboo Grove* by Yoko Kawashima Watkins
- *When My Name Was Keoko* by Linda Sue Park

Connecting with the War—Time Travel

- *Anne Frank and Me* by Cherie Bennett and Jeff Gottesfeld
- *The Devil's Arithmetic* by Jane Yolen
- *Dreaming in Black and White* by Reinhardt Jung
- *If I Should Die before I Wake* by Han Nolen

The World Following World War II

- *The Book of Everything* by Guus Kuijer
- *Briar Rose* by Jane Yolen
- *The Legend of Buddy Bush* by Sheila Moses
- *Time Bomb* by Nigel Hinton

Nonfiction Connections

Making connections between historical fiction and nonfiction books about the time period can have enormous benefits. Students who become excited about a topic or an era can continue investigating and students might explore the accuracy of the historical fiction or even use the historical information to create their own fictional narrative. With World War II there is a wide range of nonfiction available.

Holocaust

- *Displaced Persons: The Liberation and Abuse of Holocaust Survivors* by Ted Gottfried
- *My Secret Camera: Life in the Lodz Ghetto* by Frank Dabba Smith with photographs by Mendel Grossman
- *Rescued Images: Memories of a Childhood in Hiding* by Ruth Jacobsen

War Front

- *The Belly Gunner* by Carol Hipperson
- *Darkness over Denmark: The Danish Resistance and the Rescue of the Jews* by Ellen Levine
- *Fighting for Honor: Japanese Americans and World War II* by Michael Cooper

- *Remember Pearl Harbor: American and Japanese Survivors Tell Their Stories* by Thomas Allen

Home Front

- *Farewell to Manzanar* by Jeanne Wakatsuki Houston and James Houston
- *Remembering Manzanar: Life in a Japanese Relocation Camp* by Michael Cooper
- *Rosie the Riveter: Women Working on the Home Front in World War II* by Penny Colman

Germany

- *Hitler Youth: Growing Up in Hitler's Shadow* by Susan Campbell Bartoletti
- *Nazi Olympics* by Susan Bachrach

Author Spotlight

Photo courtesy of Eleanora Tate.

Eleanora E. Tate

Eleanora E. Tate is an author, folklorist, and creative writing teacher. She was born in Canton, Missouri, where she attended a one-room school. She grew up in Des Moines, Iowa. She graduated from Drake University with a bachelor of science in journalism. In 1999, she received the Zora Neale Hurston Award from the National Association of Black Storytellers. She has taught children's literature at North Carolina Central University, Durham, and is an instructor with the Institute of Children's Literature.

Additional honors she has received include the North Carolina Book Award for Juvenile Literature, an International Reading Association "Teachers' Choice Award" in 2008, a Notable Children's Trade Book in the Field of Social Studies, an American Booksellers Association Pick of the Lists, Parents Choice Gold Seal Award, and the Iowa Author Award. Visit her website at www .eleanoraetate.com.

SELECTED BOOKLIST

African American Musicians (Wiley, 2000)
A Blessing in Disguise (Delacorte, 1995)
Celeste's Harlem Renaissance (Little, Brown, 2007)
Don't Split the Pole: Tales of Down-Home Folk Wisdom (Delacorte, 1997)
Front Porch Stories at the One-Room School (Random House, 1992)
Just An Overnight Guest (Dial, 1980)
The Minstrel's Melody (Pleasant Company, 2001)
Retold African Myths (Perfection Learning, 1993)
The Secret of Gumbo Grove (Watts, 1987)
Thank You, Dr. Martin Luther King, Jr.! (Watts, 1990)
To Be Free (Steck-Vaughn/Harcourt, 2003)

ON WHAT SHE ENJOYED READING AS A YOUNG ADULT

I define the young adult period as being between the ages of 13 to 18. By that time I was living in Des Moines, Iowa, and reading James Baldwin, Gwendolyn Brooks, James Joyce, Lorraine Hansberry, and other authors, poets, and playwrights of adult literature, the *Iowa Bystander, Saturday Review,* the *New Yorke*r and *New York* magazines, and the early Scholastic magazines. I think the only books I read that dealt with teenagers were Des Moines authors Henry Gregor Felsen (*Hot Rod*) and Jeanette Eyerly.

When I was a child in Canton, Missouri, and attending elementary school, I loved *Grit* newspaper, comic books, and the works of L. Frank Baum, Lewis Carroll, and Laura Ingalls Wilder (though I realize now that her books were very negative toward Native Americans). I wasn't aware of any children's books by African Americans in those days, probably because there really weren't any, at least not within my reach as a child in tiny Canton. In both Canton and Des Moines I read *Jet* and *Ebony* magazines, and the *Kansas City Call* newspaper—all African American publications—along with *Bronze Thrills* and *True Confession* magazines.

ON HOW SHE AS AN AUTHOR OF HISTORICAL FICTION CAN WRITE AUTHENTICALLY ABOUT A TIME PERIOD SHE DID NOT EXPERIENCE

I've asked myself the same thing with each of my books. I do a lot of primary research into materials produced during the period that I'm writing about. Sense of place is equally important to me. This gives me a flavor of the times. Since most of my books involve African and African American history, I read the WPA slave narratives from the states where my stories take place, particularly Missouri and North and South Carolina. These formerly enslaved persons' narratives told their memories to mostly white writers primarily during the 1930s. These folks lived and died, by now, well over a hundred years or more before my time. Their white interviewers may have reinterpreted some of what those old folks told them, of course. When I read, "Slavery was good to me and I were better off being a slave than I is now," I must remember that the conversations took place during the Depression. In addition, some of those old Black folks were very guarded and protective in their responses because they were talking to members of the same race that had had total control over their lives and, in many respects, still did.

The purpose of this kind of research is to give me a sense of flavor of the times. Plus, as an African American, I can look back into my own family's and neighbors' histories and feel a certain kinship with their shared experience, their triumphs and tragedies, their failures, and their pride in accomplishments. Human emotion has always been us, regardless of the situation, regardless of the century.

I have racial memory, long memory. I know about racism and prejudice, successes and failures in every day living because I still have to deal with racism and prejudice, enjoying the roses despite the thorns, so to speak. I've never been physically whipped or had my children sold away from me, but that's where the primary research comes in. From it I can get printed descriptions about the physical treatment African Americans received. Internally I can certainly imagine the anger, the degradation, humiliation, helplessness, and sense of loss. I know what's happened to me.

I can get printed accounts of the enslaved or sharecropper family's activities during holidays and celebrations at the Big House. But unlike some writers outside (and a few within) my culture, I remember always that these folks were human beings whose happiness, joy, hope, etc. during these times were *despite* slavery. They had these positive feelings of "good times" *despite* slavery, and that's what makes my stories authentic.

I continue my research through conversations. Oral history. People talk to me wherever I go. I have this glazed "deer in headlights" look through my bifocals when folks begin to talk to me, and they keep on talking because I guess I look like I'm mesmerized. When I first moved to South Carolina, for example, and loving community history, I was enthralled by the true stories people told me, by their use of the language (regional vernacular), their intonation, their unique experiences. These folks, my neighbors, acquaintances, their ancestors lived the very history that I wanted to explore. I loved to listen and they loved having an audience. In addition to the printed version, the oral history from the folk is the real living history, and that's why *The Secret of Gumbo Grove* still rings with so much authenticity.

Physical primary source material includes old newspapers, old history books, courthouse papers, wills and deeds of the times, and I study photos, paintings, drawings, and read the novels of the times. I can glean bits of concrete information from those old books, which include descriptions of place and culture as the writer back then saw it around him or her. I read "secondary" source material—often scholarly material written more recently *about* the times—but I have to be careful with that because sometimes it's revisionist. The authors didn't experience firsthand what they were writing about, either, so this material is through those authors' life experiences and interpretations, and not objective.

ON WHY SHE HAS CHOSEN TO WRITE FOR RELUCTANT READERS OR READERS WHO ARE NOT AT GRADE LEVEL AND WHETHER THERE IS ANY DIFFERENCE IN HOW SHE WRITES, KNOWING THE AUDIENCE

To Be Free is my fourth book to be part of a series. It is 28 pages long and less than 4,000 words, is physically the smallest book I've ever written—and the quickest.

I wrote it in about 3 weeks. Series books are not exactly formulaic, but they do require approval of outlines, and you have to conform to the overall theme that the editors want the series or your book to promote. Sometimes that can be hard to follow. Like I mentioned before, the editors tell you what they want, and how and when, and that's what you do.

I just wanted to write the story of how a determined African American teen-aged boy overcame the treachery of slavery on coastal North Carolina by hiding on a smoke-filled ship and escaping his captors. I didn't find many books for reluctant middle school and high school readers that describe the freedom efforts of enslaved teenagers, especially by escaping via the Maritime Underground Railroad.

Middle school and high school reluctant readers will not bother to struggle through a long book that includes words they can't understand or infer from complex context. They have enough challenges getting through their textbooks! You want to maintain their respect by writing about a character their own age, who has maturity comparable to their own age group, yet keep the words and sentence structure simple so that they will read on to the end.

I keep my audience in mind when I write all of my books, though many other writers do not. I constantly ask myself how my target audience might react to what my characters are doing. I respect my audience, and I want them to empathize with my characters and travel on the journey that my characters travel. I want my readers to remember my characters after they've finished the book.

Literary and Social Issues

Historical fiction might be used in the curriculum simply as a literary work, as an introduction to genre, or it might be used in connection with social studies, but it might also be used to explore literary and historical issues. For example, how is one to write authentically about the lives of people who lived thousands of years ago, especially people who lived during times without written records. One method authors use is to draw extensively on the same materials that archeologists seek out, the artifacts left behind. The most significant factor for historical fiction is that, based on what is known about the time, the story is within the realm of the possible. Peter Dickinson's *The Kin,* for example, is set 200,000 years ago. A group of children get separated from their kin, the Moonhawks, when they are attacked by violent strangers. The early development of society and human behavior is beautifully depicted, though there is no written account that allows us to attest to the narrative's authenticity.

Often historical fiction set in ancient times draws on myth and legend as well as historical and archeological sources. Joseph Bruchac's *Dawn Land* and *Pharaoh's Daughter* by Julius Lester each draws on story as well as on the archeological and historic records we have.

Another big issue that arises in reconstructions of the past is the extent to which our own outlook on the world influences our writing about the time period. For instance, when looking at women's roles in society in the Middle Ages, there are some wonderful narratives of brave heroines who defy society and family to find their own way. One might question whether an independent-minded girl like Catherine in *Catherine, Called Birdy* would have been likely in the Middle Ages.

Author Spotlight

Photo courtesy of Pam Muñoz Ryan.

Pam Muñoz Ryan

Pam Muñoz Ryan is the National Education Association's Author recipient of the Civil and Human Rights Award, and the 2010 Virginia Hamilton Literary Award for Multicultural Literature. She has written over thirty books for young people, from picture books to novels, which include *Esperanza Rising, Becoming Naomi León, Riding Freedom, Paint the Wind,* and *The Dreamer,* awarded the Boston Globe-Horn Book Honor. Her books have garnered many accolades including the Pura Belpre Medal, the Jane Addams Peace Award, the Americas Award Honor, the ALA Schneider Award, the Tomás River Award, the Siebert Honor, and the Orbis Pictus Award. She was born and raised in Bakersfield, California, received her bachelor's and master's degrees at San Diego State University, and now lives in North San Diego County. Visit her website at www.pammunozryan.com.

SELECTED BOOKLIST

Amelia and Eleanor Go For A Ride (Scholastic, 1999)
Becoming Naomi León (Scholastic, 2004)
The Dreamer (Scholastic, 2010)
Esperanza Rising (Scholastic, 2000)
Paint the Wind (Scholastic, 2007)
Riding Freedom (Scholastic, 1998)
When Marian Sang (Scholastic, 2002)

ON HOW SHE BECAME AN AUTHOR OF YOUNG ADULT LITERATURE

The summer before fifth grade my family moved across town. I didn't know anyone in the neighborhood so I began riding my bike to the small East Bakersfield Branch Library. Books took me away from the feeling that I didn't quite belong. I became what most people would consider obsessive about books. Books allowed me to "try on" many lives different from my own. But it never occurred to me then that I might write them someday. In high school, I knew that I wanted a profession that was affiliated with literature and I thought that would be teaching. I became a bilingual teacher, married, and years later, as a mom with four young children, went back to school to get my master's degree in postsecondary education. One day after a class, one of my professors asked me if I'd ever considered writing professionally. When I told her I hadn't, she encouraged me to consider it. Coincidentally, a few weeks later, a colleague asked me if I would help her write a book for adults and I jumped at the opportunity. I began taking baby steps on an unknown path. But from the moment I started working on that first book for adults, I knew that I wanted to try a story for children, maybe because books had such an impact on me as a young adult. One thing led to another. Many years down the road, after a number of my picture books had been published, an editor at Scholastic, Tracy Mack, encouraged me to try a novel. That's when I started another journey—to becoming someone I'd never been before.

What I've discovered is that part of the appeal of writing is similar to the enchantment of reading. They are both quests, except that when I write, I'm the creator and choose the path. I can be as strong as Charlotte in *Riding Freedom*. I can begin as one type of character and evolve into another, like Esperanza in *Esperanza Rising* and Naomi in *Becoming Naomi León*. Or, I can sort out the issues of life by way of the unexpected journey, as I did with Maya in *Paint the Wind*. Through travel and research, I can recreate another time and place, for instance, the childhood of Neftalí Reyes in Temuco, Chile, for the novel, *The Dreamer*.

ON CREATING AN AUTHENTIC HISTORICAL NARRATIVE

My first approach to recreating a time and place is through extensive research. Then I corroborate with first person accounts if they are still available. Or I travel to the place and use the local history rooms of libraries. If the book is about a historical figure, I read memoirs, biographies and articles about the person. In the case of *The Dreamer,* I immersed myself in Neftalí Reyes's (Pablo Neruda's) poetry, living with his work every day. After my manuscripts are written, they are sent to consultants and academic experts to vet. For instance, after *Esperanza Rising* had gone to copyedit but before it was published, it was examined by two consultants, one an expert on Mexico and the Spanish language, to determine that my Spanish and my research was correct. The other was an academic expert on the Great Depression. Then, my editor and I gratefully consider, discuss, and change according to the experts' recommendations. When I write, I try to give the most accurate suggestion possible, the most precise illusion of what it might have been like for my characters.

Nonfiction Literature for the Young Adult

In recent years, high-quality nonfiction books have been published in record numbers. Perhaps we should start by exploring what exactly is meant by *nonfiction trade books*. The International Reading Association's *Literacy Dictionary* provides the definition: "prose literature designed primarily to explain, argue or describe rather than to entertain; specifically a type of prose other than fiction" (1995). This definition stresses the difference between fiction and nonfiction but several other aspects of nonfiction trade books need to be emphasized as well. The distinction between informational text and nonfiction literature is equally significant. Informational text can be found in dictionaries, instruction manuals, and even on cereal boxes, but trade books are not just information; they should also have quality of narrative and aesthetics. In fact there is a distinct need to disentangle the terms *information* and *nonfiction*—the difference being that as trade books these works of

The Astonishing Life of Octavian Nothing (2008) provides a very different perspective on the American Revolution. Reprinted by permission of Candlewick.

literature have to be aesthetically pleasing and well written to attract readers to choose them and to keep readers interested enough to finish them.

Terms such as *creative nonfiction* and *literary journalism* are often used when speaking of nonfiction literature that has engaging prose. Though creative nonfiction about historical topics and historical fiction can be similar in many ways, there is a definite distinction between the two genres. Although creative nonfiction might use beautiful flowing narrative, with distinct voice and style, it remains "writing about reality in which nothing is made up" (Colman, 2004, n.p.). Historical fiction uses real detail in the storyline to create context; creative nonfiction uses the narrative to explore factual detail. As Penny Colman asserts of her nonfiction narratives, "I do not make up dialogue, use composite characters, invent scenes, attribute thoughts or feelings, imagine motives, or in any other way cross the line between fact and fiction" (Colman, 1988).

Still nonfiction trade books have to be aesthetically pleasing and well written in order to be successful. So the best nonfiction has "the excitement of the adventure story, inspiration of the quest, the drama of the pathway into the unknown, and the unique satisfaction of offering nuggets of insight that allow readers to understand the world around them" (Aronson, 2003, p. 115). Although there is certainly creativity involved in writing effective nonfiction, this creativity does not extend to exaggeration or elaboration of the facts. Of course there are fuzzy border genres like fictionalized biography in which scenes are invented and thoughts and feelings might be attributed to an actual historical figure.

Studies have shown that whereas nonfiction makes up around a third of what the general population reads for pleasure, for remedial readers and especially reluctant male readers, nonfiction makes up more than 50 percent of what young people choose to read (Carter and Abrahamson, 1990). Another interesting finding is that young adults choose the majority of the nonfiction they read based not on curriculum but on interests they already have. Recent surveys from the ALA (www.ala.org/teenread) as well as from the International Reading Association (www.reading.org) support the idea that teens enjoy reading nonfiction but not just any nonfiction; young adults enjoy reading nonfiction books that connect in some way to their own interests.

A commonsense response to this might be to have a wide variety of quality nonfiction (based on teen interests) available in the classroom and the media center. Yet action research done by teacher candidates in my classes shows nonfiction as a genre that is sorely missing in many middle school and high school classrooms. One reason for this is teacher preference. Despite the emphasis in national and regional language arts standards on multiple formats and genres, fictional narratives have been traditionally favored by teachers of literature. Many teachers feel that the study of literature *is* the study of fiction. Symbolism, point of view, and all of the literary techniques that make quality literature tend to be associated with fiction.

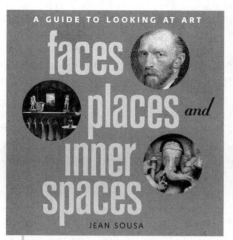

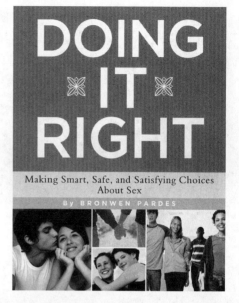

Faces, Places, and Inner Spaces (2006) by Jean Sousa highlights works from the Art Institute of Chicago with accessible observations and questions that lead to inquiry. Reprinted by permission of Abrams. *Doing it Right: Making Smart, Safe, and Satisfying Choices about Sex* by Bronwen Pardes (2007) gives down-to-earth advice about sex in this teen-oriented book. Reprinted by permission of Simon Pulse.

Moreover, unlike textbooks that can be ordered at the school system level and instructional materials, which go with specific products, nonfiction trade books have to attract and engage a reader's attention enough to actually read the book. Furthermore nonfiction trade books deal with history, science, art, and sports. There is a feeling among some teachers of literature that these nonfiction books belong in their curricular areas rather than in literature classes. Yet the social studies teacher and the science teacher have full course loads of textbooks and hands-on experiments to cover. Finding literature for students to read is often not at the top of the content area teacher's list.

Criteria for Evaluating and Selecting Nonfiction Trade Books

When evaluating nonfiction trade books accuracy is of course vital. Understandings and theories about the world are constantly changing. A book from just a few years back might present global warming as an unlikely theory, whereas today most books treat global warming as a reality; names of countries and their leaders, even seemingly solid scientific information like the number of planets in our solar system, can and do change over time.

How does the reader know what is well researched and up to date? Teachers and librarians can scrutinize author's notes, acknowledgments, prefaces, and bibliographies—or better yet teach students themselves to scrutinize these sources of information to explore the extent of the author's research.

Accuracy is key, but as has been stated over and over, if the book is well written, readers will be more likely to stick with it and become more excited—not just about the content but also about reading itself. Most of the same literary techniques that make for good prose, including point of view, tone, pace, syntax, and voice (Colman 1999), can make

Nic Bishop presenting on *Quest for the Tree Kangaroo*. The photographs in this book provide invaluable contextual information. Photo © Doug Wechsler. Reprinted by permission.

a nonfiction narrative more engaging. Penny Colman (1999) asserts, "Well-written nonfiction which goes beyond facts to present an eloquent, informed, and well-crafted discussion of those facts can generate" the same "involved enthusiastic responses" as fiction (p. 39).

Nonfiction books should be used throughout the curriculum as read-alouds, for reading assignments, and on reading lists in order to explore the genre, to learn the content, and to introduce or reinforce elements of style and literary devices. Nonfiction narrative can model effective debate and effective storytelling for different content areas. One of the greatest potentials of nonfiction is to get readers to think about how an argument is put together. As the language of politics, business, the news, debate, and of science, nonfiction narrative comes in many styles and rhetorics that will be encountered in the real world.

Inquiry and Investigation

Of all the possible nonfiction trade books teachers might choose to have in the classroom, one of the most interesting types for teachers comprise books that promote inquiry and investigation. Some of the best nonfiction stimulates curiosity in the reader. For example, *Troy: Unearthing Ancient Worlds* (Kerns) looks at the evidence around Heinrich Schliemann's 20-year search for the historical city of Troy. In addition to learning all about Troy and archeology, readers must decide for themselves whether the evidence suggests Schliemann found the actual Troy spoken of in the *Iliad* and the *Odyssey*.

Peggy Colman in *Thanksgiving: The True Story* investigates 12 competing claims for where the first Thanksgiving took place. Surprisingly these claims vary from 1541 in Texas to 1631 in Boston. The Plymouth Colony's 1621 claim became popular after a book by Alexander Young elaborated on this assertion in 1841. Some of the other claims were first published around the same time. Why would this matter? Colman (2008) writes, "This is the true story of Thanksgiving—as true as it can be, based on the available evidence. New evidence, of course, might be discovered, or old evidence might be reinterpreted. I am open to that and am hopeful that you are too. Because what we believe matters. It matters because it shapes our identity and actions, as individuals and as a nation" (p. 5).

In *Witch Hunt: Mysteries of the Salem Witch Trails* Marc Aronson presents the theories and interpretations surrounding the Salem witch trails and challenges readers to use the evidence to come to their own conclusions about what actually led to 25 executions. "We are not likely to ever know, with certainty, why the events at Salem unfolded as they did. Yet looking for new clues about Salem, re-examining old ones, formulating theories and testing them is ever the more fascinating just because it is an ongoing process." In addition to using new evidence to reevaluate the past, historical examinations provide a context in which to reflect on human nature, "to use your own experience . . . your own sense of yourself as a modern teenager, to try to picture them, your ancestors centuries ago" (p. xiii). Simi-

THE PHYSICS OF
/////// NASCAR.

HOW TO MAKE
STEEL+GAS+RUBBER=SPEED

Diandra Leslie-Pelecky
Foreword by Ray Evernham

Physics professor Diandra L. Leslie-Pelecky created *The Physics of NASCAR* for an adult audience, but it is an exciting read for any NASCAR enthusiast, filled with information about science explained in a user-friendly way. Reprinted by permission of Penguin Group (USA).

larly, Russell Freedman in *Who Was First? Discovering the Americas* notes that "as new evidence has come to light, our understanding of history has changed." Indeed he goes on to explore the evidence of various visits to the Americas by Native Americans, Vikings, and Chinese explorers. He ends with the idea that new discoveries are constantly being made about human navigation to the New World.

Though history-related trade books are perhaps most conducive to inquiry, even a sports book like *The Science of NASCAR: NASCAR in the Pits* (Stewart) can led to interesting investigations. Although written to be accessible to many fifth graders the subject matter of this series will also appeal to many older teens who might be reading below grade level. At the same time the short narrative bits lead into all sorts of math and science investigations about friction, pressure, and weight.

New Perspectives and Multiple Views

Connected to the idea of inquiry is the introduction to new perspectives and alternate views. For example, few teens will know that young women were active in rodeos until the 1940s when they were banned from participating. Candace Savage discusses this history in *Born to Be a Cowgirl*. The role women played and the circumstances for the banning will certainly get students thinking.

Accept No Substitutes: The History of American Advertising by Chistina Mierau looks at the shaping of the American mind by advertisements starting with those that lured Europeans to the New World. Likewise *The Body Project: An Intimate History of American Girls* (Brumberg) explores the history of body image for young women. Despite the advances in gender equity, 53 percent of 13-year-olds in the United States are already dissatisfied with their bodies. This information both connects with adolescent developmental needs and stimulates patterns of lifelong curiosity and inquiry.

Other Books That Make You Think
- *Children of the Indian Boarding Schools* by Holly Littlefield
- *The Crusades: Christians at War* by Christine Hatt
- *How We Know What We Know about Climate Change* by Lynne Cherry and Gary Brauch
- *Masterpieces Up Close* by Claire d'Harcourt.
- *Muckrackers* by Ann Bausum
- *Those Extraordinary Women of World War I* by Karen Stanchak
- *Voices from the Fields* by S. Beth Atkin
- *War Is: Soldiers, Survivors, and Storytellers Talk about War* ed. by Marc Aronson and Patty Campbell

Guidelines for Selecting and Evaluating Nonfiction

In addition to the general criteria for selecting books for young adult readers you likely want to consider the following when choosing nonfiction for young adults:

- *Choice of subject.* Does the text provide interest and meaning for contemporary children? Does it add to students' knowledge of past or present? Will it widen possibilities for the student?
- *Accuracy and authenticity.* Is there evidence of careful research? How is the research documented? How do the facts compare with those found in other books? Does it give a balanced picture of the subject?
- *Style.* Is dialogue used to bring the subject to life? What point of view is used? Does it add to the story? How readable is the story?
- *Characterization.* Is the subject believable? Does the author present multiple sides of the subject?
- *Theme.* Are the facts oversimplified? What are the author's biases? What themes is the author developing?

Technology Links

Digital Booktalk for *We Beat the Street*

The term *booktalk* was first coined by author Aidan Chambers, describing a talk about a text that makes the audience more interested in actually reading it. The Department of Digital Media and the Educational Technology program at the University of Central Florida have been using video book trailers since 2002 on the Internet at http://digitalbooktalk .com/?p=47. These digital narratives expand on Chambers's booktalk model by providing short book trailers to grab the attention of young viewers and helping them locate books that excite them about reading. There are close to 50 trailers on the website currently and a process for young readers to follow while creating their own digital booktalk. A "UB-the-Director Curriculum Model" is also provided.

Several good trailers for biographical narratives are included on the site. *We Beat the Street: How a Friendship Led to Success* by Sampson Davis tells the stories of three kids from poor, single-parent urban homes who overcame incredible odds, making a pact that they would all attend college and then medical school. The digital booktalk is hip and meaningful and will certainly grab the attention of many viewers.

Catering to Teen Interests

One advantage that many nonfiction trade books have that is rarely addressed in textbooks is that of offering discussions about topics that are actually of interest to young adults. For example, we have sports books, books that provide advice aimed at teens, and disaster books like *The Perfect Storm* by Sebastian Junger and *Close to Shore* by Michael Capuzzo.

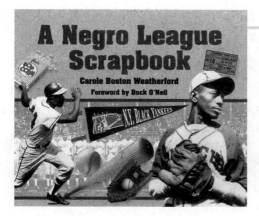

In *A Negro League Scrapbook* (2005) the scrapbook concept allows primary source documents to become an integral part of the narrative. *A Negro League Scrapbook* by Carole Boston Weatherford. Published by Boyds Mills Press. Reprinted by permission.

Sports

There are many exciting books on sports, some quite well written. For rock climbing there is *Rock and Ice Climbing: Top the Tower!* by Jeremy Roberts. Swimmers shouldn't miss *Gold in the Water* by P. H. Mullin, which is a fascinating account of Olympic hopefuls preparing for Sidney in 2000. Interested in women's basketball? *A History of Basketball for Girls and Women: From Bloomers to Big Leagues* by Joanne Lannin introduces the whole history of females playing the sport. The following list shows a few other sports books that should be mentioned.

- *Baseball: Best Shots: The Greatest Baseball Photographs* from DK Publishing
- *Bicycle Stunt Riding: Catch Air* by Chris Hayhurst
- *Hawk: Occupation Skateboarder* by Tony Hawk and Sean Martinez
- *Rookie: Tanika Whitman: First Year in the NBA* by Jim Anderson
- *Uncommon Champions: Fifteen Athletes Who Battled Back* by Marty Kaminsky

Birds and the Bees

Of course some teen interests involve the same issues for which books are being challenged. Often these are among the most popular titles. Carol Weston in *Girltalk: All the Stuff Your Sister Never Told You* introduces all sorts of problems that girls confront. The narrative is filled with tips, many dealing with sexuality. Likewise *Sista, Girlfren' Breaks It Down . . . When Mom's Not Around* by Francheska Ahmed-Cawthorne provides advice on dating and other issues of particular interest to teenage girls. Of course it is not just young women who are interested in finding out about these issues. Many librarians can recount stories of teen boys caught stealing books that discuss sexuality from the library; they are embarrassed by the idea of checking these books out, but they are dying to read them. *Doing It Right* by Bronwen Pardes has disappeared from my collection several times, taken by college students who are intrigued by the questions and answers explored in this insightful book. Similarly, *The Underground Guide to Teenage Sexuality* by Michael J. Basso is a handbook of answers to the important questions about sexuality that many young adults face.

One approach to history that often captivates young adults is the stories of people their own age and the roles they have played. One of the best examples is *We Were There Too! Young People in History* by Phillip Hoose. This is a great introduction to the roles that many teens and children have played in history. In *Girls Who Rocked the World: Heroines from Sacagawea to Sheryl Swoopes* Alice Weldon introduces 35 women who were younger than 20 years of age when they managed to have a major impact on history. These historical figures are interspersed with contemporary teen girls answering the question "How will you rock the world?" G. Clifton Wisler focuses on teen roles in a particular historical event in *When Johnny Went Marching: Young Americans Fighting the Civil War.* Each of these books presents events that are relevant because they concern young adults.

Disaster, Adventure, and Survival Stories

Books that deal with the excitement and adventure of action stories are among the most frequently chosen nonfiction. Here is a short list of some high-interest titles:

- *888½ Amazing Answers to Your Questions about the Titanic* by Hugh Brewster and Laurie Coulter
- *Black Potatoes: The Story of the Great Irish Famine, 1845–1850* by Susan Campbell Bartoletti
- *Close to Shore: The Terrifying Shark Attacks of 1916* by Michael Capuzzo
- *The Great Fire* by Jim Murphy
- *Left for Dead: A Young Man's Search for Justice for the USS Indianapolis* by Peter Nelson
- *Meltdown: A Race Against Nuclear Disaster at Three Mile Island* by William Hampton
- *A Nation Challenged* by the staff of the *New York Times*
- *The Perfect Storm* by Sebastian Junger
- *Phineas Gage* by John Fleischman
- *Shipwreck at the Bottom of the World* by Jennifer Armstrong
- *Understanding September 11th* by Mitch Frank

Literature across the Curriculum

One of the most effective ways to bring nonfiction into the English/language arts classroom is to pair nonfiction and fiction together in a literature across the curriculum approach. This can be effective in getting readers to discuss narrative techniques, and provides a context for better understandings of the fiction, while being extremely educational.

An American Plague by Jim Murphy would make a perfect book to pair with *Fever 1793*, a novel by Laurie Halse Anderson. The historical research that has gone into *Plague* will provide context for the reading and information for students who want to know more about this calamity after reading Anderson's fictional account.

Revenge of the Whale by Nathaniel Philbrick tells the story of the whale ship *Essex*, which was far from any shore in the Pacific Ocean in 1820 when an angry sperm whale turned on the ship and sank it. Of the 20 men (many of them teens) on board, only eight survived. The story was big news at the time and supposedly served as the inspiration for *Moby Dick*. A pairing of the two books could be quite effective.

Several excellent books about the Lewis and Clark expedition are aimed at YA readers. *The Saga of Lewis and Clark* by Thomas and Jeremy Schmidt and both *Plants on the Trail with Lewis and Clark* and *Animals on the Trail with Lewis and Clark* by Dorothy Hinshaw Patent would make great interdisciplinary studies paired with *Sacajawea* by Joseph Bruchac or *The Captain's Dog* by Roland Smith.

Other Nonfiction/Fiction Pairings

- *Coping with Cancer* by Holly Cefrey paired with *Drums and Dangerous Pie* by Jordan Sonnenblick
- *Hitler Youth* by Susan Campbell Bartoletti paired with *Traitor* by Gudrun Pausewang
- *The Kid Who Climbed Everest* by Bear Grylls paired with *Peak* by Roland Smith
- *Medieval Muck* by Vince Reid paired with *The Silver Cup* by Constance Leeds
- *There Comes a Time: The Struggle for Civil Rights* by Milton Meltzer paired with *Fire from the Rock* by Sharon Draper
- *To the Top: The Story of Everest* by Stephen Venables paired with *Peak* by Roland Smith
- *Witch-Hunt* by Marc Aronson paired with *Witch Child* by Celia Rees

Audio Books

Nonfiction and Life Stories

An American Plague: The True and Terrifying Story of the Yellow Fever Epidemic of 1793 by Jim Murphy; narrated by Pat Battino. (Recorded Books, 2005)

Bad Boy: a Memoir by Walter Dean Myers; read by Joe Morton. (Harper Audio, 2001) (Y)

Dear Author: Letters of Hope by Joan Kaywell; narrated by multiple readers. (Penguin/Audible, 2008)

Down to Earth Guide to Global Warming by Laurie David and Cambria Gordon; narrated by Polly Lee. (Recorded Books, 2008)

In My Hands: Memories of a Holocaust Rescuer by Irene Gut Opdyke with Jennifer Armstrong; read by Hope Davis. (Bantam Doubleday Audio, 1999) (Y)

Lives of the Presidents by Kathleen Krull; read by John C. Brown. (Audio Bookshelf, 1998) (Y)

Mao's Last Dance by Li Cunxin; narrated by Paul English. (Bolinda Audio, 2006) (Y)

Red Scarf Girl: A Memoir of the Cultural Revolution by Ji Li Jiang; read by Christina Moore. (Recorded Books, 1999) (Y)

Shipwreck at the Bottom of the World by Jennifer Armstrong; read by Taylor Mali. (Audio Bookshelf, 2000) (Y)

Sitting Bull and His World by Albert Marvin; read by Ed Sala. (Recorded Books, 2001) (Y)

Yes We Can: A Biography of Barack Obama by Gavin Thomas; narrated by Roscoe Orman. (Audible, 2008)

Y—YALSA Selected List of Audiobooks

Formatting in Nonfiction

One of the most interesting aspects of nonfiction can be found in the formatting and aesthetics of the genre. Although there are many straightforward textual narratives that will appeal primarily by topic and fine writing, many nonfiction trade books also include graphics, primary source documents, photographs, maps, graphs, and other enhancements that add tremendously to the reader's understandings and transactions with the text. Also, the inclusion of graphics in some nonfiction effectively supports visual learning styles. Yann Arthus-Bertrand's photographs in *Our Living Earth* are more significant than the text. These amazing images offer insights on the topic and attract readers who would not otherwise engage with this narrative. Nonfiction also often has structures and substructures that include sidebars, chronologies, boxed inserts, and primary source voices. For example, short bits of narrative make many of these books less daunting for reluctant readers.

Pyramids and Mummies (Simon) for example will capture the attention of many readers and draw them to the narrative by its unusual formatting. *Knights and Castles* (Osborne) is not heavy on text but the timeline, the diagrams showing how a "trebuchet" actually works, and the cut-away views of castles all make the book a valuable resource.

Lincoln Shot (Denenberg) uses the format of 19th-century newspapers very effectively. In fact, in addition to the wonderful retellings of this historical event, the book could serve as a model for a cross-curricular writing activity in which students create a newspaper telling the story of another historical event.

Historical Nonfiction

There is such a wide range of historical nonfiction that multiple books addressing a time period or a subject can generally be found. The following sets demonstrate both the range and the depth of this type of book.

A Wide Range of Historical Nonfiction

- *Black Potatoes: The Story of the Great Irish Famine, 1845–1850* by Susan Campbell Bartoletti gives a detailed account of the Great Irish Famine and its effect on the Irish people.
- *Born to Be a Cowgirl: A Spirited Ride through the Old West* by Candace Savage is an action-packed story of Americas cowgirls who bucked with the best of them until women were barred from rodeos in the 1940s. Actual diary entries and photographs add to the story.
- *Bound for America: The Story of the European Immigrants* by Milton Meltzer tells the story of the immigration of 30 million people from Europe to America between the 1820s and 1920s.
- *Civil War* from the DK Eyewitness Books series by John Stanchak provides an accurate overview of the war with excellent graphics and photographs.
- *The Crusades: Christians at War* by Christine Hatt is a beautifully illustrated overview of the Crusades, highlighting the connections between politics and religion.
- *Hidden Secrets* by David Owen provides a history of espionage and its technologies.
- *Medieval Muck* by Mary Dobson concentrates on daily life in medieval times.

Lincoln Shot: A President's Life Remembered (2008) is quite factual in the information presented although the newspaper format is fictitious. Based on the premise of a newspaper printing a commemorative edition after the assassination of Abraham Lincoln using archival material, the book would serve as an excellent model for teens using research and archival sources to create their own headlines. It is also a really good read. Reprinted by permission of Feiwel and Friends.

- *Phineas Gage* by John Fleischman tells the story of a construction foreman who had a 13-pound steel rod shot through his head and lived for another 10 years, a case that led to advances in knowledge about the human brain.
- *Piracy & Plunder: A Murderous Business* by Milton Metzler provides a broad overview of the history of crime on the high seas in a stimulating narrative that debunks the romantic myth of pirates.
- *Plants on the Trail with Lewis and Clark* and an earlier book *Animals on the Trail with Lewis and Clark* by Dorothy Hinshaw Patent make for a great cross-disciplinary study and present an interesting context for understanding Lewis and Clark's expedition.
- *Rediscovering Easter Island* by Kathy Pelta looks at what explorers, scientists, and scholars have conjectured about Easter Island over the centuries.
- *Slave Spirituals and the Jubilee Singers* by Michael Cooper recounts the story of the Jubilee Singers and connects the spirituals to our understanding of slavery.
- *Ten Queens: Portraits of Women in Power* by Milton Meltzer provides brief bios of 10 powerful women in the medieval world.
- *This Our Dark Country: The American Settlers of Liberia* by Catherine Reef tells the story of the American Colonization Society formed in the early 19th century.
- *Those Extraordinary Women of World War I* by Karen Zeinart utilizes photographs and first-person accounts to present the wide variety of roles women played during the war.
- *Till Year's Good End: A Calendar of Medieval Labors* by W. Nikola-Lisa highlights the day-to-day activities of peasants in this well-researched text.
- *We Were There Too! Young People in History* by Phillip Hoose provides an excellent window on children and young adults who have made a difference in history.
- *When Johnny Went Marching Home: Young Americans Fight the Civil War* by G. Clifton Wisler takes a hard-hitting look at young people in war.
- *Wounded Knee* by Neil Waldman looks at the events that led to this confrontation from different perspectives.

Focus on World War II

- *After the Holocaust* by Howard Greenfield
- *Air Raid—Pearl Harbor: The Story of December 7, 1941* by Theodore Taylor
- *Another River, Another Town: A Teenage Tank Gunner Comes of Age in Combat—1945* by John Irwin

- *Attack on Pearl Harbor: The True Story of the Day America Entered World War II* by Shelley Tanaka; illus. by David Craig
- *The Belly Gunner* by Carol Hipperson
- *Darkness over Denmark: The Danish Resistance and the Rescue of the Jews* by Ellen Levine
- *Farewell to Manzanar* by Jeanne Wakatsuki Houston and James Houston
- *Fighting for Honor: Japanese Americans and World War II* by Michael Cooper
- *Forging Freedom* by Hudson Talbatt
- *My Secret Camera: Life in the Lodz Ghetto* by Frank Dabba Smith
- *Nazi Germany: The Face of Tyranny* by Ted Gottfried
- *Remembering Manzanar: Life in a Japanese Relocation Camp* by Michael Cooper
- *Remember Pearl Harbor: American and Japanese Survivors Tell Their Stories* by Thomas Allen
- *Rescued Images: Memories of a Childhood in Hiding* by Ruth Jacobsen
- *A Special Fate: Chiune Sugihara: Hero of the Holocaust* by Alison Leslie Gold
- *Surviving Hitler: A Boy in the Nazi Death Camps* by Andrea Warren
- *The Yellow Star: The Legend of King Christian X of Denmark* by Carmen Agra Deedy

Holocaust

- *Anne Frank in the World* by The Anne Frank House
- *Auschwitz: The Story of a Nazi Death Camp* by Clive A. Lawton
- *Behind the Secret Window* by Nelly Toll
- *Displaced Persons: The Liberation and Abuse of Holocaust Survivors* by Ted Gottfried
- *The Hidden Children of the Holocaust* by Esther Kustanowitz
- *In My Hands: Memories of a Holocaust Rescuer* by Irene Gut Opdyke
- *Liberation: Teens in the Concentration Camps and the Teen Soldiers Who Liberated Them* by Tina E. Tito
- *My Brother's Keeper: The Holocaust through the Eyes of an Artist* by Israel Bernbaum
- *No Pretty Pictures* by Anita Lobel
- *Tell Them We Remember: The Story of the Holocaust* by Susan D. Bachrach
- *We Are Witnesses: Five Diaries of Teenagers Who Died in the Holocaust* ed. by Jacob Boas

The Green Earth Book Award

One trend that has definitely impacted the publishing industry is the green movement. The Green Earth Book Awards have existed since 2005, given annually to a book that inspires young readers "to grow a deeper appreciation, respect and responsibility for his or her natural environment" (www.newtonmarascofoundation .org). The awards include both a young adult and nonfiction category, both of which provide examples that have great potential for literature across the curriculum investigations.

The logo of the Green Earth Book Award, the first book award in the United States to promote environmental stewardship. Copyright Newton Marasco Foundation. Reprinted with permission.

Nonfiction (appropriate for YA)

Earth in the Hot Seat: Bulletins from a Warming World by Marfe Ferguson Delano (winner 2010)

Heroes of the Environment by Harriet Rohmer, illus. by Julie McLaughlin (honor 2010)

The Frog Scientist by Pamela S. Turner, photographs by Andy Comis (honor 2010)

My Space/Our Planet by the Myspace Community, Jeca Taudte, and Dan Santat (winner 2009)

Generation Green: The Ultimate Teen Guide to Living an Eco-Friendly Life by Linda Siversten and Tosh Siversten (honor 2009)

How We Know What We Know about Our Changing Climate: Scientists and Kids Explore Global Warming by Lynne Cherry and Gary Braasch (honor 2009)

Science Warriors: The Battle Against Invasive Species by Sneed B. Collard III (honor 2009)

The Down to Earth Guide to Global Warming, by Laurie David and Cambria Gordon (winner 2008)

An Inconvenient Truth: The Crisis of Global Warming by Al Gore, adapted by Jane O'Connor (honor 2008)

A Place for Butterflies by Melissa Stewart, illus. by Higgins Bond (winner 2007)

Quest for the Tree Kangaroo by Sy Montgomery, illus. by Nic Bishop (honor 2007)

YA Fiction

The Carbon Diaries: 2015 by Saci Lloyd (winner 2010)

A Summer of Silk Moths by Margaret Willey (honor 2010)

Blind Faith Hotel by Pamela Todd (co-winner 2009)

Write Naked by Peter Gould (co-winner 2009)

Whirlwind by David Klass (honor 2009)

The Light-Bearer's Daughter by O. R. Melling (winner 2008)

Secrets of the Sirens by Julia Golding (honor 2008)

Flash Point by Sneed B. Collard III (winner 2007)

Firestorm: The Caretaker Trilogy: Book 1 by David Klass (honor 2007)

Past Green Earth Book Award honor books include *Generation Green* (2008) and *Quest for the Tree Kangaroo* (2006). These honor books are great for getting young readers to think about environmental stewardship. Cover from *Generation Green* reprinted by permission of Simon Pulse. Cover from *Quest for the Tree Kangaroo* by Sy Montgomery, photographs by Nic Bishop. Jacket photograph copyright © 2006 by Nic Bishop. Reprinted by permission of Houghton Mifflin Harcourt Publishing. All rights reserved.

These books can be examined for their literary and aesthetic qualities, investigated for scientific validity, used to inspire students to engage in service learning and activism, read for information, or read for pleasure.

Life Stories: Biography, Autobiography, Memoirs, and Journals

> An autobiography that leaves out the little things and enumerates only the big ones is no proper picture of the man's life at all; his life consists of his feelings and his interests, with here and there an incident apparently big or little to hang the feelings on.
>
> —Mark Twain's *Autobiography,* 1906

The term *life stories* is used here to encompass the various forms of biography, memoir, and autobiography. These life stories can be a wonderful way to introduce readers to history, providing them "with a lens through which we can view another world, and

Female Force: Stephenie Meyer (2009) is part of a series of graphic biographies of strong female figures. The scene depicted tells the story of Meyer's dream that led to the writing of *Twilight*. The visual storytelling brings a very different interaction to the reader's understanding of her life. Reprinted by permission of Bluewater Productions. Bluewater Productions is a full-service publishing company specializing in comic books, graphic novels, and multimedia. Dedicated to pairing high-quality art with innovative storytelling, Bluewater creates a wide variety of intellectual properties that engage a growing readership and bridge the gap between comic books and the diverse multimedia marketplace. www.bluewaterprod.com

way to understand it better" (Foreword by John Haworth of the American Indian to *Painting the Wild Frontier*, p. xiv). Milton Meltzer's biographies of Willa Cather, Thoreau, Emily Dickinson, and Edgar Allen Poe, for example, have first-rate writing and memorable photographs that together create an understanding not only of the subject's life and accomplishments but also of the society in which they wrote. Most of these narratives also fall under the broad category of nonfiction trade books, though there are also certainly those that like historical fiction add detail and dialogue of the author's invention.

Trends in social studies curriculum greatly influence the types of life stories being written, as do contemporary events. On the centennial of Lincoln's assassination, many biographies about him appeared. Multicultural and female biographies have become more popular in recent years. The format of biographies has also changed. As more schools use biographies in the classroom they have become both more attractive and more accurate in their detail. More photographs and primary source materials are being integrated with the narratives. Life stories being published now tend to include extensive notes, bibliographies, and information about the author's research. These biographies are also more likely to tell the good as well as "ugly" about a person.

All biographical narratives take a perspective on a person's life. John DiConsiglio in *Francisco Pizarro: Destroyer of the Inca Empire* definitely sets Pizarro up in a context of violence, but at the same time he wisely asserts an understanding of history as a process. "So who was Pizarro? A soldier? An adventurer? A murderer?" DiConsiglio asks. "History tells us that he was all of the above. But history also tells us that his story isn't over yet" (p. 128). As with nonfiction in general, readers tend to choose life stories that reflect their interests. *Dropping In with Andy Mac* (Macdonald) for example is always off the shelves at local middle schools. This story by and about one of the premiere skateboarders in the world is well written and filled with sidebars of anecdotes, but it is the kids who are already into skating who constantly check it out.

Author Spotlight

Photo courtesy of Ted Lewin.

Sheldon Oberman
1949–2004

Sheldon Oberman studied literature at the University of Winnipeg and the University of Jerusalem. He worked as an English and drama teacher for nearly 30 years. Oberman published 12 books and was an accomplished storyteller. *The Always Prayer Shawl* was the recipient of the American Jewish Book Award. Because he was a teacher he also was interested in providing resources for young people and other educators, including a wonderful process for gathering life stories. This was one of the last interviews conducted with Sheldon Oberman. For more information visit www.sheldonoberman.com/index.shtml.

SELECTED BOOKLIST

The Always Prayer Shawl, Illus. by Ted Lewin (Boyds Mills, 1994)
Island of the Minotaur (Tradewind Books, 2003)
The Shaman's Nephew with Simon Tookoome (FitzHenry and Whiteside, 2000)

ON WHAT YOU SUGGEST FOR YOUNG ADULTS TO HELP THEM BE SUCCESSFUL WRITERS

Live intensely, read extensively, and write with everything you've got.

ON WHETHER HIS OWN LIFE APPEARS IN HIS WRITING

Everyone and every incident that has deeply impressed me seems to submerge into some part of my consciousness. I don't know what happens to them down there but they all somehow float up again in dreams, impulses, fantasies, and yes, as I write. I shape and reconstitute all of that drifting, swirling messy stuff as I try to create interesting characters and events. Am I there in my stories? How can I not be in one form or another?

However, I am never there as you might think. Even when I try to tell a true story as accurately as I can, the events and characters slip away; they submerge and merge in my imagination and when they emerge they have changed at least to some degree. I am a professional observer and writer, but I can never retell the same story without details changing. I am always being corrected by friends and family. I never seem to get the story right. (Neither do they, as far as I am concerned.) So I can't really say that my life accurately appears in my writing. As an artist, I know how to rework life experiences into something interesting, perhaps at times inspiring, but I have to admit that none of it would ever count as testimony that could hold up in court.

ON WHETHER AN AUTHOR CAN WRITE CONVINCINGLY ABOUT CHARACTERS FROM A DIFFERENT CULTURE AND BACKGROUND

It depends on who the writer is trying to convince. There are many writers who create wonderfully interesting characters who are from other cultures, even characters who are animals or ghosts or aliens. I may be convinced by them but I am not from that culture, nor am I that animal or, thank heavens, that ghost or alien. I suspect if those beings were able to read those books, they would be far less impressed.

However, some writers pull it off. *The Red Badge of Courage,* which is about the American Civil War, was written by a man who was not even alive at the time. However, he interviewed veterans so carefully that he could fabricate a tale out of the true cloth of their experiences. The war veterans were amazed at his accuracy, but that writer was not inventing; he was creatively assembling a story based on their experiences.

When I went up north, people often referred with disdain to Farley Mowat as "Hardly Knowit." Farley spent a great deal of time up north and wrote many very impressive books about it. I don't know if their criticism was at all fair but it certainly was a warning to me that I had better not try to act like an expert about Northern culture.

ON THE COLLABORATIVE PROCESS THAT WENT INTO *THE SHAMAN'S NEPHEW; A LIFE IN THE FAR NORTH* (FITZHENRY AND WHITESIDE IN CANADA)

I was on a book tour in the Arctic. I asked to stay with a traditional Inuit because I was fascinated by that culture, which people know so little about. When I arrived in Rankin Inlet near the Arctic Circle I was picked up by Simon Tookoome, a hunter and artist, who took me by dogsled to his home, which was almost completely buried in snow drifts. He did not speak a word of English and all we ate was raw caribou meat, sliced off the back end of the "deceased." This was an authentic Inuit!

Eventually a translator showed up and Simon and I shared stories of our lives. He was one the last of the Inuit to live in the ancient ways of his people. He asked me to tell his life story, the story of his people's ancient ways, because they were disappearing very fast and otherwise his stories and the Inuit way of life would be lost even to his own children.

I agreed but I did not want to pretend that I knew anything. So I had him tell me all his stories through the translator. Then after I studied them and learned more about the culture we met again with a different translator. The stories came out differently with each translator. The stories also developed as I asked questions and he thought more about them.

We worked together over a 10-year period with many translators, translating back and forth until I really understood what he wanted to say and knew how to say it. The book came out in both English and Inuktitut and, thankfully, he and other Inuit people tell me that even though I am no expert, I got it "right."

We have become close friends and our families have become very close though we live far away. When my youngest son was being born, Simon Tookoome went out onto the ice and caught a seal. He used its hide to make my son a dog sled whip. That whip has become a family heirloom just as precious as my grandfather's prayer shawl. My youngest son's middle name is Tookoome and because of that, according to Inuit tradition, Simon Tookoome has now become my son.

ON WHERE HIS INTEREST IN LIFE STORIES CAME FROM

Like many people who became "observers and expressers," I grew up feeling rather alone and unnoticed in the world. I felt very close to my grandfather but I never really knew him very well. I thought about him from a distance and wanted to know about his life. When he died and his prayer shawl came to me it was like a sign, an invitation, to get closer to him in some way. The way I chose was to write about him. I didn't have a lot of details but I wanted to honor his life. So I told his story, a simple but profound story which honors a simple but profound man.

Writing *The Always Prayer Shawl* changed my life. So many people were so moved by it and many told me their stories or stories of someone they loved. People also asked me to teach them how to gather and tell their stories. So that is one of the things I now do. I teach and give workshops on gathering and writing family and personal tales. I was also asked to tell my story very often. I have performed it as a storyteller hundreds of times and every time it has affected in some good way. I write many different kind of stories but the "life story" has become one of the important ways I look at people and write about the world.

ON HOW YOUNG READERS BENEFIT FROM THESE LIFE STORIES

I think it is important to see the larger pattern at times, the big map. Some momentary event that seems trivial or terribly important looks quite different when you see it in that larger framework.

Also, you discover you are not alone, others have gone your way before and others will come that way after you. We all live the role of the hero in our own life journey. When young people can glimpse their lives in a larger pattern, they can see how they are similar to all the rest of us who share the same pattern. It can be a way to feel closer to friends, to parents and grandparents, even to people long gone or from a distant culture. You can see where you are heading and the real challenges that lie ahead. You can understand where you have been, where you are going, and what is truly important.

Authentic Biography versus Fictionalized Biography

Given the wide range of life stories available, making some distinctions might help in our exploration. The term *authentic biography* has been used to denote those life stories that are well documented and carefully researched. In books identified this way generally nothing is invented in the retelling of the subject's life, and sources are provided to allow the reader to know where information is coming from. In Caroline Lazo's book *Alice Walker: Freedom Writer,* for example, the subject's own quotations are used to trace her life from early childhood to the present day. *Tree Shaker: The Story of Nelson Mandela* (by Bill Keller, the *New York Times* executive editor) includes a collection of articles about Mandela published in the *New York Times,* which are interconnected with the narrative. Timelines, source notes, and an extensive index all add to the credibility of the story.

On the other hand, in fictionalized biography, although the basic storyline may be grounded in research, the story structure often includes invented dialogue and dramatizations that are created by the author. The character of the subject in this case is more important than every word being "true." *Behind Rebel Lines: The Incredible Story of Emma Edmonds, Civil War Spy* by Seymour Reit is a good example of this. In 1861, Emma Edmonds refused to sit on the sidelines during the Civil War, so she enlisted disguised as a man in the Union Army. Soon she became a spy behind Confederate lines. The basic story follows the events as they are known, but all of the dialogue and the interactions are invented.

The extreme fictionalized biography is that of a fabricated character. *Lemony Snicket: The Unauthorized Autobiography* stays in zany character the whole way through, bring-

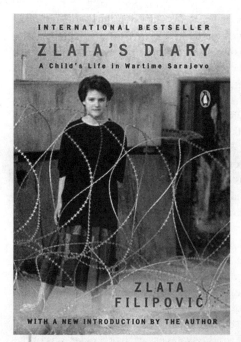

Zlata's Diary (2006) is the autobiography of Zlata Filipović, a young woman who lived through war in Sarajevo and kept a diary of her life and the turmoil around her. Reprinted by permission of Penguin Group (USA).

ing you into the fictional universe of Lemony Snicket. Photos, minutes from secret meetings, and diary entries all add to the story (though they often just confuse you more). Strange connections to the Series of Unfortunate Events books will keep fans happy. *The Unauthorized Autobiography* is obviously fully fictional but some other "biographies" are more along the lines of historical fiction. *A Coal Miner's Bride: The Diary of Anetka Kaminska* (Bartoletti) is beautifully written and quite accurate in its depiction of coal mining immigrants to Pennsylvania at the turn of the century. The central focus of the narrative is the strike of 1897—but this is really historical fiction written in a diary format. The characters are realistic but created by the author. This series actually caused a bit of a stir because many young people and even teachers and librarians assumed the manuscripts were authentic—that there really was a Anetka Kaminska who lived this life and wrote these words. Why is this problematic if it is all based on historical research? Isn't autobiography also somewhat fictional anyway? Perhaps the larger problem was that the readers were not making the choice themselves. A reader had to be observant to find the information that these books were actually written by a contemporary author.

The issue was highlighted when Ann Rinaldi wrote a book in the series from the perspective of a fictional Native American girl who attended an Indian School. Native American critics and many other readers took offense at the depiction—in part because the boarding school (where children often endured great cruelty) did not seem to be such a bad place in the book. If an actual person had written a diary describing the school this way we could assume that either the cruelty had been exaggerated in other accounts or that this school was different from others, but to have a cultural outsider present a benign version of these schools—and then pass it off as an authentic diary was taken as a double slap in the face for many readers. In a different case in 2008, a reprint of Laurie Friedman's *Angel Girl* was canceled after it was discovered that at least part of the story of this Holocaust survivor was completely fabricated. In fact the publisher recalled already purchased copies of the book for a full refund.

Partial Biographies versus Complete Biographies

Another distinction that might be made is between those books that focus on only a part of the subject's life and those that span the subject's whole life. Books such as *Alone across the Arctic: One Woman's Epic Journey by Dog Team* by Pam Flowers and Ann Dixon recount only a particular episode, in this instance a

To Consider

What factors would you take into account when choosing from the multitude of life stories about a famous figure like Abraham Lincoln or Christopher Columbus? How important do you think it would be to your readers to know whether the words being spoken could actually be attributed to the subject? Do authors and publishers have an obligation to provide information about the authenticity of the life being portrayed?

1923–24 expedition across the Arctic, in the subject's life. The retelling is authentic and well-documented, including a glossary, an index, and primary source documents such as the actual expedition supply list, but the focus makes it a partial biography, the story of just a portion of the subject's life. Other times the focus is on one aspect of life during the chosen time period. *John and Abigal Adams: An American Love Story* by Judith St. George focuses solely on the love letters written by the two when they were separated. David Colbert's 10 Days That Shook Your World series takes a different approach. Each book looks at 10 of the most significant days in the lives of subjects like Martin Luther King, Anne Frank, and Benjamin Franklin.

Because these books are presenting historical and contemporary figures to a young audience, many of the partial biographies focus on subjects in their youth. *Jack: The Early Years of John F. Kennedy* by Ilene Cooper provides great insight into John Kennedy's childhood. Aspects such as John's feelings of being overshadowed by his older brother Joe will be relevant to many teens.

Complete biographies on the other hand not only cover the subject's entire life (and sometimes their ancestry), they also tend to be more balanced and have greater depth and complexity. A book like *Johannes Gutenberg and the Printing Press* by Diana Childress discusses primary source research and includes a timeline, a glossary, source notes, bibliography, recommendations for further research, and an extensive index. The thorough research is evident in the treatment of the subject. Not only is Gutenberg's complete life portrayed, it is done in a way that "enhances readers' awareness of the complexities of the materials and helps bring to life rich stories from which we draw our understanding of our shared history" (Childress, p. 127). In fact, most of the better written complete biographies cover not only the subject's whole life but also their sociocultural milieux.

Painting the Wild Frontier (Reich) explores George Caitlin's impact on American history and art. The graphics and the archival documents (as well as the timeline, extensive source notes, index, and bibliography) are amazing. The author's exploration of art, anthropology, and aesthetic philosophy are beautifully integrated with the story of Caitlin's life. Likewise, *E. E. Cummings: A Poet's Life* by Catherine Reef is carefully documented with nine pages of source notes and a seven-page index. Cummings's life and writings are explored and contextualized within political and artistic movements of the time.

Collective Biographies

A collective biography tells the story of two or more people whose lives are connected by a theme like "women writers," "baseball players," or "children who survived the Holocaust," for instance. *Bound for the North Star: True Stories of Fugitive Slaves* by Dennis Fradin tells 12 stories of enslaved people who pursued freedom. *Nobel's Women of Peace* (Benjamin and Mooney) explores the lives of 11 Nobel Prize recipients and the commitment and hope they represent. The collective biography allows the author to explore a theme through multiple lenses and in various contexts. *Countdown to Independence: A Revolution of Ideas in England and Her American Colonies 1760–1776* by Natalie Bober provides portraits of both well-known and virtually unknown patriots. Each of these subjects has a different experience, which together provides a deeper understanding of the time period.

Author Spotlight

Photo courtesy of Jack Gantos.

Jack Gantos

After receiving a B.F.A. in creative writing from Emerson College in 1976 and an M.A. in literature/creative writing from Emerson College in 1984, Jack Gantos became a tenured professor at Emerson College. He has written several adult novel and around a dozen novels for middle-grade through YA readers. Most of his novels, including the Jack Henry books and the Joey Pigza books, can be appreciated by many readers at the sixth-grade level. *Hole in My Life* is more appropriate for ninth-grade readers and older. He has received numerous awards and citations, including the Newbery Honor and the Nasen Award: Best Book for Special Needs Education in the United Kingdom, both for *Joey Pigza Loses Control*. His autobiographical *Hole in My Life* was a Printz Honor book.

SELECTED BOOK LIST

Desire Lines (Farrar, Straus and Giroux, 1997)
Hole in My Life (Farrar, Straus and Giroux, 2002)
Jack Adrift (Farrar, Straus and Giroux, 2003)
Jack on The Tracks (Farrar, Straus and Giroux, 1999)
Jack's Black Book (Farrar, Straus and Giroux, 1997)
Joey Pigza Loses Control (Farrar, Straus and Giroux, 2000)
Joey Pigza Swallowed The Key (Farrar, Straus and Giroux, 1998)
What Would Joey Do? (Farrar, Straus and Giroux, 2002)

ON BECOMING A WRITER FOR YOUNG PEOPLE

I went to college for creative writing. Throughout my reading history I always gravitated to books that had strong main characters—or as we would say in the writing field, "character driven" books. With this in mind just pause and think of the great "character driven" books in children's literature that make up the canon of classics. This is what I grew up with, and as a student I was compelled to write stories that were told by characters, or were closely aligned to the character's point of view.

So when it came to writing I wasn't so much thinking about the age of the reader as I was thinking about the imaginative possibility of the narrator character. And when you think of it this way, then writing for young people becomes the most imaginative landscape possible to inhabit. And I found this landscape entirely enchanting and challenging.

ON WHAT HE ENJOYED READING AS A TEENAGER

I read widely and wildly as a teenager. But mostly I read all my Dad's manly war and manly romance novels. My sister read the classics of English literature so I read what she read and then I stumbled into the Beat writers and loved their world of sensorial indulgence and just couldn't wait until I could run my own life and throw off my middle class trappings and adopt a beat life like Ginsburg or Ferlingetti or Kerouac or Burroughs.

ON FAVORITE AUTHORS AND GENRES CURRENTLY

Currently I'm on a Bruce Chatwin, Paul Auster, Don Delillo, George Orwell, and Paul Bowles kick. Some time ago I was walking through the Southwest Corridor Park in Boston, on my way to the Boston Public Library, when I ran into my poet friend, Bill Corbett. He was with two men and said to me, "Let me introduce you to Paul Auster and Don Delillo." Well, my jaw dropped because I admire them tremendously. Naturally, I had to reread all of their work and tackle the work I had not yet read. I am reading the other three writers on my list because they have all written tremendous travel writing pieces and pieces of social commentary. At present I am toying with a book of essays on my travels through the children's field and so am reading writers who have really managed the essay form.

ON WHETHER HE WRITES WITH A PARTICULAR AUDIENCE IN MIND (AN IMPLIED READER)

When I wrote *Hole in My Life* I had a more mature teen audience in mind. Because I write up and down the age groups (from Rotten Ralph picture books to adult material) I often find students reading work of mine that I perceive as inappropriate. Sure, some second graders can read all my work because they can read, but that does not mean the work is appropriate for their age. I think some measure of common sense should be called upon to match book content to student comprehension and maturity.

ON SUGGESTIONS FOR YOUNG ADULTS TO HELP THEM DEVELOP AS WRITERS

First, I think schools should make a commitment to add creative writing to the basic school curriculum. And just as they support sports activities I think they should support publishing activities. Schools should have writing clubs and publishing centers. They should have a series of author visits and should make certain the library has a fully stocked collection of the best contemporary writing. What I am suggesting is not radical, but reasonable—simply, if you want students to excel at writing you have to develop a fertile environment where they feel confident to create and share their ideas and creative projects.

ON THE EXTENT TO WHICH HIS OWN LIFE STORY APPEARS IN HIS FICTIONAL WORKS

First, just as a blanket statement, I think whatever a writer creates will contain some measure of that writer's life. So, when looking at Rotten Ralph I see in each book some feeling or set of feelings that I had as a child; only now I filter those feelings through Rotten Ralph. My strong feelings of jealousy and fear that my brother was going to receive greater gifts than I was at Christmas are found in the Ralph Christmas book. My fear that my father was going to send me to military academy is found in *Not So Rotten Ralph*. Basically, whenever I write a Ralph book I have to find some emotional element about the story which is true to me; otherwise the story seems false when I write it. In the Jack Henry books it is very clear that Jack is me, and so many of the themes are related to my life. As for Joey Pigza, I think his journey from problem child to winner echoes back through the Jack books. In fact, in all my work there seems to be a shared theme: from violation to redemption.

Autobiographies can provide insight into an author's life and work, but they are often also excellent works of literature. Jacket design by Nicole Licht Urbanic from *Hole in My Life* by Jack Gantos. Jacket design © 2002 by Nicole Licht Urbanic. Reprinted by permission of Farrar, Straus and Giroux, LLC.

ON HIS COMMENTS AS A WRITER OF PICTURE BOOKS, NOVELS, AND BIOGRAPHY ABOUT THE DISTINCTIONS (OR SIMILARITIES) AMONG THESE FORMS OF NARRATIVE

What all writing shares is the mandate to make the subject fresh, insightful, and entertaining. On the surface of the writing I have to make certain that sentence by sentence the material has some attractive and purposeful value, and that it is entirely convincing. If the work is biography then the facts and motivations have to parse and if it is fictional then the inner reality of the work must remain airtight.

Honestly, I think the forms have more in common—from a writer's point of view—than not. The craft and intent of the work requires the same writing skills and clarity of purpose, and above all must plunge the reader into some state of irresistible, imaginative pleasure.

Autobiographies and Memoirs

To an extent autobiographies are by their very nature authentic. The accuracy of the personal detail is in synch at least with how the author understands his or her life. At the same time the autobiography is also inherently biased. Why would someone write a book about their own life in which they focus on the negative aspects? So although these books are often intense, lively, and filled with intimate information, generally only one perspective will be provided.

It can certainly be argued that in *Three Little Words* by Ashley Rhodes-Courter the power of this story of a young girl lost in the foster care system is all the more moving and inspiring because it is true. In this case the author did not rely simply on her own understanding of her life. She writes:

> In recreating events described, I relied on my memory as well as extensive research, which included review of court records, legal depositions, social service files, other government records, newspaper accounts, and photographs. I also conducted personal interviews and traveled to former foster homes and other places I lived. (p. 298)

Even so Rhodes-Courter did alter some of the detail. She changes names, especially of minors, and some of the characters are composites.

For Rhodes-Courter the story takes on more significance than simply the narrative of one person. She asserts that she wrote the story because so many foster children's voices are suppressed or ignored. "I represent thousands, probably tens of thousands of children who have been lost in the system. We are a chorus of voices that need to be heard" (p. 298). So although an effort is made to get the detail correct, the themes are equally important.

For other authors the reality of their past carries less import than the storylines. In his epilogue to *King of the Mild Frontier,* Chris Crutcher responds to his editor's suggestion that something is missing from his autobiography by writing, "Hey nobody told me an autobiography had to contain the truth. Jeez" (p. 249). It is not so much that he has made up stories about himself but rather that he chooses specific details that will tell a good story.

One thing that autobiographies accomplish better than most other genres is expressing the authentic voices and worldviews of cultural insiders. *The Other Side of the Sky* by Farah Ahmedi and *A Long Way Gone* by Ishmael Beah open up our understandings of other ways of life and inspiring stories of survival. *Breaking Through* by Francisco Jimenez is the story of a migrant worker struggling for education in the 1960s in southern California. It is also a beautiful description of love and a family's desire to stay together.

The fact that these things happened to a real person who allows others to live vicariously though the telling of experiences is one of the most significant aspects of autobiography. *The Burn Journals* by Brent Runyon is

Student working on a photobiography.
Photo by Jennifer Seay.

written by a young man who tried to commit suicide at age 14. The teen angst, the guilt he feels, and the desolation are so real—as is the fact that looking back he cannot remember why he did it in the first place. *No Pretty Pictures* by Anita Lobel recounts events in Poland during the Nazi occupation, including the author's internment and eventual escape from the concentration camps. The intensity of the emotions are strong in any story about the Holocaust, but for kids who have grown up with Lobel's picture books, the immediacy of her experiences really hits home.

Letters, memoirs, and diary entries are sometimes edited together with biographical information, framing the subject's own words with contextual and historical information. Nelly Toll was 6 years old when the Nazis came to Poland. Within 2 years she was alone and scared until she was taken in and hidden by a Gentile couple. For over a year she hid away, writing in her diary and painting pictures of happy families and open skies. Her story is recounted in *Behind the Secret Window*.

These memoirs can incorporate all types of text, including poetry, for example in *At the End of Words: A Daughter's Memoir* by Miriam Stone, a collection of poetic reflections from a teenager whose mother is dying of cancer made up of journal entries and poems reflecting both love, grief, and self-discovery. *Farewell to Manzanar* by Jeanne Wakatsuki Houston and James Houston tells the story of Jeanne's time in the internment camp for Japanese Americans during World War II. *Please Don't Kill the Freshman* by Zoe Trope was written by an actual teen during her freshman year of college.

Technology Links

"The Unwritten"—Saving Your Photo Story

Most people have old family photos that have been saved but that they know hardly anything about. These photos might serve as windows on the stories that are a family's personal history. The narratives that surround those stories could tell us so much about who we are and where we have been. The thinkquest website The Unwritten was created to help people capture their own photo stories.

The Unwritten was created by three young women ages 12, 14, and 16 who live in Alaska, Minnesota, and Arizona. Although they are all related, the two younger teens have never even met their older cousin except through the Internet. The website they have created will show teens how to research, write, and save their own photo stories with captions, poems, short stories, or even as a complete biography. In the process young adults might discover personal connections to world history.

http://library.thinkquest.org/C001313

Some Other Good Life Stories
- *Bad Boy* by Walter Dean Myers. Myers writes about growing up in Harlem in the 1950s.
- *Bull's Eye: A Photobiography of Annie Oakley* by Sue Macy. Fast action-packed read enhanced with archival photographs and quotes.
- *Carver: A Life in Poems* by Marilyn Nelson. Beautiful use of poetry to recount George Washington Carver's life.

- *Elizabeth Cady Stanton: The Right Is Ours* by Harriet Sigerman. Includes a chronology, further reading, a list of museums and other historic sites, and biographies of other women's rights leaders.
- *Geeks* by Jon Katz. Jesse and Eric, two 19-year-old geeks, take a ride on the Internet to escape from Caldwell, Idaho.
- *Heroine of the Titanic: The Real Unsinkable Molly Brown* by Elaine Landau. Compares legendary and factual accounts of this survivor's life.
- *Ida B. Wells: Mother of the Civil Rights Movement* by Dennis Brindell Fradin and Judith Bloom Fradin. Explores Wells's life and her impact on civil rights.
- *John Steinbeck* by Catherine Reef. Great introduction to Steinbeck with over 70 supplementary black-and-white photos.
- *King of the Mild Frontier* by Chris Crutcher. Very cool autobiographical stories about the childhood of this author of young adult fiction.
- *The Longitude Prize* by Joan Dash; illus. by Dusan Petricic. The dramatic story of John Harrison, a clockmaker, who competed against the likes of Isaac Newton to develop a device for measuring longitude in the 18th century. The social context and the scientific concepts are explained in ways that make them interesting and accessible.
- *Paul Laurence Dunbar: Portrait of a Poet* by Catherine Reef. Good introduction to the poet's life. Shows his influence on American poetry and culture.
- *Pick and Shovel Poet: The Journeys of Pascal D'Angelo* by Jim Murphy. Beautifully written biography of the poet who immigrated from Italy in 1910. Explores the harsh treatment of Italians in the New World and the experiences that influenced D'Angelo's poetry. Illustrated with archival photographs.
- *Rescued Images: Memories of a Childhood in Hiding* by Ruth Jacobsen. Story of a family during the Holocaust focused on the visuals of the author's collage work.
- *Shakespeare: His Work and His World* by Michael Rosen; illus. by Robert Ingpen. An inviting look at the Bard, his life, his plays, and his time period.
- *Shipwrecked! The True Adventures of a Japanese Boy* by Rhoda Blumberg. Adventure of the first recorded Japanese person to visit the United States.
- *Sitting Bull and His World* by Albert Marrin. A comprehensive look at the Lakota Sioux leader's life and the culture of his people.
- *Vincent Van Gogh: Portrait of an Artist* by Jan Greenberg and Sandra Jordan. Compelling story of the artist with detailed research.
- *Walt Whitman* by Catherine Reef. Great use of his poetry to help tell his life story, supplemented by photos.

In the Field: *Erin Gruwell on the Freedom Writers*

Erin Gruwell is the author of The Freedom Writers Diary, *a compilation of her own diary during her first year teaching intertwined with the diary entries of students from her English class at Woodrow Wilson High School. After noting the disinterest many of her students*

Photo courtesy of Erin Gruwell.

had with the literature they were reading in school and hearing about their life experiences, Gruwell made a decisive change in how she taught, a change that involved helping her students connect with meaningful life stories—a change that really impacted their education and their lives. For more information visit http://gruwellproject.org.

ON WHY SHE STARTED INCORPORATING LIFE STORIES INTO WHAT SHE WAS DOING IN THE CLASSROOM

Actually two statements by two different students triggered me. One was "I feel like I live in an undeclared war." And another statement was "I've been to more funerals than birthday parties." And it just triggered an intuitive thought that when a student is faced with violence and they're back up against the wall they either fight or flight. And in that time my students were experiencing one of the most violent episodes in an urban area; there had been about 125 murders the summer before their freshman year in high school. And my feel was that these students were always picking up their fists, or a gun, or a spray can as a way of fighting back. And I wanted to find books and stories written by real students who had lived in wartime and really might have gone to more funerals than birthdays, and instead of fighting back with weapons, they fought back with words. They picked up a pen in an attic like Anne Frank or in a basement like Zlata F.

So I decided initially to use those two books. The school did not have the copies of them nor did we have the budget to get them. So I had to get the money on my own and I ended up buying the books for the students. I thought what a great way to use those life stories to teach the students about the similarities to the situations they were going through: the pain, being disenfranchised, and stereotyped, but simultaneously being able to realize that when you chronicle what you see with words, you have a way of stopping rather than perpetuating the violence.

ON WHY HER STUDENTS WERE IMPACTED SO MUCH BY THE LIFE STORIES THEY READ

I think because we tried to bring the stories to life. I always had this intuitive fear that I was competing against Game Boy, PS3, MP3, and TV culture, and so for me I think it was really important to make these stories useful and palpable. I went out of my way to bring in video clips and photographs and actual survivors and I took them on trips to museums. Anything that would play on modalities that would make the black-and-white words on the page come to life.

ON HOW THIS LED TO STUDENTS DOING THEIR OWN WRITING

One of our first projects was to actually write letters to the woman who helped Anne Frank. Writing a standard five-paragraph essay can seem pretty boring to kids, but in these letters they were making these incredible comparisons between their lives and Zlata's life and Nikki's life. So these letters were gritty and very profound and they started seeing the power of storytelling, and it seemed relevant, it made more sense because they had a goal to convey to Nikki as to why these books had such a powerful impact on them.

ON HOW THIS PROCESS HAS IMPACTED HER STUDENTS

For a few of them it was really giving a voice to the voiceless. Through writing it became an unbelievably cathartic moment for them. To be able to put all of their fears and aspirations and tragedies and triumphs onto the page. And it started becoming second nature to them. So by writing they became better speakers, and they became better critical thinkers.

There was a beauty of not being constrained by a test, or a number 2 pencil, or a scantron. I think there was this liberation with writing, also the ability to see the similarities with other people, other cultures, other economic groups. Once the words were on the page (we initially wrote anonymously) there was an unbelievable metamorphosis where people were saying, "That could have been my story, even though I didn't write it, that could have been my story." With a lot of illumination along the lines of "Oh my God, someone else in this group has been through what I went through."

ON ADVICE FOR USING LIFE STORIES WITH TEENS

I would say the most powerful thing for me was to really know about where your students come from and to incorporate that into where you want them to go. I use a three-pronged approach: engaging them based on who they are and where they come from, enlightening them with the stories and testimonials of other kids, and encouraging them to take the lessons of the past, incorporate these with academia to empower them to write their own stories. If they can't change the beginning of their stories, they at least have the ability to rewrite the ending of their own story

LITERARY THEORY

From Literary History and Biographical Criticism to New Historicism

The theory and practice of literary history has been a significant part of criticism over the years. One trend in literary history looked at individual works as classic works of genius. Another trend, historicism, tended to explore literary history as part of the larger cultural, political, and social history. Both historicism and biographical criticism are commonsense approaches that have sought to understand literature as a reflection of the author's life and times. Of course, sociocultural events and personal experiences will shape any work of literature to a certain context. Though far from popular in the works of cutting-edge theorists, these are likely among the first forms of criticism young adults become familiar with.

In the 1980s a "New Historicism" gained some prominence. Building off of the writings of Foucault, this was a non-truth-oriented historicism. The general assumptions of the new historicist include the following:

- History is always textualized, always narrated. We do not see the real event; we are privy to a retelling of a past event.
- Historical periods are not unified; there are numerous conceptions of the present, not just one cultural understanding
- The historian cannot transcend their own historical situation.
- Writing literature about the past involves retelling stories, and all of these retold stories come together as intertexts for a new history.

So the literary theorist might explore how political, cultural, and popular discourses are manifest in a particular book. Key to this discourse would be an examination of how meanings and understandings contemporary to the literary work in question have influenced the text. The critic might explore the social milieu of the author but also all of the intertextual relations that influenced the narrative and the understandings of the world that are being retold.

A good example of this can be found in a comparison between two novels of enslavement: *Nightjohn* by Gary Paulsen and *The Captive* by Joyce Hansen. The question might be asked, how does the author achieve historical accuracy about a period they cannot know firsthand?

Joyce Hansen did most of her research using written slave narratives—Frederick Douglas's narrative, for example. The story that had the strongest impact on her writing was *The Interesting Narrative of Olaudah Equiano* or *Gustavas Vassa the African Written by Himself*. The slave narratives she drew on were part of a literary tradition that built on the picaresque novel in the context of being published by abolitionists for the purpose of showing in large part that those enslaved were human. So standard English was used to emphasize the slave's intellect. Written slave narratives were not just a record of what it was like to be enslaved, they were also a literary genre that built on other books. Also there were a number of literary motifs: the trickster character, learning to read and write, escaping to the North. Interestingly, Hansen's book reflects not just the history from these slave narratives but also the stylistic elements.

Gary Paulsen for *Nightjohn* on the other hand had used as his primary source the oral slave narratives collected by the Works Progress Administration during the Depression. Under the WPA people were hired to collect the stories of those who had lived under slavery. Seventeen volumes of these narratives exist in the Library of Congress. The style, the dialect, and even the types of details emphasized in the oral narratives are quite different from those in the written slave narratives. The oral narratives emphasize daily activities, they are often in strong dialect, and there are folkloric and storytelling elements mixed in. These differences are reflected in how history is retold in *Nightjohn* and *The Captive*.

The new historicist would likely go a step beyond looking at how the primary source intertexts relate to these novels. They would also be interested in how the narrative's social and historical context impacts the retelling. For example, in *The Captive* the friendship between the main character and an indentured servant becomes a key part of the story. In a 19th-century slave narrative this friendship might have developed as a way for the main character to learn to write (usually with some trickery involved), but it would likely have become problematic at some point in the storyline. So one question might center on Hansen's contemporary views about race relations and how this issue should be presented to young readers.

For Further Reading

To begin an investigation into New Historicism as it applies to a young adult literature you might commence with the following readings:

Barnhouse, Rebecca. *Recasting the Past: The Middle Ages in Young Adult Literature.* Boynton/Cook, 2000.

Cox, J. N., and L. J. Reynolds (eds.). *New Historical Literary Study: Essays on Reproducing Texts, Representing History.* Princeton University Press, 1993.

Culver, Stuart. "Growing Up in Oz." *American Literary History, 4*(4), Winter 1999, 607–628.

Culver, Stuart. "What Manikins Want: *The Wonderful Wizard of Oz* and the Art of Decorating Dry Goods Windows." *Representations, 21,* Winter 1988, 97–116.

McGillis, Roderick. "The Opportunity to Choose a Past: Remembering History." *Children's Literature Association Quarterly, 25*(1), Spring 2000, 49–55.

Veeser, H. Aram (ed.). *The New Historicism.* Routledge, 1989.

Watkins, Tony. "The Setting of Children's Literature: History and Culture." In Peter Hunt (ed.), *Understanding Children's Literature.* Routledge, 2005.

Westbrook, D. David. "Readers of Oz: Young and Old, Old and New Historicist." *Children's Literature Association Quarterly, 21*(3), Fall 1996, 111–119.

Zornado, Joseph. "A Poetics of History: Karen Cushman's Medieval World." *Lion and the Unicorn, 21*(2), April 1997, 251–266.

8
Poetry

Poetry Anthology Text Set

19 Varieties of Gazelle: Poems of the Middle East by Naomi Shihab Nye

Behind the Wheel: Poems about Driving by Janet Wong

Black Cat Bone by J. Patrick Lewis

Blue Lipstick by John Grandits

Cool Salsa: Bilingual Poems on Growing Up Latino in the United States ed. Lori Carlson

A Fire in My Hands by Gary Soto

Jazz by Walter Dean Myers; illus. by Christopher Myers

Keeping the Night Watch by Hope Anita Smith

Movin': Teen Poets Take Voice ed. Dave Johnson

Seeing the Blue Between ed. Paul Janeczko

Slow Dance Heart Break Blues by Arnold Adoff

Waiting to Waltz by Cynthia Rylant

What Have You Lost? by Naomi Shihab Nye

You Are Here, This Is Now ed. by David Levithan

You Hear Me? Poems and Writing by Teenage Boys ed. Betsy Franco

Poetic Novel Text Set

Becoming Billie Holiday by Carole Weatherford

Bronx Masquerade by Nikki Grimes

Carver: A Life in Poems by Marilyn Nelson

CrashBoomLove: A Novel in Verse by Juan F. Herrera

Girl Coming In for a Landing by April H. Wayland

Jinx by Margaret Wild

Keesha's House by Helen Frost

Locomotion by Jacqueline Woodson

Love That Dog by Sharon Creech

343

Names Will Never Hurt Me by Jaime Adoff

Shakespeare Bats Cleanup by Ron Koertge

Sister Slam by Linda Oatman High

Splintering by Elreann Corrigan

The Surrender Tree by Margarita Engle

What My Mother Doesn't Know by Sonya Sones

Worlds Afire by Paul Janeczko

Your Own Sylvia by Stephanie Hemphill

Is There Such a Thing as Young Adult Poetry?

Poetry can be an exciting and powerful form of expression for young adults. Poetic text can serve as an invitation to celebrate language, enhancing and enriching our appreciation for the power of words to capture the essence of things. It is also an able conveyer of emotions—extending and intensifying everyday experiences. As such, poetry can touch our hearts, heighten our awareness, or simply fill us with delight. Poetry is also significant for the classroom, as it by its very nature invites responses from the reader/listener.

Poetry for younger children is sometimes referred to simply as verse because of its use of rhyme, repetition, and humor is seen as setting it apart from real "Poetry." At the same time, there is an underlying assumption that good poetry is good poetry regardless of audience, resulting in a lack of scholarly discussion of poetry specifically for young readers (Nodelman and Reimer, 2002). This absence of scholarly discussion might lead one to think that poems for young adults are virtually nonexistent, though as shall be demonstrated in this chapter, there is a wide array of high-quality poetry available that is marketed for and appeals to YA audiences.

As with other literature for young adults, some great crossovers from children's literature will appeal to teens. There are also certainly many poems typically thought of as adult poetry that have become staples in school (and some that have become sought out by teens). More than a few teens have responded on a personal level to Emily Dickinson's "I'm Nobody, Who Are You" despite the 150 years that have passed since it was written.

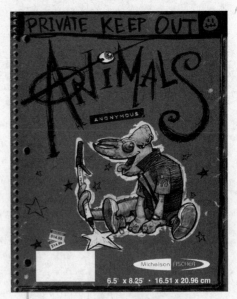

Animals Anonymous (2008) merges teen personas with animal species in irreverent poems and illustrations that read like doodlings in a notebook. Reprinted by permission of Simon and Schuster.

I'm nobody! Who are you?
Are you nobody, too?
Then there's a pair of us—Don't tell!
They'd banish us, you know.

How dreary to be Somebody!
How public like a frog
To tell your name the livelong June
To an admiring bog!

1861 Project Gutenberg Ebook Poems.
Three Series Complete, 2004; Ebook 12242

It's not unheard of to find a young reader enthralled by Arthur Rimbaud, the Beat poets, Native American poet/musician John Trudell, or any of a number of poets whose works were not published specifically with YA audiences in mind. Some excellent collections of poetry originally written for a general (adult) audience, but that have special appeal for YA, have been republished with a young audience in mind. Some of these anthologies focus on a specific poet (*Voyages: Poems by Walt Whitman* ed. Lee Bennett Hopkins), others provide an array of poems (*Shimmy Shimmy Shimmy Like My Sister Kate: Looking at the Harlem Renaissance through Poems* ed. Nikki Giovanni), and others intermingle poems for young readers with those written for a general audience (*Cool Salsa: Bilingual Poems on Growing Up Latino in the United States* ed. Lori Carlson).

In the years since *Joyful Noise* (Fleischman) won the Newbery in 1989, followed by *Out of the Dust* (Hesse), a novel in free verse, receiving the award in 1998, and as young adults actively participate in open mic nights and poetry slams, YA poetry has become harder for critics to ignore. In 2003, YALSA held its annual preconference workshop on "Slam! Poetry," the competitive art of performance poetry, and October of the same year was declared Slam Poetry month. For the first time, publishers have actively begun seeking out fresh teen-oriented poetry. Edgier picture book poems, collections focused on themes relevant to young adults, and poetic novels with teen protagonists are now all the rage.

> **To Consider**
>
> Although young adults who will admit to liking poetry are few and far between in some schools, numerous young adults will get excited about looking at and even writing song lyrics. How might this excitement be exploited in the teaching of poetry?

Author Spotlight

Photo by Ha Lam, courtesy of Naomi Shihab Nye.

Naomi Shihab Nye

Naomi Shihab Nye was born in St. Louis, Missouri, in 1952. She received her B.A. from Trinity University in San Antonio, Texas. She has authored poetry and prose for children, young adults, and adults. She has also edited some of the most critically acclaimed anthologies of poetry for the YA crowd. Today she resides with her family in San Antonio, Texas. Visit her website at www.poets.org/poet.php/prmPID/174.

SELECTED BIBLIOGRAPHY

19 Varieties of Gazelle: Poems of the Middle East (Greenwillow Books, 2002)

A Maze Me (HarperTeen, 2005)

The Flag of Childhood: Poems from the Middle East (Greenwillow, 1999)

Habibi (Simon & Schuster, 1997)

I Feel a Little Jumpy around You with Paul Janeczko (Simon & Schuster, 1996)

This Same Sky: A Collection of Poems from around the World (Macmillan, 1992)

What Have You Lost? (Greenwillow, 1999)

ON THE AUDIENCE SHE WRITES FOR

I write with a friendly audience in mind. No particular age, no particular ethnicity or location. I try to imagine I am speaking to interested ears.

They have time for whatever I am saying. They are not rushing away. The other day I visited with a bunch of gregarious seventh graders who had read *Habibi* and asked me the most intelligent questions about it—staring into their caring, lively faces, I thought, you are the ones I have been speaking to all along. You are my people!

ON THE INSPIRATION FOR HER WORKS

From everywhere around me, inside me, from the people I meet, from memory and hope, from trouble, from the frustration that comes on a daily basis, considering what the world is and what it could be.

ON THE EXTENT TO WHICH HER OWN LIFE STORY APPEARS IN HER WORKS

Alas, very much. But it is also a changed, selected story that I am always working with, not just a recounting of actual fact.

ON WHAT SHE ENJOYED READING AS A TEENAGER

Henry David Thoreau! I got goosebumps yesterday when my son's tenth-grade English teacher said they would be reading Thoreau next. And Emerson of course. All the transcendentalists. Also and especially Jack Kerouac. William Stafford. I always enjoyed contemporary poetry of all kinds, 20th-century poetry. *Catcher in the Rye* did not do as much for me as for everyone else, but I liked *Franny and Zooey* a lot. I read constantly. I spent my high school lunch breaks in the library, browsing.

ON WHAT SHE ENJOYS READING CURRENTLY

Again, nonstop, I am reading in many genres, poetry, short stories, biography, creative nonfiction, novels. The one thing I never read was fantasy. No interest at all. Tolkien for example? No way. Left me cold. If you paid me one million dollars I could probably not get through a science fiction book. Also, crime novels, lawyer books—no way. Everything else though! I also end up reading many unpublished books because generous writers send them to me. I am currently reading Amy Wilentz's *Martyr's Crossing* about the Middle East, Kim Stafford's *Early Morning* memoir about his father, William Stafford, and an unpublished, terrific novel about China by Susie Van de Ven, basketball player Steve Kerr's sister! Also *West Wind* by poet Mary Oliver. I read in each of these every day. I have always read this way.

ON WHAT MIGHT HELP YOUNG ADULTS DEVELOP AS POETS

Believe in yourselves. Write daily, even if it is only for 7 minutes. Read constantly. Share your work.

ON THE IDEA THAT TEENS ONLY READ POETRY UNDER DURESS

Teens are always under duress, so maybe. No, truthfully, I don't think it is true. I meet many teens who carry poetry books with them everywhere, like wallets.

ON THE PROCESS OF SELECTING POEMS TO BE INCLUDED IN HER ANTHOLOGIES

It is instinct, organic, elemental instinct that guides me in selection of the poems. I have a very clear memory of what it was like being a teenager. I am the mother of a teenager. Teenagers hang out at our house all the time. It is a great and difficult age. I admire them. So I try to be inside their eyes when I am reading poems and think, is this interesting to me? Would I care about this? Is the language accessible and engaging? Can I *see* what is happening here?

Many teenagers are more fond of abstract thought than I was at that age or am now. I sometimes feel the poems I select want to be a tangible grounding device.

ON MIDDLE EASTERN THEMES AND THE 9/11 BACKLASH

Arab Americans will work overtime for the rest of our lives, I guess. We have a lot to balance.

ON THE ROLE THAT LITERATURE MIGHT PLAY IN CREATING EMPATHY, UNDERSTANDING, AND EVEN RESPECT ACROSS BOUNDARIES SUCH AS CULTURE, CLASS, AND RELIGION

The most important role possible! I place a huge faith in it. How may we ever come to know one another and care about one another? When young readers tell me that they care about Liyana and her brother and Omer in *Habibi,* I think, this is my politics. They will never read headlines about the Middle East in quite the same way.

Poetry and the Young Adult Reader

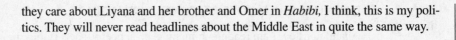

It is often suggested that young children tend to be very receptive to poetry, but something happens around the time they become young adults that causes them to quit reading the genre (Benton, 1999; Wade and Sideway, 1990). Although more teenagers than one might imagine write and read poetry outside of school, many do seem to quit reading poetry in public. I remind myself of this every semester when I ask students in my college courses how many have read a poem for pleasure in the past year and only one or two hands go up. Peter Benton (1999) has described what happens to older students, especially boys, as "a suddenly acquired built-in resistance to the possibility of enjoying poetry" (p. 522).

In the introduction to *A Fury of Motion: Poems for Boys* (Ghigna, 2003), X. J. Kennedy describes how poetry "suddenly became awful" for him when he reached sixth grade:

> We had to read a long, long poem by Henry Wadsworth Longfellow about some lady named Evangeline who got lost in the woods, or something. I couldn't get interested. Every night, when I had to read a few pages of it, I felt like somebody eating his way through a haystack. . . . I didn't much like any of the other poems the teacher liked, either. She seemed to believe that all the poets worth reading had died fifty or more years ago. (p. ix)

Certainly one of the reasons young adults quit reading poetry is because many poems they read in class were written for an audience who were adults long before the young adults were even born. The poems Kennedy introduces are written for, marketed for, and appeal to many young readers. Take, for example, "Tackle":

Tackle

by Charles Ghigna

A grizzly bear in shoulder pads,
He growls at the line of scrimmage,
Snarls into the face of the offense,
And glares into the eyes
Of the opposing quarterback.

Hike!
And he explodes
Over the line,
Bursts through
The whirling blitz
Of cracking helmets,
His legs churning forward
In a fury of motion,
His arms flailing
Through the backfield
For anything that moves.

Used by permission of Charles Ghigna. Boyds Mills Press, 2003.

The theme, the imagery, and the style of this poem will all find a ready young adult audience. Though not all teens will be interested in the same poem, "Tackle" will certainly strike a chord with a segment of the YA crowd.

As becomes quite clear in most young adult literature classes, a majority of college students who plan on becoming English teachers do not enjoy reading poetry on their own time! This is nothing new, but it is depressing food for thought to those of us who see poetry as an important part of our literary universe. Teachers who do not especially like poetry generally either do not teach it very well or use as little poetry as possible (Andrews, 1991; Heard, 1999; Lipsett, 2001).

An additional problem, Perry Nodelman suggests, is that we do not teach young people to read poetry. Children in elementary school listen to and enjoy poetry because it is perceived as personal, and finding pleasure in reading is understood as the single most important benefit of poetry. However, many teachers in elementary school never discuss the significance of sounds, imagery, or possible interpretations. Then in high school all of a sudden students are told to search for the hidden meaning of the poem, or to analyze the rhyme scheme. Both of these approaches to poetry lack perspective. Discussing the poetic craft can add pleasure to the reading and it is certainly necessary if readers are going to think critically or if they are going to write their own poetry. At the same time, poems are not necessarily puzzles to be solved and there is certainly no one correct interpretation to a poem. Poetry evokes images and elicits deep personal responses, but it also "keeps alive the instinct for linguistic play" (McGillis, 1996, p. 202). The orality of poetry and the "verbal pyrotechnics" are often left unexplored because we read them silently or they are read aloud by students encountering the poem for the first time. Without reflection and practice the intricacies of audience, intonation, and rhythm are lost.

This brings us to the question of what it is that makes a poem a poem. Rhyme and in particular ending rhyme is the most common response to this question from students in elementary school through college. However, most of them do know, especially when they start thinking of actual examples, that rhyme is just a part of the equation and in some poems not a significant factor at all. So what are the elements that differentiate poetry from prose?

Elements of Poetry

If there is one element that best distinguishes poetry from prose it might well be the musicality of the language used. Perhaps the most essential component of this musicality is rhythm. It has been suggested that rhythm is at the foundation of all biological pleasure (Havelock, 1988). Most poetry will exhibit some rhythmic quality explicitly or implicitly, what Jane Hirschfield has referred to as the "foundational heartbeat" of the poem (1997). Some of these rhythms are consciously crafted by the poet using the metered rhythm of a poetic form or the beat of a musical tradition.

Jaime Adoff deftly captures the rhythms of different musical forms in his anthology, *The Song Shoots Out of My Mouth*. In this excerpt from "Flames shoot," for example, you can feel the rhythm of the congas in the tempo and even in the spacing on the page:

Otra vez:
Flames shoot out of taped fingertips,
Hard hands hit tougher skin.
Worn from years of getting beats fly through the air,
beats
       fly
              through the air
beats
       fly
            through
                   the
                      air

Similarly, Walter Dean Myers taps into the blues tradition in his collection *Blues Journey.* The call and response, the repetition, and the beat all reflect a blues rhythm. In other poems there may be no identifiable melody, but the natural rhythms of oral language itself are captured. Although that might sound like poetic fluff, recent ideas from theoretical physics refer to "string" theory, a concept involving the rhythmic pulse found between the smallest particles of matter that are understood to hold everything in the universe together!

Of course, when young readers think of poetry, one of the first ideas that comes to mind is rhyme. A quick look at the poetry being written for young adults will show that rhyme when it appears at all is used in more complicated ways than simple end rhymes. Often rhyme is one part of the word play that makes a poem appealing. Other ways of playing with words and sounds include alliteration (the repetition of consonants), assonance (the repetition of vowel sounds), and repetition of words and phrases, all of which might be used in poetry to enhance both pleasure and meaning.

B-Ball Be

by Charles R. Smith, Jr.

B-ball be
Aquaboogie dunks
Filled with old-school funk
Rocking rims with rage
While mouths talk junk.

B-ball be
A microphone for mouths
Too timid to speak
But bounce their words
Loud on concrete.

Note. For the full poem visit www.charlesrsmithjr.com/activities-poems.htm where you can listen to and read the poem in its entirety. Reprinted by permission of Charles R. Smith, Jr.

Many readers and listeners of all ages will enjoy this poem as much for word play as for the narrative images it calls forth. Initially readers might not be able to say exactly what about the poem's sounds make it pleasurable. There is a lot of word play going on: end

To Consider
At what point does discussing how a poem works kill the pleasure of reading the poem for you as a reader? Is it because of discussion or because of how the discussion is framed?

rhymes (*dunks, funk, junk*), assonance (*mouth, bounce, loud*), and alliteration (*rocking, rims, rage*). The poem could certainly be read simply for pleasure, but this is a good example of a poem where looking at sounds and rhymes might actually add to the pleasure. Sounds are significant here, like the images conveyed; the very beat of the poem reflects the dribbling of a basketball on a court.

Among the many sound elements that might be discussed, one could look at the first stanza quoted and how various sound relations are interwoven. In addition to the abbcb end rhyme, there is an incredible amount of assonance and alliteration creating a tapestry of sound, or as Smith refers to it, "a drum solo dribble that grooves futuristic." The court sounds become the music, the beat, the words that do not need to be spoken. This is of course only part of the alliterative play that takes place, but the interlacing of sounds is definitely part of the reason why many readers find the poem so pleasurable.

A teacher walks a fine line with this type of analysis. Picking apart a poem is one of the factors that so many teen readers assert has killed the pleasure of poetry for them, but at the same time, being able to notice and talk about what happens with words and sounds in a poem that has given you pleasure can add to the enjoyment. The student who wants to write poetry of this sort would certainly benefit from exploring what it is that makes a particular poem so effective.

Poetry often utilizes imagery, similes, metaphors, and figurative language, methods by which words or phrases, by virtue of association, signify something else. Of course not all readers will discover the same meanings in the words. The imagery in Langston Hughes's "Harlem" is rather straightforward, one might assume, yet readings of the poem can differ significantly.

Many students understand the poem as referring to a deferred dream, causing frustration or anger. One eleventh grader read the imagery of the poem quite specifically—"Yeah, it's about how being denied his dream might ruin him or even lead him to be a junkie, an Uncle Tom, a drop-out, or a gangbanger." A teacher listening suggested *revolutionary* rather than *gangbanger,* but the student was adamant, and they discussed this for a few minutes until the student said something extraordinary: "When people without dreams explode, they kill their own!" Imagery is understood within a context; the student's reading of "Harlem" may not have been the same as that of Hughes or the teacher, but it was a perfectly valid and insightful reading of the imagery.

The shape and design of a poem, the positioning of words on the page, can impact the reading of and the meanings evoked. Charles Smith in *Rimshots* adds to the effect in "School's Out" by having the poem itself fake to the left and then spin out to the right, around the defender and into the hoop. Arnold Adoff is a poet who has consistently used shape to enhance his poetry, often in very subtle ways.

At This Age,
This Time
of Young Age
I
walk
down
the
up escalator
backwards

                          into
               the west
                          coast
               sunrise
               at evening,
               forward into
               the east
                          coast
               sunset
               at
               morning,
                          rocks
               in my back
                          pack.

"At This Age" by Arnold Adoff, from *Slow Dance Heart Break Blues* (Lothrop, Lee & Shepard Books)

The layout on the page in this instance subtly affects the reading of the poem. Other writers utilize shape in particular ways to recreate or add to the meaning of the images evoked in the poem. John Grandits in the collection *Blue Lipstick* offers an assortment of concrete poems such as "The Secret," "Pep Rally," and "Blue Lipstick," in which the imagery conveyed by the formatting of the words on the page becomes an important poetic element that adds to the meaning.

The concrete poetry in *Blue Lipstick* (2007) appeals most specifically to teen readers. Cover from *Blue Lipstick: Concrete Poems* by John Grandits. Copyright © 2007 by John Grandits. Reprinted by permission of Clarion Books, an imprint of Houghton Mifflin Harcourt Publishing Company. All rights reserved.

Throughout history it has been asserted about poetry both that it allows the poet a forum for "the spontaneous overflow of powerful feelings" (Wordsworth) and that it amplifies the reader's emotions—"If I feel physically as if the top of my head were taken off, I know that is poetry" (Emily Dickinson). Either way, it is often the case that poems contain a strong emotional force. Liz Rosenberg suggests that the emotional force of poetry is something particularly suited for young adults—that "poetry and adolescence make a perfect pair" precisely because of the intensity involved (Rosenberg, 1998, p. xii).

Take for example teenager Amy Peltz's poem from the collection *Movin': Teen Poets Take Voice.*

At the Sidewalk Café,
Wednesday Evening, 10:00 P.M.

Launching into notes
her guitar ripping
as if her fingers were teeth
my friend is ten times life size
and speaking in tongues.
Sizzling like hot grease her music spits and
hits its mark.

I imagine everyone is stopped,
paused at their wobbly tables
looking up at her and amazed . . .
But they're not and I'd like to shut them all up:

extinguish their cigarettes,
make the tall guy in front of me scrunch down,
if only I could breathe through the smoke
and see past the spotlight, exploding in the dark.

A teen who can relate to that sense of frustration and anger will pick up on the emotions and connect in many ways to the surrounding stories without the pages of prose narrative that might have led into similar connections.

The emotions conveyed are rather straightforward, though the imagery is intense. In contrast the emotional force of Pat Mora's "Fences" is like an undercurrent that sneaks up on you at the end of the poem, not just in the mother's eruption but also in the reader's potential response.

Fences

Mouths full of laughter
the *turistas* come to the tall hotel
with suitcases full of dollars

Every morning my brother makes
the cool beach sand new for them
with a wooden board he smooths
away all footprints

I peak through the cactus fence
And watch the women rub oil
Sweeter than honey into their arms and legs
While their children jump waves
Or sip drinks from long straws
Coconut white, mango yellow

Once my little sister
Ran barefoot across the hot sand
For a taste

My mother roared like the ocean,
"No. No. It's their beach.
It's their beach."

The readers' response might reflect the mother's sentiments, but they are more likely to react against the assumption that it is "their beach." So the emotional force is not really expressed in the words so much as evoked through the poetry. Of course, young readers without particular background knowledge and experiences may not interpret the poem in this way.

Young adults can look at word play and discover that all sorts of things are occurring—some probably unconsciously on the author's part. If the teacher looks in the instructor's manual to see whether students are correctly analyzing the poem's structure to discover the "true meanings," this can quickly kill the pleasurable experience of the poem. But if you say, "Hey look at this, does this make the poem work better for you as a reader/listener? What else can we discover?" then students might get excited about reading and discussing the work.

Author Spotlight

Photo courtesy of Arnold Adoff.

Arnold Adoff

Arnold Adoff was born in the East Bronx, New York City. It was while working as a teacher in Harlem in the 1960s that Adoff discovered the need for an anthology of poetry focused on African American authors, and this was the impetus for *I Am the Darker Brother* (1968, revised 1997). He has since authored and anthologized over 30 books for young people. He is well known for his use of shaped speech stylings in his poetry. In 1988 he was the recipient of the NCTE Award for Excellence in Poetry for Children. He has received numerous other distinctions and awards, including an American Library Association Best Book for Young Adults citation for *Slow Dance Heart Break Blues*. Visit his website at www.arnoldadoff.com.

SELECTED BIBLIOGRAPHY
All the Colors of the Race (William Morrow, 1982)
The Basket Counts (Simon & Schuster, 2000)
Chocolate Dreams (Lothrop, Lee, and Shepard, 1989)
I Am the Darker Brother (Collier, 1968)
Love Letters illus. by Lisa Desimini (Blue Sky Press, 1997)
OUTside/Inside Poems (Harcourt Brace, 1981)
Slow Dance Heart Break Blues (Lothrop, Lee, and Shepard, 1995)

ON CHANGES IN YOUNG ADULT POETRY OVER THE YEARS

Young adult poetry is still a rare thing to see published. When I did *Slow Dance Heart Break Blues,* which I'm very proud of, in 95, I did research and I saw very few titles of young adult poetry, and I myself had written mostly poetry for younger children. I think in the last 5 or 6 years I can safely say in an unscientific way that young adult poetry is changing and is catching up with the multiplicity of issues that young people are dealing with. Maybe it's the post-Columbine effect, I don't know. But you have books that deal with girls with anorexia, with girls scarring themselves, mutilation, with anger, with shootings, with whatever, you name it. To a large degree, I think, some of the black writers who write for older audiences have opened things up just as African American culture has opened up a lot of pop culture in terms of music, fashion.

Our son Jaime had a rock band for 8 or 9 years, a singer/songwriter, and now he's writing for children, young adults. And his first book is called *The Song Shoots Out of My Mouth,* and it's a selection of poems about different kinds of music, and it's YA poetry. They classify it as 12 and up. Several other projects of his have started out as poetry he is now turning into novels, and immediately they get gobbled up and signed up even though the process is going to take another year or longer. So that's the other trend.

You can make a list of 30 or more "novels" that are interconnected poems, the narrative comes out of verse, poetry, diaries, journals, so the innovative is becoming a norm. I myself have a couple young adult books coming out in the next couple of years and they're young adult poetry, and I have to say that one of them deals with blues and jazz. I've been promised Gregory Kristie, who is an incredible new black illustrator, but also a 96-page book, and that's unheard of for a collection of poetry for young people, particularly for teenagers.

ON THE PERCEPTION THAT YOUNG ADULTS SHY AWAY FROM POETRY

No, absolutely not. They all "read" poetry, even if that just means listening to Eminem's lyrics when they're 11 or 12. They stay up late and they watch Defjam, even if they're white kids from the all-white suburbs. By the way, there is a new show on Broadway now, it just opened the other day, and these poets, these rap artists, these performance artists, these slam people—granted their audience is primarily college and on up adults, but also young adults in high school. I have met with some here and there around the country, lately at Ohio State, at a coffeeshop, they look as all kids do, a generation of the age a few years beyond themselves.

The thing is high school kids, young adults do not ordinarily buy books and if they do by and large they buy copies of novels that they have to do for assignments. But I don't believe that they are not interested in poetry. They all write. They all write letters, they all write love letters, they are all concerned with death and the randomness of death and chaos. And it's just the teachers who don't want to exploit this interest in school because they're still doing the dead white poets or they're still attempting to hold on to what they consider the final shreds of their "American" culture, you know those values that William Bennett and those other right-wing ideologues have presented to America as what culture is, in other words, a Eurocentric British focused kind of literature.

The other thing is, there is energy and power in young adult poetry if it's done well in terms of writing and I always see that because there really is a poetry for change. And it's easier for novelists because there is a tradition from the sixties and so they can get their work published and not be censored and not be toned down by most editors and there is a tradition of studying novels in classrooms but when it comes to schoolwork in poetry, they'll go back to Whitman and Shakespeare and there is nothing wrong with Whitman and Shakespeare but they don't study Ginsberg. If they studied Ginsberg's 1960 *Howl*—"Fuck You America With Your Atom Bomb"—it would be so powerful! That opening line alone takes you into Bush, Iraq, the war and the life and death situation that these very teenagers will face if they're in college or will be facing very shortly. So the interest is there—it's the adults who are either afraid or not willing to till that vineyard I guess you could say.

ON HAMILTON AND ADOFF'S INFLUENCE ON THEIR SON JAIME ADOFF'S WRITING

I kid around sometimes. You know the Dutch poets, the elder and the younger. Sometimes I'll say "Adoff the elder, Adoff the younger" because you'll get a little blurb and it says Mr. Adoff and I'll say, "Who are they talking about?" Oh, man, that's my kid he's 35, he's a Mr. Adoff. You know, that kind of thing.

One of his (Internet) screen names was End Rhyme. He knows how I hate end rhymes and how I struggle against this Hickory Dickory Dock kind of end rhyme all these years. But he loves rhyming much more than I do and he loves internal rhyme schemes and he's not concerned neurotically perhaps as I am with the flushings on the right and the shapings and he doesn't have the kind of aesthetic that I've developed. But he has an extraordinary voice that's very much his own. It isn't just that he was a singer/songwriter for all those years and he fronted his own band and you know he really was a musician. He writes about other stuff besides music. But he has no self-censorship and he has no filter. And so when he writes in the voice of a high school boy or even a high school girl, that's it, he is that 16 year old. And that's the crucial thing about his writing. And that's what is so wonderful and that's what writers, editors have been seeing. The only thing in terms of the gene pool is he's immediately working on novels and trying to support his wife with prose although he loves to write poetry. But he is fortunately starting books with poems because publishers now are saying it's OK to do a connected narrative with poetry, with poetic prose and have it called a novel. So he's getting the benefit of that. But in general he has read all of Virginia's stuff, he's read all of mine, and we discuss it. Virginia worked on one of his novel manuscripts this past fall (2001). And he is very much his own person as well. You know our daughter is an opera singer. And mostly we're playing blues and rock 'n roll and jazz. (I managed Charlie Mingus a million years ago.) She grew up in a jazz and R&B scene, you know, and she goes to college and studies opera! So the kids are very, very independent. That's their way of rebelling, I guess. And he is like that himself in terms of his writing. They are respectful, they love it, they love what we have done, and what we do, and I think you can see it in his poetry because his work is startlingly fresh.

Poetic Forms

A narrative poem relates a particular event or tells a story—generally with plot, characters, and theme. Typically, when exploring the poetry preferences of young children, a majority

Jabberwocky by Lewis Carroll is famous for creating a meaningful narrative from nonsensical words. Illustration by Bryan Talbot from *Alice in Sunderland* (Dark Horse, 2007). Reprinted by permission of Bryan Talbot.

of favorites will be narrative. Narrative poems have often been republished in a picture book format, and many picture books are written as narrative poems. Young adults also often find narrative poems to be the most accessible form, so to a certain extent they remain high on the preference scale for many teens.

Some classic narrative poems have appeal for young adult readers. Works such as "The Highwayman" (1913) by Alfred Noyes and "The Pied Piper of Hamelin" (1842) by Robert Browning are often regarded as poems for all ages. Narrative poems can be lengthy, like "Casey at the Bat" by Ernest Thayer, which has been turned into an appealing picture book (Morse, 2006), or they can be short dramatic scenarios, like many of the free verse poems of Gary Soto._

Even novel-length narrative poems have become trendy of late and are discussed later in this chapter. *Splintering* for example tells of the aftermath of a terrible event. It is the story of how a stranger breaks into a family's house one night and the effect it has had on them ever since.

Closely related to narrative poems are ballads, which are basically narrative folk songs. Samuel Coleridge's "The Rime of the Ancient Mariner" (1798) is a good example. "John Henry," which is both a blues ballad and a tall tale, has been beautifully retold as a picture book by Julius Lester and Jerry Pinkney. Although most ballads are historical works, Jane Yolen uses the historical mood evoked by ballads to good effect in *The Ballad of the Pirate Queen,* about two women aboard the ship *Vanity.*

A lyric poem implies a story rather than tells one, and in terms of rhythm, tends to be melodic or songlike, which makes sense because (as the Greek root of the word indicates) they were in the past often chanted or recited to the accompaniment of a lyre or other musical instrument (Lentz, 1980). Lyric poetry captures a movement or a feeling. As Northrup Fyre describes it, a lyric poem is "a poem, brief and discontinuous, emphasizing sound and picture imagery rather than narrative or dramatic movement" (1985, p. 274).

The works of William Blake and Robert Louis Stevenson are classic examples of lyric poetry, with an emphasis on mood or feeling and rhyme schemes and alliteration that add to the melody. "Athena Speaks of Ares" by Kate Hovey captures the attributes of Ares and the feelings he inspires in a rhythmic language that could easily be part of a praise song sung by a minstrel.

A limerick is a five-line verse. The first, second, and fifth lines rhyme and have three prominent beats. The third and fourth tend to rhyme, so there is generally an AABBA pattern. There also generally tends to be a surprise ending. Limericks were popularized by

Athena Speaks of Ares

Olympians despise
his chiseled features,
stony eyes,
the way his chest swells when he stands,
his bloodied hands.

Olympians revile
his frozen heart
and crooked smile.
In his laughter echo sounds
of distant battlegrounds.

Kate Hovey's poem "Athena Speaks of Ares" from *Ancient Voices* (2004) evokes timeless emotions, while the illustrations by Murray Kimber tie the Greek myth to a contemporary paradigm. Reprinted by permission of Margaret McElderry.

Edward Lear in the 19th century, especially in his *Book of Nonsense,* which includes the following:

There was a Young Lady whose eyes,
Were unique as to colour and size;
When she opened them wide,
People all turned aside,
And started away in surprise.

1846, Edward Lear

Many collections of poetry for young readers include a limerick or two. There are several anthologies, including John Ciardi's *The Helpful Trout and Other Limericks* and X. J. Kennedy's *Uncle Switch: Loony Limericks,* that are made up entirely of limericks. These two anthologies are really aimed at younger readers but they might serve as good models for young adults.

Haiku is often taken to be a simple form of poetry because of its length and structured format. Haiku is a lyric unrhymed poem of three lines, with a syllable count of 5-7-5. But this poetic form is more complicated than one might first imagine. Haiku creates images through natural description and conveys a feeling or mood while maintaining a relationship between the image described and the mood conveyed. John Drury (1995) writes, "The essential elements of haiku are brevity, immediacy, spontaneity, imagery, the natural world, a season, and sudden illumination" (p. 125). Because all of these intricacies must be captured in so few words, the form can be very demanding to write.

Haiku by one of the best-known Japanese poets are collected in *Cool Melons Turn to Frogs!: The Life and Poems of Issa* (story and translation by Matthew Golub). A biography of the 18th-century Japanese poet Issa is nicely intertwined with 33 poems. Inspiring illustrations by Kazuko Store and Japanese calligraphy on the side of the page greatly enhance the translations. Other excellent collections include J. Patrick Lewis's *Black Swan/ White Crow,* an anthology of 13 poems with woodcut illustrations by Chris Manson that are reminiscent of classic Japanese prints, and *In the Eyes of the Cat: Japanese Poetry for All Seasons* by various poets, translated by Tze-Si Huang and illustrated by Demi.

The following haiku was written by Issa in 1795.

green plums—
the baddest of bad boys
bare-chested

青梅や餓鬼大将が肌ぬいで
aoume ya gaki-daishô ga hada nuide

Translation courtesy of David Lanoue.

The translation does not strive for the syllable count but rather for the movements and the meanings of the original. Translator David G. Lanoue, also known as the "haikuguy," runs a website called Haiku of Kobayashi Issa featuring over 9,000 haikus by Issa (http://haikuguy.com/issa).

Some wonderful contemporary poetry is written in the format of haiku, or the more visual addition of haiga (which involves brush art coupled with haiku usually written in calligraphy), but without all of the traditional elements, such as the focus on the natural world. People often make the assumption that because haiku is short and has a fixed form it will make an easy starting place for young people to begin writing their own poetry. Indeed, some youth do enjoy the puzzling and contemplation involved, but for many this can be a frustrating experience. Finding just the right word to not only fit the pattern but also convey the appropriate sentiments is a demanding process.

Free verse poems are unrhymed, with irregular patterns, and are often abstract. Though they do not consistently have rhyme, they involve a degree of rhythm and cadence. Using this form young adults can write about everyday experiences and often have a wonderful, perhaps even transformative experience expressing themselves through poetry. Teen writer Eva Lou wrote the following poem, which later appeared in *Movin': Teen Poets Take Voice,* while engaged in a poetry writing workshop sponsored by the New York Public Library.

Chopsticks

Hold the chopsticks gently
between your fingers. They should lie
weightless upon your hand, and your
knuckles should be flat. Not
protruding. Your thumb, yes, your
thumb should almost be a straight
line. And the rest of your fingers . . . Watch!
Like this: the first joints peeking like
timid hills, the second joints standing
like calm mountains. Then
let the tips (just the tips) dip
into the bowl, swiftly
but not abruptly. Pick up
a grain of rice. It should rest
delicately between the two sticks.
Bring the chopsticks toward you, not
Your face towards the chopsticks.
That grain of rice should become
the tip of your tongue,
Now, swallow.

The joy of this poem is that it makes the commonplace poetic and graceful. Eva has continued writing poetry and fiction, publishing her first book, *D'extases*, in 2006.

Free verse is a very popular format for young adults, found both in collections of poetry and in verse narratives that have become quite popular in recent years. Carole Weatherford recounts in bluesy rhythm the young life of Billie Holiday:

How Deep Is the Ocean

Without the microphone
there would be no spotlight,
no band backing me
with bluesy swing.

My voice was too small,
barely an octave,
but the mic enlarged my songs,
let me hold listeners close.

With the microphone,
my voice was an ocean,
deep as my moods,
and audiences dove in.

> "How Deep Is the Ocean" from *Becoming Billie Holiday*
> by Carole Boston Weatherford. Wordsong, an imprint of Boyds
> Mills Press, 2008. Reprinted with permission of Boyds Mills Press.
> Text copyright © 2008 by Carole Boston Weatherford.

Free verse allows for the beauty, rhythm, and figurative use of language without the constraint of rhyme schemes and syllable counts. As already mentioned some poets use the layout of the words to enhance the meanings. Arnold Adoff is well known for his shaped poetry. In anthologies such as *The Basket Counts* and *Slow Dance Heart Break Blues,* the positioning of the words on the page is integral to the effect on the reader. In one form of shaped poetry, known as concrete poetry, the words of the poem actually take on the shape connected to an image conveyed.

Lewis Carroll included an early concrete poem in *Alice's Adventures in Wonderland,* which is commonly referred to as the "The Mouse's Tale." A teen at the Pennington School in New Jersey actually discovered interesting puns in the poem when comparing the final published manuscript to an early draft written by Carroll. Most interesting of these was the fact that the format of a "tail rhyme" was used in the published version of the poem. This obviously was a conscious decision, but one that scholars had not discovered in over a century of analysis. In a tail rhyme two lines that rhyme are followed by a third rhyme of a different length. Traditionally the third line was shorter. Carroll made his longer so that the mouse's tale would become a tail. So the rhymes follow a pattern: mouse, house, you; denial, trail, do; sir, cur, breath; jury, fury, death. . . a pattern that is called a tail rhyme (connecting to the mouse theme), with a lengthened "tail" (connected to the mouse theme), recreated on the page in the shape of a tail. Carroll is well known for his puns but no one had noted this one until these two teens and their teacher published their article in *Jabberwocky,* the journal of the Lewis Carroll Society.

                              Fury said to a
                            mouse, That he
                         met in the
                      house,
                   "Let us
                   both go
                      to law: *I* will
                         prosecute
                            you.—Come
                               I'll take no
                               denial: We
                               must have a
                               trial: For
                            really this
                         morning I've
                      nothing
                   to do."
                   Said the
                   mouse to the
                   cur, "Such
                      a trial,
                         dear Sir,
                            With
                            no jury
                            or judge,
                            would be
                         wasting
                      our
                   breath."
                   "I'll be
                   judge, I'll
                   be jury,"
                      said
                         cunning
                         old Fury:
                         "I'll
                            try the
                            whole
                            cause,
                         and
                      condemn
                   you
                to
             death."

Poem from Lewis Carroll's *Alice's Adventures in Wonderland,* 1865.

Some great collections of concrete poetry targeted to young readers include

- *Doodle Dandies: Poems That Take Shape* ed. J. Patrick Lewis
- *Flicker Flash* ed. John Graham
- *A Poke in the I* ed. Paul Janescko

These anthologies have appeal for children but can also serve as good models for young adults. Other collections such as *Blue Lipstick* and *Technically It's Not My Fault,* both by John Grandits, are specifically aimed at young adults.

Choral poetry is poetry written for multiple voices. Jane Yolen and her daughter Heidi Stemple have a delightful collection called *Dear Mother/Dear Daughter,* in which one writes a short poem to which the other responds in poetry. But the term *choral poetry* generally refers to works in which the voices interact within a single poem. The best-known examples are from the Newbery Medal–winning collection by Paul Fleischman, *Joyful Noise.* Choral poetry is obviously meant to be oral and has a highly performative quality. In fact, choral poems with two or more readers are difficult to read effectively without actually rehearsing.

Other poetic formats are occasionally used in works for young audiences. A sestina, for example, is a patterned rhyme scheme that was favored by the troubadours. In a sestina the same six end words are used throughout, but in a varied order in each of the 6 six-line stanzas. In the seventh stanza all six words are used again in just three lines. This form works beautifully in "My Choice (Katie)" from *Keesha's House* by Helen Frost.

my choice (KATIE)

I sleep in my sleeping bag in a room
with a lock in the basement of the place
on Jackson Street. And I feel safe.
If Keesha wants to talk to me, she knocks
first, and if I want to let her in, I do.
If I don't, I don't. It's my choice.

There's not too much I really have a choice
about. Mom would say I chose to leave my room
at home, but that's not something anyone would do
without a real good reason. There's no place
for me there since she got married. Like, one time, I knocked
her husband's trophy off his gun safe,

and he twisted my arm—hard. I never feel safe
when he's around. I finally asked my mom to make a choice:
him or me. She went, Oh, Katie, he'll be fine. Then she knocked
on our wooden table. I blew up. I stormed out of the room
and started thinking hard. In the first place,
I know he won't be fine. I didn't tell her what he tries to do

to me when she works late. In a way, I want to, but even if I do,
she won't believe me. She thinks we're safe
in that so-called nice neighborhood. Finally, Katie, a place
of our own. And since she took a vow, she thinks she has no choice
but to see her marriage through. No room
for me, no vow to protect me if he comes knocking

on my door late at night. He knocks
and then walks in when I don't answer. Or even when I do
answer: Stay out! This is my room
and you can't come in! I could never be safe
there, with him in the house. So, sure, I made a choice.
I left home and found my way to this place,

where I've been these past two weeks. And I found a place
to work, thirty hours a week. Today Mom knocked
on the door here. She wanted to talk. I told her, You made your choice;
I made mine. She wondered what she could do
to get me to come home. But when I said, It's not safe
for me as long as he's there, she left the room.

My choice is to be safe.
This room is dark and musty, but it's one place
I do know I can answer no when someone knocks.

> Copyright © 2003 by Helen Frost. Reprinted by permission of Farrar,
> Straus and Giroux, LLC.

The words *room, place, safe, knock, choice,* and *do* (which imply action on the part of the doer) repeated over and over drives home the sentiments of the character. This is in fact a perfect example of how a quick discussion of form can enhance the pleasure and understanding of the poem. "My Choice" can be read without knowing anything about sestinas, but understanding that the echo of words (which some readers only pick up on subconsciously) is actually an ordered pattern of repetition might enhance both pleasure in and comprehension of the poem.

Guidelines for Selecting and Evaluating Poetry for Young Adults

When working with poetry for young adults you may want to consider the following questions:

Pleasure

- Will the poem/anthology appeal to young adults?
- Does the poem/anthology share traits with other literature young adults you work with have enjoyed in the past?
- Does the poem/anthology have themes that might be of interest to young adults?
- How do the poetic elements (tone, rhyme, rhythm, sounds, figurative language, imagery, and so on) enhance meaning in and enjoyment of the poems?

Quality

- Is the poetry well written and engaging?
- Does the writing contain an authenticity of voice and setting?
- Do style, theme, tone, point of view, mood, pace, and design enhance the poetry?

- How does the work compare to other works by the author?
- How has the book been received by reviewers (professional as well as young people)? Do you agree with these reviews?
- Does the poem allow the reader to see things in a fresh way?
- Do the rhythm, rhyme, and sounds used add to the meanings?
- If there are illustrations, do these work well with the words?
- For an anthology, are the poems effectively arranged? (How are they organized? Are they indexed?)
- For an anthology, is any additional information given about the poets and themes?

Appropriateness

- Is this the right poem/anthology for the context?
- Will it appeal to this individual or group?
- Will it provide a pleasurable and/or educational experience?
- Are the topics or language too difficult/simple/banal so that reading becomes frustrating?
- Are stereotypes avoided?
- Are language, themes, and symbolism accessible for the intended age group?

Technology Links

Favorite Poem Project

Robert Pinsky, when he was Poet Laureate of the United States, had a wonderful idea for reinvigorating an interest in poetry in the nation's schools, libraries, and communities. His idea came to be known as the Favorite Poem Project. The key component of the project is the 50 short video documentaries showcasing a variety of Americans speaking about their personal connections with a favorite poem, available along with a forum for teachers to share lesson plans at www.favoritepoem.org.

In the classroom the video documentaries can be an excellent source of inspiration and they are especially valuable for bringing out the personal connections people might have with poetry. A young adult from South Boston reads Gwendolyn Brooks's "We Real Cool" and discusses why he chose this poem as a personal favorite. Another teen from Decatur, Georgia, reads Dickinson's "I'm Nobody! Who Are You." The adult readers range from Hillary Clinton to a construction worker to a retired anthropologist. All of the poems are presented in a way that makes the personal transactions with the readers come to life.

The project has also served as the inspiration for over a thousand Favorite Poem readings around the country. These events involve bringing together a wide range of people from a particular community to each read a poem and discuss their personal connections to it. Information on how to put these events together is available at the Favorite Poem Project website (www.favoritepoem.org).

Author Spotlight

Photo courtesy of Janet Wong.

Janet Wong

Janet Wong was born in Los Angeles and spent her childhood in California. While attending UCLA, she started the Immigrant Children's Art Project, which taught refugee children to express themselves through art. Wong received a law degree from Yale Law School and practiced corporate law for several years before making the decision to write full time for young people. Her poetry has been widely celebrated, receiving the IRA "Celebrate Literacy Award." She has read at the White House and also appeared on the Oprah Winfrey Show. Visit her website at www.janetwong.com.

SELECTED BIBLIOGRAPHY
A Suitcase of Seaweed and other Poems (McElderry, 1996)
Buzz (Sandpiper, 2002)
Me and Rolly Maloo (Charlesbridge, 2010)
Twist: Yoga Poems (McElderry, 2007)

ON HOW SHE STARTED WRITING POETRY FOR YOUNG PEOPLE

In 1991, I decided I no longer wanted to be a lawyer; I wanted to write children's picture books. Not poetry collections; I hated poetry.

My start as a poet was quite accidental: I heard Myra Cohn Livingston speak at a writing seminar at UCLA, and the children's poems she read made a big impression on me. I didn't know much poetry, then, certainly not enough to justify my dislike of it. Myra's talk made me aware of how powerful children's poetry can be. But I didn't want to write poetry, so I continued working on my own, on picture books. Later, dejected by dozens of rejection letters, I decided I really needed to learn to write for young children; what I knew about writing was not enough. I signed up for Myra's poetry class, to sharpen my prose. Months later, I came to love reading and writing poems, and had written my first collection, *Good Luck Gold*.

ON THE PERCEPTION THAT YOUNG ADULTS ONLY READ POETRY UNDER DURESS

I think the stress of poetry comes with having to memorize it or interpret it. I have a hard time memorizing poems, and I can remember how rotten it feels to stand in front of the class and forget a (supposedly memorized) poem. Not very many teachers require memorizing poems nowadays. I think that task should be optional, maybe extra credit, for those who enjoy reciting poems from memory.

How to read a poem is a difficult subject. So much can be read into a poem that wasn't "meant" to be there; people seem compelled to do this. I don't analyze poems too much, but I am guilty of analyzing too much with contemporary art. This obsession with "what does it mean?" and "how was it done?" can enhance a person's enjoyment of a particular work, but can also ruin it. The trick, of course, is finding some balance.

About the popularity of YA poetry: teens like rhythmic and rhyming verse, and rich imagery; look at songs and music videos. I think more teens would read poems if not for the requirement to analyze. I have an idea that would really get teens motivated to read poetry: Teachers should require their students to read 25 pages a day of any book; 25 pages of a novel might take over an hour, while 25 pages of short poems might take only 15 minutes. Books would start to fly off the 811 shelves! More teens would return to picture books this way, too, which would be a good thing. The world would be a friendlier place if adults read a picture book a day. Probably the best new thing in terms of YA poetry, though, is the novel in verse, which is easy to read and gets readers used to enjoying writing that "looks awfully like a poem" (but might not be).

ON WHETHER SHE WRITES WITH A PARTICULAR AUDIENCE IN MIND

I usually don't think too much about the intended audience while I am writing, but some of my books clearly are most appropriate for specific age groups. A few of my picture books are for very young children—*Buzz,* for instance, about a child's busy morning routine, and *Grump,* about a grumpy mother trying to make her baby take a nap. Some of the books are clearly YA books, too, such as *Behind the Wheel: Poems about Driving.* But I would like to think that my best writing works for readers of any age. "Old Friend" in *Night Garden: Poems from the World of Dreams,* for example, should speak to anyone who misses an old friend, whether that person is a kindergartner or a grandmother.

ON WHAT MIGHT HELP YOUNG ADULTS DEVELOP AS WRITERS

Write tons. Write lots of drafts of everything. I take the lottery approach to writing. Each draft is another ticket, another chance to win. Work, work, work—and some of what you do is bound to work out.

Poetry in the Classroom

There are certain types of poetry that will have the broadest appeal for the widest audience of young readers. Humorous light verse with rhyme, word play, and distinctive beats tends to be the top preference. In terms of format, narrative poems are likely to be favorites. But

 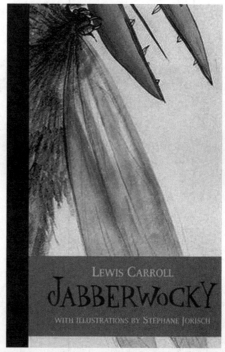

In Ernest Thayer's *Casey at the Bat* (2006) the poem is totally reenvisioned with a modern twist. Lewis Carroll's *Jabberwocky* (2004) is filled with symbolism and critical commentary on society. Cover image and material from *Casey at the Bat* by Ernest L. Thayer with illustrations by Joe Morse. Used by permission of Kids Can Press, Ltd., Toronto. Illustration © 2006 Joe Morse. Cover image from *Jabberwocky* by Lewis Carroll with illustrations by Stéphane Jorisch. Used by permission of Kids Can Press, Ltd., Toronto. Illustration © 2004 Stéphane Jorisch.

as with other forms of literature, it is hard to pigeonhole who will be drawn to certain types of poetry, and the best choice is to have a wide array of poetry available in the classroom and to try to introduce the poems in diverse ways.

One important idea to keep in mind is that poetry does not always need to be used for direct instruction! Poetry can be read aloud, hung up on the wall, included in the classroom library, or displayed in the school library. You can have poetry slams or open mic events and students can collect favorite poems for pleasure or to use as models for their own writing. Occasionally, you will find that you would like to focus on a particular poem or a set of poems and have students actually respond to or interact with the themes/images/language of that poem. As Janet Wong suggests, the trick is to find a balance between exploring poetic craft and simply enjoying the pleasures of a good poem. Because of the emotional force and imagery involved, some poems work especially well with artistic interpretation or creative writing extensions. Other poetry with strong rhythm might allow for connections with music and dance. There are poems and anthologies related to almost any theme one might imagine, which means for any area of the curriculum there are works that could be used to enhance what is being studied. Janet Wong's "Gong Gong and Susie," for example would be an excellent addition to discussions of the Depression era. Naomi Shihab Nye's poem "Trenches and Moats and Mounds of Dirt" is one of many that might open up dialogue about the Middle East.

Audio Books

Poetry Selections

Blues Journey by Walter Dean Myers. (Live Oak, 2005) (Y)

Frenchtown Summer by Robert Cormier; read by Rene Auberjanois. (Listening Library, 2000)

Heartbeat by Sharon Creech; read by Mandy Siegfried. (HarperChildren's Audio, 2004)

Joyful Noise and *I Am Phoenix* by Paul Fleischman; performed by John Bedford Lloyd and Anne Twomey. (HarperChildren's Audio, 2001)

Love That Dog by Sharon Creech; read by Scott Wolf. (HarperChildren's Audio, 2006)

Out of the Dust by Karen Hesse; read by Marika Mashburn. (Listening Library, 1998) (Y)

True Believer by Virginia Euwer Wolff; read by Heather Alicia Simms. (Random House, 2002) (N)

Witness by Karen Hesse; read by a full cast. (Listening Library, 2001) (N)

> N—ALSC Notable Children's Recording
>
> Y—YALSA Selected List of Audiobooks

Formats of Poetry

Picture Book Poems

As with picture books in general, there is an incredible variety of poetry published in picture book format that might be used effectively with young adults. There is also a very real possibility that if not approached carefully, teens might assume that the format is for children and feel that they are not being challenged. One need look no further than e. e. cummings's *may I feel said he,* illustrated with paintings by Chagal, to convince most readers of the fact that illustrated does not necessarily mean for the very young.

Some Excellent Picture Book Poems for Young Adults

Alice Yazzie's Year by Ramona Maher; illus. by Shonto Begay

Amiri and Odetta by Walter Dean Myers; illus. by Javaka Steptoe

Arachne Speaks by Kate Hovey; illus by Blair Drawson

Blues Journey by Walter Dean Myers; illus. by Christopher Myers

Casey at the Bat by Ernest Thayer; illus. by Joe Morse

Harlem: A Poem by Walter Dean Myers; illus. by Christopher Myers

I Live in Music by Ntozake Shanghe; illus. by Romare Bearden

Jabberwocky by Lewis Carroll; illus. by Christopher Myers

Poem from *My Name is Jason, Mine Too* (HarperTeen, 2009).

Jabberwocky by Lewis Carroll; illus. by Stéphane Jorisch

Patrol: An American Soldier in Vietnam by Walter Dean Myers; illus. by Ann Grifalconi

A Visit to William Blake's Inn by Nancy Willard; illus. by Alice and Martin Provensen

Picture books such as *Patrol: An American Soldier in Vietnam* have themes and a sophistication of story and imagery that make them relevant and interesting to some young adults. With many of these books the vocabulary might be understandable to an upper-elementary student, but the possible meanings and the discussions that follow might be more relevant to young adults. As discussed in Chapter 3, in these narratives the illustrations play an integral part in the creation of meaning.

Anthologies

Much of the poetry aimed at young adult audiences is collected in anthologies. There are currently such a wide variety of anthologies that for just about any subject, poems can be found to suit a reader's interest or to use across the curriculum. Anthologies can be either collections of works authored by a single poet or edited anthologies.

Some excellent collections specifically address the hassles and joys of adolescence. In Jane Yolen and Heidi Stemple's *Dear Mother, Dear Daughter: Poems for Young People,* a mother and daughter converse through poetry each has written. The book is ideally suited for middle school girls but will resonate with many older teens. In Angela Johnson's *Running Back to Ludie* a teenage girl voices her feelings about her absentee mother in 34 free verse vignettes. Gary Soto's *Fearless Fernie: Hanging Out with Fernie and Me* appeals to the humorous side of middle school boys. Likewise *A Fury of Motion* is loaded with poems that might have special attraction for middle school boys.

Some of the best received poetry anthologies are focused on specific topics that hold special interest for the age group. For older teens *Slow Dance Heart Break Blues* beautifully captures the various guises of love. Many single author collections are thematically based, like the poems in *Hoop Queens* by Charles R. Smith (which are all about professional female basketball players), Janet Wong's *Behind the Wheel: Poems about Driving,* and Jaime Adoff's *The Song Shoots Out of My Mouth: A Celebration of Music.*

Other collections are of interest to many teachers because they create a broad tapestry depicting a particular community. Gary Soto's *Neighborhood Odes,* for example, is filled with poignant slices of life from a Chicano neighborhood. In *19 Varieties of Gazelle: Poems of the Middle East,* Naomi Shihab Nye has collected her own poems that relate to the Middle East—about peace, about the region and its people, about being an Arab American. In "Trenches and Moats and Mounds of Dirt" she writes

> There is a language between two
> languages
> called Mean but who would admit
> they are speaking it?
>
> 'Let's change places,' the teenagers said.
> 'For a week, I'll be you and you be me.'
> Knowing if they did, they could never fight again.
>
>   Reprinted by permission of Naomi Shihab Nye.

Ancient Voices by Kate Hovey presents the world as seen by Ganymede, the cupbearer to the Olympian gods. Some of the poems are from Ganymede's perspective; others are voices overheard by this former shepherd from Troy who now suffers as an immortal servant. The illustrations by Murray Kimber add another layer to these sophisticated poems. Even in shorter poems such as "Athena Speaks of Ares" Hovey and Kimber evoke mythic intertexts and psychological depth.

Edited Anthologies

Many readers are truly astonished when they discover the wide range of topics and issues covered in poetry anthologies. Baseball is the subject of Paul Janeczko's collection *That Sweet Diamond: Baseball Poems;* love is the focus of *I Am Wings: Poems about Love* edited by Ralph Fletcher; the subject of mortality concerns *Stopping for Death: Poems about Death and Loss* edited by Carol Duffy; for teen angst there is *The Pain Tree and Other Teenage Angst-Ridden Poetry* edited by Esther Watson and Mark Todd; and for art we have *Heart to Heart* by Jan Greenberg. The poems in *What Have You Lost?* by Naomi Shihab Nye are all related to things that have been lost, both the physical and the ephemeral. Patrice Vecchione edits *The Body Eclectic,* an anthology of poems celebrating bodies and the things we do with them, a sure fire hook for teens, in verses that range from silly to serious, from classical to contemporary, all centered on the body.

Some collections center on presenting the voices of a certain demographic. In *I Wouldn't Thank You for a Valentine: Poems for Young Feminists* editor Carol Ann Duffy has collected poems about being a young woman. *Cool Salsa* is a wonderful collection of 36 diverse Latino/a voices. One demographic that is receiving more attention in the publishing world is poetry actually written by young adults. Several high-quality anthologies of poetry written by teenagers have been published in recent years. Dave Johnson in *Movin': Teen Poets Take Voice* has collected 36 poems by teens who participated in workshops facilitated by New York Public Library and the Poetry in the Branches teen program. Wonderful poems, some extremely mature, are included in collections like *You Hear Me? Poems and Writing by Teenage Boys* (ed. Betsy Franco) and *Broken Heart . . . Healing: Young Poets Speak Out on Divorce* (ed. Tom Worthen).

The NCTE has a wonderful collection called *Poems by Adolescents and Adults: A Thematic Collection for Middle School and High School* edited by James Brewbaker and Dawnelle Hyland. The anthology includes selections by well-known authors such as Gary Soto and Nikki Giovanni, but its strength comes from the inclusion of beautifully crafted poems by young adults.

Movin': Teen Poets Take Voice anthologizes poems collected by young people who engaged in writing poetry with New York Public Library's Poet's House. These very individual poems all address themes that reflect the lives of many young adults. Take for example teenager Toni-Ann Fischetti's poem "Nothing Could Be Better":

> I am saddened to realize
> I am in math.
>
> on a rainy bad-luck Friday
> with a drip faucet nose and no umbrella.
>
> I don't want to be here.
> I want to be eating falafel
> wrapped in waxed paper
> and foil to go.
> And mushroom barley soup
> served to me by
> the waitress
> with incredibly long tresses
> across from Poets House.
>
> That's all I really want in life—
> Falafel and mushroom barley soup,
> to be consumed in my own quiet place.
>
> Nowhere near the shadow of math.
>
> > Copyright Toni-Ann Fischetti. Reprinted with permission.

When young adults find poetry they can relate to and discover that poets as young as they are might be taken seriously, they are more likely to write their own poetry for an audience. They might consider publishing in *Teen Ink,* one of the most established venues for young writers. Or they might prefer publishing on one of the many websites that feature poetry written by young adults. Or they might take part in spoken word events such as open mic nights or poetry slams.

Spoken word poetry has seen enormous growth in recent years. How does a slam differ from an open mic event? Generally "slams" involve competition and entertainment, with readings judged on

Jason Reynolds and Jason Griffin's performance poetry. Photo courtesy of Reynolds and Griffin.

both the quality of the poetry and the performance itself. In a slam, members of the audience often act as judges, and react verbally. The open mic is more about support and a sense of literary community. Poetry at a slam tends to have a style that is very performance based. For good examples, take a look at *Listen Up! Spoken Word Poetry* edited by Zoe Anglesey. Poems by nine slam masters from Brooklyn Moon Café and Nuyorican Poets Café are included, with a bio of each poet and four spoken word poems by each.

Novels in Verse and Verse in Novels

Writing narrative in verse is not a new concept. From epics and sagas to Dante's *Inferno* to Shakespeare, verse has been used to tell many of the most significant stories in the history of literature. Now novels in verse are one of the hot trends in literature for young adults. Since Karen Hesse's *Out of the Dust* received the Newbery Medal in 1998 an ever increasing number of poetic novels have been published. One even hears rumors of publishers actively seeking authors who can write in verse. Fortunately, many of these novels are beautifully crafted. Sonya Sones, Juan Felipe Herrare, Ann Turner, Mel Glenn, Margaret Wild, Helen Frost, April Wayland, Jaimie Adoff, Sharon Creech . . . the list of must reads is growing almost daily. These novels fall into several overlapping categories: free verse or stream of consciousness narratives, narrative poems written in multiple poetic forms, and collections of poems tied together by a narrative thread that focuses as much on poetry itself as on the storyline.

Sonya Sones's *What My Mother Doesn't Know* has the appeal of contemporary realistic fiction. Sophie has a sexy boyfriend, a cyber fling, and a secret crush on a geek. Her angst-ridden voice tells the story of her freshman year in high school and especially her relationships, in this series of short free verse poems.

And just before we got to my house,
I thought I felt him
give my waist an almost squeeze.

Then the car rolled to a stop
and I climbed out
with my whole body buzzing.
I said good night,
headed up the front walk,
and when I heard the car pulling away,
I looked back over my shoulder
and saw Dylan look back over his shoulder
at me.

"WINNING." —*Entertainment Weekly*

what my mother doesn't know

SONYA SONES

Free verse works beautifully in Sonya Sones's *What My Mother Doesn't Know* (2001), where the stream of consciousness style fits with the inner thoughts of the narrator. Reprinted by permission of Simon and Schuster.

When our eyes connected,
this miracle smile lit up his face
and I practically had a religious experience.

Then I went upstairs to bed
and tried to fall asleep,
but I felt permanently wide awake.
And I kept on seeing that smile of his
and feeling that almost squeeze.

Copyright Sonya Sones. Reprinted with permission.

The emotions, the concerns, and the perspectives on life will definitely appeal to many teen readers. The flow of the narrative is like poetic stream of consciousness, but sometimes it is not so clear whether this type of narrative is poetry or simply a free flow of thought. *Make Lemonade* by Virginia Euwer Wolff and its sequel *True Believer* follow the efforts of a teenage girl named LaVaughn to reach her dream of making it into college in spite of numerous obstacles. Wolff does not regard her work as free verse, but rather as stream of consciousness narrative. Discerning the difference between the two forms would be an interesting assignment for young adults, investigating this question with no set answer.

There are a growing number of books written this way, not seeking any particular poetic form but writing the thoughts of characters in free verse. Some of these novels add the dimension of multiple perspectives, and the best of them include as part of that the distinct voices of individual characters. Mel Glenn has a number of books written in this way: *Who Killed Chippendale? A Mystery in Poems, The Taking of Room 114,* and *Split Image* each looks at an intense situation through a variety of perspectives. These books and several others by Glenn all focus on an urban school, the fictional Tower High School.

In Terri Fields's *After the Death of Anna Gonzales,* various voices reflect the reactions of different people at a school to the suicide of a classmate. *Keesha's House* by Helen Frost tells the story of a safe house where kids start to hang out, such as Stephie, who is pregnant; her boyfriend, who has a chance at a college basketball career (a chance that the baby would complicate); Dontay, whose parents are in prison; Harris, whose father kicked him out when he found out he was gay; and Katie, who has an abusive stepfather. The house actually belongs to Joe who inherited it from his Aunt Annie but Keesha is the one who has put out the word about the house. Now everyone calls it Keesha's House and the new arrivals are surprised to meet Joe. In the long run some of these kids choose to return home. Others don't.

Most readers in America who know Australian author Margaret Wild know her picture books, so *Jinx* might come as a surprise. This is a sophisticated story of Jen (who refers to herself as Jinx) and her relationships with friends, parents, and stepparents, as they

To Consider

Is there a difference between free verse and stream of consciousness writing? Are the differences to be found in the format? The meanings? Or the intent of the author?

all try to find their way. One of the most intriguing characters in the book is Grace, Jen's sister whose Down syndrome was detected early enough that her mom had the option of terminating the pregnancy. That Jen's mom chose not to do so caused Jen's father to leave them. Ms. Wild deals with all sorts of issues including peer and parental relationships, love, lust, forgiveness, death, and self-image, all with a forthrightness and deep joy in this poetic tale.

In *The Surrender Tree* Margarita Engle captures the devastating intensity of uprising and healing in Cuba, told in the lyrical voices of those involved. The narrative in this compelling story alternates between characters, including a natural healer, the fearsome Lieutenant Death, the rebel Jose, and young Silvia. The style, rhythms, and patterns of each voice are distinct, and together an evocative and vivid portrait of the past is created.

Three recent titles show the power and versatility of verse literature when its focus turns to poetry itself. *Love That Dog* by Sharon Creech, *Locomotion* by Jacqueline Woodson, and *Shakespeare Bats Cleanup* by Ron Koertge, though quite different in voice and style, are similar in many ways. Woodson's character, Lonnie, reflects on memories of his parents, life with his foster mother, the younger sister he does not want to lose track of, and being poor and black in urban America. The story would certainly be accessible to younger students but it is beautifully written and would be of interest to many young adults as well. Koertge's novel is about Kevin, the most valuable player on the baseball team, who worries primarily about not being able to play because he has mono and is stuck at home. Bored, he finds himself writing poetry and soon he is hooked. Though it sounds contrived out of context, the narrative really pulls the reader in and the poetry Kevin writes deals with the things he is interested in.

So what do these two narratives have in common? Each of these boys, reluctantly at first, turns to poetry as a release and eventually finds joy in expressing himself in verse. This sort of *Kunstlerroman* (a novel about an artist or author's coming of age) runs the danger of becoming overly didactic, but in both of these novels the voice of the narrator brings the poetry to life. Koertge has been writing novelized poetry for years whereas Woodson is better known for her prose, but both have created works that will entice many reluctant readers.

The following poem was written by media specialist Lynn Postell in response to her reading of *Shakespeare Bats Cleanup:*

I am slowly, but surely, changing my mind about poetry,
Who knew poetry didn't have to rhyme?
That it could just say what you wanted to say,
    But better, more succinct,
Who knew that it could be in novel form?
That it could reveal so much about a kid's life, his feelings,
    all in a very few verses.
Feelings ranging from funny to sweet to poignant:
    missing baseball, hating to be sick;
    not having a girlfriend; having a girlfriend
    awkwardness with dad;

missing a mom who has died;
And finally realizing that writing poetry,
Putting feelings into words on paper,
Is a very cool thing to do!
Almost as cool as baseball.

Poem used courtesy of Lynn Postell.

Similarly in *Love That Dog* Jack is not at all interested in poetry until his teacher introduces him to the poems of Walter Dean Myers. Jack eventually begins to read and even write his own poetry and is instrumental in getting Walter Dean Myers to visit his school. Each of these books introduces the idea that boys do not write poetry, or black people don't write poetry, or cool people don't write poetry, which is then deconstructed by the end.

Nonfiction: Memoirs and Biography

Authors of life stories including autobiographies, biographies, and memoirs (discussed in Chapter 7) have occasionally used poetry to good effect in telling their stories. That choice often comes about as a result of the intense emotions the author wishes to convey, like the images of fear, desperation, and abuse in Ann Turning's *Learning to Swim.* In *You Remind Me of You* Eireann Corrigan writes of her battle with eating disorders, her boyfriend's suicide, and her fears and dreams. When well done the poetic language adds an intensity to the sentiments conveyed. On the other hand the poetic form of Marilyn Nelson's *Carver: A Life in Poems* makes perfect sense given the subject. In *Your Own, Sylvia: A Verse Portrait of Sylvia Plath,* Stephanie Hemphill creates a series of biographical poems styled after Plath's own poetry. "Manic Depression" for instance is written in imitation of Plath's own poem "Aerialist," and "Your Own Sylvia" is modeled on "Child."

Stephanie Hemphill's *Your Own, Sylvia* illustrates the life of Sylvia Plath through a series of chronologically arranged poetry. The collection reflects on Plath's life's struggles, her failing marriage, and her love of writing. Copyright © 2008. Reprinted by permission of Random House.

She could not help burning herself
From the inside out,
Consuming herself

Like the sun.
But the memory of her light blazes
Our dark ceiling.

From *Your Own, Sylvia: A Verse Portrait of Sylvia Plath* by Stephanie Hemphill, copyright © 2007 by Stephanie Hemphill. Used by permission of Alfred A. Knopf, an imprint of Random House Children's Books, a division of Random House, Inc.

The poems not only provide great insight into Plath's life and work, they are also evocative poems in their own right.

Bronx Masquerade

In *Bronx Masquerade* Nikki Grimes takes a different approach to connecting prose and verse. The novel is written in internal monologue and poetry in the voices of 18 urban high school students who get inspired by a new open mic event in their English class. The thoughts of the characters give insight into their poetry and provide a narrative thread connecting otherwise disparate verse. So before the reader encounters the title poem "Bronx Masquerade," for example, she is exposed to the thoughts of Devon Hope:

> It's not much better at home. My older brother's always after me to hit the streets with him, calls me a girly man for loving books and jazz. Don't get me wrong. B-ball is all right. Girls like you, for one thing. But it's not you they like. It's Mr. Basketball. And if that's not who you are inside, then it's not you they're liking. So what's the point?

One of the things that Grimes does so well is to capture the voices of these diverse characters in both the prose and the poetry, and she maintains a consistency of voice, so much so that the characters feel real. Devon writes in his poem:

I woke up this morning
exhausted from hiding
the me of me
so I stand here confiding
there's more to Devon
than jump shot and rim.
I'm more than tall
and lengthy of limb.
I dare you to peep
behind these eyes,
discover the poet
in tough-guy disguise.
Don't call me Jump Shot.
My name is Surprise.

"Open Mike by Devon Hope" from *Bronx Masquerade* by Nikki Grimes, copyright © 2002 by Nikki Grimes. Used by permission of Dial Books for Young Readers, a division of Penguin Young Readers Group, a member of Penguin Group (USA) Inc., 345 Hudson St., New York, NY 10014. All rights reserved.

Nikki Grimes's *Bronx Masquerade* (2002) alternates between the narrative thoughts of the characters and the poetry that they write and perform in Mr. Ward's English class. Reprinted by permission of Penguin Group (USA).

The interwoven thoughts and poems make for great character development and might contribute to a young writer's understandings of possible sources of poetic voice. As the students get involved in writing the poems and reading them to the class on what turns into "Open Mic" Fridays, they reveal their dreams, nightmares, and how they relate to each other.

From not living up to a father's expectations to fears about their physical appearances, from violence and teen motherhood to friendship and alienation, you gain an incredibly intimate understanding of these teenagers. The story itself is inspirational enough to excite many teachers to try more student-written poetry in the classroom.

Author Spotlight

Reprinted by permission of Penguin Putnam.

Nikki Grimes

Nikki Grimes is an author, poet, lecturer, and educator who was born and raised in New York City. She is the author of more than two dozen books for children and young adults. Among her numerous awards and citations, Grimes was the recipient of the 2006 NCTE Award for Excellence in Poetry for Children. She also was presented with the Coretta Scott King Award for *Bronx Masquerade.* She also writes for *Essence, Booklinks,* and other journals. Grimes lives in Corona, California.

SELECTED BIBLIOGRAPHY

Bronx Masquerade (Dial, 2003)
Dark Sons (Hyperion, 2005)
Jazmin's Notebook (Dial, 1998)
My Man Blue illus. by Jerome Lagarrigue (Dial, 1999)
Talkin' about Bessie illus. by E. B. Lewis. (Orchard, 2002)

ON HOW SHE BECAME AN AUTHOR OF YOUNG ADULT LITERATURE

I've been writing books for young readers since 1977. Since that time, I've written everything from board books up to YA novels. Writing YAs was just part of the natural progression of my work.

ON WHETHER SHE WRITES WITH A PARTICULAR AUDIENCE IN MIND

I write for a general audience, but I always have at the back of my mind those readers who are at-risk children or teens. I relate, because I was one of them!

ON THE INSPIRATION FOR HER STORIES

The inspiration for my narratives come from my own childhood, the childhoods of others I've known, and from young people I know today.

ON THE EXTENT TO WHICH HER OWN LIFE STORY APPEARS IN HER WORKS

A bit of my life story works its way into almost everything I write. I just never reveal which element of a story is fact and which is fiction. That's for me to know.

ON WHAT SHE ENJOYED READING AS A TEENAGER

My favorite authors as a teen included, first and foremost, James Baldwin, Doris Lessing, and Kahlil Gibran. You'll notice the first two are not poets. However, Baldwin was a master wordsmith, and Lessing's work flows on the page. That's what I responded to and wanted most to emulate.

ON WHAT SHE ENJOYS READING CURRENTLY

Some of my favorite YA authors today are authors who write for both adults and young adults—Lucille Clifton, Gary Soto, Naomi Shihab Nye. Paul Fleischman is also on my list. (The list of authors whose work I adore would be too long to include here, or in any other article! Favorite adult authors include California J. Cooper, Mari Evans, Toni Morrison, Pablo Neruda, and Yeats)

You'll notice, I'm partial to poetry. I love a good novel, too—don't get me wrong. Katherine Paterson, Bruce Brooks, Walter Dean Myers, and Avi, to name a few novelists, can write for me any day of the week. But poetry is my first love. Poetry is the language of the heart and, in my work, I am always after the emotional jugular. Poetry gets me going, what can I say.

ON WHAT DISTINGUISHES YOUNG ADULT LITERATURE

Literature for young readers, besides being accessible, is a literature with hope at its center. A book that is dark, through and through, is, I believe, a book strictly for adults. I'm all for realism and edginess, as my own work indicates. But realism is one thing and hopelessness is another.

ON WHAT MIGHT HELP YOUNG ADULTS DEVELOP AS WRITERS

1. Anyone who wants to write needs first to read, and read ravenously. Your writing is only as good as the quality and quantity of your reading. However, reading for pleasure is not the end of the story. Read with a critical mind. Study a piece of fiction to figure out what makes it work.
2. Write. Writing is like muscle. If you don't exercise, you won't be able to perform well.

ON THE NOTION THAT TEENS SHY AWAY FROM POETRY

Teens may, in fact, pretend to shy away from poetry, but the truth is, the teen years are when people write poetry the most. Generally, the poetry ends up in the dresser drawer, but it is being written. If a teen, or any other reader, is presented with poetry with which they can connect, poetry that reaches them where they live, they will respond to it. If they're shown, by way of example, that their own lives can be the fodder for poetry, that poetry can express what's closest to their own hearts, they will risk attempting it.

ON WHY SHE HAS WRITTEN NOVELS THAT INTEGRATE POETRY

I write many books of poetry, but my novels have other things going on in them. In my novels, poetry is either an element of storytelling, or a tool for exploring the interior landscapes of my characters.

ON HOW SHE ACHIEVES ALL THE DIFFERENT POETIC VOICES IN *BRONX MASQUERADE*

I have a strong background in theatre, and I fall back on that when I do character studies for books like *Bronx Masquerade*. I climb into the skins of my characters the same way an actor climbs into the skin of a character in a play or a film. I work the same way. When I write poetry in the voice of a character, I do so by looking at the world through that character's eyes. It's one of my favorite things to do as a storyteller!

Topic Focus

Writing Poetry

Reading poetry certainly does not always lead to writing poetry, nor should it. However some poems open the door to creative writing. *Bronx Masquerade* might inspire or challenge young adults to write. Encountering poems written by other young adults can also be inspirational. Even reading what poets have to say about why they write, how they write, and what inspires them can help demystify the process.

Kathi Appelt in *Poems from Homeroom: A Writer's Place to Start* provides beautifully written teen-oriented poems followed by the inspiration and motivation for each poem. Similarly, Paul Janeczko offers an exceptional collection in *Seeing the Blue Between* with poems by about three dozen poets. The poems are accompanied by essays written by these same authors about writing poetry, sharing words of inspiration and providing insights into getting it right. The ideas expressed in these essays are as wonderfully diverse as the styles of the writers.

There are also some wonderful collections of student-written poetry that inspire by the very fact that they are written by kids the same age as the readers. Anthologies such as *Movin': Teen Poets Take Voice* (Johnson), *You Hear Me? Poems and Writing by Teenage Boys* (Franco), and *Salting the Ocean: 100 Poems by Young Poets* (Nye) can go a long way toward motivating young adults to make the attempt.

In the Field   *Virtual Open Mic at Washington High School*

Reading poetry out loud can be both an enjoyable actvity and a learning experience, but some students do not enjoy performing in front of an audience, especially if they are new to the idea of reading poetry orally. Preservice teachers doing their field experience at Washington High School therefore decided that they would help the students create a virtual open mic event.

After students had chosen or written, revised, and practiced their poems, the preservice teachers brought in a digital video camera. Students read their poems to the camera. Many students who had been shy about reading in front of an audience had no problems performing in front of the camera. Another advantage was that students could then watch and listen to themselves read. Many revised a poem after hearing that an effect they had hoped for did not work or that the rhythm was off. Others struggled more with reading their poems. Watching the video helped them understand the idea of audience in a new way. They could see that they never made eye contact or hear that they mumbled or read too quickly for the poem to have good effect. Most significantly, understanding the orality and the presentation of the poem became part of the writing process.

Background music and titles were added and the edited poetry event was warmly received at several school events. The low pressure atmosphere, the ability to view and revise, and the enthusiastic reception helped excite these students about the possibilities of writing and performing poetry.

Author Spotlight

Photo courtesy of April Wayland.

April Halprin Wayland

April Halprin Wayland is an author of poetry, picture books in verse, and a novel in verse for young adults. Her works are included in numerous anthologies. Wayland graduated with a B.S. in human development from the University of California at Davis. She attributes much of her success as a writer for young people to having studied with Myra Cohn Livingston for 12 years. She has worked as a walnut farmer, a governess (for Joan Rivers's daughter), a teacher, and a marketing manager, among other things. She is a founding member of The Santa Monica Traditional Folk Music Club, Positive Education Inc. (a nonprofit tutorial agency), and the Children's Author Network. She has also backpacked with her fiddle through Europe and the Middle East. She and her husband Gary Wayland have one son.

SELECTED BOOKLIST

Girl Coming In for a Landing (Knopf, 2002)
It's Not My Turn to Look for Grandma! (Knopf, 1995)
New Year at the Pier—A Rosh Hashanah Story (Dial, 2009)
To Rabbittown (Scholastic, 1989)

ON HOW SHE BECAME AN AUTHOR OF YOUNG ADULT LITERATURE

I have always written, but my writing life—staying up to write poems and stories deep into the night—began when I was 13.

As an adult, I explored a variety of careers (farmer, governess, teacher, marketing manager of a Fortune 500 corporation, greeting card designer) but fell in love with writing for children.

On the way to writing for young adults, I published three picture books—*To Rabbittown* (Scholastic), *The Night Horse* (Scholastic), and *It's Not My Turn to Look for Grandma!* (Knopf)—and numerous poems in anthologies and *Cricket Magazine*.

I studied for more than 10 years with renowned poet Myra Cohn Livingston. It was Myra who pulled the teenager out of me and insisted I put together a collection of poems in that voice.

We tried to sell the book for *ten* years! Editors wrote, "We love your writing, but teens don't read—and if they did read, they *certainly* wouldn't be reading *poetry*." Now, they say, "You write poetry? For *teens?* Do you have any more?"

ON WHETHER SHE WRITES WITH A PARTICULAR AUDIENCE IN MIND

I write for that one teen who needs to read my words. I get quiet and dive down to that alpha state where I *am* a teen. One of the poems in *Girl Coming In for a Landing* describes it:

> I let out a sigh, take a deep breath, and dive down into this
> familiar lagoon.
>
> I haven't swum here since summer started,
> this place where we are all treading water just over our desks,
> diving down to rummage around
> pulling things up from the deep
> and placing them on the page
>
> It's that place where I am finally focused
> completely

and totally
on the sound of the words,
on the idea,
on solving the word puzzle. . .
where I am focused on creating a poem
that sends the feeling I am having
or the mood I'm in
from my pen to my reader's heart.

Reprinted by permission.

ON THE INSPIRATION FOR HER POETIC NOVEL

My inspiration comes from the struggles I had as a young adult. Many of the poems in *Girl Coming In for a Landing* are from journals when I was a teen. I also get inspiration from observing my teenage son's journey, and from my own current demons. I'm particularly inspired to write when confronted by those horrid self-esteem issues we all experience.

ON THE EXTENT TO WHICH HER OWN LIFE STORY APPEARS IN HER WORKS

All of my books are little parts of me. Sharing my poems from *Girl Coming In for a Landing* is like lifting up my dress and showing people my underwear. It's very, very personal and very scary. I have a poem about this in the book. It's short. It's called

Poetry Is My Underwear
My sister found them.

Read them out loud.
She's so proud,

she's running to our parents
waving my poems in the air.

Doesn't she know
she's waving my underwear?

Reprinted by permission.

And the book I'm writing now, *Thirteen, Fourteen, Fatteen*—also a novel in verse—is even closer to my life. Very scary to write, and at the same time, very exciting.

ON WHAT SHE ENJOYED READING AS A TEENAGER

I loved reading Sir Arthur Conan Doyle, Lawrence Ferlinghetti, Joni Mitchell, Leon Uris. My girlfriend and I both read Uris's *Exodus* and were stunned by it. She became a practicing Jew and lived in Israel for several years. I was just inspired.

ON WHAT SHE ENJOYS READING CURRENTLY

It's always what I just finished reading. I love Bruce Balan's Cyber.kdz, a six-book series from Avon. They involve six teens (from Brazil, France, India, Amsterdam, New York, and California) who solve crimes together via the Internet. It's a brilliantly interwoven series using email and chat sessions and narrative. I also love Virginia Euwer Wolff's *Make Lemonade* and *True Believer.* There are so many wonderful YAs now! I also read adult novels—I was crazy about *The Time Traveler's Wife.* And I love well-written nonfiction, such as *Three Cups of Tea* and *Blink.*

What else do I read for inspiration outside my field? Picture books and political cartoons. They are both a kind of haiku—

A political
cartoon says so much in such
a limited space

And comics. And poetry. I also read columnists who write with humanity. Fervent political columns. Humor. I especially like a newspaper called *Funny Times,* which has nothing but comics, political cartoons, and humorous commentary. Wonderful. Pithy.

Political cartoons take an idea and make it into a metaphor. Like picture book authors and poets, cartoonists have to say something quickly, clearly, and leave by the back door.

ON WHAT MIGHT HELP YOUNG ADULTS DEVELOP AS WRITERS

I think young people want to know how to begin sharing their work without fear of rejection. I know I was a closet poet. I hid my poems. So I would encourage them to find a friend or a teacher or a group where they can share their work.

For me the most challenging part is sitting down and focusing. I give myself an hour of "circling the chair" time. During that time I answer email, clean my office, water my plants—anything but write. Then I settle down and write. It doesn't have to be brilliant. It just has to be words.

Also, I think the most important thing I learned from my mentor, Myra Cohn Livingston, was to really observe before I write a poem. Do I want to a write a poem about a tree? Then I go outside and study a tree for ten solid minutes by the clock, taking notes about all the things I see, smell, hear, feel about it—I count the leaves, listen to the birds on it, touch the bark, etc. Next, I think about the emotions and memories that come up when I look at this tree and jot those down, too. *Then* I go inside and write a poem about a tree. In the same way, I went to a middle school on the first day of school and observed students and interviewed them on their thoughts that day. Then I went home and wrote a poem for my book about my main character's first day of school. All of those real details that I may not remember without observation help make a poem.

ON THE IDEA THAT YOUNG ADULTS ONLY READ POETRY UNDER DURESS

I was a teen who read and wrote poetry. I know that my librarian friend says that books of poetry never stay on the shelves in the juvenile hall library—they're always checked out.

I think we all have shorter attention spans these days and poetry is a small chunk of literature that teens can cup their hands around.

ON WRITING A NOVEL IN POEMS

Once Paul Fleischman won the Newbery for *A Joyful Noise,* poetry in children's literature took off. And when *Out of the Dust* got the Newbery, the novel in poems was discovered.

Writing a novel in poems is wonderful and freeing—it's like watching a party lit by a strobe light. You can tell the story in patches, and the audience gets it. You don't have to fill in all the blanks. It implies a tremendous respect for the audience's ability to stay with you.

One of my friends said there should be a word for novels in poems. Maybe "noem"?

Ten Tips for Teens on Writing (Dare-I-Say-It?) Poetry

A candle. That's what writing is for me. It lights up dark places in my life so that I can see them clearly. Writing poetry, usually late at night in my journal, is a way of sorting out emotions I can't express any other way.

If you want to write and be published, try this:

1. Read. Read to escape. Read for inspiration. When you don't know how to say what you want to say, search for a poem you love. Then imitate its pattern. Fit your idea into that form.
2. Use all five senses. Observe yourself, a bird, the scuffed curb, how someone prepares food, opens a door, or plays guitar. Crumble a leaf in your fist. How does root beer feel going down?
3. Live! Play! Be a little crazy. Take a few deep breaths. *Be present.*
4. Write in your journal. Even if it's just for 1 minute. Describe one memorable thing. Take a day or two off from writing each week.
5. Then *make a mess.* Throw all your raw material onto the page and see what sticks. It doesn't have to be good. It just has to be words.
6. Now close in on your topic. Focus. Eliminate distractions (unneeded words, other ideas). Include specific details you've observed. Rearrange the words. Play with them on the page. Rewrite like crazy.
7. *Take*

        your

               time.
8. When it's ready, read it aloud. Does it work? Send it out.
9. Revise it. Send it out again. Don't give up. I'll tell you a secret—*Girl Coming In for a Landing* was rejected by publishers for *ten years* before it was finally accepted.

10. Not yet ready for (or interested in) publication? That's okay. Plenty of people write but don't want to be published. Or they want to be published, but not yet. Maybe you just love to write. Maybe it helps you sort out your thoughts and feelings.

Writing's my way of sorting out emotions I don't know how to express any other way. It will always be my candle in the dark.

May it be your candle, too.

From *Girl Coming In for a Landing—A Novel in Poems*

The Orality of Poetry

It cannot be stressed enough with young readers that much of the beauty and significance of poetry is to be found in its orality. Some poems work perfectly well on the printed page and the sounds and intonations are secondary to the format or the quiet contemplation they arouse, but many poems are meant to be spoken. The alliteration, the pauses, the *double entendres,* the beat, and the tone of voice do more than simply enhance the poem when read orally; these elements work with the words in much the same way illustrations do in picture books. The reading changes the meanings, the mood, and the characters.

There is not one "right" way to read a poem. Still it can be a wonderful experience for young readers to hear the poet interpret his or her own work. More and more authors are including audio versions of their works on their websites. Charles R. Smith, Jr. for example allows visitors to listen to a half dozen poems on his website. Smith really performs his poems. Readers will not be able to look at his poems as simply words on the page after listening to his interpretations. Likewise Janet Wong has a handful of her poems on her website. Wong adds to the educational benefits by including the story behind the poem.

Understanding what is actually meant by a poetry slam can be difficult for young adults who have never witnessed the oral and dramatic aspects of this sort of poetry. Youth Speaks is a slam poetry site that includes audio of slam poetry on podcasts and even video of slams. Young adults can learn much about performance poetry from this site.

Chales R. Smith's website (www.charlesrsmithjr.com)

Janet Wong's website (http://www.janetwong.com)

Youth Speaks website (http://www.youthspeaks.org)

Technology Links

LITERARY THEORY

The Concept of Deconstruction in Literary Theory

In Western cultures we have a tendency to think in terms of binary oppositions—good/bad, black/white, male/female, beginning/end. Structuralist theorists, such as the new critics, envision these binary oppositions as providing a network of relations within a text that ultimately gives it a unity and a meaning. For the structuralists any ambiguities in the text serve a literary function. Deconstructionist thought turns this on its head, rather than provide a unity, the ambiguities allow the reader to recognize the inconsistencies in a text and reveal it as a construct rather than a truth.

Though deconstruction has evolved in numerous directions and influenced various other literary theories its foundation really lies in the philosophy of language put forth by Jacques Derrida that focuses on the "free play of meaning." Deconstructionists argue that all signifiers are social constructs and ambiguities exist in texts because language (and thought) itself has gaps, contradictions, and varying levels of arbitrariness. So the concept of deconstruction focuses on the disunity inherent in all verbal constructs. The preeminent American deconstructionist J. Hillis Miller asserts: "Deconstruction is not a dismantling of the structure of a text, but a demonstration that it has already dismantled itself." Of course this is part of the "play." Deconstruction like new criticism presumes to be an objective criticism, yet deconstruction has a tongue in check objectivity, because it is aware of the radical turn it has given to interpretation. In deconstruction, the interpretation replaces the work of art.

The realities of a text are constructed realities that reflect the author's presuppositions, ideologies, prejudices, and experiences. So the deconstructionist might look more closely at the way reality is constructed, finding the gaps and contradictions. Many poets consciously play around with the ambiguities of language. In *Patrol,* Walter Dean Myers uses the signifier *enemy* in ways that keep shifting. One minute the enemy is the people that the soldier is supposedly there to help, then a baby, an old man, the next someone trying to kill him. The reader is even given the chance to see that perhaps the young man (enemy) on the other side may be having a similar experience. The concept of *enemy* is actively dismantled because it is always shifting. Sometimes the deconstructive process borders on reader response; if the poem or even a single word in the poem can be read differently by each reader, then the arbitrariness of the language quickly becomes apparent.

But in the endless play of language a text can be deconstructed in many ways. The initial sense of *deconstruct* has been stretched to include aspects of critical theory, or perhaps some critics merge deconstruction with critical theory. When looking at a poem that on the surface speaks with a patriarchal voice, the reader might find that there are other voices and absences in the text that demonstrate inconsistencies in the poem. Charles Carryl, who has often been called the American Lewis Carroll, wrote a poem entitled "Robinson Crusoe's Story," part of which goes like this:

> Oh! twas very sad and lonely
> When I found myself the only
> Population on this cultivated shore;
> But I've made a little tavern
> In a rocky little cavern,
> And I sit and watch for people at the door.
>
> I spent no time in looking
> For a girl to do my cooking,
> As I'm quite a clever hand at making stews;
> But I had that fellow Friday,
> Just to keep the tavern tidy,
> And to put a Sunday polish on my shoes.

Carryl was noted for his nonsense verse, so it is difficult to discern which elements are meant to be contradictory and which are simply inconsistent. If the island is uninhabited why is the shore "cultivated," and where does Friday come from? Obviously for the narrator racial preconceptions preclude some people from counting as inhabitants of the island. And why, one might ask, would the narrator assert that he hadn't even bothered looking for a girl to cook his food? Are we to assume that a girl would generally be a better cook? There are obviously many opportunities here for deconstruction, with racial and gender preconceptions being at the top of the list.

Topic Focus

Dialogue Journals

Dialogue journals are a wonderful form of assessment because the process involves reflection, evaluation, and creative response at the same time as it provides rich information about the reader's understandings of and reactions to the text. Dialogue journals are often a process in which the student and teacher communicate through the student's journal. Generally the journaling involves the student writing a response to a reading, followed by the teacher responding both to what the student has written and to the text, to which the student in turn responds in an ongoing dialogue. Alternately the journaling might be carried out by several students reading the same book, though intergenerational dialogue journals have greater potential to cause both readers to reconsider interpretations that, in isolation, would have been maintained (Bean and Rigoni, 2001).

Sometimes the writing happens every day, and other times the teacher will only look at and respond to journals once a week. There are many variations, depending on classroom context. If the teacher is dialoguing with every student in the class, this could be very time intensive. But these journals generally provide such meaningful dialogue and such rich information about students' thought processes that many teachers find them invaluable (Greenwood and Walters, 2005). One option that has proven quite useful is for the readers to create pairs or small groups for the dialogue journal, and the teacher responds to one or two journals per day. And dialogue journals are not just beneficial for kids; teachers and librarians have found them to be wonderful tools for planning and sharing ideas (Bean, 1989).

The following is a dialogue journal involving three middle school teachers responding to Sharon Creech's novel in verse *Love That Dog:*

Hey Cathy and Angie,

I have read through page 48. The simple style of the book cover and dust jacket caught my attention right away. As I read, I find myself grinning at the things this boy writes. I like how he responds to the poetry that his class has read by identifying what he does not understand, what he likes, and his misconceptions about writing his own poetry. It is neat how he adds elements of poems that they have studied to the short poems that he nervously writes.

I can relate to Jack when he does not want his name on his work when it is posted because I can sometimes be shy or self-conscious about sharing my work and seeing how others respond to it.

I look forward to hearing back from you,
Thanks! Brandy

To Brandy and Angie,

At first it didn't seem like poetry to me. It's written in a poetic form, but simply sounds like half a conversation. I wonder what the teacher is saying. It would be fun to have your students respond to the "conversation" by having them write from the other side.

Cathy

Girls,

Your responses to the books are great! I would have to say I was reluctant to read a poetic novel because I did not have many positive experiences with poetry growing up. I found the poems in the back useful; I was beginning to feel a little dopey since I couldn't remember some of the poems Jack referred to in the beginning with his teacher. The author does an excellent job of integrating humor with the struggles and experiences of a young boy and his teacher.

I intend to use it this year because I've been very neglectful in exploring poetry beyond their readers. Shame on me! I would also like to do more with dialoging during my students' attempts at poetry. They enjoy writing in their journals and having me write back to them in response to their work and questions.

Talk with you again soon! Angie

Cathy and Angie,

I enjoyed reading both of your responses. I agree that reading this story aloud to our classes and discussing it would allow our reluctant poets to see that poetry does not always have to rhyme. More importantly, students would be able to relate to Jack and his comical struggles with understanding and writing poetry. This story would make children who are unsure of their poetic abilities more willing to experiment with their writing and get their creative juices flowing. Angie—your idea of dialoguing with students during their attempts at poetry is great. Last year I always wrote responses to students' journal entries, but this year I will try extending dialogue to their poetry.

Poor Sky! All of Jack's short poems come together to explain what happened to his big yellow dog! I thought that was very creative writer's craft on the author's part. Just getting chunks of the poem at a time throughout the story left me guessing about what happened to Sky and made me cry, but when I read about Sky getting hit by the blue car I could not stop the tears from coming. It is funny how you (or at least I) can get attached to a character in such a short book!

I look forward to hearing your thoughts. Brandy

Brandy and Angie,

Great dialogue! Isn't it interesting how we have so much to say about a book that probably has less words than we are writing in this journal? The power of poetry.

Cathy

For Further Reading

To begin an investigation into dialogue journals as they apply to young adult literature, you might commence with the following readings:

Burton, Jill, and Michael Carroll, eds. *Journal Writing.* Teachers of English to Speakers of Other Languages, 2001.

Cooper, J. David, and Nancy D. Kiger. *Literacy: Helping Students Construct Meaning.* Houghton Mifflin, 2008.

Greenwood, Claudia M., and Cynthia E. Walters. *Literature-Based Dialogue Journals:* Reading, Writing, Connecting, Reflecting. Christopher Gordon, 2005.

Kreeft, J. *Student and Teachers Writing Together.* Teachers of English to Speakers of Other Languages, 1990.

Peyton, J., and L. Reed. *Dialogue Journals Writing with Nonnative English Speakers: A Handbook for Teachers.* Teachers of English to Speakers of Other Languages, 1990.

To begin an investigation into deconstruction as it applies to young adult literature, you might commence with the following readings:

Culler, Jonathan. *On Deconstruction.* Cornell University Press, 1982.

Hourihan, Marger. *Deconstructing the Hero: Literary Theory and Children's Literature.* Routledge, 1997.

Nodelman, Perry. "Hidden Meaning and the Inner Tale: Deconstruction and the Interpretation of Fairy Tales." *Children's Literature Association Quarterly, 14*(3), Fall 1989, 143–148.

Touponce, William F. "Children's Literature and the Pleasures of the Text." *Children's Literature Association Quarterly, 20*(4), Winter 1995–1996, 175–182.

APPENDIX

Chronologies of Books by Genre

Young Adult Literature

1387	*Canterbury Tales* by Geoffrey Chaucer
1477	*A Book of Courtesy* (the first book for young people published in English)
1484	*The Fables of Aesop* by William Caxton
1484	*Le Morte d'Arthur* by Sir Thomas Malory
1719	*The Life and Strange Surprising Adventures of Robinson Crusoe* by Daniel Defoe
mid-1700s	John Newbery in England publishes pleasure literature for young readers
1823	*Grimm's Popular Stories*
1824 to 1880s	American Sunday School Union books
1850	*The Wide, Wide World* by Susan Warner (aka Elizabeth Wentwell)
1850s	Domestic novels become popular
1858	*The Coral Island* by R. M. Balantyne
1860s	Dime novels: *Deadwood Dick, Nick Carter*
1865	*Alice's Adventures in Wonderland* by Lewis Carroll
1867	Elsie Dinsmore series by Martha F. Finley
1867	*Ragged Dick* by Horatio Alger
1867	*St. Elmo* by Augusta Jane Evans Wilson
1876	**American Library Association founded**
1868	*Little Women* by Louisa May Alcott
1870	*The Story of a Bad Boy* by Thomas Bailey Aldrich
1872	*Twenty Thousand Leagues under the Sea* by Jules Verne
1876	*The Adventures of Tom Sawyer* by Mark Twain
1877	*Black Beauty* by Anna Sewell
1883	*Treasure Island* by Robert Louis Stevenson
1883	*The Merry Adventures of Robin Hood* by Howard Pyle
1885	*Adventures of Huckleberry Finn* by Mark Twain
1892	*Adventures of Sherlock Holmes* by Arthur Conan Doyle
1894	*Jungle Book* by Rudyard Kipling
1900–1906	Soldiers of Fortune series by Edward Stratemeyer
1903	*Rebecca of Sunnybrook Farm* by Kate Douglas Wiggin
1904	*The Bobbsey Twins* by Laura Lee Hope
1906	*Peter Pan in Kensington Garden* by J. M. Barrie
1908	*The Wind in the Willows* by Kenneth Grahame
1912	Zane Grey novels: *Riders of the Purple Sage*
1930	Nancy Drew series by Carolyn Keene begins
1922	**Newbery Medal established**
1932	*Little House in the Big Woods* by Laura Ingalls Wilder
1937	*The Hobbit* by J. R. R. Tolkien
1942	*Seventeenth Summer* by Maureen Daly

1942	*All-American* by John Tunis
1944	*Johnny Tremain* by Esther Forbes
1945	*Call Me Charlie* by Jesse Jackson
1948	*The Story of the Negro* by Arna Bontemps (Newbery Honor)
1950	*Hot Rod* by Henry Felsen
1951	*The Catcher in the Rye* by J. D. Salinger
1957	**Young Adult Services Division (YASD) of ALA established**
1959	*A Raisin in the Sun* by Lorraine Hansbery
1960	*To Kill a Mockingbird* by Harper Lee
1964	*Tituba of Salem Village* by Ann Petry
1965	*North Town* by Lorenz Graham
1966	**Mildred Batchelder Award established**
1967	*The Contender* by Robert Lipsyte
1967	*The Outsiders* by S. E. Hinton
1967	*Zeeley* by Virginia Hamilton
1968	*The Pigman* by Paul Zindel
1968	*The Soul Brothers and Sister Lou* by Kristine Hunter
1969	**Coretta Scott King Award established**
1969	*Where the Lilies Bloom* by Bill and Vera Cleaver
1969	*Sounder* by William Armstrong
1970	*Are You There God? It's Me, Margaret* by Judy Blume
1971	*Go Ask Alice* by anonymous (Beatrice Sparks)
1972	*Dinky Hocker Shoots Smack!* by M. E. Kerr

1973	*A Hero Ain't Nothing But a Sandwich* by Alice Childress
1974	*The Chocolate War* by Robert Cormier
1975	*Dragonwings* by Laurence Yep
1976	*Roll of Thunder, Hear My Cry* by Mildred Taylor
1977	*I Am the Cheese* by Robert Cormier
1978	*Killing Mr. Griffin* by Lois Duncan
1978	*Beauty* by Robin McKinley
1980	*Jacob Have I Loved* by Katherine Paterson
1981	*The Friends* by Rosa Guy
1981	*Hoops* by Walter Dean Myers
1983	*Running Loose* by Chris Crutcher
1985	*The Moves Make the Man* by Bruce Brooks
1987	**Young Adult Choices Awards established**
1988	**Margaret A. Edwards Award established**
1992	**YASD becomes Young Adult Library Services Association (YALSA)**
1996	**Pura Belpré Award established**
1996	**National Book Award Young People's Literature category established**
1996	*Parrot in the Oven* by Victor Martinez
1999	*Monster* by Walter Dean Myers
2000	**Printz Award established**
2002	YALSA focus on graphic novels
2003	YALSA focus on slam poetry

This list includes crossovers from children's and adult literature.

Comic Books and Graphic Novels

1895	"Yellow Kid" by Richard Outcault appears for the first time in the *New York World*.
1934	The first modern comic book, *Famous Funnies,* a 68-page compilation costing 10 cents, was published.
1938	Debut of Superman (Action Comics); by 1945 over 400 superheroes had appeared!

1939	Introduction of Batman in *Detective Comics* (later known as DC).
1940	First science fiction comic is published.
1941	True crime comics become extremely popular. First appearance of *Archie*.
1947	First horror comic and first romance comic.

1948	The anticomic book crusade begins in earnest, including comic book burnings. Western comics become popular.
1950	"New trend" comics with war, crime, and horror are big. Superheroes lose popularity and many are canceled.
1952	First *Mad* magazine.
1953	80% of kids read comic books! 1.3 billion copies are sold per year. Superman gets first TV show.
1954	The influential book *Seduction of the Innocent* (Frederick Wertham) asserts that comic books cause juvenile delinquency. The Senate holds public hearings. The Comics Code Authority is created. Within a year the industry drops from 35 publishers to 9.
1956	*The Flash* reappears and ushers in a resurgence in superheroes.
1961	With the *Fantastic Four,* Marvel presents the first superheroes with real-world problems
1966	Batman gets a TV show. The underground comix movement is in full swing, typified by Robert Crumb's *Zap.*
1977	*Cerebus the Aardvark* (by Dave Sim) is the first successful self-published comic book.
1978	The first modern graphic novel *A Contract with God* (Will Eisner) is published.
1987	Comics/graphic novels for a more mature audience appear, including works such as *Batman: The Dark Knight Returns* and *Watchmen.*
1987	Art Spiegelman's *Maus: A Survivor's Tale* is published. The Comic Book Legal Defense fund is founded.
1992	Spiegelman's *Maus: A Survivor's Tale* receives a Pulitzer.
1996	Joe Sacco wins an American Book Award for *Palestine.*
1999	The Pokemon movie is evidence of the growing popularity of Japanese-style animé and manga.
2001	Marvel on the upswing (after a 1996 bankruptcy) drops its association with the Comics Code Authority.
2002	An ALA preconference on graphic novels signals an interest in and acceptance of the format by librarians

Note. This chronology draws heavily on Michael Lavin's presentation "Chronology of Comic Book Milestones" at the 2002 ALA preconference "Getting Graphic @ Your Library," though any inaccuracies are my own.

Young Adult and Children's Fantasy

1726	*Gulliver's Travels* by Jonathan Swift
1865	*Alice's Adventures in Wonderland* by Lewis Carroll
1871	*Through the Looking Glass* by Lewis Carroll
1871	*At the Back of the North Wind* by George MacDonald
1872	*The Princess and the Goblins* by George MacDonald
1885	*King Solomon's Mines* by H. Rider Haggard
1889	*Pinocchio* by Carlo Collodi
1900	*The Wonderful Wizard of Oz* by Lyman Frank Baum
1904	*Peter Pan* by James Mathew Barrie
1907	*The Enchanted Castle* by Edith Nesbitt
1908	*The Wind in the Willows* by Kenneth Grahame
1922	*The Voyage of Dr. Dolittle* by Hugh Loffy
1922	*The Worm Ouroboros* by Eric Rucker Eddison
1930s	The Inklings (a group of aspiring fantasy authors in England that included J. R. R. Tolkien, C. S. Lewis, and Charles Williams) is formed.

1932	*Conan the Barbarian* by Robert Howard
1937	*The Hobbit* by J. R. R. Tolkien
1950	*The Lion, the Witch, and the Wardrobe* by C. S. Lewis
1953	*The Borrowers* by Mary Norton
1954	*The Lord of the Rings* by J. R. R. Tolkien
1958	*The Once and Future King* by T. H. White
1962	*A Wrinkle in Time* by Madeline L'Engle
1964	*The Book of Three* by Lloyd Alexander
1968	*The High King* by Lloyd Alexander
1968	*A Wizard of Earthsea* by Ursula Le Guin
1968	*The Last Unicorn* by Peter Beagle

1969	*Dragonflight* by Anne McCaffrey
1974	*Watership Down* by Richard Adams
1974	*The Prince of Annwn* by Evangeline Walton
1975	*The Grey King* by Susan Cooper
1983	*Alanna: The First Adventure* by Tamora Pierce
1984	*The Hero and the Crown* by Robin McKinley
2001	*Fire Bringer* by David Clement-Davis
2001	*The Ropemaker* by Peter Dickinson
2004	*Airborn* by Ken Oppel

Science Fiction for Young Adults

1516	*Utopia* by Thomas More
1628	*New Atlantis* by Sir Francis Bacon
1818	*Frankenstein* by Mary W. Shelley
1864	*Journey to the Center of the Earth* by Jules Verne
1870	*Twenty Thousand Leagues under the Sea* by Jules Verne
1895	*The Time Machine* by H. G. Wells
1898	*War of the Worlds* by H. G. Wells
1932	*Brave New World* by Aldous Huxley
1948	*Space Cadet* by Robert Heinlein
1948	*Catseye* by Andre Norton
1950	*I Robot* by Isaac Asimov (Foundation series)
1950	*The Martian Chronicles* by Ray Bradbury
1953	*Childhood's End* by Arthur C. Clarke
1958	*Have Space Suit Will Travel* by Robert Heinlein
1967	*The White Mountains* by John Christopher
1968	*Do Androids Dream of Electric Sheep?* by Philip K. Dick

1975	*Z is for Zachariah* by Robert O'Brien
1976	*The Boys from Brazil* by Ira Levin
1981	*Return to Earth* by H. M. Hoover
1985	*Ender's Game* by Orson Scott Card
1988	*Eva* by Peter Dickinson
1993	*The Giver* by Lois Lowry
1994	*The Ear, the Eye, and the Arm* by Nancy Farmer
1997	*Intersellar Pig* by William Sleator
2000	*Dancing with an Alien* by Mary Logue
2001	*Mortal Engines* by Philip Reeve
2002	*The House of the Scorpion* by Nancy Farmer
2002	*Feed* by M. T. Anderson
2004	*Dragon and Thief* by Timothy Zahn
2007	*Unwind* by Neil Schusterman
2008	*Hunger Games* by Suzanne Collins
2008	*Little Brother* by Cory Doctorow
2009	*Leviathan* by Scott Westerfeld

Horror for Young Adults

1321	*The Divine Comedy* by Dante Alighieri	1923	*Weird Tales* magazine debuts
1589	*Dr. Faustus* by Christopher Marlowe	1927	*The Call of Cthulhu* by H. P. Lovecraft
1714	*A Night-Piece on Death* by Thomas Parnell (First work of the Graveyard Poets)	1930s	Pulp horror—*Terror Tales* and *Horror Stories*
1765	*The Castle of Otranto* by Horace Walpole (First Gothic novel)	1933	*The Werewolf of Paris* by Guy Endore
1773	*Leonore* by Gottfried Bürger (trans. to English as *The Hunt* in 1844)	1942	*Something Different This Way Comes* by Ray Bradbury
1776	*Tales of Moonlight and Rain* by Uneda Akinari (Ugetsu Monogatari)	1947– 1954	Horror Comics—such as *Tales from the Crypt*
1794	*The Mysteries of Udolpho* by Ann Radcliffe	1951	*The Day of the Triffids* by John Wyndham
1818	*Frankenstein—or the Modern Prometheus* by Mary Shelley	1954	*I Am Legend* by Richard Matheson
1819	*The Vampyre* by Dr. Polidori	1954	*Invasion of the Body Snatchers* by Jack Finney
1831	*Notre Dame de Paris* by Victor Hugo	1959	*The Haunting of Hill House* by Shirley Jackson
1835	"The Red Shoes" by Hans Christian Andersen	1959	*Psycho* by Robert Bloch
1839	"The Fall of the House of Usher" by Edgar Allan Poe	1967	*Rosemary's Baby* by Ira Levin
1840s	The Penny Bloods (Dime novels of the horror genre)	1971	*The Exorcist* by William Peter Blatty
1885	*The Strange Case of Doctor Jekyll and Mister Hyde* by Robert Louis Stevenson	1973	*I Know What You Did Last Summer* by Lois Duncan
1893	*Can Such Things Be?* by Ambrose Bierce	1974	*Carrie* by Stephen King
1896	*The Island of Doctor Moreau* by H. G. Wells	1976	*Interview with the Vampire* by Anne Rice
1897	*Dracula, or The Un-Dead* by Bram Stoker	1984	*The Books of Blood* by Clive Barker
1898	*The Turn of the Screw* by Henry James	1992	*Goosebumps* by R. L. Stine
1902	"The Monkey's Paw" by W. W. Jacobs	1992	*The Last Vampire* by Christopher Pike
1911	*Le Fantome de l'Opéra* by Gaston Leroux	1997	*Blood and Chocolate* by Annette Curtis Klause
		2005	*Twilight* by Stephenie Meyer

Historical Fiction

1820	*Ivanhoe* by Sir Walter Scott	1891	*Men of Iron* by Howard Pyle
1871	*Caged Lion* by Charlotte Yonge	1928	*The Trumpeter of Krakow* by Eric Kelly (Newbery)
1883	*Treasure Island* by Robert Louis Stevenson		

1943	*Johnny Tremain* by Esther Forbes		1964	**Laura Ingalls Wilder Award founded**
1949	*The Door in the Wall* by Marguerite de Angeli		1975	*Dragonwings* by Laurence Yep
1958	*The Witch of Blackbird Pond* by Elizabeth George Speare (Newbery)		1976	*Roll of Thunder, Hear My Cry* by Mildred Taylor
1960	*Island of the Blue Dolphin* by Scott O'Dell		1981	**Scott O'Dell Award founded**
1961	*The Bronze Bow* by Elizabeth Spears (Newbery)		1995	*Catherine, Called Birdy* by Karen Cushman
			2003	*A Northern Light* by Jennifer Donnelly

Timeline of Historical Fiction

Ancient Worlds

1992	*Shiva: An Adventure of the Ice Age* by J. H. Brennan		1998	*Fire, Bed, and Bone* by Henrietta Branford
1993	*Dawn Land* by Joseph Bruchac		1998	*The Shakespeare Stealer* by Gary Blackwood
1997	*The Bronze Bow* by Elizabeth George Speare		1999	*Anna of Byzantium* by Tracy Barnett
1997	*The Wadjet Eyes* by Jill Rubalcuba		1999	*The Fated Sky* by Henrietta Branford
2000	*Pharoah's Daughter* by Julius Lester		1999	*Mary Bloody Mary: A Young Royals Book* by Carolyn Meyer
2003	*The Kin* by Peter Dickinson		2000	*The Book of the Lion* by Michael Cadnum
			2000	*The Kite Fighters* by Linda Sue Park

Medieval/Renaissance

2008	*The Caged Lion* by Charlotte Mary Yonge (Original work published 1870)		2000	*Matilda Bone* by Karen Cushman
1891	*Men of Iron* by Howard Pyle		2000	*Nzingha: Warrior Queen of Matamba* by P. McKissack
1973	*A Proud Taste of Scarlet and Miniver* by E. L. Konigsburg		2000	*Shakespeare's Scribe* by Gary Blackwood
1978	*The Second Mrs. Giaconda* by E. L. Konigsburg		2001	*The Edge of the Sword* by Rebecca Tingle
1990	*The Shining Company* by Rosemary Sutcliff		2001	*The Passion of Artemisia* by Susan Vreeland
1992	*Morning Girl* by Michael Dorris		2001	*A Single Shard* by Linda Sue Park
1994	*Catherine, Called Birdy* by Karen Cushman		2002	*Girl in a Cage* by Jane Yolen and Robert J. Harris
1994	*The Ramsey Scallop* by Francis Temple		2002	*Crispin: The Cross of Lead* by Avi
1995	*The Midwife's Apprentice* by Karen Cushman		2002	*Daughter of Venice* by Donna Jo Napoli
			2002	*The Kite Rider* by Geraldine McCaughrean
			2003	*Daughter of the Wind* by Michael Cadnum
			2003	*Feast of Fools* by Bridget Crowley

2003	*Shakespeare's Spy* by Gary Blackwood
2003	*To the Edge of the World* by Michelle Torrey
2005	*The Blood Red Horse* by K. M. Grant

War and Plague

1973	*A Proud Taste of Scarlet and Miniver* by E. L. Konigsburg
1998	*Fire, Bed, and Bone* by Henrietta Branford
1999	*The Fated Sky* by Henrietta Branford
2000	*The Book of the Lion* by Michael Cadnum
2000	*The Devil and His Boy* by Anthony Herowitz
2000	*Shakespeare's Scribe* by Gary Blackwood
2002	*A Company of Fools* by Deborah Ellis
2003	*The Warhorse* by Don Bolognese

17th Century

1999	*SeeSaw Girl* by Linda Sue Park
2000	*Girl with a Pearl Earring* by Tracy Chevalier
2000	*Queen's Own Fool* by Jane Yolen and Robert Harris
2000	*Stowaway* by Karen Hesse
2000	*Witch Child* by Celia Rees
2002	*Bloody Jack* by Louis Meyer
2003	*Pocahontas* by Joseph Bruchac
2005	*Curse of the Blue Tattoo* by Louis Meyer

18th Century

1946	*Johnny Tremain* by Esther Forbes
1974	*My Brother Sam Is Dead* by James Collier and Christopher Collier
1984	*The Fighting Ground* by Avi
1990	*The True Confessions of Charlotte Doyle* by Avi
1993	*The Fifth of March: A Story of the Boston Massacre* by Ann Rinaldi
1995	*The Secret of Sarah Revere* by Ann Rinaldi

1998	*Cast Two Shadows: The American Revolution in the South* by Ann Rinaldi
1998	*The Arrow over the Door* by Joseph Bruchac
1999	*The Ghost in the Tokaido Inn* by Dorothy Hoobler and Thomas Hoobler
2000	*Stowaway* by Karen Hesse
2002	*Fever 1793* by Laurie Halse Anderson
2002	*The Winter People* by Joseph Bruchac
2003	*Death and the Arrow* by Chris Priestley
2003	*Or Give Me Death: A Novel of Patrick Henry's Family* by Ann Rinaldi
2004	*Finishing Rebecca: A Story about Peggy Shippen and Benedict Arnold* by Ann Rinaldi

19th Century

1998	*The Dark Light* by Mette Newth
1998	*Lyddie* by Katherine Paterson
1999	*The Birchbark House* by Louise Erdrich
1999	*The Smugglers* by Iain Lawrence
2000	*The Buccaneers* by Iain Lawrence
2000	*Nory Ryan's Song* by Patricia Reilly Giff
2000	*Sacajawea* by Joseph Bruchac
2000	*The Wreckers* by Iain Lawrence
2001	*In the Shadow of the Alamo* by Sherry Garland
2001	*The Shakeress* by Kimberly Heuston
2002	*The Voyage of Patience Goodspeed* by Heather Vogel Frederick
2003	*This Vast Land: A Young Man's Journal of the Lewis and Clark Expedition* by Stephen Ambrose
2005	*An Innocent Soldier* by Josef Hollub

Slavery

| 1973 | *The Slave Dancer* by Paula Fox |
| 1981 | *Jump Ship to Freedom* by James Collier and Christopher Collier |

1989	*My Name Is Not Angelique* by Scott O'Dell
1990	*Underground Man* by Milton Meltzer
1991	*Ajeemah and His Son* by James Berry
1992	*Letters from a Slave Girl: The Story of Harriet Jacobs* by Mary Lyons
1993	*Nightjohn* by Gary Paulsen
1994	*The Captive* by Joyce Hansen
1999	*Stealing Freedom* by Elisa Carbonne
2000	*Run the Blockade* by G. Clifton Wisler
2005	*Day of Tears* by Julius Lester

Civil War

1986	*Which Way to Freedom?* by Joyce Hansen
1988	*Behind Rebel Lines: The Incredible Story of Emma Edmonds, Civil War Spy* by Seymour Reit
1993	*Bull Run* by Paul Fleischman
1997	*Soldier Boy* by Brian Burks
1998	*Soldier's Heart: A Novel of the Civil War* by Gary Paulsen
2003	*Before the Creeks Ran Red* by Carolyn Reeder
2003	*Hear the Wind Blow* by M. D. Hahn

Gold Rush

1983	*Beyond the Divide* by Kathryn Lasky
1985	*Mountain Light* by Laurence Yep
1996	*Ballad of Lucy Whipple* by Karen Cushman
2000	*The Journal of Wong Ming Chung* by Laurence Yep
2001	*Down the Yukon* by Will Hobbs
2001	*Seeds of Hope: Gold Rush Diary of Susanna Fairchild* by Kristiana Gregory

Reconstruction

1984	*The Serpent's Children* by Laurence Yep
1985	*Mountain Light* by Laurence Yep

1993	*Dragon's Gate* by Laurence Yep
1997	*I Thought My Soul Would Rise and Fly: The Diary of Patsy, a Freed Girl* by Joyce Hansen
1999	*The Coffin Quilt: The Feud between the Hatfields and the McCoys* by Ann Rinaldi
2000	*A Coal Miner's Bride: The Diary of Anetka Kaminska* by Susan Bartoletti
2000	*The Boxer* by Kathleen Karr
2001	*Fair Weather* by Richard Peck
2001	*Theodore Roosevelt: Letters from a Young Coal Miner* by Jennifer Armstrong
2003	*The Traitor: Golden Mountain Chronicles* by Laurence Yep

20th Century
1900–1909

1977	*Dragonwings* by Laurence Yep
1992	*The Ellis Island Trilogy: Land of Hope* by Joan Lowery Nixon
1996	*Jip: His Story* by Katherine Paterson
2001	*Fair Weather* by Richard Peck
2001	*The Land* by Mildred Taylor
2003	*Earthquake at Dawn* by Kristiana Gregory
2003	*January 1905* by Katharine Boling
2003	*A Northern Light* by Jennifer Donnelly
2003	*The Silent Boy* by Lois Lowry

1910–1919

1983	*The Dreadful Future of Blossom Culp* by Richard Peck
1986	*After the Dancing Days* by Margaret Rostkowski
1992	*Letters from Rifka* by Karen Hesse
1998	*Pictures—1918* by Jeanette Ingold
1999	*Strawberry Hill* by A. Lafaye
1999	*Summer Soldiers* by Susan Hart Lindquist
2000	*Forgotten Fire* by Adam Bagdasarian
2000	*The Likes of Me* by Randall Platt

2001	*Lord of the Nutcracker Men* by Iain Lawrence
2002	*The Big Burn* by Jeanette Ingold
2003	*Ghosts I Have Been* by Richard Peck

1920–1929

1991	*Arly* by Robert Newton Peck
1993	*White Lilacs* by Carolyn Meyer
1994	*The Jazz Kid* by James Lincoln Collier
1998	*Choosing Up Sides* by John Ritter
1999	*Dave at Night* by Gail Carson Levine
2001	*The Secret School* by Avi
2001	*Witness* by Karen Hesse
2003	*The Grape Thief* by Kristine Franklin

1930–1939

1976	*Roll of Thunder, Hear My Cry* by Mildred D. Taylor
1991	*Airfield* by Jeanette Ingold
1991	*Nothing to Fear* by Jackie French Koller
1997	*A Part of the Sky* by Robert Newton Peck
1997	*Out of the Dust* by Karen Hesse
1997	*Treasures in the Dust* by Tracey Porter
1999	*All We Know of Heaven* by Sue Ellen Bridgers
1999	*A Long Way from Chicago* by Richard Peck
1999	*Bud, Not Buddy* by Christopher Paul Curtis
1999	*Nowhere to Call Home* by Cynthia DeFelice
2004	*Walking on Air* by Kelly Easton

Depression Era

1986	*Ivy Larkin* by Mary Stolz
1988	*Borrowed Children* by George Ella Lyon
1991	*Out of the Dust* by Karen Hesse
2000	*Esperanza Rising* by Pam Muñoz Ryan
2001	*Clem's Chances* by Sonia Levitan
2002	*Horse Thief* by Robert Newton Peck

1940–1949, World War II Era

1973	*Summer of My German Soldier* by Bette Greene

1980	*Jacob Have I Loved* by Katherine Paterson
1981	*Grace in the Wilderness: After the Liberation 1945–1948* by Aranka Siegel
1981	*Upon the Head of the Goat: A Childhood in Hungary 1939–1944* by Aranka Siegel
1985	*Sirens and Spies* by Janet Taylor Lisle
1989	*Number the Stars* by Lois Lowry
1991	*The Man from the Other Side* by Uri Orlev
1991	*Year of Impossible Goodbyes* by S. N. Choi
1994	*My Brother, My Sister, and I* by Yoko Watkins
1994	*Under the Blood Red Sun* by Graham Salisbury
1995	*The Bomb* by Theodore Taylor
1996	*Keep Smiling Through* by Ann Rinaldi
1997	*Lily's Crossing* by Patricia Giff
1997	*Stones in Water* by Donna Jo Napoli
1997	*The War in Georgia* by Jerrie Oughton
1998	*Bat 6* by Virginia Euwer Wolff
1999	*Good Night, Maman* by Norma Fox Mazer
2000	*The Art of Keeping Cool* by Janet Taylor Lisle
2001	*All the Way Home* by Patricia Giff
2001	*Don't You Know There's a War On?* by Avi
2001	*Slap Your Sides* by M. E. Kerr
2001	*Solider Boys* by Dean Hughes
2001	*Soldier X* by Don Wulffson
2002	*Blizzard's Wake* by Phyllis Reynolds Naylor
2002	*When My Name Was Keoko* by Linda Sue Park
2003	*Aleutian Sparrow* by Karen Hesse
2003	*Malka* by Mirjam Pressler
2003	*Milkweed* by Jerry Spinelli
2003	*Room in the Heart* by Sonia Levitin
2003	*Run, Boy, Run* by Uri Orlev

2003	*Shadows on the Sea* by Joan Harlow
2003	*The Journal of Ben Uchida* by Barry Denenberg
2003	*When the War Is Over* by M. Attema
2005	*Code Talker* by Joseph Bruchac
2005	*Eyes of the Emperor* by Graham Salisbury

1950–1959

1995	*How Far Would You Have Gotten If I Hadn't Called You Back?* by Valerie Hobbs
1996	*Belle Prater's Boy* by Ruth White
1997	*What I Know Now* by Rodger Larson
1998	*My Louisiana Sky* by Kimberly Willis Holt
1998	*Rocket Boys* by Homer H. Hickam Jr.
2001	*Memories of Summer* by Ruth White
2002	*Mississippi Trail, 1955* by Chris Crowe
2007	*Fire from the Rock* by Sharon Draper

1960–1969

1968	*Dancing in the Cadillac Light* by Kimberly Willis Holt
1988	*Fallen Angels* by Walter Dean Myers
1994	*Come in from the Cold* by Marsha Qualey
1994	*Jesse* by Gary Soto
1996	*Don't Think Twice* by Ruth Pennebaker
1996	*Spite Fences* by Trudy Krisher
1996	*The Cuckoo's Child* by Suzanne Freeman
1997	*Leon's Story* by Leon Walter Tillage
1997	*Long Time Passing* by Linda Crew
1999	*Saying It Out Loud* by Joan Abelove
1999	*The Watsons Go to Birmingham—1963* by Christopher Paul Curtis
2002	*A Corner of the Universe* by Ann Martin
2002	*Before We Were Free* by J. Alvarez
2002	*Sonny's War* by Valerie Hobbs (Original work published 1968)
2005	*Search and Destroy* by Dean Hughes

1970–1979

1988	*Park's Quest* by Katherine Paterson
1995	*The Road Home* by Ellen Emerson White
1997	*Little Miss Strange* by Joanna Rose
1999	*Strawberry Hill* by A. Lafaye
2000	*McKendree* by Sandra Belton
2002	*Beacon Hill Boys* by Ken Mochizuki
2002	*Gold Dust* by Chris Lynch
2002	*Sonny's War* by Valerie Hobbs

1980–1989

1995	*Quake!* by Joe Cottonwood
2002	*A Stone in My Hand* by C. Clinton

1990–1999

1993	*Linger* by M. E. Kerr
1994	*Armageddon Summer* by Jane Yolen and Bruce Coville
1994	*Gulf* by Robert Westall
1995	*Hometown* by Marsha Qualey

Time Travel

1981	*Jeremy Visick* by David Wiseman
1994	*If I Should Die before I Wake* by Han Nolan
1997	*Both Sides of Time* by Caroline Cooney
1999	*King of Shadows* by Susan Cooper
2000	*Roughing It on the Oregon Trail* by Diane Stanley
2000	*The Grave* by James Heneghan
2001	*Anne Frank and Me* by Cherie Bennett and Jeff Gottesfeld
2003	*Dreaming in Black and White* by Reinhardt Jung, translated by Anthea Bell
2003	*The House on Hound Hill* by Maggie Prince
2005	*Black Canary* by Jane Carry
2005	*Black Powder* by Staton Rabin

BIBLIOGRAPHY

Aardema, Verna. *Why Mosquitoes Buzz in People's Ears.* Illustrated by Jeo and Diane Dillon. Dial, 1975.

Abbott, Tony. *Crushing on a Capulet.* Volo Books, 2003.

Abdel-Fattah, Randa. *Does My Head Look Big in This?* Orchard, 2007.

Abelove, Joan. *Saying It Out Loud.* Dorling Kindersley, 1999.

Acosta, Belinda. *3 Girls and Clorox.* New Plays for Children, 1995.

Adams, Douglas. *Hitchhiker's Guide to the Galaxy.* Harmony, 1979.

Adams, Richard. *Watership Down.* Macmillan, 1972.

Adler, C. S. *Kiss the Clown.* Houghton Mifflin, 1986.

Adler, David. *Lou Gehrig: The Luckiest Man.* Illustrated by Terry Widener. Harcourt Brace, 1997.

Adler, David. *B. Franklin, Printer.* Holiday House, 2001.

Adlington, L. J. *Diary of Pelly D.* Greenwillow, 2005.

Adoff, Arnold. *All the Colors of the Race.* William Morrow, 1982.

Adoff, Arnold. *Chocolate Dreams.* Lothrop, Lee, and Shepard, 1989.

Adoff, Arnold. *I Am the Darker Brother.* Collier, 1968/1997.

Adoff, Arnold. *Love Letters.* Illustrated by Lisa Desimini. Blue Sky Press, 1997.

Adoff, Arnold. *Outside/Inside Poems.* Harcourt Brace, 1981.

Adoff, Arnold. *Slow Dance Heart Break Blues.* Lothrop, Lee, and Shepard, 1995.

Adoff, Arnold. *The Basket Counts.* Simon & Schuster, 2000.

Adoff, Jaime. *Names Will Never Hurt Me.* Dutton, 2004.

Adoff, Jaime. *The Song Shoots Out of My Mouth: A Celebration of Music.* Illustrated by Martin French. Dutton, 2002.

Aesop's Fables. Illustrated by Jerry Pinkney. SeaStar Books, 2000.

Aesop's Fables: A Classic Illustrated Edition. Compiled by R. Ash. Chronicle, 1990.

Ahmed-Cawthorne, Francheska. *Sista, Girlfren' Breaks It Down . . . When Mom's Not Around.* Fireside, 1996.

Aikin, Lucy. *The Pilgrim's Progress in Words of One Syllable.* McLoughlin Brothers, 1869.

Alcott, Louisa May. *Little Women.* Roberts Brothers, 1868.

Aldrich, Thomas Bailey. *The Story of a Bad Boy.* Book Jungle, 1870.

Alexie, Sherman. *The Absolutely True Diary of a Part Time Indian.* Scholastic, 2002.

Alford, Jan. *I Can't Believe I Have to Do This.* Putnam, 1997.

Alger, Horatio. *Ragged Dick.* Loring, 1868.

Allen, Thomas. *Remember Pearl Harbor: American and Japanese Survivors Tell Their Stories.* National Geographic, 2001.

Almond, David. *Kit's Wilderness.* Doubleday, 2001.

Almond, David. *Skellig.* Knopf, 1999.

Alonzo, Sandra. *Riding Invisible.* Illustrated by Nathan Huang. Hyperion, 2010.

Alverez, J. *Before We Were Free.* Knopf, 2002.

Alvarez, Lynn. *Eddie Mundo Edmundo* in *Collected Plays: Volume I.* Smith and Kraus, 1998.

Ambrose, Stephen. *This Vast Land: A Young Man's Journal of the Lewis and Clark Expedition.* Simon & Schuster, 2003.

Ames, Mildred. *Anna to the Infinite Power.* Scribner's, 1981.

Andersen, Hans Christian. *The Emperor's New Clothes.* Illustrated by Angela Barrett. Candlewick, 1997.

Andersen, Hans Christian. *The Little Match Girl.* Fogelman, 1999.

Andersen, Hans Christian. *The Little Match Girl.* Illustrated by Kveta Pacovska. Minedition, 2005.

Andersen, Hans Christian. *The Little Mermaid.* Illustrated by Charles Santore. Running Press Kids, 2009.

Andersen, Hans Christian. *The Little Mermaid.* Illustrated by Lazlo Gal. Methuen, 1984.

Andersen, Hans Christian. *The Little Mermaid.* Illustrated by Lisbeth Zwerger. Minedition, 2004.

Andersen, Hans Christian. *The Little Mermaid.* Illustrated by Sulamith Wulfing. Amber Lotus, 1996.

Andersen, Hans Christian. *The Nightingale.* Illustrated by Jerry Pinkney. Fogelman, 2002.

Andersen, Hans Christian. *The Ugly Duckling.* Illustrated by Jerry Pinkney. Morrow, 1999.

Andersen, Hans Christian. *The Ugly Duckling.* Illustrated by Robert Ingpen. Penguin, 2005.

Anderson, Ho Che. *King.* Fantagraphic, 1993.

Anderson, Joan. *Rookie: Tamika Whitmore: First Year in the WNBA.* Puffin, 2000.

Anderson, Laurie Halse. *Fever 1793.* Aladdin, 2002.

Anderson, Laurie Halse. *Speak.* Farrar, Straus & Giroux, 1999.

Anderson, M. T. *Burger Wuss.* Candlewick, 1999.

Anderson, M. T. *Feed.* Candlewick, 2002.

Anderson, M. T. *Thirsty.* Candlewick, 1997.

Anderson, Maggie, and David Hassler (eds.). *Learning by Heart: Contemporary American Poetry about School.* University of Iowa Press, 1999.

Andronik, Catherine. *Hatshepsut, His Majesty, Herself.* Illustrated by Joseph Daniel Fiedler. Atheneum, 2001.

Anglesey, Zoe. *Listen Up! Spoken Word Poetry.* Ballantine, 1999.

Anonymous. *Go Ask Alice.* Prentice-Hall, 1971.

Appelt, Kathi. *Poems from Homeroom: A Writer's Place to Start.* Henry Holt, 2002.

Applegate, K. A. *Remnants* series. Scholastic, 2001 and on.

Armstrong, Jennifer. *In My Hands: Memories of a Holocaust Rescuer.* Knopf, 1999.

Armstrong, Jennifer. *Shattered: Stories of Children and War.* Knopf, 2002.

Armstrong, Jennifer. *Shipwreck at the Bottom of the World.* Crown Publishers, 1998.

Armstrong, Jennifer. *Dear Mr. President: Theodore Roosevelt: Letters from a Young Coal Miner.* Winslow House, 2001.

Armstrong, Jennifer, and Nancy Butcher. *The Kindling: Fire-Us.* HarperCollins, 2002.

Armstrong, William. *Sounder.* Harper & Row, 1969.

Arnold, Ann. *Sea Cows, Shamans, and Scurvy: Alaska's First Naturalist: Georg Wilhelm Steller.* Farrar, Straus, and Giroux, 2008.

Arnold, Katherine. *The Amazing "True" Story of a Teenage Single Mom.* Hyperion, 1998.

Artell, Mike. *Petite Rouge: A Cajun Red Riding Hood.* Illustrated by Jim Harris. Dial, 2001.

Ashabranner, Brent. *Always to Remember: The Vietnam Veterans Memorial.* Putnam, 1988.

Ashby, Ruth (ed.). *Herstory: Women Who Changed the World.* Viking, 1995.

Asher, Sandra F. *A Woman Called Truth.* Dramatic Publishing, 1993.

Asher, Sandy. "Workout." In Don Gallo (ed.). *Centerstage: One Act Plays for Teenage Readers and Actors.* Harper & Row, 1990.

Atkins, Catherine. *Alt Ed.* Putnam, 2003.

Atkins, Catherine. *When Jeff Comes Home.* Putnam, 1999.

Attema, M. *When the War Is Over.* Orca, 2003.

Atwater-Rhodes, Amelia. *Demon in My View.* Delacorte, 2002.

Atwater-Rhodes, Amelia. *In the Forests of the Night.* Delacorte, 1999.

Atwood, Margaret. The *Handmaid's Tale.* Houghton Mifflin, 1986.

Auch, Mary Jane. *Ashes to Roses.* Henry Holt, 2002.

Auch, Mary Jane. *Peeping Beauty.* Holiday House, 1993.

Avi. *Blue Heron.* Simon & Schuster, 1992.

Avi. *Crispin: The Cross of Lead.* Hyperion, 2002.

Avi. *Don't You Know There's a War On?* HarperCollins, 2001.

Avi. *Ereth's Birthday.* HarperCollins, 2000.

Avi. *Nothing but the Truth.* Orchard, 1991.

Avi. *Poppy and Rye.* Avon, 1998.

Avi. *Silent Movie.* Illustrated by C. B. Mordin. Atheneum, 2003.

Avi. *The Fighting Ground.* Lippincott, 1984.

Avi. *The Secret School.* Harcourt, 2001.

Avi. *The True Confessions of Charlotte Doyle.* Orchard, 1990.

Avi. *Wolf Rider.* Bradbury, 1986.

Aylesworth, Jim. *Goldilocks and the Three Bears.* Illustrated by Barbara McClintock. Scholastic, 2003.

Aylesworth, Jim. *Old Black Fly.* Illustrated by Stephen Gammel. Henry Holt, 1992.

Aylesworth, Jim. *The Gingerbread Man.* Illustrated by Barbara McClintock. Scholastic, 1998.

Babbitt, Natalie. *Tuck Everlasting.* Farrar, Straus, and Giroux, 1975.

Bachrach, Susan. *Tell Them We Remember: The Story of the Holocaust.* Little, Brown, 1994.

Baird, Thomas. *Smart Rats.* Harper & Row, 1990.

Bang, Molly. *Picture This: How Pictures Work.* Sea Star, 1991.

Bang, Molly. *When Sophie Gets Angry—Really, Really Angry. . . .* Scholastic, 1999.

Banyai, Istvan. *Zoom.* Puffin, 1998.

Bardi, Abby. *The Book of Fred: A Novel.* Pocket, 2001.

Barnett, Tracy. *Anna of Byzantium.* Delacorte, 1999.

Barrett, Angela. *Snow White.* Knopf, 1991.

Barrie, Barbara. *Adam Zigzag.* Delacorte, 1994.

Barrie, J. M. *Peter Pan in Kensington Garden.* Scribner's Sons, 1906.

Barron, T. A. *The Lost Years of Merlin.* Philomel, 1996.

Bartoletti, Susan. *A Coal Miner's Bride: The Diary of Anetka Kaminska.* Dear America Series. Scholastic, 2000.

Bartoletti, Susan Campbell. *Black Potatoes: The Story of the Great Irish Famine, 1845–1850.* Houghton Mifflin, 2001.

Bass, L. G. *Sign of the Oin.* Hyperion, 2004.

Basso, Michael J. *The Underground Guide to Teenage Sexuality.*

Bauer, Cat. *Harley Like a Person.* Winslow Press, 2000.

Bauer, Joan. *Hope Was Here.* Putnam, 2000.

Bauer, Joan. *Rules of the Road.* Putnam, 1998.

Bauer, Joan. *Squashed.* Delacorte, 1992.

Bauer, Marion Dane (ed.). *Am I Blue? Coming Out from the Silence.* HarperCollins, 1994.

Beah, Ishmael. *A Long Way Gone.* Farrar, Straus, and Giroux, 2007.

Beale, Fleur. *I Am Not Ester.* Hyperion, 2004.

Beals, Melba Pattillo. *Warriors Don't Cry.* Pocket Books, 1995.

Bechard, Margaret. *Hanging on to Max.* Roaring Brook Press, 2002.

Bedard, R. L. (ed.). *Dramatic Literature for Children: A Century in Review.* Anchorage, 1984.

Bedard, Tony, and Paul Pelletier. *Negation, Book 1: Bohica.* CrossGen, 2002.

Bell, Hilari. *A Matter of Profit.* HarperCollins, 2001.

Belton, Sandra. *McKendree.* Greenwillow, 2000.

Bendis, Brian Michael, et al. *Ultimate Spider-Man.* Marvel Comics, 2001.

Bendis, Brian Michael, and Marc Andreyke. *Torso.* Image Comics, 1998.

Bendis, Brian Michael, and Michael Oemig. *Powers: Who Killed Retro Girl.* Image Comics, 2001–present.

Bennett, Cherie, and Jeff Gottesfeld. *Anne Frank and Me.* Putnam, 2001.

Bernbaum, Israel. *My Brother's Keeper: The Holocaust through the Eyes of an Artist.* G. P. Putnam's Sons, 1985.

Berry, James. *Ajeemah and His Son.* HarperCollins, 1991.

Berry, James. *When I Dance: Poems.* HBJ, 1991.

Billingsley, Frannie. *The Folkkeeper.* Atheneum, 1999.

Blacker, Terence. *The Angel Factory.* Simon & Schuster, 2002.

Blackwood, Gary. *Shakespeare's Scribe.* Dutton, 2000.

Blackwood, Gary. *Shakespeare's Spy.* Dutton, 2003.

Blackwood, Gary. *The Dying Sun.* Atheneum, 1989.

Blackwood, Gary. *The Shakespeare Stealer.* Dutton, 1998.

Blackwood, Gary. *Wild Timothy.* Atheneum, 1987.

Blackwood, Gary. *Year of the Hangman.* Dutton, 2002.

Block, Francesca Lia. *Hanged Man.* HarperCollins, 1994.

Block, Francesca Lia. *Weetzie Bat.* HarperCollins, 1989.

Bloor, Edward. *Tangerine.* Scholastic, 1997.

Blumberg, Rhoda. *Shipwrecked! The True Adventures of a Japanese Boy.* HarperCollins, 2001.

Blume, Judy. *Are You There God? It's Me, Margaret.* Bradbury, 1970.

Blume, Judy. *Forever.* Bradbury, 1973.

Boas, Jacob (ed.). *We Are Witnesses: Five Diaries of Teenagers Who Died in the Holocaust.* Henry Holt, 1995.

Bober, Natalie. *Countdown to Independence: A Revolution of Ideas in England and Her American Colonies 1760–1776.* Atheneum, 2001.

Bodanis, David. *Secret House: 24 Hours in the Strange and Unexpected World in Which We Spend Our Nights and Days.* Simon & Schuster, 1986.

Bodkin, Odds. *The Crane Wife.* Illustrated by Gennady Spirin. Harcourt, 1998.

Boling, Katharine. *January 1905.* Harcourt, 2003.

Bolognese, Don. *The Warhorse.* Simon & Schuster, 2003.

Bond, Nancy. *A String in the Harp.* HarperCollins, 2000.

Bontemps, Arna. *The Story of the Negro.* Knopf, 1948.

Bova, Ben. *Duelling Machine.* Faber and Faber, 1971.

Bradley, Kimberly. *For Freedom.* Delacorte, 2003.

Bradley, Marion Zimmer. *The Mists of Avalon.* Ballantine, 1987.

Brande, Robin. *Evolution, Me, and Other Freaks of Nature.* Knopf, 2007.

Branford, Henrietta. *Fire, Bed, and Bone.* Candlewick, 1998.

Branford, Henrietta. *The Fated Sky.* Candlewick, 1999.

Brashares, Ann. *The Second Summer of the Sisterhood.* Random House, 2003.

Brashares, Ann. *The Sisterhood of the Traveling Pants.* Delacorte Press, 2001.

Bray, Libba. *Going Bovine.* Delacorte, 2009.

Breaver, Barbara (ed.). *Voices: Poetry and Art from around the World.* National Geographic Society, 2000.

Brennan, J. H. *Shiva: An Adventure of the Ice Age.* HarperCollins, 1992.

Brennan, Michael. *Electric Girl.* Mighty Gremlin/AiT/PlanetLar, 2000.

Brett, Jan. *Beauty and the Beast.* Clarion, 1989.

Brett, Jan. *The Gingerbread Baby.* Putnam, 1999.

Brett, Jan. *The Mitten.* Putnam, 1989.

Brewbaker, James, and Dawnelle Hyland (eds.). *Poems by Adolescents and Adults: A Thematic Collection for Middle School and High School.* NCTE, 2002.

Brewster, Hugh, and Laurie Coulter. *888½ Amazing Answers to Your Questions about the Titanic.* Scholastic, 1998.

Bridgers, Sue Ellen. *All We Know of Heaven.* Banks Channel Books, 1999.

Bridgers, Sue Ellen. *Permanent Connections.* HarperCollins, 1987.

Briggs, Raymond. *Ethel and Ernest.* Pantheon Books, 1998.

Briggs, Raymond. *Jim and the Beanstalk.* Coward, McCann & Geohegan, 1970.

Briggs, Raymond. *The Snowman.* Random House, 1978.

Brooke, Michael. *Concrete Waves: The History of Skateboarding.* Warwick, 1999.

Brooke, William J. *Teller of Tales.* HarperCollins, 1994.

Brooks, Bruce. *Asylum for Nightface.* Laura Geringer, 1996.

Brooks, Bruce. *Dolores.* HarperCollins, 2001.

Brooks, Bruce. *No Kidding.* HarperCollins, 1986.

Brooks, Bruce. *The Moves Make the Man.* ABC-CLIO, 1985.

Brooks, Kevin. *Lucas.* Scholastic, 2003.

Brooks, Kevin. *Martyn Pig.* Scholastic, 2001.

Brooks, Laurie. *The Wrestling Season.* Dramatic Publishing, 2000.

Brooks, Martha. *Being with Henry.* Dorling Kindersley, 2000.

Brooks, Martha. *Traveling On into the Light and Other Stories.* Orchard, 1994.

Brooks, Polly S. *Beyond the Myth: The Story of Joan of Arc.* Lippincott, Williams and Wilkins, 1990.

Brooks, Terry. *Magic Kingdom for Sale—Sold!* Ballantine, 1987.

Brooks, Terry. *Sword of Shannara.* Del Rey, 1991.

Brous, Elizabeth. *How to Be Gorgeous: The Ultimate Beauty Guide to Hair, Makeup, and More.* HarperTeen, 2000.

Browne, Anthony. *Willy the Dreamer.* Candlewick, 1998.

Bruchac, Joseph. *A Boy Called Slow.* illus. Rocco Baviera. Philomel, 1994.

Bruchac, Joseph. *Arrow over the Door.* Dial, 1998.

Bruchac, Joseph. *Between Earth and Sky: Legends of Native American Sacred Places.* Harcourt, 1996.

Bruchac, Joseph. *Bowman's Store.* Sagebrush, 2001.

Bruchac, Joseph. *Code Talker.* Dial, 2005.

Bruchac, Joseph. *Crazy Horse's Vision.* Lee & Low, 2000.

Bruchac, Joseph. *Dawn Land.* Fulcrum, 1993.

Bruchac, Joseph. *Pocahontas.* Harcourt, 2003.

Bruchac, Joseph. *Sacajawea.* Harcourt, 2000.

Bruchac, Joseph. *Skeleton Man.* HarperCollins, 2001.

Bruchac, Joseph. *The Arrow over the Door.* Dial, 1998.

Bruchac, Joseph. *The Heart of a Chief.* Sagebrush, 2001.

Bruchac, Joseph. *The Winter People.* Dial, 2002.

Bruchac, Joseph, and Murv Jacob. *The Boy Who Lived with the Bears and Other Iroquois Stories.* HarperCollins, 1995.

Brumberg, Joan Jacobs. *The Body Project: An Intimate History of American Girls.* Vintage, 1998.

Buchholz, Quint. *Collector of Moments.* Farrar, Straus, and Giroux, 1997.

Buckley, Gail. *American Patriots: The Story of Blacks in the Military.* Adapted by Tonya Bolden. Crown, 2003.

Bunting, Eve. *Night of the Gargoyles.* Illustrated by David Weisner. Clarion, 1999.

Bunting, Eve. *Smoky Night.* Illustrated by David Diaz. Harcourt Brace, 1994.

Bunting, Eve. *So Far from the Sea.* Illustrated by Chris Soentpiet. Clarion, 1998.

Burdett, Lois. *A Midsummer Night's Dream.* Firefly, 1997.

Burgess, Melvin. *Bloodtide.* Tor, 2001.

Burgess, Melvin. *Smack.* Avon, 1993.

Burkert, Nancy Ekholm. *Snow White and the Seven Dwarfs.* Farrar, Straus, and Giroux, 1972.

Burks, Brian. *Soldier Boy.* Harcourt, 1997.

Burleigh, Robert. *Hoops.* Illustrated by Stephen Johnson. Voyager, 2001.

Burleigh, Robert, and Bill Wylie. *Amelia Earhart: Free in the Skies.* Silver Whistle, 2003.

Burnett, Frances. *The Secret Garden.* Frederick Stokes, 1911.

Burns, Khephra. *Mansa Musa: The Lion of Mali.* Illustrated by Leo and Diane Dillon. Harcourt, 2001.

Bush, Max (ed.). *Plays for Young Audiences.* Meriwether, 1995.

Bush, Max. *Sarah.* Dramatic Publishing, 2000.

Busiak, Kurt, and Brent Anderson. *Astro City.* DC, 2000/1996.

Buss, Fran Leeper. *Journey of the Sparrows.* Dutton, 1991.

Cabot, Meg. *The Princess Diaries.* HarperCollins, 2000.

Cadnum, Michael. *Daughter of the Wind.* Orchard, 2003.

Cadnum, Michael. *Forbidden Forest the Story of Little John and Robin Hood* Orchard, 2001.

Cadnum, Michael. *In a Dark Wood.* Scholastic, 2000.

Cadnum, Michael. *The Book of the Lion.* Viking, 2000.

Caniff, Milton. *Dragon Lady.* ACG Comics, 2000.

Cappo, Nan Willard. *Cheating Lessons.* Atheneum, 2001.

Capuzzo, Michael. *Close to Shore: The Terrifying Shark Attacks of 1916.*

Carbonne, Elisa. *Stealing Freedom.* Knopf, 1999.

Carbonne, Elisa. *Storm Warriors.* Knopf, 2001.

Card, Orson Scott. *Ender's Game.* Tor, 1985.

Card, Orson Scott. *Ender's Shadow.* Tor, 1999.

Carlson, Lori (ed.). *Cool Salsa: Bilingual Poems on Growing Up Latino in the United States.* Henry Holt, 1994.

Carlson, Lori Marie (selector). *You're On! Seven Plays in English and Spanish.* Morrow, 1999.

Carney, Gene. *Romancing the Horsehide: Baseball Poems on Players and the Game.* McFarland, 1993.

Carroll, Lewis. *Alice in Wonderland.* Illustrated by Robert Sabuda. Little Simon, 2003.

Carroll, Lewis. *Alice's Adventures in Wonderland.* Illustrated by Barry Moser. University of California Press, 1982. (Original work published 1865)

Carroll, Lewis. *Alice's Adventures in Wonderland.* Illustrated by Ralph Steadman. Crown, 1973.

Carroll, Lewis. *Alice's Adventures in Wonderland: A Pop-Up Adaptation.* Illustrated by Robert Sabuda. Little Simon, 2003.

Cart, Michael (ed.). *Love and Sex: Ten Stories of Truth.* Simon & Schuster, 2001.

Cart, Michael. *Tomorrowland: Ten Stories about the Future.* Scholastic, 1999.

Carter, Alden. *Bull Catcher.* Scholastic, 1997.

Carter, Alden. *Crescent Moon.* Holiday House, 1999.

Carvell, Marlene. *Who Will Tell My Brother?* Hyperion, 2001.

Catonese, P. W. *The Thief and the Beanstalk.* Aladdin, 2005.

Ceccoli, Nicoletta. *Rapunzel.* Brighter Child, 2001.

Cefrey, Holly. *Coping with Cancer.* Rosen, 2003.

Chabon, Michael. *Summerland.* Hyperion, 2002.

Chadwick, Paul. *The Complete Concrete.* Dark Horse, 1996.

Chambers, Aidan. *Breaktime.* HarperCollins, 1979.

Chambers, Aidan. *Postcards from No Man's Land.* Dutton, 2002.

Chandler, Elizabeth. *Dark Secrets.* Simon Pulse, 2008.

Chaucer, Geoffry. *The Canterbury Tales.* Selected and retold by Barbara Cohen. Illustrated by Trina Schart Hyman. Lothrop, Lee & Shepard, 1988.

Chbosky, Stephen. *The Perks of Being a Wallflower.* Pocket Books, 1999.

Che, Dia. *Dia's Story Cloth.* Stitched by Chue and Nhia Cha. Lee and Low, 1998.

Cheaney, C. B. *The Playmaker.* Knopf, 2000.

Cheripko, Jan. *Rat.* Boyds Mills, 2002.

Cherry, Lynne, and Gary Braasch. *How We Know What We Know About Our Changing Climate: Scientists and Kids Explore Global Warming.* Dawn, 2008.

Chevalier, Tracy. *Falling Angels.* Dutton, 2001.

Chevalier, Tracy. *Girl with a Pearl Earring.* Dutton, 2000.

Childress, Alice. *A Hero Ain't Nothing but a Sandwich.* Coward, McCann & Geoghegan, 1973.

Choi, S. N. *Year of Impossible Goodbyes.* Houghton Mifflin, 1991.

Chotjewitz, David. *Daniel Half Human: And the Good Nazi.* Atheneum, 2004.

Chrisp, Peter. *Welcome to the Globe: The Story of Shakespeare's Theatre.* Illustrated by Peter Dennis. Dorling Kindersley, 2000.

Christopher, M. *Soccer Duel.* Little, Brown, 2000.

Christopher, M. *Tennis Ace.* Little, Brown, 2000.

Church, Jeff. *Pied Piper of New Orleans.* Anchorage, 1993.

Ciardi, John. *The Helpful Trout and Other Limericks.* Illustrated by Sara Meddaugh. Houghton Mifflin, 1992.

Cisneros, Sandra. *My Wicked, Wicked Ways.* Random House, 1992.

Cisneros, Sandra. *The House on Mango Street.* McGraw-Hill, 2000.

CLAMP. *Chobits.* TokyoPop, 2002.

Clarke, Judith. *One Whole and Perfect Day.* Front Street, 2007.

Cleary, Beverly. *Girl from Yamhill: A Memoir.* Morrow, 1988.

Cleaver, Vera, and Bill Cleaver. *Where the Lillies Bloom.* Lippincott, 1969.

Clements, Andrew. *The Janitor's Boy.* Simon & Schuster, 2000.

Clements, Andrew. *Things Not Seen.* Penguin, 2002.

Climo, Shirley. *Atlanta's Race: A Greek Myth.* Clarion, 1995.

Clinton, Catherine (ed.). *I, Too, Sing America: Three Centuries of African American Poetry.* Illustrated by Stephen Alcorn. Houghton Mifflin, 1998.

Clinton, Cathryn. *A Stone in My Hand.* Candlewick, 2002.

Clowes, Daniel. *Ghost World.* Fantagraphics, 2001.

Cochran, Thomas. *Roughnecks.* Harcourt, 1997.

Cofer, Judith Ortiz. *An Island Like You: Stories of the Barrio.* Penguin, 1995.

Cofer, Judith. *Call Me Maria.* Orchard, 2004.

Cohen, Daniel. *Cloning.* Millbrook, 1998.

Cohn, Rachel. *Gingerbread.* Simon & Schuster, 2002.

Cohn, Rachel. *Pop Princess.* Simon & Schuster, 2004.

Cole, Babette. *Prince Cinders.* Putnam, 1988.

Cole, Brook. *The Facts Speak for Themselves.* Hand Print, 1993.

Colfer, Eoin. *Artemis Fowl.* Hyperion, 2001.

Collard, Sneed B. *Flash Point.* Peachtree, 2006.

Collard, Sneed B. *Science Warriors: The Battle Against Invasive Species.* Houghton Mifflin, 2008.

Collier, Bryan. *Visiting Langston.* Henry Holt, 2002.

Collier, James Lincoln. *The Jazz Kid.* Henry Holt, 1994.

Collier, James, and Christopher Collier. *Jump Ship to Freedom.* Delacorte, 1981.

Collier, James, and Christopher Collier. *My Brother Sam Is Dead.* Four Winds, 1974.

Collins, David. *Farmworker's Friend: The Story of Cesar Chavez.* Carolrhoda, 1996.

Collins, Max, and Dick Locher (eds.). *The Dick Tracy Casebook: Favorite Adventures 1931–1990.* St. Martin's Press, 1990.

Collins, Max Allen. *Road to Perdition.* Illustrated by Richard Payner. Pocket Books, 2002.

Collins, Suzanne. *The Hunger Games.* Scholastic, 2008.

Colman, P. *A Woman Unafraid: The Achievements of Frances Perkins.* Atheneum, 1993.

Colman, P. *Breaking the Chains: The Crusade of Dorothea Lynde Dix.* Betterway Books, 1992.

Colman, P. *Corpses, Coffins, and Crypts: A History of Burial.* Henry Holt, 1997.

Colman, P. *Fannie Lou Hamer and the Fight for the Vote.* The Millbrook Press, 1993.

Colman, P. *Girls! A History of Growing Up Female in America.* Scholastic, 2000.

Colman, P. *Madam C. J. Walker: Building a Business Empire.* The Millbrook Press, 1994.

Colman, P. *Mother Jones and the March of the Mill Children.* The Millbrook Press, 1994.

Colman, P. *101 Ways to Do Better in School.* Troll, 1993.

Colman, P. *Rosie the Riveter: Women Working on the Home Front in World War II.* Crown, 1995.

Colman, P. *Spies! Women in the Civil War.* Cincinnati: Betterway Books, 1992.

Colman, P. *Strike! The Bitter Struggle of American Workers from Colonial Times to the Present.* The Millbrook Press, 1995.

Colman, P. *Toilets, Bathtubs, Sinks, and Sewers: A History of the Bathroom.* Atheneum, 1994.

Colman, P. *Women in Society: United States of America.* Marshall Cavendish and Times International, 1994.

Colum, Padric. *The Trojan War and the Adventures of Odysseus.* Illustrated by Barry Moser. Morrow, 1997.

Compton, Joanne. *Ashpit.* Holiday House, 1994.

Connelly, Neil. *St. Michael's Scales.* Arthur Levine, 2001.

Compestine, Ying Chang. *A Banquet for Hungry Ghosts.* Henry Holt, 2009.

Conrad, Liza. *High School Bites.* Nal, 2006.

Cooke, Kaz. *Real Gorgeous: The Truth about Body and Beauty.* Norton, 1996.

Cooney, Barbara. *Miss Rumphius.* Viking, 1982.

Cooney, Caroline. *Flight #116 Is Down.* Demco, 1993.

Cooney, Caroline. *Goddess of Yesterday.* Delacorte, 2002.

Cooney, Caroline. *The Face on the Milk Carton.* Bantam Doubleday Dell, 1990.

Cooney, Caroline. *The Ransom of Mercy Carter.* Delacorte, 2001.

Cooney, Caroline B. *Both Sides of Time.* Delacorte, 2001.

Cooney, Caroline B. *Operation Homefront.* Starfire, 1992.

Cooper, Ilene. *Jack: the Early years of John F. Kennedy.* Dutton, 2003.

Cooper, Michael. *Fighting for Honor: Japanese Americans and World War II.* Clarion, 2000.

Cooper, Michael. *Remembering Manzanar: Life in a Japanese Relocation Camp.* Clarion, 2000.

Cooper, Michael. *Slave Spirituals and the Jubilee Singers.* Clarion, 2001.

Cooper, Susan. *King of Shadows.* McElderry, 1999.

Cooper, Susan. *The Dark Is Rising.* Atheneum, 1973.

Cormier, Robert. *Beyond the Chocolate War.* Bantam Doubleday Dell, 1985.

Cormier, Robert. *Fade.* Bantam Doubleday Dell, 1988.

Cormier, Robert. *Frenchtown Summer.* Delacorte, 1999.

Cormier, Robert. *I Am the Cheese.* Knopf, 1977.

Cormier, Robert. *Tenderness.* Bantam Doubleday Dell, 1997.

Cormier, Robert. *The Chocolate War.* Panthcon, 1974.

Cormier, Robert. *We All Fall Down.* Bantam Doubleday Dell, 1991.

Corrigan, Eireann. *You Remind Me of You.* Scholastic, 2002.

Cottonwood, Joe. *Quake!* Scholastic, 1995.

Couloumbis, Audrey. *Getting Near to Baby.* Putnam, 1999.

"Count Alaric's Lady." Retold by Barbara Picard. *Selected Fairy Tales.* Oxford University Press, 1995.

Coville, Bruce. *William Shakespeare's Romeo and Juliet.* Illustrated by Dennis Nolan. Dial, 1999.

Coville, Bruce. *William Shakespeare's Twelfth Night.* Illustrated by Tim Raglin. Dial, 2003.

Covington, Dennis. *Lizard.* Delacorte, 1991.

Cowley, J. *Starbright and the Dream Eater.* HarperCollins, 2000.

Cowley, Lorinda. *Pancake Boy: An Old Norwegian Folktale.* Putnam, 1988.

Craddock, Sonia. *Sleeping Boy.* Illustrated by Leonid Gore. Atheneum, 1999.

Craft, K. Y. *Cinderella.* Chronicle, 2000.

Craft, Mahlon. *Sleeping Beauty.* Illustrated by Kinuko Craft. Sagebrush, 2002.

Crane, Walter. *The House That Jack Built.* Ward, Lock, and Tyler, 1865.

Crawford, Elizabeth. *Little Red Cap.* Illustrated by Lisbeth Zwerger. Minedition, 2006.

Creech, Sharon. *Absolutely Normal Chaos*. HarperCollins, 1995.

Creech, Sharon. *Chasing Redbird*. HarperCollins, 1997.

Creech, Sharon. *Love That Dog*. Harper Trophy, 2001.

Creech, Sharon. *The Wanderer*. HarperCollins, 2000.

Crew, Linda. *Children of the River*. Delacorte, 1989.

Crew, Linda. *Long Time Passing*. Delacorte, 1997.

Crilley, Mark. *Akiko*. Sirius Entertainment, 1998–present.

Cronin, Doreen. *Click, Clack, Moo*. Illustrated by Betsy Lewin. Simon & Schuster, 2000.

Cross, Gillian. *New World*. Holiday House, 1995.

Crossley-Holland, Kevin. *Beowulf*. Illustrated by Charles Keeping. Oxford University Press, 1999.

Crossley-Holland, Kevin. *The Seeing Stone: Arthur Trilogy, Book One*. Arthur Levine, 2001.

Crowe, Chris. *Mississippi Trail, 1955*. Dial, 2002.

Crowley, Bridget. *Feast of Fools*. McElderry, 2003.

Crumb, Robert. *Introducing Kafka*. Kitchen Sink Press, 1994.

Crutcher, Chris. *Angry Management*. Greenwillow, 2009.

Crutcher, Chris. *Athletic Shorts: Six Short Stories*. Greenwillow, 1991.

Crutcher, Chris. *Chinese Handcuffs*. Greenwillow, 1989.

Crutcher, Chris. *Crazy Horse Electric Game*. Bantam Doubleday Dell, 1987.

Crutcher, Chris. *Ironman*. Greenwillow, 1995.

Crutcher, Chris. *King of the Mild Frontier*. Greenwillow, 2003.

Crutcher, Chris. *Running Loose*. Greenwillow Books, 1983.

Crutcher, Chris. *Staying Fat for Sarah Byrnes*. Greenwillow, 1993.

Crutcher, Chris. *Stotan!* Bantam Doubleday Dell, 1986.

Crutcher, Chris. *The Crazy Horse Electric Game*. Greenwillow, 1987.

Crutcher, Chris. *Whale Talk*. Greenwillow, 2001.

Cullum, Albert. *Shakespeare in the Classroom: Plays for Intermediate Grades*. Fearon, 1995.

Cummings, Priscilla. *A Face First*. Dutton, 2001.

Cummings, Priscilla. *Red Kayak*. Puffin, 2006.

Cummings, Pat. *Talking With Artists: Conversations with Illustrators*. Simon & Schuster, 1992.

Cummins, Julie. *Children's Book Illustration and Design II*. PBC International, 1997.

Cummins, Julie. *Wings of an Artist: Children's Book Illustrators Talk about Their Art*. Henry Abrams, 1999.

Curley, Marianne. *Old Magic*. Bloomsbury, 2000.

Curry, Jane Louise. *Dark Shade*. Margaret McElderry, 1998.

Curtis, Christopher Paul. *Bud, Not Buddy*. Delacorte, 1999.

Curtis, Christopher Paul. *The Watsons Go to Birmingham—1963*. Delacorte, 1999.

Cushman, Karen. *Ballad of Lucy Whipple*. Clarion, 1996.

Cushman, Karen. *Catherine Called Birdy*. Clarion, 1994.

Cushman, Karen. *Matilda Bone*. Clarion, 2000.

Cushman, Karen. *The Midwife's Apprentice*. Clarion, 1995.

Da Chen. *China's Son: Growing Up in the Cultural Revolution*. Delacorte, 2001.

Daly, Maureen. *Seventeenth Summer*. Dodd, 1942.

Danticot, Edwidge. *Behind the Mountains*. Scholastic, 2003.

Danziger, Paula, and Ann Martin. *P.S. Longer Letter Later*. Scholastic, 1998.

Danziger, Paula, and Ann Martin. *Snail Mail No More*. Scholastic, 2000.

Darnton, Robert. *The Great Cat Massacre*. Basic Books, 2000.

Dash, Joan. *The Longitude Prize*. Illustrated by Dusan Petricic. Farrar, Straus, and Giroux, 2000.

Datlow, Ellen, and Terri Windling (eds.). *The Green Man: Tales from the Mythic Forest*. Viking, 2001.

David, Laurie, and Cambria Gordon. *The Down to Earth Guide to Global Warming*. Orchard, 2007.

Davis, Rebecca Fjelland. *Jake Riley: Irreparably Damaged*. HarperTempest, 2003.

Dean, Carolee. *Comfort*. Houghton Mifflin, 2002.

DeClements, Barthe. *Sixth Grade Can Really Kill You*. Scholastic, 1985.

Deedy, Carmen Agra. *The Yellow Star: The Legend of King Christian X of Denmark*. Peachtree, 2000.

Deem, James. *3 NBs of Julien Drew*. Houghton Mifflin, 1994.

DeFelice, Cynthia. *Death at Devil's Bridge*. Farrar, Straus, and Giroux, 2000.

DeFelice, Cynthia. *Nowhere to Call Home*. Farrar, Straus, and Giroux, 1999.

Defoe, Daniel. *The Life and Strange Surprising Adventures of Robinson Crusoe*. W. Taylor, 1719.

Delacre, Lulu. *Golden Tales: Myths, Legends, and Folktales from Latin America*. Scholastic, 1996.

Delano, Marfe Ferguson. *Earth in the Hot Seat: Bulletins from a Warming World*. National Geographic, 2009.

Delany, Joseph. *Revenge of the Witch*. HarperCollins, 2005.

Delany, Mark. *The Kingfisher's Tale*. Misfits, Inc. series. Peachtree, 2000.

Delany, Mark. *The Protestor's Song*, Misfits, Inc. series. Peachtree, 2001.

de la Pena, Matt. *Ball Don't Lie*. Delacorte, 2005.

Delessert, Etienne. *Beauty and the Beast*. Creative Education, 1984.

De Lint, Charles. *Waifs and Strays*. Viking, 2002.

Demi. *In the Eyes of the Cat: Japanese Poetry for All Seasons*. Translated by Tze-Si Huang. Illustrated by Demi. Henry Holt, 1997.

Denenberg, Barry. *The Journal of Ben Uchida*. Scholastic, 1999.

Denenburg, Barry. *Lincoln Shot: A President's Life Remembered*. Feiwel and Friends, 2008.

dePaola, Tomie. *Oliver Button Is a Sissy*. Harcourt Brace, 1979.

Desjarlait, Patrick. *Conversations with a Native American Artist*. Runestone, 1995.

Dessen, Sarah. *Dreamland*. Viking, 2000.

Dessen, Sarah. *This Lullaby: A Novel*. Viking, 2001.

Deuker, Carl. *Night Hoops*. Houghton Mifflin, 2000.

DiCamillo, Kate. *Because of Winn Dixie*. Candlewick, 2000.

Dickinson, Emily. *I'm Nobody! Who Are You?* Stemmer House, 1978.

Dickinson, Peter. *Eva*. Bantam, 1988.

Dickinson, Peter. *The Kin.* Putnam, 2003.

Dickinson, Peter. *The Ropemaker.* Delacorte, 2001.

Dobson, Mary. *Medieval Muck.* Illustrated by Vince Reid. Oxford, 1999.

Doctorow, Cory. *Little Brother.* Tor, 2008.

Doherty, Berlie. *Daughter of the Sea.* Dorling Kindersley, 1997.

Donnelly, Jennifer. *A Northern Light.* Harcourt, 2003.

Donovan, John. *I'll Get There, It Better Be Worth the Trip.* Harper & Row, 1969.

Doran, Colleen. *A Distant Soil.* Image Comics, 1997–present.

Dorris, Michael. *Morning Girl.* Hyperion, 1992.

Dowell, Frances O'Roark. *Dovey Coe.* Atheneum, 2000.

Dowell, Frances O'Roark. *Where I'd Like to Be.* Atheneum, 1993.

Doyle, Sir Arthur Conan. *Adventures of Sherlock Holmes.* Burt Company, 1892.

Draper, Sharon. *Darkness before Dawn.* Simon Pulse, 2002.

Draper, Sharon. *Double Dutch.* Atheneum, 2002.

Draper, Sharon. *Fire from the Rock.* Dutton, 2007.

Draper, Sharon. *Forged by Fire.* Simon & Schuster, 1997.

Draper, Sharon. *Just Another Hero.* Atheneum, 2009.

Draper, Sharon. *Romiette and Julio.* Simon Pulse, 2001.

Draper, Sharon. *Tears of a Tiger.* Atheneum, 1994.

Draper, Sharon. *The Battle of Jericho.* Atheneum, 2003.

Duane, D. *A Wizard Alone.* Delacorte, 2002.

Duane, D. *So You Want to Be a Wizard.* Delacorte, 1983.

Duffy, Carol. *Stopping for Death: Poems of Death and Loss.* Holt, 1996.

Duffy, Carol, and Trisha Rafferty. *I Wouldn't Thank You for a Valentine: Poems for Young Feminists.* Henry Holt, 1994.

Dumas, Alexandre. *Count of Monte Cristo.* Little, Brown, 1894.

Dunbar, Paul Lawrence. *Jump Back Honey: The Poems of Paul Lawrence Dunbar.* Compiled by Bryan Ashly and Andrea Davis Pinkney. Hyperion, 2000.

Duncan, Lois. *Don't Look Behind You.* Delacorte, 1989.

Duncan, Lois. *Gallows Hill.* Delacorte, 1997.

Duncan, Lois. *I Know What You Did Last Summer.* Little, Brown, 1978.

Duncan, Lois. *Killing Mr. Griffin.* Little, Brown, 1978.

Duncan, Lois. *Locked in Time.* Bantam Doubleday Dell, 1985.

Duncan, Lois (ed.). *On the Edge: Stories from the Brink.* Simon & Schuster, 2000.

Duncan, Lois. *Songs from Dreamland.* Knopf, 1989.

Duncan, Lois. *Stranger with My Face.* Little, Brown, 1981.

Duncan, Lois. *The Terrible Tales of Happy Days School.* Little, Brown, 1983.

Duncan, Lois. *The Twisted Window.* Bantam Doubleday Dell, 1987.

Duncan, Lois. *Who Killed My Daughter.* Delacorte, 1992.

Durrant, Lynda. *The Sun, the Rain, and the Appleseed.* Houghton Mifflin, 2003.

Early, Margaret. *Sleeping Beauty.* Abrams, 1993.

Easton, Kelly. *Walking on Air.* Margaret K. McElderry, 2004.

Edelman, Bernard. *Dear America: Letters Home from Vietnam.* Norton, 1985.

Edwards, Wallace. *Alphabeasts.* Kids Can Press, 2002.

Egielski, Richard. *The Gingerbread Boy.* HarperCollins, 2000.

Ehlert, Lois. *In My World.* Harcourt, 2002.

Eisner, Will. *Fagin the Jew.* Doubleday, 2003.

Eisner, Will. *The Princess and the Frog.* NBM, 1999.

Eisner, Will, P. Craig Russell, and Tom Moth. *9–11: Artists Respond.* Dark Horse Comics, 2002.

Elliott, Laura. *Under a War Torn Sky.* Hyperion, 2001.

Ellis, Deborah. *A Company of Fools.* Fitzhenry and Whiteside, 2002.

Ellis, Deborah. *Parvana's Journey.* Illustrated by Pascal Milleli. Groundwood Books, 2002.

Ellis, Deborah. *The Breadwinner.* Douglas & MacIntrye, 2001.

Ellis, Roger. (ed.). *Audition Monologues for Student Actors: Selections from Contemporary Plays.* Meriwether, 1999.

Elwin, Rosamund, and Michelle Paulse. *Asha's Mums.* Women's Press, 1990.

Emond, Stephen. *Happy Face.* Little Brown, 2010.

Equiano, Olaudah. *The Kidnapped Prince: The Life of Olaudah Equiano.* Adapted by Ann Cameron. Knopf, 1995.

Erdrich, Louise. *The Birchbark House.* Hyperion, 1999.

Ernst, Lisa Campbell. *Goldilocks Returns.* Aladdin, 2000.

Ernst, Lisa Campbell. *Little Red Riding Hood: A Newgangled Prairie Tale.* Simon & Schuster, 1995.

Falconer, Ian. *Olivia.* Atheneum, 2000.

Falconer, Ian. *Olivia and the Missing Toy.* Atheneum, 2003.

Farmer, Nancy. *The Ear, the Eye, and the Arm.* Orchard, 1994.

Farmer, Nancy. *The House of the Scorpion.* Atheneum, 2002.

Farmer, Nancy. *The Sea of Trolls.* Atheneum, 2004.

Feelings, Tom. *Middle Passage: White Ships/Black Cargo.* Harcourt Brace, 1994.

Ferris, Jean. *Bad.* Farrar, Straus, and Giroux, 1999.

Ferris, Jean. *Of Sound Mind.* Farrar, Straus, and Giroux, 2001.

Fiedler, Lisa. *Dating Hamlet: Ophelia's Story.* Holt, 2002.

Fields, Terri. *After the Death of Anna Gonzales.* Holt, 2002.

Filipi and Boiscommun. *The Book of Jack.* Humanoids, 2002.

Filipovic, Zlata. *Zlata's Diary: A Child's Life in Sarajevo.* Viking, 1994.

Finley, Martha Farquhar. *Elsie Dinsmore.* Garland, 1977. (Original work published 1867)

Finn, Alex. *Breathing Underwater.* Perfection Learning, 2002.

Finney, Jack. *Time and Again.* Simon & Schuster, 1970.

Fisher, Leonard. *Jason and the Golden Fleece.* Holiday House, 1990.

Fisher, Leonard. *Theseus and the Minotaur.* Holiday House, 1992.

Fisher, Leonard Everett. *Theseus and the Minotaur.* Holiday, 1988.

Fitzhugh, Louise. *Harriet the Spy.* Harper & Row, 1964.

Flake, Sharon. *The Skin I'm In.* Hyperion, 1999.

Fleischman, John. *Phineas Gage.* Houghton Mifflin, 2002.

Fleischman, Paul. *Breakout.* Cricket Books, 2003.

Fleischman, Paul. *Bull Run.* HarperCollins, 1993.

Fleischman, Paul. *Dateline Troy.* Illustrated by Gwen Frank-feldt and Glen Narrow. Candlewick, 1996.

Fleischman, Paul. *I Am Phoenix: Poems for Two Voices.* Harper Trophy, 1985.

Fleischman, Paul. *Joyful Noise: Poems for Two Voices.* Harper Trophy, 1988.

Fleischman, Paul. *Mind's Eye.* Henry Holt, 1999.

Fleischman, Paul. *Seek.* Cricket Books, 2001.

Fleischman, Paul. *Shadow Play.* Illustrated by Eric Beddors. Harper & Row, 1990.

Fleischman, Paul. *Whirligig.* Henry Holt, 1999.

Fleischman, Sid. *The Abracadabra Kid: A Writer's Life.* Greenwillow, 1996.

Fletcher, Ralph (ed.). *I Am Wings: Poems about Love.* Bradbury, 1995.

Fletcher, Susan. *Shadow Spinner.* Atheneum, 1998.

Flinn, Alex. *Breaking Point.* HarperCollins, 2001.

Flinn, Alex. *Breathing Underwater.* HarperCollins, 2001.

Florian, Douglas. *Lizards, Frogs, and Polliwogs.* Harcourt, 2001.

Flowers, Pam, and Ann Dixon. *Alone Across the Arctic: One Woman's Epic Journey by Dog Team.* Alaska Northwest, 2001.

Foon, Dennis. *Skud.* Groundwood Books, 2003.

Forbes, Esther. *Johnny Tremain.* Houghton Mifflin, 1943.

Fox, Paula. *The Slave Dancer.* Bradbury, 1973.

Fradin, Dennis Brindell. *Bound for the North Star: True Stories of Fugitive Slaves.* Clarion, 2000.

Fradin, Dennis, and Judith Bloom Fradin. *Ida B. Wells: Mother of the Civil Rights Movement.* Clarion, 2000.

Frampton, David. *Rhyolite: The True Story of a Ghost Town.* Clarion, 2003.

Francis, Temple. *Tonight by Sea.* Scholastic, 1995.

Franco, Betsy. *Metamorphosis: Junior Year.* Candlewick, 2009.

Franco, Betsy (ed.). *Things I Have to Tell You: Poems and Writing by Teenage Girls.* Candlewick, 2001.

Franco, Betsy (ed.). *You Hear Me? Poems and Writing by Teenage Boys.* Candlewick, 2002.

Frank, E. R. *America.* New York: Atheneum, 2002.

Frank, E. R. *Life is Funny.* Dorling Kindersley, 2000.

Frank, Mitch. *Understanding September 11th.* Viking, 2002.

Franklin, Kristine. *The Grape Thief.* Candlewick, 2003.

Fraustino, Lisa Dowe (ed.). *Dirty Laundry: Stories about Family Secrets.* Viking, 1998.

Frederick, Heather Vogel. *The Voyage of Patience Goodspeed.* Simon & Schuster, 2002.

Fredericks, Mariah. *The True Meaning of Cleavage.* Atheneum, 2003.

Freedman, Russell. *Confucius: The Golden Rule.* Illustrated by Frederic Clement. Arthur Levine, 2002.

Freedman, Russell. *Eleanor Roosevelt: A Life of Discovery.* Sandpiper, 1994.

Freedman, Russell. *Lincoln: A Photobiography.* Clarion, 1987.

Freedman, Russell. *Wright Brothers: How They Invented the Airplane.* Holiday House, 1992.

Freeman, Suzanne. *The Cuckoo's Child.* Greenwillow, 1996.

French, Fionna. *Snow White in New York.* Oxford University Press, 1987.

Freymann-Weyr, Garret. *My Heartbeat.* Houghton Mifflin, 2001.

Freyman-Weyr, Garret. *Stay with Me.* Houghton Mifflin, 2006.

Friedman, D. Dina. *Escaping into the Night.* Simon & Schuster, 2006.

Fritz, Jean. *Homesick: My Own Story.* Yearling, 1982.

Fritz, Jean. *Leonardo's Horse.* Illustrated by Hudson Talbott. Putnam, 2001.

Froese, Deborah. *Out of the Fire.* Sumach Press, 2001.

Frost, Helen. *Keesha's House.* FSG/Frances Foster Books, 2003.

Frost, Robert. *Birches.* Henry Holt, 1988.

Fujishima, Kosuke. *Oh My Goddess!* Dark Horse Comics, 2005.

Funke, Cornelia. *Inkheart.* The Chicken House, 2003.

Funke, Cornelia. *Thief Lord.* Scholastic, 2002.

Gaiman, Neil. *The Day I Swapped My Dad for Two Goldfish.* Illustrated by Dave McKean. White Wolf, 1998.

Gaiman, Neil. *The Graveyard Book.* Illustrated by Dave McKean. HarperCollins, 2008.

Gaiman, Neil. *The Wolves in the Walls.* Illustrated by Dave McKean. HarperCollins, 2003.

Gaiman, Neil, Sam Keith, Mike Dringenberg, and Malcolm Jones. *Sandman, Vol. 1.* DC, 1993.

Galdone, Paul. *Hansel and Gretel.* McGraw-Hill, 1982.

Galdone, Paul. *Little Red Riding Hood.* McGraw-Hill, 1974.

Gallo, Don. *Center Stage: One Act Plays for Teenage Readers and Actors.* HarperCollins, 1990.

Gallo, Don (ed.). *On the Fringe.* Dial, 2001.

Gallo, Don (ed.). *Ultimate Sports: Short Stories by Outstanding Writers for YA.* Delacorte, 1995.

Galloway, Priscilla. *Snake Dreamer.* Delacorte, 1998.

Galloway, Priscilla. *Truly Grim Tales.* Delacorte, 1995.

Gammell, Stephen. *Ride.* Harcourt, 2001.

Gantos, Jack. *Hole in My Life.* Farrar, Straus, and Giroux, 2002.

Gantos, Jack. *Joey Pigza Loses Control.* Farrar, Straus, and Giroux, 2000.

Gantos, Jack. *Joey Pigza Swallowed the Key.* Farrar, Straus, and Giroux, 1998.

Garcia, Laura Gallego. *The Legend of the Wandering King.* Arthur Levine, 2005.

Garden, Nancy. *Annie on My Mind.* Farrar, Straus, and Giroux, 1982.

Gardner, John. *Grendel.* Knopf, 1971.

Garland, Sherry. *In the Shadow of the Alamo.* Gulliver Books, 2001.

Geisert, Arthur. *The Etcher's Studio.* Houghton Mifflin, 1997.

George, Jean Craighead. *Julie of the Wolves.* HarperCollins, 1972.

George, Jean Craighead. *My Side of the Mountain.* Dutton, 1959.

Geras, Adele. *Pictures of the Night.* Harcourt Brace Jovanovich, 1993.

Geras, Adele. *The Tower Room.* Harcourt Brace Jovanovich, 1992.

Geras, Adele. *Troy.* Harcourt, 2001.

Geras, Adele. *Watching the Roses.* Harcourt Brace Jovanovich, 1992.

Getchell, Scott. *Ritchie Kill'd My Toads.* Skidmark Press, 1995.

Ghigna, Charles. *A Fury of Motion: Poems for Boys.* Boyds Mills, 2003.

Giardino, Vittorio. *A Jew in Communist Prague: Loss of Innocence.* NBM, 1997

Giff, Patricia Reilly. *All the Way Home.* Delacorte, 2001.

Giff, Patricia Reilly. *Lily's Crossing.* Delacorte, 1997.

Giff, Patricia Reilly. *Nory Ryan's Song.* Delacorte, 2000.

Giff, Patricia Reilly. *Pictures of Hollis Woods.* Wendy Lamb Books, 2002.

Giles, Gail. *Shattering Glass.* Roaring Brook Press, 2001.

Gilmore, Kate. *The Exchange Student.* Houghton Mifflin, 1999.

Giovanni, Nikki (ed.). *Grand Fathers: Reminiscences, Poems, Recipes, and Photos of the Keepers of Our Traditions.* Henry Holt, 1999.

Giovanni, Nikki (ed.). *Grand Mothers: Reminiscences, Poems, Recipes, and Photos of the Keepers of Our Traditions.* Henry Holt, 1994.

Giovanni, Nikki. *Shimmy Shimmy Shimmy Like My Sister Kate: Looking at the Harlem Renaissance through Poems.* Holt, 1996.

Glazher, Gary Max. *Poetry Slam: The Competitive Art of Performance Poetry.* Penguin, 2000.

Glenn, Mel. *Back to Class.* Clarion, 1988.

Glenn, Mel. *Class Dismissed II: More High School Poems.* Clarion, 1986.

Glenn, Mel. *Foreign Exchange: A Mystery in Poems.* Morrow, 1999.

Glenn, Mel. *Jump Ball: A Basketball Season in Poems.* Dutton, 1997.

Glenn, Mel. *My Friend's Got This Problem, Mr. Candler: High School Poems.* Clarion, 1991.

Glenn, Mel. *Split Image,* Clarion, 2000.

Glenn, Mel. *The Taking of Room 114.* Dutton, 1997.

Glick, Susan. *One Shot.* Henry Holt, 2003.

Glovach, Linda. *Beauty Queen.* HarperTeen, 1998.

Godall, John. *Little Red Riding Hood.* Margaret McElderry, 1988.

Gold, Alison Leslie. *A Special Fate: Chiune Sugihara: Hero of the Holocaust.* Scholastic, 2000.

Goldberg, Moses. *The Analysis of Mineral #4.* Anchorage, 1982.

Goldin, Barbara Diamond. *Journeys with Elijah: Eight Tales of the Prophet.* Illustrated by Jerry Pinkney. Harcourt, 1999.

Golding, Julia. *Secrets of the Sirens.* Oxford University Press, 2007.

Golding, Theresa Martin. *The Secret Within.* Boyds Mills, 2002.

Golding, William. *Lord of the Flies.* Coward-McCann, 1954.

Goldman, William. *The Princess Bride.* Harcourt Brace Jovanovich, 1973.

Golub, Matthew. *Cool Melons Turn to Frogs! The Life and Poems of Issa.* Illustrated by Kazuko Store. Lee and Low Books, 1998.

Gonick, L. *The Cartoon History of the Universe II.* Main Street, 1994.

Gonsalves, Rob. *Imagine a Night.* Text by Sarah Thompson. Atheneum, 2003.

Goodman, Alison. *Singing the Dogstar Blues.* Viking, 2003.

Gordon, Sheila. *Waiting for the Rain.* Bantam Doubleday Dell, 1987.

Gore, Al, adapted by Jane O'Connor. *An Inconvenient Truth: The Crisis of Global Warming.* Viking, 2007.

Gottfried, Ted. *Displaced Persons: The Liberation and Abuse of Holocaust Survivors.* Twenty-First Century Books, 2001.

Gottfried, Ted. *Nazi Germany: The Face of Tyranny.* Twenty-First Century Books, 2000.

Gould, Peter. *Write Naked.* Farrar, Straus, and Giroux, 2008.

Graham, John. *Flicker Flash.* Illustrated by Nancy Davies. Houghton Mifflin, 2003.

Graham, Kenneth. *The Wind in the Willows.* Methuen, 1908.

Graham, Lorenz. *North Town.* Boyds Mills, 2003. (Original work published 1965)

Graham, Rosemary. *My Not-So-Terrible Time at the Hippie Hotel.* Viking, 2003.

Grahame-Smith, Seth. *Pride and Prejudice and Zombies.* Quirk, 2009.

Grandits, John. *Blue Lipstick.* Clarion, 2007.

Grant, K. M. *The Blood Red Horse.* Walker, 2005.

Green, John. *Looking for Alaska.* Dutton, 2005.

Green, John. *Abundance of Katherines.* Dutton, 2006.

Greenberg, Jan (ed.). *Heart to Heart: New Poems Inspired by 20th Century American Art.* Harry Abrams, 2001.

Greenberg, Jan, and Sandra Jordan. *Vincent Van Gogh: Portrait of an Artist.* Delacorte, 2001.

Greene, Bette. *The Drowning of Stephan Jones.* Bantam Doubleday Dell, 1991.

Greene, Bette. *Summer of My German Soldier.* Dial, 1973.

Greenfeld, Howard. *After the Holocaust.* Greenwillow, 2001.

Gregory, Kristiana. *Earthquake at Dawn.* Gulliver, 2003.

Gregory, Kristiana. *Seeds of Hope: Gold Rush Diary of Susanna Fairchild.* Scholastic, 2001.

Greif, Jean-Jacques. *The Fighter.* Bloomsbury, 2006.

Griffin, Adele. *Amandine.* Hyperion, 2001.

Grimes, Nikki. *Bronx Masquerade.* Dial, 2002.

Grimes, Nikki. *My Man Blue.* Illustrated by Jerome Lagarrigue. Dial, 1999.

Grimly, Gris. Poe, *Edgar Allan Poe's Tales of Death and Dementia.* Atheneum, 2009.

Grimly, Gris. Poe, *Edgar Allan Poe's Tales of Mystery and Madness.* Atheneum, 2004.

Grimm Brothers. *Kinderund Hausmärchen.* Erstertheil, 1812.

Grimm Brothers. *Little Red Riding Hood.* Illustrated by Trina Schart Hyman. Holiday House, 1982.

Grove, Vicki. *Destiny.* Putnam, 2000.

Guarnaccia, Steven. *Goldilocks and the Three Bears: A Tale Moderne.* Abrams, 2000.

Gurney, James. *Dinotopia: A Land Apart from Time*. Turner, 1992.

Gutman, Dan. *Babe and Me: A Baseball Card Adventure*. HarperCollins, 2000.

Gutman, Dan. *Virtually Perfect*. Hyperion, 1999.

Guy, Rosa. *Disappearance*. Delacorte, 1979.

Haddix, Margaret. *Among the Hidden*. Simon & Schuster, 1998.

Haddix, Margaret. *Just Ella*. Simon & Schuster, 1999.

Haddix, Margaret Peterson. *Leaving Fishers*. Simon & Schuster, 1997.

Haddix, Margaret Peterson. *Among the Betrayed*. Simon & Schuster, 2002.

Haddix, Margaret Peterson. *Takeoffs and Landings*. Simon & Schuster, 2001.

Haddix, Margaret Peterson. *Turnabout*. Simon & Schuster, 2000.

Hahn, M. D. *Dead Man in Indian Creek*. Clarion, 1990.

Hahn, M. D. *Hear the Wind Blow*. Clarion, 2003.

Halam, Ann. *Taylor Five*. Wendy Lamb, 2004.

Halliday, John. *Shooting Monarchs*. McElderry, 2003.

Hamilton, Virginia. *A Ring of Tricksters: Animal Tales from America, the West Indies, and Africa*. Illustrated by Barry Moser. Blue Sky Press, 1997.

Hamilton, Virginia. *Bluish: A Novel*. Blue Sky Press, 1995.

Hamilton, Virginia. *Bruh Rabbit and the Tar Baby Girl*. Illustrated by James Ransome. Blue Sky Press, 2003.

Hamilton, Virginia. *Her Stories: African American Folktales, Fairy Tales, and True Tales*. Blue Sky Press, 1995.

Hamilton, Virginia. *M. C. Higgins the Great*. Macmillan, 1974.

Hamilton, Virginia. *Second Cousins*. Blue Sky Press, 1998.

Hamilton, Virginia. *Sweet Whispers, Brother Rush*. Philomel, 1982.

Hamilton, Virginia. *The Girl Who Spun Gold*. Illustrated by Leo and Diane Dillon. Blue Sky Press, 2003.

Hamilton, Virginia. *The House of Dies Drear*. Macmillan, 1968.

Hamilton, Virginia. *The People Could Fly: American Black Folktales*. Knopf, 2000.

Hamilton, Virginia. *The Planet of Junior Brown*. Macmillan, 1971.

Hamilton, Virginia. *Timepieces*. Blue Sky Press, 2002.

Hamilton, Virginia. *Zeely*. Macmillan, 1967.

Hampton, William. *Meltdown: A Race against Nuclear Disaster at Three Mile Island*. Candlewick, 2001.

Hansberry, Lorraine. *A Raisin in the Sun*. Random House, 1959.

Hansen, Joyce. *I Thought My Soul Would Rise and Fly: The Diary of Patsy, A Freed Girl*. Scholastic, 1997.

Hansen, Joyce. *The Captive*. Scholastic, 1994.

Hansen, Joyce. *Which Way to Freedom?* Walker, 1986.

Hardy, P. Stephen, and Sheila Jackson Hardy. *Extraordinary People of the Harlem Rennaissance*. Extraordinary People series. Children's Press, 2000.

Harlow, Joan. *Shadows on the Sea*. Margaret McElderry, 2003.

Harris, Aurand. (ed.). *Short Plays of Theatre Classics*. Anchorage, 1991.

Hart, Elva Trevino. *Barefoot Heart*. Bilingual Press, 1999.

Hart, Philip. *Up in the Air: The Story of Bessie Coleman*. Carolrhoda, 1996.

Hartman, Bob. *The Wolf Who Cried Boy*. Illustrated by T. Raglin. Grosset & Dunlap, 2002.

Hartman, Rachel. *Amy Unbounded: Belondweg Blossoming*. Pug House, 2002.

Hatt, Christine. *The Crusades: Christians at War*. Watts, 2000.

Hautman, Pete. *Hole in the Sky*. Simon & Schuster, 2001.

Hautman, Pete. *Rash*. Simon & Schuster, 2006.

Hautzig, Deborah. *Second Star to the Right*. Greenwillow Books, 1981.

Hawk, Tony and Sean Martinez. *Hawk: Occupation Skateboarder*. Harper Entertainment, 2000.

Haworth-Attard, Barbara. *Theories of Relativity*. Henry Holt, 2005.

Hawthorne, Nathaniel. *The Scarlet Letter*. Chelsea, 1986.

Hayhurst, Chris. *Bicycle Stunt Riding: Catch Air*. Rosen, 1999.

Heinlein, Robert. *Have Space Suit Will Travel*. Scribner's, 1958.

Heinlein, Robert. *Space Cadet*. Scribner's, 1948.

Heisler, Gail. *Jack and the Bean Tree*. Knopf, 1986.

Hemphill, Stephanie. *Your Own Sylvia: A Verse Portrait of Sylvia Plath*. Knopf, 2007.

Hendershot, Judith. *In Coal Country*. Illustrated by Thomas Allen. Random House, 1987.

Heneghan, James. *The Grave*. Farrar, Straus, and Giroux, 2000.

Hennessey, B. G. *The Boy Who Cried Wolf*. SeaStar Books, 2006.

Hentoff, Nat. *The Day They Came to Arrest the Book*. Delacorte, 1982.

Henty, George Alfred. *Orange and Green*. Blackie and Son, 1888.

Heo, Yumi. *The Rabbit's Escape*. Henry Holt, 1995.

Herge. *The Adventures of Tintin*. Little, Brown, 1992.

Hernandez, Jaime. *Death of Speedy*. Fantagraphics Books, 1989.

Herowitz, Anthony. *The Devil and His Boy*. Philomel, 2000.

Herrera, Juan Felipe. *CrashBoomLove: A Novel in Verse*. University of New Mexico Press, 1999.

Herrera, Juan Felipe. *Laughing Out Loud, I Fly: Poems in English and Spanish*. HarperCollins, 1998.

Herrick, Steven. *A Place Like This*. Simon Pulse, 2004.

Herrick, Steven. *Love, Ghosts, and Facial Hair*. Simon Pulse, 2004.

Hesse, Karen. *Aleutian Sparrow*. Margaret McElderry, 2003.

Hesse, Karen. *Letters from Rifka*. Henry Holt, 1992.

Hesse, Karen. *Out of the Dust*. Scholastic, 1997.

Hesse, Karen. *Stowaway*. McElderry, 2000.

Hesse, Karen. *Witness*. Scholastic, 2001.

Hesser, Terry. *Kissing Doorknobs*. Delacorte, 1998.

Hettinga, Donald. *The Brothers Grimm: Two Lives, One Legacy*. Clarion, 2001.

Heuston, Kimberly. *The Shakeress*. Front Street, 2001.

Hickam, H. *Rocket Boys: A Memoir*. Delacorte 1999.

Hickam, Homer H., Jr. *Rocket Boys*. Delta, 2000.

Hicyilmaz, Gaye. *Smiling for Strangers*. Farrar, Straus, and Giroux, 2000.

Hidier, Tanuja Desai. *Born Confused*. Scholastic, 2002.

Higginson, William J. *Haiku Handbook: How to Write, Share, and Teach Haiku*. Kodansha, 1992.

Highwater, Jamake. *Rama: A Legend*. Henry Holt, 1994.

Hinton, S. E. *The Outsiders*. Viking, 1967.

Hipperson, Carol. *The Belly Gunner*. Millbrook, 2001.

Hite. *Stick and Whittle*. Scholastic, 2000.

Hobbs, Valerie. *Charlie's Run*. Farrar, Straus, and Giroux, 2000.

Hobbs, Valerie. *How Far Would You Have Gotten If I Hadn't Called You Back?* Orchard, 1995.

Hobbs, Valerie. *Sonny's War*. Farrar, Straus, and Giroux, 2002. (Original work published 1968)

Hobbs, Valerie. *Tender*. Farrar, Straus, and Giroux, 2001.

Hobbs, Will. *Crossing the Line*. HarperCollins, 2006.

Hobbs, Will. *Downriver*. Bantam Doubleday Dell, 1991.

Hobbs, Will. *Down the Yukon*. HarperCollins, 2001.

Hobbs, Will. *Far North*. HarperCollins, 1996.

Hobbs, Will. *Ghost Canoe*. HarperCollins, 1997.

Hobbs, Will. *Go Big or Go Home*. HarperCollins, 2008.

Hobbs, Will. *Jackie's Wild Seattle*. HarperCollins, 2003.

Hobbs, Will. *Jason's Gold*. HarperCollins, 1999.

Hobbs, Will. *River Thunder*. Bantam Doubleday Dell, 1997.

Hobbs, Will. *The Maze*. Morrow Junior, 1998.

Hobbs, Will. *Wild Man Island*. HarperCollins, 2001.

Hodges, Margaret. *Gulliver in Lilliput*. Illustrated by Kimberly Root. Holiday, 1995.

Hodges, Margaret. *Making a Difference: The Story of an American Family*. Beech, 1989.

Hodges, Margaret. *Saint George and the Dragon*. Illustrated by Trina Schart Hyman. Little, Brown, 1984.

Hoeye, Michael. *The Sands of Time*. Putnam, 1999.

Hoeye, Michael. *Time Stops for No Mouse*. Putnam, 1999.

Hoffman, Alice. *Aquamarine*. Scholastic, 2001.

Hogrogian, Nonny. *Cinderella*. Greenwillow, 1981.

Holland, Isabelle. *Heads You Win, Tails I Lose*. Dell, 1973.

Hollub, Josef. *An Innocent Soldier*. Arthur Levine, 2005.

Holt, Kimberly Willis. *Dancing in the Cadillac Light*. Putnam, 2001.

Holt, Kimberly Willis. *My Louisiana Sky*. Henry Holt, 1998.

Holt, Kimberly Willis. *Zachary Beaver Came to Town*. Henry Holt, 1999.

Hoobler, Dorothy and Thomas. *The Ghost in the Tokaido Inn*. Philomel, 1999.

Hook, William. *The Three Little Pigs and the Fox*. Illustrated by S. D. Schindler. Aladdin, 1997.

Hoose, Phillip. *It's Our World Too! Stories of Young People Who are Making a Difference*. Farrar, Straus, and Giroux, 2002.

Hoose, Phillip. *We Were There Too! Young People in U.S. History*. Farrar, Straus, and Giroux, 2001.

Hope, Laura Lee. *The Bobbsey Twins*. Mershon, 1904.

Hopkins, Jackie Mims. *The Horned Toad Prince*. Illustrated by Michael Austin. Peachtree, 2000.

Hopkins, L. B. (ed.) *Opening Days: Sports Poems*. HarperCollins, 1999.

Hopkins, L. B. *Sports! Sports! Sports! A Poetry Collection* HarperCollins, 1999.

Hopkins, Lee Bennett (ed.). *Voyages: Poems by Walt Whitman*. Harcourt, 1992.

Hornby, Nick. *Slam*. Putnam, 2007.

Horowitz, Anthony. *Point Blank*. Philomel, 2002.

Hosler, Jay. *Clan Apis*. Active Synapse, 2000.

Hotta, Yumi, and Takeshi Obata. *Hikaru No Go*. Viz, 2004.

Houghton, Norris (ed.). *Romeo and Juliet*. Laurel Leaf, 1965.

Houghton, Norris (ed.). *West Side Story*. Laurel Leaf, 1965.

Houston, Jeanne Wakatsuki, and James Houston. *Farewell to Manzanar*. Houghton Mifflin, 2002.

Howard, Richard. *Beauty and the Beast*. Illustrated by Hillary Knight. Simon & Schuster, 1990.

Howarth, Lesley. *MapHead*. Candlewick, 1994.

Howarth, Lesley. *MapHead: The Return*. Candlewick, 1997.

Howe, James. *The Color of Absence: 12 Stories about Loss and Hope*. Atheneum, 2001.

Howe, James. *The Misfits*. Atheneum, 2001.

Howe, James. *The Watcher*. Atheneum, 1997.

Howe, John. *Jack and the Beanstalk*. Little, Brown, 1989.

Howland, Naomi. *The Matzah Man: A Passover Story*. Clarion, 2002.

Hrdlitschka, Shelly. *Dancing Naked*. Orca Book Publisher, 2001.

Hughes, Dean. *Search and Destroy*. Atheneum, 2005.

Hughes, Dean. *Solider Boys*. Atheneum, 2001.

Hughes, Langston. *The Block*. Illustrated by Romare Bearden. Viking, 1995.

Hughes, Langston. *The Dreamkeeper and Other Poems*. Knopf, 1996. (Original work published 1932)

Hughes, Monica. *The Keeper of the Isis Light*. Hamish Hamilton, 1980.

Hughes, Monica. *Invitation to the Game*. Simon & Schuster, 1990.

Hunter, Mollie. *A Stranger Came Ashore*. Hamilton, 1975.

Hunter, Mollie. *The Mermaid Summer*. Harper & Row, 1988.

Hurst, Carol Otis, and Rebecca Otis. *A Killing In Plymouth Colony*. Houghton Mifflin, 2003.

Hurwin, Davida Wills. *A Time for Dancing*. Little, Brown, 1995.

Hutton, Warwick. *Beauty and the Beast*. Atheneum, 1985.

Hutton, Warwick. *Sleeping Beauty*. Atheneum, 1979.

Hutton, Warwick. *Theseus and the Minotaur*. McElderry, 1989.

Huxley, Aldous. *Brave New World*. Perennial Classics, 1998. (Original work published 1932)

Hyman, Trina Schart. *Snow White*. Little, Brown, 2000.

Ibbotson, Eva. *The Secret of Platform 13*. Dutton, 1998.

Igus, Toyomi. *I See the Rhythm*. Children's Book Press, 1998.

Ingold, Jeanette. *Airfield*. Harcourt Brace, 1999.

Ingold, Jeanette. *Mountain Solo*. Harcourt, 2003.

Ingold, Jeanette. *Pictures, 1918*. Harcourt Brace, 1998.

Ingold, Jeanette. *The Big Burn*. Harcourt, 2003.

Innocenti, Roberto. *Cinderella*. Creative Editions, 2000.

Irwin, John. *Another River, Another Town: A Teenage Tank Gunner Comes of Age in Combat—1945.* Random House, 2002.

Jackson, Ellen B. *Cinder Edna.* Lothrop, Lee & Shepard, 1994.

Jackson, Jack. *Lost Cause: The True Story of Famed Texas Gunslinger John Wesley Hardin.* Kitchen Sink Press, 1998.

Jackson, Jesse. *Call Me Charlie.* HarperCollins, 1945.

Jacobsen, Ruth. *Rescued Images: Memories of a Childhood in Hiding.* Mikaya Press, 2001.

Janeczko, Paul. *A Poke in the I.* Illustrated by Chris Rashka. Candlewick, 2001.

Janeczko, Paul (ed.). *Blushing: Expressions of Love in Poems and Letters.* Orchard, 2003.

Janeczko, Paul. *Favorite Poetry Lessons.* Scholastic, 1998.

Janeczko, Paul (ed.). *Home on the Range: Cowboy Poetry.* Dial, 1997.

Janeczko, Paul. *How to Write Poetry.* Scholastic, 1999.

Janeczko, Paul. *Place My Words Are Looking for: What Poets Say about and through Their Work.* Candlewick, 1991.

Janeczko, Paul. *Seeing the Blue Between: Advice and Inspiration for Young Poets.* Candlewick, 2002.

Janeczko, Paul. *That Sweet Diamond: Baseball Poems.* Atheneum, 1998.

Janeczko, Paul. *The Music of What Happens: Poems That Tell Stories.* Orchard, 1988.

Janeczko, Paul (ed.). *Very Best (Almost) Friends: Poems of Friendship.* Candlewick, 1999.

Janover, Caroline. *How Many Days Until Tomorrow?* Woodbine House, 2000.

Janover, Caroline. *The Worst Speller in Junior High.* Free Spirit, 1995.

Jansen, Hannah. *Over a Thousand Hills I Walk with You.* Carolrhoda, 2006.

Jarvis, Robin. *The Dark Portal.* Seastar Books, 2000.

Jeffers, Susan. *Hansel and Gretel.* Dial, 1980.

Jenkins, A. M. *Damage.* HarperCollins, 2001.

Jenkins, A. M. *Repossessed.* HarperTeen, 2007.

Jennings, Coleen. *Playing Juliet.* Dramatic Publishing, 1999.

Jennings, Coleman (ed.). *Eight Plays for Children: The New Generation Play Project.* University of Texas, 1999.

Ji-Li. *Red Scarf Girl: Memoir of the Cultural Revolution.* HarperCollins, 1997.

Jimenez, Francisco. *Breaking Through.* Houghton Mifflin, 2001.

Johnson, Angela. *Heaven.* Simon & Shuster, 1998.

Johnson, Angela. *The First Part Last.* Simon & Schuster, 2003.

Johnson, Angela. *The Other Side: Shorter Poems.* Orchard, 1998.

Johnson, Dave (ed.). *Movin': Teen Poets Take Voice.* Orchard, 2000.

Johnston, Antony, and Drew Gilbert. *Rosemary's Backpack.* Cyberosia, 2003.

Jones, Bruce, and Christopher Schenck. *Tarzan.* Dark Horse, 1996.

Jones, Carol. *The Gingerbread Man: A Peep-Through Picture Book.* Houghton Mifflin, 2002.

Jones, Diana Wynne. *Castle in the Air.* Greenwillow, 1991.

Jones, Diana Wynne. *Howl's Moving Castle.* Greenwillow, 1986.

Jordan, Sherryl. *The Hunting of the Last Dragon.* HarperCollins, 2002.

Josephs, Rebecca. *Early Disorder.* Farrar, Straus, and Giroux, 1980.

Jung, Reinhardt. *Dreaming in Black and White.* Translated by Anthea Bell. Mammoth, 2000.

Junger, Sebastian. *The Perfect Storm.* Norton, 1997.

Jurgas, Dan, James Bonny, Andy Park, and Billy Tan. *Lara Croft: Tomb Raider.* Top Cow, 1999.

Kaaberbol, Lene. *Shamer's Daughter.* Henry Holt, 2004.

Kadohata, Cynthia. *Weedflower.* Atheneum, 2006.

Kaeser, Gigi. *Love Makes a Family.* University of Massachusetts Press, 1999.

Kafka, Franz. *Give it Up! And Other Stories.* Illustrated by Peter Kuper. ComicsLit, 2005.

Kaminsky, Marty. *Uncommon Champions: Fifteen Athletes Who Battled Back.* Boyds Mills, 2000.

Kanari, Yozaburo. *The Kindaichi Case Files: The Opera House Murders.* Tokyopop, 2003.

Karr, Kathleen. *The Boxer.* Farrar, Straus, and Giroux, 2000.

Katz, Jon. *Geeks: How Two Lost Boys Rode the Internet Out of Idaho.* Villard Books, 2000.

Kay, Elizabeth. *Back to the Divide.* The Chicken House, 2004.

Kay, Elizabeth. *The Divide.* The Chicken House, 2003.

Kaye, Marilyn. *Amy, Number Seven* (Replica Series). Bantam, 1998.

Kaye, Marilyn. *Real Heroes.* Harcourt Brace, 1993.

Keenan, Sheila. *Gods, Goddesses, and Monsters: An Encyclopedia of World Mythology.* Illustrated by Belgin Wedman. Scholastic, 2000.

Keene, Carolyn (Wirt, Mildred Benson). *The Hidden Staircase.* Grosset and Dunlap, 1930.

Keller, Bill. *Tree Shaker: The Story of Nelson Mandela.* Kingfisher, 2008.

Keller, Emily. *Sleeping Bunny.* Illustrated by Pamela Silin-Palmer. Random House, 2003.

Kellogg, Steven. *Jack and the Beanstalk.* Morrow Junior, 1991.

Kelly, Joe. *I Kill Giants.* Image Comics, 2009.

Kennedy, Joseph. *Lucy Goes to the Country.* Alyson, 1998.

Kennedy, X. J. *Uncle Switch: Loony Limericks.* Illustrated by John O'Brien. McElderry, 1997.

Kennerly, Karen. *The Slave Who Bought His Freedom.* Dutton, 1971.

Kerley, Barbara. *The Dinosaurs of Waterhouse Hawkins.* Illustrated by Brian Selznick. Scholastic, 2001.

Kerr, M. E. *Dinky Hocker Shoots Smack!* Harper, 1972.

Kerr, M. E. *Linger.* HarperCollins, 1993.

Kerr, M. E. *Me Me Me Me: Not a Novel.* Harper & Row, 1983.

Kerr, M. E. *Slap Your Sides.* HarperCollins, 2001.

Kersjes, Mike, with Joe Layden. *A Smile as Big as the Moon.* St. Martin's Press, 2001.

Kesel, Barbara. *Meridian: Flying Solo.* CrossGen, 2001.

Kesel, Barbara, Joshua Middleton, Dextor Vines, and Michael Atiyeh. *Meridian: Flying Solo.* CrossGeneration, 2002.

Kimmel, Eric. *Rimonah of the Flashing Sword: A North African Tale.*

Kindl, Patrice. *Goose Chase: A Novel.* Houghton Mifflin, 2001.

Kindl, Patrice. *Owl in Love.* Puffin, 1994.

King, Stephen. *The Girl Who Loved Tom Gordon.* Scribner's, 1999.

Kinney, Jeff. *Diary of a Wimpy Kid.* Amulet, 2007.

Kipling, Rudyard. *A Collection of Rudyard Kipling's Just So Stories.* Candlewick, 2004.

Kipling, Rudyard. *Just So Stories.* Foreword by Janet Taylor Lisle. Aladdin, 2002.

Kipling, Rudyard. *Rudyard Kipling's Jungle Book.* Illustrated by P. Craig Russell. NBM, 1997.

Kirby, Jack. *Jack Kirby's New Gods.* DC, 1998.

Kiyama, Henry Yoshitaka. *The Four Immigrants Manga.* Stone Bridge, 1999.

Klass, David. *Firestorm: The Caretaker Trilogy: Book I.* Farrar, Straus, and Giroux, 2006.

Klass, David. *Home of the Braves.* Farrar, Straus, & Giroux, 2002.

Klass, David. *Whirlwind: The Caretaker Trilogy: Book II.* Farrar, Straus, and Giroux, 2008.

Klass, David. *You Don't Know Me.* Frances Foster Books, 2001.

Klause, Annette Curtis. *Blood and Chocolate.* Delacorte, 1997.

Klause, Annette Curtis. *The Silver Kiss.* Delacorte, 1990.

Klein, Lisa. *Ophelia.* Bloomsbury, 2006.

Klein, Norma. *Breaking Up: A Novel.* Random House, 1980.

Klein, Norma. *It's OK If You Don't Love Me.* Fawcett Crest, 1977.

Klise, Kate. *Trial by Journal.* Illustrated by M. Sarah Clise. HarperCollins, 2001.

Knight, Michael. *In Chains to Louisiana.* Dutton, 1971.

Knudson, R. R., and May Swenson. *American Sports Poems.* Orchard, 1995.

Kochalka, James. *Monkey vs. Robot.* Top Shelf, 2000.

Koertge, Ron. *Shakespeare Bats Cleanup.* Candlewick, 2003.

Koertge, Ron. *Stoner and Spaz.* Candlewick. 2001.

Koertge, Ron. *The Arizona Kid.* 1988.

Koertge, Ron. *The Brimstone Journals.* Candlewick, 2001.

Koja, Kathe. *Buddha Boy.* FSG/Frances Foster Books, 2003.

Koja, Kathe. *Straydog.* Farrar, Straus, and Giroux, 2001.

Koller, Jackie French. *Nothing to Fear.* Harcourt Brace Jovanovich, 1991.

Konigsburg, E. L. *A Proud Taste of Scarlet and Miniver.* Atheneum, 1973.

Konigsburg, E. L. *Silent to the Bone.* Atheneum, 2000.

Konigsburg, E. L. *The Second Mrs. Giaconda.* Macmillan, 1978.

Korman, Gordon. *Born to Rock.* Hyperion, 2006.

Korman, Gordon. *No More Dead Dogs.* Hyperion, 2000.

Korman, Gordon. *Son of the Mob.* Hyperion, 2002.

Koss, Amy. *Stranger in Dadland.* Dial, 2001.

Koss, Amy. *Strike Two.* Dial, 2001.

Koss, Amy. *The Cheat.* Dial, 2003.

Krisher, Trudy. *Spite Fences and Kinship.* Delacorte, 1997.

Kubert, Joe. *Fax From Sarajevo.* Dark Horse, 1996.

Kunkel, Mike. *Herobear and the Kid: The Inheritance.* Astonish Comics, 2003.

Kushner, Tony. *Brundibar.* Illustrated by Maurice Sendak. Hyperion, 2003.

Kustanowitz, Esther. *The Hidden Children of the Holocaust.* Rosen Publishing, 1999.

LaFaye, A. *Strawberry Hill.* Simon & Schuster, 1999.

Laird, Elizabeth. *A Little Piece of Ground.* Haymarket, 2006.

Laird, Roland, Tanishia Laird, and Elihu Bey. *Still I Rise: A Cartoon History of African Americans.* Norton, 1997.

Lamb, Charles, and Mary Lamb. *Tales from Shakespeare.* Unicorn, 1989. (Original work published 1807)

Lamb, Wally. *She's Come Undone.* Pocket Books, 1992.

Landau, Elaine. *Heroine of the Titanic: The Real Unsinkable Molly Brown.* Clarion, 2001.

Langley, John. *Little Red Riding Hood.* Barrows, 1996.

Langton, Jane. *The Diamond in the Window.* Harper & Row, 1962.

Lanier, Shannon, and Jane Feldman. *Jefferson's Children: The Story of One American Family.* Random House, 2000.

Lannin, Joanne. *A History of Basketball for Girls and Women: From Bloomers to Big Leagues.* Lerner Sports, 2000.

Larson, Rodger. *What I Know Now.* Henry Holt, 1997.

Lasky, Kathryn. *Beyond the Divide.* Macmillan, 1983.

Lasky, Kathryn. *Star Split.* Hyperion, 2001.

Lattany, Kristin Hunter. *The Soul Brothers and Sister Lou.* Scribner, 1968.

Lawlor, Laurie. *Helen Keller: Rebellious Spirit.* Holiday.

Lawrence, Iain. *Lord of the Nutcracker Men.* Delacorte, 2001.

Lawrence, Iain. *The Buccaneers.* Delacorte, 2000.

Lawrence, Iain. *The Smugglers.* Delacorte, 1999.

Lawrence, Iain. *The Wreckers.* Delacorte, 2000.

Lawton, Clive A. *Auschwitz: The Story of a Nazi Death Camp.* Candlewick Press, 2002.

Lazo, Caroline. *Alice Walker: Freedom Writer.*

Lee, Harper. *To Kill a Mockingbird.* Lippincott, 1960.

Lee, Marie. *F Is for Fabuloso.* Avon Books, 1999.

Lee, Marie. *Saying Goodbye.* Houghton Mifflin, 1994.

Lee, Nancy, Lonnie Schlein, and Mitchel Levitas. *A Nation Challenged.* Callaway, 2002.

Lee, Stan, Chris Claremont, and John Byrne. *The Dark Phoenix Saga.* Marvel, 1990.

Lee, Stan, and Steve Dirko. *The Essential Spiderman.* Marvel, 1996.

LeGuin, Ursula. *A Wizard of Earthsea.* Parnassus, 1968.

Lelooska, Chief. *Spirit of the Ceder People.* D.K. Publishers/Callaway Editions, 1998.

Lesser, Rika. *Hansel and Gretel.* Dodd Mead, 1984.

Lester, Julius. *Cupid.* Harcourt, 2007.

Lester, Julius. *Day of Tears: A Novel in Dialogue.* Hyperion, 2005.

Lester, Julius. *Guardian.* Amistad, 2008.

Lester, Julius. *The Old African.* Illustrated by Jerry Pinkney. Dial, 2005.

Lester, Julius. *Othello: A Novel.* Scholastic, 1995.

Lester, Julius. *Pharoah's Daughter.* Harcourt Brace, 2000.

Lester, Julius. *Sam and the Tigers.* Illustrated by Jerry Pinkney. Dial, 1996.

Lester, Julius. *Shining.* Silver Whistle, 2003.

Lester, Julius. *To Be a Slave.* Longman, 1968.

Lester, Julius. *What a Truly Cool World.* Illustrated by Joe Cepeda. Scholastic, 1999.

Lester, Julius. *When Dad Killed Mom.* Harcourt, 2000.

Lester, Julius. *Why Is Heaven So Far Away.* Illustrated by Joe Cepeda. Scholastic, 2002.

LeTord, Bijou. *A Blue Butterfly: A Story about Claude Monet.* Doubleday, 1995.

Levenkron, Steven. *The Best Little Girl in the World.* Warner Books, 1991.

Levin, Ira. *The Boys from Brazil.* Random House, 1976.

Levine, Ellen. *Darkness Over Denmark: The Danish Resistance and the Rescue of the Jews.* Holiday House, 2000.

Levine, Gail Carson. *Dave at Night.* HarperCollins, 1999.

Levine, Gail Carson. *Ella Enchanted.* HarperCollins, 1997.

Levitin, Sonia. *Clem's Chances.* Orchard Books, 2001.

Levitin, Sonia. *Room in the Heart.* Dutton, 2003.

Levitin, Sonia. *The Singing Mountain.* Simon & Schuster, 1998.

Levy, Marilyn. *Rumors and Whispers.* Fawcett Juniper, 1990.

Lewin, Ted. *Sacred River: The Ganges of India.* Clarion, 1994.

Lewin, Waldtraut. *Freedom beyond the Sea.* Delacorte, 2001.

Lewis, J. Patrick. *Black Swan/White Crow.* Illustrated by Chris Manson. Atheneum, 1995.

Lewis, J. Patrick. *Doodle Dandies: Poems That Take Shape.* Illustrated by Lisa Desimmi. Atheneum, 1998.

Lewis, J. Patrick. *Freedom Like Sunlight: Praisesongs for Black Americans.* Illustrated by John Thompson. Creative Editions, 2000.

Lewis, Richard. *The Killing Sea.* Simon & Schuster, 2006.

Lindquist, Susan Hart. *Summer Soldiers.* Delacorte, 1999.

Lipsyte, Robert. *The Contender.* HarperCollins, 1967.

Lisle, Janet Taylor. *Sirens and Spies.* Bradbury Press, 1985.

Lisle, Janet Taylor. *The Art of Keeping Cool.* Atheneum Books, 2000.

Littlefield, Holly. *Children of the Indian Boarding Schools.* Carolrhoda, 2001.

Liu, Jae-Soo. *Yellow Umbrella.* Kane Miller, 2002.

Lively, Penelope. *In Search of a Homeland.* Illustrated by Ian Andrew. Delacorte, 2001.

Livingston, Myra Cohn (ed.). *Call Down the Moon: Poems of Music.* McElderry, 1995.

Livingston, Myra Cohn. *I Am Writing a Poem about . . . A Game of Poetry.* McElderry, 1997.

Lloyd, Saci. *The Carbon Diaries: 2015.* Holiday House, 2009.

Lobel, Anita. *No Pretty Pictures.* Greenwillow, 1998.

Loddell, Scott, Daniel Rendon, and Lea Hernandez. *The Hardy Boys: Undercover Brothers.* Papercutz, 2005.

Logue, Mary. *Dancing with an Alien.* HarperCollins.

London, Jack. *The Call of the Wild.* Illustrated by Barry Moser. Macmillan, 1994.

London, Jack. *The Call of the Wild.* Illustrated by Wendell Minor. Atheneum, 1999.

Louie, Ai-Ling. *Yeh Shin: A Cinderella Story from China.* Philomel, 1982.

Low, Alice. *The Macmillan Book of Greek Gods and Heroes.* Macmillan, 1985.

Lowachee, Karin. *Warchild.* Warner Aspect, 2002.

Lowell, Susan. *CindyEllen.* Illustrated by Jane Manning. HarperCollins, 2000.

Lowell, Susan. *Dusty Locks and the Three Bears.* Henry Holt, 2001.

Lowell, Susan. *The Three Little Javelinas.* Northland, 1992.

Lowery, Linda. *Wilma Mankiller.* Carolrhoda. 1996.

Lowry, Lois. *Gathering Blue.* Houghton Mifflin, 2000.

Lowry, Lois. *Number the Stars.* Houghton Mifflin, 1989.

Lowry, Lois. *The Giver.* Houghton Mifflin, 1993.

Lowry, Lois. *The Messenger.* Houghton Mifflin, 2004.

Lowry, Lois. *The Silent Boy.* Houghton Mifflin, 2003.

Loya, Olga. *Momentos Magicos/Magic Moments.* August House, 1997.

Lubar, David. *Hidden Talents.* Tom Doharty, 1999.

Luby, Thia. *Yoga for Teens.* Clear Light, 2000.

Luge-Lason, Lise. *The Troll with No Heart in His Body and Other Tales of Trolls from Norway.* Illustrated by Betsy Boner. Houghton Mifflin,1999.

Lynch, Chris. *Extreme Elvin.* HarperCollins, 1999.

Lynch, Chris. *Freewill.* HarperCollins, 2001.

Lynch, Chris. *Gold Dust.* HarperCollins, 2000.

Lynch, Chris. *Gypsy Davey.* HarperCollins, 1994.

Lynch, Chris. *Inexcusable.* Ginee Seo, 2005.

Lynch, Chris. *Slot Machine.* HarperCollins, 1995.

Lynn, Sanford. *Ten-Second Rainshowers: Poems by Young People.* Simon & Schuster, 1996.

Lynn, Tracy. *Snow.* Simon & Schuster, 2003.

Lyon, George Ella. *Borrowed Children.* Orchard Books, 1988.

Lyon, George Ella. *Where Poems Come From.* Abbey & Co., 1999.

Lyon, George Ella. *With a Hammer for My Heart.* Dorling Kindersley, 1997.

Lyons, Mary. *Letters from a Slave Girl: The Story of Harriet Jacobs.* Scribner, 1992.

Lyons, Mary. *Sorrow's Kitchen: The Life and Folklore of Zora Neale Hurston.* Collier, 1990.

Macaulay, David. *Black and White.* Houghton Mifflin, 1990.

Mack, Tracy. *Drawing Lessons.* Scholastic, 2000.

MacLeod, Joan. *The Shape of a Girl.* Talon Books, 2002.

MacLeod, Ken. *Cydonia.* Orion, 1999.

Macy, Sue. *Bull's Eye: A Photobiography of Annie Oakley.* National Geographic Society, 2001.

Mah, Adeline Yen. *Chinese Cinderella.* Longman, 2004.

Mahy, Margaret. *Aliens in the Family.* Scholastic, 1986.

Mahy, Margaret. *The Changeover: A Supernatural Romance.* Atheneum, 1984.

Mahy, Margaret. *The Tricksters.* Macmillan, 1987.

Mandela, Nelson. *Favorite African Folktales.* Norton, 2002.

Marcantonio, Patricia. *Red Riding in the Hood.* Farrar, Straus, and Giroux, 2005.

Marchetta, Melina. *Jellicoe Road.* HarperTeen, 2008.

Marcos, Subcomandante. *The Story of Colors/La Historia de los Colores.* Illustrated by Domitila Dominguez. Cinco Puntas, 1999.

Marcus, Leonard. *A Caldecott Celebration: Six Artists and Their Paths to the Caldecott Medal.* Walker, 1998.

Marcus, Leonard. *Author Talk.* Simon & Schuster, 2000.

Marcus, Leonard. *Side by Side: Five Favorite Picture-Book Teams Go To Work.* Walker, 2001.

Marcus, Leonard. *Ways of Telling: Conversations on the Art of the Picture Book.* Dutton, 2002.

Mark, Jan. *Handles.* Atheneum, 1985.

Marrin, Albert. *Sitting Bull and His World.* Dutton, 2000.

Marsden, John. *So Much to Tell You.*

Marsden, John. *Tomorrow, When the War Began.* Houghton Mifflin, 1995.

Marshal, Rita. *Little Red Riding Hood.* Creative Education, 1983.

Marshall, James. *Goldilocks and the Three Bears.* Dial, 1988.

Marshall, James. *Hansel and Gretel.* Dial, 1990.

Marshall, James. *Little Red Riding Hood.* Dial, 1987.

Marshall, James. *The Three Little Pigs.* Dial, 1989.

Martin, Ann. *A Corner of the Universe.* Scholastic, 2002.

Martin, Jacqueline Briggs. *Snowflake Bentley.* Illustrated by Mary Azarian. Houghton Mifflin, 1998.

Martin, Rafe. *Mysterious Tales of Japan.* Illustrated by Tarsuro Kiuchi. Putnam, 1996.

Martin, Rafe. *The Rough Faced Girl.* Illustrated by David Shannon. Putnam, 1992.

Martin, Rafe. *The World before This One.* Arthur Levine, 2002.

Martinet, Jeanne. *Truer Than True Romance.* Watson-Gutpill, 2001.

Marz, Ron, Greg Land, Drew Geraci, and Caesar Robriguez. *Sojourn: From the Ashes.* CrossGen, 2003.

Marzollo, Jean. *Happy Birthday, Martin Luther King.* Illustrated by Brian Pinkney. Scholastic, 1993.

Mason, Jeff, Will Eisner, Harvey Pekar, and Ted Roll. *9–11: Emergency Relief.* Alternative, 2002.

Mason, Prue. *Camel Rider.* Charlesbridge, 2007.

Matas, Carol. *After the War.* Scholastic, 1996.

Matas, Carol. *Cloning Miranda.* Scholastic Canada, 1999.

Matthaei, Gay, and Jewel Grutman. *The Sketchbook of Thomas Blue Eagle.* Chronicle Books, 2001.

Maynard, Bill. *Pond Fire.* Putnam, 2000.

Mazar, Harry. *I Love You, Stupid!* Crowell, 1981.

Mazer, Anne. *Going Where I'm Coming From: Memoirs of American Youth.* Persea Books, 1995.

Mazer, Anne. *Working Days: Short Stories about Teenagers and Work.* Persea Books, 1997.

Mazer, Norma Fox. *Girlhearts.* HarperCollins, 2001.

Mazer, Norma Fox. *Good Night, Maman.* Harcourt Brace, 1999.

Mazer, Norma Fox. *Out of Control.* Avon Books, 1993.

McCaffrey, Anne. *Dragonsinger.* Atheneum, 1977.

McCall, Nathan. *Makes Me Wanna Holler: A Young Black Man in America.* 1995.

McCaughrean, Geraldine. *Not the End of the World.* Harper-Teen, 2005.

McCaughrean, Geraldine. *Odysseus.* Cricket, 2004.

McCaughrean, Geraldine. *The Kite Rider.* HarperCollins, 2002.

McCaughrean, Geraldine. *The Pirate's Son.* Scholastic, 1999.

McCaughrean, Geraldine. *The Stones Are Hatching.* Harper-Collins, 2000.

McCloud, Scott. *Understanding Comics.* Kitchen Sink Press, 1993.

McCloud, Scott. *Zot!* Eclipse Comics, 1984–1990.

McCormick, Patricia. *Cut.* Front Street, 2000.

McCully, Emily Arnold. *Mirette on the High Wire.* Putnam, 1992.

McDonald, Janet. *Spellbound.* Frances Foster, 2001.

McDonald, Joyce. *Swallowing Stones.* Laurel Leaf, 1998.

McDonell, Nick. *Twelve: A Novel.* Grove Press, 2000.

McKay, Hillary. *Indigo's Star.* Margaret K. McElderry, 2004.

McKinley, Robin. *Beauty: A Retelling of the Story of Beauty and the Beast.* HarperCollins, 1978.

McKinley, Robin. *Rose Daughter.* Greenwillow, 1997.

McKinley, Robin. *Spindle's End.* Putnam's Sons, 2000.

McKinley, Robin. *The Blue Sword.* Greenwillow, 1982.

McKinley, Robin. *The Outlaws of Sherwood.* Greenwillow, 1988.

McKinley, Robin, and Peter Dickinson. *Water: Tales of Elemental Spirits.* Putnam, 2002.

McKissack, P. *Nzingha: Warrior Queen of Matamba.* Scholastic, 2000.

McKissack, Patricia, and Fredrick McKissack. *Rebels Against Slavery: American Slave Revolts.* Scholastic, 1997.

McKissack, Patricia, and Fredrick McKissack. *Sojourner Truth: Ain't I a Woman.* Scholastic, 1992.

McKissack, Patricia. *Flossie and the Fox.* Illustrated by Rachel Isadora. Dial, 1986.

McKissack, Patricia. *The Dark Thirty: Southern Tales of the Supernatural.* Illustrated by Brian Pinkney. Knopf, 1992.

McLaren, Clemence. *Inside the Walls of Troy.* Atheneum, 1996.

McLaren, Clemence. *Waiting for Odysseus.* Atheneum, 2000.

McNaughton, Janet. *The Secret Under My Skin.* HarperTeen, 2005.

Medearis, Angela Shelf. *Skin Deep and Other Teenage Reflections.* Macmillan, 1995.

Medley, Linda. *Castle Waiting: The Curse of Brambly Hedge.* Olio, 1996.

Medley, Linda. *Castle Waiting: The Lucky Road.* Olio, 2000.

Melling, O. R. *The Light-Bearer's Daughter.* Amulet, 2007.

Meltzer, Milton. *Bound for America: The Story of the European Immigrants.* Benchmark Books, 2002.

Meltzer, Milton (ed.). *Hour of Freedom: American History in Poetry.* Boyds Mills, 2003.

Meltzer, Milton. *Lincoln: In His Own Words.* Harcourt Brace, 1993.

Meltzer, Milton. *Piracy & Plunder: A Murderous Business.* Dutton, 2001.

Meltzer, Milton (ed.). *The Black Americans: A History in Their Own Words 1619–1983.* Crowell, 1984.

Meltzer, Milton. *Ten Queens: Portraits of Women in Power.* Illustrated by Berthanne Anderson. Dutton, 1998.

Meltzer, Milton. *There Comes a Time: The Struggle for Civil Rights.* Random House, 2001.

Meltzer, Milton. *Underground Man.* Harcourt, 1990.

Melville, Herman. *Moby Dick.* Retold by Lew Sayre Schwartz and Richard Giordano. Illustrated by Richard Giordano. Houghton Mifflin, 2002.

Merrell, Billy. *Talking in the Dark.* Push, 2003.

Meyer, Carolyn. *Mary Bloody Mary: A Young Royals Book.* Gulliver, 1999.

Meyer, Carolyn. *White Lilacs.* Harcourt Brace Jovanovich, 1993.

Meyer, Louis. *Bloody Jack.* Harcourt, 2002.

Meyer, Louis. *Curse of the Blue Tattoo.* Harcourt, Turtleback, 2005.

Meyer, Stephenie. *Twilight.* Little, Brown, 2005.

Meyer, Stephenie. *Twilight: The Graphic Novel.* Illustrated by Young Kim. Yen, 2010.

Michaels, Judith Rowe. *Risking Intensity: Reading and Writing Poetry with High School Students.* NCTE, 1999.

Mierau, Christina. *Accept No Substitutes: The History of American Advertising.* Lerner, 2000.

Mignola, Mike. *Hellboy.* Dark Horse, 1994–present.

Mikaelsen, Ben. *Red Midnight.* Rayo, 2002.

Mikaelsen, Ben. *Rescue Josh McGuire.* Hyperion, 1991.

Mikaelsen, Ben. *Touching Spirit Bear.* HarperCollins, 2001.

Mikolaycak, Charles. *Orpheus.* Harcourt Brace Jovanovich, 1992.

Millar, Mark, and Adam Kubert. *Ultimate X-Men.* Marvel Comics, 1997.

Miller, Frank. *Batman: Year One.* DC, 1997.

Miller, Frank, and Geoff Darrow. *Big Guy and Rusty the Boy Robot.* Dark Horse, 1996.

Miller, Frank, and Klaus Janson. *Batman: The Dark Knight Returns.* DC, 1997/1987.

Miller, Mary Beth. *Aimee.* Penguin Putnam, 2001.

Milligan, Peter, and Mike Alred. *X-Force: New Beginnings.* Marvel Comics, 2001.

Millionaire, Tony. *The Adventures of Tony Millionaire's Sock Monkey.* Dark Horse, 1999.

Mills, Claudia. *Lizzie at Last.* Farrar, Straus, and Giroux, 2000.

Min, Anchee. *Wild Ginger.* Houghton Mifflin, 2001.

Minters, Frances. *Sleepless Beauty.* Illustrated by G. Brian Karas. Viking, 1996.

Miyazaki, Hayao. *Miyazaki's Spirited Away.* Viz Comics, 2002.

Miyazaki, Hayao. *Nausicaa of the Valley of the Wind.* Tokuma, 1993.

Mochizuki, Ken. *Beacon Hill Boys.* Scholastic Press, 2002.

Mollel, Tololwa. *Ananse's Feast.* Clarion, 1997.

Montgomery, Sy. *Quest for the Tree Kangaroo.* Illustrated by Nic Bishop. Houghton Mifflin, 2006.

Montresor, Beni. *Little Red Riding Hood.* Doubleday, 1991.

Moore, Alan, and Eddie Campbell. *From Hell.* Top Shelf, 2000.

Moore, Alan, and Dave Gibbons. *Watchmen.* Warner Books, 1995.

Moore, Alan, and Kevin O'Neil. *League of Extraordinary Gentlemen.* America's Best Comics, 2003.

Moore, Perry. *Hero: A Novel.* Hyperion, 2007.

Moore, Terry. *Strangers in Paradise.* Abstract Studio, 1994–1999.

Morgenstern, S. A. *Book of Coupons.* Viking, 2001

Morley, Jacqueline. *Egyptian Myths.* Illustrated by Giovanni Caselli. Peter Bednick, 1999.

Morpurgo, Michael. *Arthur, High King of Britain.* Illustrated by Michel Foreman. Harcourt Brace, 1995.

Morpurgo, Michael. *Robin of Sherwood.* Harcourt Brace, 1996.

Morris, Gerald. *Parsifal's Page.* Houghton Mifflin, 2001.

Morrison, Lillian. *Way to Go! Sports Poems.* Boyds Mills, 2001.

Morse, Scott. *The Barefoot Serpent.* Top Shelf, 2003.

Morse, Scott. *Soulwind: The Kid from Planet Earth.* Oni, 2000.

Morvan, Jean, and Phillip Buchet. *Wake: Fire and Ash.* NBM, 2003.

Moss, Marissa. *Hannah's Journal: The Story of an Immigrant Girl.* Harcourt, 2000.

Mowry, Jess. *Babylon Boyz.* Aladdin, 1997.

Mullen, P. H. *Gold in the Water.* Houghton Mifflin, 2001.

Murphy, Jim. *The Great Fire.* Scholastic, 1995.

Murray, Jaye. *Bottled Up: A Novel.* Dial, 2003.

Muten, Burleigh. *Grandmother Stories: Wise Woman Tales from Many Cultures.* Barefoot Books, 1999.

Myers, Christopher. *Wings.* Scholastic, 2000.

Myers, Walter Dean. *Amiri and Odette: A Love Story.* Scholastic, 2009.

Myers, Walter Dean. *Bad Boy: A Memoir.* HarperCollins, 2001.

Myers, Walter Dean. *Fallen Angels.* Scholastic, 1988.

Myers, Walter Dean. *Fast Sam, Cool Clyde, and Stuff.* Puffin, 1988.

Myers, Walter Dean. *Handbook for Boys: A Novel.* HarperCollins, 2001.

Myers, Walter Dean. *Harlem: A Poem.* Illustrated by Christopher Myers. Scholastic, 1997.

Myers, Walter Dean. *Hoops: A Novel.* Delacorte, 1981.

Myers, Walter Dean. *Malcolm X.* Scholastic, 1993.

Myers, Walter Dean. *Monster.* HarperCollins, 1999.

Myers, Walter Dean. *Patrol: An American Soldier in Vietnam.* Illustrated by Ann Grifalconi. HarperCollins, 2001.

Myers, Walter Dean. *Scorpions.* Harper & Rowe, 1988.

Myers, Walter Dean. *Shadow of the Red Moon.* Scholastic, 1995.

Myers, Walter Dean. *Slam.* Scholastic, 1996.

Myers, Walter Dean. *Somewhere in the Darkness.* Scholastic, 1992.

Myers, Walter Dean. *Sunrise over Fallujah.* Scholastic, 2008.

Myers, Walter Dean. *The Beast*. Scholastic, 2003.

Myers, Walter Dean. *The Glory Field*. Scholastic, 1995.

Myers, Walter Dean, and Christopher Myers. *A Time to Love: Stories from the Old Testament*. Scholastic, 2003.

Myracle, Lauren. *Bliss*. Amulet, 2008.

Na, An. *A Step from Heaven*. Front Street, 2001.

Na, An. *The Fold*. Putnam, 2008.

Naidoo, Beverly. *The Other Side of Truth*. HarperCollins, 2001.

Naifeh, Ted. *Courtney Crumrin and the Night Things*. Oni, 2003.

Namioka, Lensey. *An Ocean Apart, A World Away*. Random House, 2001.

Napoli, Donna Jo. *Bound*. Atheneum, 2004.

Napoli, Donna Jo. *Crazy Jack*. Delacorte, 1999.

Napoli, Donna Jo. *Daughter of Venice*. Random House, 2002.

Napoli, Donna Jo. *Sirena*. Scholastic, 1998.

Napoli, Donna Jo. *Spinners*. Dutton, 1999.

Napoli, Donna Jo. *Stones in Water*. Dutton, 1999.

Napoli, Donna Jo. *The Great God Pan*. Wendy Lamb, 2003.

Napoli, Donna Jo. *The Magic Circle*. Dutton Children's Books, 1993.

Napoli, Donna Jo. *The Prince of the Pond*. Puffin Books, 1992.

Napoli, Donna Jo. *Zel*. Dutton's Children's Books, 1996.

Nathan, Amy. *Yankee Doodle Gals: Women Pilots of World War II*. National Geographic Society, 2001.

National Museum of American Art, Smithsonian Institution. *Celebrate America In Poetry and Art*. Hyperion, 1994.

Naylor, Phyllis Reynolds. *Blizzard's Wake*. Atheneum, 2002.

Naylor, Phyllis Reynolds. *Jade Green: A Ghost Story*. Atheneum, 2000.

Naylor, Phyllis Reynolds. *Reluctantly Alice*. Atheneum, 1991.

Naylor, Phyllis Reynolds. *Shiloh*. Atheneum, 1991.

Naylor, Phyllis Reynolds. *Simply Alice*. Atheneum, 2002.

Nelson, Marilyn. *Carver: A Life in Poems*. Front Street, 2001.

Nelson, Peter. *Left for Dead: A Young Man's Search for Justice for the USS Indianapolis*. Bantam Doubleday Dell, 2002.

Neri, Greg. *Chess Rumble*. Illustrated by Jesse Watson. Lee and Low, 2007.

Nesbit, E. *The Book of Dragons*. Random House, 2010.

Ness, Evaline. *Tom Tit Tot*. Scribner, 1965.

Ness, Patrick. *The Knife of Never Letting Go*. Candlewick, 2008.

Neufield, John. *Boys Lie*. Dorling Kindersley, 1999.

Newbery, John. *The History of Little Goody Two Shoes*. John Newbery, 1765.

Newman, Leslea. *Fat Chance*. Paperstar/Putnam and Grosset Group, 1994.

Newth, Mette. *The Dark Light*. Farrar, Straus, and Giroux, 1998.

Niane, D. T. *Sundiata: An Epic of Old Mali*. Longman, 1995.

Nicholson, Jeff. *Colonia*. AiT/Planet Lar, 1998.

Nikola-Lisa, W. *Till Year's Good End: A Calendar of Medieval Labors*. Illustrated by Christopher Manson. Simon & Schuster, 1997.

Niles, Steve. *Thirty Days of Night*. Illustrated by Ben Templesmith. Idea and Design Works, 2003.

Nishiyama, Yuriko. *Harlem Beat*. TokyoPop, 1999.

Nix, Garth. *Abhorson*. HarperCollins, 2003.

Nix, Garth. *Lireal*. HarperCollins, 2001.

Nix, Garth. *Sabriel*. HarperCollins, 1997.

Nix, Garth. *Shade's Children*. HarperCollins, 1997.

Nixon, Joan Lowery. *The Christmas Killer*. Scholastic, 1991.

Nixon, Joan Lowery. *The Ellis Island Trilogy: Land of Hope*. Bantam, 1992.

Nolan, Han. *Born Blue*. Harcourt, 1994.

Nolan, Han. *If I Should Die Before I Wake*. Harcourt, 1995.

Nolan, Han. *Send Me Down a Miracle*. Harcourt, 1996.

Nolan, Han. *When We Were Saints*. Harcourt, 2003.

Norton, Andre. *Catseye*. Harcourt Brace and World, 1961.

Norton, Mary. The "Borrower and the Boy." Adapted from *The Borrowers* by Aaron Shepard. www.aaronshep.com/rt/RTE29.html

Nye, Naomi Shihab. *19 Varieties of Gazelle: Poems of the Middle East*. Greenwillow, 2001.

Nye, Naomi Shihab. *Salting the Ocean: 100 Poems by Young Poets*. Greenwillow, 2001.

Nye, Naomi Shihab (ed.). *The Flag of Childhood: Poems from the Middle East*. Greenwillow, 1999.

Nye, Naomi Shihab (ed.). *This Same Sky: A Collection of Poems from Around the World*. Macmillan, 1992.

Nye, Naomi Shihab. *What Have You Lost?* Greenwillow, 1999.

Nye, Naomi Shihab, and Paul Janeczko (eds.). *I Feel a Little Jumpy Around You: A Book of Her Poems and His Poems Presented in Pairs*. Simon & Schuster, 1996.

Nye, Robert. *Beowulf: A New Telling*. Farrar, Straus, and Giroux, 1963.

Oates, Joyce Carol. *Big Mouth & Ugly Girl*. HarperTempest, 2002.

Oberman, Sheldon. *The Always Prayer Shawl*. Illustrated by Ted Lewin. Boyds Mills, 1994.

O'Brien, Judith. *Mary Jane*. Marvel, 2003.

O'Brien, Robert. *Z for Zachariah*. Simon & Schuster, 1974.

Ochoa, Annette Pina, Betsy Franco, and Traci Gourdine. *Night Is Gone, Day Is Still Coming: Stories and Poems by American Indian Teens and Young Adults*. Candlewick, 2003.

O'Dell, Scott. *Island of the Blue Dolphins*. Houghton Mifflin, 1960.

O'Dell, Scott. *My Name Is Not Angelique*. Dell, 1989.

Okutoro, Lydia Onolola (ed.). *Quiet Storm: Voices of Young Black Poets*. Jump Sun, 1999.

O'Malley, Kevin. *Mount Olympus Basketball*. Walker and Co., 2003.

Opdyke, Irene Gut. *In My Hands: Memories of a Holocaust Rescuer*. Random House, 2001.

Oppel, Kenneth. *Sunwing*. Simon & Schuster, 2000.

Orgel, Dorris. *Ariadne, Awake*! Illustrated by Barry Moser. Viking, 1994.

Orlev, Uri. *Run, Boy, Run*. Houghton Mifflin, 2003.

Orlev, Uri. *The Man from the Other Side*. Puffin, 1991.

Osborne, Mary Pope, and Will Osborne. *Sleeping Bobby*. Illustrated by Giselle Potter. Atheneum, 2005.

Osborne, Mary Pope. *Favorite Greek Myths*. Illustrated by Troy Howell. Scholastic, 1989.

Osborne, Mary Pope. *Favorite Norse Myths.* Illustrated by Troy Howell. Scholastic, 1996.

Osborne, Mary Pope. *Kate and the Beanstalk.* Illustrated by Giselle Potter. Atheneum, 2000.

Ostrander, John, and Leonardo Manco. *Apache Skies.* Marvel, 2003.

Ostrander, John, and Leonardo Manco. *Blaze of Glory: The Last Ride of the Western Heroes.* Marvel, 2002.

Ottaviani, Jim. *Dignifying Science.* Illustrated by Donna Barr. G. T. Labs, 1999.

Ottaviani, Jim. *Fallout: Robert Oppenheimer, Leo Sziland and the Political Science of the Atom Bomb.* GT Labs, 2001.

Ottaviani, Jim. *Two Fisted Science.* San Val, 2001.

Oughton, Jerrie. *The War in Georgia.* Houghton Mifflin, 1997.

Owen, David. *Hidden Secrets.* Firefly Books, 2002.

Packer, Tina. *Tales from Shakespeare.* Scholastic, 2004.

Pak, Soyung. *A Place to Grow.* Illustrated by Marcellino Truong. Arthur Levine, 2002.

Paolini, Christopher. *Eragon (Inheritance).* Knopf, 2003.

Park, Linda Sue. *A Single Shard.* Clarion, 2001.

Park, Linda Sue. *SeeSaw Girl.* Clarion, 1999.

Park, Linda Sue. *The Kite Fighters.* Clarion, 2000.

Park, Linda Sue. *When My Name Was Keoko.* Clarion, 2002.

Parker, Jeff. *The Interman.* Octopus, 2003.

Parkinson, Siobhan. *The Leprechaun Who Wished He Wasn't.* Illustrated by Donald Teskey. San Val, 1997.

Partridge, Elizabeth. *This Land Was Made for You and Me: The Life & Songs of Woody Guthrie.* Viking, 2001.

Partridge. *Oranges on Golden Mountain.* Dutton, 2001.

Patent, Dorothy Hinshaw. *Animals on the Trail with Lewis and Clark.* Photographs by William Munoz. Clarion, 2002.

Patent, Dorothy Hinshaw. *Biodiversity.* Photographs by William Munoz. Clarion, 1996.

Patent, Dorothy Hinshaw. *Plants on the Trail with Lewis and Clark.* Clarion, 2003.

Paterson, Katherine. *Jacob Have I Loved.* Crowell, 1980.

Paterson, Katherine. *Jip: His Story.* Lodestone, 1996.

Paterson, Katherine. *Lyddie.* Lodestar, 1998.

Paterson, Katherine. *Park's Quest.* Dutton, 1988.

Paterson, Katherine. *Parzival: A Quest of the Grail Knight.* Lodestar, 1998.

Pattou, Edith. *East.* Harcourt, 2003.

Paulsen, Gary. *Brian's Return.* Delacorte, 1999.

Paulsen, Gary. *Brian's Winter.* Delacorte, 1996.

Paulsen, Gary. *Guts.* Delacorte, 2001.

Paulsen, Gary. *Hatchet.* Penguin, 1987.

Paulsen, Gary. *Nightjohn.* Delacorte, 1993.

Paulsen, Gary. *Sisters.* Harcourt Brace, 1993.

Paulsen, Gary. *Soldier's Heart: A Novel of the Civil War.* Delacorte, 1999.

Paulsen, Gary. *Woodsong.* Simon & Schuster, 1990.

Pausewang, Gudrun. *Traitor.* Carolrhoda, 2006.

Paver, Michelle. *Wolf Brother.* Katherine Tegen Books, 2005.

Pawlak, Mark, and Dick Lourie (eds.). *Bullseye: Stories and Poems by Outstanding High School Writers.* Hanging Loose, 1995.

Peck, Richard. *A Long Way from Chicago.* Dial, 1999.

Peck, Richard. *A Year Down Yonder.* Dial, 2000.

Peck, Richard. *Fair Weather.* Dial, 2001.

Peck, Richard. *Ghosts I Have Been.* Viking, 1977.

Peck, Richard. *The Dreadful Future of Blossom Culp.* Delacorte, 1983.

Peck, Robert Newton. *A Part of the Sky.* Knopf, 1994.

Peck, Robert Newton. *Arly.* Walter, 1989.

Peck, Robert Newton. *Horse Thief.* HarperCollins, 2002.

Pelta, Kathy. *Rediscovering Easter Island.* Lerner, 2001.

Pennebaker, Ruth. *Don't Think Twice.* Henry Holt, 1996.

Perham, Molly. *King Arthur and the Legends of Camelot.* Belitha, 1993.

Perkins, Mitali. *The Sunita Experiment.* Little, Brown, 1993.

Perlman, Janet. *Cinderella Penguin.* Viking, 1993.

Perrault, Charles. *Cinderella.* Illustrated by Susan Jeffers. Dial, 1985.

Perrault, Charles. *Cinderella: A Fairy Tale.* Translated by Anthea Belt. Illustrated by Lock Koopmans. North-Scott Books, 1999.

Perrault, Charles. *Little Red Riding Hood.* Illustrated by Beni Montresor. Doubleday, 1991.

Peters, Julie Anne. *Keeping You a Secret.* Little, Brown, 2003.

Petrie, Doug, and Ryan Sook. *Buffy the Vampire Slayer: Ring of Fire.* Dark Horse, 2000.

Petry, Ann. *Tituba of Salem Village.* Crowell, 1964.

Pfeffer, Susan. *Life As We Knew It.* Harcourt, 2006.

Philbrick, Nathaniel. *Revenge of the Whale: The True Story of the Whaleship Essex.* Putnam, 2002.

Philbrick, Rodman. *The Last Book in the Universe.* Scholastic, 2000.

Philip, Neil. *Odin's Family: Myths of the Vikings.* Orchard, 1996.

Pierce, Tamora. *First Test: Protector of the Small.* Random House, 1999.

Pierce, Tamora. *Trickster's Choice.* Random House, 2003.

Pini, Richard, and Wendy Pini. *Elfquest: The Hidden Years.* Warp Graphics, 1994.

Placide, Jaira. *Fresh Girl.* Wendy Lamb, 2002.

Platt, Kin. *A Mystery for Thoreau.* Farrar, Straus, and Giroux, 2008.

Platt, Randall. *The Likes of Me.* Delacorte, 2002.

Plum-Ucci, Carol. *What Happened to Lani Garver.* Harcourt, 2002.

Plum-Ucci, Carol. *The Body of Christopher Creed.* Harcourt, 2000.

Polacco, Patricia. *Chicken Sunday.* Philomel, 1992.

Polacco, Patricia. *January's Sparrow.* Philomel, 2009.

Polacco, Patricia. *Pink and Say.* Philomel, 1994.

Polacco, Patricia. *Thank You, Mr. Falker.* Philomel, 1998.

Polacco, Patricia. *The Butterfly.* Philomel, 2000.

Polacco, Patricia. *The Keeping Quilt.* Simon & Schuster, 1988.

Politzer, Anie, and Michel Politzer. *My Journals and Sketchbooks.* Harcourt, Brace, Jovanovich, 1974.

Poole, Josephine. *Snow White.* Illustrated by Angela Barrett. Knopf, 1991.

Pope, Elizabeth Marie. *The Sherwood Ring.* Houghton Mifflin, 1989.

Porcellino, John. *Thoreau at Walden.* Hyperion, 2008.

Porter, Conni. *Imani All Mine.* Houghton Mifflin, 1999.

Porter, Tracey. *Treasures in the Dust.* HarperCollins, 1997.

Potter, Beatrix. *The Tale of Peter Rabbit.* Frederick Warne, 1902.

Pratchett, Terry. *The Amazing Maurice and His Educated Rodents.* HarperCollins, 2001.

Pratchett, Terry. *Nation.* HarperCollins, 2008.

Pressler, Mirjam. *Malka.* Philomel, 2003.

Price, Susan. *The Sterkarm Handshake.* HarperCollins, 2000.

Priceman, Marjorie. *Little Red Riding Hood.* Little Simon, 2001.

Priestley, Chris. *Death and the Arrow.* Knopf, 2003.

Prince, Maggie. *The House on Hound Hill.* Houghton Mifflin, 2003.

Proddow, Penelope. *Art Tells a Story: Greek and Roman Myths.* Doubleday, 1979.

Proust, Marcel. *Remembrance of Things Past: Combray.* Adapted by Stanislas Brezet and Stephanie Heuet. NBM, 2003.

Pullman, Philip. *The Amber Spyglass.* Knopf, 2000.

Pullman, Philip. *The Ruby in the Smoke.* Peter Smith, 2002.

Pullman, Philip. *Clockwork: Or All Wound Up.* Scholastic, 1999.

Pullman, Philip. *I Was a Rat.* Knopf, 1997.

Pullman, Philip. *The Golden Compass.* Knopf, 1996.

Pullman, Philip. *The Subtle Knife.* Knopf, 1997.

Pyle, Howard. *Men of Iron.* Harper and Brothers, 1891.

Pyle, Howard. *The Merry Adventures of Robin Hood of Great Renown in Nottinghamshire.* Scribner's, 1883.

Pyle, Howard. *The Story of King Arthur and His Knights.* Scribner's, 1903.

Qualey, Marsha. *Come in from the Cold.* Houghton Mifflin, 1994.

Qualey, Marsha. *Hometown.* Houghton Mifflin, 1995.

Qualey, Marsha. *One Night.* Penguin Putnam, 2001.

Rabin, Staton. *Black Powder.* McElderry, 2005.

Rapp, Adam. *33 Snowfish.* Candlewick, 2003.

Rapp, Adam. *Copper Elephant.* Front Street, 1995.

Raschka, Chris. *John Coltrane's Giant Steps.* Atheneum, 2002.

Raskin, Ellen. *The Westing Game.* Dutton, 1978.

Raven. *Night Boat to Freedom.* Illustrated by E. B. Lewis. Farrar, Straus, and Giroux, 2006.

Ray, Jane. *Shakespeare's Romeo and Juliet.* Illustrated by Michael Rosen. Candlewick, 2004.

Reeder, Carolyn. *Before the Creeks Ran Red.* HarperCollins, 2003.

Reef, Catherine. *John Steinbeck.* Clarion, 1996.

Reef, Catherine. *Paul Laurence Dunbar: Portrait of a Poet.* Enslow, 2000.

Reef, Catherine. *This Our Dark Country: The American Settlers of Liberia.* Clarion, 2002.

Reef, Catherine. *Walt Whitman.* Clarion, 1995.

Rees, Celia. *Witch Child.* Bloomsbury, 2000.

Reeve, Philip. *Mortal Englines.* Scholastic, 2001.

Reger, Rob, Jessica Gruner, and Buzz Parker. *Emily the Strange: The Lost.* HarperCollins, 2009.

Reich, Susanna. *Painting the Wild Frontier.* Clarion, 2008.

Reid, Vince. *Medieval Muck.* Oxford University Press, 1998.

Reilly, Matthew. *Crash Course.* Simon & Schuster, 2005.

Reiss, Kathryn. *Sweet Miss Honeywell's Revenge.* Harcourt, 2004.

Reit, Seymour. *Behind Rebel Lines: The Incredible Story of Emma Edmonds, Civil War Spy.* Harcourt Brace, 1988.

Rennison, Louise. *Angus, Thongs, and Full Frontal Snogging.* HarperCollins, 2000.

Rhodes-Courter, Ashley. *Three Little Words.* Atheneum, 2008.

Rice, David. *Crazy Loco.* Dial, 2001.

Rider, C. *The Boy Who Cried Wolf.* Illustrated by D. Catchepole. Oxford University Press, 2000.

Rieber, John, and Peter Gross. *The Books of Magic: Bindings.* Vertigo, 1995.

Rieber, John Ney, Gary Amaro, and Peter Gross. *The Books of Magic: Bindings.* DC/Vertigo, 1995.

Rinaldi, Ann. *Cast Two Shadows: The American Revolution in the South.* Gulliver, 1998.

Rinaldi, Ann. *Finishing Rebecca: A Story about Peggy Shippen and Benedict Arnold.* Gulliver, 2003.

Rinaldi, Ann. *Keep Smiling Through.* Harcourt Brace, 1996.

Rinaldi, Ann. *Or Give Me Death: A Novel of Patrick Henry's Family.* Gulliver, 2003.

Rinaldi, Ann. *The Coffin Quilt: The Feud Between the Hatfields and the McCoys.* Harcourt, 1999.

Rinaldi, Ann. *The Fifth of March: A Story of the Boston Massacre.* Gulliver, 1993.

Rinaldi, Ann. *The Secret of Sarah Revere.* Gulliver, 1995.

Rinaldi, Ann. *Wolf by the Ears.* Scholastic, 1991.

Ringold, Faith. *Tar Beach.* Crown, 1991.

Ritter, John. *Choosing Up Sides.* Philomel, 1998.

Roberts, Jeremy. *Rock and Ice Climbing: Top the Tower!* Rosen, 2000.

Roberts, Willo Davis. *Rebel.* Atheneum, 2003.

Robertson, Bruce. *Marguerite Makes a Book.* Paul Getty Museum, 2002.

Robinson, James, and Jackson Grice. *Terminator: End Game.* Dark Horse, 1992.

Robinson, James, and Paul Smith. *Leave it to Chance.* Image, 1996.

Rochelle, B. (ed.). *Words with Wings: A Treasury of African American Poetry and Art.* HarperCollins, 2001.

Rodda, E. *Rowan of Rin.* Greenwillow, 2001.

Rogasky, Barbara. *Rapunzel.* Illustrated by Trina Hyman Schart. Holiday House, 1982.

Rohmann, Eric. *My Friend Rabbit.* Roaring Brook, 2002.

Rohmann, Eric. *Time Flies.* Crown, 1994.

Rohmer, Harriet. *Heroes of the Environment.* Illustrated by Julie McLaughlin. Chronicle, 2009.

Roman, Dave, and John Green. *Jax Epoch and the Quicken Forbidden: Borrowed Magic.* Pantheon, 2003.

Rose, Joanna. *Little Miss Strange.* Algonquin Books, 1997.

Rosen, Michael. *Classic Poetry: An Illustrated Collection.* Candlewick, 1998.

Rosen, Michael. *Shakespeare: His Work and His World.* Illustrated by Robert Ingpen. Candlewick Press, 2001.

Rosen, Michael. *Shakespeare's Romeo and Juliet*. Illustrated by Jane Ray. Candlewick, 2004.

Rosenberg, Liz (ed.). *Earth Shattering Poetry*. Holt, 1998.

Rosoff, Meg. *How I Live Now*. Wendy Lamb, 2004.

Ross, Gayle. *How Turtle's Back Was Cracked*. Dial, 1995.

Rostkowski, Margaret. *After the Dancing Days*. Harper & Row, 1986.

Rottman, S. L. *Stetson*. Viking, 2001.

Rounds, Glen. *The Three Little Pigs and the Big Bad Wolf*. Holiday House, 1992.

Rousseau, Jean Jacques. *Emile ou de l'education* (1765). Garnier, 1999.

Rowling, J. K. *Harry Potter and the Half Blood Prince*. Scholastic, 2005.

Rowling, J. K. *Harry Potter and the Sorcerer's Stone*. Arthur Levine, 1998.

Rubalcuba, Jill. *The Wadjet Eyes*. Clarion, 1997.

Ruby, Lois. *Skin Deep*. Scholastic, 1994.

Ruby, Lois. *Soon Be Free*. Simon & Schuster, 2000.

Russell, Janice. *Goldilocks*. Boyds Mills, 1997.

Rutsky, Joshua. *Beyond the Bard: Fifty Plays for Use in the English Classroom*. Allyn & Bacon, 2001.

Ryan, Carrie. *The Forest of Hands and Teeth*. Delacorte, 2009.

Ryan, Pam Muñoz. *Esperanza Rising*. Scholastic, 2000.

Ryan, Pam Muñoz. *When Marian Sang*. Illustrated by Brian Selznick. Scholastic, 2002.

Ryan, Sara. *Empress of the World*. Viking, 2001.

Rylant, Cynthia. *A Fine White Dust*. Atheneum, 1986.

Rylant, Cynthia. *But I'll Be Back Again*. Beech, 1993.

Sabuda, Robert. *Tutankhana's Gift*. Maxwell Macmillian, 1994.

Sacco, Joe. *Palestine*. Fantagraphics, 2002.

Sacco, Joe. *Safe Area Gorazde*. Fantagraphics, 2000.

Saijyo, Shinji. *Iron Wok Jan!* ComicsOne, 2005.

Sakai, Stan. *Usagi Yojimbo: Demon Mask*. Fantagraphics/Dark Horse Comics, 1987.

Salinger, J. D. *The Catcher in the Rye*. Little, Brown, 1951.

Salisbury, Graham. *Eyes of the Emperor*. Delacorte, 2005.

Salisbury, Graham. *Island Boyz: Short Stories*. Wendy Lamb, 2002.

Salisbury, Graham. *Lord of the Deep*. Delacorte, 2001.

Salisbury, Graham. *Under the Blood Red Sun*. Delacorte, 1994.

San Jose, Christine. *Cinderella*. Boyds Mills, 1994.

San Souci, Robert. *Faithful Friend*. Illustrated by Brian Pinkney. Simon & Schuster, 1995.

San Souci, Robert. *Fa Mulan*. Illustrated by Jean and Mou-Sien Tseng. Hyperion, 1998.

Sanchez, Alex. *Rainbow Boys*. Simon & Schuster, 2001.

Satrapi, Marjane. *Persepolis*. Pantheon, 2003.

Savage, Candace. *Born to Be a Cowgirl: A Spirited Ride through the Old West*. Tricycle Press, 2001.

Say, Allen. *Grandfather's Journey*. Houghton Mifflin, 1994.

Say, Allen *Home of the Brave*. Houghton Mifflin, 2002.

Schlee, Ann. *The Vandal*. Crown, 1979.

Schmidt, Gary. *Straw into Gold*. Clarion, 2001.

Schmidt, Thomas, and Jeremy Schmidt. *The Saga of Lewis and Clark*. D.K. Children, 1999.

Schmook, Kathy Grizzard (ed.). *Poetry for Guys Who Thought They Hated Poetry*. Willow Creek, 1996.

Schusterman, Neal. *The Schwa Was Here*. Dutton, 2004.

Schwartz, Lew Sayre. *Moby Dick* by Herman Melville. Illustrated by Dick Giordano. Sandpiper, 2002.

Scieszka, Jon. *Squids Will Be Squids*. Illustrated by Lane Smith. Penguin, 1998.

Scieszka, Jon. *The Stinky Cheese Man and Other Fairly Stupid Fairy Tales*. Illustrated by Lane Smith.

Scieszka, Jon. *The True Story of the Three Little Pigs*. Illustrated by Lane Smith. Viking, 1989.

Scott, Michael. *The Alchemyst*. Delacorte, 2007.

Sedgewick, Marcus. *Floodland*. Delacorte, 2001.

Seely, Debra. *Grasslands*. Holiday House, 2002.

Sendak, Maurice. *We're All in the Dumps with Jack and Guy*. HarperCollins, 1993.

Sendak, Maurice. *Where the Wild Things Are*. HarperCollins, 1963.

Seto, Andy. *Crouching Tiger Hidden Dragon*. Comics One, 2005.

Seuss, Dr. *Oh the Places You'll Go*. Random House, 1990.

Severance, John. *Gandhi: Great Soul*. Clarion, 1997.

Sewell, Anna. *Black Beauty*. Jarrokis and Sons, 1877.

Shakespeare, William. *Under the Greenwood Tree: Shakespeare for Young People*. Stemmer House, 1986.

Shan, Darren. *Cirque du Freak*. Little, Brown, 2001.

Shange, Ntozake. *Ellington Is Not a Street*. Simon & Schuster, 2004.

Shanghe, Ntozake. *I Live in Music*. Tabori & Chang, 1994.

Shannon, David. *A Bad Case of Stripes*. Blue Sky, 1998.

Shanower, Eric. *Age of Bronze: A Thousand Ships*. Image Comics, 2001.

Sheldon, Dyan. *Planet Janet*. Candlewick, 2003.

Shepard, Aaron. *Resthavn*. Adapted from Nancy Farmer's *The Ear, the Eye, and the Arm*. Orchard, 1994. www.aaronshep.com/rt

Shigeno, Shuichi. *Initial D*. TokyoPop, 2002.

Sidman, Joyce. *The World According to Dog: Poems and Teen Voices*. Houghton Mifflin, 2003.

Siebert, Diane. *Mississippi*. Illustrated by Greg Harlin. HarperCollins, 2001.

Siegal, Aranka. *Grace in the Wilderness: After the Liberation 1945–1948*. Farrar, Straus, and Giroux, 1985.

Siegal, Aranka. *Upon the Head of the Goat: A Childhood in Hungary 1939–1944*. Farrar, Straus, and Giroux, 1981.

Silverberg, Robert (ed.). *Legends: Stories by the Masters of Modern Fantasy*. Tor, 1998.

Sís, Peter. *Messenger: Galileo Galilei*. Farrar, Straus, and Giroux, 1996.

Sís, Peter. *Tibet: Through the Red Box*. Farrar, Straus, and Giroux, 1998.

Shields, Charles. *I Am Scout: A Biography of Harper Lee*. Henry Holt, 2008.

Siversten, Linda, and Tosh Siversten. *Generation Green: The Ultimate Teen Guide to Living an Eco-Friendly Life*. San Val, 2008.

Skurzynski, Gloria. *Spider's Voice*. Simon & Schuster, 1999.

Skurzynski, Gloria. *Virtual War*. Simon & Schuster, 1997.

Sleator, William. *Interstellar Pig*. Dutton, 1984.

Sleator, William. *Parasite Pig*. Dutton, 2002.

Sleator, William. *Strange Attractors*. Dutton, 1990.

Smith, Anita Hope. *Keeping the Night Watch*. Henry Holt, 2008.

Smith, Charles R. *Hoop Queens*. Dutton, 2003.

Smith, Charles R. *Rimshots: Basketball Pix, Rolls, and Rhythm*. Dutton, 1999.

Smith, Cynthia Leitich. *Eternal*. Candlewick, 2009.

Smith, Cynthia Leitich. *Jingle Dancer*. Illustrated by Cornelius Van Wright and Ying-Hwa Hu. Morrow, 2000.

Smith, Cynthia Leitich. *Rain Is Not My Indian Name*. HarperCollins, 2001.

Smith, Jeff. *Bone: Out from Boneville*. Cartoon Books, 1994–present.

Smith, Roland. *Elephant Run*. Hyperion, 2007.

Smith, Roland. *Peak*. Harcourt, 2007.

Smith, Sherri. *Lucy the Giant*. Delacorte, 2001.

Sneed, Brad. *Aesop's Fables*. Phyllis Fogleman Books, 2003.

Snyder, Dianne. *The Boy of the Three Year Nap*. Illustrated by Allen Say. Houghton Mifflin, 1988.

Sones, Sonya. *Stop Pretending: What Happened When My Big Sister Went Crazy*. HarperCollins, 1999.

Sones, Sonya. *What My Mother Doesn't Know*. Simon & Schuster, 2002.

Soryo, Fuyumi. *Mars*. TokyoPop, 2002.

Soto, Gary. *Body Parts in Rebellion: Hanging Out with Fernie and Me*. Putnam, 2002.

Soto, Gary. *Chato and the Party Animals*. Illustrated by Susan Guevara. Putnam, 2000.

Soto, Gary. *Jesse*. Harcourt, 1994.

Soto, Gary. *Nerdlandia: A Play*. Penguin, 1999.

Soto, Gary. *New and Selected Poems*. Chronicle, 1995.

Souhami, Jessica. *Rama and the Demon King*. Dorling Kindersley, 1997.

Speare, Elizabeth George. *The Bronze Bow*. Houghton Mifflin, 1997.

Spiegelman, Art. *The Complete Maus*. Pantheon Books, 1997.

Spiegelman, Art. *Maus: A Survivor's Tale*. Pantheon, 1986–1991.

Spinelli, Jerry. *Milkweed*. Knopf, 2003.

Spinelli, Jerry. *Stargirl*. Knopf, 2000.

Spinner, Stephanie. *Be First in the Universe*. Delacorte, 2000.

Spinner, Stephanie. *Quiver*. Knopf, 2002.

Springer, Nancy. *I Am Mordred*. Philomel, 1998.

Springer, Nancy. *I Am Morgan LeFay*. Philomel, 2001.

Springer, Nancy. *Lionclaw: A Tale of Rowan Hood*. Philomel, 2002.

Springer, Nancy. *Rowan Hood: Outlaw Girl of Sherwood Forest*. Philomel, 2001.

Springer, Nancy. *The Friendship Song*. Atheneum, 1992.

Stanchak, John. *Civil War*. Dorling Kindersley, 2001.

Stanchak, Karen. *Those Extraordinary Women of World War I*. Lerner, 2001.

Stanley, Diane. *Petrosinella: A Neopolitan Rapunzel*. Puffin, 1997.

Stanley, Diane. *Roughing It on the Oregon Trail*. HarperCollins, 2001.

Stephenson, Neal. *Snow Crash*. Bantam, 1992.

Stevenson, Robert Louis. *Treasure Island*. Cassell, 1883.

Stevermer, Caroline. *River Rats*. Harcourt, 1992.

Stewart, Melissa. *A Place for Butterflies*. Illustrated by Higgins Bond. Peachtree, 2006.

St. George, Judith. *John and Abigail Adams: An American Love Story*. Holiday House, 2001.

St. George, Judith. *So You Want to Be An Inventor*. Illustrated by David Small. Philomel, 2002.

Still, James. *And Then They Came for Me: Remembering the World of Anne Frank*. Dramatic Publishing, 1999.

Stolz, Mary. *Ivy Larkin*. Houghton Mifflin, 1986.

Stone, Jeff. *Tiger*. Random House, 2005.

Stone, Miriam. *At the End of Words: A Daughter's Memoir*. Candlewick, 2003.

Stowe, Harriet Beecher. *Uncle Tom's Cabin*. Aladdin, 2002.

Strasser, Todd. *Boot Camp*. Simon & Schuster, 2007.

Strasser, Todd. *Give a Boy a Gun*. Simon Pulse, 2002.

Straczynski, J. Michael, and John Romita, Jr. *Amazing Spider-Man: Coming Home*. Marvel Comics, 2002.

Strather, Allan. *Leslie's Journal*. Annick Press, 2008.

Stratton, Allan. *Chanda's Wars*. HarperTeen, 2008.

Stren, Patti. *I Was a 15-Year-Old Blimp*. Harper & Row, 1985.

Stroud, Jonathan. *The Amulet of Sumarkind*. Hyperion, 2003.

Surface, Mary Hall. *Most Valuable Player: And Four Other All-Star Plays for Young Audiences*. Smith and Kraus, 1999.

Sutcliff, Rosemary. *Black Ships before Troy: The Story of the Iliad*. Illustrated by Alan Lee. Delacorte, 1993.

Sutcliff, Rosemary. *The Light beyond the Forrest*. Dutton, 1981.

Sutcliff, Rosemary. *The Shining Company*. Farrar, Straus, and Giroux, 1990.

Sutcliff, Rosemary. *The Sword and the Circle*. Dutton, 1981.

Swortzell, Lowell. *Theatre for Young Audiences: Around the World in 21 Plays*. Applause Theatre Books Publishers, 1997.

Taback, Sims. *Joseph Had a Little Overcoat*. Random House, 1977.

Takahashi, Kazuki. *Yu-Gi-Oh*. Viz, 2003.

Talbatt, Hudson. *Forging Freedom*. Putnam, 2000.

Talbot, Bryan. *Age of Reptiles: Tribal Warfare*. Dark Horse, 1996.

Talbot, Bryan. *Tale of One Bad Rat*. Dark Horse Comics, 1995.

Tamaki, Hisao. *Star Wars: A New Hope* (adapted). Dark Horse, 1998.

Tan, Shaun. *The Arrival*. Arthur Levine, 2007.

Tan, Shaun. *The Red Tree*. Lothian, 2001.

Tan, Shaun. *Tales from Outer Suburbia*. Arthur Levine, 2009.

Tanaka, Shelley. *Attack on Pearl Harbor: The True Story of the Day America Entered World War II*. Illustrated by David Craig. Hyperion, 2001.

Tashjian, Janet. *The Gospel According to Larry*. Henry Holt, 2001.

Tate, Eleanora. *Celeste's Harlem Renaissance*. Little, Brown, 2007.

Taudte, Jeca, MySpace Community, and Dan Santat. *My Space/Our Planet*. HarperCollins, 2008.

Taylor, Mildred D. *Roll of Thunder, Hear My Cry*. Dial, 1976.

Taylor, Mildred D. *The Land*. Fogelman, 2001.

Taylor, Mildred D. *Song of the Trees*. Dial, 1975.

Taylor, Theodore. *Air Raid—Pearl Harbor: The Story of December 7, 1941*. Ty Crowell, 1971.

Taylor, Theodore. *Lord of the Kill*. Blue Sky Press, 2002.

Taylor, Theodore. *The Bomb*. Harcourt, 1995.

Taylor, Theodore. *The Sniper*. Avon, 1989.

Tejima, Keizaburo. *Owl Lake*. Philomel, 1987.

Temple, Frances. *Tiger Soup: An Anansi Story from Jamaica*. Orchard, 1994.

Temple, Francis. *The Ramsey Scallop*. Orchard, 1994.

Testa, Maria. *Almost Forever*. Candlewick, 2003.

Tezuka, Osamu. *Astro Boy*. Dark Horse, 2002.

Thayer, Ernest. *Casey at the Bat*. Illustrated by Christopher Bing. Handprint Books, 2000.

Thayer, Ernest. *Casey at the Bat*. Illustrated by Joe Morse. Kids Can Press, 2006.

The National Museum of the American Indian (compiler). *When the Rain Sings: Poems by Young Native Americans*. Simon & Schuster, 1999.

Thimmesh, Catherine. *Girls Think of Everything*. Houghton Mifflin, 2000.

Thomas, Rob. *Rats Saw God*. Simon & Schuster, 1996.

Thompson, Kate. *Creature of the Night*. Roaring Brook, 2009.

Thoms, Annie (ed.). *With Their Eyes: September 11th: The View from a High School at Ground Zero*. HarperTeen, 2002.

Tillage, Leon Walter. *Leon's Story*. Farrar, Straus, and Giroux, 1997.

Tingle, Rebecca. *The Edge of the Sword*. Putnam, 2001.

Tito, Tina E. *Liberation: Teens in the Concentration Camps and the Teen Soldiers Who Liberated Them*. Rosen Publishers, 1999.

Todd, Pamela. *Blind Faith Hotel*. Margaret McElderry, 2008.

Tolhurst, Marilyn. *Somebody and the Three Blairs*. Orchard Books, 1990.

Tolkien, J. R. R. *The Hobbit*. Adapted by Sean Deming. Illustrated by David Wenzel. HarperCollins, 2000.

Tolkien, J. R. R. *The Hobbit: Or There and Back Again*. Allen & Unwin, 1937.

Toll, Nelly. *Behind the Secret Window*. Dial, 1993.

Tomlinson, Theresa. *Child of May*. Orchard, 1998.

Tomlinson, Theresa. *The Forest Wife*. Orchard, 1995.

Torres, J., and Mike North. *Jason and the Argobots*. Oni, 2002.

Torres, J., and Scott Chandler. *Days Like This*. Oni, 2003.

Torres, J., and Takeshi Miyazawa. *Sidekicks: The Transfer Student*. Oni, 2002.

Torrey, Michelle. *To the Edge of the World*. Knopf, 2003.

Toten, Teresa. *The Game*. Red Deer Press, 2001.

Trembath, Don. *Popsicle Journal*. Orca, 2001.

Trivizas, Eugene. *The Three Little Wolves and the Big Bad Pig*. Illustrated by Helen Oxenbury. Scholastic, 1994.

Trondheim, Louis. *LaMouche*. Seuil, 1995.

Trope, Zoe. *Please Don't Kill the Freshman*. HarperCollins, 2003.

Trueman, Terry. *Cruise Control*. HarperCollins, 2004.

Trueman, Terry. *Inside Out*. HarperTempest, 2003.

Trueman, Terry. *Stuck in Neutral*. HarperCollins, 2000.

Turkle, Brinton. *Deep in the Forest*. Dutton, 1976.

Turner, Ann. *Abe Lincoln Remembers*. Illustrated by Wendell Minor. HarperCollins, 2000.

Turner, M. W. *Queen of Attolia*. Greenwillow, 2000.

Turner, Pamela. *A Life in the Wild*. Farrar, Straus, and Giroux, 2008.

Turner, Pamela S. *The Frog Scientist*. Photographs by Andy Comis. Houghton Mifflin, 2009.

Turning, Ann. *Learning to Swim*. Scholastic, 2002.

Twain, Mark. *Adventures of Tom Sawyer*. Kingfisher Classics, 2002. (Original work published 1876)

Twain, Mark. *The Adventures of Huckleberry Finn*. New York: Signet Classic, 1959.

Uehashi, Nahoke. *Moributo: Guardian of the Spirit*. Arthur Levine, 2008.

Vaes, Alain. *The Princess and the Pea*. Little, Brown, 2001.

van Allsburg, Chris. *The Polar Express*. Houghton Mifflin, 1985.

van Allsburg, Chris. *The Widow's Broom*. Houghton Mifflin, 1992.

van der Rol, Ruud, and Rian Verhoeven. *Anne Frank: Beyond the Diary*. Viking, 1993.

Vande Velde, Vivian. *Being Dead*. Harcourt, 2001.

Vande Velde, Vivian. *Companions of the Night*. Harcourt, 1995.

Vande Velde, Vivian. *The Rumpelstilskin Problem*. Houghton Mifflin, 2000.

Vande Velde, Vivian. *User Friendly*. Harcourt, 1991.

Van Draanen, Wendelin. *Flipped*. Knopf, 2001.

Van Draanen, Wendelin. *Sammy Keyes and the Hollywood Mummy*. Knopf, 2001.

Van Meter, Jen, and Christine Norris. *Hopeless Savages*. Oni, 2002.

Vecchione, Patrice (ed.). *The Body Eclectic: An Anthology of Poems*. Henry Holt, 2002.

Vecchione, Patrice (ed.). *Truth & Lies*. Henry Holt, 2001.

Veitch, Tom, and Cam Kennedy. *Star Wars: Dark Empire*. Dark Horse, 1995.

Verheiden, Mark. *Aliens*. Dark Horse, 1989.

Verheiden, Mark, Dan Barry, Christopher Warren, and Ron Randall. *Predator*. Dark Horse, 2007.

Verne, Jules. *Twenty Thousand Leagues Under the Sea*. Sampson Low, Marston, Low and Searle, 1872.

Vincent, Gabrielle. *A Day, a Dog*. Front Street, 1999.

Vizzini, Ned. *Be More Chill*. Hyperion, 2004.

Voigt, Cynthia. *Bad Girls in Love*. New York: Atheneum, 2002.

Voigt, Cynthia. *Orfe*. Atheneum, 1992.

Voigt, Cynthia. *Runner*. Atheneum, 1985.

Voigt, Cynthia. *When She Hollers*. Scholastic, 1985.

Von Ziegesar, Cecily. *SLAM*. Alloy/Putnam, 2002.

Vozar, David. *Yo Hungry Wolf: A Nursery Rap.* Doubleday, 1992.

Vreeland, Susan. *The Passion of Artemisia.* Viking, 2001.

Vrettos, Adrienne Maria. *Sight.* Margaret McElderry, 2007.

Wade, Mark, Scott Beatty, Butch Grice, and Paul Ryan. *Ruse.* CrossGen, 2003.

Wagner, Matt. *Mage: The Hero Discovered.* Donning Co., 1987–1988.

Waid, Mark, and Alex Ross. *Kingdom Come.* DC, 1998/1996.

Waldman, Neil. *Wounded Knee.* Atheneum, 2001.

Walker, Paul Robert. *Giants: Stories from Around the World.* Illustrated by James Bernardin. Harcourt, 1995.

Walker, Richard. *The Barefoot Book of Trickster Tales.* Illustrated by Claudio Munoz. Barefoot Books, 1998.

Wallace, Rich. *Wrestling Sturbridge.* Knopf, 1996.

Walter, Virginia. *Making Up Megaboy.* Dorling Kindersley, 1998.

Walters, Eric. *Northern Exposure.* HarperCollins, 2001.

Ware, Chris. *Jimmy Corigan: The Smartest Kid on Earth.* Pantheon, 2002.

Warner, Susan (Elizabeth Wentwell). *The Wide, Wide World.* Tauchnitz, 1850.

Warren, Andrea. *Surviving Hitler: A Boy in the Nazi Death Camps.* HarperCollins, 2001.

Waters, Daniel. *Generation Dead.* Hyperion, 2008.

Watkins, Yoko. *My Brother, My Sister, and I.* Bradbury, 1994.

Watson, Andi. *The Complete Geisha.* ONI Press, 2003.

Watson, Esther Pearl (ed.). *The Pain Tree and Other Teenage Angst-Ridden Poetry.* Houghton Mifflin, 2000.

Watts, Bernadette. *Snow White.* Faber and Faber, 1983.

Watts, Irene. *Goodbye Marianne.* Scirocco Drama, 1995.

Waugh, Sylvia. *Space Race.* Dell Yearling, 2000.

Wayland, April Halprin. *Girl Coming In for a Landing—A Novel in Poems.* Illustrated by Elaine Clayton. Knopf, 2002.

Wegman, William. *Cinderella.* Hyperion, 1993.

Wegman, William. *Little Red Riding Hood.* Hyperion, 1993.

Wein, Elizabeth. *The Winter Prince.* Atheneum, 1993.

Weinstein, Howard. *Star Trek.* DC, 2001.

Weisner, David. *Sector 7.* Clarion, 1999.

Weisner, David. *The Three Pigs.* Clarion, 2001.

Weisner, David. *Tuesday.* Clarion, 1997.

Weldon, Alice. *Girls Who Rocked the World: Heroines from Sacajewea to Sheryl Swoopes.* Gareth Stevens, 1999.

Werlin, Nancy. *Black Mirror.* Dial, 2001.

West, Terry, and Steve Ellis. *Confessions of a Teenage Vampire: The Turning.* Scholastic, 1997.

Westall, Robert. *Gulf.* Heinemann, 1994.

Westerfield, Scott. *Leviathan.* Simon Pulse, 2009.

Westerfield, Scott. *Pretties.* Simon Pulse, 2005.

Westerfield, Scott. *Uglies.* Simon Pulse, 2005.

Weston, Carol. *Girltalk: All the Stuff Your Sister Never Told You.* HarperCollins, 1994.

Weston, Tamsa. *Hey, Pancakes.* Illustrated by Stephen Gammell. Silver Whistle, 2003.

Weyn, Suzanne. *The Bar Code Tattoo.* Scholastic, 2004.

Whincup, G. *The Heart of Chinese Poetry.* Anchor, 1987.

Whipple, L. *If the Shoe Fits: Voices from Cinderella.* Illustrated by L. Beingessner. McElderry, 2002.

White, Ellen Emerson. *The Road Home.* Scholastic, 1995.

White, Ruth. *Belle Prater's Boy.* Farrar, Straus, and Giroux, 1996.

White, Ruth. *Memories of Summer.* Farrar, Straus, and Giroux, 2000.

White, T. H. *The Once and Future King.* Ace, 1987.

Wieler, Diana. *Bad Boys.* Delacorte, 1992.

Wiggin, Kate Douglas. *Rebecca of Sunnybrook Farm.* Houghton Mifflin, 1903.

Wilbur, Richard. *The Disappearing Alphabet.* Illustrated by David Diaz. Harcourt, 1998.

Wild, Margaret. *Jinx.* Simon Pulse, 2004.

Wild, Margaret. *Woolvs in the Sitee.* Illustrated by Anne Spudvilas. Boyds Mills, 2009.

Wilder, Laura Ingalls. *Little House in the Big Woods.* HarperCollins, 1932.

Wildsmith, Brian, and Rebecca Wildsmith. *Jack and the Meanstalk.* Knopf, 1994.

Willard, Nancy. *A Visit to William Blake's Inn.* Illustrated by Alice and Martin Provensen. Harcourt, 1981.

Willard, Nancy. *Beauty and the Beast.* Illustrated by Barry Moser. Harcourt, 1992.

Willard, Nancy. *Cinderella's Dress.* Illustrated by Jane Dyer. Blue Sky Press, 2003.

Willard, Nancy. *Pish, Posh said Hieronymous Bosch.* Illustrated by Leo and Diane Dillon. Harcourt, 1991.

Willey, Margaret. *A Summer of Silk Moths.* Flux, 2009.

Williams, Laura E. *The Executioner's Daughter.* Henry Holt, 2000.

Williams, Lori. *Shayla's Double Brown Baby Blues.* Simon & Schuster, 2001.

Williams, Lori. *When Kambia Elaine Flew in from Neptune.* Simon & Schuster, 2000.

Williams-Garcia, Rita. *Every Time a Rainbow Dies.* HarperCollins, 2001.

Willis, Jeanne. *The Truth or Something: A Novel.* Holt, 2002.

Wilson, Augusta Jane Evans. *St. Elmo.* Indypublish, 2002. (Original work published 1867)

Wilson, Jacqueline. *The Illustrated Mum.* Delacorte, 2005.

Winick, Judd. *Adventures of Barry Ween, Boy Genius.* ONI, 1999.

Winick, Judd. *Pedro and Me: Friendship, Loss, & What I Learned.* Henry Holt, 2000.

Winter, Barbara. *Plays from Hispanic Tales: One Act, Royalty-Free Dramatizations for Young People from Hispanic Stories and Folktales.* Plays Inc., 1998.

Wiseman, David. *Jeremy Visick.* Houghton Mifflin, 1981.

Wisler, G. Clifton. *Run the Blockade.* HarperCollins, 2000.

Wisler, G. Clifton. *When Johnny Went Marching Home: Young Americans Fight the Civil War.* HarperCollins, 2001.

Wisniewski, David. *Golem.* Clarion, 1996.

Withers, Pam. *Raging River.* Take It to the Extreme series. Walrus, 2003.

Withrow, Sarah. *Box Girl.* Groundwood, 2001.

Wittlinger, Ellen. *Gracie's Girl.* Simon & Schuster, 2000.

Wittlinger, Ellen. *Hard Love.* Aladdin, 1999.

Wittlinger, Ellen. *Razzle.* Simon & Schuster, 2001.

Wittlinger, Ellen. *The Long Night of Leo and Bree.* Simon & Schuster, 2001.

Wittlinger, Ellen. *Zig Zag.* Simon & Schuster, 2003.

Wolff, Virginia Euwer. *Bat 6.* Scholastic, 1998.

Wolff, Virginia Euwer. *Make Lemonade.* Holt, 1993.

Wolff, Virginia Euwer. *True Believer.* Atheneum, 2001.

Wong, Janet. *A Suitcase of Seaweed and Other Poems.* McElderry, 1996.

Wong, Janet. *Behind the Wheel: Poems about Driving.* McElderry, 1999.

Wong, Janet. *Good Luck Gold and Other Poems.* McElderry, 1999.

Wong, Janet. *Night Garden: Poems from the World of Dreams.* McElderry, 2000.

Wooding, Chris. *Kerosene.* Scholastic, 2001.

Woodson, Jacqueline. *From the Notebooks of Melanin Sun.* Scholastic, 1995.

Woodson, Jacqueline. *Hush.* G. P. Putnam's Sons, 2001.

Woodson, Jacqueline. *If You Come Softly.* Putnam, 1998.

Woodson, Jacqueline. *Locomotion.* Putnam, 2003.

Woodson, Jacqueline. *Miracle's Boys.* G. P. Putnam's Sons, 2000.

Woodson, Jacqueline. *The House You Pass on the Way.* Laurel-Leaf, 1999.

Woodson, Jacqueline. *The Other Side.* Illustrated by E. B. Lewis. Putnam, 2001.

Worthen, Tom (ed.). *Broken Heart . . . Healing: Young Poets Speak Out on Divorce.* Illustrated by Kyle Hernandez. Poet Tree, 2001.

Wrede, Patricia. *Book of Enchantments.* Harcourt, 1996.

Wrede, Patricia. *Dealing with Dragons.* Harcourt Brace, 1990.

Wulffson, Don. *Soldier X.* Viking, 2001.

Wyeth, Sharon. *Something Beautiful.* Illustrated by Chris Soenpiet. Doubleday, 1998.

Wynne-Jones, T. *The Boy in the Burning House.* Farrar, Straus, and Giroux, 2001.

Wynne-Jones, Tim. *Dracula.* Illustrated by Laszlo Gal. Key Porter, 1997.

Wynne-Jones, Tim. *The Hunchback of Notre Dame.* Illustrated by Bill Slavin. Orchard, 1996.

Yaccarino, Dan. *First Day on a Strange New Planet.* Harper-Collins, 2000.

Yagawa, Sumiko. *The Crane Wife.* Illustrated by Akaba Suekichi. Morrow, 1981.

Yancey, Rick. *Monstrumologist.* Simon & Schuster, 2009.

Yang, Gene Luen. *American Born Chinese.* First Second, 2007.

Yasuhiko, Yoshikazu. *Joan: Book 1.* ComicsOne, 2001.

Yen Mah, Adeline. *Chinese Cinderella.* Delacorte, 1999.

Yep, Laurence. *Dragon's Gate.* HarperCollins, 1993.

Yep, Laurence. *Dragonwings.* Harper & Row, 1977.

Yep, Laurence. *Dream Soul.* HarperCollins, 2000.

Yep, Laurence. *Mountain Light.* Harper & Row, 1985.

Yep, Laurence. *The Amah.* Putnam, 1999.

Yep, Laurence. *The Dragon Prince: A Chinese Beauty and the Beast Tale.* Illustrated by Kam Mak. HarperCollins, 1997.

Yep, Laurence. *The Journal of Wong Ming Chung.* Scholastic, 2000.

Yep, Laurence. *The Magic Paintbrush.* HarperCollins, 2000.

Yep, Laurence. *The Serpent's Children.* Harper & Row, 1984.

Yep, Laurence. *The Traitor.* HarperCollins, 2003.

Yolen, Jane. *Briar Rose.* Tor, 1992.

Yolen, Jane. *Dragon's Blood.* Delacorte, 1982.

Yolen, Jane. *Dragon's Boy.* HarperCollins, 1990.

Yolen, Jane. *Encounter.* Illustrated by David Shannon. Harcourt Brace Jovanovich, 1992.

Yolen, Jane. *Least Things: Poems about Small Natures.* Boyds Mills, 2003.

Yolen, Jane. *Merlin. The Young Merlin Trilogy, Book Three.* Harcourt, 1997.

Yolen, Jane. *Not One Damsel in Distress: World Folktales for Strong Girls.* Harcourt, 2000.

Yolen, Jane (ed.). *Sherwood: Original Stories from the World of Robin Hood.* Illustrated by Dennis Nolan. Philomel, 2000.

Yolen, Jane. *Sleeping Ugly.* Illustrated by Diane Stanley. Coward-McCann, 1981.

Yolen, Jane. *Sword of the Rightful King.* Harcourt Brace, 2003.

Yolen, Jane. *The Devil's Arithmetic.* Viking, 1988.

Yolen, Jane. *Wings.* Illustrated by Dennis Nolan. Hampton Brown, 1990.

Yolen, Jane, and Heidi Stemple. *Dear Mother, Dear Daughter: Poems for Young People.* Boyds Mills, 2001.

Yolen, Jane, and Robert J. Harris. *Girl in a Cage.* Philomel, 2002.

Yolen, Jane, and Robert J. Harris. *Queen's Own Fool.* Philomel, 2000.

Yolen, Jane, with Bruce Coville. *Armageddon Summer.* Harcourt Brace, 1998.

Yonge, Charlotte Mary. *The Caged Lion.* Illustrated by W. J. Hennessy. Macmillan, 1870.

Yorinks, Arthur. *Hey Al.* Illustrated by Richard Egielski. Farrar, Straus, and Giroux, 1986.

Young, Cathy (ed.). *One Hot Second: Stories about Desire.* Knopf, 2002.

Young, Ed. *Lon Po Po.* Philomel, 1989.

Young, Ed. *The Lost Horse.* Sandpiper, 2004.

Young, Ed. *The Turkey Girl: A Zuni Cinderella.* Little, Brown, 1996.

Zahn, Timothy. *Dragon and Slave.* Starscape, 2005.

Zahn, Timothy. *Dragon and Soldier.* Starscape, 2004.

Zahn, Timothy. *Dragon and Thief.* Tor, 2003.

Zeder, Suzan. *Mother Hicks.* Anchorage, 1986.

Zeifert, Harriet. *Little Red Riding Hood.* Viking, 2000.

Zeinart, Karen. *Those Extraordinary Women of World War I.* Lerner, 2001.

Zelinsky, Paul. *Hansel and Gretel.* Dutton, 1999.

Zelinsky, Paul. *Rapunzel.* Dutton, 1997.

Zelinsky, Paul. *Rumplestiltskin.* Dutton, 1986.

Zema, Ludmila. *Gilgamesh the King.* Tundra, 1999.

Zema, Ludmila. *The Last Quest of Gilgamesh.* Tundra, 1998.

Zema, Ludmila. *The Revenge of Ishtar.* Tundra, 1993.

Zemach, Harve. *Duffy and the Devil: A Cornish Tale.* Illustrated by Margot Zemach. Farrar, Straus, and Giroux, 1973.

Zemach, Margaret. *Three Little Pigs: An Old Story.* Farrar, Straus, and Giroux, 1988.

Zenatti, Valerie. *When I Was a Soldier.* Bloomsbury, 2005.

Ziegesar, Cecily. *Slam.* Alloy Books, 2000.

Zindel, Paul. *Pigman and Me.* HarperCollins, 1992.

Zindel, Paul. *Rats.* Hyperion, 1999.

Zindel, Paul. *The Effect of Gamma Rays on Man in the Moon Marigolds.* Harper & Row, 1991.

Zindel, Paul. *The Pigman.* Harper & Row, 1968.

Zipes, Jack. *Don't Bet on the Prince.* Routledge, 1986.

Zusak, Markus. *Fighting Ruben Wolfe.* Arthur Levine, 2001.

Zusak, Markus. *Getting the Girl.* Arthur Levine, 2003.

Zusak, Markus. *The Book Thief.* Knopf, 2006.

Zweger, Lisbeth. *Hansel and Gretel.* Minedition, 2008.

Zweger, Lisbeth. *Little Red Cap.* Morrow, 1983.

Secondary Sources

Abbott, Charles. *Howard Pyle: A Chronicle.* Harper & Brothers, 1925.

Adams, Gillian. "Medieval Children's Literature: Its Possibility and Actuality." *Children's Literature, 26,* 1998, 1–24.

Adamson, Lynda. *Recreating the Past: A Guide to American and World Historical Fiction for Children and Young Adults.* Greenwood, 1987.

A History of Sequential Art. www.comic-art.com/history/history0.htm

Allie, Scott. "Afterword." In Doug Petrie and Ryan Sook, *Buffy the Vampire Slayer: Ring of Fire.* Dark Horse, 2000.

Alsup, Janet. "Politicizing Young Adult Literature: Reading Anderson's *Speak* as a Critical Text." *Journal of Adolescent and Adult Literacy,* October 2003, 158–167.

Altman, Anna, and Gail van de Vos. *Tales, Then and Now: More Folktales as Literary Fictions for Young Adults.* Libraries Unlimited, 2001.

Amidon, Rick. "Toward a Young Adult Drama." *English Journal, 76*(5), 1987, 58–60.

Anderson, Sheila. *Extreme Teen: Library Services to Nontraditional Young Adults.* Libraries Unlimited, 2005.

Anderson, Sheila. *Serving Older Teens.* Libraries Unlimited, 2004.

Anderson, Sheila (ed.). *Serving Young Teens and 'Tweens.* Libraries Unlimited, 2005.

Andrews, Richard. *The Problem with Poetry.* Open University Press, 1991.

Andrews, Sharon E. "Using Inclusive Literature to Promote Positive Attitudes towards Disabilities." *Journal of Adolescent and Adult Literacy, 41*(6), 1998, 420–426.

Applebee, Arthur. "A Study of Book Length Works Taught in High School English Courses." Report Series 1.2, Center for the Learning and Teaching of Literature. ERIC, 1989.

Applebee, Arthur. *Shaping Conversations: A Study of Continuity and Coherence on High School Literacy Curriculum.*

National Research Center on Literature Teaching and Learning, 1994.

Archie Comics. www.archie.com

Arizona State University Libraries. "Child Drama Collection." www.asu.edu/lib/speccoll/drama/links.htm

Aronowitz, Stanley, and Henry Giroux. *Education under Siege.* Bergin-Garvey, 1985.

Aronson, Marc. *Beyond the Pale: New Essays for a New Era.* Scarecrow Press, 2003.

Aronson, Marc. "Exploding the Myths about Teenagers and Reading." *Studies in Young Adult Literature, 4,* 2001.

Artbomb.net. www.artbomb.net

Ayala, E. C. " 'Poor Little Things,' and 'Brave Little Souls': The Portrayal of Individuals with Disabilities in Children's Literature." *Reading Research and Instruction, 39,* 1999, 103–117.

Bainbridge, Joyce, and Sylvia Pantaleo. "Filling the Gap in Text: Picture Book Reading in the Middle Years." *The New Advocate, 14*(4), 2001, 401–411.

Bamford, Rosemary, and Janice Kristo (eds.). *Making Facts Come Alive: Choosing Quality Nonfiction Literature K–8.* Christopher-Gordon, 2003.

Barchers, Suzanne. *Reader's Theater for Beginning Readers.* Teacher Ideas Press, 1993.

Battiscombe, Georgina. *Charlotte Mary Yonge: The Story of an Uneventful Life.* Constable and Co., 1943.

Baxter, Kathleen. "Nonfiction Booktalker" (column). *School Library Journal.*

Baxter, Kathleen, and Marcia Agness Kochel. *Gotcha Again! More Nonfiction Booktalks . . .* Libraries Unlimited, 2002.

Baxter, Kathleen, and Marcia Agness Kochel. *Gotcha! Nonfiction Booktalks To Get Kids Excited about Reading.* Libraries Unlimited, 1999.

Beach, R. *A Teacher's Introduction to Reader-Response Theories.* NCTE, 1993.

Bean, Joy. "A Fresh Look at YA Literature." *Publishers Weekly, 250*(27), 2003, 21–23.

Bean, T. W. "Using Dialogue Journals to Foster Reflective Practice with Preservice, Content-Area Teachers." *Teacher Education Quarterly, 16*(1), 1989, 33–40.

Bean, T. W., and N. Rigoni. "Exploring the Intergenerational Dialogue Journal Discussion of a Multicultural Young Adult Novel." *Reading Research Quarterly, 36*(3), 2001, 232–248.

Beers, Kylene, and Barbara G. Samuels (eds.). *Into Focus: Understanding and Creating Middle School Readers.* Christopher-Gordon, 1998.

Bennett, Cherie. *Life in the Fast Lane.* Random House, 1998.

Bennett, Kathleen. "Joe Sacco's Palestine: Where Comics Meets Journalism." *The Stranger,* 1994. www.thestranger.com

Benton, Mike. *The Comic Book in America.* Taylor, 1993.

Bettleheim, Bruno. *The Uses of Enchantment: The Meaning and Importance of Fairy Tales.* Knopf, 1976.

Biamonte, Christina. "Crossing Culture in Children's Book Publishing." *Publishing Research Quarterly, 18*(3), September, 2002.

Black, Alison, and Anna M. Stave. *A Comprehensive Guide to Readers Theatre: Enhancing Fluency and Comprehension in Middle School and Beyond.* IRA, 2007.

Blagg, Dorothy. "Charlotte Mary Yonge and Her Novels." In Muriel Masefield, *Women Novelists: From Fanny Burney to George Eliot.* Books for Libraries Press, 1967, 191–201. (Original work published 1934)

Blaska, Joan K. *Using Children's Literature to Learn about Disabilities and Illness.* Educators International Press, 1996.

Blassingame, John. *The Slave Community: Plantation Life in the Anti-Bellum South.* Oxford University Press, 1972.

Blatt, Gloria (ed.). *Once upon a Folktale: Capturing the Folkloric Process with Children.* Teacher's College, 1993.

Blume, Judy (ed.). *Places I Never Meant to Be.* Simon and Schuster, 1999.

Bodart, Joni. *Radical Reads 2: Working with the Newest Edgy Titles for Teens.* Scarecrow, 2010.

Bolton, Gavin. *Drama as Education.* Longman, 1984.

Booth, David. *Story Drama: Reading, Writing, and Roleplaying across the Curriculum.* Pembroke, 1994.

Booth, David. *Whatever Happened to Language Arts.* Pembroke, 2009.

Booth, David, and Charles. Lundy. *Improvisation: Learning through Drama.* Academic Press Canada, 1985.

Bosmajian, Hamida. "Reading the Unconscious: Psychoanalytic Criticism." In Peter Hunt (ed.), *Understanding Children's Literature,* 2nd ed. Routledge, 2005, 100–111.

Brent, Linda (Harriet Jacobs). *Incidents in the Life of a Slave Girl.* Dover, 2001. (1861)

Brockman, Bennett. "Children and Literature in Late Medieval England." *Children's Literature, 4,* 1975, 58–63.

Brockman, Bennett. "The Juvenile Audiences of Sir Orfeo." *Children's Literature Association Quarterly, 10*(1), 1985, 18–20.

Broderick, Dorothy. *Image of the Black in Children's Fiction.* R. R. Browker, 1973.

Brumberg, Joan Jacobs. *The Body Project: An Intimate History of American Girls.* Random House, 1997.

Bucher, Katherine T., and M. Lee Manning. "Taming the Alien Genre: Bringing Science Fiction into the Classroom." *The ALAN Review, 28*(2), Winter 2001.

Bucher, K. T., and M. L. Manning, "Creating Safe Schools." *The Clearing House, 79,* 2005, 55–60.

Burke, Kay, Robin Fogarty, and Susan Belgrad. *The Mindful School: The Portfolio Connection. K–College.* Allyn & Bacon, 1994.

Burns, Eila. "Pause, Prompt and Praise—Peer Tutored Reading for Pupils with Learning Difficulties." *British Journal of Special Education, 33*(2), 2006, 62–67.

Burton, Hester. "The Writing of Historical Novels." In Virginia Haviland (ed.), *Children and Literature.* Scott Foresman, 1973.

Bushman, John. "Young Adult Literature in the Classroom—Or Is It?" *English Journal, 86*(3), 1997, 35–40.

Bushman, John, and Kay Parks Bushman. *Using Young Adult Literature in the English Classroom.* Merrill, 1993.

Bushman, John, and Shelly McNerny. "Moral Choices: Building a Bridge between YA Literature and Life." *The ALAN Review, 32*(1), Fall 2004.

Cai, Migshui. "Variable and Values in Historical Fiction for Children." *The New Advocate, 5*(4), Fall 1992, 279–291.

Cam, Helen. *Historical Novels.* Historical Association, 1964.

Campbell, Joseph. *The Hero with a Thousand Faces.* New World Library, 1949.

Campbell, Joseph. *The Masks of God: Primitive Mythology.* Viking, 1959.

Card, Orson Scott. *How to Write Science Fiction and Fantasy.* Writer's Digest Books, 1990.

Carey-Webb, Allen. *Literature and Lives: A Response-Based, Cultural Studies Approach to Teaching English.* National Council Teachers of English, 2001.

Carr, J. *Beyond Fact: Nonfiction for Children and Young People.* American Library Association, 1982.

Cart, Michael. *From Romance to Realism: 50 Years of Growth and Change in Young Adult Literature.* HarperCollins, 1996.

Carter, Betty, and Richard F. Abrahamson. *Nonfiction for Young Adults: From Delight to Wisdom.* Oryx Press, 1990.

Cartoon Books. www.boneville.com

Cassady, J. K. "Wordless Books: No-Risk Tools for Inclusive Middle-Grade Classrooms." *Journal of Adolescent and Adult Literacy, 41,* 1998, 428–432.

Center for Disease Control. "Injury Research Agenda: Preventing Suicidal Behavior 2006." www.cdc.gov/ncipc/pub-res/research_agenda/08_suicide.htm

Center for Media Literacy. "Media Literacy: A Definition . . . and More." 2007. www.medialit.org/reading_room/rr2def.php

Children's Literature. "Chris Raschka: Following Ideas in Music and Art." 2005. www.childrenslit.com/childrenslit/mai_raschka_chris.html

Cianciolo, Patricia. "Folktale Variants: Links to the Never-Ending Chain." In Gloria Blatt (ed.), *Once Upon a Folktale.* Teacher's College Press, 1993.

Cobb, Nancy J. *Adolescence: Continuity, Change, and Diversity,* 2nd ed. Mayfield, 1995.

Cofer, Judith Ortiz. "Introduction." In *Riding Low on the Streets of Gold.* Arte Publico, 2003.

Cohn, Rachel. "Teens, Teachers and Controversial Text." *The ALAN Review,* Summer 2004. http://scholar.lib.ut.edu/ejournals/ALAN/v31n3/cohn.html

Colman, Penny. "Adventures in Nonfiction." *Journal of Children's Literature, 28*(2), Fall 2002, 58–61.

Colman, Penny. "Hooked on Nonfiction: How About You?" Speech at The Ohio State University's Children's Literature Conference, Columbus, Ohio, 2004. www.pennycolman.com/art2.htm

Colman, Penny. "Nonfiction Is Literature, Too." *The New Advocate, 12*(3), Summer 1999, 215–223.

Comic Book Legal Defense Fund. www.cbldf.org

Comic Book Resources. www.comicbookresources.com

Comic Page Guide to the History of the American Comic Book. www.dereksantos.com/comicpage/

Comics Archive. www.execpc.com/~icicle/main.html

Comics Get Serious: Graphic Novel Reviews. www.rational magic.com/Comics/Comics.html

Comics Newsarama. www.comicon.com/newsrama

CPM Manga. www.centralparkmedia.com

Crew, Hilary. "Not So Brave a World: The Representation of Human Cloning in Science Fiction for Young Adults." *The Lion and the Unicorn, 28*(2), 2004, 203–221.

Daniels, Harvey. "Expository Text in Literature Circles." *Voices in the Middle, 9*(4), 2002, 7–14.

Daniels, Harvey. *Literature Circles: Voice and Choice in Book Clubs and Reading Groups,* 2nd ed. Stenhouse, 2001.

Dark Horse Comics. www.darkhorse.com

Davies, Bronwyn. *Frogs and Snails and Feminist Tales.* Allen and Unwin, 1989.

Davies, Bronwyn. *Shards of Glass: Children Reading and Writing beyond Gendered Identities.* Hampton Press, 1993.

Davis, Charles, and Henry Louis Gates, Jr. (eds.). *The Slave's Narrative.* Oxford University Press, 1985.

DC Comics. www.dccomics.com

Degh, Linda. *American Folklore and the Mass Media.* Indiana University Press, 1994.

Derrickson, Teresa. " 'Cold/Hot, English/Spanish': The Puerto Rican American Divide in Judith Ortiz Cofer's *Silent Dancing.*" *MELUS, 28*(2), 2003, 21–37.

Dixon, Neill, Ann Davies, and Colleen Politano. *Learning with Reader's Theatre: Building Connections.* Peguis, 1996.

Doiron, R. "Using Nonfiction in a Read-Aloud Program: Letting the Facts Speak for Themselves." *The Reading Teacher, 47*(8), 1994, 616–624.

Donelson, Kenneth I., and Alleen P. Nilsen. *Literature for Today's Young Adults,* 5th ed. Allyn & Bacon, 2005.

Doran, Colleen. *Getting Graphic @ Your Library Preconference.* ALA Annual Conference, 2002.

Dorson, Richard. *Folklore and Fakelore: Essays toward a Discipline of Folk Studies.* Harvard University Press, 1976.

Douglass, Frederick. *Narrative of the Life of Frederick Douglass, an American Slave, Written by Himself.* Boston Anti-Slavery Office, 1845.

Doyle, Robert. *Banned Books: 2001 Resource Guide.* American Library Association, 2001.

Drabble, Margaret. *The Oxford Companion to English Literature.* Oxford University Press, 2005.

Drury, John. *The Poetry Dictionary.* Story Press, 1995.

Duin, Steve, and Mike Richardson. *Comics between the Panels.* Dark Horse, 1998.

Dundes, Alan (ed.). *Mother Wit from the Laughing Barrel.* Prentice Hall, 1973.

Dyches, Tina Taylor, Mary Anne Prater, and S. Cramer. "Characterization of Mental Retardation and Autism in Children's Books." *Education and Training in Mental Retardation and Developmental Disabilities, 36,* 2001, 230–243.

Edelsky, Carole. *With Literacy and Justice for All: Rethinking the Social in Language and Education: Critical Perspectives on Literacy and Education.* Falmer, 1991.

Edwards, Paul (ed.). *Equiano's Travels.* Heinemann, 1986. (Original work published 1789)

Egan, Keiran. *Teaching as Storytelling.* University of Chicago Press, 1989.

Eisner, Will. *Comics and Sequential Art.* Poorhouse, 1985.

Eisner, Will. *Graphic Story Telling and Visual Narrative.* Poorhouse Press, 1996.

Ellis, Alec. *A History of Children's Reading and Literature.* Pergamon Press, 1963.

Ellis, Sarah. "Rob Crue, or the Classics Revised." *Horn Book.* January/February 2000, 55–58.

Farrel, E., and Squires, J. (eds.). *Transactions with Literature: A Fifty Year Perspectiv*e. NCTE, 1990.

Feinberg, Barbara. *Welcome to Lizard Motel: Children, Stories, and the Mystery of Making Things Up.* Beacon Press, 2004.

Fish, Stanley. *Is There a Text in This Class? The Authority of Interpretative Communities.* Harvard University Press, 1980.

Fisher, Leona. "Closing the Hermeneutic Circle on George MacDonald: For the Child or the Childlike?" *Children's Literature Association Quarterly, 20*(1), 1995, 47–48.

Fleischman, Avrom. *The English Historical Novel.* John Hopkins Press, 1971.

Flynn, R. M., and G. A. Carr. "Exploring Classroom Literature through Drama: A Specialist and a Teacher Collaborate. *Language Arts, 71,* 1994, 38–43.

Foster, Warren. "Why the Stories Are Told" from *Stories of the Dreaming* [Video]. Australian Museum, 2004.

Fox, M. *Teaching Drama to Young Children.* Heinemann, 1987.

Freud, Sigmund. Excerpts from "On Dreams." In Charles Harrison and Paul Wood (eds.), *Art in Theory.* Blackwell, 1993, 26–34.

Frye, Northrop. "Approaching the Lyric." In Chaviva Hosek and Patricia Parker (eds.) *Lyric Poetry: Beyond New Criticism.* Cornell University Press, 1985.

Frye, Northrop, Sheridan Baker, and George Perkins. *The Harper Handbook to Literature.* Harper and Row, 1985.

Gerard, Philip. *Creative Nonfiction: Researching and Crafting Stories of Real Life.* Story Press, 1996.

Glasgow, Jacqueline. "Teaching Social Justice through Young Adult Literature." *English Journal, 90,* 2001, 54–61.

Going, K. L. "Interview." *Totally YA,* 2007. http://fictionfor youngadults.blogspots.com

Goldsmith, Francisca. "Earphone English—An Old Standby (the Audiobook) Has Become a Hip Tool for Teaching Teens a Second Language." *School Library Journal, 48*(5), May 2002, 50–53.

Graves, Donald, and Bonnie Sunstein. *Portfolio Portraits.* Heinemann, 1992.

Greenacre, Phyllis. "Further Considerations Regarding Fetishism." In *Psychoanalytic St. Child, 10,* 1955, 187–194.

Greenwood, Claudia M., and Cynthia E. Walters. *Literature-Based Dialogue Journals: Reading, Writing, Connecting, Reflecting.* Christopher-Gordon, 2005.

Griswold, Jerry. *The Meaning of "Beauty and the Beast": A Handbook.* Broadview Press, 2004.

Guild, Sandy, and Sandra Hughes-Hassell. "The Urban Minority Young Adult As Audience: Does Young Adult Literature Pass the Reality Test?" *New Advocate, 14*(4), Fall 2001, 361–377.

Haase, Donald. "Response and Responsibility in Reading Grimms' Fairy Tales" in *The Reception of Grimms Fairy Tales.* Wayne State Press, 1993, 23–49.

Hallden, Ola. "Learning History." *Oxford Review of Education, 12,* 1986, 53–66.

Hamilton, Martha, and Mitch Weiss. *Children Tell Stories: A Teaching Guide.* Richard C. Owen, 1990.

Hansen, Joyce. "Whose Story Is It?" *The New Advocate, 3*(3), 1990, 167–173.

Harrill, J. L., J. J. Leung, R. A. McKeag, and J. Price. *Portrayal of Handicapped/Disabled Individuals in Children's Literature: Before and after Public Law 94–142.* University of Wisconsin–Oshkosh, 1993. (ERIC Document Reproduction Services No. ED 357557)

Harris, Theodore, and Richard Hodges. *The Literary Dictionary: The Vocabulary of Reading and Writing.* International Reading Association, 1995.

Harryhausen, Ray, and John Landis. "Introduction." In Ricardo Delgado, *Age of Reptiles: Tribal Warfare.* Dark Horse, 1996.

Havelock, Eric. *The Muse Learns to Write: Reflecting on Orality and Literacy from Antiquity to the Present.* Yale University Press, 1988.

Haven, Kendall. *Great Moments in Science: Experiments and Reader's Theatre.* Teacher Ideas Press, 1996.

Haviland, Virginia (ed.). *Children and Literature.* Scott Foresman, 1973.

Heard, Georgia. *Awakening the Heart: Exploring Poetry in Elementary and Middle School.* Heinemann, 1999.

Hewitt, Geof. *A Portfolio Primer: Teaching, Collecting, and Assessing Student Writing.* Heinemann, 1995.

Heyking, Amy von. "Historical Thinking in the Elementary Years: A Review of Current Research." *Canadian Social Studies, 39*(1), Fall 2004. http://www.quasar.ualberta.ca/Css/Css_39_1/ARheyking_historical_thinking_current_research.html

Hill, Bonnie Campbell, Katherine Noe, and Janine King. *Literature Circles in Middle School: One Teacher's Journey.* Christopher Gordon, 2003.

Hill, Bonnie Campbell, Katherine Noe, and Nancy Johnson. *Literature Circles Resource Guide.* Christopher Gordon, 2001.

Hillman, Judith. *Discovering Children's Literature.* Prentice Hall, 1995.

Hirschfield, Jane. *Nine Gates: Entering the Mind of Poetry.* HarperCollins, 1997.

Holland, Norman. *Five Readers Reading.* Yale University Press, 1975.

Horn, Maurice. *The World Encyclopedia of Comics,* 2nd ed. Chelsea House, 1999.

Horovitz, Carolyn. "Dimensions in Time: A Critical View of Historical Fiction for Children." *Horn Book,* June 1962, 137–150.

Huck, Charlotte, Susan Hepler, and Janet Hickman. *Children's Literature in the Elementary School.* Holt, Rinehart, and Winston, 1987.

Hunt, Peter. *Criticism, Theory, and Children's Literature.* Blackwell, 1991.

Hurmence, Belinda. *Before Freedom When I Can Just Remember.* John Blair, 1989.

Image Comics. www.imagecomics.com

International Reading Association. *Literacy Dictionary.* IRA, 1995.

International Reading Association. "The Young Adults' Choices Project." 1994. www.reading.org/libraries/choices/yac_flyer.sflb.ashx

Isaacs, Kathleen T. "Reality Check." *School Library Journal, 49*(10), 2003, 50–51.

Iser, Wolfgang. *The Implied Reader: Patterns of Communication in Prose Fiction from Bunyan to Beckett.* Johns Hopkins University Press, 1974.

Jacobson, J., L. Thrope, D. Fisher, D. Lapp, N. Frey, and J. Flood. "Cross-Age Tutoring: A Literacy Improvement Approach for Struggling Adolescent Readers." *Journal of Adolescent and Adult Literacy, 44,* 2001, 528–536.

Jennings, Kevin (ed.). *Becoming Visible: A Reader in Gay and Lesbian History for High School and College Students.* Alyson, 1994.

Jett-Simpson, Mary. "Creative Drama and Story Comprehension." In J. W. Stewig and S. L. Sebasta (eds.). *Using Literature in the Elementary Classroom.* National Council of Teachers of English, 1989, 91–109.

Johnson, Nancy, and Cyndi Giorgis. "Stepping Back, Looking Forward." *Reading Teacher, 55*(4), Dec/Jan 2001–2002, 400–408.

Jones, Patrick. "True Grit: The New Edge in YA Fiction." In *Connecting Young Adults and Libraries,* 2nd ed. Neal-Schuman Publishers, 1998.

Jung, Carl. *Man and His Symbols.* Doubleday, 1964.

Kaeser, Gigi. *Love Makes a Family.* University of Massachusetts Press, 1999.

Kan, Kat. "Graphically Speaking" column on graphic novels. *VOYA: Voice of Youth Advocates.* Scarecrow Press, 1994–present.

Kaplan, J. S. "Nonfiction Books in the Classroom: Undervalues, Underused, and Oversimplified." *The English Journal, 93*(2), 2003, 91–94.

Kaplan, Jeffrey. "Contrasting Points of View (and Then Some): Politicizing Young Adult Literature." *The ALAN Review,* Winter 2004, 16–24.

Kaplan, Jeffrey. "New Perspectives in Young Adult Literature." *The ALAN Review,* Fall 2003. http://scholar.lib.vt.edu/ejournals/ALAN/v31n1/kaplan.html

Kardash, C. A. M., and L. Wright. "Does Creative Drama Benefit Elementary School Students: A Meta-Analysis." *Youth Theatre Journal, 1*(3), 1987, 11–18.

Kaywell, Joan. *Adolescent Literature as a Complement to the Classics.* Christopher Gordon, 1993.

Kennedy, X. J. "Introduction." In Charles Wordsong, *A Fury of Motion: Poems for Boys.* Ghigna, 2003.

Klemin, Diana. *The Art of Art for Children's Books: A Contemporary Survey.* Clarkson N. Potter, 1966.

Larson, M. R. "Comic Books and Graphic Novels for Librarians: What to Buy." *Serials Review, 24*(2), 1998, 31–46.

Lasky, Kathryn. "The Fiction of History: Or, What Did Miss Kitty Really Do?" *The New Advocate,* Summer 1990, 157–166.

Lathey, Gillian. "Children's Books in Translation." *Paper Tigers, Pacific Rim Voices Project.* http://www.papertigers.org/personalViews/archiveViews/GLathey.html, 2004.

Laughin, Mildred, and Kathy Howard. *Reader's Theater for Children: Scripts and Script Development.* 1992.

Lavin, Michael. "Comic Books for Young Adults." http://ublib.buffalo.edu/libraries/units/lml/comics/pages

Lavin, M. R. "Comicbooks and Graphic Novels for Librarians: What to Buy." *Serials Review, 24*(2), 31–46.

Lentz, Tony. "The Rhapsodes Revisited: Notes Regarding Their Divine Inspiration, Success and Recognition." *Text and Performance Quarterly, 1*(1), November 1980, 45–50.

Lester, Julius. "Morality and Adventure of Huckleberry Finn." In James Phelan and Gerald Graff, *Adventures of Huckleberry Finn: A Case Study in Critical Controversy.* St. Martins, 1995, 340–347.

Letts, William J., and James T. Sears (eds.). *Curriculum, Cultures, and (Homo) Sexualities: Queering Elementary Education: Advancing the Dialogue about Sexualities and Schooling.* Rowman and Littlefield, 1999.

Levstik, Linda. "I Wanted to Be There: The Impact of Narrative on Children's Historical Thinking." In Michael Tunnell and Richard Ammon (eds.), *The Story of Ourselves: Teaching History Through Children's Literature.* Heinemann, 1992, 65–77.

Lieberman, Marcia. " 'Some Day My Prince Will Come': Female Acculturation through the Fairy Tale." In Jack Zipes (ed.), *Don't Bet on the Prince: Contemporary Feminist Fairy Tales in North America and England,* Routledge, 1989, 383–395.

Lipsett, Laura. "No Need to 'Duck, Run and Hide': Young Adult Poetry That Taps into You." *The ALAN Review, 28*(3), Spring/Summer 2001, 58.

Lochhead, Marion. "Clio Junior: Historical Novels for Children." In Sheila Egoff, G. T. Stubbs, and L. F. Ashley (eds.), *Only Connect.* Oxford University Press, 1980, 1727.

Lukacs, George. *The Historical Novel.* Translated by Hannah and Stanley Mitchell. Beacon Press, 1963.

Manning, Rita. *Speaking from the Heart: A Feminist Perspective on Ethics.* Rowman, 1992.

Marvel Comics. www.marvel.com

McCarty, H., and L. Chalmers. "Bibliotherapy: Intervention and Prevention." *Teaching Exceptional Children, 29*(6), 1997, 12–13, 16–17.

McCaslin, Nellie. *Creative Drama in the Classroom.* Longman, 1980.

McClure, A. "Choosing Quality Nonfiction Literature: Examining Aspects of Writing Style." In R. Bamford and J. Kristo (eds.), *Making Facts Come Alive: Choosing Quality Nonfiction Literature K–8.* Christopher-Gordon, 1998, 260–267.

McDermott, Gerald. "Caldecott Award Acceptance." *Horn Book,* August 1975, 349–354.

McGillis, Roderick. *The Nimble Reader: Literary Theory and Children's Literature.* Twayne, 1996.

McMunn, William Robert. "The Literacy of Medieval Children." *Children's Literature, 4,* 1974, 36–40.

Mendlesohn, Farah. "Is There Any Such Thing as Children's Science Fiction?" *The Lion and the Unicorn, 28*(2), 2004, 284–313.

Miall, David. "Empowering the Reader: Literary Responses and Classroom Learning." In Roger Kreuz and Susan MacNealy (eds.), *Empirical Approaches to Literature and Aesthetics.* Ablex, 1996, 363–378.

Mikolayzak, Charles. *Orpheus.* Harcourt Brace Jovanovich, 1992.

Moffett, James, and Betty Wagner. *Student-Centered Language Arts, K–12,* 4th ed. Boynton-Cook, 1992.

Moore, David W., Thomas Bean, Deanna Birdyshaw, and James Rycik. "Adolescent Literacy: A Position Statement." *Journal of Adolescent and Adult Literacy, 43,* 1999, 97–112.

Morrell, Jessica Page. *Between the Lines: Master the Subtle Elements of Fiction Writing.* Writer's Digest Books, 2006.

Mozzocco, Caleb. "Palestine in Pen and Ink." *Columbus Alive,* 2002.

Nardi, Peter M., and Beth E. Schneider (eds.). *Perspectives in Lesbian and Gay Studies: A Reader.* Routledge, 1998.

National Council for Family Literacy. *Talking about Wordless Picture Books: A Tutor Strategy Supporting English Language Learners.* NCFL, 2006.

National Council of Teachers of English. *Best in Children's Nonfiction: Reading, Writing and Teaching Orbis Pictus Award Books.* NCTE, 1999.

National Endowment for the Humanities. "Summertime Favorites." NEH, 2003. www.neh.gov/projects/summertimefavorites.html

Nodelman, Perry. *The Pleasures of Children's Literature,* 2nd ed. Longman, 1996.

Nodelman, Perry. "Reading against Text." In Rise Axelrod and Charles Cooper (eds.), *Reading Critically, Writing Well,* 3rd ed. St. Martin's Press, 1993.

Nodelman, Perry, and Mavis Reimer. *Pleasures of Children's Literature,* 3rd ed. Allyn & Bacon, 2003.

Nussbaum, Martha C. *Cultivating Humanity: A Classical Defense of Reform in Liberal Education.* Harvard University Press, 1997.

Obbink, Laura Apol, Joy Kreeft Petyon, and Jana Staton. *Dialogue Journal Bibliography: Published Works about Dialogue Journal Research and Use.* CAELA, 2000.

O'Neil, Cecily. *Drama Worlds: A Framework for Process Drama.* Heinemann, 1995.

Oittinen, Riitta. *Translating for Children.* Garland, 2000.

Opie, Iona, and Peter Opie. *The Lore and Language of Schoolchildren.* Oxford University Press, 1959.

O'Quinn, Elaine. "Vampires, Changelings, and Radical Mutant Teens." *The ALAN Review, 3*(3), 2004, 50–56.

Orenstein, Peggy. *Schoolgirls: Young Women, Self-Esteem and the Confidence Gap.* Doubleday, 1994.

Osborn, Sunya. "Picture Books for Older Readers." *ALAN Review, 28*(3), 2001, 24.

Ostry, Elaine. " 'Is He Still Human? Are You?': Young Adult Science Fiction in the Posthuman Age." *The Lion and the Unicorn, 28*(2), 2004, 222–246.

Ostry, Elaine, and Carrie Hintz (eds.). *Utopian and Dystopian Writing for Children and Young Adults.* Routledge, 2002.

Pappas, C. "Fostering Full Access to Literacy by Including Information Books." *Language Arts, 68,* 1991, 449–462.

Paterson, Katherine. "Cultural Politics from a Writer's Point of View." *The New Advocate, 7*(2), Spring, 1994, 85–91.

Phelan, James, and Gerald Graff. *Adventures of Huckleberry Finn: A Case Study in Critical Controversy.* St. Martins, 1995.

Pipher, Mary. *Reviving Ophelia: Saving the Selves of Adolescent Girls.* Putnam, 1994.

Porter, Carol, and Janell Cleland. *The Portfolio as a Learning Strategy.* Heinemann, 1995.

Prater, Mary Anne. "Characterization of Mental Retardation in Children's and Adolescent Literature." *Education and Training in Mental Retardation and Developmental Disabilities, 34,* 1999, 418–431.

Prater, Mary Anne. "Learning Disabilities in Children's and Adolescent Literature: How Are Characters Portrayed?" *Learning Disability Quarterly, 26*(1), 2003, 47–62.

Prater, Mary Anne. "Using Juvenile Literature with Portrayals of Disabilities in Your Classroom." *Intervention in School and Clinic, 35*(3), 2000, 167–176.

Provost, Gary. *Beyond Style: Mastering the Finer Points of Writing.* Writer's Digest Books, 1988.

Purves, Alan C., Joseph A. Quattrini, and Christine I. Sullivan. *Creating the Writing Portfolio.* NTC Publishing Group, 1995.

Rabinowitz, Peter. *Before Reading: Narrative Conventions and the Politics of Interpretation.* Cornell University Press, 1987.

Rahn, Suzanne. "An Evolving Past." *The Lion and the Unicorn, 15*(1), 1991, 1–26.

Raiteri, Steve. "Recommended Graphic Novels for Public Libraries." http://my.voyager.net/~sraiteri/graphicnovels .htm

Ramsay, Richard. *Gay, Lesbian, Bisexual & Transgender "Attempted Suicide" Incidences/Risks Suicidality Studies from 1970 to 2006.* 2007. www.ucalgary.ca/%7Eramsay/ attempted-suicide-gay-lesbian-all-studies.htm

Rawick, George. *The American Slave: A Composite Autobiography.* Greenwood, 1972.

Reese, C. (1996). Story Development Using Wordless Picture Books. *The Reading Teacher, 50,* 172–173.

Reid, Calvin. "The Literature of Comics." *Publisher Weekly,* October 16, 2000, 44–45.

Reid, S. E. *Presenting Young Adult Science Fiction.* Twayne, 1998.

Robbins, Trina. *From Girls to Grrrlz: A History of Women's Comics from Teens to Zines.* Chronicle Books, 1999.

Rochman, Hazel. "Is That Book Politically Correct? Truths and Trends in Historical Literature for Young People." *Youth Services in Libraries, 7*(2), Winter 1994, 159–175.

Rogers, Teresa. "No Imagined Peaceful Place." In *Reading Across Culture: Teaching Literature in a Diverse Society.* Teachers College Press, 1997, pp. 95–115.

Rosenblatt, Louise. *Literature as Exploration,* 5th ed. Appleton-Century, 1995. (Original work published 1938)

Rowe, Karen. "Feminism and Fairy Tales." In Jack Zipes (ed.), *Don't Bet on the Prince: Contemporary Feminist Fairy Tales in North America and England.* Routledge, 1989.

Rudman, Masha. "An Educator Speaks . . ." *Youth Services in Libraries, 7*(2), 1994, 164–172.

Sabin, Roger. *Comics, Comix, and Graphic Art: A History of Comic Art.* Phaidon Press, 1996.

Schectman, Jacqueline. *The Stepmother in Fairy Tales: Bereavement and the Feminine Shadow.* Sigo Press, 1993.

Shepard, Aaron. *Stories on Stage: Scripts for Reader's Theater.* W.H. Wilson, 1993.

Simpson, Jacqueline. *European Mythology.* Peter Bedrick, 1987.

Sims, Rudine. *Shadow and Substance: Afro-American Experience in Contemporary Children's Fiction.* National Council of Teachers of English, 1982.

Sims Bishop, Rudine. "Foreword." In Lorenz Graham, *Northtown.* Boyds Mills, 2003.

Singer, Eliot A. *Fakelore, Multiculturalism, and the Ethics of Children's Literature.* www.msu.edu/user/singere/fakelore .htm

Smith, Barbara. "Homophobia: Why Bring It Up?" In *The Truth That Never Hurts: Writings on Race, Gender, and Freedom.* Rutgers University Press, 1999, 111–115.

Smith, Gail G. "Stimulating Critical Thinking with Wordless Books." *Ohio Reading Teacher, 26*(1), 2003–2004, 4–10.

Smith, John, Jay Monson, and Dorothy Dobson. "A Case Study on Integrating History and Reading Instruction through Literature." *Social Education, 56*(7), 370–375, 1992.

Smith, Michael W., and Jeffrey D. Wilhelm. *Reading Don't Fix No Chevys: Literacy in the Lives of Young Men.* Boynton/ Cook, 2002.

Snyder, Louis. *Roots of German Nationalism.* Indiana University Press, 1978.

Soter, Anna. "Reading Literature of Other Cultures: Some Issues in Critical Interpretation." In *Reading Across Culture: Teaching Literature in a Diverse Society.* Teachers College Press, 1997, 213–229.

Spiegelman, Art. *Getting Graphic @ Your Library Preconference.* ALA Annual Conference, 2002.

Spivak, Charlotte, and Roberta Staples. *The Company of Camelot: Arthurian Characters in Romance and Fantasy.* Greenwood, 1994.

Springer, Nancy. *The Friendship Song.* Atheneum, 1992.

Sridhar, Deepha, and Sharon Vaughn. "Bibliotherapy for All: Enhancing Reading Comprehension, Self-Concept, and Behavior." *Teaching Exceptional Children, 33*(2), 2000, 74–82.

Stanley, Diane. "A Writer Speaks . . ." *Youth Services in Libraries, 7,* 1994, 172–175.

Steiner, Stanley, and Linda Marie Zaerr. "The Middle Ages." *Book Links, 4*(2), November 1994, 11–15.

Stephens, J., and R. McCallum. *Retelling Stories, Framing Culture: Traditional Story and Metanarratives in Children's Literature.* Garland, 1998.

Stevenson, Deborah. "'If You Read This Last Sentence, It Won't Tell You Anything': Postmodernism, Self-Referentiality, and the Stinky Cheese Man." *Children's Literature Association Quarterly, 19*(1), Spring 1994, 32–34.

Stewig, John Warren. *Exploring Language Arts in the Elementary Classroom.* Henry Holt, 1983.

Stott, Jon. " 'Will the Real Dragon Please Stand Up?' Convention and Parody in Children's Stories." *Children's Literature in Education, 21*(4), 1990, 219–228.

Stringer, Sharon A. *Conflict and Connection: The Psychology of Young Adult Literature.* Boynton/Cook, 1997.

Sullivan, C. W., III. *Young Adult Science Fiction.* Greenwood, 1999.

Sullivan, Ed. "Some Teens Prefer the Real Thing: the Case for Young Adult Nonfiction." *English Journal, 90*(3), January 2001, 43–47.

Sutcliff, Rosemary. "History Is People." In Virginia Haviland (ed.), *Children and Literature: Views and Reviews.* Scott Foresman, 1973, 305–312.

Swartz, Patti Capel. "Bridging Multicultural Education: Bringing Sexual Orientation into the Children's and Young Adult Literature Classrooms." *Radical Teacher, 66,* 2003, 11–16.

Tabers-Kwak, Linda, and Timothy Kaufman. "Shakespeare through the Lens of a New Age." *English Journal, 92*(1), 2002, 69–73.

Talbot, C. H. "Children in the Middle Ages." *Children's Literature, 6,* 1977, 17–33.

Talbot, Bryan. "Rat's Tail." In *Tale of One Bad Rat.* Dark Horse, 1995.

Taxel, Joel. "Historical Fiction and Historical Interpretation." *The ALAN Review, 10*(1), 1983, 32–36.

Taxel, Joel. "The American Revolution in Children's Fiction." *Research in the Teaching of English, 17*(1), 1983, 61–83.

Thrall, William, Addison Hibbard, and C. H. Holman. *A Handbook to Literature,* 8th ed. Prentice Hall, 1999.

Tierney, Robert J., Mark A. Carter, and Laura E. Desai. *Portfolio Assessment in the Reading-Writing Classroom.* Christopher-Gordon, 1991.

TokyoPop. www.tokyopop.com

Tomlinson, Carl, and Carol Lynch-Brown. *Essentials of Children's Literature.* Allyn & Bacon, 1993.

Trites, Roberta Seelinger. *Waking Sleeping Beauty: Feminist Voices in Children's Novels.* University of Iowa Press, 1997.

Versaci, Rocco. "How Comic Books Can Change the Way Our Students See Literature: One Teacher's Perspective." *The English Journal, 91*(2), November 2001.

Virtualit Interactive. "Definition of Character." In *Elements of Fiction Interactive Fiction Tutorial.* Bedford/St Martin's, 2007. http://bcs.bedfordstmartins.com/virtualit/fiction/elements.asp?e=2

Viz Communications. www.viz.com

Wagner, Betty. Research Currents: Does Classroom Drama Affect the Arts of Language? *Language Arts, 65,* 1988, 46–55.

Walker, Lois. *Readers Theatre Strategies in the Middle and Junior High Classroom.* Take Part Productions, 1997.

Walsh, Jill Paton. "History Is Fiction." *Horn Book, 4,* February 1972, 17–23.

Watson, Jinx Stapleton. "Appreciating Gantos' Jack Henry as an Archetype." *The New Advocate, 14*(4), 2001, 379–385.

Weiner, Stephen. *101 Best Graphic Novels.* NBM, 2001.

Wertham, Frederic. *Seduction of the Innocent.* Reinhart, 1954.

Whaley, Liz, and Liz Dodge. *Weaving in the Women: Transforming the High School English Curriculum.* Boynton/Cook, 1993.

Whang, Gail, Mary Pippett, and Katherine Davies Samway. *Buddy Reading: Cross-Age Tutoring in a Multicultural School.* Greenwood, 1995.

Wilder, Ann, and Alan Teasley. "High School Connections YA: FAQ (We're Glad You Asked!)." *The ALAN Review, 28*(1), 2000, 55–57.

Wilder, Ann, and Alan Teasley. "Young Adult Literature in the High School." *The ALAN Review, 26*(1), 1998, 42–45.

Wilhelm, Jeffrey, and Brian Edmiston. *Imagining to Learn: Inquiry, Ethics, and Integration through Drama.* Heinemann, 1998.

Windling, Terri. "White as Snow: Fairy Tales and Fantasy." In Ellen Datlow and Terri Windling, *Snow White, Blood Red.* William Morris, 1993.

Wright, Bradford W. *Comic Book Nation: The Transformation of Youth Culture in America.* Johns Hopkins University Press, 2001.

Yagelski, Robert. *Literacy Matters: Writing and Reading the Social Self.* Teachers College Press, 2000.

Yetman, N. R. *Voices from Slavery.* Holt, Rinehart, and Winston, 1978.

Yonge, Charlotte. "Class Literature of the Last Thirty Years." In Virginia Haviland (ed.), *Children and Literature: Views and Reviews.* Scott Foresman, 1973, 25.

Younger, Beth. "Pleasure, Pain, and the Power of Being Thin: Female Sexuality in Young Adult Literature." *National Women's Studies Association Journal, 15*(2), 2003, 45–56.

Zinsser, William. *On Writing Well. 30th Anniversary Edition: The Classic Guide to Writing Nonfiction.* HarperCollins, 2006.

Zipes, Jack. *Breaking the Magic Spell.* Metheun, 1979.

Zipes, Jack. *Don't Bet on the Prince: Contemporary Feminist Fairy Tales in North America and England.* Routledge, 1986.

Zipes, Jack. *Happily Ever After: Fairy Tales, Children, and the Culture Industry.* Routledge, 1997.

Zipes, Jack (ed.). *The Trials and Tribulations of Little Red Riding Hood,* 2nd ed. Routledge, 1993.

INDEX